Handbook of
Parent Training

Handbook of Parent Training

Helping Parents Prevent and Solve Problem Behaviors

Third Edition

Edited by

James M. Briesmeister

Charles E. Schaefer

John Wiley & Sons, Inc.

Published by John Wiley & Sons, Inc., Hoboken, New Jersey.
Published simultaneously in Canada.

Wiley Bicentennial Logo: Richard J. Pacifico

For general information on our other products and services please contact our Customer Care Department within the United States at (800) 762-2974, outside the United States at (317) 572-3993 or fax (317) 572-4002.

Wiley also publishes its books in a variety of electronic formats. Some content that appears in print may not be available in electronic books. For more information about Wiley products, visit our web site at www.wiley.com.

Library of Congress Cataloging-in-Publication Data:

  Handbook of parent training : helping parents prevent and solve problem behaviors / edited by James M. Briesmeister, Charles E. Schaefer. -- 3rd ed.
        p.   cm.
    Includes bibliographical references and index.
    ISBN-13: 978-0-471-78997-0 (cloth : alk. paper)
    1. Behavior disorders in children—Study and teaching. 2. Child psychotherapy—Study and teaching. 3. Child psychotherapy—Parent participation. I. Briesmeister, James M.   II. Schaefer, Charles E.
  RJ506.B44H26   2007
  618.92'89—dc22
                                                                2006052496

Printed in the United States of America.

10 9 8 7 6 5 4 3 2

Contents

Preface

The Handbook of Parent Training was first published in 1989. It was an impressive compilation and review of some of the most relevant empirical research and clinical applications of behavioral parent training available at that time. Since then the field of parent training and intervention has evolved significantly as evidenced by the offerings in the Second Edition of the *Handbook*, published in 1998. This educational and instructional format for parents continues to demonstrate positive results using parents as strategic agents of constructive change for their children's disruptive and dysfunctional behaviors. In this format, the therapist/practitioner coaches and instructs parents in new parenting skills and ways of relating to their children, ways that reduce conflict and enhance the likelihood of reciprocal respect, acceptance, and contentment within the family.

The Third Edition of the *Handbook* continues the journey and gives even further proof of the value of this innovative and highly successful intervention strategy. With time and experience, parent training approaches have become immensely diversified and applicable to an array of problematic situations. Not only does this format reduce problems and conflicts within the parent-child relationship it also fosters self-efficacy in the children and a sense of competence in the parents. Children, even those with problems, learn that they are capable of self-control and self-management. Similarly, parents, even those who have experienced persistent struggles to gain a sense of integrity and mastery within their respective families, learn that they can develop healthy and effective child management skills. Furthermore, there is unquestionable evidence that these newly acquired skills, in the parents and the children, can be generalized to a myriad of different situations and circumstances. These skills can be beneficially applied in the home, at play, in the school, and in relating with peers and adults. These skills are grounded in the behavioral principles of operant conditioning and in social learning theory. They address and modify behaviors; enhance social and interpersonal relationships; and encourage self-growth, self-control, and self-esteem.

The Third Edition continues to clarify, assess, and resolve difficulties experienced by children, adolescents, and their parents. In addition, the authors in this *Handbook* focus on the key variable of prevention. Undoubtedly, it is preferable and less stressful to prevent problems rather than try to solve them once they have taken root within the parent-child relationship and within the family and school. Unfortunately, problems, too, have a way of generalizing; they are contagious and spread beyond the constraints of the individual child and parent. The resultant malady can infect schools, neighborhoods, the extended family, and the community, in general.

The contributing authors in this text are experts and pioneers in the areas of parent training and intervention, child and adolescent therapy, and child and adolescent development. They share their expertise in the formation and implementation of effective parent training programs. They clearly demonstrate the importance and impact of an essential premise, namely, parent training is a collaborative endeavor involving parents, children, and mental health professionals. In this scientifically and clinically grounded format practical and replicable skills are learned, practiced, and developed to the advantage of all the members of this collaborative process.

This book is intended as a practical and comprehensive guide for practitioners in a number of areas of child care, including the fields of psychology, psychiatry, social work, nursing, pediatrics, education, those working with a special needs population, and related areas. Although each chapter is based on scientific evidence, the authors do not describe and discuss their respective intervention strategies in an empirical vacuum. Each approach has been clinically tested, evaluated, and reappraised. The authors are also mental health consultants and practitioners. They illustrate techniques that they have developed and implemented. They offer case studies, clinical vignettes, and outcome studies that support the benefits and efficacy of their various formats and demonstrate how the applied techniques can prevent disruptive and at-risk behaviors. The readers are invited to adopt these intervention perspectives and strategies to their own unique parent-child scenarios. When appropriate, these programs can be combined and integrated with other treatment alternatives. The authors not only educate, they also offer appealing challenges and directives for further professional research and collaboration, the continued development of new and creative parent training approaches, and the ongoing discovery of practical and applicable strategies to prevent and resolve problems and foster the well-being of parents, children, and family members.

JAMES M. BRIESMEISTER
Shelby Township, Michigan
CHARLES E. SCHAEFER
Teaneck, New Jersey

January 2007

Acknowledgments

WE WOULD like to express our gratitude to Carlos J. Quinones, professor at the University of Detroit Mercy, and Janet Lynn Briesmeister, computer analyst, for sharing their computer expertise. Their patient direction and technical advice was invaluable and genuinely appreciated.

Contributors

Paula Barrett, PhD, is an adjunct professor at the University of Queensland (Australia) and Pathways Health and Research Center. Her research interests focus on behavioral intervention strategies and evidence-based treatment for childhood anxiety disorders.

Steven A. Branstetter, PhD, is an assistant professor of Child Clinical Psychology at West Virginia University. His research focuses on the onset and development of tobacco use and other substance use in adolescence, with particular emphasis on the influence of parents and peers.

James M. Briesmeister, PhD, is a clinical psychologist in private practice and a consultant for the State of Michigan Department of Labor and Economic Growth. He is an adjunct professor at Macomb College. His research focuses on rehabilitation psychology, family and child therapy, and parenting. He has coauthored four books and authored numerous chapters and articles.

Monica Campbell, PhD, is an assistant professor of Special Education at the University of North Carolina, Wilmington. Her research interests include improving outcomes for individuals with disabilities in the areas of reading and social communication through the development, identification, implementation, and evaluation of effective interventions for teachers and families.

Timothy A. Cavell, PhD, is a professor and director of Clinical Training at the University of Arkansas. His research focuses on parent- and mentor-based interventions for high-risk children and the prevention of delinquency and adolescent substance abuse. He is the author of two books on childhood aggression.

Jeffrey S. Danforth, PhD, is a professor in the Department of Psychology at Eastern Connecticut State University. He teaches in the Children and Youth Studies Program. He conducts research on parent training for families of children with comorbid ADHD/ODD. He is also a licensed psychologist in private practice.

Joseph M. Ducharme, PhD C Psych, is an associate professor in the Human Development and Applied Psychology Department at the University of Toronto (Ontario Institute for Studies in Education). His research focuses on proactive treatment of child psychopathology in residential education and classroom environments.

L. Christian Elledge, MA, is a doctoral candidate in clinical psychology at the University of Arkansas. His research interests include the etiology of childhood aggression, intervention strategies, and the development of relationship-based interventions that incorporate different levels of the family system.

Lara Farrell, PhD, is a postdoctoral research fellow at the University of Queensland, Australia, and Pathways Health and Research Center. Her research focuses on family and behavioral intervention approaches for the treatment of childhood anxiety.

Louis Fogg, PhD, is a professor at Rush University in the Psychology Department and College of Nursing with a 20-year history of scholarly research and publication, he is the past president of the local Chicago chapter of the American Statistical Association.

Christine Garvey, DNSc, RN, is an assistant professor in the Department of Community and Mental Health Nursing at Rush University. She is the coauthor of the Chicago Parent Program at Rush University and co-investigator on the NIH study that supported its development and testing.

Lisa Greene, MS, is a doctoral candidate in Child Clinical Psychology at West Virginia University whose research and clinical interests lie broadly in the area of childhood trauma and how trauma exposure affects both children and their families.

Deborah Gross, DNSc, RN, FAAN, is a professor and associate dean for Research and Scholarship at Rush University College of Nursing in Chicago and Robert Wood Johnson Nurse Executive Fellow. She serves on the Early Childhood Committee of the Illinois Children's Mental Health Partnership and on the editorial board of Research in Nursing and Health. She published extensively on various issues regarding children's mental health.

Amy D. Herschell, PhD, is a postdoctoral research fellow at Western Psychiatric Institute and Clinic, University of Pittsburgh School of Medicine. Her research focuses on the implementation of evidence-based treatment for child physical abuse and externalizing behavioral problems.

Arthur C. Houts, PhD, is retired from the position of professor and director of Clinical Training at the University of Memphis in 2003. He currently works as the vice president for Scientific Analysis and Development with the Supportive Oncology Services (SOS) and accredited Community Oncology Research Network (ACORN).

Wrenetha A. Julion, DNSc, MPH, RN, is an assistant professor in the Department of Women and Children's Health Nursing at Rush University College of Nursing, Chicago, Illinois. Appointed commissioner to Governor Rod Blagojevich's Council on Responsibility Fatherhood, he is a member of the board of directors of the Illinois Fatherhood Initiative.

Christopher A. Kearney, PhD, is a professor of Psychology and director of the UNLV Child School Refusal and Anxiety Disorders Clinic at the University of Nevada, Las Vegas. His primary research interests are youths with internalizing behavior problems in general and school refusal behavior in particular.

Martin Kozloff, PhD, is a Watson distinguished professor at the University of North Carolina, Wilmington. Since 1967, he has been developing, evaluating, and disseminating curricula and instruction for children with autism and training programs for teachers and families.

Marcus T. LaSota, MA, is a doctoral candidate in Clinical Psychology at the University of Nevada, Las Vegas.

Amie Lemos-Miller, MA, is a doctoral candidate in Clinical Psychology at the University of Nevada, Las Vegas.

Joshua Masse, MS, is a doctoral candidate in Child Clinical Psychology at West Virginia University. His interests focus on the development and treatment of externalizing behavior disorders in children and adolescents. He researched parent-child interaction and their influence on the development and maintenance of externalizing behavior.

Cheryl B. McNeil, PhD, is a professor of psychology in the child clinical program at West Virginia University. Her research focuses on program development and evaluation, specifically with regard to abusive parenting practices and managing the disruptive behaviors of young children in both home and school settings. She coauthored two books.

Michael W. Mellon, PhD, is a consultant and pediatric psychologist in the Department of Psychiatry and Psychology at Mayo Clinic. He serves as co-director of the Mayo Clinic-Dana Development and Learning Disorders Program and director of the Enuresis and Encopresis Clinic.

Matthew R. Sanders, PhD, is a professor of Clinical Psychology and director of the Parenting and Family Support Center at the University of Queensland, Australia. He is the founder of the internationally recognized Triple P–Positive Parenting Program. He is also a fellow of the Australian Psychological Society and the Academy of Experimental Criminology. He published extensively in the field of children's mental health.

Irwin Sandler, PhD, is a regent's professor in and director of the Program Prevention Research at Arizona State University. He has been the director of an NIMH supported Preventive Intervention Research Center. His research focuses on the studies of resilience in children who have experienced major life stressors.

Charles E. Schaefer, PhD, is a professor of Psychology at Fairleigh Dickinson University in New Jersey. He has authored and coauthored over 50 books and written extensively on child therapy, family therapy, and parenting. His lectures and training programs on play therapy, parent training, and clinical-developmental issues are in high demand.

Kate Sofronoff, PhD, is a member of the academic staff in the School of Psychology at the University of Queensland, Australia, she is the director of Clinical Training and her research is focused on intervention for parents of children and adolescents with Asperger syndrome who experience significant anxiety and anger management problems.

Jennifer Vecchio, MA, is a doctoral candidate in Clinical Psychology at the University of Nevada, Las Vegas.

Carolyn Webster-Stratton, PhD, is a professor and director of the Parenting Clinic at the University of Washington. She is a licensed clinical psychologist and a nurse-practitioner. She produced the Incredible Years: Parents, Teachers, and Children training series that consists of over 36 videotapes to promote social competence and reduce behavior problems. She has been the recipient of the prestigious National Mental Health Research Scientist Award.

Lillie Weiss, PhD, is a clinical psychologist doing private practice using empirically-based interventions. Her research interests include bulimia and preventive programs for children from divorced families.

Koa Whittingham, MA, is a doctorate candidate in the School of Psychology at the University of Queensland, Australia. Her area of research is evaluating the Stepping Stone Triple P Parenting Program with parents of children diagnosed with autism or Asperger syndrome.

Emily Winslow, PhD, is an assistant research professor at the Prevention Research Center in the Department of Psychology at Arizona State University. She is currently principal investigator on a 5-year, NIMH-supported training and research grant to develop and evaluate preventive parenting programs.

Sharlene Wolchik, PhD, is a professor in the Department of Psychology at Arizona State University. She has been involved in multiple federally funded grants that have supported the development and evaluation of prevention programs for children in at-risk situations.

Introduction

HISTORICAL ANTECEDENTS OF PARENT TRAINING

The notion of parents as agents of change in their childrens' lives is not a novel or surprising concept. After all, throughout history, it is typically the parents who have been the caregivers, educators, disciplinarians, managers, and primary agents of change and socialization for their children. One of the earliest recorded cases of therapeutic intervention with a child occurred at the turn of the last century. In his analysis and treatment of a young boy, under the age of 5, Freud (1955/1909) uncovered the etiology, development, and resolution of a phobia in the historic case of Little Hans. A review of this famous case reveals a noteworthy phenomenon. Freud did not treat Little Hans directly. Instead, he instructed the boy's father in techniques for resolving the child's underlying fears. This approach laid the foundations for a therapeutic intervention modality that seeks to effect positive change within the framework of the child-parent relationship.

In the 1960s (Hawkins, Peterson, Schweid, & Bijou, 1966; Wahler, Winkel, Peterson, & Morrison, 1965) we saw the emergence of an effective trend in working with troubled children, known as parent training or parent intervention. Throughout the 1970s and 1980s, a number of researchers investigated and compared the effectiveness of differential parent training programs in reducing childhood conflicts (e.g., Blechman, 1985; Flanagan, Adams, & Forehand, 1979; Forehand & McMahon, 1981; O'Dell, Flynn, & Benlolo, 1979). Nay (1975) conducted one of the earliest systematic comparisons of differential instructional formats. An in-depth analysis was made among five different methods of instructing mothers of young children in time-out procedures: written, lecture, and videotape presentations; videotape modeling coupled with role-playing; and a no-treatment condition. The results of this comparison indicated that the parents benefited from all the training techniques. The results did not show any statistically significant differences among the divergent instructional formats.

Parent training as an effective method of intervention certainly fared very well in these early reviews and critiques.

The growing success of the parent training approach continued into the 1990s. It spawned numerous empirical, comparative, and outcome studies and prompted a broader application of the methods and principles involved in training parents as cotherapists. Researchers and clinicians progressed in their discovery of the advantages and applicability of the parent training format. Zacker (1978) points out that parents are able to quickly master and apply the essential principles of social-cognitive learning and behavioral modification. Because behavior therapy is based on natural and observable phenomena, it is readily accepted by parents without any resistance or hesitation. There is also a good deal of research and experimental evidence indicating that parental practices and styles of parenting have a direct effect on the child's development (Collins, Maccoby, Steinberg, Hetherington, & Bornstein, 2000). Given the unquestionable influence of parents on children and, conversely, children on parents, it is logical that parent training has become established as a viable, multifaceted, and innovative forum for managing the disruptive behaviors of children and adolescents. Parent training not only offers techniques for modifying and controlling negative behaviors, it also strengthens the resolve and self-assurance of parents in their parenting skills. With parent training, practitioners now have an avenue for instructing parents in various aspects of child development and behavioral management. These programs are designed to enable parents to become agents of change in their children's lives and patterns of behaving. Parent intervention formats teach parents how to effect change through the implementation of behavioral engineering, the application of social learning principles, the development of parental monitoring skills, and the proper application of operant principles such as reinforcement contingencies and extinction to modify disruptive behaviors (Ducharme, & Van Houten, 1994). The parent training formats are quite versatile. The needs of the target child, the unique parent-child relationship, the idiosyncratic needs inherent in the family structure, and the nature of the presenting problem typically determine the intervention strategy. All interventions share in the common goal of teaching parents how to modify and remedy destructive and dysfunctional patterns of family interaction to produce lasting and constructive changes. All interventions involve the parents in a collaborative treatment process (Braswell, 1991). Parent training particularly aims to modify the reciprocal patterns of antecedents and consequences of problematic child behavior as well as faulty styles of child management. The behavioral parent training format may also involve didactic measures and verbal instructions that teach parents the ways of communicating and interacting with their children which are most likely to result in a positive relationship and desirable behaviors for all involved (Sanders & Dadds, 1993; Sanders & Glynn, 1981; Webster-Stratton & Herbert, 1994).

ADVANCEMENTS IN PARENT TRAINING

Increasingly, there has been a growing recognition that constructive behavior changes might be most effectively accomplished by working with children in their natural environment (Moreland, Schwebel, Beck, & Wells, 1982). Family therapy approaches and multisystemic intervention modals (e.g., Haley, 1976; Minuchin, 1974) propose that behavioral problems of the child are best understood and treated within the context of the family as an interrelated system. In an early review of parent training approaches, for example, Graziano (1977) proposes that training parents to effect behavior changes in their children may be one of the most significant achievements within the field of child therapy. Traditionally, mental health practitioners who work with children and adolescents have sought to effect change directly with their young patients. In the parent training format, however, the professional educates the parents in the most appropriate and effective application of procedures that elicit socially desirable changes in behavior and the elimination of socially undesirable actions. Parent training has steadily evolved into a highly systematic, empirically-based, and widely-applied intervention strategy. Usually, it is the parents who are in a position to determine the nature, structure, and content of the childrens' immediate environment. The parents decide what school the youngsters attend. The parents decide what pediatricians, dentists, educators, and counselors will be in their children's lives. It is the parents who are in the best position to influence the youngsters' social and peer relationships. It follows logically that it is the parents who ought to determine what influences will or will not be exerted and which behaviors will or will not be encouraged and tolerated within the family. A review of the extensive and evolving body of literature on parent training and intervention procedures makes it clear that the behavioral training approach using parents as agents of change does not merely serve as an adjunct to child therapy. In fact, it is an intervention maneuver that is at the very core of the intervention process. Given this, the parent-child relationship is clearly the most essential and integral variable within the therapeutic endeavor. The parents and their parenting and management skills are the most essential factors in the intervention and therapeutic paradigm. Their role is that of an active therapeutic agent of change.

Any discussion of parent training must take into accurate account the age and developmental level of the target child. Any intervention, if it hopes to be relevant and effective, must be age- and stage-appropriate.

Parent training strategies are, by nature, child-focused. Intervention ploys that are too young or too old for the child's level of intellectual, cognitive, and social functioning will miss their mark. The techniques will not only fall on deaf ears, they will also be rejected, met with a good deal of noncompliance and resistance, or simply ignored. Bemporad (1978) wisely notes that any consideration of therapeutic intervention with young children must of necessity identify, evaluate, and treat the symptoms within the context of the developmental process. Parent training approaches must be developed, structured, and implemented within the viable parameters of the target child's age and developmental level.

Parent training and intervention has been and continues to be based on empirical and applied concepts of behaviorism as well as the tenets of social learning theory. These principles are imparted to the parents in several divergent ways. Each modality, however, involves instructing parents in such a way that they can use the knowledge, instruments, skills, and techniques that may have once been solely the province of the professional mental health practitioner and educator. Although individually designed and equipped to meet the idiosyncratic needs of each target parent, child, and family, the approaches share a common denominator, to help parents remedy their children's destructive behaviors and help the youngsters develop, embellish, and express their positive and constructive behaviors. In particular, parent training strategies seek to modify the reciprocal patterns of antecedents and consequences of difficult and problematic child behavior as well as faulty patterns of child management in order to achieve lasting and constructive changes (Patterson, 1969).

The First and Second Editions of this book focused on parents as cotherapists for children's behavior problems. While posing the same premise, this Third Edition also centers on helping parents prevent as well as solve problem behaviors. Parent training has made significant strides over the past few decades. The behavioral-social-cognitive instructional format has exceeded many more traditional procedures and even some earlier expectations. The strategies involve a combination of social learning and behavioral principles and techniques that have been used in a myriad of creative and highly practical ways. In this current edition, the contributors certainly continue to emphasize approaches that are grounded in empirical theory and research. They also demonstrate behavioral intervention strategies that are practical and applicable. They offer a "hands on" instructional format that guides the parents through the initial identification of their children's problem areas, an assessment of the levels of severity of these targeted problem issues, and the development and implementation of appropriate intervention modalities, and techniques for monitoring and managing these conflicts. The chapters in this book offer multimodal and multifaceted programs that can be individually tailored to meet a variety of unique needs and address a myriad of specific problems and conflictual parent-child relationships. In fact, an essential priority of the parent training format is to determine which type of parenting technique is most appropriate for the training of different parents, children, and conflicts (Blechman, 1981). Even though the parent training modes are individualized, these behavioral instructional approaches can also be generalized and effectively applied to a wide facet of problematic situations. The authors in this *Handbook* not only expertly address these issues and concerns, they also emphasis clear and specific strategies to prevent the formation of problems. Few people would argue that it's more effective and significantly less stressful to prevent problems rather than attempt to ameliorate them once they have developed and had a chance to wreck havoc upon the children, parents, family, and community.

PREVENTION AS INTERVENTION

Increasingly, the research and approaches to resolving childhood, parental, and familial problems have emphasized prevention as intervention (Stambor, 2006). Programs that prioritize prevention as an intervention strategy within the family structure have been developed and implemented in a variety of situations. For example, preventive intervention programs have been used to reduce substance abuse within the family (Ashery, Robertson, & Kumpfer, 1998; Corby & Russell, 1997), conduct disorders and acting-out behaviors in early adolescents (Ducharme, Atkinson, & Poulton, 2000; Ialongo, Poduska, Werthamer, & Kellam, 2001), and conduct disorders within a Head Start population (Webster-Stratton, 1998; Webster-Stratton & Lindsay, 1999; Webster-Stratton, Reid, & Hammond, 2001). Obviously, parent intervention has run the age and developmental gamut, from the earliest of preschool levels to adolescence.

Preventive programs have been extremely flexible and adaptive. They have been employed in the home, school, and within various arenas of the larger community. Whatever the program and wherever it is applied, an essential goal of a preventive program should include specific ploys to enhance protective factors within the family and the parent-child dyad. An effective intervention program must also aim to modify or eliminate risk factors within the family and the child-parent relationship. The protective and risk factors must be identified and assessed within the parameters of the target child's age and developmental level. A review of the various chapters in this *Handbook* will quickly disclose that the authors also place a premium on the development and strengthening of parental skills and self-confidence. Too often parents of children who experience behavioral problems and disorders experience a sense of embarrassment or even shame. They feel that their children's disruptive and dysfunctional patterns reflect their incompetence as a parent. The intervention programs within this book also seek to prevent or modify these negative parental perceptions and images. The various intervention techniques are designed to give the parents a sense of efficacy and competence as parents as well as providing concrete, replicable, and generalizable parenting skills. Parents need the reassurance that they possess viable skills to identify, assess, control, and change their children's current and future problem behaviors. This *Handbook* covers an array of inventive and invaluable instructional techniques that are multivariate and multifaceted. They include a wide and diverse range of parenting and learning tools, such as: role-playing, video demonstrations, interviewing, problem-assessment protocols, group dialogue, modeling positive and effective parenting styles, instructional homework and handouts, and others. In the final analysis, each of these maneuvers are carefully designed to help parents and children improve the quality of their lives and relationships. They address, manage, and change problematic behaviors and situations. In addition, they instill in the parents a well-earned sense of parental competence. When effectively applied, they also impart to the children a sense of self-efficacy, self-control, and integrity. The programs and strategies for preventive intervention are also strategies that facilitate empowerment in the parent, child, and family.

THE FORMAT OF THIS BOOK

Often, books that focus on therapy with children open with a broad theoretical orientation and then attempt to relate the theory to maladaptive, disruptive, and dysfunctional behaviors. Our approach, in contrast, identifies some prevalent and specific childhood behavioral problems. We then offer parent training programs to address, manage, and modify these particular behavioral difficulties. Each of the contributors to this *Handbook* present unique and innovative multifaceted parent training formats. Many of the authors are acknowledged pioneers and specialists in the fields of parent training, developmental issues, and child therapy. They embody an impressive array of well-versed and experienced researchers, clinicians, and professionals. They are practitioners who teach, train, assess, evaluate, and contribute to the growing body of parent intervention and parent training literature. The book has five parts, each of which focuses on specific areas of parent-child stressors, problematic behaviors, and childhood disorder categories.

The parent training strategies of the authors in Part One of the *Handbook* specifically address the central theme of the book, prevention. They have developed and implemented intervention formats that reduce at-risk behaviors and enhance the existing skills and protective elements, factors that strengthen the family members, that may already exist within the parent-child relationship and family structure but need to be identified and revitalized.

In Chapter 1, the authors offer compelling reasons why parent training programs should extend beyond middle-class socioeconomic strata. They offer a preventive program that was created in collaboration with a Parent Advisory Council that was composed of African American and Latino parents from various neighborhoods in Chicago. The program instructs parents of 2- to 5-year-old children in nonmaternal care. They counter the ways in which parents and children unknowingly reinforce each others' negative and destructive behaviors and offer insights and practical strategies to prevent the development of conflicts and stressors.

Chapter 2 focuses on preventing and ameliorating the damaging long-term effects that divorce can have on children and families. The authors give an interesting and detailed description of the New Beginnings Program, an empirically-based format for children from divorced families that uses custodial mothers as agents of constructive change. They present an interesting notion of the divorce equation. It focuses on the synergistic effects that occur when taking into account the difficulties children have adjusting to divorce plus the problems mothers have adjusting. It is a preventive strategy that teaches a number of relationship-building skills that can be generalized to an array of situations and harbors a good deal of promise and hope in preventing and resolving parent, child, family problems.

In Part Two, the authors tackle the difficulties and challenges that confront parents with children who experience developmental disorders. The contributors in this section identify and address problems that may interfere with the natural process of physical, cognitive, emotional, social, and psychological growth and development.

Chapter 3 presents a comprehensive program for providing training to parents of children with autism. The authors differentiate the goals of various types of parent training programs that deal with this disorder. Their chapter centers on a group program connected to a school. They offer a number of guidelines to help develop, structure, and implement intervention strategies to address and modify the unique problems experienced by the parents of children with the autism spectrum disorder and to prevent a resurgence of parent-child conflicts.

In Chapter 4, the authors discuss and describe an inventive program that centers on relieving the major problems that parents of children with Asperger syndrome face on a daily basis. The program they elucidate covers some primary and essential components of their intervention strategy and seeks to instill a sense of competence in the parents and reduce the immediate and long-term problems that typically surface in children with Asperger syndrome.

The authors in Part Three of the *Handbook* direct attention to internalizing disorders. They apply treatment maneuvers aimed at preventing, reducing, and modifying the negative impact and problems associated with childhood anxiety and school refusal issues.

In Chapter 5, the authors present the inventive FRIENDS for life program, providing an in-depth session-by-session description of an approach that can help children control stress and instruct parents in anxiety-reducing ploys that can be conveyed to their children. The authors offer strategies that can help children gain self-awareness, foster reciprocity, and facilitate problem-solving and coping skills.

Chapter 6 uses a muticomponent assessment process and intervention modality that identifies and modifies some of the primary factors that lead to children's school refusal. The authors' approach addresses the divergent and specific reasons why children may refuse school. An extensive spectrum of school refusal problems are discussed. The authors identify a number of variables that have been associated with school refusal. They, then, employ a program that can be generalized effectively in intervening in a wide range of school refusal situations.

Part Four of this *Handbook* focus on externalizing disorders. This category of disorders typically include behaviors that turn against others. By their very nature, these disorders negatively affect the child, the family, the school, and society as a whole. The impact of these externalizing disorders have far-reaching and, at times, devastating effects. This part of the book describes creative intervention programs that seek to prevent, modify, and control the disruptive behaviors associated with physically abusive families, oppositional behavior, comorbid Attention-Deficit/Hyperactivity Disorder and Oppositional Defiant Disorder, and aggressive and maladaptive behaviors.

Chapter 7 introduces an empirically-based and systematic treatment, the Triple P–Positive Parenting Program. It is a multilevel public health approach that aims to enhance family protective factors and reduce family risk factors. The strategy uses clear-cut positive parenting principles to instruct parents in meeting the unique needs of their children and family. The approach is dedicated to helping parents become autonomous agents of positive change for their children and themselves.

In Chapter 8, the authors offer a timely parent-child intervention format focused on reducing physical abuse within families. The authors develop a treatment program that includes coaching and coding parents as they interact with their children. Their approach involves two treatment phases, the Child Directed Interaction (CDI) phase and the Parent Directed Interaction (PDI) phase. The parents are instructed in the use of nonaggressive and noncoercive behavioral management skills. In addition, the authors demonstrate the value and efficacy of applying specific practical skills and tools, such as relaxation techniques and time-out procedures.

Chapter 9 gives us an intervention strategy that prevents and modifies problems through a format designed to reduce the need for punishment and power assertion in the treatment of children with oppositional behavior and related problems. The author presents a success-focused intervention approach that incorporates "errorless" management techniques based on the principles of operant conditioning. The parents benefiting from this approach learn to use the Compliance Probability Checklist. They learn the value of praise and reinforcement in issuing requests that increase the probability of compliance and success.

Chapter 10 presents a well-documented and practical intervention approach, the Incredible Years Parent Program. The author spells out the structure, function, and format of the program, emphasizing the flexibility of the intervention strategy and the ways in which it can be tailored to the individual developmental needs of the children and their families. Parents are taught how to identify viable goals for themselves and their children. The author discusses the impact of various attachment patterns and styles, also focusing on the particular challenges of parenting children with oppositional defiant disorder or conduct disorder and the added problems of parenting children who are comorbid with an Attention Deficit Disorder or an Attention-Deficit/Hyperactivity Disorder.

Chapter 11 continues the discussion of the complexities and challenges involved in treating comorbid issues. The author describes a thorough and systematic treatment strategy for training parents of children with comorbid Attention-Deficit/Hyperactivity Disorder and Oppositional Defiant Disorder. This complex interaction of behavioral problems compounds and exacerbates parental stressors and heightens the urgency for immediate and effective preventive and intervention modalities. The author discusses a number of crucial objectives that can help parents in their struggles, offering a helpful behavioral management flowchart that aids parents in the formation and application of a logical sequence of skills that parents can learn to help them manage the disruptive and disturbing behaviors of ADHD/ODD children.

In Chapter 12, the authors spell out an innovative treatment approach to address and prevent the problems that parents encounter in working with school age children who act-out aggressively. The authors discuss some of the major underlying premises and differences in using responsive parent training (RPT) in contrast to parent management training (PMT). The responsive parent-training modal offers an organized framework and set of principles for working with parents of aggressive children. The authors give essential tips and techniques for facilitating listening skills between practitioners and parents and between parents and children.

Part Five focuses on some childhood disorders that do not readily fit into the internalizing/externalizing categories but, nevertheless offer their own set of unique and demanding challenges for parents and clinicians. These include some of the problems characteristically associated with primary enuresis, substance use and delinquent behaviors, and children's sleep problems.

Chapter 13 offers a home-based treatment intervention for primary enuresis. The authors open their chapter by emphasizing the necessity for a close collaboration between behavioral psychologists, pediatricians, and parents. They then demonstrate how this alliance accomplishes significant and positive benefits and results for children and families. The authors offer some direction for building and using strategies that can eliminate bed wetting, such as: instructional and treatment approaches, wall charts, and monitoring devices like the urine alarm. Essentially, the authors focus on an innovative and empirically-based Full Spectrum Home Training Program and the development of self-control training and damage-control methods for reinstating the child's faltering sense of self-esteem.

In Chapter 14, the authors present a practical and timely program that is grounded in empirical research and experience. Their intervention aims at training parents of adolescents with substance use and delinquent problems. They offer instructional tables and charts that help parents recognize, access, and develop protective factors as well as identify and eliminate potential risk factors with their child and in their particular situation. In addition, they offer specific and proven strategies for building relationships as well as techniques for praising adolescents, reducing negative behaviors, and improving parent-child communication. These are skills that can certainly generalize and benefit the child, parent, and family unit in a number of situations and circumstances.

In each of the chapters in this *Handbook,* the various authors offer empirically-based methodological intervention approaches that are melded with their own expertise and treatment experiences. The parent invention training formats that are found in this book are grounded in behavioral principles and social learning theory. Relying on these principles as their backdrop, the various authors have developed and implemented their own specific intervention formats to identify, clarity, assess, evaluate, and treat a myriad of disruptive, disturbing, and dysfunctional childhood behavioral problems. They have also designed parent intervention training programs that not only reduce and mollify childhood conflicts and troubled behaviors but also help parents to identify essential protective factors as well as risk factors within their respective families. The authors use divergent parent training intervention formats that seek to improve the relationship between parent and child as well as establish a format for constructive relationships. The various treatment approaches in this book also aim to impart a sense of competence, pride, achievement, and self-efficacy in parents as well as children. With self-assurance, determination, and the support gleaned through the different and unique intervention approaches, parents and children can learn how to generalize the newly acquired skills and intervention strategies and effectively apply them in a variety of problematic situations. The authors in this *Handbook* not only aim to help parents resolve their children's problems but also prevent these problems before they have a chance to develop, ferment, and undermine the integrity and fabric of the family and the immediate and long-term well-being of the parents and the children.

REFERENCES

Ashery, R. S., Robertson, E. B., & Kumpfer, K. L. (Eds.). (1998). Drug abuse prevention through family interventions. *NIDA Research Monograph No. 177.* Washington, DC: U.S. Government Printing Office.

Bemporad, J. (1978). Psychotherapy of depression in children and adolescents. In S. Arieti & J. Bemprad (Eds.), *Severe and mild depression* (pp. 344–357). New York: Basic Books.

Blechman, E. A. (1981). Toward comprehensive behavioral family intervention: An algorithm for matching families and interventions. *Behavior Modifications, 5,* 221–236.

Blechman, E. A. (1985). *Solving child behavior problems: At home and at school.* Champaign, IL: Research Press.

Braswell, L. (1991). Involving parents in cognitive-behavioral therapy with children and adolescents. In P. C. Kendall (Ed.), *Child and adolescent therapy.* New York: Guilford Press.

Collins, W. A., Maccoby, E. E., Steinberg, L., Hetherington, E. M., & Bornstein, M. H. (2000). Contemporary research on parenting: The case for nature and nurture. *American Psychologist, 55,* 218–232.

Corby, E. A., & Russell, J. C. (1997). Substance abuse risk reduction: Verbal mediational training for children by parental and non-parental models. *Substance Abuse, 18,* 145–164.

Ducharme, J. M., Atkinson, L., & Poulton, L. (2000). Success-based non-coercive treatment of oppositional behavior in children from violent homes. *Journal of the American Academy of Child and Adolescent Psychiatry, 39,* 995–1003.

Ducharme, J. M., & Van Houten, R. (1994). Operant extinction in the treatment of severe maladaptive behavior: Adapting research to practice. *Behavior Modification, 18,* 139–170.

Flanagan, S., Adams, H. E., & Forehand, R. (1979). A comparison of four instructional techniques for teaching parents how to use time-out. *Behavior Therapy, 10,* 94–102.

Forehand, R. L., & McMahon, R. (1981). *Helping the noncompliant child.* New York: Guilford Press.

Freud, S. (1955). The analysis of a phobia in a 5-year-old boy. In J. Strachey (Ed. & Trans.), *The standard edition of the complete psychological works of Sigmund Freud* (Vol. 10, pp. 149–289). London: Hogarth Press. (Original work published 1909)

Graziano, A. M. (1977). Parents as behavior therapists. *Progress in Behavior Modification, 4,* 252–298.

Haley, J. (1976). *Problem solving therapy.* San Francisco: Jossey-Bass.

Hawkins, R. P., Peterson, R. F., Schweid, E., & Bijou, S. W. (1966). Behavior therapy in the home: Amelioration of problem parent-child relations with the parent in a therapeutic role. *Journal of Experimental Child Psychology, 4,* 99–107.

Ialongo, N., Poduska, J., Werthamer, L., & Kellam, S. (2001). The distal impact of two first-grade preventive interventions on conduct problems and disorder in early adolescence. *Journal of Emotional and Behavioral Disorders, 9,* 146–160.

Minuchin, S. (1974). *Families and family therapy.* Cambridge, MA: Harvard University Press.

Moreland, J. R., Schwebel, A. J., Beck, S., & Wells, R. (1982). Parents as therapists: A review of the behavior therapy parent training literature—1975 to 1981. *Behavior Modification, 6,* 250–276.

Nay, W. R. (1975). A systematic comparison of instructional techniques for parents. *Behavior Therapy, 6,* 14–21.

O'Dell, S. L., Flynn, J. M., & Benlolo, L. A. (1979). A comparison of parent training techniques in child behavior modification. *Journal of Behavior Therapy and Experimental Psychiatry, 8,* 261–268.

Patterson, G. R. (1969). Behavioral techniques based on social learning: An additional base for developing behavioral modification technologies. In C. M. Franks (Ed.), *Behavior therapy: Appraisal and status* (pp. 341–374). New York: McGraw-Hill.

Sanders, M. R., & Dadds, M. R. (1993). *Behavior family interventions.* Needham Heights, MA: Allyn & Bacon.

Sanders, M. R., & Glynn, T. (1981). Training parents in behavioral self-management: An analysis of generalization and maintenance. *Journal of Applied Behavior Analysis, 14,* 223–227.

Stambor, Z. (2006, June). Monitor on psychology. *American Psychological Association,* 30–31.

Wahler, R. C., Winkel, G. H., Peterson, R. F., & Morrison, D. C. (1965). Mothers as behavior therapists for their own children. *Behaviour Research and Therapy, 3,* 113–134.

Webster-Stratton, C. (1998). Preventing conduct problems in Head Start children: Strengthening parenting competencies. *Journal of Consulting and Clinical Psychology, 66,* 715–730.

Webster-Stratton, C., & Herbert, M. (1994). *Troubled families-problem children: Working with parents: A collaborative process.* Chichester, England: Wiley.

Webster-Stratton, C., & Lindsay, D. W. (1999). Social competence and early-onset conduct problems: Issues in assessment. *Journal of Child Clinical Psychology, 28,* 25–93.

Webster-Stratton, C., Reid, J., & Hammond, M. (2001). Preventing conduct problems, promoting social competence: A parent and teacher training partnership in Head Start. *Journal of Clinical Child Psychology, 30,* 282–302.

Zacker, J. (1978). Parents as change agents. *American Journal of Psychotherapy, 37*(4), 572–582.

PART ONE

PREVENTION

WITHOUT QUESTION, the goal of all the chapters in this book is to prevent the development of disruptive, dysfunctional, and destructive behaviors among children and adolescents. The aim is to eliminate behaviors that put a rift between parent-child interactions and relationships, lead to negative and undesirable behaviors, and, in general, place children at risk for problems at home, in school, and with peers, and have the potential to contribute to current and future stressors. The authors in Part One address prevention as the central theme of their approaches. It is easier and certainly more preferable to prevent problems rather than attempt to resolve them once they have infected the child, parents, and family. In a very real sense, prevention is the best and most effective means of parenting.

In Chapter 1, Gross, Garvey, Julion, and Fogg present a preventive parent training strategy that addresses the specific needs of ethnic minority parents. As the authors point out, many parent training strategies were developed using middle-class socioeconomic strata and European-American populations. Their program seeks to extend the advantages of parent training beyond the constraints of these parameters. Their preventive program, created in collaboration with a Parent Advisory Council that was composed of African American and Latino parents, takes great efforts to ensure that the data included are culturally and contextually relevant for the minority and low-income parents in their study.

Their chapter describes the theory that underlies the Chicago Parent Training Program. The authors acknowledge their debt to the pioneering research of Patterson, Webster-Stratton, and Hancock. They emphasize the implementation of the community-based program to facilitate

1

constructive and effective intervention for parents of 2- to 5-year-old children in nonmaternal care. The study focuses on a day-care population and indicates that parent training in child care centers may moderate any possible effects of child care on the development of potential behavioral difficulties. Their approach prevents the ways in which parents and children, without realizing it, engage in behaviors that facilitate conflict in parent-child interactions. They discuss ways in which children and parents unwittingly reinforce each others' negative behaviors. Behaviors that are rewarded with attention tend to be repeated, even negative behaviors.

Gross, Garvey, Julion, and Fogg employ inventive and contemporary techniques. For example, they use videotapes that reenact real life vignettes as training tools. They offer four problem-solving scenarios to help parents develop effective parenting skills. Parents are given opportunities to practice and hone their new skills. They are given handouts, homework, and other useful instructional tools. Finally, it is worth noting that the preventive Chicago Parent Program was designed and implemented in collaboration with the parents who participated in, and benefited from, the program. Indeed, everyone who works with children and parents can benefit from this empirically based and practical study.

In the second chapter, Wolchik, Sandler, Weiss, and Winslow discuss some of the devastating and long-term effects of divorce on children and families. They describe the New Beginnings Program, an empirically validated program for children from divorced families that use custodial mothers as agents of change. The New Beginnings Program was designed to reduce mental health problems and promote competencies following divorce by reducing risk factors. It also endeavors to increase the children's protective resources. This cognitive-behavioral program places a strong emphasis on the development and enhancement of skill acquisition.

After describing the theoretical framework of their approach, the authors provide a general overview, followed by a description of multiple and invaluable sessions. They employ a variety of techniques to enhance the quality of the mother-child relationship. The newly acquired skills build on each other. The authors offer us a glimpse into the didactic and experiential skills that are taught within the various group sessions. They give a clear description of the purpose and content of each session.

The authors pose an interesting notion of the divorce equation. It is used to graphically illustrate the idea that the difficulties children have adjusting to divorce plus the problems mothers have adjusting to divorce have synergistic effects that create a sum greater than the total of its parts. It conveys to mothers that the problems they experience with their youngsters are understandable, predictable, and, in fact, common following divorce. This approach offers mothers in the New Beginnings Program a good deal of hope and promise for improvements and constructive modifications.

In presenting solutions to the problems that follow divorce, the authors use and illustrate relationship building skills, such as family fun time, home-practice assignments, one-on-one time, "catch 'em being good," and related skills. Their approach also emphasizes and teaches the art of effective listening. A number of strategies are used to impart these skills, including group leaders role-playing and video demonstrations. When those occasions occur when listening is not enough, mothers are taught how to protect children from witnessing and being overwhelmed by interparental conflicts. Every safeguard is employed to ensure that children do not feel that they are caught in the middle, feeling torn between an alliance to both parents. The mothers are also shown how to identify and form realistic expectations for the misbehaviors they want to address and decrease. Mothers learn how to monitor and modify their children's misbehaviors. All the cognitive-behavioral maneuvers are aimed at instilling effective discipline and decreasing unwanted behaviors.

The authors also describe the training, supervision, and general guidelines for group leaders. These practical training directives are complemented by a discussion of research findings on the efficacy of the New Beginnings Program. A case study illustrates how the strategies of the program effected significant positive changes, improved the relationships between mothers and children, and facilitated constructive and desirable behaviors in the children.

It is not difficult to see the positive wide range of implications and applications of the innovative programs offered by the Chicago Parent Program (Chapter 1) and the New Beginnings Program (Chapter 2).

CHAPTER 1

Preventive Parent Training with Low-Income, Ethnic Minority Families of Preschoolers

DEBORAH GROSS, CHRISTINE GARVEY,
WRENETHA A. JULION, and LOUIS FOGG

[Parenthood] is the biggest on-the-job training program ever.
—Erma Bombeck, *Motherhood:*
The Second Oldest Profession

To OBTAIN a driver's license in the state of Illinois, one must complete up to 25 hours of supervised driving and pass a vision, written, and practical driving test under the watchful eye of government evaluators. The vehicle must also pass inspection showing evidence of working headlights, brake lights, turn signals, and back-up lights and proof of insurance. The theory behind this costly and lengthy effort is to create safe and competent drivers. In contrast, parents receive no training. Yet, the need to become a safe and competent parent is no less critical. In this chapter, we describe the Chicago Parent Program, designed to train safe and competent parents capable of negotiating the often difficult road of raising very young children.

This study was supported by the grant from the National Institute for Nursing Research, #R01 NR004085.

Numerous reviews of parent training research have supported this model as an effective method for reducing child behavior problems (Barlow & Stewart-Brown, 2000; Lundahl, Risser, & Lovejoy, 2006; Serketich & Dumas, 1996). However, most parent training programs were developed using middle-class European-American samples (Forehand & Kotchick, 1996; Martinez & Eddy, 2005). This bias in parent training programs may be one reason why socioeconomic disadvantage is consistently identified as a predictor of drop out and diminished intervention effectiveness (Dumas & Wahler, 1983; Reyno & McGrath, 2006). To address this limitation, the Chicago Parent Program was created in collaboration with a Parent Advisory Council (PAC) comprised of African American and Latino parents from different Chicago neighborhoods. Using an advisory council ensured that the information included in this program would be culturally and contextually relevant for ethnic minority and low-income parents raising children in urban communities.

Many outstanding parent training programs were originally created for the purposes of treating children with or at high risk for developing disruptive behavior disorders. The Chicago Parent Program was originally developed as a health promotion/prevention intervention. There were three reasons for this decision. First, if we target only parents of behaviorally disordered preschoolers, we address the needs of a small, highly select group of children and miss a much larger population of children and parents with varying degrees of behavioral difficulty.

Second, epidemiologic data suggests that 5% to 13% of all preschool children are rated as having moderate to high levels of externalizing behavior problems (Lavigne et al., 1996). Among low-income preschool children, behavior problem rates are twice as high (Gross, Sambrook, & Fogg, 1999; Rose, Rose, & Feldman, 1989). Most of these children will not receive mental health services to treat the behavior or the underlying family issues that support the problematic behavior (Forness et al., 1998; Razzino, New, Lewin, & Joseph, 2004; U.S. Public Health Service, 2000). However, parents may be more willing to seek guidance about accessing appropriate services when they are engaged in community-based interventions that focus on strengths and skill-building rather than parent-child deficits.

Third, our ability to accurately identify which toddlers and preschool children have behavior disorders remains limited. The diagnostic criteria for distinguishing developmentally appropriate behavior from pathological defiance, hyperactivity, and aggression are not well established (Campbell, Shaw, & Gilliom, 2000; Egger & Angold, 2006; Wakschlag & Keenan, 2001). Though many will outgrow their behavior problems, a significant portion of young children with externalizing problems will continue to exhibit difficulties in elementary school (Campbell, 1997). Thus, parent training during the toddler/preschool years is likely to have the greatest benefit when a wide net is cast and is offered in the community as a health promotion/prevention intervention.

This chapter describes the (a) theory underlying the Chicago Parent Program, (b) role of the PAC in the development of the program, and (c) implementation of the Chicago Parent Program as a community-based health promotion/prevention intervention for parents of 2- to 5-year-old children in day care. The results of a randomized clinical trial evaluating its effectiveness for reducing behavior problems among young children in day care is also presented.

PARENT TRAINING IN CHILD CARE CENTERS

According to data from the U.S. Census Bureau (Overturf Johnson, 2005), approximately 11 million (59%) children under 5 years of age are in nonmaternal care. The largest portion, over 4 million children, receive care in center-based facilities such as day care, preschool, and Head Start centers. Among low-income families, almost 30% of preschool children are enrolled in child care centers. Thus, child care centers serve a large number of young children, providing an unparalleled opportunity for reaching low-income families and providing health promotion and prevention services.

A recent study sponsored by the National Institute of Child Health and Human Development (NICHD) provided one of the most extensive examinations to date of early child care and developmental outcomes in the first 5 years of life (NICHD Early Child Care Research Network, 2006; Patterson, 1982). Based on their longitudinal assessments of children from birth to 4.5 years, young children engaged in more child care hours had more classroom behavior problems and more caregiver-child conflict than children with fewer child care hours. However, positive parenting behavior (defined by observed maternal sensitivity and responsiveness) was an important moderator of these effects. Indeed, when positive parenting was added into the analytic model, it emerged as the strongest predictor of positive outcome among children in day care.

These results suggest that (a) the use of center-based child care in the United States is extensive, (b) effective parent training programs delivered in child care centers may moderate the negative effects of extensive child care on the development of behavior problems, and (c) imbedding parent training programs in child care centers has the potential for reaching a large number of young children and their families who could benefit from this powerful health promotion/prevention intervention. In addition, day care centers provide a natural point of contact for families with young children who might not otherwise seek mental health services. Although the Chicago Parent Program was not solely designed for use in child care centers, this chapter describes the implementation of this program in day care centers serving low-income families in Chicago.

THEORETICAL BACKGROUND

The development of the Chicago Parent Program was heavily influenced by the work of Gerald Patterson, Carolyn Webster-Stratton, and our Parent Advisory Council. Patterson (1982) proposed that parents and children inadvertently behave in ways that promote conflictual parent-child interactions. According to his coercive family process model, young children use high rates of aversive behaviors to stimulate parent attention. Parental attention to these aversive behaviors tends to reinforce the negative child behavior and increase the likelihood of reoccurrence. For example, parents may give into the behavior (e.g., give the child what she wants) or use negative tactics to coerce the child to stop the behavior (e.g., scolding, nagging, threatening, spanking). With both types of management strategies, children's aversive behaviors are reinforced by the parent's attention.

According to Patterson's theory, children simultaneously reinforce their parents' use of coercive management strategies. For example, a young child may momentarily stop the aversive behavior in response to a threatened spanking. This reinforces the parent's reliance on threats and spankings. When the child resumes the aversive behavior to regain the parent's attention, the parent is most likely to threaten the child again with possible escalation into acting on the threat. A "reinforcement trap" ensues whereby the child's negative behaviors escalate while the parent's management strategies become increasingly more punitive and coercive.

Consistent with the coercive family process model, the core objective of the Chicago Parent Program is to teach parents principles of effective child behavior management that avoid reinforcement traps and promote positive parent-child interactions. For example, the guiding principle emphasized throughout the program is: *If you want to see a behavior again, give it your attention. If you do not want to see a behavior again, do not give it your attention.* Typically, parents do the exact opposite. That is, parents say very little to their children when they comply with requests, share their toys, or help their siblings. But they say a great deal to their children when they are noncompliant, horde their toys, and fight with siblings.

It is important to note that the two primary antecedents to the reinforcement traps are (a) coercive interchanges initiated by children to gain parental attention and (b) coercive interchanges initiated by parents to gain child compliance. Therefore, the Chicago Parent Program includes training sessions addressing each antecedent. There are four sessions that focus on using positive parent attention to reinforce desired child behavior and four sessions on discipline strategies that encourage child cooperation without nagging, scolding, or hitting.

Research suggests that stress can exacerbate parents' reliance on coercive discipline strategies (Eamon & Zuehl, 2001; Mistry, Vandewater, Huston, & McLloyd, 2002). Parents may learn new techniques for managing their children's misbehavior but high stress and faulty problem-solving skills can diminish their ability to effectively and consistently use them. Therefore, two sessions are also included on stress management and problem-solving strategies.

Although the theoretical content of the Chicago Parent Program is consistent with the groundbreaking work led by Patterson, the structure of the program is largely modeled after the highly innovative work of Carolyn Webster-Stratton (Webster-Stratton & Hancock, 1998). This includes the use of videotaped vignettes for stimulating group discussion among parents, the use of a "collaborative process model" for engaging parents in the intervention, and weekly practice assignments for applying at home what they learned in the parent group.

Webster-Stratton pioneered the use of videotape modeling with group discussion (Webster-Stratton, 1982). Videotape modeling capitalizes on the strengths of live modeling approaches and direct therapist coaching but at much lower cost. Parents watch and discuss brief vignettes of parent and child models engaged in multiple situations typical of families with young children. The vignettes are shown to parents by trained group leaders who facilitate group discussion of the relevant aspects of the modeled interactions and encourage parents' ideas and problem solving. The vignettes are used to stimulate group discussion rather than model "correct" ways of interacting with children. Group leaders help parents tailor the ideas they learn during the parent group discussion to their parenting goals and values. A manual standardizes the discussion questions and reminds group leaders of important points parents should glean from each vignette. Parents also receive weekly handouts summarizing each session and homework assignments designed to help parents practice what they have learned (see Components of the Chicago Parent Program).

This intervention structure has been shown to be highly effective in numerous parent training studies (Gross, Fogg, & Tucker, 1995; Gross et al., 2003; Kumpfer & Alvarado, 2003; Webster-Stratton, 1990, 1998b). However, parents' efforts to use parenting programs can be derailed if the modeled scenes do not resonate with their lives and the strategies promoted in the program do not have social validity. This led us to conclude that the most useful parent training program for low-income and ethnic minority families will have to be developed in collaboration with parents from the target population. Thus, the third key influence in the development of the Chicago Parent Program was the PAC. The PAC guided us in the development of relevant topics, strategies, vignettes, group discussion questions, and handouts. The following section will describe the role of the PAC in the development of the Chicago Parent Program.

DEVELOPMENT OF THE CHICAGO PARENT PROGRAM

In 2001, we were funded to develop and test a parent program that would be culturally and contextually relevant for low-income ethnic minority parents of young children. We convened a PAC of seven African American and five Latino parents from different Chicago communities. This group advised us on the kinds of situations they found most challenging as parents, the kinds of videotaped scenes they wanted to see that truly resonated with their lives, and admonished us about advocating parenting strategies they believed were steeped in White, middle-class thinking. Although the principles taught in the Chicago Parent Program are empirically supported, the PAC was instrumental in helping us shape and present these principles in ways that were culturally and contextually relevant.

The situations our PAC thought were most challenging for parents included children having tantrums, children misbehaving in public, parents trying to get children dressed and ready for school and themselves to work on time in the morning, parents coming home after work at the end of the day and getting dinner ready when children are demanding of their time and attention, sibling rivalry, and getting children to bed at night. These situations were the daily, stressful scenes of their lives during which their children were most likely to misbehave and they were most likely to feel inadequate as parents.

The PAC explained their skepticism about common, empirically-supported strategies such as time-outs and parent-child play. Next, we discuss some examples of concepts and strategies the PAC discussed with us and how their ideas were incorporated into the Chicago Parent Program.

CHILD-CENTERED TIME

In the 1960s, Connie Hanff (1969) described child-directed play as an innovative technique for promoting positive parent-child interaction. The principle behind child-directed play is that these interactions build positive relationships between parents and children by teaching parents how to "follow the child's lead." When "following the child's lead," parents might describe aloud what the child is doing, imitate the child's behavior, or praise the child's efforts. Child-directed play is intended to create a fun experience at the child's level of interest that promotes exploration, learning, and self-esteem and reduces parents' control over the interaction. It is a popular strategy built into many parent training programs including the Incredible Years and Parent-Child Interaction Therapy (Eyberg & Boggs, 1989; Uzgiris & Raeff, 1995; Webster-Stratton & Hancock, 1998).

However, the parents in our advisory group said that they did not support the idea that parents should play with children. Rather, they believed that children should play with children. As a result, the important principle of "following the child's lead" for building positive parent-child rapport would be lost if it focused solely on parent-child play. Instead, we developed the concept of "child-centered time" in which parents followed their child's lead but in a variety of situations parents might normally find themselves with their children. For example, one vignette shows a father following his 3-year-old daughter's lead while making chocolate milk. Another scene shows a mother following her children's lead while making pancakes.

Spanking versus Time-Out

The PAC was very vocal about their beliefs about spanking and time-outs. These parents reported that most families they know spank their children and their children have not become aggressive or delinquent. They told us that if you communicate to parents in a parent training program that spanking is not acceptable, you will lose the parents' interest. Moreover, the parents will still spank their children but not disclose it. The PAC viewed time-outs as ineffective and a prime example of why they think White children are "spoiled" and "ill-mannered."

These views are not unique to our PAC. Research has shown that low-income and ethnic minority parents tend to view time-outs as less acceptable and spanking as a more acceptable form of discipline than do middle-income and European-American parents (Corral-Verdugo, Frias-Armenta, Romero, & Munoz, 1995; Heffer & Kelley, 1987). Moreover, the PAC's views about spanking have received some support in the research literature. Although some studies show positive correlations between physical discipline and child behavior problems (Strassberg, Dodge, & Pettit, 1994; Strauss, Sugarman, & Giles-Sims, 1997), other research suggests nonabusive physical discipline has no association with child behavior problems among African American children (Deater-Deckard, Dodge, Bates, & Pettit, 1996; Gunnoe & Mariner, 1997), particularly when maternal emotional support is high (McLloyd & Smith, 2002).

Nonetheless, there are many studies demonstrating the effectiveness of time-out procedures for reducing negative child behavior (Fabiano et al.,

2004; Jones, Sloane, & Roberts, 1992; Walle, Hobbs, & Caldwell, 1984). We asked the advisory council what they disliked about time-out and why they thought it was an ineffective discipline strategy. According to the PAC, time-outs were ineffective for three reasons: (1) they believed children did not care about being sent to a corner or a chair for a few minutes; (2) giving a time-out was seen as being too lenient and failing to communicate to the child the seriousness of the infraction; (3) Finally, time-outs were viewed as ineffective because they could not be used in public which is where many children misbehave.

These concerns led to the inclusion of two vignettes in which an African American mother gives her 5-year-old son a time-out in a laundromat. Of particular note is the obvious look of sadness and disappointment on this child's face as he is sent to a different part of the laundromat (but within the mother's view) to take a 5-minute time-out. It is followed by a second vignette showing his delight at being brought back into the playful interaction his mother is having with his younger brother when the time-out is over.

Since every parent in the advisory council had been spanked as a child, we asked the group the following question: "When you were spanked as a child, how did you know that you were still loved?" This question led to a frank and emotional discussion about how they had been disciplined as children, what was painful and should never have been allowed to happen, and what was effective and why. The outcome was the development of a list of Eight Keys to Effective Discipline now incorporated into the program. These eight keys to effective discipline are:

1. *Discipline is tied to a specific behavior:* Children need to know the specific thing they did wrong and what needs to change.
2. *The punishment should fit the crime:* Harsh punishments make children angry and hopeless and make behavior worse.
3. *Discipline is predictable:* The discipline should happen whenever the misbehavior happens, not just when parents have had a bad day.
4. *Discipline is controlled:* Parents should never lose control over what they are saying or doing.
5. *Discipline without rage:* Parents should never lose control over what they are feeling.
6. *Discipline without humiliation:* Even when children are being disciplined, parents should always respect a child's dignity.
7. *Discipline with a positive ending:* When it's over, it's over. Children need to be allowed to reconnect with the parent in a positive and loving way.
8. *Children should know they are loved even though the misbehavior is not:* Children need to know that, no matter what, they are loved.

ROUTINES AND TRADITIONS

In our prior research, we worked with several day care centers located in housing projects managed by the Chicago Housing Authority. One day care teacher explained to us that over the 35 years she had been working with children, one of the biggest changes she had witnessed was the loss of routines and traditions in the children's lives. Many children in her classroom had no experience with eating together as a family. In addition, some came to day care exhausted because there was no set bedtime or bedtime routine at home. Bedtime occurred haphazardly, often based on when the parent was tired. As a result, she believed that many of the children's behavior problems could be traced to sleep deprivation.

We brought this information to the PAC. They agreed that many of the families they knew had few routines or traditions in their lives. Routines seem to require too much energy and traditions were being lost; life was too stressful and schedules were too unpredictable. Yet, research has shown that routines and traditions in children's lives tend to decrease stress and increase predictability, and are associated with more positive outcomes in young children (Fiese, 2002; Kliewer & King, 1998; Kubicek, 2002). The advisory council agreed that routines and traditions were very important in family life and each could recall a routine or tradition that had been important to them while growing up. We discussed what made those experiences meaningful to them and incorporated those ideas into a session on family routines and traditions.

RECREATING REAL LIFE ON VIDEOTAPE

Once we had the information we needed from the PAC on the content of the program, we hired a local production company to help us cast and film 13 Chicago families in their homes, the grocery store, and a laundromat. Of these families, 46% were African American, 23% were Latino, and 31% were non-Latino White. The on-screen narrator is a Latina. All of the families had at least one preschool child and all had at least two children ranging in age from 6 months to 12 years.

We edited over 50 hours of film to obtain 157 vignettes of parents and children engaged in a range of situations the PAC advised us to record. These include mealtimes, bedtimes, children misbehaving in public, children misbehaving at home, parents disciplining their children, parents under stress, getting children ready in the morning for day care, homework rituals, children being uncooperative in the grocery store, parents dealing with bored children in a laundromat, sibling rivalry, family disagreements about child rearing, and parents working with teachers to address behavior problems in the classroom. There are also many scenes of cooperative children and families having fun together.

There are four problem-solving scenarios used to help parents develop effective problem-solving skills toward the end of the program series. The first situation includes a married couple arguing about money in front of the children. As the discussion progresses, the children's play becomes louder and more frantic. This scene is used to help parents understand the effect of parental arguments on children's behavior and the importance of finding appropriate times for these problem-solving discussions.

The second scenario is of a mother and nonresident father problem solving their conflicts related to visitation schedules. The couple initially gets off to a rocky start but then begin working on a plan for communicating more clearly about child visits.

The third problem-solving scenario is of a mother and day care teacher discussing their disagreement on how the child's misbehavior is managed in the classroom. In this situation, the mother's 4-year-old child is not tired after lunch when all of the children are expected to lie down for a two-hour nap. As a result, the girl becomes disruptive to the other children around her and the teacher ultimately places her on a time-out. The mother believes that the teacher's expectation that her daughter should lie quietly for two hours is unrealistic and that she should not be punished. The teacher believes the expectation is appropriate and, based on years of teaching experience, believes the child is capable of better behavior. This problem-solving situation stimulates a great deal of conversation about how to work with teachers when parents disagree with their classroom rules.

The fourth problem-solving situation includes a grandmother and her daughter, a teen mother, discussing their disagreements on how the teen mother harshly disciplines the 4-year-old grandchild. The grandmother and mother each describe the problems as they see them. As the situation evolves, the problems are clarified and together they create a plan for how the grandmother will support the mother's efforts to assume a more maternal role and how the mother will use more positive strategies to discipline her 4-year-old. This situation is highly relevant for many of the families who live in multigenerational homes.

To ensure that the selected scenes would generate discussion in parents groups, the PAC rated each vignette along two dimensions: (a) usefulness (i.e., would teach parents something important and/or stimulate discussion among parents in a group) and (b) relevance (i.e., shows a situation to which people they knew would be able to relate). All scenes were ranked by PAC members on a scale of 1 (not useful or not relevant) to 5 (very useful or very relevant). Only scenes receiving mean scores of 4 (useful or relevant) or greater were selected for inclusion in the program.

COMPONENTS OF THE CHICAGO
PARENT PROGRAM

In addition to the vignettes, a group leader manual standardizes the group sessions. The manual includes transcriptions of all narration and dialogue in the vignettes, group leader discussion questions, and notes to the group leader highlighting select aspects of scenes and suggestions on how to respond to some of the most common concerns parents may raise during the discussion of the scene. Handouts summarizing the important points from each session are included as well as weekly practice assignments for parents to try at home.

Two-hour parent group sessions are conducted once a week over 11 consecutive weeks at the child's day care center on week day evenings. Free child care and food are provided at all sessions to reduce barriers to attendance. At the eleventh session, parents and group leaders schedule a booster session to be held about 2 months later. The purpose of the booster session is to discuss challenges parents have faced using the program without the ongoing support of the parent group. A topical outline of the 12 sessions is presented in Table 1.1.

Although the vignettes become the focal point for each group session, the key ingredient to effective delivery of the Chicago Parent Program is the group leader. This is the person who expertly facilitates the discussion, encourages an open exchange of ideas among the parents, and is

Table 1.1
Topical Outline of the Chicago Parent Program

Program Topic	Session/Week
Unit 1: The Value of Your Attention	
Part 1: Child-centered time	1
Part 2: Family routines and traditions	2
Part 3: Praise and encouragement	3
Part 4: Using rewards for challenging behaviors	4
Unit 2: Using Your Authority Wisely	
Part 1: Say what you mean and mean what you say	5
Part 2: Threats and consequences	6
Part 3: Ignore and distract	7
Part 4: Using time-outs	8
Unit 3: Managing Your Stress	
Part 1: Reducing your stress	9
Part 2: Problem-solving	10
Unit 4: Sticking with the Program	
Part 1: Putting it all together	11
Part 2: Booster session	(2 months after week 11)

most knowledgeable about the program principles. Group leaders also support the parents as the experts about their children and partner with them in helping parents tailor the program principles to their individual needs, values, and childrearing goals. According to Webster-Stratton (1998a), this "collaborative process model" is essential for strengthening parents' knowledge and self-efficacy. It has been our experience that this kind of collaboration between group leaders and parents is critical for participant engagement and program effectiveness. However, collaborative group facilitation is a high level skill. Extensive group leader training and supervision is needed to ensure that group leaders fully understand and "buy into" the program principles, are competent but empathic facilitators of group discussion, and fully engage in a collaborative relationship with parents. To assess whether group leaders are helping parents meet their goals, parents complete weekly satisfaction surveys rating the helpfulness of the group discussion and the group leaders' facilitation so adjustments can be made accordingly.

EVALUATING THE EFFICACY OF THE CHICAGO PARENT PROGRAM

We have been evaluating the effectiveness of the Chicago Parent Program with parents of toddlers and preschoolers in seven Chicago day care centers serving low-income families. These centers were matched on size, racial/ethnic composition, median income, and percent single-family households and randomly assigned to an intervention or waiting-list control condition. We recruited 292 families between 2002 and 2004 when the target child was between 2 and 4 years of age. From baseline to postintervention, complete data is available on 253 (86.6%) families. Parents with complete data at postintervention were more likely to be younger than those who did not complete the postintervention assessments [M parent age = 29.13 years ($SD = 7.6$) for completers and 32.13 years ($SD = 7.4$) for noncompleters, $t(290) = 2.14$, $p < .05$]. There were no other differences related to parent or child demographic background or child behavior problems. This chapter presents data from the sample of 253 parents and their children.

Inclusion criteria were (a) being a parent or legal guardian of a 2- to 4-year-old child enrolled in the participating day care center and (b) ability to speak English. One hundred and thirty-five families participated in the intervention condition and 118 families participated in the waiting-list control condition. Most of the participating parents (88.9%; $n = 225$) were mothers. Approximately 92% ($n = 232$) of the parents were African American or Latino. Mean parent age was 30.3 years ($SD = 7.77$) and mean child age was 2.9 years ($SD = .74$). Seventy-four percent of the children were living in single-parent households. Approximately 21% of parents were immigrants, primarily from Mexico. All families were considered low-income based on state eligibility criteria for receiving subsidized child care.

There were two significant demographic differences between parents and children by experimental condition. There were more Latino parents, χ^2 (3, n = 253) = 11.4, p < .01 and girls, χ^2 (1, n = 253) = 5.5, p < .05 in the intervention than in the waiting-list control condition. The demographic characteristics of the sample by experimental condition are displayed in Table 1.2. For a fuller description of the sample and participation rates, see Garvey, Julion, Fogg, Kratovil, and Gross (2006).

Table 1.2
Demographic Characteristics of the Sample by Experimental Condition

Variable	Intervention Group (n = 135)		Waiting-List Control Group (n = 118)	
	n	(%)	n	(%)
Parent Race/Ethnicity[a]				
African American	70	51.9	79	66.9
Latino	50	37.0	33	28.0
Non-Latino White	11	8.1	1	0.8
Other	4	3.0	5	2.0
Employment Status				
Full time	71	52.6	79	66.9
Part time	23	17.0	16	13.6
In school	13	9.6	7	5.9
Work and school	13	9.6	5	4.2
Unable to work	2	1.5	1	0.8
Looking for work	8	5.9	10	8.5
Other	5	3.7	0	0
Marital Status				
Married	33	24.4	34	28.8
Single	82	60.7	74	62.7
Partnered	15	11.1	8	6.8
Other	5	3.7	2	1.7
Parent Immigrant Status				
Parent U.S. Immigrant	24	17.8	28	23.7
Child Sex[b]				
Male	66	48.9	75	63.9
Female	69	51.1	54	48.9

Note: n = 253.

[a] The intervention group included more Latino and non-Latino White parents while the waiting-list control group included more African American parents, χ^2 (3, n = 253) = 11.4, p < .01.

[b] There were more boys in the waiting-list control group than in the intervention group, χ^2 (1, n = 253) = 5.5, p < .05.

To examine the effects of the Chicago Parent Program on children's behavior in the day care classroom, teachers completed the Caregiver-Teacher Rating Form (C-TRF) for ages 1.5 to 5 (Achenbach & Rescorla, 2000). The C-TRF is a checklist completed by the child's day care teacher rating the extent to which 99 behaviors listed on the form are not true (rating of 0), somewhat or sometimes true (rating of 1), or very true or often true (rating of 2) of the child's behavior in the classroom. The C-TRF measures two broad dimensions of child behavior: internalizing and externalizing problems. The Internalizing scale includes 32 items indicative of anxiety, depression, and withdrawal. The Externalizing scale includes 34 items representing symptoms of inattention and aggression.

The C-TRF was normed on a sample of 1,192 preschool children (56% European American, 44% ethnic minority). Achenbach and Rescorla (2000) report that 8-day test-retest reliability scores for the C-TRF were .88. For the current sample, alpha reliability scores for the Internalizing and Externalizing scales were .88 and .94, respectively. Interrater reliabilities were .80 for the Internalizing scale and .83 for the Externalizing scale (Gross, Fogg, Garvey, & Julion, 2004). The validity of the C-TRF has been supported by its ability to discriminate referred from nonreferred children (Achenbach & Rescorla, 2000).

The C-TRF uses raw scores and T scores demarcating borderline (93rd to 97th percentile) and clinical (greater than 97th percentile) ranges. In the current study, T scores at or above the 93rd percentile were used to identify children with significant behavior problems and to examine the effectiveness of the Chicago Parent Program for reducing behavior problems in the day care classroom. Teachers were asked to complete the C-TRF on the target child at baseline and at postintervention (3 to 4 months later).

Intervention parents completed an end-of-program satisfaction survey at the eleventh parent group session. This survey asked parents to rate the extent to which the program was helpful and useful to them, how difficult it was to attend the program and to complete weekly assignments, and their overall satisfaction with the program.

To examine the efficacy of the Chicago Parent Program for reducing behavior problems among 2- to 4-year-old children in day care, we examined the number of children with scores in the borderline and clinical ranges at baseline and how many of those children had scores in the normal range at postintervention. At baseline, 9.1% ($n = 23$) of the children had C-TRF scores in the borderline/clinical range on the Externalizing or the Internalizing scale and 2% ($n = 5$) had baseline C-TRF scores in the borderline/clinical range on both scales. Thirteen of the children with high C-TRF scores were in the intervention group and 15 were in the waiting-list control group.

At postintervention, most children's behavior improved. Only 5.1% ($n = 13$) of the children with high baseline C-TRF scores continued to have scores in the borderline/clinical range 3 to 4 months later. However, there was a significant difference in C-TRF improvement rates by experimental condition, χ^2 (1, $n = 23$) = 3.49, $p < .05$. As shown in Table 1.3, 50% of the intervention group children with baseline externalizing scores in the borderline/clinical range had scores in the normal range at postintervention compared to 37.5% of the waiting-list control group children. For the Internalizing scale, 85.7% of the intervention children with baseline internalizing behavior problem scores in the borderline/clinical range had postintervention scores in the normal range whereas only 28.5% of the waiting-list control group children's internalizing scores improved. There were no differences in improvement rates on the C-TRF by parent race/ethnicity or child gender.

Parents rated the program highly on the end-of-program satisfaction surveys. Ninety-six % reported that the concerns they had about their child's behavior were better (44%) or much better (52%) than when they started the program. Interestingly, 62% of parents thought the program helped them with concerns not directly related to their child such as with family members or coworkers. At the end of the program, 72% of parents rated themselves as "very confident" about talking with their child's day care teacher about their child's behavior. Overall, 88% of the parents said they would "highly recommend" and 12% said they would "recommend" the program to another parent.

However, some parents found it difficult to attend the program (39%) and to complete the weekly homework assignments (37%). Nonetheless, 87% of parents rated the homework assignments as "very helpful." There were no differences in parent satisfaction ratings by race/ethnicity

Table 1.3

Improvement Rates from Baseline to Postintervention among Children with Classroom Behavior Problem Scores in the Borderline/Clinical Range by C-TRF Scale and Condition

Scale	Intervention Group ($n = 135$)			Waiting-List Control Group ($n = 118$)		
	Baseline n	Post-intervention n	Improved (%)	Baseline n	Post-intervention n	Improved (%)
Externalizing	6[a]	3[b]	50.0	8[a]	5[b]	37.5
Internalizing	7[a]	1[b]	85.7	7[a]	5[b]	28.5

[a] Number of children with T scores in the borderline/clinical range on the Caregiver-Teacher Report Form at baseline.

[b] Number of children with T scores in the borderline/clinical range at baseline and postintervention.

although many Latino parents requested that the program be made available in Spanish.

CONCLUSION

The findings suggest that the Chicago Parent Program is effective and relevant for low-income and ethnic minority families with preschool children. Specifically, children of intervention parents showed significantly greater improvement in teacher ratings of their classroom behavior. It is noteworthy that although improvements were found on scores for the Externalizing as well as the Internalizing scales, greater improvements were evident for children's internalizing problems. This suggests that the parent training intervention may have had the greatest impact by reducing young children's anxiety.

Parents also rated the program highly. This is one of the few, empirically-tested parenting programs created in collaboration with parents. Moreover, it was specifically designed to address many of the concerns relevant for low-income and ethnic minority families. Child rearing occurs in context and the advisory council was adamant that the context they needed to see had to include the stressful elements they felt on a daily basis. Per their recommendations, all of the scenes captured real families interacting in their homes or in public places in real-life situations. Most scenes include multiple children. All were rated as useful and relevant by the PAC before being included in the intervention program.

Intervention parents found the Chicago Parent program helpful not only for addressing concerns they had with their children but also with concerns unrelated to their children. There is a significant therapeutic effect of simply being with other parents and learning that they share many of the same concerns. Since all of the parents in this study had low incomes and most were single, working parents, many functioned in isolation from other parents going through the same experiences they were having.

However, some parents found it difficult to get to the parent groups. One of the disadvantages of delivering parenting interventions in a group format is that participation rates are often low (Garvey et al., 2006; Heinrichs, Bertram, Kuschel, & Hahlweg, 2005; Perrino, Coatsworth, Briones, Pantin, & Szapocznik, 2001). Therefore, future research might evaluate alternative methods for providing parent training and compare their effectiveness against group-based parent training. Examples might include delivering the program during home visits, as a self-administered intervention, or making it available on television.

Research is continuing to examine the effectiveness of the Chicago Parent Program on parent and child behavior up to a year postintervention.

In addition, plans are underway to translate the program into Spanish so it will be available to more immigrant parents. The growth rate of the Latino population in the United States exceeds that of any other ethnic minority group and the overall growth rate for the United States. By the year 2020, an estimated one in five children living in the United States will be Latino (Zambrana & Logie, 2000). Thus, empirically-supported parenting programs for ethnic minority parents of young children are greatly needed.

REFERENCES

Achenbach, T., & Rescorla, L. (2000). *Manual for the ASEBA forms and profiles.* Burlington: University of Vermont.

Barlow, J., & Stewart-Brown, S. (2000). Behavior problems and group-based education programs. *Developmental and Behavioral Pediatrics, 21,* 356–370.

Campbell, S. B. (1997). Behavior problems in preschool children: Developmental and family issues. In T. H. Ollendick & R. J. Prinz (Eds.), *Advances in clinical child psychology* (Vol. 9, pp. 1–26). New York: Plenum Press.

Campbell, S. B., Shaw, D. S., & Gilliom, M. (2000). Early externalizing behavior problems: Toddlers and preschoolers at risk for later maladjustment. *Development and Psychopathology, 12,* 467–488.

Corral-Verdugo, V., Frias-Armenta, M., Romero, M., & Munoz, A. (1995). Validity of a scale of beliefs regarding the 'positive' effects of punishing children: A study of Mexican mothers. *Child Abuse and Neglect, 19,* 669–679.

Deater-Deckard, K., Dodge, K. A., Bates, J. E., & Pettit, G. S. (1996). Physical discipline among African-American and European-American mothers: Links to children's externalizing behaviors. *Developmental Psychology, 32,* 1065–1072.

Dumas, J. E., & Wahler, R. G. (1983). Predictors of treatment outcome in parent training: Mother insularity and socioeconomic disadvantage. *Behavioral Assessment, 5,* 301–313.

Eamon, M. K., & Zuehl, R. M. (2001). Maternal depression and physical punishment as mediators of the effect of poverty on socioemotional problems of children in single-mother families. *American Journal of Orthopsychiatry, 71,* 218–226.

Egger, H. L., & Angold, A. (2006). Common emotional and behavioral disorders in preschool children: Presentation, nosology, and epidemiology. *Journal of Child Psychology and Psychiatry, 47,* 313–337.

Eyberg, S. M., & Boggs, S. R. (1989). Parent training for oppositional-defiant preschoolers. In C. E. Schaefer & J. M. Briesmeister (Eds.), *Handbook of parent training: Parents as co-therapists for children's behavior problems* (pp. 105–132). New York: Wiley.

Fabiano, G. A., Pelham, W. E., Manos, M. J., Gnagy, E. M., Chronis, A. M., Onyango, A. N., et al. (2004). An evaluation of three time-out procedures for children with attention deficit/hyperactivity disorder. *Behavior Therapy, 35,* 449–469.

Fiese, B. H. (2002). Routines of daily living and rituals in family life: A glimpse at stability and change during the early child-raising years. *Zero to Three, 22*(4), 10–13.

Forehand, R., & Kotchick, B. A. (1996). Cultural diversity: A wake-up call for parent training. *Behavior Therapy, 27,* 187–206.

Forness, S. T., Cluett, S. E., Ramey, C. T., Ramey, S. L., Zima, B. T., Hsu, C., et al. (1998). Special education identification of Head Start children with emotional and behavioral disorders in second grade. *Journal of Emotional and Behavioral Disorders, 6,* 194–204.

Garvey, C., Julion, W., Fogg, L., Kratovil, A., & Gross, D. (2006). Measuring participation in a prevention trial with parents of young children. *Research in Nursing and Health, 29,* 212–222.

Gross, D., Fogg, L., Garvey, C., & Julion, W. (2004). Behavior problems in young children: An analysis of cross-informant agreements and disagreements. *Research in Nursing and Health, 27,* 413–425.

Gross, D., Fogg, L., & Tucker, S. (1995). The efficacy of parent training for promoting positive parent-toddler relationships. *Research in Nursing and Health, 18,* 489–499.

Gross, D., Fogg, L., Webster-Stratton, C., Garvey, D., Julion, W., & Grady, J. (2003). Parent training with multi-ethnic families of toddlers in day care in low-income urban communities. *Journal of Consulting and Clinical Psychology, 71,* 261–278.

Gross, D., Sambrook, A., & Fogg, L. (1999). Behavior problems among young children in low-income urban day care centers. *Research in Nursing and Health, 22,* 15–25.

Gunnoe, M. L., & Mariner, C. L. (1997). Toward a developmental-contextual model of the effects of parental spanking on children's aggression. *Archives of Pediatric and Adolescent Medicine, 151,* 768–775.

Hanff, C. A. (1969). *A two-staged program for modifying maternal controlling during mother-child (M-C) interaction.* Western Psychological Association, Vancouver, CA.

Heffer, R. W., & Kelley, M. L. (1987). Mothers' acceptance of behavioral interventions for children: The influence of parent race and income. *Behavior Therapy, 2,* 153–163.

Heinrichs, N., Bertram, H., Kuschel, A., & Hahlweg, K. (2005). Parent recruitment and retention in a universal prevention program for child behavior and emotional problems: Barriers to research and program participation. *Prevention Science, 6,* 275–286.

Jones, R. N., Sloane, H. N., & Roberts, R. W. (1992). Limitations of "don't" instructional control. *Behavior Therapy, 23,* 131–140.

Kliewer, W., & King, E. (1998). Family moderators of the relation between hassles and behavior problems in inner-city youth. *Journal of Clinical Child Psychology, 27,* 278–292.

Kubicek, L. F. (2002). Fresh perspectives on young children and family routines. *Zero to Three, 22*(4), 4–9.

Kumpfer, K. L., & Alvarado, R. (2003). Family-strengthening approaches for the prevention of youth problem behaviors. *American Psychologist, 58,* 457–465.

Lavigne, J. V., Gibbons, R. D., Christoffel, K. K., Arend, R., Rosenbaum, D., Binns, H., et al. (1996). Prevalence rates and correlates of psychiatric disorders among preschool children. *Journal of the American Academy of Child and Adolescent Psychiatry, 35,* 204–214.

Lundahl, B., Risser, H. J., & Lovejoy, M. C. (2006). A meta-analysis of parent training: Moderators and follow-up effects. *Clinical Psychology Review, 26,* 86–104.

Martinez, C. R., & Eddy, M. J. (2005). Effects of culturally adapted parent management training on Latino youth behavioral health outcomes. *Journal of Consulting and Clinical Psychology, 73,* 841–851.

McLloyd, V. C., & Smith, J. (2002). Physical discipline and behavior problems in African-American, European-American, and Hispanic children: Emotional support as a moderator. *Journal of Marriage and Family, 64,* 40–53.

Mistry, R. S., Vandewater, E. A., Huston, A. C., & McLloyd, V. C. (2002). Economic well-being and children's social adjustment: The role of family process in an ethnically diverse low-income sample. *Child Development, 73,* 935–951.

NICHD Early Child Care Research Network. (2006). Child care effect sizes for the NICHD study of early child care and youth development. *American Psychologist, 61,* 99–116.

Overturf Johnson, J. (2005). *Who's minding the kids? Child care arrangements.* Washington, DC: U.S. Census Bureau.

Patterson, G. R. (1982). *Coercive family process.* Eugene, OR: Castalia.

Perrino, T., Coatsworth, J. D., Briones, E., Pantin, H., & Szapocznik, J. (2001). Initial engagement in parent-centered preventive interventions: A family systems perspective. *Journal of Primary Prevention, 22,* 21–44.

Razzino, B. E., New, M., Lewin, A., & Joseph, J. (2004). Need for and use of mental health services among parents of children in the Head Start program. *Psychiatric Services, 55,* 583–586.

Reyno, S. M., & McGrath, P. J. (2006). Predictors of parent training efficacy for child externalizing behavior problems: A meta-analytic review. *Journal of Child Psychology and Psychiatry, 47,* 99–111.

Rose, S. L., Rose, S. A., & Feldman, J. F. (1989). Stability of behavior problems in very young children. *Development and Psychopathology, 1,* 5–19.

Serketich, W. J., & Dumas, J. E. (1996). The effectiveness of behavioral parent training to modify antisocial behavior in children: A meta-analysis. *Behavior Therapy, 27,* 171–186.

Strassberg, Z., Dodge, K. A., & Pettit, G. S. (1994). Spanking in the home and children's subsequent aggression toward kindergarten peers. *Development and Psychopathology, 6,* 445–461.

Strauss, M. A., Sugarman, D. B., & Giles-Sims, J. (1997). Spanking by parents and subsequent antisocial behavior of children. *Archives of Pediatric and Adolescent Medicine, 151,* 761–767.

U.S. Public Health Service. (2000). *Report of the surgeon general's conference on children's mental health: A national action agenda.* Washington, DC: Department of Health and Human Services.

Uzgiris, I. C., & Raeff, C. (1995). Play in parent-child interactions. In M. Bornstein (Ed.), *Handbook of parenting* (Vol. 4, pp. 353–376). Mahwah, NJ: Erlbaum.

Wakschlag, L. S., & Keenan, K. (2001). Clinical significance and correlates of disruptive behavior in environmentally at-risk preschoolers. *Journal of Clinical Child Psychology, 30,* 262–275.

Walle, D. L., Hobbs, S. A., & Caldwell, H. S. (1984). Sequencing of parent training procedures: Effects on child noncompliance and treatment acceptability. *Behavior Modification, 8,* 540–552.

Webster-Stratton, C. (1982). Teaching mothers through videotape modeling to change their children's behavior. *Journal of Pediatric Psychology, 7,* 279–294.

Webster-Stratton, C. (1990). Long-term follow-up of families with young conduct-problem children: From preschool to grade school. *Journal of Clinical Child Psychology, 19,* 144–149.

Webster-Stratton, C. (1998a). Parent training with low-income families: Promoting parental engagement through a collaborative approach. In J. R. Lutzker (Ed.), *Handbook of child abuse research and treatment* (pp. 183–210). New York: Plenum Press.

Webster-Stratton, C. (1998b). Preventing conduct problems in Head Start children: Strengthening parenting competencies. *Journal of Consulting and Clinical Psychology, 66,* 715–730.

Webster-Stratton, C., & Hancock, L. (1998). Training for parents of young children with conduct problems: Content, methods, and therapeutic processes. In J. M. Briesmeister & C. E. Schaefer (Eds.), *Handbook of parent training* (2nd ed., pp. 98–152). New York: Wiley.

Zambrana, R. E., & Logie, L. A. (2000). Latino child health: Need for inclusion in the U.S. national discourse. *American Journal of Public Health, 90,* 1827–1833.

CHAPTER 2

New Beginnings: An Empirically-Based Program to Help Divorced Mothers Promote Resilience in Their Children

SHARLENE WOLCHIK, IRWIN SANDLER,
LILLIE WEISS, and EMILY WINSLOW

PARENTAL DIVORCE is one of the most prevalent stressors experienced by children. Over 1.5 million youth experience parental divorce each year in the United States (National Center for Health Statistics, 1995). Currently, 10 million children (14% of the population) live in divorced or separated households (U.S. Census Bureau, 2005), and it is estimated that 34% of children in the United States will experience parental divorce before reaching age 16 (Bumpass & Lu, 2000).

It is well documented that parental divorce can have serious negative effects on child and adolescent functioning. Meta-analyses of 92 studies published through the 1980s (Amato & Keith, 1991) and 67 studies in the 1990s (Amato, 2001) showed that youth in divorced families have more conduct, internalizing, social, and academic problems than those in non-divorced families. These differences occurred across age and gender and were slightly larger for more recent studies. Although less well studied, divorce has also been shown to relate to children's physical health problems (see Troxel & Matthews, 2004). Adolescents in divorced families are more likely than those in nondivorced families to report elevated levels of drug and alcohol use (e.g., Furstenberg & Teitler, 1994; Hoffmann & Johnson, 1998) and are two to three times more likely than their counterparts in nondivorced families to experience clinically significant levels of mental health problems, receive mental health services (e.g., Hetherington et al., 1992), drop out of school (McLanahan, 1999), leave home early, cohabitate, and experience premarital childbearing (Goldscheider & Goldscheider, 1998; Hetherington, 1999). Illustratively, Hetherington and coworkers (1992) reported that 35% of adolescent girls and 20% of the boys whose parents divorced in childhood scored in the clinical range on mental health problems versus 4% of girls and 4% of boys in nondivorced families. McLanahan's (1999) analysis of 10 national probability samples revealed school dropout rates of 31% and teen birth rates of 33% for adolescents in divorced families versus 13% and 11%, respectively, for adolescents in nondivorced families.

A large body of research has also shown that exposure to parental divorce in childhood increases risk for an array of problems in adulthood. Multiple prospective studies with epidemiologic samples have shown that parental divorce is associated with substantial increases in clinical levels of mental health problems, substance abuse, mental health services use, and psychiatric hospitalization in adulthood (Chase-Lansdale, Cherlin, & Kiernan, 1995; Kessler, Davis, & Kendler, 1997; Maekikyroe et al., 1998; Rodgers, Power, & Hope, 1997; Zill, Morrison, & Coiro, 1993). Although the effect sizes in studies comparing the functioning of youth and adults who grew up in divorced homes with those from two-parent families are generally modest, the high prevalence of divorce means that its impact on population rates of problem outcomes is substantial (Scott, Mason, & Chapman, 1999). Thus, facilitating children's postdivorce adjustment is an important focus for preventive mental health programs that has substantial public health implications.

In this chapter, we describe New Beginnings, an empirically validated program for children from divorced families that uses custodial mothers as change agents. The program of research in which this theory-driven, research-based program was developed and evaluated has been funded by the National Institute of Mental Health. Our description of the program primarily focuses on the "nuts-and-bolts" of the program, although we also briefly discuss the research that guided the design of the program and the evaluations of its short-term and long-term effects. First, we briefly describe the theoretical framework and research findings on which the program was based. Next, we provide a general overview of the program, followed by a description of each session. Then, we discuss the results of two randomized experimental field trials of the program, one of which included a 6-year follow-up assessment. A case illustration is then presented. We end the chapter with a discussion of some general guide-lines for group leaders.

THEORY BEHIND THE NEW
BEGINNINGS PROGRAM

Making the link between research findings and an intervention program is a complex task. The development of New Beginnings involved four steps: (1) Examining the literature for theory and empirical research on factors associated with the development of adjustment problems in chil-dren from divorced families; (2) conducting generative studies to provide further insight into the processes that may lead to adjustment problems; (3) developing intervention strategies designed to affect the critical processes identified in the research; and (4) evaluating the intervention using a randomized field trial.

The conceptual model underlying our research on the prevention of postdivorce problems combines elements from a person-environment transactional framework and a risk and protective factor model. Person-environment transactional models posit dynamic person-environment processes underlying individual development across time. Changes in the social environment (e.g., parenting) affect the development of problems and competencies in an individual, which in turn influence the social environ-ment and development of competencies and problems at later developmental stages (e.g., Cicchetti & Schneider-Rosen, 1986; Sameroff, 1975, 2000). De-rived from epidemiology (Institute of Medicine, 1994), the risk and protec-tive factor model posits that the likelihood of mental health problems is affected by exposure to risk factors and the availability of protective re-sources. Although not available at the time the New Beginnings Program was developed, Cummings, Davies, and Campbell's (2000) "cascading path-way model" integrates these two models into a developmental framework that we have employed in our research on the long-term effects of the New Beginnings Program. From this perspective, stressful events such as divorce can lead to an unfolding of failures to resolve developmental tasks and in-crease susceptibility to mental health problems and impairment in develop-mental competencies. In this framework, parenting is viewed as playing a central role in facilitating children's successful adaptation following divorce, and the skills and resources developed in successful resolution of early post-divorce developmental tasks are important tools for coping with future chal-lenges. Dynamic interactions between the child's successful adaptation, skills, and resources are hypothesized to lead to a positive cascade of adap-tive functioning in multiple domains of functioning over time.

The New Beginnings Program, which was designed to reduce mental health problems and promote competencies following divorce by reducing children's exposure to risk factors and increasing their protective resources, was developed using a "small theory" approach (Lipsey, 1990). Our use of the term *small theory* is based on two features. First, the practical public health objective of reducing problems is the central goal. Thus, program developers are primarily concerned with maximizing impact on outcomes by identifying multiple factors to target for change by the programs (Rothman, 1980) and so evaluation focuses on assessing program effects on outcomes and the mediators of these effects (West & Aiken, 1997). Second, small theory specifies a model of precursors of problem behaviors based on previous theory and empirical (usually correlational) evidence (West & Aiken, 1997). To maximize the chances of impacting significant public health outcomes, multiple factors are targeted based on evidence that they are related to outcomes and are modifiable. These factors are called *putative mediators* because changing them is predicted to lead to the reduction or prevention of behavior problems and promotion of competencies.

There are important advantages of using a small theory approach to program design. First, identification of potentially modifiable mediators allows for efficient program design by targeting processes that are most likely to impact desired outcomes. Second, empirical evidence of processes that mediate program effects can be used to identify the "core components" to be preserved in adaptations for other cultural groups and disseminated versions (West & Aiken, 1997). Finally, evidence that experimentally induced change in putative mediators accounts for program effects on outcomes provides stronger support for causal effects of these variables than that from passive correlational studies (Patterson & Fisher, 2002; Sandler, Wolchik, MacKinnon, Ayers, & Roosa, 1997).

The small theory articulates both a psychosocial theory (links between the putative mediators and outcomes based on theories of problem development and psychosocial research) and a program theory (links between the putative mediators and change strategies based on theories of behavior change and intervention research; West & Aiken, 1997). The psychosocial theory of the New Beginnings Program was based on the transitional events perspective (Felner, Farber, & Primavera, 1983; Felner, Terre, & Rowlinson, 1988; Hetherington, 1979; Kurdek, 1981) and empirical work on the modifiable correlates of children's postdivorce adjustment problems. From this perspective, divorce is viewed as a process in which multiple stressors occur in children's social and physical environments, and the adjustment problems of children are viewed as a consequence of both the stressful environmental events that may occur during this transition in family structure and the interpersonal and intrapersonal protective resources available to the child (e.g., Felner et al., 1983; Kurdek, 1981; Sandler, Wolchik, & Braver, 1988).

This framework was used to organize the results of research that showed consistent empirical support for significant associations between children's adjustment after divorce and the following environmental and interpersonal factors: (a) the quality of the child's relationship with the custodial parent (e.g., Fogas, Wolchik, & Braver, 1987; Guidubaldi, Cleminshaw, Perry, Nastasi, & Lighel, 1986; Stolberg & Bush, 1985); (b) discipline strategies (e.g., Baldwin & Skinner, 1989; Fogas et al., 1987; Santrock & Warshak, 1979); (c) amount of contact between the child and the noncustodial parent (e.g., Guidubaldi et al., 1986; Hetherington, Cox, & Cox, 1981; Warren et al., 1984); and (d) interparental conflict (e.g., Guiduabaldi et al., 1986; Hetherington, Cox, & Cox, 1978; Long, Forehand, Fauber, & Brody, 1987; Sandler et al., 1988; Stolberg & Anker, 1984). A parent-based intervention was designed to affect these putative mediators, with changes in these mediating variables, in turn, being expected to lead to positive changes in children's psychological adjustment.

The specific intervention procedures used to modify each of these constructs are shown in Table 2.1. Whenever possible, techniques were used that previously have been shown to be effective in changing these processes. For example, in selecting techniques to enhance the quality of the mother-child relationship, we relied heavily on Forehand's and Patterson's work with families (Forehand & McMahon, 1981; Patterson, 1975). The specific change techniques included: positive family activities (Family Fun Time), one-on-one time, monitoring and reinforcing children's

Table 2.1
Theory of the Intervention

Putative Mediators	Intervention Techniques
Quality of mother-child relationship	Family fun time
	One-on-one time
	Catch 'em being good
	Listening skills
Effective discipline	Setting clear and realistic expectations
	Monitoring misbehaviors
	Selecting appropriate consequences
	Using consequences consistently
	Increasing consistency
Father-child relationship	Education about importance of child's relationship with father
	Reduction of obstacles to visitation
Interparental conflict	Anger management skills
	Listening skills

positive behaviors, and listening skills. Discipline was enhanced by self-monitoring discipline strategies and using fair and consistent consequences to change the frequency of two specific behaviors. Anger management training (Novaco, 1975) was used to decrease interparental conflict. Contact with the noncustodial father was addressed by discussion of the impact of this relationship on children's well-being and by identification and removal of obstacles to visitation, such as inflexible visitation arrangements and fighting during visitation exchanges.

The orientation of the program is cognitive-behavioral, with a strong emphasis on skills acquisition or enhancement. It consists of ten 1.75-hour, weekly group sessions and two 1-hour individual sessions. Each group is led by two masters' level counselors and is composed of 8 to 10 custodial or primary residential mothers.

The skills in the program build on each other. The first half of the program teaches skills to enhance the quality of the mother-child relationship and to reverse the negative cycle of interaction between mothers and children that frequently accompanies divorce. Improving mother-child communication early in the program helps reduce children's misbehaviors so there is less need to address those in later sessions. It prevents little problems from turning into big ones and eliminates many problem behaviors altogether. As mothers spend more time doing fun activities with and listening to their children, they avoid many current and potential discipline issues later on. As shown in Table 2.2, in session 1 and 2, we teach three relationship building skills (family fun time, one-on-one time, and catch 'em being good) that mothers implement each week of the program and indefinitely following the program. This is followed by the Listening module in sessions 3, 4, and 5. Session 6 focuses on shielding children from interparental conflict. This session is followed by the Discipline module in sessions 7, 8, and 9. The last session includes a review of program skills, discussion of ways to keep using program skills and a closure activity.

The group sessions are both didactic and experiential. The didactic material is presented in a conversational, interactive learning style, allowing time for participation. Much of the skill acquisition is experiential, with active learning exercises (e.g., role-play) aimed at learning the skills accurately and applying them outside the group session. An old proverb states: "*Tell* me and I may forget. *Show* me and I may remember. *Involve* me and I will learn." As much as possible, we use active learning principles to maximize *involvement*, which promotes effective learning. We also *show* via videotapes, demonstrations, and modeling rather than *tell*. We tell or lecture as little as possible, and even in the didactic components, we often ask questions and use participants' responses to make key teaching points.

Table 2.2
Central Topics Covered in Each Session

Session Number	Overview
1	Introductions, making sense of children's problems after divorce, and family fun time
2	Changing negative cycles into positive ones, one-on-one time, and catch 'em being good
3	Why learning to listen is important, and Listening step one: Getting children to talk
Individual Session	Troubleshooting use of program activities
4	Listening step two: Taking time to think before responding
5	Listening step three: Responding effectively
6	Shielding kids from interparental conflict
Individual Session	Removing obstacles to the father-child relationship
7	Effective discipline step one: Setting clear and realistic expectations
8	Effective discipline step two: Developing a change plan
9	Effective discipline step three: Seeing how the change plan is working and making revisions if needed
10	What mothers have accomplished and how to keep the changes going

The format for each session is essentially the same. Except for session 1 that starts out in a large group, the sessions begin with splitting into two subgroups for home-practice review with one of the co-leaders. The two subgroups then join and meet as a large group for the bulk of the session, where new material is introduced and skills are practiced in dyads or small groups. At the beginning of every session for home-practice review, mothers meet with the same subgroup of mothers and their assigned group leader. However, for skills practice, group leaders chose different groups at each session. The composition of these groups is usually planned before each session and strategized by group leaders to maximize effective learning of skills (e.g., subgroups are formed based on ages of children).

SESSION 1. INTRODUCTIONS, MAKING SENSE OF CHILDREN'S PROBLEMS AFTER DIVORCE, AND FAMILY FUN TIME

The purpose of session 1 is to provide an overview of the program and to help parents understand how the skills being taught in the program address the issues that children and mothers face following divorce. In addition, the first program skill, family fun time, is taught and mothers rehearse how they will implement it with their family in the coming week. Other goals include building rapport, trust, and group cohesion; establishing group leader credibility; and motivating mothers to attend sessions on time and to do home-practice every week.

This is probably the most important session because it sets the tone for future sessions. This is where group norms begin to be established (e.g., punctuality, attendance, commitment to following through with the program and completing home-practice assignments). Leaders stress the importance of attending every session and completing all home-practice assignments. By being role models themselves (e.g., being prepared, following through on assignments, and "going the extra mile"), leaders can set good group norms. Because there is a great deal of material to cover, leaders try to limit off-task discussion and adhere to the time schedule as much as possible. The group leaders establish norms for adhering to the schedule by starting sessions *exactly* on time and letting group members know that sometimes they will need to end a discussion and move on to the next part of the session to cover all the material.

In this and subsequent sessions, leaders build *group cohesion* and give *hope* along with providing information. We want mothers to recognize that they can change their children's behavior problems by using program skills. We use every opportunity to link changes in children's behavior to mothers' hard work and effort. Providing hope and encouragement is essential because the program requires a great deal of work from mothers, and it may take some time before they see the results of their efforts.

Introductions

Leaders introduce themselves and talk about their training, background, and experience to establish credibility. When talking about themselves, they keep in mind that mothers are asking themselves, "Why should I listen to and believe what she or he has to say?" Then mothers introduce themselves, giving their names, length of time since the divorce, and names and ages of their children. Some mothers may want to talk about their divorces or ex-husbands and may see the introductions as an opportunity to "vent" or elicit support. We try to limit this type of discussion because it can be confusing to other group members if a mother begins to do the work that properly belongs in group therapy. When this happens, group leaders acknowledge the mother's feelings and try to redirect her back to answering the questions that the leaders have posed for the introductions.

Participation Agreement

Following introductions, mothers sign a participation agreement stating that they agree not to discuss other mothers' personal issues outside of the meetings, they will attend every meeting, be on time, and do all of the home-practice assignments. In addition, they agree to let group leaders know when they are having trouble with the assignments, and the leaders in turn agree to work with mothers to tailor the material to their children's needs.

Providing Program Information

The leaders then provide information about the program, stating that its purpose is to help children adjust to divorce, and that children are the targets of the program. Mothers are told that the program is based on years of working with families and learning what helps children. They are told that the program is *not* a divorce adjustment group for mothers, although if children are coping well, parents will experience less stress and will feel better. They are also told that the program is MOTHER-driven—the program works with mothers because they are the most powerful agents of change in their families. In addition, leaders stress that home-practice *IS* the program and that mothers who do the home-practice *will* see changes in their families and those who don't *won't*.

Goal Setting

Mothers are then asked what changes they would like to see in their families as a result of participating in the program. This exercise helps to normalize problems mothers are experiencing, shape their expectations to fit with the program goals, and instill hope by showing a good fit between their expectations and the program. Leaders reinforce realistic expectations (e.g., reducing the stress level at home, helping children share their concerns with mothers, decreasing fighting) and screen out unrealistic expectations (e.g., getting the ex-husband to be more responsible). Mothers' expectations are linked to program activities that will address them. For example, if a mother mentions that she hopes to get her children to talk to her more, leaders point out that there are three sessions on effective listening that focus on getting children to share their concerns and feelings with their mothers. Each mother's expectations are written on a flipchart. Also, leaders record these expectations in the front of their manual so they use this information to personalize session content in later sessions. For example, leaders may state, "As I recall, Maria, you mentioned in our first week that one of your goals was to get Juan to stop fighting with his brothers. Tonight's session on discipline will teach you skills to help make that happen."

Impact of Divorce: 2 + 2 = 5

This exercise provides the foundation and rationale for the whole program and lays the groundwork for the next nine sessions. The first purpose of the exercise is to normalize the stressors that accompany divorce, emphasizing that there are valid reasons why divorce is a difficult time for families. The second purpose is to instill hope that the program can provide solutions to mothers' problems.

The divorce equation—$2 + 2 = 5$—is used to graphically illustrate the idea that the problems children have adjusting to divorce plus the problems mothers have adjusting to divorce have synergistic effects that create a sum greater than the total of its parts; in this case, a family situation characterized by stress, fighting, and other problems. It conveys to mothers that these problems are understandable, predictable, and are very common following divorce. After leaders state that divorce is a period of transition and change, group members are asked what problems and changes have occurred in their worlds and in their children's. Their responses are written on flipcharts and augmented with a prepared flipchart listing other problems and changes. Leaders use mothers' responses to deliver the punch line at the end of the exercise that with so much change, mothers get more than they bargained for: $2 + 2$ doesn't equal 4; it equals 5!

Hope is instilled by providing solutions to the problems mothers listed, laying the groundwork and rationale for the rest of the program. The solutions are the skills they will learn: increasing warm and positive contact between mothers and children, shielding children from interparental conflict, supporting father-child contact and using effective discipline strategies. The presentation of solutions leads into the rationale for using the first relationship building skill, family fun time.

Family Fun Time

Family fun time increases positive and warm contact with children. This is a skill that mothers are asked to do every week so that it becomes a positive family routine that children can count on. Many divorced families think of themselves as "broken" or "incomplete" families. Doing a pleasurable activity as a family every week provides children with a sense of family and helps create a new family tradition. Just as the name connotes, family fun time has two essential components: it includes only the *family* and it has to be *fun*. It happens once a week, every week, and children decide what to do. In addition, it has to be an *activity* where interaction between family members occurs (e.g., playing games together) rather than a *passive activity or passivity* such as watching a movie together. The activity must be inexpensive and cannot include any problem solving, complaining, teasing, or fighting. Examples of family fun time activities include going out for ice cream, playing basketball or board games, or going to the park. We have been impressed with the many creative and inexpensive ways children have come up with to have fun. Leaders role-play how to introduce family fun time to children and answer questions about how to introduce this activity. Then, the group is split into two subgroups where mothers role-play introducing this activity to their children and give and receive feedback.

Home-Practice Assignment

The home-practice for this week is to introduce family fun time to the children, plan what to do, and do it. Mothers are also asked to fill out a sheet listing their children's positive qualities, which they will use in session 2. They are given a home-practice diary sheet to write down the family's experiences doing family fun time and are asked to bring this sheet to the next session. Leaders read the diaries each week, make comments, and give them back to the mothers. This is an effective way for mothers to communicate with leaders about problems or questions they experienced and for leaders to provide feedback, help problem solve, and give encouragement to mothers.

SESSION 2.　CHANGING NEGATIVE CYCLES INTO POSITIVE ONES, ONE-ON-ONE TIME, AND CATCH 'EM BEING GOOD

The goals of this session are to teach mothers how to change negative cycles into positive ones and introduce two more relationship building skills that mothers will do weekly: one-on-one time and catch 'em being good. We continue to build group cohesion so that mothers see the group as a place to problem solve and feel comfortable practicing skills in a group setting.

Cycles: Negative and Positive

After reviewing home-practice activities in assigned subgroups and collecting home-practice diaries, leaders discuss how the changes resulting from divorce can lead to a negative cycle of stress, with children's behavior affecting mothers and vice versa. These changes sometimes lead children to be aggressive, mind less, act angry, talk back, and sometimes lead mothers to ignore good behaviors, yell, use less consistent discipline, control with power and authority, and make fewer demands for responsible behavior from their children. These negative ways of interacting escalate, and the negative cycle feeds off itself. Mothers are told that *they* are the ones who can change the negative cycle into a positive one and that when they change their behaviors, their children will begin to respond differently to them, although this *won't happen overnight*. As mothers recognize good behaviors, ignore bad behaviors, give lots of attention, and have fewer power struggles, they reverse the negative cycle. Mothers are told that by doing the activities they will learn in the group, they can make the bond with their children stronger. The next two skills taught in the session—one-on-one time and catch 'em being good—help do that.

One-on-One Time

One-on-one time is a regular, *short* (15 minutes) period of scheduled time that mothers spend with each of their children where the child experiences pure acceptance. During this time, the mother gives undivided positive attention to the child. Children choose the activity. Common choices include participating in the child's hobby, playing a card game, or having the child teach the parent to play a video game. The mother does not compete or try to win, criticize, ask questions, or teach. Rather, she gives the child her full attention, follows the child's lead and comments on the positive things the child does. Group leaders show a video of one-on-one time and also demonstrate the skill using role-play. Leaders discuss how the nature of one-on-one time differs depending on the child's age, with younger children choosing games and older children and adolescents choosing walks or going out for a snack. Leaders emphasize that the key to achieving positive effects from one-on-one time is expressing an *attitude* of warmth, caring, and unconditional acceptance rather than just the *rote* application of the skill, and that it takes *work*. Leaders also stress that this is one of the most powerful activities and that children love it. Mothers get a chance to experience the power of this tool when they practice the skill, playing the part of mother and also of the child. When asked how it feels to play the part of the child, they use terms like "special," "the focus of attention," and "important." This helps them understand the goal of this skill, which is to make their children feel loved and valued. We tell mothers that it often feels awkward at first but that one-on-one time becomes more natural and comfortable with practice.

Catch 'em Being Good

The second skill, catch 'em being good, also helps children feel valued and is an important step in creating the positive cycle. It involves providing positive attention to children when they show good behavior. It is a positive discipline method that increases desirable behaviors mothers want their children to exhibit. Mothers are shown a video that demonstrates this skill. Leaders encourage mothers to notice their children's behaviors, ideas, or personal characteristics and to "catch 'em being good" in both physical (e.g., a hug) and verbal (e.g., "nice going!") ways. They learn to praise the behavior rather than the child and to be careful to not give backhanded compliments such as "it's about time you did such a nice job of cleaning your room." Mothers practice using this skill in the group, with one mother role-playing a child and another playing the part of a mother. For home-practice, they do one-on-one time once with each child (or twice if they have only one child) and catch 'em being good as often as they can.

SESSION 3. WHY LEARNING TO LISTEN IS IMPORTANT, AND LISTENING
STEP ONE: GETTING CHILDREN TO TALK

This is the first of three sessions devoted to improving listening skills. Its goals are to provide a rationale for good listening, to introduce the three parts of effective listening (listen, think, respond) and to teach the first part—the five talk-to-me's.

Good listening tells children "I love you," "I'm here for you," and "What you have to say is valuable." These messages are major factors in promoting children's adjustment after a divorce. Good listening raises children's self-esteem, and when parents listen, children feel comfortable sharing their concerns with them and feel closer to them. Mothers are told that good listening is not easy and requires a lot of practice.

Mothers view two videos that demonstrate the difference between bad and good listening and introduce "The Big Picture" or three parts of effective listening. Mothers are told that good listening is circular, continuous, and ongoing.

The Five Talk-to-Me's

We discuss five ways for mothers to let their children know that they are interested in what they are saying and to keep them talking. These are:

(1) *Big ears:* being "all ears" and tuning in to what their child is saying;
(2) *Good body language:* facing the speaker and making eye contact;
(3) *Good openers:* using open-ended questions rather than closed-ended;
(4) *Mmm-Hmms:* nodding and using phrases such as "uh-huh," "really?"; and
(5) *Say mores:* using phrases such as "tell me more about that" or "what else happened?" that encourage the child to continue talking.

The first three "talk-to-me's" get the conversation off to a good start; the last two keep it going. Leaders first demonstrate these skills; then mothers practice them in small groups.

The First Individual Session

The first individual session is held between sessions 3 and 4. In it, leaders review and troubleshoot the skills taught so far in the program.

SESSION 4. LISTENING STEP TWO: TAKING TIME TO
THINK BEFORE RESPONDING

The goals of this session are to teach mothers to think before they respond and to use summary responses.

Think Before You Respond

Stopping to think before responding allows time to "tailor" responses to the child's needs and helps mothers form responses that make their child feel heard and understood. Parents frequently rush into a response in an attempt to "fix" the situation. When mothers rush into a response without thinking, they miss important information, frustrate their children by giving advice unnecessarily, and undermine their child's self-esteem and competence by solving a problem that children could have solved themselves with encouragement. Mothers are taught to ask themselves two questions before responding: (1) Am I able to use the five talk-to-me's? and (2) what did I hear? If they are unable to give their child their full attention, they are taught how to postpone listening until a later time. In response to the second question, mothers are taught to reflect on what they heard their child say.

Summary Responses

After teaching parents to stop and think, we move on to the third part of effective listening—responding. We start with summary responses. Summary responses condense the child's message and ask the question, "Did I get it right?" To summarize accurately, mothers need to reflect on what the child said, then condense the message in a way that asks, "Is this what you mean?" This approach invites children to correct any misunderstandings. Accurate summary responses do not add anything, guess at feelings, or interpret what is going on—they simply summarize. After leaders demonstrate summary responses, mothers practice this skill, receiving corrective feedback.

Learning to summarize is not easy, and there is a strong tendency for mothers to give advice or offer a solution immediately (i.e., "quick fix"). Initially, mothers often are not aware of the tendency to quick fix, so group leaders need to point this out when it happens. Soon, mothers learn to catch themselves when they want to offer a quick fix. In this and other sessions, leaders model listening skills in their interactions with group members, so mothers experience the positive feelings of being heard and have multiple opportunities to observe good listening.

SESSION 5. LISTENING STEP THREE: RESPONDING EFFECTIVELY

The goals of this session are to teach mothers how to use feeling responses, provide opportunities to practice using the listening skills all together, and teach mothers guided problem solving for those times when listening is not enough.

Feeling Responses

Feeling responses ask the question "Is this how you feel?" They are used sparingly when the child is talking about an emotional issue. When making feeling responses, mothers try to identify what their child might be feeling, using their intuition, previous experience or consideration of how they would feel in that situation. Feeling responses, like summary responses, are tentative responses that allow the child the opportunity to correct the listener. Leaders role-play and use videos to demonstrate summary and feeling responses; then mothers practice using them. These are *not* easy skills to learn. When mothers have difficulty reaching for the feelings underneath the message, they are encouraged to use global responses such as "feel bad" or "feel upset."

Putting It All Together: Listen, Think, Respond

Mothers break up into small groups to practice putting all the skills together by role-playing scenarios of situations that elicit feeling responses. Some of the scenes deal with tough issues like feelings about the father or the father's new partner. Mothers are encouraged to use their listening skills to help their children with their feelings about the divorce and the changes that have occurred in their lives.

When Listening Isn't Enough

Sometimes children bring up problems that require mothers to do more than just listen. Group leaders do a role-play to demonstrate the steps involved in effectively guiding children through problem solving: (a) using good listening skills to clarify the problem; (b) asking the child to come up with possible solutions; (c) giving a list of options if the child has difficulty identifying solutions, and (d) allowing the child to select an option to try, if all options are possible and equally good, or helping the child evaluate positive and negative outcomes for each if some solutions are better than others.

SESSION 6. SHIELDING CHILDREN FROM INTERPARENTAL CONFLICT

The purpose of this session is to educate mothers about how to shield children from interparental conflict and teach mothers anger management skills to prevent children from witnessing interparental conflict.

Being Caught in the Middle

We try to help mothers see interparental conflict through their children's eyes. Leaders first give mothers a list of conflict experiences, such as arguing with the ex-spouse while the child is in the room and saying negative things about the ex-spouse to the child. Mothers circle those that their child has experienced in the past couple of months. After mothers briefly share their experiences, leaders stress that of all the negative things that children experience during divorce, *being caught in the middle of interparental conflicts is the most stressful.*

Leaders then show a video illustrating how children feel when they are caught in the middle: responsible, angry, anxious, and unsure about whether they should love their mother or father. We provide mothers with information on the many ways that children get caught in the middle and how stressful these situations are for them. Mothers are sometimes surprised to learn that sometimes even a simple question such as, "What did you do at Dad's house?" can be very stressful.

Because saying negative things about the ex-spouse to their children is particularly stressful, we have each mother choose a self-statement that she can use to stop from making such statements. We encourage mothers to find "adult ears" to listen to their anger and frustration. We do not ask them to stop saying negative things about the ex-spouse altogether—*only to stop saying negative things in front of the children.* Although mothers cannot control what their ex-spouse says, they can control their own behavior by not responding when their children talk about the negative things that their ex-spouses say about them. Many mothers feel that they need to defend themselves by saying negative things about the ex-spouse or telling their children the truth. Group leaders acknowledge that it is difficult not to respond in these situations and help mothers recognize that when they retaliate, their child pays too big a price and that saying nothing is in the best interest of their children. Mothers generate a self-statement such as "I'm not going to put my child in the middle" or "Just because he's a jerk, I don't have to be one" that can help them ignore negative statements made by their ex-spouse and limit the damage. Sometimes it is helpful for mothers to hear that their children will learn the "truth" about their father on their own, when they are developmentally and emotionally ready. Group leaders tell them that one of the biggest gifts that mothers can give children during divorce is the message that it is okay to love both parents. Although they cannot prevent their ex-spouse from saying negative things about them, they can choose not to retaliate for their child's benefit.

Parents are not the only ones who say negative things about the ex-spouse. Grandparents and other relatives are often angry at the mother's ex-spouse as well. Leaders role-play how to make respectful requests to relatives to keep them from saying negative things about the ex-spouse in front of the children.

Anger Management

Research clearly shows that watching parents argue is extremely stressful and leads to aggression, depression, and anxiety. When parents argue in private, the effects are not as harmful. We teach anger management skills to keep mothers from arguing with their ex-spouse in front of their children. The goal of anger management is not to swallow anger but to *control* it. Mothers learn to use self-talk to keep their anger under control and to use "I messages" to communicate effectively with their ex-spouse in private. Group leaders role-play using anger management self-statements to keep from arguing in front of the children. Mothers identify self-statements that will help them before, during, and after a confrontation with their ex-spouse. Then they practice using anger management skills as leaders role-play their ex-spouse.

The Second Individual Session

The second individual session is scheduled after the sixth group session to discuss the child's relationship with the father. Obstacles to visitation are discussed, such as mothers restricting phone calls and being inflexible about changing visitation plans. Working together, the leader and mother develop strategies to remove these obstacles.

Session 7. Effective Discipline Step One: Setting Clear and Realistic Expectations

This is the first of three sessions devoted to managing children's misbehavior more effectively. It provides an introduction to discipline and teaches the first step of effective discipline: setting clear and realistic expectations for behavior. Sessions 8 and 9 teach the next two steps: developing and using a change plan and evaluating and changing the plan if needed.

Discipline When Half the Team Is Gone

Discipline presents a big challenge for divorced mothers for several reasons. Unlike two-parent families, parents cannot work together to discipline. In addition, the stress mothers and children experience may lead to negative cycles of interaction that lead to less cooperation. After divorce, mothers often need their children to take on more responsibilities around the house but have less time and energy to supervise. Consequently, there are more opportunities for discipline problems. In families where children have some input in family decision making, it may be difficult for children to accept the mother as the disciplinarian. Thus, after divorce, mothers have less help in discipline and more complex discipline problems.

The first step in helping mothers make some positive changes in their discipline practices is having them conduct a self-assessment. Mothers record their responses to five discipline scenarios to assess which of three discipline styles is most similar to their own. Leaders then use role-plays to demonstrate the three styles: Dana Drill Sergeant, Pam Permissive, and Freida Fair 'N Firm. Leaders also explore some of the myths about children's misbehavior (e.g., that children are punishing the mother for the divorce, that they are rotten or bad children) and point out the realities: that children may not be getting enough of their mother's positive attention, they may be "testing the limits," or they may be unsure of the rules.

Adopting Clear and Realistic Expectations

Clear expectations provide children with structure and help them know what parents want them to do. Clear expectations involve specific behaviors ("my child should not talk back when told to do something") rather than broad qualities ("she should not be sassy"). Also, expectations should be realistic and age-appropriate. In this session, mothers evaluate whether expectations are clear and realistic. Leaders help them change the unrealistic expectations into more realistic ones and the unclear expectations into clear ones.

Mothers then identify a clear and realistic expectation for a misbehavior they want to decrease for each of their children, and leaders help each mother develop a plan for monitoring the misbehaviors. Mothers are told that it is important to monitor and evaluate a problem before trying to change it. If the behavior is one that occurs many times every hour, mothers pick an hour per day to count the misbehavior. If the behavior is only associated with a certain event (e.g., arguing at the dinner table) mothers keep track of how many times it happens at each dinner for that week. If it occurs only a few times per day, mothers count how many times the behavior happens on each of several days. Mothers frequently choose misbehaviors such as fighting with siblings, not completing homework, or not going to bed when instructed.

SESSION 8. EFFECTIVE DISCIPLINE STEP TWO:
DEVELOPING A CHANGE PLAN

Session 8 teaches the second step of effective discipline: developing a change plan for decreasing a misbehavior. Mothers learn how to choose consequences for misbehaviors and how to communicate their expectations to children.

Demonstration of Effective and Ineffective Discipline

After reviewing each mother's counting plan, the group leader helps mothers decide whether the misbehavior they counted is troublesome enough to develop a change plan for or whether mothers should count another misbehavior the coming week. Mothers then watch two brief videos that demonstrate the difference between effective and ineffective discipline. Following the videos, leaders discuss the second step of effective discipline: developing a change plan that includes reasonable and easy to use consequences, communicating expectations and consequences clearly to children, and planning to use the consequences consistently.

Kinds of Consequences

We review the types of consequences to use when children meet expectations and when they do not, relating these to the problem behaviors mothers have counted. Mothers are told that positive attention is one of the easiest and most powerful tools for getting children to meet their parents' expectations. Positive attention can be in the form of compliments, thank you's or providing special privileges like staying up late.

We provide a menu of six choices of negative consequences to use when children do not meet expectations. We encourage mothers to choose the consequence that is the least harsh but is still likely to decrease her child's misbehavior. The goal is to make discipline as easy and pleasant as possible for both mothers and children. The consequences are presented in an interactive lecture format, using role-play and examples from the group to illustrate each of the following types of consequences:

- *Ignoring* misbehavior that the child does to get attention and *rewarding* appropriate behavior instead.
- *Increasing supervision* (e.g., calling home from work to check on child's whereabouts).
- *Allowing natural consequence to occur* (e.g., if Kayla is late for dinner, the family begins to eat without her).
- *Taking away or restricting meaningful privileges* (e.g., television time).
- *Giving something unpleasant* (e.g., extra chores).

Leaders role-play communicating expectations and consequences to children and emphasize the importance of being consistent in implementing consequences. Many parents experiencing high levels of stress discipline according to their emotional state. They tend to punish more often and more severely when they are angry or anxious and allow misbehaviors to occur without consequences when they are happy or worn down. This inconsistency increases child behavior problems. Mothers are taught how to use self-statements such as "I don't need to lose it" or "I can choose not to let her push my buttons" to help them calm down before implementing negative consequences.

Leaders help each mother select a consequence for the misbehavior she recorded last week and commit to a time when she will talk to her child about the change plan. In choosing a consequence for a misbehavior, mothers ask themselves several questions: (a) Is it is a fair consequence? (b) Can I give the consequence consistently? (c) Will it help my child learn the negative consequences of misbehavior? and (d) Is it the least harsh consequence that will decrease the misbehavior?

At the end of the session, leaders schedule a phone appointment with each mother for the middle of the week to evaluate how the change plan is working and problem solve any difficulties the mother is experiencing implementing the plan.

SESSION 9. EFFECTIVE DISCIPLINE STEP THREE: SEEING HOW THE CHANGE PLAN IS WORKING AND MAKING REVISIONS IF NEEDED

Session 9 introduces the third step of effective discipline: Evaluating the change plan and revising it if necessary. In this session, leaders also help parents develop change plans to increase a positive behavior and to address misbehaviors they may want to decrease in the future.

Using the Change Plan, Seeing if It Is Working, and Revising It if Needed

Managing children's behavior is an ongoing process—it is not something mothers do once and forget about. If misbehaviors that mothers are managing are not decreasing, they can ask several questions to figure out why the plan is not working: (a) Are my expectations realistic and clear? (b) Are the consequences easy to use and meaningful to the child? (c) Did I communicate the consequences clearly to my child? (d) Have I been consistent in giving positive attention when my child meets the expectation and negative consequences when my child does not meet the expectation? Group leaders tell mothers that some misbehaviors take more time than others to change and sometimes things get worse before they get better. Leaders also tell them that as children mature, the expectations for their behaviors should be re-evaluated for appropriateness at regular intervals.

Creating Change Plans for Positive Behaviors and Other Misbehaviors

In this session, leaders help parents develop a change plan for increasing a positive behavior in the next week. Positive behaviors are *not* the opposite of misbehaviors. Rather, positive behaviors are the "extra credit" behaviors that do not cause problems when they do not occur. These are the "it would be nice if they did" behaviors. Some examples of positive behaviors that mothers have used change plans to increase include picking flowers and putting them in a vase, doing homework before being reminded, helping with meal preparation. Mothers also develop a change plan for another misbehavior that they will address in the future.

SESSION 10: WHAT MOTHERS HAVE ACCOMPLISHED AND HOW TO KEEP THE CHANGES GOING

This session includes a review of all the skills that mothers learned in the group as well as exercises to help mothers reflect on the positive changes they have seen in their families and identify ways to maintain these changes.

Leaders tell mothers that setbacks and problems are an inherent part of making change and to use future problems as a cue to review and renew the skills they have learned. Mothers identify several ways to maintain the changes they have made in the program, such as putting notes about the skills on the refrigerator. Mothers are given home-practice diaries for the next 6 months so that they can continue to monitor their use of the program skills. Leaders also help them plan ahead by anticipating and planning how to handle future problems.

After a brief closure exercise where mothers share the changes they and their children have made, there is a brief graduation ceremony where leaders hand out diplomas as they make personalized, positive comments about each mother. The session culminates with eating cake to celebrate a job well done.

TRAINING, SUPERVISION, AND GENERAL GUIDELINES FOR LEADING THE GROUPS

Training and supervision are critical components of the program. Leaders receive 20 hours of training before they begin implementing the program and 1 hour of training per week prior to delivering each session. They also receive 1 hour of supervision per week after delivering each session.

INITIAL TRAINING

The purpose of the initial 20 hours of training is to provide a broad overview of the program and to orient the group leaders to the program's approach for working with divorced parents. The group leaders are provided with readings to give them background on the program. The scientific foundations for the program are described by reviewing the family processes the program is developed to change and the theoretical reasons why these processes are targeted. The findings from evaluations of the effectiveness of the program are presented to engender a sense of confidence in the ability of the program to affect meaningful and lasting changes in children's behavior problems. The group leaders quickly come to understand that the program activities were carefully constructed to change empirically supported mediating processes and that implementing the program with fidelity can significantly affect children's lives. A brief review of each session is presented to show how the sessions build on each other, and how they teach the processes that are targeted for change. Most importantly, we emphasize that mothers' practice of the program skills with their children is the essence of the program. "The home-practice is the program" is a phrase the leaders hear again and again.

The manualized nature of the program is then described, and we review the session outline for one session. Group leaders' prior experiences with and feelings about manualized interventions are discussed. We describe several key reasons for using a detailed manual. First, the manual provides a way for leaders to teach mothers skills that have been carefully selected and have been shown to lead to changes in children's behaviors. Second, the manual provides a resource for the group leader to use in anticipating potential problems in implementation. The "Tips and Traps" section of each session describes common difficulties in implementing program activities and solutions for dealing with these problems.

We emphasize that effective delivery of the program requires good clinical skills. Group leaders must be able to implement active learning strategies, tailor each program skill to the needs of individual families, and provide specific positive feedback that shows a thorough understanding of program theory and skill implementation in response to mothers' comments and experiences using program skills. Role-play is used extensively in sessions to allow mothers to practice program skills with each other before they use them with their children. Leaders reinforce successful use of program skills and problem-solve any difficulties mothers experience using program skills. To enhance mothers' sense of efficacy, leaders routinely attribute changes that mothers see in their children to changes that the mother is making in her behavior.

Weekly Training

Prior to weekly training, the leaders review the session for the coming week and complete a brief self-assessment quiz on the session. They are expected to know all the activities prior to the meeting. The weekly training is an opportunity to rehearse delivery of the session. Leaders take turns delivering sections of the session and receive feedback from the supervisors and other group leaders. We also discuss questions about each activity and common problems in implementing them. Emphasis is placed on building the group leaders' sense of efficacy through positive feedback from the supervisors and other group leaders. Feedback on role-play typically includes positive comments about specific things the group leader did well, and comments about things that might be done differently. Essentially, we model the way we want group leaders to provide feedback to the parents.

SUPERVISION

One hour of supervision is provided following each session. The supervision focuses mainly on reviewing how the mothers are implementing the program skills with their children, reinforcing the message that "the home-practice is the program." The supervisor and other group leaders help problem-solve difficulties that leaders are experiencing in helping mothers successfully use program skills. Supervision also focuses on issues that arose in the delivery of the session. The supervisor reviews brief sections of videotapes of the session and provides feedback on specific aspects that were done well and those that might be improved. In the same way we want group leaders to work with parents, supervision focuses on building a sense of efficacy in implementing the program by reinforcing specific positive behaviors and helping the leaders devise solutions to the difficulties they or the mothers are having.

GENERAL GUIDELINES FOR EFFECTIVE PROGRAM DELIVERY

In our training and supervision, we have found the following guidelines help leaders create an atmosphere that facilitates mothers' effective learning and implementation of program skills. Many of these guidelines involve basic psychotherapeutic and active learning principles:

Be Prepared

- *Know the session material.* No matter how experienced or clinically skilled, a group leader cannot implement the sessions effectively without adequate preparation. Each group session requires several hours of preparation before conducting it. A group leader must read and learn the session material thoroughly, rehearse parts of the session with the co-leader, and actively participate in the training sessions.
- *Practice the skills.* We have found that one of the best ways to become familiar with the program is for group leaders to practice the skills with their own children, if applicable, or with a "borrowed" child.

Many of the listening and anger management skills can also be practiced with adults, and one-on-one time can be practiced with a pet.

- *Anticipate possible problems.* To ensure the session flows *smoothly,* group leaders must think about what can possibly go wrong. Also, leaders should make certain that all supplies are available and ready to use so they do not spend session time rewinding tapes or looking for papers.

Stay Focused on the Goal of the Program— To Teach Mothers Skills

- *Remember that the program is designed to teach mothers skills that will improve their children's mental health.* It is *not* a therapy group for divorced mothers. Group leaders might be tempted to adopt the role of the mother's therapist. However, the goal of the program is to help mothers improve parenting skills so their children can benefit. Remember that the program is primarily to benefit the children.
- *Remember that this is not group therapy.* This is a *psychoeducational* group with both *psychological* and *educational* components. The emphasis is *not* on catharsis for mothers, but on learning and practicing skills in a group environment. Group principles are used to facilitate effective learning of these skills and motivating mothers to use them at home with their children. Although group principles are very important (e.g., promoting cohesion, instilling hope, providing support, sharing), group leaders must keep in mind that their primary job is to help mothers *learn* the skills and *practice* them at home.
- *Make certain that the program is delivered as written.* This is an empirically-based program, and it is *critical* that it is delivered as it is outlined in the manual. Although we do not expect group leaders to memorize the lines, we expect them to present the material in such a way that all the *points* in the session outline are made. We want to make certain that group leaders follow this script, even if they have had a great deal of experience working with divorced mothers.
- *Do not get sidetracked.* Unlike an unstructured therapy group where there is flexibility to follow the group members if they want to discuss one topic instead of another, group leaders do not have the same flexibility in this program. If group members want to talk about other relevant divorce topics, group leaders can tell them that these issues will come up in another session or they can be discussed individually with the group leader after the session.
- *Stick to the schedule.* Group leaders should always come *at least* 10 minutes early to each session, start the session *exactly* on time and

end on time. Leaders should always plan ahead the strategy for the best possible flow of the session, so they do not waste group time moving chairs, rewinding videos, or organizing handouts.

- *Use active learning methods:*
  - —*Use group members' comments to illustrate key points.*
  - —*Set up skills practice with plenty of structure.* Group leaders should always begin by modeling the skill they are teaching. Whenever possible, have a highly competent group member follow for additional modeling and learning.
  - —*Reinforce mothers for small gains.* Some mothers may have a lot of difficulty with the skills and may feel a reduced sense of efficacy if they do not perform well. Leaders need to give a lot of genuine and specific positive reinforcement to each mother after she role-plays.
  - —*Use modeling to maximize learning.* Leaders can model appropriate group norms (e.g., being on time, being prepared). In addition, they can model program skills in interactions with mothers. For example, they should use summary and feeling responses, make good eye contact and use open-ended questions frequently when interacting with mothers.
- *Emphasize the importance of home-practice.* It is essential *not* to create a group culture which allows members to forego home-practice. Preventing such group norms can be accomplished by:
  - —Emphasizing the importance of doing the home-practice assignments.
  - —Assessing whether each mother did the assignment during home-practice review and problem solving if a mother did not get it done.
  - —Reviewing how each mother did with the home-practice assignments in home-practice reviews and reinforcing mothers over and over for all their efforts.
  - —Frequently making the link between completing the home-practice and changes in children's behaviors.
  - —Using other mothers' success experiences to emphasize the importance of practicing the skills at home.
  - —Making written comments on home-practice sheets to reinforce and problem solve. If leaders put a lot of effort into giving written input to mothers, mothers are more likely to complete their home-practice diaries. Mothers look forward to getting individualized written feedback each week.
  - *Emphasize attendance and commitment.* Set up group norms for attendance. Follow up when a group member does not attend and problems solve obstacles to attending so that she is able to attend

regularly. Group leaders schedule and conduct make-up sessions immediately before the next group session for mothers who missed a session. Parents are warned that if they miss more than three sessions, they will probably not benefit from the program.

- *Convey a belief in the program's ability to improve mothers' relationships with their children and change children's behavior problems.*
- *Remember that all the hard work is to benefit the children.*

Be Attentive to Process Issues

- *Create an atmosphere that encourages participation.* Leaders can do much in the first few sessions to encourage sharing among mothers (e.g., point out similarities among mothers' experiences, reinforce mothers for participating). Environmental factors can also do a great deal to create a comfortable atmosphere (e.g., comfortable seating, refreshments) or inhibit participation (e.g., classroom-like set-up). Try to make the physical setting as pleasant as possible within the existing limitations. We have found that arranging the chairs in a circle without tables in the middle encourages participation.
- *Use basic clinical skills to establish group cohesion.* The following suggestions can be used to increase group member interaction:
  —Tempting as it may be to give a long monologue when asked a question, involving the group can increase cohesion. Comments such as "Can anyone else relate to that?," "Let's have a show of hands," or "How many of you have experienced that?," can quickly change a didactic group structure to a more interactive one and prevent one member from monopolizing the session.
  —Point out similarities between group members ("This sounds like what happened to Latisha"; "We're all mothers") to promote cohesion and bridge ethnic and social class differences.
  —Normalize divorce-related experiences as common occurrences so that mothers do not feel that they are abnormal.
  —Comment on the group process to increase interaction. ("It looks like we're having a difficult time coming up with ideas.")
  —Recognize and validate in a warm and supportive way the difficult feelings mothers are having.

  It is important to note that although these suggestions can increase group participation, it may not always be appropriate to do so, especially when time is a factor. Group leaders need to balance how much attention is paid to group process and how much to content, because there is a great deal of content to cover in each session.

It is normal for groups to bond at different rates, and certain factors such as group composition may make it easier for some groups to become cohesive earlier than others. It is not unusual, particularly in beginning sessions, for most mothers to be quiet. If there are still many uncomfortable silences after several group sessions, group leaders should talk with their supervisor to try to understand what is inhibiting interaction and problem-solve ways to increase participation.

- *Empower mothers.* After divorce, many mothers feel depressed and have negative feelings about themselves as mothers. Group leaders' comments can make a real difference in how mothers feel about their parenting abilities and themselves. Leaders can help mothers change how they view themselves by repeatedly making the link between changes in mothers' behaviors and the changes they are seeing in their children and by reinforcing them for practicing the program skills at home. It is also important to be vigilant for small changes in the children. Group leaders should point these out to mothers as signs that they are making the program work.

- *Be aware of any unresolved issues with an ex-spouse or children that may make it difficult to teach or model some of the skills.* Group leaders should discuss these issues with their supervisor to make certain they do not interfere with their ability to teach and help the mothers.

- *Self-disclosure.* Group leaders should disclose personal information about themselves only if it benefits the mothers. A rule of thumb is to disclose only resolved issues and not unresolved ones. For example, it may be helpful for leaders to share how they have used program skills to solve similar problems with their own children or ex-spouses, but it would not be helpful to disclose problems that leaders are currently having trouble solving. Mothers may either lose hope or feel that leaders are incompetent if they are unable to use the skills they are teaching!

- *Inform the supervisor of any potential clinical problems or crises as they arise.* Some problems or issues, such as domestic violence or child abuse, may come up from time to time that need additional intervention. In such cases, it is important to contact the supervisor immediately so that appropriate referrals and resources can be provided to the family.

Does the New Beginnings Program require a lot of work on the part of group leaders? Yes! But it is well worth it. When group leaders work hard and deliver the program with fidelity, mothers learn and use skills that lead to meaningful improvements in their children's mental health problems and social adaptation. All the leaders' and mothers' work is being done to benefit the children.

RESEARCH FINDINGS

The efficacy of the New Beginnings Program has been evaluated in two randomized, experimental field trials (Wolchik et al., 1993, 2000). The first small-scale trial ($N = 70$) used an experimental versus delayed intervention control group design. Using a design that included follow-up assessments and a larger sample ($N = 240$), the second trial had several aims: (a) to assess whether the positive effect the program achieved in the first trial could be replicated; (b) whether a combined program involving concurrent, separate groups for mothers and their children produced additive effects; and (c) whether the benefits for children persisted long-term. In the second trial, a literature control condition was used and the follow-up assessments occurred at 3 months, 6 months, and 6 years after program completion. We are currently conducting a 15-year follow-up with mothers and their offspring who are now young adults.

Although the second trial included a condition in which the mothers' program was combined with a separate group for children, our analyses showed that the children's group component did not increase program benefits on mental health outcomes beyond the effects of the mothers' program alone. Therefore, we focus on the findings of the analyses that compared the mother-only program to the literature control condition and those in which the mother-only program and the mother plus child programs were combined and then compared to the literature control condition.

Participants in both trails were recruited primarily through random sampling of court records for divorce filings. Media articles, presentations to school personnel, and word of mouth were also used to recruit families. Eligibility criteria in both studies included divorce within the past 2 years, the mother did not plan to remarry during the course of the study, and neither the mother nor the child was in treatment for psychological problems at the time. In the first trial, families were eligible if there was at least one child between 8 and 15 years old. Because of the child component in the second trial, the age range was narrowed to 9 to 12 years old. See Wolchik et al. (1993, 2002) for additional eligibility criteria. Because the intervention was designed to be preventive, families were excluded if the child had test scores indicating clinical levels of depression or extreme levels of externalizing problems or endorsed an item about suicidal ideation. These families were referred for treatment.

The program was highly similar in the trials. However, in addition to the four putative mediators described earlier, in the first trial, the program targeted increases in the amount and quality of support children received from nonparental adults. The focus on nonparental adult support was deleted in the second trial to accommodate an expanded discipline section. The child component in the second trial was designed to increase effective coping, reduce negative thoughts about divorce stressors, and improve mother-child relationship quality.

In both trials, several steps were taken to ensure high levels of intervention fidelity. First, sessions were delivered using detailed descriptions of content and format. Second, extensive training (20 hours prior to the start of the program and 2 hours/week during program delivery) and supervision (1.5 hours/week) were provided. Training included readings and didactic presentations about the theoretical and empirical bases for the program, videotapes of prior program sessions, and role-plays of session material. Weekly supervision addressed problems encountered in conducting the previous session, including skill acquisition and home-practice compliance difficulties. Third, extensive process evaluation data, including observer ratings of adherence to the program components using videotapes of all sessions, were collected. These efforts led to exceptionally high levels of program fidelity.

The evaluation in the first trial showed positive program effects at posttest on the putative mediators of mother-child relationship quality, divorce stressors, discipline, and the father-child relationship (i.e., mother's willingness to change visitation). In addition, program effects occurred on children's mental health outcomes. For mother-child relationship quality, divorce stressors, discipline, and mental health problems, the magnitude of intervention effects differed depending on preintervention functioning, with effects being most marked among those with the poorest initial levels. Analyses indicated that changes in mother-child relationship quality partially mediated the program effects on children's mental health outcomes.

The results of the second trial replicated these positive effects of the mother program on children's mental health outcomes at posttest. Program effects also occurred on three putative mediators: effective discipline, relationship quality, and maternal attitudes toward the father-child relationship. Analyses showed that program effects on internalizing problems at posttest were mediated by improvements in mother-child relationship quality and that the program effects on externalizing problems at posttest were mediated by program-induced improvements in mother-child relationship quality and effective discipline. Analyses of the 6-month follow-up data showed program effects on mother/child and teacher reports of externalizing problems, which were mediated by improvements in mother-child relationship quality and effective discipline. As in the first trial, several of the program effects were moderated by initial level of functioning; those with poorer functioning at baseline showed greater program benefit. Comparison of the mother-only program and mother plus child program indicated that the child component did not increase program benefits on mental health outcomes relative to the mother program alone.

The 6-year follow-up occurred when the youth were mid-to-late adolescents. The retention rate for the sample was exceptional; 91% of the families participated in this assessment. Because only one significant difference emerged when the mother-only and the mother-plus-child conditions were compared on mental health outcomes at posttest, 3-month and 6-month follow-up, we combined the mother-only condition and mother-plus-child condition in analyses to provide a more parsimonious view of the program effects at the 6-year follow-up. In addition, because analyses of the earlier waves had consistently shown that program benefit was greater for those families who had poorer functioning at baseline, we developed a composite risk index that was used in all the analyses. This risk index included those variables that were significant predictors of adolescent outcomes in the literature control group. The index consisted of standardized scores on baseline externalizing and environmental stress (i.e., interparental conflict, negative life events that occurred to the child, maternal distress, reduced contact with father, current per capita income).

As shown in Table 2.3, positive program effects occurred for a wide range of developmentally salient outcomes at the 6-year follow-up. Illustratively, 23.5% of the adolescents in the control group had a mental disorder in the past year, as assessed with the DIS-C, versus 14.8% of those whose mothers participated in the New Beginnings Program ($OR = 2.7$). Positive program effects also occurred on number of sexual partners, externalizing problems, internalizing problems, symptoms of mental disorder, alcohol use, marijuana use, other drug use, polydrug use, self-esteem, and activities involvement. Similar to the findings in the earlier assessments, several of the program effects on these outcomes were stronger for those with the greatest level of risk for developing problems when they entered the program. Examination of the putative mediators showed significant interactive effects for active coping and mother-adolescent relationship quality, with greater program benefits occurring for those with higher baseline risk.

Mediational analyses were conducted to assess which variables targeted for change in the program accounted for program benefits on outcomes 6 years later. The findings indicated that program effects to improve effective discipline at the posttest partially mediated program effects to improve grade point average at the 6-year follow-up. Program effects to improve mother-child relationship quality partially mediated program effects to reduce total symptoms of mental health problems, internalizing problems and externalizing at the 6-year follow-up for the high-risk group.

Table 2.3
Combined MP and MPCP versus LC at 6-Year Follow-Up
with Risk as Covariate

	6-Year Follow-Up Adjusted Means[a]		p Value		Effect Size (Cohen's d/OR)[b]
			Program Main Effect	Program by Baseline Interaction	
	MP	LC			
Externalizing (P/Ad)	—	—	.04	<.001	.67
Internalizing (P/Ad)	—	—	.16	<.001	.48
Externalizing (Teacher)	—	—	.01	.04	.51
Internalizing (Teacher)	−.03	.09	.46	NA	—
Diagnosis of mental disorder in the past year	14.8%	23.5%	.02	NA	2.70[c]
Diagnosis of drug abuse or dependence	4.7%	2.9%	.79	NA	—
Symptoms of mental disorder	—	—	.41	<.001	.47
Drug dependence or abuse symptom count	—	—	.52	.08	—
Polydrug use	—	—	.64	.02	.30
Alcohol use	—	—	.60	.005	.28
Marijuana use	—	—	.001	.05	.20
Other drug use			.82	.02	.23
Number of sexual partners	.65	1.68	.02	NA	.37
Grade point average	2.96	2.70	.01	NA	.26
Competence[d]	—	—	.03	<.001	.57

Note: NA = Not applicable because models with nonsignificant interactions were rerun without this term; P/Ad = Composite of parent and adolescent report.

[a] Means are not reported when interaction is significant.

[b] When interaction is significant, effect size is evaluated at 1 *SD* above the mean of the covariate.

[c] Effect size for dichotomous variables was calculated as an odds ratio.

[d] Competence is a composite of academic competence, social competence, activities involvement, and self-esteem; follow-up analyses showed that this effect was accounted for by self-esteem and activities involvement.

Additional details of these trials can be found in Wolchik et al. (1993, 2000, 2002), Sandler, Zhou, Millsap, and Wolchik (2006), Dawson-McClure, Sandler, Millsap, and Wolchik (2004), and Tein, Sandler, MacKinnon, and Wolchik (2004).

The cascading pathway models (Cummings et al., 2000; Masten, Obradović, & Burt, in press; Sameroff, 2000) suggest that the skills and resources achieved at posttest should provide important tools for coping with future challenges and that dynamic interactions across areas of functioning should occur, leading to a positive cascade of program benefits over time. To examine whether there were increases in the program effects over time, we plotted effect sizes for key outcome and mediator variables for the high risk group at posttest, short-term (3- and 6-month) follow-up, and 6-year follow-up. As shown in Figure 2.1a, for discipline

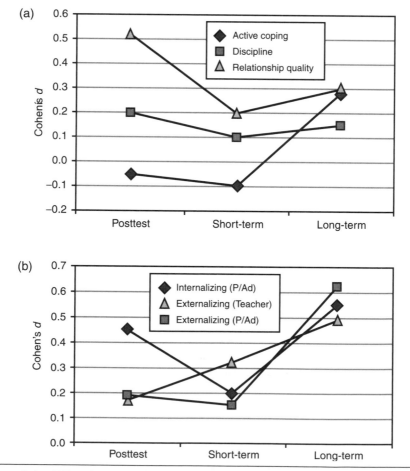

Figure 2.1 Effect Sizes (Cohen's *d*) (a) on Putative Mediators and (b) on Outcomes.

and relationship quality the effect sizes decreased from posttest to short-term follow-up (discipline, $d = .20$ to $d = .09$; quality $d = .52$ to $d = .19$), and then increased somewhat from short-term to 6-year follow-up (discipline $d = .15$, quality $d = .30$). For active coping, the effect size showed a sizeable increase from short-term ($d = -.09$) to 6-year follow-up ($d = .27$). As shown in Figure 2.1b, the short-term decline in effect size for parent/adolescent report of internalizing (posttest $d = .45$, short-term $d = .20$) was followed by an increase from short-term to 6-year follow-up ($d = .54$). For both parent/adolescent and teacher reports of externalizing, effect sizes at 6-year follow-up were considerably larger (parent/adolescent $d = .63$, teacher $d = .49$) than at posttest (parent/child $d = .19$, teacher $d = .16$) or short-term follow-up (parent/child [3- and 6-month] $d = .15$, teacher [6-month only] $d = .32$). These findings are consistent with a cascading pathways model in which program-induced changes increase over time.

CASE STUDY

Olivia is a 35-year-old woman whose husband left her for another woman. She has two children, Jose, 9 and Maria, 8. When she started the New Beginnings Program, she was particularly concerned about Jose. Since the separation, he had become increasingly rude and defiant to her. Olivia tried to get Jose to mind her, but the more she tried, the angrier and more defiant he became. She reported that he treated her "pretty much the way my ex-spouse does"—with little respect and much belittlement. She felt that she did not have any control over Jose. At times, she was so frustrated with him that she resorted to spanking, which only escalated the negative cycle. Olivia's daughter Maria had become increasingly quiet and distant since the divorce. She was not interested in playing with her friends, and her grades had fallen from high Bs to low Cs. Olivia's ex-husband called her frequently and berated her in front of the children.

Although Olivia was overwhelmed, distressed, and demoralized when she entered the program, she could readily see that her family was in a negative cycle, and that it was up to her to change the cycle to improve family life for herself and her children. After getting encouragement from the leaders and other group members, she decided to try the family fun time activity assigned for the first home-practice. In the second session, she reported that the family was able to agree on an activity, and she noted with some surprise that even Jose seemed to enjoy it. This early success gave her confidence to try the other relationship building activities of one-on-one time and catch 'em being good, and as she used them she reported a marked positive change in the "atmosphere" in the house. Olivia initially found it hard to use the listening skills. She felt that she needed to be a strong parent, and to her this meant giving a "quick fix" to any problem Jose or Maria presented or being defensive when they expressed negative emotion toward her. The group leader empathized with her concerns but urged her to refrain from the quick fix and to use the listening skills to make sure she really heard what her children were saying and understood what they were feeling. These skills were particularly helpful in dealing with Jose's anger and kept Olivia from getting into a shouting match with him when he expressed anger about the divorce. She reported that rather than being defensive, she felt that she was able to show him that she understood his feelings and that this seemed to draw them closer together. Maria also looked forward to the program activities, and as Olivia changed how she listened to Maria, Maria began to share more of her feelings and concerns about the divorce. Olivia learned some anger management skills and used them to stop the fights with her ex-spouse in front of the children.

Before participating in the New Beginnings Program, Olivia had alternated between being Pam Permissive and Dana Drill Sergeant in her discipline style. Olivia was not happy with her methods of discipline. In Olivia's words, both her children were a "bit out of control." She picked very simple behaviors, but ones that really "got under her skin," for her change plans. Both children used the bedroom floor as a hamper, so Olivia was constantly picking up after them. Counting these misbehaviors, developing a change plan and calmly explaining the plan to her children gave her a real sense of being a "mom in charge" rather than one being run ragged by ungrateful children. Even though the children continued to test limits and "things got worse before they got better," Olivia became more consistent in the consequences she used for misbehaviors and used anger management skills to keep herself from implementing negative consequences when she was angry. By the end of the program, both Maria and Jose were regularly putting their dirty clothes in the hamper, and Olivia reported that they minded her more often.

Olivia and her children did not make these changes overnight. Olivia needed a great deal of support and instruction from the group leaders and other mothers in her group to affect these changes in herself and her children. Her story is similar to other mothers who have participated in the New Beginnings Program, with many reporting significant changes in their own behaviors, their relationships with their children and their children's behaviors by the end of the program.

CONCLUSION

Rigorous evaluations of the New Beginnings Program have demonstrated that it leads to clinically significant and lasting benefits in multiple domains of children's functioning. Teaching parents skills and helping them to make these skills a regular part of their family life can help mitigate and cushion many of the potentially harmful effects of divorce. Although mothers cannot prevent or "fix" the stressors that happen in their children's lives during and after the divorce, they can learn lifelong skills to build a protective armor and secure base for children to withstand those stressors. Whereas much of the success of the program is because its content is based on sound theoretical and empirical principles, process issues are also very important in helping mothers make changes. Like Olivia, many mothers feel out of control and need support to learn and use the program skills. Providing mothers with warmth and acceptance and empowering them at the same time that we are teaching them skills helps them be more effective mothers to their children and gives them skills to prevent future problems.

For further information on the development and continuing evaluation of the New Beginnings Program, several resources are available. Articles by the program developers that are cited in this chapter provide further details on the randomized trials of the program. A more complete list of references concerning the program and the theory underlying it can be found at www.asu.edu/clas/asuprc. For those interested in implementation of the New Beginnings Program, training and supervision are provided periodically by the authors of this chapter. Certification as a group leader requires successful completion of the 20-hour training program and participation in supervision while delivering a group.

REFERENCES

Amato, P. R. (2001). Children of divorce in the 1990s: An update of the Amato and Keith (1991) meta-analysis. *Journal of Family Psychology, 15,* 355–370.

Amato, P. R., & Keith, B. (1991). Parental divorce and the well-being of children: A meta-analysis. *Psychological Bulletin, 110,* 26–46.

Baldwin, D. V., & Skinner, M. L. (1989). Structural model for anti-social behavior: Generalization to single-mother families. *Developmental Psychology, 25,* 45–50.

Bumpass, L., & Lu, H.-H. (2000). Trends in cohabitation and implications for children's family contexts in the United States. *Population Studies, 54,* 29–41.

Chase-Lansdale, P. L., Cherlin, A. J., & Kiernan, K. K. (1995). The long-term effects of parental divorce on the mental health of young adults: A developmental perspective. *Child Development, 66,* 1614–1634.

Cicchetti, D., & Schneider-Rosen, K. (1986). An organizational approach to childhood depression. In M. Rutter, C. E. Izard, & P. B. Read (Eds.), *Depression in young people: Developmental and clinical perspectives* (pp. 71–134). New York: Guilford Press.

Cummings, E. M., Davies, P. T., & Campbell, S. B. (2000). New directions in the study of parenting and child development. In E. M. Cummings, P. T. Davies, & S. B. Campbell (Eds.), *Developmental psychopathology and family process: Theory, research, and clinical implications* (pp. 200–250). New York: Guilford Press.

Dawson-McClure, S. R., Sandler, I. N., Wolchik, S. A., & Millsap, R. E. (2004). Prediction and reduction of risk for children of divorce: A 6-year longitudinal study. *Journal of Abnormal Child Psychology, 32,* 175–190.

Felner, R. D., Farber, S. S., & Primavera, J. (1983). Transitions and stressful life events: A model for primary prevention. In R. D. Felner, L. A. Jason, J. N. Moritsugu, & S. S. Farber (Eds.), *Preventive psychology: Theory, research and practice* (pp. 199–215). New York: Pergamon Press.

Felner, R. D., Terre, L., & Rowlinson, R. T. (1988). A life transition framework for understanding marital dissolution and family reorganization. In S. A. Wolchik & P. Karoly (Eds.), *Children of divorce: Empirical perspectives on adjustment* (pp. 35–65). New York: Gardner Press.

Fogas, B. S., Wolchik, S. A., & Braver, S. L. (1987, August). *Parenting behavior and psychopathology in children of divorce: Buffering effects.* Paper presented at the American Psychological Association convention, New York.

Forehand, R., & McMahon, R. J. (1981). *Helping the noncompliant child: A clinician's guide to parent teaching.* New York: Guilford Press.

Furstenberg, F. F., Jr., & Teitler, J. O. (1994). Reconsidering the effects of marital disruption: What happens to children of divorce in early adulthood? *Journal of Family Issues, 15,* 173–190.

Goldscheider, F. K., & Goldscheider, C. (1998). The effects of childhood family structure on leaving and returning home. *Journal of Marriage and Family, 60,* 745–756.

Guidubaldi, J., Cleminshaw, H. K., Perry, J. D., Nastasi, B. K., & Lightel, J. (1986). The role of selected family environment factors in children's post-divorce adjustment. *Family Relations, 35,* 141–151.

Hetherington, E. M. (1979). Divorce: A child's perspective. *American Psychologist, 34,* 851–858.

Hetherington, E. M. (1999). Social capital and the development of youth from nondivorced, divorced, and remarried families. In B. Laursen & W. A. Collins (Eds.), *Minnesota Symposia on Child Psychology: Vol. 30. Relationships as developmental contexts* (pp. 177–209). Mahwah, NJ: Erlbaum.

Hetherington, E. M., Clingempeel, W. G., Anderson, E. R., Deal, J. E., Stanley-Hagan, M., Hollier, E. A., et al. (1992). Coping with marital transitions: A family systems perspective. *Monographs of the Society for Child Development, 57*(Serial No. 227), 2–3.

Hetherington, E. M., Cox, M., & Cox, R. (1978). The aftermath of divorce. In J. H. Stevens Jr. & M. Matthews (Eds.), *Mother-child, father-child relations* (pp. 149–176). Washington, DC: National Association for the Education of Young Children.

Hetherington, E. M., Cox, M., & Cox, R. (1981). Effects of divorce on parents and children. In M. Lamb (Ed.), *Nontraditional families* (pp. 233–288). Hillsdale, NJ: Erlbaum.

Hoffmann, J. P., & Johnson, R. A. (1998). A national portrait of family structure and adolescent drug use. *Journal of Marriage and Family, 60,* 633–645.

Institute of Medicine. (1994). *Reducing risks for mental disorders: Frontiers for preventive intervention research.* Washington, DC: National Academy Press.

Kessler, R. C., Davis, C. G., & Kendler, K. S. (1997). Childhood adversity and adult psychiatric disorder in the U.S. National Comorbidity Survey. *Psychological Medicine, 27,* 1101–1119.

Kurdek, L. A. (1981). An integrative perspective on children's divorce adjustment. *American Psychologist, 36,* 856–866.

Lipsey, M. W. (1990). Theory as method: Small theories of treatments. In L. Sechrest, E. Perrin, & J. Bunker (Eds.), *Research methodology: Strengthening causal interpretations of nonexperimental data* (DHHS Publication No. 90-3454; pp. 33–51). Washington, DC: U.S. Department of Health and Human Services, Agency for Health Care Policy and Research.

Long, N., Forehand, R., Fauber, R., & Brody, G. (1987). Self-perceived and independently observed competence of young adolescents as a function of parental marital conflict and recent divorce. *Journal of Abnormal Child Psychology, 15,* 15–27.

Maekikyroe, T., Sauvola, A., Moring, J., Veijola, J., Nieminen, P., Jaervelin, M. R., et al. (1998). Hospital-treated psychiatric disorders in adults with a single-parent and two-parent family background: A 28-year follow-up of the 1966 Northern Finland Birth Cohort. *Family Process, 37,* 335–344.

Masten, A. S. Obradović, J., & Burt, K. B. (in press). Resilience in emerging adulthood: Developmental perspectives on continuity and transformation. In J.J. Arnett & J. Tanner (Eds.), *Emerging adults in America: Coming of age in the 21st century.* Washington, DC: American Psychological Association.

McLanahan, S. (1999). Father absence and the welfare of children. In E. M. Hetherington (Ed.), *Coping with divorce, single parenting, and remarriage* (pp. 117–144). Mahwah, NJ: Erlbaum.

National Center for Health Statistics. (1995). Births, marriages, divorces, and deaths for April 1995. *Monthly Vital Statistics Report, 4,* 1–20.

Novaco, R. A. (1975). *Anger control: The development and evaluation of an experimental treatment.* Lexington, MA: Heath.

Patterson, G. R. (1975). *Families: Application of social learning to family life.* Champaign, IL: Research Press.

Patterson, G. R., & Fisher, P. A. (2002). Recent developments in our understanding of parenting: Bidirectional effects, causal models, and the search for parsimony. In H. B. Marc (Ed.), *Handbook of parenting: Vol. 5. Practical issues in parenting* (2nd ed., pp. 59–88). Mahwah, NJ: Erlbaum.

Rodgers, B., Power, C., & Hope, S. (1997). Parental divorce and adult psychological distress: Evidence from a national cohort: A research note. *Journal of Child Psychology and Psychiatry and Allied Disciplines, 38,* 867–872.

Rothman, J. (1980). *Social R&D: Research and development in the human services.* Englewood Cliffs, NJ: Prentice-Hall.

Sameroff, A. J. (1975). Early influences on development: Fact or fancy? *Merrill-Palmer Quarterly, 21,* 267–294.

Sameroff, A. J. (2000). Developmental systems and psychopathology. *Development and Psychopathology, 12,* 297–312.

Sandler, I. N., Wolchik, S. A., & Braver, S. L. (1988). The stressors of children's postdivorce environments. In S. A. Wolchik & P. Karoly (Eds.), *Children of divorce: Empirical perspectives on adjustment* (pp. 111–143). New York: Gardner Press.

Sandler, I. N., Wolchik, S. A., MacKinnon, D. P., Ayers, T. S., & Roosa, M. W. (1997). Developing linkages between theory and intervention in stress and coping processes. In S. A. Wolchik & I. N. Sandler (Eds.), *Handbook of children's coping: Linking theory and intervention* (pp. 3–40). New York: Plenum Press.

Sandler, I. N., Zhou, Q., Millsap, R., & Wolchik, S. (2006). *Mediation of the 6-year outcomes of the New Beginnings Program.* Manuscript in preparation.

Santrock, J. W., & Warshak, R. (1979). Father custody and social development in boys and girls. *Journal of Social Issues, 35,* 112–125.

Scott, K. G., Mason, G. A., & Chapman, D. A. (1999). The use of epidemiological methodology as a means of influencing public policy. *Child Development, 70,* 1263–1272.

Stolberg, A. L., & Anker, J. M. (1984). Cognitive and behavioral changes in children resulting from parental divorce and consequent environmental changes. *Journal of Divorce, 7,* 23–41.

Stolberg, A. L., & Bush, J. P. (1985). A path analysis of factors predicting children's divorce and adjustment. *Journal of Clinical Child Psychology, 14,* 49–54.

Tein, J.-Y., Sandler, I. N., MacKinnon, D. P., & Wolchik, S. A. (2004). How did it work? Who did it work for? Mediation and mediated moderation of a preventive intervention for children of divorce. *Journal of Consulting and Clinical Psychology, 72,* 617–624.

Troxel, W. M., & Matthews, K. A. (2004). What are the costs of marital conflict and dissolution to children's physical health? *Clinical Child and Family Psychology Review, 7,* 29–57.

U.S. Census Bureau. (2005). *Current population survey* (2004 Annual Social and Economic Supplement). Available from http://www.census.gov/population/socdemo/hh-fam/cpps2004/tabC3-all.csv.

Warren, N. J., Grew, R. S., Ilgen, E. L., Konans, J. T., Bourgoondien, M. E., & Amara, I. A. (1984, June). *Parenting after divorcing: Preventive programs for divorcing families.* Paper presented at the meeting of the National Institute of Mental Health, Washington, DC.

West, S. G., & Aiken, L. S. (1997). Toward understanding individual effects in multicomponent prevention programs: Design and analysis strategies. In K. J. Bryant, M. Windle, & S. G. West (Eds.), *The science of prevention: Methodological advances from alcohol and substance abuse research* (pp. 167–209). Washington, DC: American Psychological Association.

Wolchik, S. A., Sandler, I. N., Millsap, R. E., Plummer, B. A., Greene, S. M., Anderson, E. R., et al. (2002). Six-year follow-up of a randomized, controlled trial of preventive interventions for children of divorce. *Journal of the American Medical Association, 288,* 1874–1881.

Wolchik, S. A., West, S. G., Sandler, I. N., Tein, J.-Y., Coatsworth, D., Lengua, L., et al. (2000). An experimental evaluation of theory-based mother and mother-child programs for children of divorce. *Journal of Consulting and Clinical Psychology, 68,* 843–856.

Wolchik, S. A., West, S. G., Westover, S., Sandler, I. N., Martin, A., Lustig, J., et al. (1993). The children of divorce parenting intervention: Outcome evaluation of an empirically based program. *American Journal of Community Psychology, 21*(3), 293–331.

Zill, N., Morrison, D. R., & Coiro, M. J. (1993). Long-term effects of parental divorce on parent-child relationships, adjustment, and achievement in young adulthood. *Journal of Family Psychology, 7,* 91–103.

PART TWO

DEVELOPMENTAL DISORDERS

MANY SITUATIONS can negatively affect the child's progression toward healthy development. At times, challenges can arise that contribute to problems with development and difficulties for the child and the family. These problems can radiate into the school, relationships, and the community at large. They leave their destructive imprint on various aspects or the child's life and that of the child's family. These situations may manifest themselves as developmental delays, deviance from the expected stages of development, or simply stagnation or inability to move forward. These struggles to achieve mastery of continuous and higher levels of development fall into the category of developmental disorders.

In Chapter 3, Campbell and Kozloff offer a comprehensive program for providing training to parents of children with autism. They propose several important reasons this type of training is crucial to parents who are trying to cope with the challenges of their youngster's autism, not the least of which include the parents' expectations for their children's realistic achievements and the fact that effective programs result in the children learning more in less time. The authors, then, discuss four types of parent training programs: (1) individual separate from a school program, (2) individual connected to school program, (3) group separate from a school program, and (4) group connected to a school program. They state that the fourth approach is the most effective and efficient. As such, their chapter focuses on comprehensive group programs connected to a school. This involves an egalitarian relationship that includes parent and professional input in decision making and educational tasks.

Campbell and Kozloff describe concrete ways in which professionals who possess necessary child care skills can convey these skills to parents, thereby instilling confidence in parents as well as a willingness on their part to try alternative and more constructive techniques for controlling and eliminating negative behaviors and relationship styles. The authors of Chapter 3 also define and clarify the most essential features necessary to establish a comprehensive training program connected with a school. This is particularly instrumental counsel for those mental health professionals who want to replicate this group intervention approach.

The authors present practical as well as empirical evidence for the effectiveness of their program. They offer myriad timely, invaluable, and proven guidelines to facilitate the development, organization, and implementation of this type of program intervention with parents of children with autism. In addition, they include a helpful list of reading materials for use by parents, schools, and professionals. These books, like the author's intervention strategy, teach parents how to instruct their children in essential survival functions, such as eye contact, cooperating, toileting, dressing, large and small motor play, imitation, functional speech, and the achievement of routine household chores. Campbell and Kozloff's intervention approach offers parents a torch to guide them through the darkness, confusion, and frustration that often accompany the challenges of training children with an autism spectrum disorder. The potential for frustration is replaced by a well-earned sense of self-reliance and efficacy in dealing with their children's issues. They also present practical tables that illustrate how to eliminate counterproductive exchanges that result in conflicts and foster productive exchanges that lead to mutual rewards.

In Chapter 4, Sofronoff and Whittingham discuss the challenges and stressors associated with Asperger syndrome, a pervasive developmental disorder that typically involves a pattern of speech development and intellectual capacity that is within the normal range. However, there are marked deficits in the child's ability to understand and empathize with the thoughts and feelings of others. These deficits often affect their development and maintenance of personal interactions and friendships. Problems may arise due to impairments in social functioning, empathy, and special interests, or a need for repetition and routine. Those with Asperger syndrome may respond inappropriately to social cues.

Sofronoff and Whittingham describe parent training and intervention programs that are theoretically grounded in social learning theory. They discuss and contrast different approaches. In what they term "Parent Training Program 1," they specifically target the needs of parents of children who have been diagnosed with Asperger syndrome by the consultant pediatrician at the Mater Children's Hospital, Queensland, Australia. The program they designed and present covers six primary components of intervention: (1) psychoeducation, (2) Comic Strip Conversations, (3) Social Stories, (4) management of problem behaviors, (5) management of rigid behaviors and speech interests, and (6) management of anxiety. They point out that in attempting to assess the usefulness and acceptability of these six components of their intervention with parents of children with Asperger syndrome, there was a good deal of variability in the strategies used and in the parents' reports of effectiveness.

The authors of Chapter 4 discuss and compare Parent Training Program 1 with "Parent Training Program 2—Stepping Stones Triple P." The Stepping Stones is a recent version of the Triple P—Positive Parenting Program that specifically targets families of children with disabilities. It is also a behavioral intervention based on social learning. The Triple P approach to parenting focuses on providing children with positive attention and managing children's behavior in a constructive, nonpunitive manner. The authors specify that the strategies offered to the parents can be grouped into four categories. These are delineated in Table 4.3. They include specific methods for the development of positive relationships, techniques for encouraging desirable behaviors, ways of teaching new skills and behaviors, and practical strategies for managing misbehavior. The authors share some interesting case studies that demonstrate the problems that might be experienced by families of children with Asperger syndrome. They then discuss the management and treatment of these problems, proving the effectiveness of their invaluable and inventive approach.

The authors of the chapters in Part Two present creative training programs for parents of children with autism (Chapter 3) and Asperger syndrome (Chapter 4). They offer theoretically based as well as practical methods for managing and controlling the problems associated with these disorders. Not only do these programs effectively modify the disruptive and negative behaviors of the children, they also instill competence, self-efficacy, and a beacon of hope for parents who deal with the immediate and long-range challenges of these childhood developmental disorders.

CHAPTER 3

Comprehensive Programs
for Families of Children
with Autism

MONICA CAMPBELL and MARTIN KOZLOFF

THIS CHAPTER reflects the authors' many years of work with families of children with autism (Kozloff, 1973, 1974, 1994a, 1994b). It presents what we think are the most important elements of programs.

WHY WORK WITH FAMILIES?

The challenges of autism do not go away. One of the authors recently spoke with an assistant principal of an elementary school. The AP explained that a newly admitted boy with autism was doing well in the school program, but not doing well at home. The AP said, "This is so hard on the parents. They don't know what's happened. They don't know what to do. The whole family is stressed out." All the careful research, differential diagnostics, educational methods, laws, and medications developed over the past 40 years don't change the fact that for every family, autism is an unexpected event for which no one is prepared. Service providers must treat each family of a child with autism as if it were the first family.

There are five important reasons for providing training to parents of children with autism:

1. Effective teachers and benevolent social policies come and go. In the long run, the family is the only group that children with autism can depend on to seek, obtain, and deliver services.
2. Families of children with autism face many stressors and challenges, including the unexpectedness of their child's disability; their child's

67

behavioral deficits and aversive behaviors; the difficulty finding answers and services; confusion from competing claims about treatment efficacy; and strained interactions with neighbors, relatives, and people in community settings. Without social support and practical child-management and instructional skills, the resources of many families (money, energy, time, coping) are increasingly strained; marital conflict and emotional problems develop; unproductive interactions with the child with autism stabilize into rigid patterns; and careers are disrupted.

3. Initial and progress assessment provided by parents contributes essential information to a comprehensive assessment and education program plan. Parents can make narrative recordings of their child's behavior in everyday settings, such as dressing, eating, cooperating, playing, and speaking. In addition, parents can collect quantitative baseline data on specific behaviors (e.g., the rate of tantrums, the average duration of play episodes, the rate of functional speech). This information can be used to develop and to sequence instructional objectives, and to decide which settings (e.g., special teaching sessions, individual versus group, incidental learning opportunities) are best for initial instruction (skill acquisition), generalization and application, fluency building, and independence.

4. Parents' knowledge of their child's educational goals instills expectations for concrete achievements and encourages parental involvement to ensure academic and social gains.

5. When parents conduct effective home educational programs, their children learn more in less time; their children's desirable behaviors can be generalized from school to home (e.g., speech) and from home to school (e.g., washing dishes); attendance increases; and families and schools can develop more coherent programs for the children. They can decide which skills will receive initial instruction in school, which in the home, and which in both environments at the same time (see Cronin, Slade, Bechtel, & Anderson, 1992; Guralnick, 1997; Hardin & Littlejohn, 1994; Newman, 2005).

TYPES OF PROGRAMS

Programs for families vary in four ways: individual program; individual program connected to school program; group program not affiliated with the child's school; group program affiliated with the child's school program. Each of the four styles has advantages and disadvantages:

1. *Individual program:* This version is a typical clinical relationship, usually with a psychologist. It provides parents with the possibility

of a close, personal relationship. However, it is expensive; there is not likely to be in-home coaching; the educational scope of the program (i.e., range of target behaviors) is likely to be narrow; and there is no group support.

2. *Individual program connected to school program:* This version makes it possible for the home program to operate along with the school program. Parents can work on generalizing functional speech to everyday activities. It also means that the family may have a close relationship with the coach. However, there is no learning from the experiences of other families (e.g., how another family solved a problem, or a method that does not work) and no group support. This is also inefficient as the same information is delivered over and over individually.

3. *Group program not affiliated with the child's school:* An organization for families with children who have autism and other disabilities may offer this type of program. The advantages are efficiency (information that all families need is provided at one time), group cohesion (the emotional and hands-on support that each family receives), and group problem solving and modeling. The disadvantage is that home programs may not be consistent with the children's programs in school.

4. *Group program affiliated with the child's school program:* This is the most effective and efficient design. It is efficient (information that all families need is provided at one time); group cohesion provides support for each family; there is group problem solving and modeling; the children's home programs and school programs will be consistent and complementary (e.g., play skills learned at school may be generalized to the home); each family can have an individual consultant as well; the program (and the interfamily contacts made in the program) can last a long time; and veteran families can help to train newer families.

The remainder of this chapter discusses comprehensive group programs connected to a school.

FEATURES OF AN EFFECTIVE PARENT-PROFESSIONAL PARTNERSHIP

Although technical proficiency is essential for professionals (teachers, family specialists) working with families, this is not enough. Given the anxiety, sadness, and chronic strain of parenting a child with autism, professionals also must be skilled at initiating and sustaining a more personal relationship (see Darch, Miao, & Shippen, 2004, for a review of this issue).

The research of Blue-Banning, Summers, Franklin, Nelson, and Beegle (2004) identifies the features of this relationship. Blue-Banning et al. held in-depth interviews and focus groups with 53 professionals and 137 adult family members of children with and without disabilities. The participants represented a wide range of ethnic groups and socioeconomic levels. The findings suggested that collaborative partnerships are defined by six dimensions—communication, personal commitment, equality, skills, trust, and respect—as shown in specific behaviors.

COMMUNICATION

Important aspects of communication include tact, openness, interest, frequency, and positive statements emphasizing the child's progress and family strengths (Spann, Kohler, & Soenksen, 2003). The teacher need not agree with everything a parent says but should convey understanding and appreciation of the parent's point of view (Wilson, 1995).

"I can see how Scott's many problem behaviors leave you feeling helpless. Anyone would feel that way. We'd feel the same way if our child had some kind of infection that we couldn't cure with commonsense remedies. Then all of a sudden we find an effective antibiotic. We're no longer helpless. This program will give you some of the tools that we use here at the school—and these tools will help you to replace many of Scott's problem behaviors at home, just as we do here."

Professionals should also respond with animation and interest (Howard, Williams, & Lepper, 2005), through facial expressions, tone of voice, and posture:

"Yes! That's an excellent idea!" rather than, "Mmm hmm. Interesting."

In addition, open-ended questioning appears to foster more communication from parents than close-ended questions: "Please tell me some of the most important things that have happened since you first suspected that something was not right with Robin's development."

This enables parents to identify what is salient for them, which enables the consultant to clarify, help parents to elaborate, and clear up misinterpretations (e.g., that they are to blame for their children's disabilities).

PERSONAL COMMITMENT

It is important for professionals to express personal commitment to the family by valuing the relationship and viewing the welfare of the child and family as more than a part of the job. Indicators of commitment include flexible meeting times and objectives, accessibility (e.g., availability for phone calls and as-needed home visits), and empathy.

EQUALITY

Features of an egalitarian relationship include parent and professional input in decision making and educational tasks, and willingness to explore suggestions made by parents:

PARENT: I really think he does it for attention. I mean, attention reinforces the behavior, like when we look at him or ask him what he wants.

CONSULTANT: I'm not sure. But you know him better than I. We could do a functional analysis to find out. For three days, you respond as usual, with attention, and count episodes of whining. Then for the next week you never attend to whining. Instead. . . .

In our experience, egalitarian relationships with families promote investment in outcomes, which is revealed in high attendance, group participation, initiative (e.g., starting home educational programs independently), and persistence in the face of difficulties:

PARENT: Hey, we are getting pretty good at this! Last week we did a functional analysis of play. We found out that we helped to initiate Jerry's play by pointing to his toys, but that we *reinforced* playing only about once in five minutes. Then we increased reinforcement to about two times per minute. Play episodes doubled in the amount of playtime.

CONSULTANT: Terrific! Excellent plan and initiative.

SKILLS

Not only must professionals *have* skills, they need clearly to *reveal* their skills. This builds parents' confidence and willingness to take risks (such as no longer giving in to their child's tantrums). In addition to using effective instructional practices, professionals can demonstrate skills in the following three ways:

1. Presenting alternatives and taking parents through the process for weighing and choosing the better one.
2. Showing parents how confusing occurrences can often be explained (made to appear rational) in fairly simple terms.
   "You are worn out *not* because you are weak, but because the demands on you exceed your resources. We can improve this by reducing the demands (for example, by decreasing Scott's problem behavior). And we can get more resources—such as respite and home assistance."

3. Accurately identifying past events:

> Ms. JONES: Well, we used to try to ignore Scott's tantrums.
> TEACHER: And he tantrumed louder and longer, didn't he?
> Ms. JONES: Yes. I thought I'd go crazy. How did you know?
> TEACHER: It's called an extinction burst. He was trying to coerce you into giving him what you used to give him to calm him down.

TRUST

Again, parents who trust their consultant are more likely to have confidence in the consultant's judgments and suggestions, to reveal more personal information ("Sometimes I want to spank her hard. I feel awful, but that's how I *feel*"), and to take risks. Professionals can foster trust through empathy, nonjudgmental responses ("Of course you sometimes feel like spanking her. Who wouldn't?! Anything to make her stop!"), maintaining parents' privacy, and fulfilling agreements.

RESPECT

Many parents of children with autism feel humiliated by the insensitive comments and stares of other persons. They may feel like outsiders in their community—the odd family. It is essential that professionals show respect for families though sensitivity when listening and responding; treating parents as *cognitively competent* (akin to the person with hearing loss saying, "I'm deaf, not stupid!"); showing appreciation for their efforts and for their personal qualities ("You are one tough bunch of people!"); and maintaining their privacy.

PROGRAM DESIGN

A comprehensive program connected with a school is feasible and, as noted, has significant benefits for the family, children, and the school. The program should have the following eight features:

1. *A workable size:* A group program should contain between 3 or 4 and 20 families. Fewer than 4 families does not have the feel of a group. More than 20 makes it difficult for families to discuss issues or for consultants to provide enough individual attention during meetings and during home visits.
2. *A carefully planned curriculum:* It should begin with general family issues and educational knowledge, move to individualized educational programs, and then shift to long-term subjects. There is flexibility in the number of weeks allotted for each unit of the curriculum:

Meeting 1: One of the consultants, acting as program moderator, states program objectives and features; families introduce themselves and their children; consultants help families to examine their experiences and to construct a partial success story.

Meetings 2 and 3: Consultants help parents replace counterproductive parent-child interaction patterns (exchanges).

Meetings 4 and 5: Consultants present features of a good individual education plan (IEP). It should assess the child's needs and identify behaviors and skills to work on that are (a) most relevant to the family (e.g., increasing compliance, reducing tantrums), and (b) connected to the child's school program (e.g., generalizing functional speech from classroom to home).

Meetings 6 and 7: These meetings focus on basic educational (behavioral) concepts, principles, and procedures (e.g., reinforcement contingencies; shaping; prompting. More is added as needed in later weeks (e.g., phases of mastery, such as fluency and generalization).

Meetings 8 and 9: Consultants and parents plan, conduct, evaluate, and revise the first home teaching program (e.g., eye contact, sitting, cooperating, simple tasks).

Meetings 10 to 17: These sessions are devoted to planning, conducting, evaluating, and revising more advanced teaching programs; (e.g., building fluency on earlier target behaviors; working on more complex behaviors such as playing, imitation, speech, social skills).

Meeting 18: Work continues on family interaction (exchanges) and earlier target skills. There is also work on new skills and on the handling of issues such as stress, the need for support and hands-on assistance, and revisions of the IEP.

3. *Weekly meetings for the first nine or so sessions:* Families need frequent and timely coaching and group support. Meetings 10 to 17 can be biweekly, but *weekly meetings are still best* to sustain momentum and to firm skills. From the 18th meeting on, the time between meetings can be gradually stretched, but should return to several consecutive weekly meetings as needed to handle common difficulties or to present new information.

4. *A general program contract:* This contract specifies the mutual obligations of families and program consultants. Families agree to attend all meetings, to arrive on time, to read all required materials, to do all written assignments, to do all agreed-on weekly home teaching assignments, and to be available for scheduled home visits. Consultants agree to begin all meetings on time; to provide written materials; to schedule home visits; to receive and return phone calls and

e-mails in a timely fashion. The contract is signed by the parents and a staff member. A copy is kept by each.

In addition to the general contract—discussed and signed during the first meeting—*weekly contracts* specify readings, home visits, home teaching assignments, and other activities (e.g., parents agree to go out to dinner; consultant agrees to find an effective program on toilet training). The weekly contract is written and signed at the end of the meeting.

Our programs that used contracts were more effective than the programs that did not. Attendance was higher; parents and staff were more serious about knowing exactly what they had to do and getting it done. Without contracts that focused attention on specific topics and agreed-on tasks, meetings quickly became opportunities to ventilate feelings and to complain.

5. *A consultant for each family:* In programs with a large number of families, three or four families with similar children (e.g., age, degree of disability and ability, educational goals, and programs) have the same consultant. During meetings, the assigned consultant sits near those families and discusses important points during breaks. At the end of the meeting, the consultants and parents plan the next week's work and write their contracts—part of which may be to telephone or to visit each other for coaching and support.

6. *Weekly home visits in conjunction with the early meetings:* The consultant and family review the contracted assignments. The family demonstrates any teaching programs they were working on. If possible, the consultant video records teaching sessions or family interactions. The consultant and family examine these recordings to identify strong and weak points: "Excellent for rewarding him so fast"; "Oooops, you just rewarded him for whining when you asked him what was wrong." They then revise and rewrite the plans as needed.

"Okay, so for the next week, you will make a list of ten different simple tasks for Tim to do. You will ask Tim to do each one each day, about one per hour. You will prompt him through the task. And you will give him a big hug and bite of snack when he finishes. If he's noncompliant, you will walk away. Let's write that out. Call me in two days to tell me how it's working."

7. *A consistent pattern for organizing meetings:* Consider the following format:
   a. First, review each family's past week's home program. Families are prompted to use concepts and principles they've been taught to describe their programs and the outcomes.

      "Last week we were increasing the duration of Jessie's eye contact. We had sit-down sessions twice a day—breakfast and afternoon snack—for 22 minutes. We sat at the kitchen table, where we hold sessions. We worked with her one at a time. I did the teaching and Bill counted the number of eye contacts that were four seconds or longer. I would hold a bite of food near my eyes and say, 'Look at me.' If she looked within three seconds and held her gaze for four seconds, I would say, 'Good for looking at Mommy!' and put the bite in her mouth. If she did not look within three seconds or if she turned away before four seconds, I would put the bite down and turn my head to the side a little. I would wait ten seconds and start again. So basically this is differential reinforcement. Next session, Bill worked with Jessie and I took data. Here's our chart. Eye contact dropped on Thursday. I think she was satiated from lunch." (See Figure 3.1.)

In programs with six or more families, it's not possible to review every family's program. Therefore, have families rotate who is on deck.

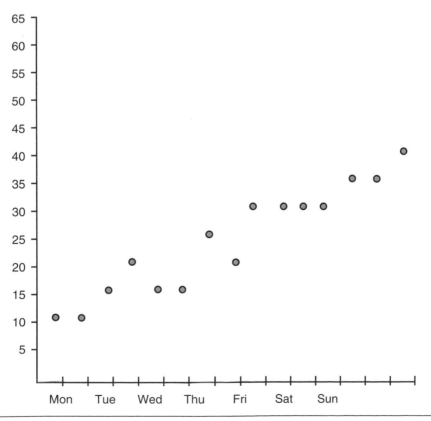

Figure 3.1 Jessie's Chart of Four or More Second Eye Contacts.

Consultants help the group to generalize each family's program—and the relevant concepts and evaluations (eye contact dropped because the child was satiated on the reinforcer)—to their own programs.

b. Next is the main business portion, in which consultants present new material (e.g., educational concepts, principles, and methods such as prompting, chaining, fluency-building via speed drills). Consultants show illustrative videos, demonstrate new methods, and have parents practice them.

c. Consultants explain next educational steps that are common to the families, such as everyone implementing a program to increase cooperation and one self-help activity—with all families using the same basic procedures. Details (reinforcers, cooperation tasks) are tailored to each family at the end of the meeting.

d. Consultants open the floor to discussion of difficulties families may be having, such as fear of depriving siblings, lack of progress in a child's program (e.g., the rate of functional speech is not increasing), fatigue, marital disagreements over best methods. Consultants should help families develop partial solutions; for example, scheduled breaks from parenting to reduce fatigue; special outings with siblings; using a checklist to see if all elements of effective instruction are used, and which elements of a procedure might be altered.

Ms. JONES: I feel so tired at the end of the day. I don't think I can be effective.

Ms. COSTA: Well, maybe what we do will work for you. From 5:30 to 7:00 P.M., Monday, Wednesday, and Friday, I am off the clock. I take a nap, sit in the yard, or go for a run. Jorge makes the supper. Two days a week, no one cooks. It's takeout or baloney sandwiches.

e. Finally, families and consultants plan the next week's home program. This could involve trying an improved teaching program plan (e.g., using a wider range of reinforcers, adding visual prompts) and incorporating suggestions for handling difficulties such as fatigue. Home visits and telephone calls are scheduled. Again, this is all written up as a weekly contract.

8. *Readings and materials:* Thirty years ago, before there were well-designed (or hardly any) schools or classrooms for children with autism, families in our programs read material written by one of the authors (Kozloff, 1974). The book taught parents how to teach eye contact, cooperating, toileting, dressing, large and small motor play, imitation, functional speech, and household chores. In fact, the book

alone was effective in teaching parents how to teach and in producing significant change in their children (Kaufman, 1976). However, parents now can employ tested materials that are also used in their children's school programs, or materials that supplement or complement the school program. Examples include *Teach Your Child to Read in 100 Easy Lessons* (Engelmann, Haddox, & Bruner, 1983); *Language for Learning* (Engelmann & Osborn, 1999); *DISTAR Arithmetic* (Engelmann & Carnine, 1975); *Behavioral Intervention for Young Children with Autism* (Maurice, Green, & Luce, 1996); *Teaching Kids and Adults with Autism* (Fad & Moulton, 1999); *Basic Skill Builders* (Beck, Anderson, & Conrad, 1999); *Activity Schedules for Children with Autism* (McClannahan & Krantz, 1998); and *Do-Watch-Listen-Say* (Quill, 2000).

EARLY MEETINGS (1 THROUGH 3 OR 4)

There are two important objectives at the beginning of a program: (1) building group cohesion—a sense of group membership and esprit de corps—which will increase parents' optimism, instill self-attributions of strength, and reduce the burden of needless guilt; and (2) improving parent-child interaction.

GROUP COHESION AND MEMBERSHIP

One way to accomplish the first objective is to guide families though an examination of what they've been through. Common experiences for many families include the following:

- Parents feel shock, bewilderment, confusion, and sorrow when they finally realize or are told by a clinician that their child has autism, that their child is not the child they expected, and that their lives are forever changed—and not for the better as they may see it.
- Parents develop feelings of guilt, shame, and remorse for having done something to cause their child's autism, or not having found proper diagnosis and treatment soon enough.

"Maybe it was because I let him cry when he was an infant."

"Why didn't I see it sooner!"

"Maybe this is punishment for something I did when I was younger."

The effects of these destructive and false notions are revealed in the worried faces, dejected postures, and timid social behavior of some parents—who see themselves marked by fate. Autism in the family is more than a matter of contingencies that need correcting. It is existential as well. Autism, like other developmental disabilities in children, confronts parents with problems that most persons in an affluent society never notice, let alone must solve; namely, the purpose of their lives, the fact that things are not and never will be as they wanted them to be, and the responsibility for creating the meaning and the value of their existence (Frankl, 1970).

- There is a perception of being different, weird, damaged. Parents know that having a "normal" child is a symbol of membership in society, and so parents often label themselves deviant. This is confirmed again and again through the distancing reactions of other persons in public, who stare at the child making bizarre hand gestures and strange noises, who steer clear of the family as they make their way through a mall, and who offer unasked for advice—as if the parents were so stupid that they didn't realize something was wrong.

- Many parents feel isolated (and are isolated) as they spend more and more time trying to manage their child in the home; as relatives withdraw; and as their energy declines.

- Families often speak of going through a fruitless search for professionals who can tell them what is wrong with their child ("Don't worry; he'll grow out of it"), who give them multiple diagnoses, or who have few concrete and worthwhile suggestions for helping their child. The result is anger, confusion, and sometimes hopelessness. But for others, the result is activation of self-reliance. Some parents say, "Well, we realized that if anyone was going to help Larry it was going to be us." Or, "We will never quit until we get the right program."

- Without timely assistance, stress in the family typically increases as the parents have to handle what become habitual disruptive behaviors and deficits (e.g., dressing) that require extra work. In time, parents may be less able to satisfy each other and work together. Both parents, but especially the mother, come to feel alone and overwhelmed. These spousal problems may end in divorce, depression, anxiety, and even less ability to satisfy their child's needs.

Ironically, these experiences are a resource that consultants can use to achieve the two objectives mentioned earlier. The group leader invites families (sitting around a table) to "describe what it has been like with your child, from the time you first thought something was wrong." The consultant probes for how these events made parents feel, how they made sense of their experiences (e.g., self-blame? biogenetic?), and how they responded (passively, actively, productively, unproductively). The consultant writes the main points, in temporal sequence, on a wall chart. The consultant emphasizes the following three points:

1. Parents did as well as anyone could do in the circumstances.
2. Parents achieved certain desirable outcomes such as skills they taught their child.
3. The families share many of the same experiences; they have always been "a group waiting to happen"; and they can help each other now and in the future.

As the discussion moves along, the consultant should help parents build on the points made.

"Think of other things you did with Larry that worked."

"Now that you have other parents who have the same needs, what might you ask of another family?" [Babysit for us once in awhile. Help during a crisis. Take a sibling with you and your other children to a movie.]

"So, you went from one professional to another. You never gave up."

"What does this say about you as parents and as persons?"

The discussion should end with general agreement that the families have been partial success stories despite the obstacles, and largely because the parents have strengths such as persistence, recognition of moral responsibility, and intelligence to see what is needed. Esprit de corps can be furthered by stressing that if families could accomplish what they have alone, *think of what they can do together.*

Improving Parent-Child Interaction, or Exchanges

This section discusses the importance of productive parent-child interaction, describes different kinds of interaction, and suggests methods for improving interaction. After the first few meetings, the first home program is to replace counterproductive interaction patterns with productive interaction patterns. This is an early, essential task for the following four reasons:

1. Counterproductive exchanges in the home weaken or even reverse beneficial behavior changes produced by proficient instruction in school or at home.
2. Replacing counterproductive exchanges reduces a child's problem behaviors and increases cooperation. These changes reduce stress in the family.
3. Learning how to replace counterproductive exchanges and how to increase productive exchanges increases parents' optimism and provides techniques (e.g., timely reinforcement, differential

reinforcement of desirable behavior) they need to teach specific skills in the home.

4. Everyday social exchanges, not teaching sessions, are the pervasive context of psychosocial development.

Early programs for families of children with problem behaviors (e.g., Allen & Harris, 1966; Patterson & Brodsky, 1966; Wahler, Winkel, Peterson, & Morrison, 1965) focused almost entirely on parent-child interactions.

What are exchanges? An exchange is simply an interaction between two or more persons, examined with respect to the reinforcement contingencies. Sometimes an exchange is a single incident:

MOM: Andy, come here, please.
ANDY: [Comes into the living room].
MOM: Thanks, Honey.

Usually, exchanges are in sequences, such as nagging—until a parent finally gives up or a child complies. Here is an example of a common sequence of exchanges between Brad (a 5-year-old boy with autism) and Brad's mother, leading to a highly counterproductive concluding exchange:

[Brad enters the kitchen, looks at Mom, and whines.]

MOM: What's the matter, Honey? [Mom reinforces the whining and provides a signal for Brad to continue.]
BRAD: Cookie. Want Cookie!
MOM: You want a cookie? [Mom reinforces the coercive demand and provides another signal for Brad to continue.]
BRAD: Cookie. [By answering, Brad reinforces Mom's asking a question at this spot in the sequence.]
MOM: I'm sorry, Honey. It's too close to supper. You can have cookies after supper. [Mom's nonreinforcement of Brad's request is aversive to Brad.]
BRAD: Cookie!!! [He screams, a response that is aversive to Mom.]
MOM: Are we supposed to scream? [This pseudoquestion inadvertently reinforces the scream.]
BRAD: [He jumps up and down and screams some more.]
MOM: [She gives Brad a cookie.] Okay, but just this one.
BRAD: [He stops screaming and starts smiling.]

Let's look at the sequence of exchanges and at what happens in each exchange:

- Each person directs behavior at the other person.
- Some of these behaviors function as unconditioned or conditioned stimuli that elicit feelings. Brad's screaming instantly raises Mom's blood pressure and elicits fear ("He might throw something next!") and perhaps anger.
- Some of these behaviors are also cues or signals for the other person to respond. Brad's whining and screaming set the occasion for Mom to reinforce these behaviors. And Mom's questions set the occasion for Brad to demand cookies.
- Each person's response functions as a reinforcer or punisher or neutral event with respect to the other person's previous response. For example, Mom positively reinforces Brad's whining by asking him another question. She reinforces Brad's screaming (escalated whining) when she verbally concedes and gives him the cookie. And Brad negatively reinforces Mom's reinforcement of Brad's screaming when he stops screaming and starts smiling. Indeed, this is strong reinforcement of Mom's escape-from-Brad's-tantrum behavior because Mom was reinforced (Brad stopped) when Mom was under duress.

You can see that each person is learning something in each exchange and over the sequence of exchanges:

- Brad whines and screams more and more often to get what he wants.
- Brad learns to escalate the aversiveness of his demands. In time, he may begin the sequence by screaming rather than asking, because screaming is closest to the reinforcement.
- Mom learns to give in to screaming because nothing else works, while giving in always and immediately enables her to escape from Brad's aversive behavior. She gives in more and more often. The more she gives in, the more Brad's aversive behaviors increase, the more stressed Mom is, and the more likely she is to do anything (reinforcing to Brad) to stop Brad's behavior.
- Whining and screaming compete with desirable behavior such as waiting, doing something else, and talking. As whining and screaming increase, desirable behavior may not increase or will decrease.
- Mom may escalate to the use of punishment. "I'll give you something to scream about!" This may start a different sequence of exchanges—mutual punishment—Brad hits, too.
- At the end of the day, Mom is exhausted. This affects interaction with her spouse. Mom may need more support and empathy than her spouse can provide. This sets the stage for counterproductive spousal exchanges.

Following is a typology of exchanges and the short-term and long-term changes that each type produces:

Counterproductive (Conflict) Exchanges	Productive (Mutual Reward) Alternative Exchanges
Rewarded coercion	Unrewarded coercion
Rewarded threat	Earning
Rewarded noncompliance, nagging	Single signals/cooperation training
Lack of opportunities for desirable behavior	Plenty of opportunities for desirable behavior
Lack of rewards for desirable behavior	Plenty of rewards for desirable behavior
Aversive methods	Proper use of aversive methods

REPLACING COUNTERPRODUCTIVE EXCHANGES WITH PRODUCTIVE EXCHANGES

We have used the following eight procedures to help families improve parent-child interactions:

1. Explain basic principles of behavior, drawing on general and family examples:

   Signals → Behavior → Consequences

Requests	Rewards (positive reinforcement)
Questions	Escape/avoidance/delay (negative reinforcement)
Gestures	Punishment by removing rewards
	Punishment through aversive events
	Not responding (extinction)

   Parents learn the following skills:
   a. How to identify different contingencies and to predict short-term and long-term behavior change.
   b. How events become effective signals versus ineffective signals.
   c. How to differentially reinforce desirable behavior.
   d. How to shape desirable behavior by reinforcing small improvements.
2. Parents read and discuss counterproductive and productive exchanges (see Table 3.1). They provide examples from family life. These examples, and other examples that have been video recorded with parents' permission, are analyzed. Parents (as a group during

Table 3.1

Counterproductive and Productive Exchanges

Counterproductive Exchange	Productive, Alternative Exchange
Rewarded Coercion	*Unrewarded Coercion*

Rewarded Coercion

In the long run, this may be the most destructive exchange. The exchange may be initiated when the parent asks the child to do something or tells the child that he can't have something. Or, it may be initiated by the child. In either case, the child performs a behavior that is aversive to the parent—whining (irritating), playing with feces (disgusting), screaming, bizarre gestures, hitting. At first, the parent typically tries to stop aversive behavior of lower intensity (e.g., bizarre gestures) by looking at the child, as if to say, "Are we supposed to flap our hands?" Or, the parent responds to more intensive behavior by telling the child to stop. These escape responses of the parent rarely stop the child's behavior—they usually reinforce the child's behavior because the rate of these behaviors increases. One reason a mere look from a parent is a reinforcer may be that the child's repertoire is so deficient that he or she is in a state of deprivation.

As the child continues to perform the aversive behavior—at a higher rate—the parent tries other ways to stop the behavior; for example, giving the child something to eat or cuddling the child. These events do interrupt the child's aversive behavior. Therefore, the parent's escape behavior is negatively reinforced. The exchange is now complete. *The child is reinforced for aversive behavior, and the parent is reinforced for reinforcing the aversive behavior.* Each person has learned how to participate in this interaction. The frequency of the exchange increases. The parent becomes more stressed. The parent may try new ways to stop the child's aversive behavior, such as giving the child baths or new toys. The more the child coerces reinforcers via aversive behavior, the less the child "needs" to use speech, cooperation, or other desirable behaviors.

Sometimes, the child becomes satiated on the reinforcing responses of the parent.

Unrewarded Coercion

When the child performs a problem behavior, the parent waits and mentally rehearses what to do. The parent either completely ignores the problem behavior, times-out the child, or if necessary, uses punishment procedures appropriately. The parent is alert to desirable behaviors to reinforce.

(continued)

Table 3.1 *(Continued)*

Counterproductive Exchange	Productive, Alternative Exchange

Rewarded Coercion (continued)

In this case, the child's aversive behavior (e.g., tantrum) continues, or the child does something even more aversive, such as hitting himself. The parent may then provide a new and even more reinforcing response. At some point, the child may perform the "last straw" behavior—hitting an infant sibling. The child may then be sent to a residential placement.

Rewarded Threat

This exchange sometimes develops after the rewarded coercion exchange. The child usually performs the behavior that is the most aversive to the parent after "working up to it" or in certain circumstances (e.g., noise, the parent makes a request, the child sees cookies). Once the parent learns the events that precede and predict the child's more aversive behavior, the parent does something to prevent this behavior by, in effect, placating the child. Instead of waiting for the child to escalate to hitting himself to coerce a snack from the parent, the parent gives a snack when the child is merely whining. Sometimes the parent is not paying attention to the child's pre-aversive signal behavior (whining). The child then tries another behavior, such as screaming. The parent notices and reinforces this behavior. The child now has two ways to evoke a placating reinforcer from the parent.

We have seen this exchange increase to the point that a child is controlling the household with a large repertoire of threatening behavior. Family members are hypervigilant for cues that predict a blowup from the child. The child's behavior and the parents' and siblings' responses have resulted in no one asking the child to do anything and no one refusing the child anything he wants.

Unrewarded Threat, Earning

The parent ignores mild problem behaviors (e.g., whining for a snack), but prompts the child to perform desirable behavior to earn the snack. As the child cooperates more often in this exchange, the parent increases the amount of desirable behavior required. The parent often signals the child with the statement, "As soon as you . . . , you (can, will) . . ."

Table 3.1 *(Continued)*

Counterproductive Exchange	Productive, Alternative Exchange
Rewarded Noncompliance/Nagging	*Single Signals/Cooperation Training*

Another common exchange involves parents asking the child to do something (come to the kitchen or do a simple task), followed by the child turning away, walking away, performing a bizarre behavior, or whining. The untrained parent is likely to repeat the request, and the child is likely to repeat the noncooperative response. It seems that each repetition of the request reinforces the child's noncooperative response. If the child finally does what the parent asks, the parent's nagging is reinforced on a variable schedule. The parent has learned a rule: "You have to ask her a thousand times." Since the parent is strongly reinforced, the parent feels inclined to reward the child. "Thank you for coming, Brad. Have a cookie." This reinforces the child for performing a series of noncooperative behaviors before the final cooperative response. On the other hand, some parents simply give up requesting anything, and the child's role in the family is "guest" or "invalid."

The parent is prepared with a set of simple tasks and requests to initiate the tasks. The parent waits until the child is attentive, prompts the child's attention, or waits until the child is about to ask for or demand something. The parent then makes the request. "As soon as you (put this wrapper in the trash, put this piece in the puzzle) you (can, will) . . ." The parent asks only once. If the child does not cooperate, the parent walks away, and gives the request again after a waiting period.

In cases where a child is extremely noncompliant, the parent gives the request and prompts the child to perform a simple action, such as stand up. This is repeated until the child responds reliably and quickly. Then the parent makes requests, as above, in a more incidental fashion.

Lack of Opportunities and Rewards for Desirable Behavior	*Plenty of Opportunities and Rewards for Desirable Behavior*

The more the child's undesirable behaviors increase (partly because of the rewarded coercion, rewarded threat, or nagging exchanges), the less the parents want to interact with their child. They are happy just to find a few minutes of peace. The result, however, is that the child receives too few opportunities to perform desirable behavior (the parents have stopped asking the child to help set the table) and too little reinforcement when the child does engage in desirable behavior (e.g., self-play), as the parents finally have a few minutes to relax. This means that there is little growth in the child's repertoire of desirable behavior and low parental expectations that the child will "get any better."

Throughout the day, parents attempt to initiate desirable behavior with simple requests that the child join family activities. For example, the child is asked to put two bowls on the table before ice cream is served. Parents reinforce these behaviors naturally (e.g., the child receives ice cream) or with praise and activity reinforcers (e.g., if the child cooperates with the request to work a puzzle).

Parents are also alert to short episodes or unskillful episodes of desirable behavior (e.g., the child nicely asks for a snack but in an ungrammatical way). The parents reinforce these behaviors immediately.

(continued)

Table 3.1 *(Continued)*

Counterproductive Exchange	Productive, Alternative Exchange
Aversive Methods	*Proper Use of Aversive Methods*
It is rare in our experience, but some parents finally use aversive methods to stop their child's aversive behaviors, for example, spanking. If this works (at least temporarily), then the parents do it more often. Unfortunately, parents seldom know how to teach desirable behaviors at the same time. Therefore, their punitive responses merely teach the child to avoid them. Most often, parents do not use aversive methods properly. They wait too long; they are not consistent; the aversive event is not intense enough to stop the child's behavior. In this case, the parents may increase the intensity of their punitive response and/or the child may use his own aversive behavior to keep the parents away or to stop the parent's delivery of punishment. For example, the child smacks herself in the face, bites herself or her parent. The combination of this exchange, rewarded coercion, and rewarded threat turns home life into a waking nightmare.	We have rarely taught parents to use aversive methods. In most cases, the preceding productive exchanges reduce problem behaviors. The few times that we have taught parents to use aversive methods, it was because the child performed a "last straw" problem behavior at a high rate; the behavior occurred in a predictable time or place; the child had alternative behaviors in his repertoire; or the child was largely nonverbal. When the child performs the targeted behavior, the parent responds, for example, with a brief but fairly painful slap on the buttocks along with the word "No!" The slap is hard enough to interrupt the response. When the child calms down, the parent presents a request that the child perform a simple task, such as sit down, and the parent reinforces this.

group programs) think of alternative, productive ways to respond to and weaken undesirable behavior and ways to respond to and increase desirable behavior.

3. Parents target one counterproductive exchange to replace with a productive alternative. One family may choose to work on nagging. Another may choose to work on whining for snacks. Parents are encouraged to select the easiest exchanges to work on; for example, the child has desirable alternative behaviors; it is feasible for the parents to try to ignore the problem behavior; it will be easy to reinforce the desirable alternative behavior.

4. Parents write a detailed plan for working on the exchange and for taking data. Table 3.2 is an example of a family's plan.

5. Parents practice their plan with other parents in a group and with their coach. They modify the plan if needed (e.g., it may be too hard for a parent to respond as planned).

6. Parents try their first plan during the week. Their coach calls to check progress and to solve problems, and makes a home visit to give more direct assistance (e.g., modeling how to reinforce) and praise.

Table 3.2
Example of Family's First Plan for Improving Parent-Child Exchanges

Counterproductive Exchange	Productive, Alternative Exchange

Rewarded Coercion

Brad screams. We go to him, sit with him, talk softly to him, ask him what is bothering him, hold him, or give him music or food—to calm him down.

Unrewarded Coercion

Brad screams. We will completely ignore this and go about our business. When he stops screaming and begins to engage in a more desirable behavior, we will then reward him with smiles, hugs, and the opportunity to play. If he plays with us, we will reward him every few minutes with praise and small bites of food.

[During teaching sessions, the parents will teach Brad to use words to ask for food, toys, music, and other things that he used to scream for. Then they will generalize his asking behavior to other times and places.]

Rewarded Noncompliance

We ask Brad over and over to do a simple task, such as open or close the door, put his plate in the sink, or take off his coat. Sometimes he finally cooperates, but most of the time, we just give up. This lets Brad get out of the task. We also give Brad requests when he isn't paying attention.

Cooperation Training

We will first make sure that Brad is looking at us when we make a request. For example, we will call his name. At first, we will reinforce him with praise and a small bite of snack when he looks at us within three seconds. When he looks at us, we will then make a request from a list of 10 different simple requests. If he cooperates, we will reinforce with praise, hugs, and a small bite of snack or an activity reward, such as wrestling. If he does not cooperate, we will walk away and try again later. He will only get the snacks and activity rewards when he cooperates.

Rewarded Coercion

Brad does things that tell us that he will soon begin to scream or throw things. For example, if he does not get what he wants, he whines and whines and then screams. Or if we go to the grocery store, he whines until we give him a snack, or else he starts to scream.

Unrewarded Coercion

Brad will have to earn all snacks, baths, wrestling, and rides on the outdoor swing. If he whines for these things, we will walk away. If he screams, we will ignore it and stay away from him. After he has stopped whining or screaming for a few minutes, we will give him an opportunity to earn the things he wanted by doing a simple task. For example, we will say, "As soon as you put this paper in the trash (right next to him), you can have snack." If he cooperates, he gets the reward. If he does not cooperate, we walk away.

(continued)

Table 3.2 *(Continued)*

Counterproductive Exchange	Productive, Alternative Exchange
Lack of Opportunities and Rewards for Desirable Behavior	*Plenty of Opportunities and Rewards for Desirable Behavior*
We are often so tired that we leave Brad alone when he is playing quietly. And we do things for him to avoid his noncompliance. For example, we put the straw in his chocolate milk.	We will be on the lookout for times when Brad is doing desirable behaviors, and we will reinforce these behaviors with praise, hugs, and activities. Also, we will expect him to at least do a small amount of everyday activities for himself: putting his plate on the table, taking his underwear and socks out of the drawer, putting some of his toys back in the toy box, putting his pillow on the bed at night, taking his favorite shirt out of the dryer, or putting his bowls and plate and utensils in the sink. He will get praise and hugs for this and rewards for natural activities. For example, when he puts his plate on the table, we will put food on the plate.

7. During the next meeting, families (in group meetings) present their original plan, and describe what they did and how well it worked. Suggestions are offered for improvements. If needed, parents are given special help (e.g., they might practice how to ignore a problem behavior, or how to make requests without sounding as if they are asking a question—"Can you pick up the candy wrapper?"

8. The first plan is worked on for several weeks. Then another plan is developed and tried. Families do not move on to programs for teaching specific skills until the child is less disruptive, more attentive, and more cooperative, and parents are more skilled at making requests, ignoring problem behavior, and reinforcing desirable behavior.

SECOND SET OF MEETINGS
(4 OR 5 THROUGH 7 OR 8)

The objectives of this set of meetings are (a) assessment; and (b) using assessment information and educational concepts, principles, and procedures to conduct, evaluate, and revise the first home programs.

ASSESSMENT

The home education program should be part of the child's IEP. In fact, the child's IEP should reflect assessment and program planning for the child in the home. School-based assessment should include standardized assessments such as the following 10 instruments:

1. The Autism Screening Instrument for Educational Planning (2nd ed.; ASIEP-2; Krug, Arick, & Almond, 1993)
2. The Vineland Adaptive Behavior Scales (VABS; Sparrow, Balla, & Cicchetti, 1984)
3. The Sequenced Inventory of Communication Development (Rev. ed.; SICD- R; Hedrick, Prather, & Tobin, 1984)
4. The Receptive One-Word Picture Vocabulary Test (Rev. ed.; Gardner, 1990)
5. The Clinical Evaluation of Language Fundamentals—Preschool (CELF-P; Wiig, Secord, & Semel, 1992)
6. The Peabody Picture Vocabulary Test-III (PPVT-III; Dunn & Dunn, 1981)
7. The Preschool Language Scale (3rd ed.; PLS-III; Zimmerman, Steiner, & Pond, 1992)
8. Scales of Infant Development (2nd ed.; BSID-II; Bayley, 1993)
9. The Wechsler Preschool and Primary Scale of Intelligence (Rev. ed.; WPPSI- R; Wechsler, 1989)
10. Wechsler Intelligence Scale for Children—Third Edition (WISC-III; Wechsler, 1991)

Information from these assessments is used to identify behaviors or skill areas to work on and to plan a sequence of instruction (e.g., scores on the Peabody Picture Vocabulary Test may suggest that a child needs instruction on receptive language). This is worked on in school. It also might be part of the family's home programs.

A second source of target behaviors and skills for home programs is simply what would make home life easier. During the second set of meetings, families are asked to list five or so desirable behaviors and skills to increase (e.g., cooperating with simple requests, putting toys away, asking for things the child wants, self-initiated play) and several undesirable behaviors to decrease (whining for things the child wants, bizarre gestures, refusing to come out of the car after a ride). Consultants can use these lists to develop general procedures (e.g., a simple program on cooperation, a procedure to model and then request functional speech, ignoring whining and reinforcing asking). These would be taught at an appropriate point in a logical-progressive sequence (e.g., parents would work on imitative speech, if needed, before expecting a child to produce functional speech).

A third source of target behaviors and skills for home (and school) programs is a model of children's psychosocial development. Such a model can assist parents and teachers to (a) identify behaviors and environments for assessing children's strengths and needs, (b) use assessment information to plan curricula (concepts and skills to teach and the sequence for teaching) and instruction (child-caregiver communication), and (c) identify behaviors and environments for evaluating a child's progress. An adequate model of psychosocial development would depict (a) the ways that elemental behaviors emerge and are assembled into complex, compound tasks and activities and response classes as children interact with their environments; and (b) how children are provided different social positions, roles, and identities as they become increasingly competent participants in social systems such as family and school. Following is a brief description of a model of psychosocial development discussed in Kozloff (1994a, 1994b).

The model of psychosocial development focuses on six competency areas (identified as Areas A through F) consisting of behaviors grouped by the similar functions they serve. Items learned in earlier competency areas contribute to a child's capacities for learning in other competency areas; that is, the model depicts psychosocial development as a cumulative logical progressive process.

Area A: Interest in, Attention to, and Orientation to the Environment

This competency area is essential to children's further psychosocial development; that is, the items in this area are necessary if a child is to participate effectively in social interaction/instruction. Items in this area include (a) visually tracking movements of hands, objects, and persons; (b) looking at objects and parts of the body spontaneously and on request, (c) turning to locate the source of sounds; and (d) attending and orienting to the speech of others.

Area B: Participation in Elementary and Early Forms of Social Interaction

This area identifies fundamental competencies in social interaction. Social interaction is the pervasive context in which children are brought into the social world; they learn to take turns and perform expected actions during their turns. Elementary social exchanges (such as greetings and good-byes, questions and answers, requests and assistance) are usually assembled into longer social sequences, such as meals, play, and lessons. Therefore, an early objective in the education of autistic children is to teach them how to participate in social exchanges. Items in this area include (a) responding to own name and to requests, such as "Look"; (b) making eye contact (spontaneous and on request) to produce natural reinforcers, such as play; (c) approaching other persons spontaneously and on request; (d) showing and giving objects (i.e., initiating interaction or taking a turn); (e) expressing needs, wants, or preferences by vocalizing, reaching, pointing, shaking the head, or placing an adult's hand on a desired object; (f) imitating an adult's movements, sounds, words, and actions; and (g) enacting greetings, good-byes, thanks, questions, answers, and descriptions.

AREA C: BODY COORDINATION AND LOCOMOTION

Items in this area bring a child into contact with objects and activities from which the child can learn about time, space, movement, cause and effect, and social norms. Items include (a) fluency at moving and using (extending, flexing, rotating) hands, arms, and legs; (b) bending and standing; (c) carrying objects; (d) throwing, kicking, and catching a ball; (e) hopping, jumping, and running, and many more.

AREA D: SIMPLE ACTIONS AND INTERACTIONS WITH OBJECTS

Items in this area build on items in the earlier areas. Examples include (a) elementary actions such as reaching, grasping, picking up, releasing, placing, switching hand-to-hand, pushing away, turning over, rotating, fitting, and squeezing; and (b) composite activities such as putting objects into containers, wrapping/covering and unwrapping/uncovering, stacking, stirring, stringing, screwing/unscrewing, turning pages, winding/unwinding, scribbling, tracing, coloring, spreading, placing (e.g., utensils on a mat), inserting (e.g., utensils into a drawer), rolling, folding, cutting, and assembling.

AREA E: COMMONSENSE KNOWLEDGE OF HOW THE WORLD WORKS AND OF THE CULTURAL CONFIGURATION

As children pay attention to their own behavior and to the activities around them (items in earlier areas) they acquire knowledge in the form of concepts, propositions, and strategies. Examples include knowledge (a) that some events signal later events; (b) that there are sequential and causal relationships; (c) of associations among objects, activities, persons, places, words/names; (d) of characteristics by which one can describe and group (e.g., color, shape, use, speed, number, distance, position);

(e) of actors (I, you, we); and (f) of rules, recipes, and strategies (first do X; then do Y).

Area F: Increasingly Competent Participation in More Complex Forms of Social Organization

As a child becomes more competent with items in earlier areas, other persons may come to see the child as increasingly attuned to what is going on and more capable of taking part. Therefore, they may provide the child with opportunities to perform more complex tasks in more complex forms of social organization such as helping to prepare meals and participating in conversations. These changes further increase a child's competence in lessons, chores, stories, play, shopping, and conversations.

The model is described to families around Meeting 4 or 5. Parents are taught the following three concepts:

1. Their child's education should begin with items in Areas A and B (Interest in, Attention to, and Orientation to the Environment and Participation in Elementary and Early Forms of Social Interaction). A child's progress in other areas depends on competence in these areas.
2. Increasing competence in one area facilitates beneficial change in other areas. For example, as their child learns to move her body from one place to another (Area C) and to interact with objects (Area D), she acquires commonsense knowledge of how the world works. This increases her competence with items in Area F.
3. If a child is not making much progress in an area, we assess the child's skills in the earlier areas. It is likely that items in these earlier areas are "tools skills," or components of behaviors in the harder areas, and must be strengthened before the child will make more progress.

The model (the competency areas, items in each area, and sequence) are then used to identify skills to work on.

A fourth source of target behaviors and skills for home (and school) programs can be an ecological analysis. The family spends several days observing and writing down what they do, where they do it, and when they do it in a typical day. They also list what their child with autism is doing, and where. The point is to (a) have a fairly detailed picture of the family round of daily life and the child's participation in it; and (b) identify spots where they can increase their child's participation. This information can then be turned into a series of program plans:

Typical Day in the Costa Family

	Activity	Suggestions
6:30–7:00 A.M.	Dad wakes everyone up. Jose and Lena get up and dress themselves. Edwardo (boy with autism) turns on TV and "relaxes." Then Lena (older sister) helps him get dressed while Mom makes breakfast and Dad checks emails from work.	Before bed, help Edwardo select clothes for next day. Put clothes on floor in the shape of a person. Practice dressing sequence. Each morning, Lena prompts Edwardo to put on each item. As he begins, she praises him several times and then leaves the room. She returns when it is about time for the next item. [Gradually chain 2 and 3 items in a sequence.]

The different sorts of assessment information assist the selection of target behaviors and skills. Standardized tests tell what must be worked on. The family's list of preferred targets also suggests what must be worked on to sustain energy and incentive. The ecological description broadens the picture and the selection of targets. *There is likely to be triangulation among this information.* If the Peabody test says that a child needs work on receptive vocabulary, it is likely that the parents are well aware of this and want to work on it. "He gives us a blank stare when we say, 'Pick up your socks.' We need to teach him what these words mean." And finally, the model of psychosocial development suggests that certain skills facilitate learning other skills, and therefore ought to be taught in a particular sequence, from elements to composites.

THIRD SET OF MEETINGS
(APPROXIMATELY 7 THROUGH 17)

This set of meetings is the bulk of a program. Parents and consultants use assessment information to plan home teaching programs.

BEHAVIORAL FOUNDATIONS

Training programs for families of children with autism were generally part of the development of the behavioral approach in education and mental health. The reader is invited to read the early work of Allen and Harris (1966); Ayllon and Michael (1959); Bijou (1967); Davison (1964); Ferster

(1968); Hart, Allen, Buell, Harris, & Wolf (1965); Lindsley (1964); Lovaas, Freitag, Gold, and Kassorla (1965); Patterson, McNeal, Hawkins, and Phelps (1967); Risley and Wolf (1967); Russo (1964); Schopler and Reichler (1971); Wahler et al. (1965); Walder et al. (1967); and Williams (1965). These and many other articles reveal the enduring commitment of behavior analysts to children and families, and their amazing skill at translating principles of learning into effective programs.

Most training programs for families are behavioral in nature. Behavioral concepts and principles guide the development of curricula (e.g., in social skills and language) and instructional methods. In addition, behavioral concepts, principles, and methods are a large part of what families are taught in programs. The following sections describe some of the more commonly used behavioral concepts, principles, and methods.

Respondent Learning

Parents need to know that certain events (unconditioned stimuli, such as food and pain) have the capacity without prior instruction to elicit emotional responses (unconditioned responses), such as smiling, attention, crying, and fear. However, most events that elicit emotional responses are learned. A child learns to experience pleasure at the words "Good job" because these words (initially neutral) are associated with food and physical contact. Through association with food and physical contact, neutral events come to elicit the same emotional responses. This has six practical implications:

1. *Parents must ensure that their child's interaction with them is associated with pleasure and the experience of success.* For example, the child finally grasps a spoon for eating ice cream. The interaction should not be associated with pain, frustration, and boredom. Otherwise, the child will attempt to escape via crying, whining, tuning out, and tantrums.
2. *Parents should pair neutral events with events that already elicit desirable attention and emotional responses.* Teaching sessions (where a child might be receiving food, affection, accomplishment, and other pleasure-eliciting responses from parents) should be held in the same place in the home, so that these places come to elicit attention and the anticipation of reward. Gradually, instructional settings can be expanded to include the kitchen table, den, and other rooms.
3. *Parents should make tasks easy enough for the child to succeed.* This assures that teaching sessions are not associated with frustration and lack of reward.

4. *Parents should end instruction before their child has had enough.* However, they should gradually increase the amount of time.

5. *Parents should use a variety of things as rewards.* They should rotate them before their child is satiated. Otherwise, the child's enjoyment will decrease and this will become associated with instruction.

6. *Parents should avoid trial-and-error instruction.* This can be highly frustrating and therefore aversive for their child. Instead, they should provide assistance (prompts—discussed later) so that their child's behavior is effective and receives rewarding consequences.

OPERANT LEARNING

Operant behavior is construed not as reflexive emotion but as volitional, goal-directed action. These terms may grate on persons who find them too mentalistic and subjective. However, the task is not to turn parents into behaviorists, but to help them to become technically proficient at interacting with their children and evaluating education plans and programs in their children's schools. It does not matter that the parents say "reward" rather than "positive reinforcement" or "Billy is trying to get attention" rather than "Billy engages in behavior that is reinforced by attention." Practically, the parents are going to reward desirable behavior and not reward undesirable behavior, no matter which words they use. This is illustrated by the remarks of one of the most successful parents we have worked with. This father, who had a homemade tattoo and rolled his pack of Camel cigarettes into the sleeve of his T-shirt, toilet-trained his 8-year-old son, taught him social play, taught him to speak in sentences (from a beginning repertoire of about 20 words), and even to read. At the end of the program, the father said to one of the authors, "Marty, you know what I really liked about this program?"

"What?"

"It was all about behavior. You taught us how to make our kids behave."

We hadn't even taught this father what "behavior" meant. And it didn't matter.

Contingencies of Reinforcement

A contingency of reinforcement is the connection between a specific class of behavior (tantrums, asking for things) and what follows (the consequence). Parents should be taught to describe the effects, to identify them in the family, and to plan how to use knowledge of the five contingencies of reinforcement.

1. *Positive reinforcement:* Some events that follow behavior result in that behavior happening more often. These events are called positive reinforcers. Good parent training programs teach parents to
   a. Identify events that are positive reinforcers for their child and for each other.
   b. Identify weak (infrequently occurring) desirable behaviors of their child and to reinforce these behaviors immediately and often.
   c. Think of ways to reinforce themselves for their efforts and achievements.

   In addition to the contingency of positive reinforcement, parents are taught about *schedules of reinforcement.* Most important, they are taught that weak behaviors and behaviors at the start of a teaching program probably should be reinforced every time (*continuous schedule*). However, as a behavior increases in strength (happens more often), reinforcement should gradually be given less often: from every time, to two out of three times, to about 50% of the time, to about one out of three times. Or, when duration is being reinforced, parents should at first reinforce very often, and gradually reinforce after longer and longer (by randomly longer) intervals. These less-often schedules are called *intermittent.*

2. *Negative reinforcement:* Some events (behaviors of other persons) are so aversive, irritating, and stressful that when a person finds that responding with a certain behavior will stop, delay, shorten, or prevent these events, the person will perform the escape, delay, or avoidance behavior more often until it becomes a habit. Many behaviors of a child with autism are aversive—tantrums, screaming, weird gestures. Parents try to stop, delay, shorten, or prevent these behaviors. For example, parents may give the child a snack to stop the child's crying. If giving the snack (escape behavior) works (the child stops), the parent uses this escape behavior more often. The problem is, the snack positively reinforces the child's crying. Therefore, the child will cry even more often—"to get snacks." Parents must be taught to
   a. Identify their child's aversive behaviors and how they react to these behaviors.
   b. Ensure that they do not "give in" in a way that reinforces these behaviors, but must teach their children desirable alternative ways to get what they want.

3. *Extinction:* Extinction is a contingency in which the consequence is a neutral event—neither reinforcing nor aversive. For example, a child plays, but no one notices. The consequence is that nothing

happens. Or the child whines and nothing happens. In effect, the behavior takes more effort than it is worth. With enough unreinforced repetitions, the behavior begins to decrease—to extinguish. It is important to teach parents to

a. "Put on extinction" (not respond to) any undesirable behaviors. The less the child is reinforced for these behaviors, the more powerful will be the reinforcement the child receives for desirable behavior.

b. Extinguish behavior in a matter-of-fact way; for example, a child screams and the parents "don't hear it." This is not the same as telling the child, "I'm not going to pay attention to that." (Obviously, the parent did just that.)

c. Couple *non*reinforcement of undesirable behavior (extinction) with positive reinforcement of desirable alternatives.

d. Be resolute about combining extinction with reinforcement of desirable behavior. When parents no longer respond as usual, the child may try harder and harder to coerce the parents to respond. For example, the child will yell louder and longer. This is called an "extinction burst." If the parents give in and reinforce the child's worsened behavior, child will act that way in the future.

e. Recognize that they will at first receive precious little reinforcement for their efforts, and therefore should support each other and reinforce themselves. "Wow, we hung in there and just let her yell."

4, 5. *Type 1 and Type 2 punishment:* There are two kinds of punishment contingencies. Type 1 punishment means that a specific behavior is followed by an aversive event, and the behavior decreases in frequency. Spanking (that works) is an example. Type 2 punishment means that a behavior is followed by the removal of a positive reinforcer. Examples include having dessert removed as a result of playing with it, or having one's computer stop working as a result of smacking it. *In the field of behavior analysis and in programs for families, punishment is not punitive.* The point is not to "teach a child a lesson" by giving the child pain. The point is rapidly to weaken behavior that is dangerous or destructive, such as self-injurious behavior.

There is an ongoing debate in the field about the use of punishment, even when it has beneficent objectives. Advocates of punishment argue that nonaversive methods (such as reinforcing alternative desirable behavior) usually take longer to work than punishment. The child could cause serious damage in the meantime. Opponents of punishment argue that punishment is difficult to use properly (immediately, every time, painful enough to stop a behavior); that its effects are unpredictable (e.g., it may evoke fear or violence toward the parent); and that it is easy to abuse ("I'll give you something to yell about!"). We cannot resolve the issues here. Suffice it to say that no procedure (in this case, aversive methods) that has been shown to stop self-injurious behavior (such as head-banging and self-mutilation) should be prohibited in all cases because there may be undesirable effects. Otherwise, surgery, dentistry, and colonoscopy would be prohibited as well.

Regardless of the outcomes of the debate, parents should be taught:

a. To use punishment in the technical sense (to suppress harmful behavior) and never to use punishment in the punitive sense—to teach the child a lesson.

b. How to use punishment properly—immediately, every time, with an aversive event that is painful enough to stop the behavior, and only after careful planning and with close monitoring by a consultant.

Differential Reinforcement

Differential reinforcement is a procedure in which one behavior (or feature of a behavior, such as skill, intensity, duration) is not reinforced and another behavior or feature of a behavior is reinforced. The result is that the reinforced behavior or feature increases while the behavior or feature that is not reinforced (is on extinction) decreases. It is essential that families learn to identify these pairs and use differential reinforcement: Ignore long tantrums but (ironically) reinforce short ones; ignore whining and reinforce asking; ignore bizarre hand movements but reinforce proper play; ignore noncompliance but reinforce cooperation with requests.

Shaping

Shaping is a procedure that is based on differential reinforcement. One aspect of a behavior is differentially reinforced. Parents can practice this in meetings using the game of hot and cold (e.g., a dollar bill is hidden. A parent comes in the room and the group says "hotter" as the parent gets closer). Parents can reinforce (a) longer durations of eye contact and play; (b) longer utterances ("I want cookie"; not "Cookie"); (c) longer chains of behavior (the child is reinforced after he puts on two items of clothing without help, no longer after each one); (d) faster responses to requests (getting dressed faster, putting away toys faster).

Chaining

Chaining is a procedure in which a person assembles steps or parts into a routine (e.g., a child might be able to put in each piece of a puzzle, but waits for a signal to put in each one). In chaining, another step is added before reinforcement is given. Chaining can be forward: The child learns to put on underpants, then underpants and socks; then underpants, socks, and shirt; then underpants, socks, shirt, and shoes. In backchaining, the child learns the last step first: the child first learns to fluff the pillow on the bed; then to pull up the cover and fluff the pillow; then to pull up the sheet, then the cover, and then the pillow. The sequence would be written on (or, if from a commercial program, it would be attached to) the family's home teaching program contract.

Prompts

Basically, prompts are something added to a setting that increase the clarity of information or assist the production of a response. Parents need to be taught how to add and how to remove or fade prompts so that their children will more easily learn otherwise difficult skills.

There are at least six kinds of prompts: accentuating, gestures, instructions, models, manual, and tools and other aids:

1. *Accentuating or highlighting cues, responses, and consequences:* The relevant features of a setting can be made more ear- and eye-catching to attract attention or increase children's understanding of what they are doing. Examples include using large letters; shining a light on important objects; marking off play versus eating areas with bright contrasting colors; increasing the loudness of requests; using food pictures taped to a refrigerator door to cue the child to open it; and placing small pictures of objects beneath the words for those objects, to assist reading. These prompts might be *faded* as a child responds to them in a more reliable and fluent fashion (e.g., the pictures beneath the printed words might be gradually covered up). The salience of instructional events can also be increased by reducing background sounds and removing distracting sights.

2. *Gestures:* Gesture prompts include nodding, pointing, or looking at places or relevant objects, to give the child information about when, how, where, or with what to respond. For example, Sam's mother points to Sam's special drawer, as though to say "Play over there." And she says "Come here" at the same time she performs the conventional arm or head gestures.

3. *Instructions:* Instructions can tell children (a) that they can respond ("There are no cars in the street; walk now"); (b) what response to

make ("Now spread the jelly"); (c) what to pay attention to ("Watch my mouth"); and (d) how to respond ("Use both hands").

Note that instructions can be full ("Now put the pillow on the bed") or partial ("Pillow"). Instructions can also be *verbal* (live or video recorded), pictorial (a series of pictures of the steps in clearing a supper table) or written (cards that recite rules such as, "First we hang up coat and then we play"). Hints or indirect prompts may also be considered a form of instruction (if Edwardo gets stuck while making his bed, Mr. Costro says, "What do you lay your head on?").

4. *Models:* Models involve demonstrating all or part of a desired performance. For example, Edwardo is holding a saw properly with his right hand, but not securing the board with his left. Mr. Costro says, "Like this," which gets Edwardo's attention. Then Mr. Costro puts his own left hand on the board and presses down (a motor model). Edwardo imitates the model and Mr. Costro gives him a pat on the back.

5. *Manual prompts:* Manual prompts involve physically helping a child correctly move his or her body. Ms. Jones gently turns Sam's head so he sees relevant *cues* in a toothbrushing task. She guides his hands with her own so he *correctly performs* the brushing movements. And she again gently turns his head so he can see how his teeth look—the relevant *consequence* of brushing.

   Manual prompts vary with respect to *completeness* and *restrictiveness.* Parents can manually prompt every movement in a sequence (e.g., from locating the toothbrush to replacing it on the shelf), or only one response (e.g., hand-over-hand help in brushing). Regarding restrictiveness, or the degree of guidance, parents can use a *partial* manual prompt allowing much leeway of movement, or a *full* manual prompt that restricts movement to a certain path.

6. *Tools and other aids:* Tools, jigs, templates, and devices refer to materials and mechanical/electrical means to simplify tasks or increase a child's closeness to objects, range of motion, strength, accuracy, and attention. Examples include eating utensils with special handles; clothing and other materials joined with Velcro; microswitches for electrical equipment; a strap for pulling open a refrigerator door; mats with outlines of plates and utensils; stools for standing; partially predrilled holes to facilitate using a screwdriver; a computer or tape recorder that gives cues, instructions, or feedback for each step; and equipment for sitting, reaching, turning, and holding things.

SETTINGS FOR INSTRUCTION

The education of many children with autism occurs during sit-down sessions in a special place and time. This is proper for certain skills and at certain (e.g., early) stages. However, early instruction in this setting may inadvertently train some teachers to teach almost solely in this setting, which inhibits generalization and independence. Parents should be taught to teach in at least three complementary settings that cover a wide sample of a child's environments. The three settings are routine tasks and activities, incidental-engineered opportunities, and special sessions.

Routine Tasks and Activities

A child's round of daily life is a recurring sequence of tasks (setting the table, eating, cleaning up) and larger activities (meals). There are at least five reasons that routine tasks and activities are an important instructional setting:

1. They provide regular and frequent opportunities to participate in social life.
2. A child's participation can vary from partial (handing someone a spoon) to lengthier contributions (stirring soup).
3. A child learns about (a) means-end relations (to accomplish Z, first do X, and Y), (b) parts and wholes (a sandwich consists of bread, filling, and condiment), and (c) social conventions (e.g., there are table manners for eating meals and rules for playing games).
4. A child's participation is likely to be noticed, reinforced, and supported by available models, which may enhance estimation of the child's competence.
5. The signals, prompts, and reinforcers are normative, natural, and reliably there; therefore generalization of a skill to other settings is easier.

Incidental-Engineered Opportunities

There are four kinds of incidental-engineered opportunities: incidental teaching, the mand-model technique, the delay procedure, and chain interruption. These can be used when teaching routine tasks and activities:

1. *Incidental teaching:* Here, the parent waits for or engineers the setting to encourage a particular response. A parent briefly opens the refrigerator door, exposing a child's favorite juice. The child pulls the door open. The parent prompts, reinforces, and/or encourages the child to expand the performance.
2. *The mand-model technique:* Here, the parent inserts a request into a child's ongoing activity, and then prompts and reinforces the child's response (Goetz & Sailor, 1988). While a child is playing

with toy cars, his mother asks what he is doing or asks him to show her a red car. This helps bring the child into contact with possibly unnoticed events and generalize into the play setting behaviors acquired elsewhere (e.g., color naming and the question-answer format). In contrast to incidental teaching, the mand-model technique involves more initiation by a caregiver.

3. *The delay procedure:* In the delay procedure, the parent identifies spots in a task or interaction where a child could make a request (Halle, Baer, & Spradlin, 1981). The caregiver participates in the interaction as usual, but at the preselected spot interrupts the flow for a few seconds, and waits for the child's request. If a request is not forthcoming, the caregiver models one.

4. *Chain interruption:* In chain interruption, a caregiver interrupts the child engaged in a sequence, and makes a request requiring the child to insert another behavior into the sequence, thus enriching it (Hunt & Goetz, 1988).

Special Teaching Sessions

Special sessions are useful and perhaps essential under certain conditions:

- For initially strengthening responsiveness and turn-taking during simple collaborative tasks; that is, bringing a child into the social world.
- To improve parent-child interaction.
- To help parents increase their teaching competence and give children with a history of slow progress the experience of success.
- For practicing weak behaviors and generalizing them to routine tasks and activities.

It is essential that parents move a child's instruction away from these sessions and into routine activities.

Home teaching program plans should specify all essential elements including (a) the objectives (what the child will do, and by what time); (b) a concrete definition of the behavior or skill; (c) the settings of instruction; (d) how the behavior or skill will be taught (models, signals to respond, prompts, chaining, shaping, reinforcers, schedules of reinforcement); handling problem behaviors; and (e) measurement.

When a program is connected to a school, parents can receive initial and continuing training in these procedures by assisting in class with close supervision and coaching—but working with children other than their own. An effective sequence is first to have parents merely reinforce desirable behavior. After becoming skilled at quick differential reinforcement, the parents can begin to signal behavior (e.g., "Look at me"). Next they can model responses for the child. Later, the parents put all the responses together into a teaching routine: gaining attention, modeling, signaling, prompting, and reinforcing. When they have become proficient with several children, parents can begin to use these methods with their own child.

Each week, as parents and consultants describe the past week's home teaching, consultants help families to evaluate the plan and the faithfulness with which it was carried out. These debriefings can be done by having the group examine video recordings.

CONSULTANT: Ms. Jones. What about that last one?
MS. JONES: I reinforced too slow. I reinforced when he looked away.
CONSULTANT: Right. Good eye. What can you do to reinforce faster?
MS. JONES: Maybe if I leaned a little closer.
MR. COSTRO: That's a good idea!

These points of evaluation are turned into a checklist that parents use to prepare and to evaluate their teaching. Did the parents reinforce, model, prompt, and chain properly? Did they rotate reinforcers? Did they end sessions before a child was fatigued? Did they ignore mild problem behaviors?

FINAL AND CONTINUING SET OF MEETINGS (APPROXIMATELY 18 TO END OF PROGRAM)

The remaining meetings involve working on fluency, generalization, and independence for older target skills; adding new target skills; and handling long-term likely difficulties, such as the need for respite, updating IEPs, summer activities, transitions to other schools.

REFERENCES

Allen, K. E., & Harris, F. R. (1966). Elimination of a child's excessive scratching by training the mother in reinforcement procedures. *Behavior Research and Therapy, 4*, 79–84.

Ayllon, T., & Michael, J. (1959). The psychiatric nurse as a behavioral engineer. *Journal of the Experimental Analysis of Behavior, 2*, 323–334.

Bayley, N. (1993). *Bayley scales of infant development* (2nd ed.). San Antonio, TX: Psychological Corporation.

Beck, R., Anderson, P., & Conrad, D. (1999). *Basic skill builders*. Longmont, CO: Sopris West.

Bijou, S. W. (1967). Experimental studies of child behavior: Normal and deviant. In L. Krasner & L. P. Ullmann (Eds.), *Research in behavior modification* (pp. 56–82). New York: Holt, Rinehart and Winston.

Blue-Banning, M., Summers, J., Franklin, H., Nelson, L., & Beegle, G. (2004). Dimensions of family and professional partnerships: Constructive guidelines for collaboration. *Exceptional Children, 70*, 167–184.

Cronin, M. E., Slade, D. L., Bechtel, C., & Anderson, P. (1992). Home-school partnerships: A cooperative approach to intervention. *Intervention in School and Clinic, 27*, 286–292.

Darch, C., Miao, Y., & Shippen, P. (2004, Spring). A model for involving parents of children with learning and behavior problems in the schools. *Preventing School Failure, 48*,(3).

Davison, G. C. (1964). A social learning therapy program with an autistic child. *Behaviour Research and Therapy, 2*, 149.

Dunn, L. M., & Dunn, L. M. (1981). *Peabody picture vocabulary test-revised: Manual for forms L and M.* Circle Pines, MN: American Guidance Service.

Engelmann, S., & Carnine, D. (1975). *DISTAR Arithmetic.* Columbus, OH: SRA/McGraw-Hill.

Engelmann, S., Haddox, P., & Bruner, E. (1983). *Teach your child to read in 100 easy lessons.* New York: Simon & Schuster.

Engelmann, S., & Osborn, J. (1999). *Language for learning.* Columbus, OH: SRA/McGraw-Hill.

Fad, K. M., & Moulton, R. (1999). *Teaching kids and adults with autism.* Longmont, CO: Sopris West.

Ferster, C. B. (1968). Positive reinforcement and behavioral deficits of autistic children. In H. C. Quay (Ed.), *Children's behavior disorders* (pp. 107–132). Princeton, NJ: Van Nostrand.

Frankl, V. (1970). *The will to meaning: Foundations and applications of logotherapy.* New York: New American Library.

Gardner, M. F. (1990). *Expressive one-word picture vocabulary test.* Austin, TX: ProEd.

Goetz, L., & Sailor, W. (1988). New directions: Communication development in persons with severe disabilities. *Topics in Language Disorders, 8*(4), 41–54.

Guralnick, M. J. (Ed.). (1997). *The effectiveness of early intervention.* Baltimore: Brookes.

Halle, J. W., Baer, D. M., & Spradlin, J. E. (1981). An analysis of caregivers' generalized use of delay in helping children: A stimulus control procedure to increase language use in handicapped children. *Journal of Applied Behavior Analysis 14*, 389–409.

Hardin, D., & Littlejohn, W. (1994). Family-school collaboration: Elements of effectiveness and program models. *Preventing School Failure, 39*, 4–9.

Hart, B. M., Allen, K. E., Buell, J. S., Harris, F. R., & Wolf, M. M. (1965). Effects of social reinforcement on operant crying. In L. P. Ullmann & L. Krasner (Eds.), *Case studies in behavior modification* (pp. 320–325). New York: Holt, Rinehart & Winston.

Hedrick, D. L., Prather, E. M., & Tobin, A. R. (1984). *Sequenced inventory of communication development* (Rev. ed.). Seattle: University of Washington Press.

Howard, V., Williams, B. F., & Lepper, C. (2005). *Very young children with special needs (3rd edition).* Columbus, Ohio: Pearson, Merrill Prentice Hall.

Hunt, P., & Goetz, L. (1988). Teaching spontaneous communication in natural settings through interrupted behavior chains. *Topics in Language Development, 9*(1), 58–71.

Kaufman, K. F. (1976). Teaching parents to teach their children: The behavior modification approach. In B. Feingold & C. Bank (Eds.), *Developmental disabilities in early childhood* (pp. 96–120). Springfield, IL: Charles C Thomas.

Kozloff, M. A. (1973). *Reaching the autistic child: A parent training program.* Champaign, IL: Research Press.

Kozloff, M. A. (1974). *Educating children with learning and behavior problems.* New York: Wiley.

Kozloff, M. A. (1994a). *Improving educational outcomes for children with disabilities: Guidelines and protocols for practice.* Baltimore: Paul H. Brookes.

Kozloff, M. A. (1994b). *Improving educational outcomes for children with disabilities: Principles for assessment, program planning, and evaluation.* Baltimore: Paul H. Brookes.

Krug, D. A., Arick, J. R., & Almond, P. (1993). *Autism screening instrument for educational planning* (2nd ed.). Austin, TX: ProEd.

Lindsley, O. R. (1964). Direct measurement and prosthesis of retarded behavior. *Journal of Education, 147,* 62–81.

Lovaas, O. I., Freitag, G., Gold, V., & Kassorla, I. (1965). Experimental studies of childhood schizophrenia: Analysis of self-destructive behavior. *Journal of Consulting and Clinical Psychology, 55,* 3–9.

Maurice, C., Green, G., & Luce, S. (1996). *Behavioral intervention for young children with autism.* Austin, TX: ProEd.

McClannahan, L., & Krantz, P. (1998). *Activity schedules for children with autism.* Bethesda, MD: Woodbine House.

Newman, L. (2005). *Family involvement in the educational development of youth with disabilities* (A special topic report of findings from the National Longitudinal Transition Study-2 [NLTS2]). Menlo Park, CA: SRI International. Available from www.nlts2.org/pdfs/familyinvolve_complete.pdf.

Patterson, G. R., & Brodsky, G. (1966). A behavior modification programme for a child with multiple problem behaviors. *Journal of Child Psychology and Psychiatry, 7,* 277–295.

Patterson, G. R., McNeal, S. M., Hawkins, N., & Phelps, R. (1967). Reprogramming the social environment. *Journal of Child Psychology and Psychiatry, 8,* 181–195.

Quill, K. (2000). *Do-watch-listen-say.* Baltimore: Paul H. Brookes.

Risley, T. R., & Wolf, M. M. (1967). Establishing functional speech in echolalic children. *Behaviour Research and Therapy, 5,* 73–88.

Russo, S. (1964). Adaptations of behavioral therapy with children. *Behaviour Research and Therapy, 2,* 43–47.

Schopler, E., & Reichler, R. J. (1971). Parents as cotherapists in the treatment of psychotic children. *Journal of Autism and Childhood Schizophrenia, 1,* 87–102.

Spann, S. J., Kohler, F. W., & Soenksen, D. (2003, Winter). Examining parents' involvement in and perceptions of special education services: An interview with families in a parent support group. *Focus on Autism and Other Developmental Disabilities, 18,*(4).

Sparrow, S., Balla, D. R., & Cicchetti, D. (1984). *Vineland adaptive behavior scales: Interview edition.* Circle Pines, MN: American Guidance Service.

Wahler, R. J., Winkel, G. H., Peterson, R. F., & Morrison, D. C. (1965). Mothers as behavior therapists for their own children. *Behavior Research and Therapy, 3,* 113–124.

Walder, L. O., Cohen, S. I., Breiter, D. E., Datson, P. G., Hirsch, I. S., & Leibowitz, J. M. (1967, April 6). Paper presented at the meeting of the Eastern Psychological Association, Boston.

Wechsler, D. (1989). *Manual for the Wechsler preschool and primary scale of intelligence* (Rev. ed.). San Antonio, TX: Psychological Corporation.

Wechsler, D. (1991). *Manual for the Wechsler intelligence scale for children* (3rd ed.). San Antonio, TX: Psychological Corporation.

Wiig, E. H., Secord, W. A., & Semel, E. (1992). *Clinical evaluation of language fundamentals: Preschool.* San Antonio, TX: Psychological Corporation.

Williams, C. D. (1965). The elimination of tantrum behavior by extinction procedures. In L. P. Ullmann & L. Kranser (Eds.), *Case studies in behavior modification* (pp. 295–297). New York: Holt, Rinehart and Winston.

Wilson, C. L. (1995). Parents and teachers: "Can we talk?" *LD Forum, 20*(2), 31–33.

Zimmerman, I. L., Steiner, V. G., & Pond, R. E. (1992). *Preschool language scale-3.* San Antonio, TX: Psychological Corporation.

CHAPTER 4

Parent Management Training to Improve Competence in Parents of Children with Asperger Syndrome

KATE SOFRONOFF and KOA WHITTINGHAM

IT IS beyond doubt that parents have an enormous impact on the well-being and functioning of their children, and it is also beyond doubt that children in turn have a major impact on their parents. Furthermore, it is widely recognized that children with developmental disabilities display behavior problems at a significantly higher rate than typically developing children (Einfeld & Tonge, 1996; Emerson, 2003). Parent reports have indicated that 40% of children diagnosed with autism spectrum disorders engage in some type of problematic behavior on a daily basis (Dunlap, Robbins, & Darrow, 1994). It has been found that those children with more severe levels of intellectual disability are more likely to display behavior problems such as self-injury, aggression, and autistic or ritualistic behaviors (Quine, 1986), whereas children with milder levels of disability (e.g., Asperger syndrome) are more likely to display common psychiatric disorders, such as Conduct Disorder or Oppositional and Disruptive Behavior Disorders (Einfeld & Tonge, 1996), anxious behaviors (Sofronoff, Attwood, & Hinton, 2005), and problems with anger management (Sofronoff, Attwood, Hinton, & Levin, in press). Additional behavior problems create a significant added burden for children with developmental disabilities since behavior problems further interfere with the child's ability to learn essential social and educational skills, which may lead to exclusion from educational and community settings and even threaten physical health (Rojahn & Tasse, 1996; Tonge, 1999).

It has also been found that most challenging behavior problems displayed by individuals with developmental disabilities originate in early childhood and without intervention are extremely persistent over time (Emerson, Moss, & Kiernan, 1999). Both parents and siblings of children with a developmental disability and disruptive behavior problems experience significant levels of stress (Cuijpers, 1999; Pakenham, Samios, & Sofronoff, 2005); and to cope with their situation, families frequently require respite services (Sloper, Knussen, Turner, & Cunningham, 1991). Parents of a child diagnosed with a pervasive developmental disorder face great challenges and demands associated with the uneven developmental progress of their child (Schuntermann, 2002) and are at increased risk of developing psychological difficulties themselves (Holroyd & McArthur, 1976; Konstantareas & Homatidis, 1988). Stoddart (2003) reported a study in which 37.7% of parents of a child with Asperger syndrome reported that they had received a diagnosis from a mental health professional. The most common diagnoses were depression and anxiety, with diagnosis more common in mothers than in fathers.

HISTORY

Children diagnosed with Asperger syndrome generally present with a pattern of speech development and intellectual capacity within the normal range. They do, however, exhibit deficits in understanding or empathizing with the thoughts and feelings of others that frequently affect their ability to develop and maintain friendships (Wing, 1981). These impairments often result in behaviors that parents, teachers, and others perceive as problematic. In some instances, poor behavior may emanate from impairments in social functioning, empathy, and special interests, or an anxiety-driven need for routine and repetitive behaviors; but at other times, the child may simply respond in an inappropriate manner to social cues.

Training programs for parents have been available for decades, but only relatively recently have specific programs been developed or trialed for parents of children with Asperger syndrome (Sofronoff, Leslie, & Brown, 2004; Whittingham, Sofronoff, & Sheffield, 2006). Many agencies around the world conduct information sessions for parents to assist them with managing emotional and behavioral problems in their children. Though the programs may be excellent, they are unlikely to be available to many parents or to have demonstrated efficacy in a controlled trial. It is widely recognized that parents are an important resource in the management and support of the child with an autism spectrum disorder such as Asperger syndrome (Howlin & Rutter, 1987; Mullen & Frea, 1995; Sofronoff et al., 2005).

Several studies have demonstrated the effectiveness of behavioral family interventions in reducing disruptive behaviors in children with developmental disabilities. Both contingency management training (CMT), which trains parents to respond contingently to desirable and undesirable behavior; and planned activities training (PAT), which trains parents to structure activities that minimize opportunities for disruptive problem behaviors, have been effective approaches in such a program (Roberts, Mazzucchelli, Taylor, & Reid, 2003). Sanders and Plant (1989) implemented a parent training program that included specific training for generalization across settings. The study was conducted with parents of children with developmental disabilities and behavior problems specifically because generalization across settings is known to be problematic for this population of children. Five intervention families successfully implemented and generalized strategies across multiple target settings and experienced significant decreases in problem behaviors.

Teaching parents effective strategies to manage the behaviors of their child and to better cope with the presentation of Asperger syndrome also results in a significant increase in parental self-efficacy (Sofronoff et al., 2005; Sofronoff & Farbotko, 2002).

In other areas dealing with childhood disorders, it is well documented that training parents to manage child behavior is effective. The effectiveness of parent training for externalizing disorders such as Attention-Deficit/Hyperactivity Disorder (ADHD), Conduct Disorder (CD), and Oppositional Defiant Disorder (ODD)has been empirically evaluated and found to be sound (Anastopoulos, 1998; Braswell, 1991; Johnston & Freeman, 1998; Sanders, 1992). Parent training for internalizing disorders such as separation anxiety, generalized anxiety, social anxiety, and phobias has also been found to be effective (Barrett, 1998; Cobham, 1998; Eisen, Engler, & Geyer, 1998; Sanders, 1992). In a recent study, parents reported greater satisfaction with and better results from a child-focused anxiety intervention program for children with Asperger syndrome when a parallel parent program was included (Sofronoff et al., 2005).

THEORY

The theoretical basis for the evidence-based parenting programs that we discuss here is social learning theory in the context of child developmental theories.

PARENT TRAINING PROGRAM 1—A PROGRAM SPECIFIC TO ASPERGER SYNDROME

This program was developed to target parents of children with Asperger syndrome (Sofronoff et al., 2004). Fifty-one families participated in the trial of the program, each with a child of primary school age recently diagnosed with Asperger syndrome by the consultant pediatrician at the Mater Children's Hospital, Queensland, Australia. All parents received a parent's manual that contained all the information covered by the following six components of the intervention package:

1. *Psychoeducation:* The nature of Asperger syndrome was outlined to parents and the difficulties likely to be experienced by the child were demonstrated. We used both video demonstration and discussion. This component was interactive: Parents were asked to give examples of aspects of the disorder affecting their own child. The heterogeneity of the disorder was emphasized, as was the importance of accessing the perspective of their child in problem situations.

2. *Comic Strip Conversations:* This technique, devised by Carol Gray (1998), is based on the belief that visualization and visual supports improve the understanding and comprehension of conversation. Simple drawings are used to portray conversations between two people. The comic strips identify what people say and do and also emphasize what people may be thinking.

3. *Social Stories:* This technique aims to facilitate social understanding through the creation of a short story about a specific situation that the target child can identify with. The stories are written according to guidelines using mostly descriptive and perspective sentences, with only one directive sentence. Thus the child is given information on what is occurring and why as the situation is described in terms of social cues and anticipated actions.

4. *Management of problem behaviors:* Some of the most common problem behaviors displayed by children with Asperger syndrome were outlined for parents. These included interrupting, temper tantrums, anger, noncompliance, and bedtime problems. Techniques were outlined for dealing with each of these issues and parents were asked to choose a particular problem behavior pertinent to their child and to outline and implement a management strategy for that behavior.

5. *Management of rigid behaviors and special interests:* This component aimed to deal with parents' experience of the child's rigid behaviors, adherence to routines, literal interpretations, and special interests. The focus of this component was to ensure that parents

understood the perspective of the child; why the child has a need for routines, and so on. From this perspective, it is a little easier to deal with some of the more extreme instances of such behaviors. It is also possible to see the potential for the child's special interest as a reward to facilitate other activities.

6. *Management of anxiety:* A child with Asperger syndrome is extremely susceptible to anxiety. Many problem behaviors are, in fact, the result of anxiety rather than real naughtiness; we emphasized that parents need to recognize when their child is anxious or is likely to become anxious and be ready to prevent and manage such behavior.

RESEARCH FINDINGS

The primary aim of the study was to evaluate the efficacy of short-term parent management training as an appropriate intervention for children diagnosed with Asperger syndrome. The second aim was to compare the treatment delivery methods—workshop format and individual sessions. The techniques that had not been previously evaluated in a controlled study were also of interest.

First, the results suggest that parent management training can be an effective intervention for parents of a child diagnosed with Asperger syndrome. On each of the measured outcome variables—number of problem behaviors, intensity of problem behaviors (Eyberg Child Behavior Inventory, Eyberg & Pincus, 1999), and ratings of social skills (Social Skills Questionnaire, Spence, 1995)—parents indicated significant improvement following parent training for both intervention groups. The wait-list control group showed no significant improvement on any of the outcome variables. This finding supports research in other areas that suggests training parents to manage child problem behaviors is effective (Sanders and Markie-Dadds, 1996). It also demonstrates the relevance of this body of literature to children with a diagnosis of Asperger syndrome (see Table 4.1).

Second, the results indicated some notable differences on the outcome variables between the workshop group and the group with individual sessions. The measure of parent ratings of the intensity of problem behaviors, which reports frequency of difficult behaviors, revealed a significant difference between the two intervention groups at postintervention and follow-up, with the parents in the individual sessions endorsing much greater change. Furthermore, the workshop group was not significantly different from the wait-list group at postintervention and follow-up on this measure.

Table 4.1

Problem Behaviors and Intensity of Problem Behaviors across
Time (ECBI Scores)

Group Scores	Preintervention		Postintervention		Follow-Up	
	M	SD	M	SD	M	SD
Workshop problem	17.44	5.77	11.78[a]	5.90	12.50[b]	6.96
Individual problem	16.89	5.84	9.22[a]	4.93	8.67[a]	4.93
Wait-list problem	18.13	5.19	17.53	5.65	18.20	6.21
Workshop intensity	149.72	29.78	130.44[a]	25.54	129.00[a]	18.13
Individual intensity	140.44	22.59	110.66[a,c]	19.85	106.44[a,d]	22.99
Wait-list intensity	144.73	26.39	148.00	31.75	144.40	31.85

[a] Significantly different from preintervention, $p < .0001$.
[b] Significantly different from preintervention, $p < .005$.
[c] Significantly different from Workshop group $p < .05$.
[d] Significantly different from Workshop group $p < .01$.

There are several possible explanations for this finding. The parents who received individualized sessions had many more opportunities to model strategies and fine-tune their approach to problem behaviors, and it is likely that this resulted in a more consistent use of the strategies and greater success in their use. It is also possible that through the ongoing individual sessions, parents became increasingly knowledgeable about the syndrome's manifestation in their child and hence became more tolerant of some behaviors. This increased tolerance may have been manifested in the lower intensity ratings for behaviors that were ongoing.

We also noted that the reported use of strategies in the workshop group was lower than in the individual sessions. This was especially noticeable with the more complex strategies such as Social Stories and Comic Strip Conversations. A possible explanation for this finding is that the presentation of such a broad range of material is too much for parents to absorb in a single day and would be better presented over two sessions and in smaller groups. Although most parents stated that they would prefer to take part in the 1-day workshop, this may not be the most effective format for training more complex strategies. The parents in the individual sessions could improve and modify their approach with the help of continued therapist support. They also could ask for clarification and discuss their strategies more thoroughly in terms of what worked and what needed further development (see Table 4.2).

In trying to assess the usefulness and acceptability of various components of the intervention, we noticed variability in the strategies that different parents used and endorsed as effective. An overwhelming number of parents, however, endorsed the usefulness of psychoeducation as a means of empowerment, and many parents rated this as the most useful

Table 4.2
Parent Ratings of Use at Home and Usefulness of Different
Components of the Intervention

	Workshop		Individual	
Component	Use at Home (%)	Usefulness (0–5)	Use at Home (%)	Usefulness (0–5)
Psychoeducation	79	4.5	87	4.4
Social Stories	50	4.2	87	4.3
Comic Strip Conversations	50	4.2	75	4.1
Behavior management	86	4.3	81	4.2
Anxiety management	64	4.1	62	4.1

component of the intervention. In a recent study in which parents were asked how they had "made meaning" or "made sense" of raising a child with Asperger syndrome and whether they had found any benefits, many parents described making meaning and finding benefits by gaining knowledge about the disorder and becoming empowered as an advocate for their child (Pakenham et al., 2005). Since the focus of this component was not only on sharing information about Asperger syndrome, but also on accessing the child's perspective in each situation, it led many parents to look at behavior from a different perspective and to try different strategies when dealing with their child's behavior.

When we looked at the ratings of the parents who used Social Stories and Comic Strip Conversations, it was apparent that they were finding them extremely helpful. While we know that these techniques will not be useful for every child with Asperger syndrome, it appears from the usefulness ratings from this study that those parents who use the techniques experience positive results.

Parents in both the workshop and individual sessions indicated that they were satisfied with the program. Although there is sparse literature related to parental satisfaction with programs that address Asperger syndrome, the few that exist in related areas seem to report similar results. Even when gains are not as great as parents may have hoped, they still report satisfaction with the gains that have been achieved (Boyd & Corley, 2001; Smith & Lerman, 1999). Several parents in the current program also indicated that they believed they could use some of the strategies in the future; they did not feel that they had wasted their time; and many were relieved to have met other parents with similar experiences.

LIMITATIONS AND FUTURE RESEARCH

It must be acknowledged that the study conducted used only small numbers and that the results should be viewed with some reservations. The trend in the workshop group to less robust results may have been even further increased by a larger sample size and by a 6- to 12-month follow-up.

It is important to note that in a skills-based intervention such as this one, parents are aware of the expected outcomes as measured by self-report questionnaires. It is also not possible to draw any conclusions about actual child behavior change since this was not measured other than by parent report. For this reason, the results should be viewed with caution. What seems certain is that parents feel as though they can better cope with their child's behaviors and reported significant improvements.

Perhaps the greatest drawback for such a program is its limited reach to parents. This program was delivered in a university setting with the help of a research grant and postgraduate clinical students who served as therapists. Although some of these students may eventually use the program in their own practice and other research teams have trialed the program in other countries, it is still not possible to readily and widely disseminate the program. For this reason, we decided to trial a widely used parent training program to evaluate the acceptability and efficacy of a program that is not specifically tailored to the diagnosis of Asperger syndrome.

PARENT TRAINING PROGRAM 2— STEPPING STONES TRIPLE P

Stepping Stones is a recent version of the Triple P (Positive Parenting Program) that targets families of children with disabilities (Sanders, Mazzucchelli, & Studman, 2003). Triple P is a behavioral family intervention with social learning principles as the theoretical basis (Sanders, 1999). The Triple P approach to parenting focuses on providing children with positive attention and managing their behavior in a constructive way that does not hurt the child (Sanders et al., 2003). To this end, parents are encouraged to develop knowledge, skills, and confidence (Sanders, 1999). Stepping Stones Triple P involves the basic Triple P strategies and includes additional strategies from the disabilities literature developed especially for this population (Sanders et al., 2003).

Triple P has an impressive evidence base and has been shown to produce statistically significant and clinically meaningful decreases in the problem behaviors of children that are maintained over time (Sanders, 1999; Sanders, Markie-Dadds, Tully, & Bor, 2000). The treatment effect of Triple P has been replicated in many studies and has been typically associated with high levels of acceptance and satisfaction on the part of participating parents (Sanders, 1999).

Components of the Program

The strategies in which parents are trained in Stepping Stones, as depicted by Sanders, Mazzuchelli, and Studman (2004), can be grouped into the four broad categories shown in Table 4.3.

Is This Program Acceptable to Parents of a Child with Asperger Syndrome?

A pilot study was conducted with parents of children with a diagnosis of Asperger syndrome to evaluate the acceptability of the Stepping Stones program. Parents were introduced to the strategies in the program via video demonstration and were asked to indicate whether they found each strategy acceptable for use with their child and also to rate the likelihood that they would participate in training if the program were available. The 42 parents involved in the pilot study rated Stepping Stones as highly acceptable and indicated a strong commitment to participating in the training program (Whittingham et al., 2006).

A randomized controlled trial of the Stepping Stones program was conducted in 2005 with parents of children diagnosed with an autism spectrum disorder. The majority of the children had received a diagnosis of Asperger syndrome, but there were a number with a diagnosis of autism. Parents were seen individually for the initial intake interview, for observation of a parent-child interaction, and for feedback of findings from these sessions and from questionnaires completed. A total of five group sessions were conducted by two therapists, with three to five families in each group. Families were grouped as far as possible by diagnosis type and age of child. The group sessions lasted approximately two hours, and in these sessions parents were trained in the skills of encouraging positive relationships and desirable behavior, teaching new skills and behaviors, and managing misbehavior.

In addition to the group sessions, three individual practice sessions were provided during which a therapist observed parents interacting with their child and using strategies that they had nominated to engage positively with the child and manage misbehavior as it occurred. Following training in individual parenting strategies, parents focused on planned activities for situations that they saw as high risk for their child engaging in problem behaviors. Parents were encouraged to nominate three such situations and to develop and trial their plan. One of the individual practice sessions involved observing the parents enact and trial a plan and giving the parent feedback. The final session was a group session that brought the training to an end and focused on maintaining gains and solving problems for the future.

Table 4.3

Strategies Included in the Stepping Stones Triple P–
(Positive Parenting Program)

Strategy	Description	Application
Developing Positive Relationships		
Spending quality time with children	Spending frequent, brief amounts of time (as little as 1 or 2 minutes) involved in child-preferred activities	Opportunities for parents to become associated with rewarding activities and events, and also for children to share experiences and practice conversational skills
Communicating with your children	Having brief conversations or interactions with children about an activity or interest of the child	Promoting vocabulary, conversational, and social skills
Showing affection	Providing physical affection (e.g., hugging, touching, cuddling, tickling, patting)	Opportunities for children to become comfortable with intimacy and physical affection
Encouraging Desirable Behavior		
Using descriptive praise	Providing encouragement and approval by describing the behavior that is appreciated	Encouraging appropriate behavior (e.g., speaking in a pleasant voice, playing cooperatively, sharing, drawing pictures, reading, compliance)
Giving attention	Providing positive nonverbal attention (e.g., smile, wink, stroke on the cheek, pat on the back, watching)	As in preceding entry
Providing other rewards	Providing tangibles desired by the child (e.g., a toy, mirror, flashlight, article of clothing, food) with praise and attention	As in preceding entry— particularly for children who do not respond to praise and attention
Providing engaging activities	Arranging the child's physical and social environment to provide interesting and engaging activities, materials, and age-appropriate toys (e.g. board games, paints, tapes, books, construction toys)	Encouraging independent play, promoting appropriate behavior when in the community (e.g., shopping, traveling)
Setting up activity schedules	Arranging a series of pictures or words representing activities that children may engage in	Prompting participation in the daily routine of activities

Table 4.3 *(Continued)*

Strategy	Description	Application
Teaching New Skills and Behaviors		
Setting a good example	Demonstrating desirable behavior through parental modeling	Showing children how to behave appropriately (e.g., speak calmly, wash hands, tidy up, solve problems)
Using physical guidance	Providing just enough pressure to gently move a child's arms or legs through the motions of a task	Teaching self-care skills (e.g., brushing teeth, making bed) and other new skills (e.g., playing with toys appropriately). Also, ensuring compliance with an instruction (e.g., "put your hands down")
Using incidental teaching	Using a series of questions and prompts to respond to child-initiated interactions and promote learning	Promoting language, problem solving, cognitive ability, independent play
Using Ask, Say, Do	Using verbal, gestural, and manual prompts to teach new skills	Teaching self-care skills (e.g., brushing teeth, making bed) and other new skills (e.g., tidying up)
Teaching backward	Using verbal, gestural, and manual prompts to teach new skills beginning with the last steps of the task	As in preceding entry
Using behavior charts	Setting up a chart and providing social attention and backup rewards contingent on the absence of a problem behavior or the presence of an appropriate behavior	Encouraging children for appropriate behavior (e.g., playing cooperatively, asking nicely) and for the absence of problem behavior (e.g., tantrums, swearing, hitting)
Managing Misbehavior		
Using diversion to another activity	Using instructions, questions, and prompts to divert a child who may soon misbehave to another activity	To prevent problem behaviors (e.g., self-injurious behavior, damaging property, running away)
Establishing ground rules	Negotiating in advance a set of fair, specific, and enforceable rules	Clarifying expectations (e.g., for watching TV, shopping trips, visiting relatives, going out in the car)
Using directed discussion for rule breaking	The identification and rehearsal of the correct behavior following rule breaking	Correcting occasional rule breaking (e.g., leaving school bag on floor in kitchen, running through the house)

(continued)

117

Table 4.3 (Continued)

Strategy	Description	Application
Managing Misbehavior (continued)		
Using planned ignoring for minor problem behavior	The withdrawal of attention while the problem behavior continues	Ignoring attention-seeking behavior (e.g., answering back, protesting after a consequence, whining, pulling faces)
Giving clear calm instructions	Giving a specific instruction to start a new task, or to stop a problem behavior, and start a correct alternative behavior	Initiating an activity (e.g., getting ready to go out, coming to the dinner table), or terminating a problem behavior (e.g., fighting over toys, pulling hair) and saying what to do instead (e.g., share, keep your hands to yourself)
Teaching children to communicate what they want	Teaching a functionally equivalent way of making needs known or met	Dealing with noncompliance, temper outbursts, self-injurious behavior, pica.
Backing up instructions with logical consequences	The provision of a specific consequence that involves the removal of an activity or privilege from the child, or the child from an activity, for a set time	Dealing with noncompliance—mild problem behaviors that do not occur often (e.g., not taking turns)
Blocking	Catching or blocking hands, legs to prevent the completion of a behavior	Dealing with dangerous behavior (e.g., reaching for an iron, running out into the street, attempting to hit themselves) or terminating a problem behavior (e.g., hitting another person)
Using brief interruption	Having a child sit quietly for a set time where a problem has occurred	Dealing with self-injurious behavior, repetitive behavior, or struggling during physical guidance
Using quiet time for misbehavior	Removing a child from an activity in which a problem has occurred and having the child sit on the edge of the activity for a set time	Dealing with noncompliance, children repeating a problem behavior after a logical consequence
Using time-out for serious misbehavior	The removal of a child to an area away from others for a set time	Dealing with children not sitting quietly in quiet time, temper outbursts, serious misbehavior (e.g., hurting others)
Planned activities	Providing engaging activities in specific high-risk situations	To prevent out-of-home disruptions (e.g., on shopping trips; visiting; traveling in a car, bus, train)

Table 4.4
Problem Behaviors and Intensity of Problem
Behaviors across Time (ECBI Scores)

Group Scores	Preintervention		Postintervention		Follow-Up	
	M	*SD*	*M*	*SD*	*M*	*SD*
Intervention problem	18.06	7.71	11.21[a]	6.77	9.97[a]	5.98
Intervention intensity	144.14	31.32	121.40[b]	25.28	118.67[b]	22.72
Wait-list problem	19.72	6.83	18.82	8.32		
Wait-list intensity	142.19	31.73	148.63	30.33		

[a] Significantly different from preintervention, *p* < .005.
[b] Significantly different from preintervention, *p* < .001.

OUTCOME STUDIES

The randomized controlled trial of Stepping Stones with parents of a child with autism or Asperger syndrome demonstrated clear and significant improvements in parent reports of child behavior problems as measured by the Eyberg Child Behavior Checklist (ECBI; Eyberg & Pincus, 1999) both in the number of problem behaviors reported and in the frequency of the occurrence of problem behaviors (see Table 4.4).

Parents also reported significant changes in their style of parenting, moving from less effective styles (e.g., giving in, reasoning with the child, or becoming angry), to more effective styles using strategies taught in the program (e.g., giving clear, calm instructions and following their instructions with either descriptive praise or reward for compliance or a consequence for noncompliance). These results are shown in Table 4.5.

These parent reports were further supported by observations conducted during the practice sessions. Parents could generalize the gains they made to different settings and situations. They endorsed the usefulness of the Planned Activities Training in increasing their confidence in

Table 4.5
Means and Standard Deviations for the Indices of Parenting Style

Group Style	Pretreatment		Posttreatment		Follow-Up	
	M	*SD*	*M*	*SD*	*M*	*SD*
Intervention laxness	2.80	0.76	2.61[a]	0.45	2.54[a]	0.71
Intervention overreactivity	2.97	0.75	2.11[b]	0.59	2.35[a]	0.80
Intervention verbosity	3.26	0.97	2.51[a]	0.84	2.65[a]	0.83
Wait-list laxness	2.87	0.75	3.30	0.60		
Wait-list overreactivity	2.90	0.86	3.01	0.85		
Wait-list verbosity	3.38	0.78	3.37	0.84		

[a] Significance = > .01.
[b] Significance = > .001.

managing their child's behavior across settings (Whittingham, Sofronoff, Sheffield, & Sanders, in preparation).

CASE STUDY

The following client, Alice, with her son Jonathon, received Stepping Stones Triple P through participating in a randomized controlled trial at the University of Queensland. They were randomly allocated to the treatment group and received the intervention in August and September 2005.

The intervention was run in groups of four or five families (although observation and practice sessions were individual). Intake interviews were conducted before the allocation of participants to groups. Two strategies that are not currently a part of Stepping Stones Triple P were added to the program: Comic Strip Conversations and Social Stories (Gray, 1998). This change was made on the basis of information received from a pilot study including a focus group (Whittingham et al., 2006).

DEMOGRAPHIC INFORMATION AND BACKGROUND

At the time of the intervention, Jonathon was 5 years of age. Alice is divorced from Jonathon's father and retains primary custody of Jonathon. Jonathon has fortnightly weekend contact and holiday contact with his father. Jonathon's father was not involved in the intervention. Alice is primarily a stay-at-home mother. Additionally, she works as a teacher's aide 4 hours a week. At the time of the intervention, Alice had not previously sought help with parenting. Jonathon was diagnosed with Asperger syndrome in June 2005, 2 months before participating in Stepping Stones Triple P. A diagnostic interview conducted as a part of the research project confirmed this diagnosis.

PRESENTING PROBLEMS AND PATTERN

Alice reported that her main goals in completing Stepping Stones Triple P were to decrease Jonathon's aggression, to improve the bedtime routine, and to find strategies to deal with his meltdowns. Additionally, she reported being concerned about noncompliance. Alice described Jonathon's aggression as typically consisting of hitting or kicking his mother, often in the context of a meltdown or impending separation from Alice. Alice described Jonathon's meltdowns as consisting of yelling, screaming, and aggression and typically lasting for 20 minutes. She reported that Jonathon's meltdowns occurred daily and were often preceded by frustration or anxiety. Additionally, she reported that after a meltdown, Jonathon usually became remorseful and sought her affection. This is consistent with independent observations of Alice and Jonathon's interactions.

Alice reported that bedtime was a particularly high-risk time for noncompliance, meltdowns, and aggression. She described Jonathon as frequently being overtired but not wanting to go to sleep. In addition, Alice and Jonathon both reported that Jonathon was afraid of the dark and anxious about going to sleep alone. Consistent with this, Jonathon was observed to be fearful of clinic rooms until a light was turned on. At the time of intake, Alice was staying with Jonathon in his bed until he fell asleep, which on a typical night would take one to two hours. In addition, Alice reported that while she was in the room with Jonathon, he would often start talking to her. She reported responding to this by explaining that it was time to go to sleep. Jonathon would become increasingly demanding and begin yelling and screaming. Frequently, this would escalate to the point of Jonathon hitting or kicking Alice. Consistent with Alice's reports of Jonathon's behavior and the observations of Jonathon's behavior, Jonathon scored in the clinical range on the Eyberg Child Behavior Inventory (ECBI) for both the Intensity Score, 149 (clinical cutoff, 131), and the Problem Score, 17 (clinical cutoff, 15).

Alice reported that she frequently responds to Jonathon's meltdowns by talking quietly to him and attempting to calm him down (e.g., putting him in a bath). Consistent with this, she was observed in session to respond to demanding behavior and noncompliance with attempts to reason with Jonathon. She was also observed to attempt to induce compliance by threatening a punishment that she did not enact. Alice also reported that using consequences backfired because Jonathon would "discipline" her by using consequences for her, too (e.g., he might hide her purse). Thus, consequences could escalate into a series of retaliations. Alice was highly creative and skillful in providing engaging activities and rewards for Jonathon. This included the use of a "boredom box" containing cards listing activities to be selected when Jonathon was bored, as well as a "reward jar" that contained described rewards for appropriate behavior. The contents of each of these was negotiated with Jonathon and changed regularly to ensure that they were both salient and reinforcing for him.

At intake, she scored above the cutoff for the Parenting Scale total score, 3.5, over-reactivity score, 3.5, and verbosity score, 4.2. Her score on the laxness scale was within the normal range, 2.9. Alice's levels of parenting satisfaction, 36, and efficacy, 29, as measured by the Being a Parent Scale as well as the total score, 65, were within the normal range. Additionally, on the Depression, Anxiety, Stress Scale (DASS; Lovibond & Lovibond, 1995) Alice scored within the normal range for depression, 1;

anxiety, 7; and stress, 11; and for family functioning on the Family Assessment Device, 1.41. All the reported scores are consistent with Alice's reports and in-session observations.

FORMULATION

It was hypothesized that Jonathon's noncompliance, meltdowns, and aggression were being positively reinforced by attention from Alice and that Alice's attempts at reasoning with Jonathon were part of this reinforcement. It was also noted that frustration or anxiety often precipitated Jonathon's meltdowns. Alice would frequently respond to the yelling or aggression with attempts to calm Jonathon. It was hypothesized that this reinforced Jonathon's yelling and aggression as it aided Jonathon in managing difficult emotions. Further, it was hypothesized that Jonathon was not being reinforced for more appropriate ways of managing anxiety and frustration. Table 4.6 represents a functional analysis illustrating how these processes created the difficulties at bedtime.

TREATMENT

At the beginning of the intervention, Alice already had many strategies in her repertoire to encourage desirable behavior in her son. However, she was unable to implement these strategies satisfactorily in her main areas of concern. Although she was aware that Jonathon's meltdowns were often precipitated by frustration or anxiety, she had not attempted to teach Jonathon more appropriate emotional regulation skills or to reinforce more appropriate ways of coping with frustration or anxiety. Thus, a major component of the intervention was helping Alice to problem-solve what she wanted Jonathon to do instead of yelling, screaming, hitting, or kicking when he was feeling frustrated or anxious and then specifically teaching and encouraging these behaviors. For example, Jonathon was observed to ask permission to "punch a pillow" while feeling frustrated; however, Alice had previously refused such requests, leading to further escalation of Jonathon's anger. Alice began instead to use descriptive praise and rewards to encourage Jonathon for appropriately managing his frustration by punching a pillow. Additionally, Alice began to use descriptive praise and rewards to increase "brave behavior" at bedtime.

Alice was observed to make many changes in how she managed misbehavior. She refined her instructions so that they were more obviously instructions as opposed to requests. In addition, she was observed to decrease the number of times that she gave instructions. Alice decided to mostly use the strategies of logical consequences and planned ignoring

Table 4.6
Functional Analysis of Jonathon's Bedtime Behavior

Stimulus	Organismic	Response	Consequences	Contingencies
Immediate: Instruction to "go to sleep"	"Overtired" Physiological response of anxiety in response to the dark and to potential separation from Alice	Talking to Alice	*Short-term:* Alice explains that it is time to go to sleep	*Positive reinforcement:* Attention from Alice
Contextual: Sleeping in the previous morning				*Negative reinforcement:* Delay of sleeping
Historical: History of falling asleep late and awakening late the next morning		Demands for Alice to stay in his bed, including yelling, screaming, and aggression	Alice stays in Jonathon's bed Alice attempts to calm Jonathon	*Positive reinforcement:* Time with Alice *Negative reinforcement:* Decrease in anxiety
History of anxiety about the dark and separation from Alice			*Long-term:* Jonathon develops an aversive behavioral repertoire	
			Jonathon is used to falling asleep late at night	
			Jonathon does not learn to cope with anxiety	

to manage misbehavior. In the past, she had not been successful in her use of logical consequences as Jonathon had complained or enacted a consequence of his own, to which she had responded with verbal explanations. In the course of the intervention, she saw that Jonathon's complaints or consequences following a logical consequence were merely behaviors that she wished to decrease. She decided that the best strategy for decreasing such behaviors was planned ignoring. Alice also reported that she found establishing clear ground rules a helpful strategy.

Alice's management of Jonathon's bedtime routine shows how Alice put the various Stepping Stones Triple P strategies together. Alice decided to reward and praise Jonathon for spending successively longer amounts of time in his darkened bedroom alone. She creatively presented this activity as a treasure hunt for a reward hidden in the darkened room. Jonathon needed to search his darkened bedroom with a small flashlight to retrieve this reward, first with Alice and then by himself. Additionally, Alice targeted the bedtime routine by providing a lava lamp as an engaging activity to occupy Jonathon and manage his anxiety while he was lying quietly in bed. Alice decided that the best strategy for managing Jonathon's talking or demanding at bedtime was planned ignoring. Additionally, she began to wake him up earlier in the morning so that he would be more tired at nighttime. She continued to stay in Jonathon's room until he fell asleep, but she sat on a chair next to his bed instead of lying in his bed.

Outcome

Following the intervention, Jonathon's scores were below the clinical cutoff on the ECBI Intensity and Problem scales. The difference between the preintervention and the postintervention scores is statistically reliable, taking a confidence interval of 90% (Evans, Margison, & Barkham, 1998; Jacobsen & Truax, 1991). Additionally, Jonathon's ECBI Intensity and Problem scores remained below the clinical cutoff at follow-up 6 months later. Following the intervention, Alice's scores on the Parenting Scale including the total score, the laxness score, the overreactivity score, and the verbosity score, were all below the clinical cutoff. The difference between the preintervention and the postintervention scores is statistically reliable, taking a confidence interval of 90% (Evans et al., 1998; Jacobsen & Truax, 1991). Further, Alice's Parenting Scale total score, laxness score, and verbosity score remained below the clinical cutoff 6 months later. However, her overreactivity score was again in the clinical range. Preintervention, postintervention, and follow-up data are presented in Table 4.7.

This is consistent with Alice's reports as well as in-session observations. At the completion of the intervention, Alice reported decreases in Jonathon's aggression and meltdowns and increases in Jonathon's compliance, as well as improvements in the bedtime routine. She stated that Jonathon's fear of the dark had decreased. This is consistent with in-session observations as Jonathon confidently walked into a darkened clinic room of which he had previously been fearful. Alice described Jonathon as now falling asleep "easily" within 20 minutes and no longer engaging in problem behavior at bedtime. Alice also reported that Jonathon was compliant with prompts to punch a pillow when he was beginning to feel frustrated and that encouraging this behavior was work-

Table 4.7
Scores on the Relevant Measures

Variable	Pretreatment	Posttreatment	Follow-Up
ECBI intensity	149*	80	128
ECBI problem	17*	2	12
Parenting scale total	3.5*	2.20	3.07
Parenting scale laxness	2.9	2.45	2.82
Parenting scale overreactivity	3.5*	2.00	3.80*
Parenting scale verbosity	4.2*	2.00	2.43

* Score is above the clinical cutoff.

ing well. Alice also reported that she is now more patient and calm with Jonathon and feels that she understands better the reasons behind his behavior. She describes the outcome in the following words, "We have 'bad' moments and not bad days. I remember when we had bad weeks—such is the improvement in our case."

CONCLUSION

What we have learned from conducting these two-parent training programs is that we can work effectively with parents of children diagnosed with Asperger syndrome to help them manage the behaviors commonly associated with that syndrome as well as those problem behaviors that occur in typically developing children. It is tremendously helpful for parents to learn how to manage issues such as the special interests, rigid behaviors, and excessive anxiety. It is also important for parents to feel confident that they can manage their child's behavior across settings and that they have useful strategies for new behaviors that might occur. A major point raised in this chapter is our ability to disseminate effective evidence-based parenting programs. A program conducted on a few occasions in a university clinic does not allow the far-reaching benefits to parents of a program that can be disseminated internationally and is available without cost to parents.

REFERENCES

Anastopoulos, A. D. (1998). A training program for parents of children with attention-deficit hyperactivity disorder. In J. M. Briesmeister & C. E. Schaefer (Eds.), *Handbook of parent training: Parents as co-therapists for children's behavior problems* (pp. 27–60). New York: Wiley.

Barrett, P. (1998). Evaluation of cognitive-behavioral group treatments for childhood anxiety disorders. *Journal of Clinical Child Psychology, 27*, 459–468.

Boyd, R. D., & Coreley, M. M. J. (2001). Outcome survey of early intensive behavioral intervention for children with autism in a community setting. *Autism, 5,* 430–441.

Braswell, L. (1991). Involving parents in cognitive-behavioral therapy with children and adolescents. In P. Kendall (Ed.), *Child and adolescent therapy: Cognitive behavioral procedures* (pp. 316–351). New York: Guilford Press.

Cobham, V. E. (1998). The case for involving the family in the treatment of childhood anxiety. *Behavior Change, 15,* 203–212.

Cuijpers, P. (1999). The effects of family interventions on relatives' burden: A meta-analysis. *Journal of Mental Health, 8,* 275–285.

Dunlap, G., Robbins, F. R., & Darrow, M. A. (1994). Parents' reports of their children's challenging behaviors: Results of a statewide survey. *Mental Retardation, 32,* 206–212.

Einfeld, S. L., & Tonge, B. J. (1996). Population prevalence of psychopathology in children and adolescents with intellectual disability: Pt. 2. Epidemiological findings. *Journal of Intellectual Disability Research, 40,* 99–109.

Eisen, A. R., Engler, L. B., & Geyer, B. (1998). Parent training for separation anxiety disorder. In J. M. Briesmeister & C. E. Schaefer (Eds.), *Handbook of parent training: Parents as co-therapists for children's behavior problems* (pp. 205–224). New York: Wiley.

Emerson, E. (2003). Prevalence of psychiatric disorders in children and adolescents with and without intellectual disability. *Journal of Intellectual Disability Research, 47,* 51–58.

Emerson, E., Moss, S., & Kiernan, E. (1999). The relationship between challenging behavior and psychiatric disorders. In N. Bouras (Ed.), *Psychiatric and behavioral disorders in developmental disabilities and mental retardation* (pp. 38–48). New York: Cambridge University Press.

Evans, C., Margison, F., & Barkham, M. (1998). The contribution of reliable and clinically significant change method to evidence-based mental health. *Evidence Based Mental Health, 1,* 70–72.

Eyberg, S. M., & Pincus, D. (1999). *Eyberg Child Behavior Inventory and Sutter-Eyberg Student Behavior Inventory-Revised: Professional manual.* Odessa, FL: Psychological Assessment Resources.

Gray, C. (1998). Social stories and comic strip conversations with students with Asperger syndrome and high functioning autism. In E. Schopler, G. B. Mesibov, & L. J. Kunce (Eds.), *Asperger syndrome or high functioning autism.* New York: Plenum Press.

Holroyd, J., & McArthur, D. (1976). Mental retardation and stress on the parents: A contrast between Down syndrome and childhood autism. *American Journal of Mental Deficiency, 80,* 431–436.

Howlin, P., & Rutter, M. (1987). *Treatment of autistic children.* Chichester, West Sussex, England: Wiley.

Jacobsen, N. S., & Truax, P. (1991). Clinical significance: A statistical approach to defining meaningful change in psychotherapy research. *Journal of Consulting and Clinical Psychology, 59*(1), 12–19.

Johnston, C., & Freeman, W. (1998). Parent training for interventions for sibling conflict. In J. M. Briesmeister & C. E. Schaefer (Eds.), *Handbook of parent train-*

ing: Parents as co-therapists for children's behavior problems (pp. 153–176). New York: Wiley.

Konstantareas, M. M., & Homatidis, S. (1988). Stress and differential parental involvement in families of autistic and learning disabled children. In E. D. Hibbs (Ed.), *Children and families: Studies in prevention and intervention* (pp. 321–336). Madison, CT: International Universities Press.

Lovibond, P. F., & Lovibond, S. H. (1995). The structure of negative emotional states: Comparison of the Depression Anxiety Stress Scales (DASS) with the Beck Depression and Anxiety Inventories. *Behavior Research and Therapy, 33,* 335–343.

Mullen, K. B., & Frea, W. D. (1995). A parent-professional consultation model for functional analysis. In R. L. Koegel & L. K. Koegel (Eds.), *Teaching children with autism* (pp. 175–188). Baltimore: Paul H. Brookes.

Pakenham, K. I., Samios, C., & Sofronoff, K. (2005). Adjustment in mothers of children with Asperger syndrome. *Autism, 9,* 191–212.

Quine, L. (1986). Behavior problems in severely mentally handicapped children. *Psychological Medicine, 16,* 895–907.

Roberts, C., Mazzucchelli, T., Taylor, K., & Reid, R. (2003). Early intervention for behavior problems in young children with developmental disabilities. *International Journal of Disability, Development and Education, 50,* 275–292.

Rojahn, J., & Tasse, M. J. (1996). Psychopathology in mental retardation. In J. W. Jacobsen & J. A. Mulick (Eds.), *Manual of diagnosis and professional practice in mental retardation* (pp. 147–156). Washington, DC: American Psychological Association.

Sanders, M. R. (1992). *Every parent: A positive approach to children's behavior.* Sydney, Australia: Addison-Wesley.

Sanders, M. R. (1999). Triple P positive parenting program: Towards an empirically validated multilevel parenting and family support strategy for the prevention of behavior and emotional problems in children. *Clinical Child and Family Psychology Review, 2,* 71–90.

Sanders, M. R., & Markie-Dadds, C. (1996). Triple P: A multi-level family intervention program for children with disruptive behavior disorders. In P. Cotton & H. Jackson (Eds.), *Early intervention and prevention in mental health* (pp. 59–85). Melbourne: Australian Psychological Society.

Sanders, M. R., Markie-Dadds, C., Tully, L. A., & Bor, W. (2000). Triple P positive parenting program: A comparison of enhanced, standard and self-directed behavioral family intervention for parents of children with early onset conduct problems. *Journal of Consulting and Clinical Psychology, 68,* 624–640.

Sanders, M. R., Mazzucchelli, T. G., & Studman, L. J. (2003). *Practitioner's manual for standard Stepping Stones Triple P.* Brisbane: Triple P International.

Sanders, M. R., Mazzucchelli, T. G., & Studman, L. J. (2004). Stepping Stones Triple P: The theoretical basis and development of an evidence-based positive parenting program for families with a child who has a disability. *Journal of Intellectual and Developmental Disability, 29,* 265–283.

Sanders, M. R., & Plant, K. (1989). Programming for generalization to high and low risk parenting situations in families with oppositional developmentally disabled preschoolers. *Behavior Modification, 13,* 283–305.

Schuntermann, P. (2002). Pervasive developmental disorder and parental adaptation: Previewing and reviewing atypical development with parents in child psychiatric consultation. *Harvard Review of Psychiatry, 10,* 16–27.

Sloper, P., Knussen, C., Turner, S., & Cunningham, C. C. (1991). Factors related to stress and satisfaction with life in families of children with Down syndrome. *Journal of Child Psychology and Psychiatry, 32,* 655–676.

Smith, M. R., & Lehrman, D. C. (1999). A preliminary comparison of guided compliance and high-probability instructional sequences as treatment for noncompliance in children with developmental disabilities. *Research in Developmental Disabilities, 20,* 183–195.

Sofronoff, K., Attwood, T., & Hinton, S. (2005). A randomized controlled trial of a CBT intervention for anxiety in children with Asperger syndrome. *Journal of Child Psychology and Psychiatry, 46,* 1152–1160.

Sofronoff, K., Attwood, T., Hinton, S., & Levin, I. (in press). A randomized controlled trial of a cognitive behavioral intervention for anger management in children diagnosed with Asperger syndrome. *Journal of Autism and Developmental Disorders.*

Sofronoff, K., & Farbotko, M. (2002). The effectiveness of parent management training to increase self-efficacy in parents of children with Asperger syndrome. *Autism, 6,* 271–286.

Sofronoff, K., Leslie, A., & Brown, W. (2004). Parent management training and Asperger syndrome: A randomised controlled trial to evaluate a parent based intervention. *Autism, 8,* 301–317.

Spence, S. H. (1995). *Social skills training: Enhancing social competence with children and adolescents* (The Social Skills Questionnaire). Windsor: NFER-Nelson.

Stoddart, K. P. (2003). Reported stress, personality and mental health in parents of children with pervasive developmental disorders. *Dissertation Abstracts International: Humanities and Social Sciences, 64,* 1411A.

Tonge, B. J. (1999). Psychopathology of children with developmental disabilities. In N. Bouras (Ed.), *Psychiatric and behavior disorders in developmental disability and mental retardation* (pp. 157–174). Cambridge: Cambridge University Press.

Whittingham, K., Sofronoff, K., & Sheffield, J. (2006). Stepping Stones Triple P: A pilot study to evaluate acceptability of the program by parents of a child diagnosed with an Autism Spectrum Disorder. *Research in Developmental Disabilities, 27,* 364–380.

Whittingham, K., Sofronoff, K., Sheffield, J., & Sanders, M. (in prep). Stepping Stones Triple P: A randomized controlled trial for parents of a child with an autism spectrum disorder.

Wing, L. (1981). Asperger's syndrome: A clinical account. *Psychological Medicine, 11,* 115–129.

INTERNALIZING DISORDERS

THE DIFFERENTIAL categories of "internalizing/externalizing" allow for a classification of troubled children on the basis of psychiatric symptoms. The chapters in Part Three address internalizing disorders. These childhood disorders typically involve symptoms of excessive inhibition or anxiety and depression in all its various and insidious modalities. In Chapter 5, Barrett and Farrell present a highly effective behavioral intervention approach for families of children with anxiety. They point out that disruptive behaviors are often given more attention since they are overt and affect a wide range of people. Anxiety, however, being an internalized disorder, often goes undetected. Nonetheless, the negative impact of anxiety is undeniable and can be catastrophic, all the more reason to focus on the etiology, development, symptoms, and intervention of this prevalent disorder.

Barrett and Farrell describe the role of parents and family in the maintenance of anxiety as well as the treatment status for childhood anxiety disorders. Parents need to be included in the treatment of their children. In fact, the authors discuss the bidirectionality and circular influence of parent-child interactions as they are relevant to anxiety and its manifold expressions. Anxiety in the child may certainly exacerbate distress in the parents. Conversely, anxiety in the parents may increase distress in the child. The authors discuss in detail a highly innovative intervention strategy, the FRIENDS for Life program—a family based cognitive-behavioral intervention for childhood anxiety disorders. After a thorough discussion of the multiple factors that may moderate the efficacy of an intervention approach, they state that the FRIENDS for Life program has been effective as an individual treatment program and as a group treatment, such as a school-based prevention program.

The program utilizes the acronym "FRIENDS" to help children remember the strategies they can use to manage and control their anxiety. Indeed, the word *friends* highlights the major objectives and themes of the program. Children are encouraged to make friends and talk to their friends. The authors give a detailed and session-by-session explanation of their invaluable format. The underlying philosophy of the FRIENDS program empowers families to effect positive changes in their lives, and it values the unique experiences that parents, siblings, and children bring to the group. It is a collaborative team approach. The authors focus on the underlying components of family training in the FRIENDS program, including (a) parenting strategies, (b) self-awareness of one's own stress and anxiety, and (c) the awareness of at-risk times in the child. Practical, specific, and applicable tools are offered including techniques that encourage relaxation, show children how to be aware of their own thoughts and inner processes, foster reciprocity, and facilitate problem-solving and coping skills. They also instruct the children in techniques for developing a coping support team. Using helpful tables, the authors illustrate how the FRIENDS program can be effectively developed and implemented.

In Chapter 6, Kearney, LaSota, Lemos-Miller, and Vecchio recount an extensive spectrum of school refusal problems ranging from those children who never attend school to those who attend intermittently to those who attend school but act out and become disruptive in school. They discuss some essential components of treatment modalities. Intervention must include all types of children who refuse school and must allow for the divergent reasons children refuse school. Each youngster has specific and unique reasons for refusing school. Therefore, we cannot assume a one-size-fits-all formula when working with children. The child's individual and subjective reasons for refusing school should serve as the basis for the nature and format of the parent intervention strategy. The authors of Chapter 6 note that children may refuse school to avoid anxiety-provoking and stressful situations, to escape aversive social situations, to gain attention from significant others, to pursue positive reinforcements outside school, or to achieve some combination of all these possible reasons for refusal. Whatever the reason, school refusal behavior has several aversive consequences that must be addressed.

Kearney, LaSota, Lemos-Miller, and Vecchio employ a multicomponent assessment process and intervention approach that identifies fundamental core variables. These variables are clinically pertinent in each instance of school refusal. They encompass a large and complex array of related factors that certainly include the individual child's reasons for refusing school, parent variables, parenting styles, components of the contingencies used with each child, and expectations. The individuality and the unique situation of each child particularly come into play when designing a viable contract between parent and child and the most effective means for implementing that contract. Therapists are encouraged to restructure parenting skills programs within the broader ecological context of the family. The authors offer an in-depth discussion of the major treatment methods for addressing the various reasons youths may refuse school. They demonstrate how relaxation and breathing retraining, modeling and role-play, and the tenets of cognitive therapy can be effective intervention techniques. They also present thorough and informative case illustrations based on comprehensive assessments that demonstrate specific ways to implement their multicomponent approach. The case studies illustrate the practical value of contingency contracting that specifically identifies the privileges and responsibilities of the target child and the parents.

CHAPTER 5

Behavioral Family Intervention for Childhood Anxiety

PAULA BARRETT and LARA FARRELL

ANXIETY DISORDERS are among the most common mental health problems affecting children and youths, with estimates indicating prevalence as high as 10% to 20% (Costello & Angold, 1995). While these estimates suggest as many as 1 in 5 children and youths are at risk for experiencing clinical anxiety, the majority of them do not come to the attention of mental health professionals (Esser, Schmidt, & Woerner, 1990; Hirschfeld et al., 1997; Olfson, Gameroff, Marcus, & Waslick, 2003; Sawyer et al., 2000). Anxiety disorders in childhood are frequently overlooked and tend to be unrecognizable, insofar as anxious children are frequently shy, cooperative, and compliant within school settings and when away from home. Children with anxiety are frequently perfectionistic in their academic pursuits, and because they are driven by the need for peer acceptance, they seek constant approval by peers, teachers, and adults in general. Disruptive behavioral disorders tend to receive more attention and are more frequently diagnosed in childhood, due to the increased impact, disruption, and interference these disorders have on family and school routines. While anxiety disorders in childhood often go undetected by comparison, they are highly prevalent, are associated with a wide range of psychosocial impairments, tend to be chronic and unremitting in course, and are linked with significant risk for other psychological disorders if left untreated (e.g., Cole, Peeke, Martin, Truglio, & Seroczynski, 1998; Harrington, Fudge, Rutter, Pickles, & Hill, 1990; Kashani & Orvaschel, 1990; Orvaschel, Lewinsohn, & Seeley, 1995).

Increased attention to childhood anxiety disorders in the literature, as well as in mental health practice and schools, has led to the recognition that anxiety disorders are not merely a phase or part of normal development and that children tend not to simply grow out of these difficulties. This recognition is in part due to our increased understanding of the implications and sequelae of anxiety disorders, and knowledge that anxiety disorders during childhood tend to be chronic and unremitting (i.e., Aschenbrand, Kendall, Webb, Safford, & Flannery-Schroeder, 2003; Cole et al., 1998). Anxiety disorders in childhood are predictive of other psychiatric disorders later in life (Last, Perrin, Herson, & Kazdin, 1996; Woodward & Fergusson, 2001); including the development of depression in adolescence and adulthood (Brady & Kendall, 1992; Cole et al., 1998; Orvashel, Lewinsohn, & Seeley, 1995; Pine, Cohen, Gurley, Brook, & Ma, 1998; Pollack, Rosenbaum, Marrs, Miller, & Biederman, 1996; Seligman & Ollendick, 1998); personality psychopathology and suicidality in young adulthood (Brent et al., 1993; Rudd, Joiner, & Rumzke, 2004); and an increased risk for substance abuse disorders in late adolescence and adulthood (Christie et al., 1988; Greenbaum, Prange, Freidman, & Silver, 1991; Kessler et al., 1996). Anxiety and the associated symptoms of excessive worry, physiological arousal, psychosomatic complaints, and extreme avoidance of specific situations (to name a few), not surprisingly cause significant disruption to life for children and teenagers. They frequently experience substantial disruption and difficulties in their peer and social relationships (e.g., Chansky & Kendall, 1997; Strauss, Forehand, Smith, & Frame, 1986) and in their academic achievement (e.g., Kessler, Foster, Saunders, & Stand, 1995; King & Ollendick, 1989), and often experience concurrent psychosocial difficulties such as immaturity, attention and concentration problems, oversensitivity, low self-esteem, and low social competence (Ialongo, Edelsohn, Werthemar-Larsson, Crockett, & Kellam, 1994; Kashani & Orvaschel, 1990; Kendall, Cantwell, & Kazdin, 1989; Strauss, Frame, & Forehand, 1987).

Anxiety disorders in childhood not only cause significant distress and impairment to the child, but also generate distress in family members and disruption in family routines. Particularly high stress times for families are in the mornings before school, when anxious children may be highly aroused and sometimes physically unwell with psychosomatic complaints because of fears associated with school. These fears may be related to separation from parents; concerns about academic performance; changes associated with school or class routines, such as a new teacher; or fears associated with the peer group. In the afternoons following school, children and youths with anxiety may be agitated, volatile, and distressed by their inability to cope with the demands of the day. The role of the family, and in particular the parents, in child anxiety has been an issue of interest for many years, with the traditional view being one that blamed parents for the anxious, avoidant symptoms of their child. The more widely accepted, contemporary perspective of parental involvement in child anxiety contends that these children and youths frequently have some degree of biological vulnerability for anxiety, and that parental and family interactional factors may be *one* mechanism through which anxiety is maintained, along with a host of other social, psychological, and situational factors. An understanding of the role parents may play in the maintenance of childhood anxiety, as well as the important role of parents and the family in treatment, is essential for practitioners who work with children and youths who have anxiety and anxiety disorders.

This chapter reviews the role of parents and the family in the maintenance of anxiety, as well as the current status of treatment for child and youth anxiety disorders, focusing in particular on the inclusion of parents in treatment. A practitioner's guide to an evidenced-based cognitive-behavioral treatment (CBT) for child anxiety is presented—the *FRIENDS for Life* program (Barrett, 2004, 2005)—with special detail to parental and family involvement in therapy. This chapter concludes with a summary of the key processes associated with a family-based intervention for child anxiety disorders, and presents the issues and challenges for practitioners and researchers in the field of child anxiety treatment.

THE ROLE OF PARENTS AND THE FAMILY IN CHILD ANXIETY

A wide range of variables in the literature have been proposed to be associated with the development or maintenance of childhood anxiety disorders including biological, familial, social, psychological, and environmental factors. The most highly studied variables that emerge from this literature are parental anxiety (Turner, Beidel, & Costello, 1987; Weissman, Leckman, Merikangas, Gammon, & Prusoff, 1984), temperamental predisposition to shyness (Kagan, Reznick, & Snidman, 1988), family interaction variables (Barrett, Rapee, Dadds, & Ryan, 1996; Krohne & Hock, 1991), and exposure to traumatic and stressful life events (Benjamin, Costello, & Warren, 1990; Goodyer & Altham, 1991). What is clear from the research literature into factors associated with the development of child anxiety disorders is that risk is based on a complex interaction among a broad range of potential risk variables and is complicated further by the interactional influences of a broad array of biological, psychological, social, and situational protective factors. Although we have some knowledge about the potential influence of specific variables on perpetuating child anxiety disorders, we know very little about causality, making it difficult to define clear etiological pathways for anxiety disorders in childhood. For the purposes of this chapter, we discuss the research and literature on the influence of parental anxiety and family interaction on childhood anxiety disorders.

Empirical research has implicated parental anxiety as being a risk factor for childhood anxiety problems, with evidence supporting both a hereditability link and environmental influences in mediating this link. Family aggregate studies indicate children of anxious parents are 2 to 7 times more likely to develop an anxiety disorder than children of nonanxious parents; and among anxious parents, research suggests up to 60% of their children meet criteria for an anxiety disorder (Capps, Sigman, Sena, & Henker, 1996; Turner et al., 1987). Parental depression has also been linked to childhood anxiety (Beidel & Turner, 1997; Kovacs, Gatsonis, Paulauskas, & Richards, 1989), suggesting more generally that parental psychopathology may be a risk for anxiety disorders in children and youths. While these studies do not indicate the relative contribution of genetic and environmental influences, a study by Thapar and McGuffin (1995) provided insight into such estimates, suggesting that heritability may account for approximately 40% to 50 % of anxiety symptoms in children and youths. Beyond hereditability, a number of studies have provided support for the reciprocal relationship between child and parent interaction characteristics in understanding the development of childhood anxiety.

High levels of anxiety in parents have been hypothesized to interfere with the development of parents' adaptive coping skills and lead to parent-child interactions that enhance anxiety (Ginsburg, 2004). It has been postulated that parental psychopathology may exert its effect through social learning processes, due to the modeling of parental maladaptive coping strategies (Barrett, Rapee, Dadds, & Ryan, 1996; Gerull & Rapee, 2002; Manassis & Bradley, 1994; Rapee, 1997; Shortt, Barrett, Dadds, & Fox, 2001; Siqueland, Kendall, & Steinberg, 1996). Additionally, parental internalizing problems may influence the quality of communication and interaction between parent and child (Krohne & Hock, 1991; Murray, Kempton, Woolgar, & Hooper, 1993; Rapee, 1997; Tarullo, DeMulder, Martinez, & Radke-Yarrow, 1994). Moreover, parental anxiety may moderate treatment outcome in the case of child anxiety. Cobham, Dadds, and Spence (1998) found that children who had a parent or parents with an anxiety disorder responded less well to treatment. Southam-Gerow, Kendall, and Weersing (2001) reported that higher levels of maternal self-reported depressive symptoms were associated with less favorable outcomes following cognitive-behavioral treatment for anxious youths.

Beyond the influence of parental psychopathology, it has also been suggested that anxiety in the child may exacerbate distress in parents, who then adjust demands, expectations and parenting practices to cope with this distress, and as a consequence through negative reinforcement, maintain anxious, avoidant behaviors' in children (Kendall & Ollendick, 2004). It is likely that parenting an anxious child, and dealing with the associated daily demands of avoidance, reassurance seeking, clinginess, and tantrums, is likely to affect and influence one's parenting approach and interactions with the child. The reciprocal influence of distress on parents and children with anxiety, and patterns of parent-child interaction, are likely to perpetuate and maintain child anxiety. Alternatively, if parents and children are equipped with positive, coping skills that are solution focused, families and parent-child interactions can also serve as protective factors against childhood anxiety.

Research has demonstrated that parent-child interactions, characterized by parental overcontrol, overprotection, less granting of autonomy, and low maternal warmth are associated with increased risk for the development of internalizing disorders in children (Dumas, LaFreniere, & Serketich, 1995; Hudson & Rapee, 2001; Krohne & Hock, 1991; Miller, Warner, Wickramaratne, & Weissman, 1999; Rapee, 1997; Siqueland et al., 1996). Studies of anxious adults have also supported a connection between anxiety and parenting styles, with retrospective reports by adults of parenting styles characterized by low levels of parental warmth and high levels of control or overprotection (e.g., Arrindell, Emmelkamp, Monsma, & Brikman, 1983). Rapee (1997) suggests that maternal overcontrol may maintain child anxiety insofar as it reinforces a child's perception of threat and therefore interferes with opportunities for a child to develop successful coping mechanisms through encouraging avoidance of potentially threatening situations. In addition to directly controlling the situations their children encounter, parents may indeed attempt to protect their anxious children by encouraging avoidance of potentially difficult situations. Barrett, Rapee, Dadds, and Ryan (1996) analyzed the degree to which parents modeled, prompted, and rewarded anxiety in their children during videotaped family discussions. The parents of anxious children were found to be more likely than parents of nonclinic and aggressive children to reciprocate avoidant solutions and less likely to encourage prosocial solutions to ambiguous social situations. Research investigating the influence of parental anxiety and parent-child interactions on child anxiety has demonstrated a link in mechanisms of maintenance. What research has not demonstrated is any causal link between parental psychopathology and parenting behaviors on child anxiety. The circular influence of parental anxiety and parent-child interactions on child anxiety highlights the importance of engaging parents, and families more broadly, in treatments for child anxiety.

The following sections examine cognitive-behavioral treatment for childhood anxiety disorders, specifically the role of parents and families in treatment and the improvement of long-term outcomes for children.

COGNITIVE-BEHAVIORAL TREATMENT OF CHILD ANXIETY DISORDERS

Randomized controlled trials (RCTs) of CBT for child and youth anxiety have consistently shown evidence of significant symptom reduction (Barrett, Dadds, & Rapee, 1996; Kendall, 1994; Kendall et al., 1997), leading to the current recognition of this intervention modality as being *"probably efficacious"* (e.g., Albano & Kendall, 2002; Ollendick & King, 1998). More than 10 years ago, Kendall (1994) published the first RCT of CBT for anxiety disorders in children, examining the efficacy of the now widely used CBT program *Coping Cat* (Kendall, 1994). This is an individual *child-focused* therapy program that teaches children skills to help them cope with difficult situations and manage their anxiety. The Coping Cat program is a 16-session protocol that teaches children affective recognition, relaxation skills, cognitive-restructuring, exposure and response prevention, and problem-solving skills. This program relies on therapist instruction of skills and in-session practice and exposure tasks. Children are also encouraged to practice skills through homework activities. In Kendall's study, (1994), parents were seen in two additional sessions in which therapists updated the parents on the program and the child's progress and addressed any concerns parents raised. In this way, Kendall describes the role of parents in his treatment as being that of consultants and collaborators for the child's individual therapy (Barmish & Kendall, 2005). Outcomes of this trial (Kendall, 1994) were positive, with results indicating that the program was effective for 64% of the children who participated.

The efficacy of *child-focused* CBT for child anxiety disorders has been extended since Kendall's first trial (1994) with several now published replication studies (Kendall et al., 1997), and long-term follow-up studies (Kendall, Safford, Flannery-Schroeder, & Webb, 2004; Kendall & Southam-Gerow, 1996). Since Kendall's first RCT for child anxiety (1994), researchers have espoused the importance of *parental involvement* in helping anxious children, and have extended the role of parents in treatment from the typically more passive role of consultants and collaborators, to engaging parents and families as coclients in therapy. Barrett, Dadds, et al. (1996) conducted the first randomized, controlled trial of CBT plus family anxiety management training (FAM). In this study (Barrett, Dadds, et al., 1996), FAM involved (a) training parents in contingency management, (b) giving parents better skills to manage their own anxiety, and (c) training parents in problem solving and communication skills. Barrett, Dadds, et al. (1996) randomly assigned 79 children (aged 7 to 14 years) to either child only CBT, CBT + FAM, or a wait-list condition. At posttreatment, 61% of children in the child only CBT group were diagnosis free compared with 88% of children in the combined treatment and less than 30% in the wait-list condition. At 12-month follow-up, the relative superiority of CBT+FAM was maintained. However at a long-term follow-up, conducted 5 to 7 years after completion of treatment, child only CBT and CBT+FAM were equally effective, with 87% and 86% of participants in these respective groups diagnosis free (Barrett, Duffy, Dadds, & Rapee, 2001).

Interestingly, in Barrett, Dadds, et al.'s (1996) family treatment study, age and gender appeared to moderate the effectiveness of the additional parent component. Specifically, younger children (ages 7 to 10 years) and girls who completed the CBT+FAM condition were more likely to be diagnosis free than their peers in the child only CBT condition. For boys, and children aged 11 to 14 years, the child alone CBT was as effective as CBT+FAM at posttreatment and at follow-up. Barrett, Dadds, et al. (1996) suggested that enhancing parenting skills and involvement in child anxiety management may be important for younger children, but for older children individual work may be sufficient to reduce anxiety, possibly because of the growing need for autonomy that occurs during adolescence.

Since Barrett, Dadds, et al.'s (1996) family treatment trial, several controlled treatment trials have included active parental involvement (Barrett, 1998; Cobham et al., 1998; Manassis et al., 2002; Mendlowitz et al., 1999; Nauta, Scholing, Emmelkamp, & Minderaa, 2003; Shortt, Barrett, & Fox, 2001; Silverman et al., 1999; Spence, Donovan, & Brechman-Toussaint, 2000). These trials have varied in the delivery of treatment (individual versus group treatment), and in the number or format of parent sessions. Barmish and Kendall (2005) completed a review and meta-analysis of nine controlled treatment trials for child anxiety that included parents as coclients. Barmish and Kendall identified that within these trials, the majority included parents for 10 to 12 sessions. Trials varied in whether parents were involved in the therapy process separate from the child or cojointly in child sessions. Parental involvement generally focused on three major therapeutic strategies: (1) removing parental reinforcement of child anxiety behavior, (2) training parents in self-anxiety management and encouraging parents to model coping behaviors, and (3) family problem solving focused on reducing family conflict (see Barmish & Kendall, 2005).

Barmish and Kendall (2005) concluded, based on their review of controlled trials and the respective effect sizes yielded for CBT plus parental involvement versus CBT alone, that the evidence to date is inconclusive on whether parental involvement as coclients in therapy is a superior treatment for anxious children, than CBT alone. Effect ranged from small, to midsize, to large, across studies for both CBT alone and CBT plus parental involvement (Barmish & Kendall, 2005). Overall, effect sizes for parental involvement appeared to be larger than CBT alone. However, the great variability in effect sizes across studies and the equally large variability in methodologies across studies make any definite conclusion impossible to make at this stage. When the results of the controlled trials conducted to date for child anxiety are taken together, the combined research evidence supports CBT plus parental involvement as a probably efficacious treatment, across both individual and group based delivery (Manassis et al., 2002), with parental involvement possibly being particularly important for children versus youths (Barrett, Dadds, et al., 1996), for children diagnosed with separation anxiety disorder, due to the central role parents play in this disorder, and in the case where parental psychopathology exists (Cobham et al., 1998).

A number of the treatment trials conducted to date with parental involvement have involved group-based CBT (Barrett, 1998; Flannery-Schroeder & Kendall, 2000; Manassis et al., 2002; Mendlowitz et al., 1999; Shortt, Barrett, & Fox, 2001). Barrett (1998) evaluated the first controlled trial of group CBT family-based intervention for childhood anxiety disorders. Sixty children ranging from 7 to 14 years old were randomly allocated to 3 treatment conditions: group CBT (GCBT), group CBT plus family management (GCBT+FAM), and wait-list control (WL). At posttreatment, 56% of children in the GCBT, 71% of children in the GCBT+FAM, and 25% of children in the WL no longer met criteria for any anxiety disorder diagnosis. At 12-month follow-up, 65% of children in the GCBT group and 85% of children in the GCBT+FAM were diagnosis free. At posttreatment and follow-up, comparison of the GCBT and GCBT+FAM conditions revealed that children in the GCBT+FAM condition showed significant improvements on measures of diagnostic status, parents' perception of their ability to deal with the child's behavior, and change in family disruption by child's behavior. These results suggest that CBT family interventions for childhood anxiety disorders can be effectively administered in a group format. In support of the findings from Barrett, Dadds, et al.'s (1996) earlier study, the addition of a family management component led to more favorable outcomes.

Since Barrett's (1998) group-based treatment study, authors have published group outcome trials for child anxiety including parental involvement in therapy with similar outcomes (Shortt, Barrett, & Fox, 2001), and with results demonstrating no significant difference between individual and group-based treatment modalities (Flannery-Schroeder, & Kendall, 2000; Manassis et al., 2002). Group interventions have always been a promising treatment alternative in psychotherapy, due to the obvious cost, time, and labor effectiveness of treating multiple clients in one session. For child anxiety, groups offer more than just resourcefulness, providing a therapeutic process that appears to foster treatment gains. While studies of therapeutic process are lacking in this field, clinical experience of working with anxious children in group therapy provides insight into the possible mechanisms that make group therapy so appealing and effective. In working with groups of children, the experience of anxiety is normalized, a support network within the group is formed for each child, individual motivation appears to increase in overcoming fears, and children can acquire and practice new skills in a safe and interactive environment that fosters supportive peer learning through experiential group exercises. Since a number of controlled trials have now demonstrated the comparable effectiveness of group CBT to individual CBT, group-based delivery of treatment including parental involvement has become the favored mode of treatment delivery for anxious children and youths. One evidence-based treatment program for child anxiety disorders that includes parental and family involvement is the FRIENDS program (Barrett, Lowry-Webster, & Turner, 2000a, 2000b), now in its fourth edition and called *FRIENDS for Life* (Barrett, 2004, 2005). (The use of the word *friends* as an acronym is discussed in detail later in this chapter.) This program comprises two components, including child-focused CBT, adapted from Kendall's Coping Cat (Kendall, 1994), and a comprehensive family training component first developed in Barrett, Dadds, et al.'s (1996) individual family treatment study. The FRIENDS for Life program has been validated as being effective as an individual treatment program (Barrett, Dadds, et al., 1996), as well as a group treatment (Barrett, 1998; Shortt, Barrett, & Fox, 2001), and more recently as a school-based prevention program for child and youth anxiety and depression at an indicated/selective level of prevention (Barrett, Moore, & Sonderegger, 2000; Barrett, Sonderegger, & Sonderegger, 2001; Barrett, Sonderegger, & Xenos, 2003; Bernstein, Layne, Egan, & Tennison, 2005; Dadds, Spence, Holland, Barrett, & Laurens, 1997; Dadds, Spence, Laurens, Mullins, & Barrett, 1999), as well as at a universal level (Barrett, Farrell, Ollendick, & Dadds, in press; Barrett & Turner, 2000; Lock & Barrett, 2003; Lowry-Webster, Barrett, & Dadds, 2001; Lowry-Webster, Barrett, & Lock, 2003).

THE FRIENDS FOR LIFE PROGRAM: CHILD TREATMENT OUTLINE

The child component of the FRIENDS for Life program (Barrett, 2004, 2005) originated with the development of the *Coping Koala* program (Barrett, Dadds, et al., 1996), an Australian adaptation of Kendall's Coping Cat program (Kendall, 1994). The program later became FRIENDS when it was adapted for group treatment delivery (i.e., Barrett, 1998; Shortt, Barrett, & Fox, 2001). The FRIENDS for Life program (4th ed.; Barrett, 2004, 2005) includes two developmentally tailored workbooks for use with either children (Barrett, 2004) or youths (Barrett, 2005; the program also consists of leader's manuals), and can be run in both group and individual settings. The program consists of 10 weekly sessions and 2 booster sessions. Each session is designed to run for approximately 1 to 1.5 hours. The initial 10 sessions are conducted weekly for optimal effectiveness, and the booster sessions are conducted 1 month and 3 months following completion of treatment. The booster sessions provide additional opportunities for children to practice the skills learned in the previous sessions and to facilitate the generalization of these skills when coping with situations encountered in everyday life.

The program utilizes the acronym FRIENDS to help children remember the strategies they can use to effectively manage their anxiety. The FRIENDS acronym (4th ed.; Barrett, 2004, 2005) stands for:

Feelings.
Remember to relax. Have quiet time.
I can do it! I can try my best!
Explore solutions and coping step plans.
Now reward yourself! You've done your best!
Don't forget to practice.
Smile! Stay calm for life!

The word *friends* also highlights the major objectives and themes of the program, which encourages children to (a) think of their *body as their friend* since it tells them when they are feeling worried or nervous by giving them special clues (physiological and somatic symptoms); (b) to *be their own friend* and to look after their body through affective regulation activities, as well as reward themselves when they try hard; (c) to *make friends,* building empathy skills and compassion for others, and finally; (d) to *talk to their friends* when they are in difficult or worrying situations, or when their friends and family members are in difficult situations, so that they build, extend, and strengthen their social support networks. The FRIENDS program has six important components that are based on skill acquisition:

1. Psychoeducation regarding feelings
2. Understanding of the physical manifestation of anxiety and how to use relaxation skills
3. Cognitive restructuring and positive self-talk
4. Problem-solving skills and graded exposure for achieving goals and facing fears

5. The importance of self-rewards for trying hard and achieving goals
6. Relapse prevention and ways to maintain skills for life. The two booster sessions are designed to facilitate generalization of skills and help children to apply the skills to challenging situations.

Tables 5.1 and 5.2 summarize the session by session content for both the child and youth programs.

Table 5.1
Outline of FRIENDS for Life—For Children

Session Number	Content of Session—Major Learning Objectives
1	Build rapport and introduce group participants Establish group guidelines Normalize anxiety and individual differences in anxiety reactions
2	Affective education and identification of various emotions Introduce the relationship between thoughts and feelings
3	**F:** Feelings (Identify physiological symptoms of worry) **R:** Remember to relax. Have quiet time. (Use relaxation activities and identify pleasant activities to do when feeling worried or sad)
4	**I:** I can do it! I can try my best! (Identify self-talk, introduce helpful green thoughts and unhelpful red thoughts)
5	Attention training (look for positive aspects in all situations) Challenge unhelpful red thoughts **E:** Explore solutions and coping step plans (introduce coping step plans/graded exposure to fear hierarchies, setting goals, and breaking problems into small steps)
6	Problem-solving skills (Six stage problem-solving plan) Coping Role models Social support plans
7	**N:** Now reward yourself. You've done your best!
8	**D:** Don't forget to practice (practice the FRIENDS skills) **S:** Smile. Stay calm for life! (Reflect on ways to cope in difficult situations)
9	Generalize skills of FRIENDS to various difficult situations Coach others in how to use the FRIENDS coping skills
10	Use new skills for maintenance of the FRIENDS strategies Prepare for minor setbacks that may occur
Booster 1	Review FRIENDS strategies and prepare for future challenges
Booster 2	Review FRIENDS strategies and prepare for future challenges

Table 5.2
Outline of FRIENDS for Life—For Youth

Session Number	Content of Session—Major Learning Objectives
1	Build rapport and introduce group participants Establish group guidelines Normalize anxiety and individual differences in anxiety reactions
2	Enhance self-esteem in self and others Recognize individual strengths
3	Affective education Introduce the relationship between thoughts and feelings Friendship skills
4	**F:** Feelings (Identify physiological symptoms of worry) **R:** Remember to relax. Have quiet time. (Use relaxation activities and identify pleasant activities to do when feeling worried or sad)
5	**I:** I can do it! I can try my best! (Identify self-talk; introduce helpful, optimistic thoughts and unhelpful, pessimistic thoughts) Attention training (environmental, intrapersonal, and interpersonal) Challenge unhelpful thoughts
6	**E:** Explore solutions and coping step plans (introduce coping step plans / graded exposure to fear hierarchies, setting goals, and breaking problems into small steps)
7	Coping Role models Social support plans Conflict and communication styles: assertive, aggressive, passive CALM: conflict resolution plan
8	Six stage problem-solving plan **N:** Now reward yourself. You've done your best! Think like a winner—focus on positive aspects in every situation
9	**D:** Don't forget to practice (practice the FRIENDS skills) **S:** Smile. Stay calm for life! (Reflect on ways to cope in difficult situations) Generalize the skills of FRIENDS to various difficult situations Coach others in how to use the FRIENDS coping skills
10	Skills for maintenance of the FRIENDS strategies Prepare for minor setbacks that may occur
Booster 1	Review FRIENDS strategies and prepare for future challenges
Booster 2	Review FRIENDS strategies and prepare for future challenges

THE FRIENDS FOR LIFE PROGRAM: PARENT AND FAMILY TRAINING OUTLINE

FRIENDS for Life includes a family skills component that involves parents in each stage of skill acquisition and provides parent training in anxiety management. In the current edition of FRIENDS (Barrett, 2004, 2005), two structured parent sessions are outlined in the leader's manuals. The reasoning behind condensing the parent and family skills training into two sessions in the current leader's manual is to facilitate its use as a prevention program in schools. In the majority of cases, it may be difficult to attract parents to parent information or training evenings within the school environment; hence, condensing the protocol into two comprehensive sessions for schools met the practicalities of this context of intervention. In treatment settings, however, involvement of parents in every session is the preferred process of therapy. Generally, individual or group child-focused sessions run for 1 to 1.5 hours (in the case of larger groups), and then parents join the group with children and youths for the last 30 minutes of the session. This process may vary to meet the needs and preferences of the groups. Youth groups tend to run best by having the parent group sessions separate from the youths, due to the increased desire for autonomy and independence in adolescence. The typical size of an effective group is between 6 and 10 children, which allows adequate time for everyone in the group to share ideas. When running group interventions, it is often helpful to offer every family the opportunity for at least one individual session during the course of the therapy to raise personal issues for discussion and guidance. The private session is usually best timed after Session 5, when children and youths have identified individual goals and have begun working on graded exposure to fears. The use of cofacilitators in group therapy is very helpful, both to manage the group process by offering reinforcement to children who are trying their best and to assist children with any reading or writing difficulties.

The underlying philosophy of the FRIENDS program empowers families to make positive change in their lives and values the unique knowledge and experiences that parents, siblings, and children and youths with anxiety bring to the group. A collaborative team approach is emphasized in which the therapist, parent/s, siblings, and the child work together with a shared goal of increasing both the child's and parent's confidence and coping skills. The family component of the FRIENDS program is aimed at empowering everyone in the family to recognize their skills and strengths, and to use these skills to help each other become braver and more confident. The family therapy component is not focused on the child, but on how the entire family can learn positive, proactive coping skills to overcome fears and challenges, and make positive choices in life. Each session involves homework activities for the children and youths to work on. These homework activities are discussed jointly with children and parents (generally youths and parents separately), and are termed "family homework." Parents are encouraged to work with the child and involve siblings on all these activities and are instructed to take responsibility for any written recording that may be required to remove the focus from reading and writing to experiential learning.

There are three major underlying components of family training in the FRIENDS program when used as a clinical intervention:

1. *Parenting strategies* including attending to and reinforcing coping, approaching behaviors in children, and parents modeling appropriate coping behavior to children
2. *Self-awareness* of own stress and anxiety and appropriate management of these experiences
3. *Awareness of at-risk times in child,* coaching children in how to use strategies to cope, and reinforcing and rewarding appropriate attempts to cope.

In each parent session, the general format remains the same: First, the skills of the child's treatment are reviewed, and then strategies for how parents can help children use these skills are discussed. Following this, the therapist discusses how families can practice these skills at home together, shifting the focus from the child working toward positive change, to the entire family working as a team toward change. The following subsections describe how parents and siblings are actively engaged in this family training, focusing on each of the major steps taught to children and youths in the FRIENDS program.

F: FEELINGS

This is the first skill taught in the treatment program. It involves affective education, focused on understanding feelings in oneself, as well as in others. The focus is on both empathy building and awareness of one's own emotional responses. This part of the program teaches children to identify physiological and behavioral indicators of anxiety. Children are taught that their body gives them special clues when they are feeling nervous or scared, such as butterflies in the stomach, heart racing, red face, and shaky knees. This is an important component of therapy as many young people with anxiety have difficulty making the connection between the physical symptoms of anxiety and the situations that scare or worry them. Children who feel sick every Monday morning before school believe they are unwell and will be unable to cope with facing school. These children are unlikely to be feeling sick from an illness, but rather are experiencing body clues, or physiological arousal associated with anxiety, possibly as a result of worry about something associated with school. It is both empowering and normalizing for children to recognize anxiety symptoms as their body's normal response to worry and stress, and to feel confident that they can repair these feelings through effective relaxation strategies that are taught under the **R** component of the program.

Family Training

Parents and siblings are encouraged to focus on their physiological responses to fear and anxiety and on learning the skills of anxiety awareness. In addition, examples are shared with families on accepting individual differences, particularly in response to feelings, and how important it is to normalize and validate each other's personal emotional responses to situations in life. A scenario may be presented to the group such as "you are asked to give a talk in front of your class/colleagues," and then group members are asked to think how they would respond to that situation. They are asked: What would you think? How would you feel? What might you do in that situation? This discussion illustrates individual differences in perceptions, as well as in actual coping strategies. It is important to highlight that all responses are normal and acceptable. Examples of validating a child's emotional response are provided: "I can see you feel very scared about talking in front of your class. That is okay, I would feel scared, too. We could practice together, and then you might feel more confident and brave."

R: REMEMBER TO RELAX. HAVE QUIET TIME

The second strategy covered in the FRIENDS program builds on the first. Children are taught that they can feel more calm and brave if they repair their body clues, improving their performance by practicing relaxation exercises. Children are encouraged to think of relaxation as a skill like riding a bike that needs to be practiced regularly before they can really enjoy it and notice the benefits of it. Relaxation strategies taught in the FRIENDS program include diaphragmatic breathing, progressive muscle relaxation, and visualization. The fourth edition of the FRIENDS program coaches children and youths in an "athletes game" relaxation exercise, whereby children are taught to manage anxiety and nerves like athletes do before a race. Children are coached to prepare their minds and bodies to be calm and in control and to perform their very best before doing something difficult (e.g., class oral presentation, musical recital, running race), through practicing breathing, muscle relaxation, and visualization. Along these lines, children are also encouraged to engage in regular exercise, as a preventive approach to stress and anxiety. Engaging in enjoyable activities, and having regular periods of quiet time, particularly when feeling worried or sad is another way to help children cope with their worries. Quiet time involves doing some activity that the child enjoys, without pressure or competition, that is calming, and that does not involve stimulation from technology (e.g., computer games, TV, or PlayStations).

Family Training

Families are encouraged to learn relaxation strategies as well, and to practice these strategies regularly as a family. Families are asked to make a weekly family schedule for relaxation, with each family member taking an important role in planning and coaching the rest of the family through relaxation activities on scheduled days. The program strongly emphasizes the importance of *quiet time,* as a preventive measure for stress and anxiety in children, youths, and parents. Parents are encouraged to ensure the family has regular periods of quiet time, whereby everyone in the family can regulate their stress and achieve relaxation. Examples of quiet time activities include lying on the grass under a tree, listening to quiet music at home, going for a walk along the beach or in the forest, giving someone in the family a massage or tickle, cuddling on the sofa or bed, floating in the pool, reading stories, writing poems, drawing pictures. Quiet time should be supported and practiced by all family members; attempts should be made to turn off television sets and computers, and to put telephones on silent or divert calls to message bank. A discussion on the importance of reinforcing and encouraging relaxation practice in children, as well as parental modeling of relaxation and quiet time, is important in this session. Parents are encouraged to focus on preventing emotional distress and misbehavior through providing and modeling adequate quiet time, and relaxation activities, and by spending quality time with each child in the family, as well as the family as a whole unit. Parents often feel overwhelmed in parenting and destitute of any time to invest as quality time with their children. Parents are supported and encouraged to look for opportunities for spending minimal but quality time with their child; for example, walking to the local shops with their child instead of driving, allowing time to talk, washing the car or watering the garden with their child, riding a bike alongside the child to school, or simply reading a story to the child at bedtime.

I: I CAN DO IT! I CAN TRY MY BEST!

This step introduces the cognitive strategies of the program. The FRIENDS program teaches children to become aware of their inner thoughts or self-talk and learn to pay attention to this inner dialogue.

Children are taught that their inner thoughts are the control center of their bodies; what they think will determine how they feel and that in turn will influence how they behave and cope in any given situation. Self-talk is described in terms of two kinds—green helpful thoughts and red unhelpful thoughts. Children are taught that green helpful thoughts make us feel good, happy, and brave. Red unhelpful thoughts make us feel sad, worried, scared, or unhappy. Children are encouraged to identify negative-self talk, or red thoughts, and to challenge these thoughts, and come up with alternative green helpful ways of thinking. Children are taught two major processes: (1) *awareness* of their self-talk; and (2) *flexibility* in their thinking—the ability to move from thinking red thoughts and feeling red feelings, to thinking positive, powerful green thoughts, and feeling braver, happier, and more confident. Under I in FRIENDS, children are also taught attention training strategies. Children and youths are encouraged to always look for and pay attention to the positive aspects, or safety signals, in every situation. In the youth version, this activity goes into more detail, with teenagers trained to look for, and pay attention to, positive aspects and safety cues at an interpersonal, intrapersonal, and environmental level within a situation. A teenager starting at a new school may be trained to focus on the positive cues of smiling faces (*interpersonal cue*), people who say hello (*interpersonal cue*), their positive green thoughts of "I can cope, I will make friends" (*intrapersonal cue*), their own smiling face (*intrapersonal cue*), the beautiful fountain at the school (*environmental cue*) and the great sporting facilities (*environmental cue*).

Family Training

Parents are encouraged to become aware of their own cognitive style and aware of how they model optimism or pessimism to their children through their own individual responses to stress and challenges. Families are encouraged to use positive, powerful green thoughts to help them cope in difficult situations, and to notice and reward each other for trying to think in helpful ways. Parents can assist children to use more positive thoughts through encouraging children with positive prompts, called encouragers in the FRIENDS program, such as "you can do it, you have done it before!," "you can be calm and brave," "just try your best, that is all you can do," and "remember your past successes!" Parents, as well as children, are encouraged to notice when they hear unhelpful or worrisome thoughts in other family members or in their friends, and to actively challenge this person by using questions. A child might notice their parents saying, "I am never going to get this work finished!" The child could help the parent challenge negative thinking through asking questions such as "have you ever *not* finished your work on time?" "Is it really true that you will never finish?" or "Did you get through all your work the last time you felt like this?"

The concept of reciprocity is discussed with families throughout the program—parents *and* children are encouraged to find ways to support *each other* and reinforce or reward each other for trying—whether it is through practicing relaxation, being solution focused, and approaching challenges, or through using positive thinking. While it is important for parents to model brave, positive, and confident coping to their children, and attend to desirable behaviors in their children, it is equally important for children to notice when parents are trying hard, working hard, and being supportive, and for children to recognize this and reinforce this through acknowledging parents' efforts; for example, saying, "Thanks Mom and Dad for helping me practice for my exam—is there something I can do to help you?" Children are encouraged to help their friends, parents, and siblings when they notice them feeling tired, sad, or worried.

E: EXPLORE SOLUTIONS AND COPING STEP PLANS

The fourth step of FRIENDS aims to teach children and youths ways to solve problems in difficult or worrying situations. FRIENDS teaches children several positive, proactive plans: (a) a problem-solving plan, (b) a coping step plan, (c) coping role models and support team plans, and (d) in the youth program, a conflict resolution plan. First, the Six Block Problem-Solving Plan involves thinking through six steps to solve a problem:

1. What is the problem—Define it!
2. Brainstorm—list all possible solutions.
3. List what might happen for each solution.
4. Select the best solution based on the consequences.
5. Make a plan for putting this solution into practice and do it!
6. Evaluate the outcome in terms of strengths and weaknesses, and if it did not work return to Step 2 and try again.

The second plan for dealing with anxiety-provoking situations is the coping step plan. The coping step plan involves children constructing a graded exposure hierarchy that they implement during the remainder of the program—it involves exposure and response prevention (ERP) to feared situations. In ERP, children are systematically exposed to a series of fear-eliciting situations or stimuli and instructed to not engage in any avoidant behavior to reduce the resulting increases in anxiety. Exposure and response prevention progresses in graded fashion with less distressing symptoms addressed first, followed by more difficult exposures as treatment progresses. If individual therapy is being delivered, exposures are typically developed and initially practiced in the therapy session (it is not possible to do in-session ERP with a group of children); however, most treatment gains accrue from ongoing practice in the natural environment—be it home or school or with friends. The most commonly proposed mechanism for the effectiveness of ERP is that with repeated exposures, associated anxiety dissipates through autonomic habituation. In addition, as children realize that the feared consequences are not going to occur, their expectations of harm disappear, which reduces anxiety even further (Foa & Kozak, 1986).

In implementing the step plan, children are encouraged to use the strategies covered in previous sessions (e.g., relaxation, deep breathing, and thinking helpful thoughts) to assist them as they climb each step. Children are encouraged to identify coping role models in their life—people they know or fictional characters who cope well in challenging situations. Children are taught to think of their coping role models when in challenging situations and to think what their role model might do to cope in that situation. Along similar lines, the FRIENDS program also teaches children to identify people in their life who could form their coping support team—a team of people who care about us and who could help us in both good and bad times. Children are encouraged to look beyond their families and immediate friends and consider all possible support people in their life, including teachers, coaches, neighbors, friends, and siblings. Children are encouraged to strengthen their own support teams through being good support people to others. CALM is a conflict resolution plan that is introduced in the youth program, and teaches teenagers in conflict situations to *(C)* calm down when in a conflict situation, as it is difficult to focus on solutions when very upset; *(A)* actively listen to what the other person wants; *(L)* list their own needs in the situation; and *(M)* make a solution that is based on a compromise between both persons' needs.

Family Training

Parents are coached in how to assist their child develop a coping step plan, based on a fear hierarchy, and how to support their child using the coping step plan to face their fears. Parents are provided with examples of coping step plans and are given the following rules to ensure the coping step plan is successful for their child:

- Ensure the child identifies a clear, specific, and achievable goal.
- Ensure the steps are small enough to be achievable.
- Ensure the steps allow the child to practice the activity regularly—exposure and response prevention work through *repeated* exposure to feared situations, preferably on a daily basis.

- The steps should gradually become more difficult as the child progresses through the step plan, approaching the goal.
- The child should be coached and encouraged to use the FRIENDS plan when trying to climb each step (e.g., breathe and think "I can do this!").
- The child should not climb the next step until feeling completely calm and confident on the current step.

An example of a coping step plan is provided in Table 5.3.

All family members are taught how to use the problem-solving and coping step plans, so that everyone can practice focusing on solutions and also setting goals and working toward outcomes. Parents and siblings are encouraged to identify their own goals (they may be based on fears or on more general challenges in life), and to use the coping step plan to break their goal down into small steps and work toward reaching their goal with practice. It is important for parents to encourage their anxious children to approach situations by modeling appropriate approach behaviors. Children and teenagers respond to events as they have seen their parents respond to them. Parents are encouraged to be positive role models for children by approaching difficult situations rather than avoiding them, encouraging their child to do the same, and by using positive self-talk to help them cope. Children "live what they learn," so it is important that parents engage in behaviors that approach situations in a positive, proactive manner. When things do not go as planned, parents are encouraged to

Table 5.3
A Coping Step Plan

Fear: Staying away from home for school camp

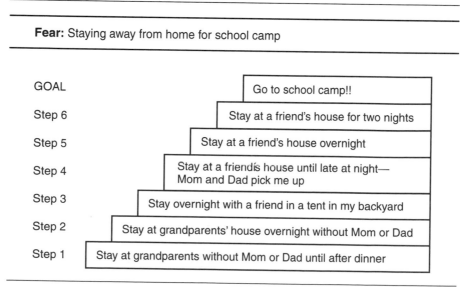

GOAL	Go to school camp!!
Step 6	Stay at a friend's house for two nights
Step 5	Stay at a friend's house overnight
Step 4	Stay at a friend's house until late at night—Mom and Dad pick me up
Step 3	Stay overnight with a friend in a tent in my backyard
Step 2	Stay at grandparents' house overnight without Mom or Dad
Step 1	Stay at grandparents without Mom or Dad until after dinner

engage the entire family in a problem-solving activity to work out acceptable solutions to the problem. To meet the emotional needs of children and adolescents, it is important for parents to accept their children for who they are, and to spend quality time talking and listening to them. Parents can encourage children or teenagers to approach situations by discussing with them their concerns, and the future situations they may face. When parents talk and listen to their children, they are helping them feel supported and understood. Parents should be active in helping their children explore plans they can use for coping, identify and problem-solve potential difficulties, and help them practice these plans in a safe and supported environment.

In encouraging children and youths to extend and strengthen their support networks, it is important for parents to welcome their child's friends into their homes, respect them for who they are, and expect their respect by setting clear and specific limits on their behavior. Parents are encouraged to become involved in their child's life through mentoring positive friendships with peers. Parents can help children to improve their social competence by modeling good social skills (eye contact), thinking positively, being aware of and interested in things going on at home and at school, and using problem-solving skills to deal with challenges and conflict. Spending quality time getting to know their children will help parents recognize when something isn't right. Parents can also assist in building their child's social support team by encouraging other safe adults to be involved in their child's life, and to welcome their own adult friends into the home, spending quality time with the children at home, not just as friends of the parents.

FRIENDS takes the positive, preventive approach to parenting, which focuses on building strengths in children and providing them with adequate quiet time and quality time to help regulate emotional distress, but it is also important for parents to have confidence in parenting strategies for dealing with misbehavior and conflict. Discipline and clear boundaries are critical for children and youths. FRIENDS addresses some of these parenting strategies and emphasizes making careful plans, modeling, explaining, making rules, and giving consequences for misbehavior and conflict. When setting boundaries, parents need to make sure (a) that they are clear and specific in their instructions and avoid giving multiple instructions in one request, (b) that both parents are consistent with instructions and ally together at all costs in front of the child, (c) that they check for understanding from the child by asking "tell me what you have heard me say," and (d) that they are prepared to back up their decision or instruction with action and a consequence if their child breaks the rules or bends the boundaries. The following tips are useful for parents in managing misbehavior:

- Set realistic limits and expectations of your child's behavior.
- Praise your child enthusiastically for behaving appropriately.
- Respond to misbehavior immediately, consistently, and decisively.
- Respond to misbehavior by describing what the child has done wrong.
- Respond to misbehavior by telling the child what would have been more acceptable.
- Model your expectations of the child.
- Remain calm but firm when speaking to a child who has misbehaved.
- Deal with the problem yourself rather than threatening someone else's action.
- Act quickly with a consequence (withdrawal of privilege), rather than threaten to act.
- Try to prevent problems by spending time building your relationship with your child.
- Listen and talk to your child and spend time with your child doing activities that your child enjoys.

N: Now Reward Yourself. You Have Done Your Best!

The fifth step of FRIENDS teaches children to evaluate their performance in terms of partial success and to set reasonable, achievable goals. Children are encouraged to reward themselves whenever they try their best (e.g., after studying for an examination or entering a singing competition at school. Children are encouraged to think of activity rewards to do with their family and friends, rather than rewards that involve purchasing material possessions or always relying on unhealthy food rewards. Learning to self-reward facilitates children's independence and teaches children to evaluate their own performance in terms of partial successes.

Family Training

All family members are encouraged to notice brave and confident behaviors of each other (or friends), and to acknowledge and reward any approach behavior that is noticed. Parents in particular are encouraged to attend to the positive and approach behaviors of their anxious children. Attending to positive behavior means giving praise or attention to children for engaging in desirable behaviors, such as approaching difficult or worrying situations and acting in brave ways. Attending to positive behavior reinforces it and increases the likelihood that the positive behavior will be repeated. Attending to positive behavior may be as simple as acknowledging a child's efforts: "Lucy, I noticed you practicing your shooting for basketball! It's really great to see you try—that will certainly help you for the game on Saturday. I'm really proud of you!" In addition, parents can reinforce their child or teenager with signs of affection, such as offering a hug or kiss, or by spending quality time doing the things the child enjoys. Hence, parents are coached to "catch their child being brave" and offer reinforcement *immediately*. In line with this, parents are also coached to ignore complaining or avoidance behaviors, since the simple act of attention acts as a powerful reinforcer that encourages the misbehavior or avoidance. Therefore, parents are taught that when they notice complaining, avoiding, or misbehavior, to first acknowledge the behavior for what it is (e.g., "You are feeling nervous and trying to get out of school today—that seems like worry to me!") and second, to prompt the child to use the FRIENDS plan (e.g., "You know what you need to do—practice your breathing, tell yourself you can do it, and get ready for school—of course you can do it"). If the complaining or avoidance continues, parents are encouraged to walk away, or simply change the topic. In summary, parents are coached to (a) acknowledge and validate all feelings, (b) redirect the child to use their FRIENDS plan, (c) shift the focus, and (d) ignore complaining and reinforce any attempt at coping.

D: Don't Forget to Practice

The sixth step of FRIENDS reminds children that the skills and strategies learned in FRIENDS need to be practiced on a regular basis. Children are encouraged to role-play difficult situations with family and/or peers. For example, if a child has a class talk to do, then role-playing in front of members of the family will allow the child to practice presentation skills as well as FRIENDS skills to help in coping with this situation. Children are encouraged to coach someone else through a challenging situation (a group member or a family member), using the FRIENDS plan. This reinforces the child's learning and provides an opportunity for developing empathy and being a supportive friend.

S: Smile! Stay Calm for Life

This last step reminds children that they can stay calm because they have effective strategies for coping, and through the experience of the program they have managed anxiety and overcome challenges using the positive, proactive coping skills taught in FRIENDS. This step also encourages children to plan ahead for challenging situations and to identify how they can use their FRIENDS plan to help them cope. Children and youths are encouraged to always evaluate their performance and coping behaviors when faced by challenges, so that they can learn from their experiences and identify new skills, or different approaches to use next time they are in a similar situation.

Family Training for "D" and "S"

Families are encouraged to always review challenging situations, as well as positive life events as a family, focusing on what everyone in the family did well, what each person may have had difficulties with, and how each person could try to be more confident and proactive next time around. As children with anxiety tend to focus on future problems and worry in advance, parents should always talk about upcoming challenges with children and teenagers, focusing on the positive aspects of the situation. They can prepare the child by discussing how to use FRIENDS to cope with any potential difficulties. Parents can assist their child by role-playing those situations, so that the child can practice using the FRIENDS skills in a controlled and safe environment. Families should regularly use the FRIENDS strategies, so that everyone continues to practice skills and build confidence. Parents should also encourage their children to support and help other friends and family members who may be feeling worried, sad, or upset by coaching them in using the FRIENDS plan to be more brave, confident, and happy. So that children continue to develop new skills, acquire mastery of fears, and increase in confidence, parents should urge them to try new activities while using their coping skills to manage the normal fear that everyone experiences to some degree when trying something new.

CONCLUSION

Cognitive-behavioral treatment for child anxiety disorders that involves parents in treatment is an effective treatment intervention, with durable outcomes (Barrett, Duffy, et al., 2001; Kendall et al., 2004; Kendall & Southam-Gerow, 1996). Treatment studies evaluating CBT plus parental involvement show favorable outcomes; however, the evidence to date is not clear in supporting a uniform superiority of CBT plus parental involvement, compared with CBT alone (Barmish & Kendall, 2005). It seems to be clear from the literature to date, that parental involvement is clinically the preferred model of treatment for child anxiety, with outcome data supporting possible benefits of this treatment over child-focused CBT for younger children, and for children who have parents with psychopathology (Barmish & Kendall, 2005).

To date, parental involvement has focused on involving parents in child CBT treatment. On closer examination of the treatment trials conducted, this typically only involves mothers in the majority of studies and in the majority of treatment sessions within studies. It seems to be a universal experience across studies and clinics that it is exceedingly difficult to gain involvement of both parents in therapy. The following reasons are frequently given: (a) Treatments are offered during working hours, (b) other siblings need to be cared for at home by the other parent, (c) there are competing extracurricular demands of other siblings (e.g., one parent is taking brother to soccer practice at the same time as therapy), and (d) fathers are absent from the child's home during the week because of work commitments or separation of parents. Because children exist within the context of a family and are greatly influenced by all family members, it is important for family treatment to engage and involve all family members; including fathers and siblings. Frequently, family involvement tends to overlook siblings; however research by our team has demonstrated the negative effects that anxiety disorders have on siblings, and the potential significance and benefits of involving siblings in therapy (Barrett, Fox, & Farrell, in press; Barrett, Rasmussen, & Healy, 2001; Fox, Barrett, & Shortt, 2002). Family involvement in therapy, including parents and siblings, increases the social support for the child with anxiety, enhances consistency in contingency management, and encourages greater practice of skills and generalization of skills because everyone is using the same strategies and approach in managing stress and anxiety. The likelihood of family attendance can be increased by offering after-hours appointments for families, including weekend sessions. Clinicians should also ensure that families are aware in advance that all members are expected to attend; strongly reinforce fathers and siblings who come to sessions, and provide specific homework tasks for every family member so that they feel their presence is valued and worthwhile; and offer a room where parents and siblings can wait comfortably (ideally with snacks and tea and coffee) and chat with other families while they wait for completion of the child group session.

The FRIENDS for Life program is a positive, family based, treatment and prevention/resilience program for all children. The philosophy of the program is on building skills and setting goals, and on families working together to achieve positive behavioral change at a family level; it is not just focused on the child with anxiety. The approach of this program is on empowering children and families to make positive choices in life to overcome fears and to build confidence. The program has a strong preventive approach to parenting and to managing anxiety by using positive coping skills to prevent escalation of anxiety and depression. Parents and children are coached in having a balanced life characterized by plenty of quiet time; adequate sleep, diet, and exercise; and an abundance of family quality time spent talking and listening to each other and focusing on solutions and positive aspects of every situation. In this way, treatment builds strengths and protective factors in children, as well as within families.

Issues for future research in child anxiety treatment include extended evaluations of family-based treatments focused on outcomes addressing the role of the family in maintaining anxiety as well as in improving outcomes for child anxiety disorders. Although parental psychopathology and family interaction variables may play a role in the maintenance of anxiety, little is known about how these issues can be addressed in treatment, and how family members and family characteristics (such as interactions) may actually improve outcomes in therapy. Controlled trials evaluating family-based CBT that include the entire family in therapy, against child-focused therapy alone, are warranted to determine the genuine effectiveness of family involvement in CBT for child anxiety disorders.

REFERENCES

Albano, A. M., & Kendall, P. C. (2002). Cognitive behavioral therapy for children and adolescents with anxiety disorders: Clinical research advances. *International Review of Psychiatry, 14,* 129–134.

Arrindell, W. A., Emmelkamp, P. M. G., Monsma, A., & Brikman, E. (1983). The role of perceived parental rearing practices in the etiology of phobic disorders: A controlled trail. *British Journal of Psychiatry, 155,* 526–535.

Aschenbrand, S. G., Kendall, P. C., Webb, A., Safford, S. M., & Flannery-Schroeder, E. (2003). Is childhood separation anxiety disorder a predictor of adult panic disorder and agoraphobia? A 7-year longitudinal study. *Journal of the American Academy of Child and Adolescent Psychiatry, 42*(12), 1478–1485.

Barmish, A. J., & Kendall, P. C. (2005). Should parents be co-clients in cognitive-behavioral therapy for anxious youth? *Journal of Clinical Child and Adolescent Psychology, 34*(3), 569–581.

Barrett, P. M. (1998). Evaluation of cognitive-behavioral group treatments for childhood anxiety disorders. *Journal of Clinical Child Psychology, 27,* 459–468.

Barrett, P. M. (2004). *Friends for life program: Group leader's workbook for children* (4th ed.). Brisbane: Australian Academy Press.

Barrett, P. M. (2005). *Friends for life program: Group leader's workbook for youth* (4th ed.). Brisbane: Australian Academy Press.

Barrett, P. M., Dadds, M. R., & Rapee, R. (1996). Family treatment of childhood anxiety: A controlled trial. *Journal of Consulting and Clinical Psychology, 64,* 333–342.

Barrett, P. M., Duffy, A., Dadds, M., & Rapee, R. (2001). Cognitive-behavioral treatment of anxiety disorders in children: Long term (6-year) follow up. *Journal of Consulting and Clinical Psychology, 69*(1), 135–141.

Barrett, P. M., Farrell, L. J., Ollendick, T. H., & Dadds, M. (in press). Long-term outcomes of an Australian universal prevention trial of anxiety and depression symptoms in children and youth: An evaluation of the FRIENDS program. *Journal of Clinical Child and Adolescent Psychology.*

Barrett, P. M., Fox, T., & Farrell, L. (in press). Parent-child interactions of anxious children and their siblings. *Behavior Change.*

Barrett, P. M., Lowry-Webster, H. M., & Turner, C. M. (2000a). *Friends for children group leader manual.* Brisbane: Australian Academic Press.

Barrett, P. M., Lowry-Webster, H. M., & Turner, C. M. (2000b). *Friends for youth group leader manual*. Brisbane: Australian Academic Press.

Barrett, P. M., Moore, A. F., & Sonderegger, R. (2000). The FRIENDS program for young former-Yugoslavian refugees in Australia: A pilot study. *Behavior Change, 17*, 124–133.

Barrett, P. M., Rapee, R., Dadds, M. R., & Ryan, S. (1996). Family enhancement of cognitive style in anxious and aggressive children. *Journal of Abnormal Child Psychology, 24*(2), 187–203.

Barrett, P. M., Rasmussen, P., & Healy, L. (2001). The effects of childhood obsessive-compulsive disorder on sibling relationships in late childhood and early adolescents: Preliminary findings. *Australian Educational and Developmental Psychologist, 17*(2), 82–102.

Barrett, P. M., Sonderegger, R., & Sonderegger, N. L. (2001). Evaluation of an anxiety-prevention and positive-coping program (FRIENDS) for children and adolescents of non-English-speaking background. *Behavior Change, 18*(2), 78–91.

Barrett, P. M., Sonderegger, R., & Xenos, S. (2003). Using FRIENDS to combat anxiety and adjustment problems among young migrants to Australia: A national trial. *Clinical Child Psychology and Psychiatry, 8*(2), 241–260.

Barrett, P. M., & Turner, C. M. (2001). Prevention of anxiety symptoms in primary school children: Preliminary results from a universal school-based trial. *British Journal of Clinical Psychology, 40*, 399–410.

Beidel, D. C., & Turner, S. M. (1997). At risk for anxiety: Psychopathology in offspring of anxious parents. *Journal of American Academy of Child and Adolescent Psychiatry, 36*, 918–924.

Benjamin, R. S., Costello, A. J., & Warren, M. (1990). Anxiety disorders in pediatric sample. *Journal of Anxiety Disorders, 4*, 293–316.

Bernstein, G. A., Layne, A. E., Egan, E. A., & Tennison, D. M. (2005). School-based interventions for anxious children. *Journal of American Academy of Child and Adolescent Psychiatry, 44*(11), 1118–1127.

Brady, E. U., & Kendall, P. C. (1992). Comorbidity of anxiety and depression in children and adolescents. *Journal of Consulting and Clinical Psychology, 111*, 244–255.

Brent, D. A., Perper, J. A., Moritz, G., Allman, C., Friend, A., Roth, C., et al. (1993). Psychiatric risk factors for adolescent suicide: A case-control study. *Journal of the American Academy of Child and Adolescent Psychiatry, 32*, 521–529.

Capps, L., Sigman, M., Sena, R., & Henker, B. (1996). Fear, anxiety, and perceived control in children of agoraphobic parents. *Journal of Child Psychology and Psychiatry, 37*, 445–452.

Chansky, T. E., & Kendall, P. C. (1997). Social expectations and self perceptions of children with anxiety disorders. *Journal of Anxiety Disorders, 11*, 347–365.

Christie, K. A., Burke, J. D., Reiger, D. A., Rae, D. S., Boyd, J. H., & Locke, B. Z. (1988). Epidemiological evidence for early onset of mental disorders and higher risk of drug abuse in young adults. *American Journal of Psychiatry, 145*, 971–975.

Cobham, V. E., Dadds, M. R., & Spence, S. H. (1998). The role of parental anxiety in the treatment of childhood anxiety. *Journal of Consulting and Clinical Psychology, 66*(6), 893–905.

Cole, D. A., Peeke, L. G., Martin, J. M., Truglio, R., & Seroczynski, A. D. (1998). A longitudinal look at the relation between depression and anxiety in children and adolescents. *Journal of Consulting and Clinical Psychology, 66,* 451–460.

Costello, E. J., & Angold, A. A. (1995). Epidemiology. In J. S. March (Ed.), *Anxiety disorders in children and adolescents* (pp. 109–124). New York: Guilford Press.

Dadds, M. R., Spence, S. H., Holland, D., Barrett, P. M., & Laurens, K. (1997). Prevention and early intervention for anxiety disorders: A controlled trial. *Journal of Consulting and Clinical Psychology, 65,* 627–635.

Dadds, M. R., Spence, S. H., Laurens, K., Mullins, M., & Barrett, P. M. (1999). Early intervention and prevention of anxiety disorders in children: Results at 2-year follow-up. *Journal of Consulting and Clinical Psychology, 67,* 145–150.

Dumas, J. E., LaFreniere, P. J., & Serketich, W. J. (1995). "Balance of power": A transactional analysis of control in mother-child dyads involving socially competent, aggressive and anxious children. *Journal of Abnormal Psychology, 104*(1), 104–113.

Esser, G., Schmidt, M. H., & Woerner, W. (1990). Epidemiology and course of psychiatric disorders in school-age children: Results of a longitudinal study. *Journal of Child Psychology and Psychiatry, 31,* 243–264.

Flannery-Schroeder, E. C., & Kendall, P. C. (2000). Group and individual cognitive-behavioral treatments for youth with anxiety disorders: A randomised clinical trial. *Cognitive Therapy and Research, 24*(3), 251–278.

Foa, E. B., & Kozak, M. J. (1986). Emotional processing of fear: Exposure to corrective information. *Psychological Bulletin, 99,* 20–35.

Fox, T., Barrett, P. M., & Shortt, A. (2002). Sibling relationships of anxious children: A preliminary investigation. *Journal of Clinical Child and Adolescent Psychiatry, 31*(3), 375–383.

Gerull, F. C., & Rapee, R. M. (2002). Mother knows best: Effects of maternal modeling in the acquisition of fear and avoidance behavior in toddlers. *Behavior Research and Therapy, 40*(3), 279–287.

Ginsburg, G. S. (2004). Anxiety prevention programs for youth: Practical and theoretical considerations. *Clinical Psychology: Science and Practice, 11*(4), 430–434.

Goodyer, I. M., & Altham, P. M. (1991). Lifetime exit events and recent social and family adversities in anxious and depressed school-aged children. *Journal of Affective Disorders, 21,* 219–228.

Greenbaum, P. E., Prange, M. E., Friedman, R. M., & Silver, S. E. (1991). Substance abuse prevalence and comorbidity with other psychiatric disorders among adolescents with severe emotional disturbances. *Journal of American Academy of Child and Adolescent Psychiatry, 30,* 575–583.

Harrington, R., Fudge, H., Rutter, M., Pickles, A., & Hill, J. (1990). Adult outcomes of childhood and adolescent depression. *Archives of General Psychiatry, 47,* 465–473.

Hirschfeld, R., Keller, M., Panico, S., Arons, B., Barlow, D., Davidoff, F., et al. (1997). The National Depressive and Manic-Depressive Association consensus statement on the undertreatment of depression. *Journal of the American Medical Association, 277,* 333–340.

Hudson, J. L., & Rapee, R. M. (2001). Parent-child interactions and anxiety disorders: An observational study. *Behavior Research and Therapy, 39,* 1411–1427.

Ialongo, N., Edelsohn, G., Werthemar-Larsson, L., Crockett, L., & Kellam, S. (1994). The significance of self-reported anxious symptoms in first-grade children. *Journal of Abnormal Child Psychology, 22*(4), 441–455.

Kagan, J., Reznick, J. S., & Snidman, N. (1988). Biological basis of childhood shyness. *Science, 240,* 161–171.

Kashani, J. H., & Orvaschel, H. (1990). A community study of anxiety in children and adolescents. *American Journal of Psychiatry, 147,* 313–318.

Kendall, P. C. (1994). Treating anxiety disorders in youth: Results of a randomised clinical trial. *Journal of Consulting and Clinical Psychology, 62,* 100–101.

Kendall, P. C., Cantwell, D. P., & Kazdin, A. E. (1989). Depression in children and adolescents: Assessment issues and recommendations. *Cognitive Therapy and Research, 13,* 109–146.

Kendall, P. C., Flannery-Schroeder, E., Panichelli-Mindel, S. M., Southam-Gerow, M., Henin, A., & Warman, M. (1997). Therapy for youths with anxiety disorders: A second randomized clinical trial. *Journal of Consulting and Clinical Psychology, 65,* 366–380.

Kendall, P. C., & Ollendick, T. H. (2004). Setting the research and practice agenda for anxiety in children and adolescence: A topic comes of age. *Cognitive and Behavioral Practice, 11*(1), 65–74.

Kendall, P. C., Safford, S., Flannery-Schroeder, E., & Webb, A. (2004). Child anxiety treatment: Outcomes in adolescence and impact on substance use and depression at 7.4-year follow-up. *Journal of Consulting and Clinical Psychology, 72*(2), 276–287.

Kendall, P. C., & Southam-Gerow, M. A. (1996). Long-term follow-up of a cognitive-behavioral therapy for anxiety disordered youth. *Journal of Consulting and Clinical Psychology, 64,* 724–730.

Kessler, R. C., Foster, J., Saunders, W. B., & Stand, P. E. (1995). Social consequences of psychiatric disorders: Pt. I. Educational attainment. *American Journal of Psychiatry, 152,* 1026–1032.

Kessler, R. C., Nelson, C., McGonagle, K., Edlund, M., Frank, R., & Leaf, P. (1996). The epidemiology of co-occurring addictive and mental disorders: Implications for prevention and service utilization. *American Journal of Orthopsychiatry, 66,* 17–31.

King, N. J., & Ollendick, T. H. (1989). Children's anxiety and phobic conditions in school settings: Classification, assessment and intervention issues. *Review of Educational Research, 59,* 431–470.

Kovacs, M., Gatsonis, C., Paulauskas, S. L., & Richards, C. (1989). Depressive disorders in childhood: Pt. IV. A longitudinal study of comorbidity with and risk for anxiety disorders. *Archives of General Psychiatry, 46,* 776–783.

Krohne, H. W., & Hock, M. (1991). Relationships between restrictive mother-child interactions and anxiety of the child. *Anxiety Research, 4,* 109–124.

Last, C. G., Perrin, S., Hersen, M., & Kazdin, A. E. (1996). A prospective study of childhood anxiety disorders. *Journal of the American Academy of Child and Adolescent Psychiatry, 35*(11), 1502–1510.

Lock, S., & Barrett, P. M. (2003). A longitudinal study of developmental differences in universal preventive intervention for child anxiety. *Behavior Change, 20*(4), 183–199.

Lowry-Webster, H. M., Barrett, P. M., & Dadds, M. R. (2001). A universal prevention trial of anxiety and depressive symptomatology in childhood: Preliminary data from an Australian study. *Behavior Change, 18*(1), 36–50.

Lowry-Webster, H. M., Barrett, P. M., & Lock, S. (2003). A universal prevention trial of anxiety symptomatology during childhood: Results at 1-year follow-up. *Behavior Change, 20*(1), 25–43.

Manassis, K., & Bradley, S. J. (1994). The development of childhood anxiety disorders: Toward an integrated model. *Journal of Applied Developmental Psychology, 15*, 345–366.

Manassis, K., Mendlowitz, S. L., Scapillato, D., Avery, D., Fiksenbaum, L., Freire, M., et al. (2002). Group and individual cognitive-behavioral therapy for childhood anxiety disorders: A randomized controlled trial. *Journal of American Academy of Child and Adolescent Psychiatry, 41*, 1423–1430.

Mendlowitz, S. L., Manassis, K., Bradley, S., Scapillato, D., Miezitis, S., & Shaw, B. F. (1999). Cognitive-behavioral group treatments in child anxiety disorders: The role of parental involvement. *Journal of American Academy of Child and Adolescent Psychiatry, 38*(10), 1223–1229.

Miller, L., Warner, V., Wickramaratne, P., & Weissman, M. (1999). Self-esteem and depression: Ten year follow-up of mothers and offspring. *Journal of Affective Disorders, 52*, 41–49.

Murray, L., Kempton, C., Woolgar, M., & Hooper, R. (1993). Depressed mothers' speech to their infants and its relation to infant gender and cognitive development. *Journal of Child Psychology and Psychiatry, 34*, 1083–1101.

Nauta, M., Scholing, A., Emmelkamp, P., & Minderaa, R. (2003). Cognitive-behavioral therapy for children with anxiety disorders in a clinical setting: No additional effect of a cognitive parent training. *Journal of American Academy of Child and Adolescent Psychiatry, 42*, 1270–1278.

Olfson, M., Gameroff, M. J., Marcus, S. C., & Waslick, B. D. (2003). Outpatient treatment in child and adolescent depression in the United States. *Archives of General Psychiatry, 60*(12), 1236–1242.

Ollendick, T. H., & King, N. J. (1998). Empirically supported treatments for children with phobic and anxiety disorders: Current status. *Journal of Clinical Child Psychology, 27*, 156–167.

Orvaschel, H., Lewinsohn, P. M., & Seeley, J. R. (1995). Continuity of psychopathology in a community sample of adolescents. *Journal of the American Academy of Child and Adolescent Psychiatry, 34*, 1525–1535.

Pine, D. S., Cohen, P., Gurley, D., Brook, J., & Ma, Y. (1998). The risk for early-adulthood anxiety and depressive disorders in adolescents with anxiety and depressive disorders. *Archives of General Psychiatry, 55*, 56–64.

Pollock, R. A., Rosenbaum, J. F., Marrs, A., Miller, B. S., & Biederman, J. (1996). Anxiety disorders of childhood: Implications for adult psychopathology. *Psychiatric-Clinics-of-North-America, 18*(4), 745–766.

Rapee, R. M. (1997). Potential role of childrearing practices in the development of anxiety and depression. *Clinical Psychology Review, 17*, 47–67.

Rudd, M. D., Joiner, T. F., & Rumzek, H. (2004). Childhood diagnoses and later risk for multiple suicide attempts. *Suicide and Life-Threatening Behavior, 34*(2), 113–125.

Sawyer, M. G., Arney, F. M., Baghurst, P. A., Clark, J. J., Graetz, B. W., Kosky, R. J., et al. (2000). *The mental health of young people in Australia: The child and adolescent component of the National Survey of Mental Health and Well-Being.* Canberra, Australian Capital Territory: Publications Production Unit (Public Affairs, Parliamentary, and Access Branch).

Seligman, L. D., & Ollendick, T. H. (1998). Comorbidity of anxiety and depression in children and adolescents: An integrative review. *Clinical Child and Family Psychology Review, 1,* 125–144.

Shortt, A., Barrett, P. M., Dadds, M. R., & Fox, T. L. (2001). The influence of family and experimental context on cognition in anxious children. *Journal of Abnormal Child Psychology, 29*(6), 585–596.

Shortt, A., Barrett, P. M., & Fox, T. (2001). Evaluating the FRIENDS program: A cognitive-behavioral group treatment of childhood anxiety disorders. *Journal of Clinical Child Psychology, 30*(4), 525–535.

Silverman, W. K., Kurtines, W. M., Ginsburg, G. S., Weems, C. F., Lumpkin, P. W., & Carmichael, D. H. (1999). Treating anxiety disorders in children with group cognitive-behavioral therapy: A randomized clinical trial. *Journal of Consulting and Clinical Psychology, 67,* 995–1003.

Siqueland, L., Kendall, P. C., & Steinberg, L. (1996). Anxiety in children: Perceived family environments and observed family interaction. *Journal of Clinical Child Psychology, 25,* 225–237.

Southam-Gerow, M. A., Kendall, P. C., & Weersing, V. R. (2001). Examining outcome variability: Correlates of treatment response in a child and adolescent anxiety clinic. *Journal of Clinical Child Psychology, 30,* 422–436.

Spence, S. H., Donovan, C., & Brechman-Toussaint, M. (2000). The treatment of childhood social phobia: The effectiveness of a social skills training-based, cognitive-behavioral intervention, with and without parental involvement. *Journal of Child Psychology and Psychiatry and Allied Disciplines, 41,* 713–726.

Strauss, C. C., Forehand, R., Smith, K., & Frame, C. (1986). The association between social withdrawal and internalizing problems of children. *Journal of Abnormal Child Psychology, 14,* 525–535.

Strauss, C. C., Frame, C. L., & Forehand, R. (1987). Psychosocial impairment associated with anxiety in children. *Journal of Clinical Child Psychology, 16,* 235–239.

Tarullo, L., DeMulder, E., Martinez, P., & Radke-Yarrow, M. (1994). Dialogues with preadolescents and adolescents: Mother-child interaction patterns in affectively ill and well dyads. *Journal of Abnormal Psychology, 22,* 33–51.

Thapar, A., & McGuffin, P. (1995). Are anxiety symptoms in childhood heritable? *Journal of Child Psychology and Psychiatry, 36,* 439–447.

Turner, S. M., Beidel, D. C., & Costello, A. (1987). Psychopathology in the offspring of anxiety disorder patients. *Journal of Consulting and Clinical Psychology, 55,* 229–235.

Weissman, M. M., Leckman, J. F., Merikangas, K. R., Gammon, G. D., & Prusoff, B. A. (1984). Depression and anxiety disorders in parents and children: Results from the Yale family study. *Archives of General Psychiatry, 41,* 845–852.

Woodward, L. J., & Fergusson, D. M. (2001). Life course outcomes of young people with anxiety disorders in adolescence. *Journal of the American Academy of Child and Adolescent Psychiatry, 40,* 1086–1093.

CHAPTER 6

Parent Training in the Treatment of School Refusal Behavior

CHRISTOPHER A. KEARNEY, MARCUS T. LaSOTA,
AMIE LEMOS-MILLER, and JENNIFER VECCHIO

OF ALL the problems parents address in their children, perhaps none is as frustrating and perplexing as school refusal behavior. School refusal behavior refers to child-motivated refusal to attend school or difficulty remaining in classes for an entire day (Kearney & Silverman, 1996). Cases of school withdrawal, where a parent deliberately withholds a child from school, are excluded here (Kahn & Nursten, 1962). School refusal behavior refers to youths aged 5 to 17 years who

- Are completely absent from school;
- Attend school but then leave during the school day;
- Attend school or arrive late to school only after intense morning misbehaviors to miss school;
- Attend school with intense distress and pleas to parents for future nonattendance.

School refusal behavior thus includes a spectrum of children from those who never attend school to those who intermittently attend school to those who attend school with many interfering behaviors. In some cases, these problems remit spontaneously after a short time. Such cases of self-corrective school refusal behavior are common and usually last less than 2 weeks. In contrast, acute school refusal behavior lasts between 2 weeks and 1 year and is marked by significant interference in a child's and family's daily routine. Chronic school refusal behavior lasts longer than 1 year and is marked by greater interference. In general, the longer a child refuses school, the less likely full-time school attendance can be restored (Kearney, 2001).

This chapter focuses on children whose primary problem is school refusal behavior. However, parents who refer a child with multiple behavior problems often wish to address school refusal behavior first. The material in this chapter may thus be useful for this latter situation as well.

PREVALENCE AND CLINICAL PICTURE

School refusal behavior affects 5% to 28% of school-age children, though absenteeism rates may be considerably higher in some urban areas. The problem occurs fairly equally in boys and girls. Peak age of onset is 5 to 6 and 10 to 13 years of age (the ages at many children enter a new school building for the first time). Entry into kindergarten, first grade, middle school, and high school may be particularly problematic for some children. Children with school refusal behavior generally have average intelligence and adequate academic achievement up to the point of initial absenteeism (Hampe, Miller, Barrett, & Noble, 1973; Kearney, 2001; Nichols & Berg, 1970). The socioeconomic status of families with a child refusing school is considerably mixed (Baker & Wills, 1978; Last & Strauss, 1990).

A hallmark of school refusal behavior is symptom heterogeneity. Common internalizing symptoms include general and social anxiety, fear, depression, social withdrawal, fatigue, worry, and somatic complaints, especially stomachaches and headaches (Last, 1991; Last & Strauss, 1990). Common externalizing symptoms include running away from home or school, verbal or physical aggression to avoid school, noncompliance, tantrums, arguing, clinging, and refusal to move (Kearney, 2001). Many youths with school refusal behavior show a mixture of these symptoms.

School refusal behavior has several aversive short-term consequences. These consequences include social alienation, declining school performance, increased family conflict, and general disruption of daily activities. These problems gradually worsen as school refusal continues, especially if the behavior persists over two academic years. Researchers have noted several long-term consequences of continued school refusal behavior. They include school dropout, occupational and marital problems, economic deprivation, anxiety and depressive disorders, and alcohol abuse and criminal behavior (Berg, 1970; Berg & Jackson, 1985; Berg, Marks, McGuire, & Lipsedge, 1974; Flakierska, Lindstrom, & Gillberg,

1988; Hibbett & Fogelman, 1990; Hibbett, Fogelman, & Manor, 1990; Tyrer & Tyrer, 1974).

CLINICAL PROCESSES FOR SCHOOL REFUSAL BEHAVIOR

The seriousness, prevalence, and consequences of school refusal behavior demand effective ways of classifying, assessing, and treating this population. These processes have been hampered by substantial confusion among researchers (Kearney, 2003). As a result, therapists and educators are often forced to rely on idiosyncratically designed strategies to address this population. Historically, the following areas of confusion have resulted:

- Several definitions of school refusal behavior
- Overemphasis of anxiety- or fear-based school refusal, or school phobia
- Failure to agree on a uniform classification system for this population
- Development of few assessment devices specific to children who refuse school
- Advocation of treatment practices that work well for some but not all children with school refusal behavior

An alternative and systematic way of conceptualizing school refusal behavior should concentrate on inclusiveness and utility. This alternative method is based on three key ideas. First, the recommended definition of school refusal behavior includes youths who are clearly anxious about attending school in addition to those with obvious delinquent or truant behaviors. Second, it is important to examine the function of school refusal behavior as well as its many forms. Although children with school refusal behavior show myriad symptoms, basic reinforcements for the behavior are relatively few. Third, a combined assessment-prescriptive treatment approach is recommended and should heavily involve parents and other family members.

In this chapter, a functional model of school refusal behavior for classifying, assessing, and treating this population is described. In doing so, a particular focus is on parent training and related practices critical to resolving school refusal behavior. Classification and assessment are discussed first.

A FUNCTIONAL APPROACH TO CLASSIFYING YOUTHS WITH SCHOOL REFUSAL BEHAVIOR

Youths refuse school primarily for one of four main reasons. First, some youths refuse school to avoid school-based stimuli that provoke anxiety and sadness (negative affectivity). Common stimuli include school buses, hallways, classroom items, teachers, schoolmates, fire alarms, cafeterias, playgrounds, gymnasiums, or specific courses or assignments. Many children are unable to say exactly what upsets them, though some report unpleasant physical symptoms at school. Children who refuse school to avoid school-based stimuli that provoke negative affectivity tend to be younger and may attend school regularly but with great dread. Absenteeism may also occur.

A second reason many youths miss school is to escape aversive social and evaluative situations. Common avoided situations include meeting new people, having conversations with friends and acquaintances, interacting with aggressive peers, taking tests, writing on the blackboard, speaking before others, performing athletically in physical education class, engaging in recitals, moving from class to class, and talking to peers or school officials (Kearney, 2005). Many of these cases involve older children and adolescents who can identify specific aversive stimuli. The level of absenteeism in this function can vary widely. These first two functional conditions refer to children missing school for negative reinforcement or to leave something unpleasant at school.

A third reason many children miss school is to pursue attention from significant others, usually a parent. These children may scream, cry, cling, hit, refuse to move, and exaggerate somatic complaints to miss school and stay home. Separation anxiety is sometimes associated with this function. These children often wish to remain home with a parent, though some parents may wish this as well. Children may call their parents several times during the school day to induce guilt and force parental acquiescence to demands to come home. Children who refuse school for attention tend to be younger and may attend school intermittently after intense morning misbehaviors or if a parent agrees to attend school with them.

A fourth reason many youths miss school is to pursue tangible reinforcement outside school. These youths skip school to have fun. Common out-of-school activities include day parties with friends, alcohol or other drug use, video games or television, sports, bicycling, sleeping, shopping, and gambling. Family conflict, poor academic performance, and delinquent acts are common in this group. Youths who refuse school for tangible reinforcement tend to be older children and adolescents and their level of absenteeism ranges widely. These last two functional conditions refer to youths missing school for positive reinforcement, or to pursue something attractive outside school. Therapists are more apt to receive referrals for children refusing school for positive than negative reinforcement.

Youths may also refuse school for a combination of these reasons. Many children miss school to avoid something upsetting and to pursue many positive aspects of staying home. Conversely, youths may skip school for an extended period and then become nervous at the prospect of returning to school and facing new classes, teachers, and peers. Clinicians should consider all possible combinations of reasons for school refusal behavior when assessing a particular case.

These four functional conditions may serve as an adequate classification system for youths with school refusal behavior (Kearney, 2006). The system assists clinicians who can become overwhelmed by the substantial number of symptoms many of these children show. Another advantage of this system is its direct link to assessment and treatment strategies.

A FUNCTIONAL APPROACH TO ASSESSING YOUTHS WITH SCHOOL REFUSAL BEHAVIOR

When assessing a child with school refusal behavior, therapists are encouraged to focus on key reinforcements. These reinforcements or functions include (a) avoiding school-based stimuli that provoke negative affectivity, (b) escaping aversive social and evaluative situations, (c) pursuing attention from significant others, and (d) pursuing tangible reinforcement outside school. To assess why a child refuses school, therapists may rely heavily on child and parent reports and direct observations of behavior.

CHILD AND PARENT REPORTS

As part of a multicomponent assessment process, parents and children may be interviewed extensively about primary symptoms and reasons for school refusal behavior. In addition, each party may be asked to complete respective versions of the School Refusal Assessment Scale-Revised (SRAS-R; Kearney, 2002b, 2006). The SRAS-R is a 24-item instrument that measures relative influence of the four functional conditions described here. A therapist solicits SRAS-R ratings from parents and child and combines the ratings into a functional profile. From this profile and in accordance with other assessment data, a therapist can decide what maintains a child's school refusal behavior. The therapist can then decide on a treatment direction.

For example, assume a child's mean SRAS-R item ratings for the four functional conditions are 1.25, 2.00, 4.25, and 3.00 and a parent's mean SRAS-R ratings for the four functional conditions are 1.75, 3.00, 4.75, and 3.00. Ratings are averaged across all parties; in this case: 1.50, 2.50, 4.50, and 3.00. The highest-scoring functional condition is considered the primary reason for a child's school refusal behavior (in this case, the third functional condition, attention-seeking). Ratings within 0.25 to 0.50 points of one another may be considered equivalent. From this profile, a therapist may also identify other functions that play a secondary or even minimal role in maintaining school refusal behavior. Therapists should confirm SRAS-R ratings via direct observations of behavior (Kearney, 2006).

DIRECT OBSERVATIONS OF BEHAVIOR

Therapists may directly observe certain child behaviors and parent-child interactions to better understand how and why a child is refusing school (Kearney & Albano, 2007). Observations may be done formally in a child's home or school as well as in the therapist's office. For children thought to be refusing school to avoid stimuli provoking negative affectivity, therapists may compare how a child attends school under normal conditions with how he attends school when certain aspects of the school are not present, such as not having to ride the school bus. In the office, therapists may watch for tearful, passive, and withdrawn child behavior and note whether and how a parent reinforces this behavior.

For children thought to be refusing school to escape aversive social and evaluative situations, therapists may compare how a child attends school under normal conditions with how she attends school without certain requirements such as tests, peer interactions, or physical education class. In the office, therapists may watch for child social anxiety when meeting new people. Parental responses to this behavior should also be closely monitored.

For children thought to be refusing school for attention, therapists may compare how a child attends school under normal conditions with how he attends school with significant others present, such as a mother in the classroom. In the office, therapists may watch for whether a child has difficulty separating from a parent (or vice versa) or displays tantrums to avoid speaking with the therapist.

For children thought to be refusing school for tangible reinforcement, therapists may compare a child's school attendance under normal conditions with attendance when increased rewards are made available and when increased punishments or restrictions on rewards are made for nonattendance. In the office, therapists may watch for youths who argue vigorously with parents to induce treatment termination or maintenance of the status quo. For children thought to be refusing school for more than one reason, an evaluation of school refusal behavior under varying circumstances is necessary.

DECIDING ON TREATMENT FOR SCHOOL REFUSAL BEHAVIOR

After determining why a child is refusing school, a treatment decision can be made. For children refusing school for negative reinforcement (first two functional conditions), relaxation training, breathing retraining, modeling, role-play, cognitive therapy, and exposure-based practices are recommended. A key aspect of treatment is to train parents to train children to use these techniques and maintain their use over time. For children refusing school for attention, parent training in contingency management may be best. This involves restructuring parental commands, establishing fixed routines for the morning and day, and applying consistent attention-based rewards for attendance and punishments for nonattendance. For children refusing school for tangible reinforcement, contracting among relevant family members is recommended. Parents are encouraged to initiate and develop effective contracts independently with their child. This allows parents and children to solve problems effectively, reduce conflict, increase tangible rewards for attendance, and decrease rewards and social activities for nonattendance. Youths who refuse school for multiple reasons are given combined treatment.

THE PARENT TRAINING PROGRAM AND CASE MATERIAL

Parent and Family Treatment Mediators

This section outlines a parent-family training program to address youths with school refusal behavior. Therapists are cautioned that restructuring parent skills without considering the broader ecological context of the family is problematic. Clinicians should use the parent training procedures prudently under certain conditions such as low parent motivation, exigent circumstances such as maltreatment, or legitimate school-based threats or curriculum problems. These conditions may make the parent training program ineffective. This section begins with a brief discussion of important parent variables that can mediate the scope and pace of treatment for youths with school refusal behavior. Each variable should be watched closely by therapists during treatment and may need to be resolved prior to parent-based treatment for school refusal behavior.

Parenting and Family Style

Parenting style affects all child cases. Therapists should be generally wary of neglectful, rejecting, overly permissive, or highly authoritarian parents. Some maladaptive parent and family patterns are especially pertinent to cases of school refusal behavior. In particular, therapists should be wary of parent-family dynamics closely associated with specific functions of school refusal behavior. Examples are provided here.

Enmeshed families are sometimes characterized by overprotective parents and are common to children who refuse school for attention or have some aspect of separation anxiety. Detached parents are generally less involved in their child's activities and provide little attention to a child's thoughts and needs. Such a dynamic is common in families of youths who refuse school for tangible reinforcement. Isolated parents or families are characterized by little extrafamilial contact with others. This dynamic is common in families of children who refuse school to escape aversive social and evaluative situations at school. Conflictive parents or families are marked by extensive hostility and poor problem-solving skills. Family conflict is related to all functions of school refusal behavior (Kearney & Silverman, 1995). Therapists should be sensitive to these familial patterns and adjust treatment accordingly. Communication skills training may need to be implemented to address family conflict during treatment for school refusal behavior.

Parent Attitudes and Expectations about Treatment

Therapists also need to be sensitive about parent attitudes and expectations for treatment. Parents are sometimes pessimistic about a child's school refusal behavior and likelihood for change. This is especially characteristic of parents of adolescents who have missed school for a long time. In this case, clinicians may wish to separate legitimate parent concerns, such as curfew-breaking, from those more suspect, such as a child's belligerence to everyone. In addition, therapists should focus first on simple behaviors such as a single chore and easier treatment practices such as a short contract to help parents experience successful outcomes and perhaps become more optimistic and motivated in therapy.

Parent Psychopathology

Parents of youths with school refusal behavior often have mental disorders themselves, especially those related to anxiety and depression. Youths who refuse school sometimes model their parents' aversive reactions, avoidance responses, negative thinking patterns, perfectionism, aggression, and even substance use. Therapists should be aware of these possibilities and perhaps seek to redress the parent's mental condition first or concurrently with a child's behavior.

Marital Conflict and Divorce

Parents of youths with school refusal behavior often disagree about disciplinary procedures in general and how to address a child's absenteeism in particular. In addition, many cases of school refusal behavior, especially those involving positive reinforcement, are marked by single-parent families and complicated family situations. Therapists are encouraged to address spousal disagreements as soon as possible, ask parents to jointly commit to a treatment plan, and make adjustments for single-parent families. Therapists should remind parents that failure to consistently provide a united front to the child will undermine the treatment process and risk relapse.

In related fashion, therapists should be aware that parents will sometimes disagree with each other and with a child about current household events. Therapists should assess whether this is a deliberate attempt to absolve oneself of blame or to fault a spouse. If so, then reframing the school refusal situation as a "family problem" that requires effort from all family members may be helpful. Developing special rapport with a parent who fears omission from the therapy process is recommended as well.

THE PARENT TRAINING PROGRAM AND CASE MATERIAL

A parent-family training program to address youths with school refusal behavior is described next. Several clinical researchers propose that parent training programs can be divided into different types (Kazdin, 1991). The most common types include treatment where (a) parents help a child implement major techniques and maintain compliance to them, (b) parents are the primary focus of treatment, with little therapist-child contact, and (c) parents learn to better monitor their child and apply specific techniques involving different family members.

In this section, primary treatment components are described for children who refuse school for (a) negative reinforcement, such as to avoid school-based stimuli that provoke negative affectivity and to escape aversive social or evaluative situations, (b) attention from significant others, or (c) tangible reinforcement outside school. Treatment for each type is related, respectively, to the parent training programs previously mentioned. A case example is provided following each section.

PARENT-CHILD TREATMENT FOR YOUTHS REFUSING SCHOOL FOR NEGATIVE REINFORCEMENT

Major treatment methods for youths who refuse school for negative reinforcement include relaxation training, breathing retraining, modeling and role-play, cognitive therapy, and exposure or gradual reintegration into the classroom. Of these, exposure is most critical. Each component is largely child-based, but parents are asked to assist training their child and maintaining treatment gains over time. A therapist gradually transfers control of therapy to the parents, who can then help the therapist transmit treatment information to the child currently and in the future (Silverman & Kurtines, 1996).

Relaxation Training and Breathing Retraining

To control aversive physiological reactions that keep a child out of school, relaxation training and breathing retraining are recommended. Relaxation training is based on a tension-release model whereby a child tenses various muscle groups, holds the tension for 5 to 10 seconds, and flexes the muscles quickly. This is done to teach a child the difference between a tense muscle and a relaxed one, help her identify which muscles are most tense in a stressful situation, and provide her with a covert strategy of controlling physiologically based anxiety. Relaxation training should be conducted directly with the child and audiotaped. The child may then practice independently at least twice per day and begin using the procedure when physically anxious during the day. This procedure is most effective for children with facial or other muscle tension, shaking or jitteriness, or butterflies in the stomach.

Breathing retraining is also used to control negative physical symptoms, especially those related to hyperventilation and dizziness. A child is asked to slowly and fully breathe in through the nose and exhale slowly and fully through the mouth. The therapist emphasizes using regular breathing in anxiety-provoking situations. For younger children, various images are encouraged as well, such as pretending to be a hot air balloon that needs regular fueling to reach its destination. As with relaxation training, youths practice this procedure during the day and especially during stressful situations.

For relaxation training and breathing retraining, parents are asked to systematically monitor and reward their child's compliance to the assigned treatment regimen. This is particularly important for younger children who have trouble remembering what to do from the therapy session. Parents should check whether a child did what was asked by the therapist, correct the child as necessary, monitor progress, and praise the child for completing the therapeutic homework assignments. Within this population, a close relationship exists between parental involvement and encouragement, a child's use of therapeutic procedures, and successful outcome.

Modeling and Role-Play

To build successful social skills, particularly in youths who refuse school to escape aversive social and evaluative situations, a combination of modeling and role-play may be useful. This skills training is designed to build a child's social competence and allow positive feedback and social reinforcement from others. In turn, this should encourage a child to initiate more social contacts and interact effectively in aversive situations.

In modeling and role-play, a therapist identifies two to three school-based social and evaluative situations most unpleasant for a child. Common examples include having to speak before others or initiating or maintaining conversations. Subsequently, the therapist asks the child to model the therapist or others who manage a social situation appropriately, such as giving a speech without fear or maintaining a productive conversation. In some cases, a child's family members or parents can act as helpful models. The child is then asked to role-play the modeled situation before others and receive constructive feedback. Most detailed feedback will come from the therapist, though family members should provide encouragement and praise the child's effort.

After a child has successfully practiced social interactions in session, practice can begin in real-life situations. As the child does so, parents and teachers should be active monitors of performance. This can be done covertly by asking parents or teachers to watch the child's interactions at school, or more overtly by asking them to place the child in progressively more challenging social situations. Praise and feedback from parents, teachers, the therapist, and relevant others should continue as well. As with relaxation training and breathing retraining, a close relationship exists between a supportive and motivating parent/family milieu and successful modeling and role-play.

Cognitive Therapy

Cognitive therapy is used to reduce irrational thinking that interferes with school performance and attendance and to enhance more realistic ways of thinking. Parents and youths are educated about cognitive distortions such as overgeneralization ("Everyone will laugh at me"), personalization ("When I hear whispers in the hall, I know they are talking about me"), all-or-none thinking ("If my speech is not perfect, it will be a disaster"), and catastrophization ("I will fail the test and get kicked out of school"). A youth's verbalizations are scrutinized in therapy for such distortions and parents and the youth are asked to maintain written logs of distorted thoughts and verbalizations at home and school.

Cognitive therapy in this population largely involves restructuring irrational thoughts and verbalizations into more realistic, logical forms. Youths are encouraged to stop themselves in the middle of cognitive or verbal distortions, avoid extremist phrases such as "always" or "never," hypothesis-test probabilities of something negative occurring, and reframe harsh thoughts or statements into more realistic ones. Because many adolescents have a long history of cognitive and verbal distortions, parents should be highly involved in this process. Parents can be particularly helpful in reminding youths about these distortions and by assisting the restructuring process. In some cases, parents can practice these procedures in conjunction with their child.

Exposure to the School Setting

To decrease behavioral avoidance of school and to help a child practice treatment techniques in key real-life situations, gradual exposure to the classroom is used. Such exposure may be imaginal if a child is already attending school with great distress or in vivo if a child is missing most days of school. In either case, exposure is likely to be the most effective treatment component for a child refusing school for negative reinforcement. Exposure is also the component most likely facilitated by parents.

Parents should encourage their child's school attendance whenever possible. This includes the morning as a child prepares for school, at the time of expected school attendance, during the morning if the child has yet to go to school, during the afternoon if a few hours of schooltime remain available, and even on weekends. Such prodding may be verbal but later may come in the form of physically assisted school attendance (see procedures for treating school refusal behavior for attention).

CASE STUDY

Presenting Client and Problem

Nathan was a 10-year-old boy referred by his parents, Mr. and Mrs. M., and the counselor at Nathan's elementary school. During the initial telephone screening, Mrs. M. said Nathan missed only 4 of the previous 40 days of school but that he complained about school nearly every day and kept asking his parents to place him in home schooling. Nathan had intermittent problems attending school in the past, but not to the extent currently shown. Mrs. M. said Nathan was complaining about tests in class and had physical symptoms, but he was reluctant to give more specific information.

During the assessment session, Nathan was initially hesitant about talking with the therapist but gradually became more expressive. He said school was not generally a problem except for test-taking situations and having to write or speak before others in class. Nathan also said these situations elicited physical symptoms of dizziness, trembling, and nausea. He indicated he had a small group of close friends at school but had recently become more distant from them as these problems developed. Nathan was quite concerned about receiving high grades and pleasing his parents. He said he wanted to be taught by a tutor at home so he would not have to be nervous about school.

Mr. and Mrs. M. confirmed most of this report but also said Nathan seemed to exaggerate some of his symptoms for attention from his parents and teacher. To this point, they resisted the idea of home schooling but felt they should consult a therapist. Mr. and Mrs. M. indicated that Nathan, the oldest of three children, had always been "fussy and nervous about things" and seemed overly concerned about his schoolwork. They also said they wished their son would be more social and enjoy school more. A telephone interview with Nathan's teacher revealed a similar pattern of excessive conscientiousness and anxiety as well as occasional attention-seeking behavior.

FORMULATION

Based on a comprehensive assessment, the therapist determined that Nathan was largely missing school to avoid situations that caused negative physical symptoms and to escape unpleasant social or evaluative situations such as tests and performing before others. This determination was supported by the facts that Nathan displayed fewer school refusal problems on days when no tests or performances were required and when he could spend substantial time with close friends. In addition, parent and child questionnaire scores and ratings from the SRAS-R indicated that negative reinforcement was the key function of Nathan's school refusal behavior. Attention-seeking behavior was deemed to be a moderate secondary function.

The therapist recommended treatment to reduce Nathan's negative physical symptoms, to build skills necessary to function well on tests and before others, and to encourage more social contact. As part of this approach, Mr. and Mrs. M. would actively participate in all techniques, encourage their use at home and in other settings, and reward Nathan's compliance with therapeutic homework assignments. In addition, Mr. and Mrs. M. were asked to take a firmer stand against Nathan's excess attention-seeking behaviors. Finally, Mr. and Mrs. M. were encouraged to refrain from home schooling at least until the therapy program ended.

COURSE OF TREATMENT

The therapist initially concentrated on helping Nathan control negative physical symptoms he experienced at school. Relaxation training and breathing retraining exercises were used to minimize muscle tension, trembling, dizziness and, to some extent, nausea. Nathan was asked to practice these exercises at least twice per day and in school-related situations that evoked his symptoms. In addition, Nathan's parents viewed the procedures and listened to the therapist's rationale about their use. Each parent was instructed about how to use and practice the procedures. This allowed the therapist to give the parents feedback on their performance and allowed them to adequately check whether Nathan was appropriately engaging in the procedures. The therapist and parents also devised rewards and punishments for Nathan's compliance or noncompliance, respectively, to practicing relaxation and better breathing.

As Nathan practiced these techniques at home and school, the therapist began modeling and role-play to enhance Nathan's test performance and ability to speak and write before others. In the office setting, the therapist asked Nathan to take a sample test provided by his teacher, give a brief reading of a newspaper article before a small audience of strangers, and write and solve some arithmetic problems on a blackboard before others. Nathan's parents were part of each audience. Following each performance over the next several sessions, Nathan was given detailed feedback about areas of strength, such as effort and articulation, as well as areas that needed improvement, such as timing and concentration. Initially, the therapist encouraged Nathan's parents to be supportive only. Later in therapy, Mr. and Mrs. M. were asked to give direct feedback to Nathan.

Following Nathan's repeated practice of these tasks, which involved incorporating feedback from his therapist and parents, a series of real-life practices were assigned. With Nathan's foreknowledge, Nathan's teacher placed him in several test-taking and performance situations at school. Nathan was also instructed to practice appropriate relaxation and breathing during these situations. In session, Nathan discussed his performance and what areas still needed improvement. Feedback from the teacher was also obtained weekly.

In the meantime, Mr. and Mrs. M. rewarded Nathan for his school attendance, particularly on days when evaluative events were scheduled for him. The therapist also worked with Mr. and Mrs. M. to increase Nathan's participation in extracurricular activities that involved substantial social interaction and performance before others.

OUTCOME AND PROGNOSIS

In cases such as Nathan's, school attendance may not be the best barometer of successful behavior change. Instead, daily child and parent ratings of anxiety and avoidance may be best. In Nathan's case, remaining problems of absenteeism and avoidance of evaluative situations were quickly resolved. However, high levels of anxiety during school performance situations remained for several weeks. By the end of therapy, these levels decreased 70% and Nathan no longer asked to be home schooled. Long-term functioning was generally good, though Nathan experienced considerable anticipatory anxiety prior to the next school year. In cases such as this, parents and school officials should arrange an orientation for the child prior to the start of school. The child can thus become well acquainted with the school's structure and required procedures.

PARENT TRAINING IN CONTINGENCY MANAGEMENT FOR YOUTHS REFUSING SCHOOL FOR ATTENTION

For children refusing school for attention or who display some aspect of separation anxiety, parent training in contingency management can be quite helpful. Key components of contingency management for this population are (a) restructuring parent commands toward clarity and brevity, (b) establishing fixed routines in the morning and throughout the day,

(c) implementing rewards for compliance and school attendance and punishments for noncompliance and school refusal behavior, and (d) forced school attendance under certain conditions.

RESTRUCTURING PARENT COMMANDS

In many cases of school refusal behavior motivated by attention, parents become frustrated and issue vague commands to their children such as "Get ready for school!" To counter this, parents may be taught to give commands in clearer, simpler, and more direct ways. Parents should compose a list of commands they gave on previous mornings and continue to do so throughout therapy.

Therapists may then work to restructure parent commands so they are clear, concise, and understood by the child. To accomplish this, parents may first be taught to avoid certain patterns in their commands. Parents should avoid question-like commands, lecturing, vagueness, criticism, interrupted commands, incomplete commands, commands with too many steps, and commands eventually completed or ignored by the parent. Therapists should look for patterns of errors parents make in their commands and provide constructive feedback as necessary.

After parents can successfully avoid certain negative patterns in their commands, a therapist may help them create more effective commands. Parents should specify exactly when a command is to be completed, such as within 5 minutes. In addition, parents should say exactly what is required of a child and keep it simple. Instead of "Go to school," a parent could say, "Put on your jacket now and walk to the bus stop." The child should be capable of complying with the command, no distractions should compete with a command, the command should not contain an option for the child, and the command should not be too long. During therapy, parents monitor their commands daily and make changes where needed. Soliciting input from the child may be useful.

ESTABLISHING ROUTINES

Because children who refuse school for attention often show most of their misbehaviors in the morning, therapists and parents should focus on establishing a set routine for the early part of the day. Such a routine will mesh nicely with straightforward parent commands and rewards and punishments to be discussed. The therapist and parents design a morning routine that will result in certain rewards if the routine is followed, or in punishments if it is not. The child should be required to rise from bed about 90 to 120 minutes prior to the start of school. Ten minutes of lead time between waking and rising may be given. Subsequent times are set for going to the bathroom and washing, dressing, and making one's bed, eating breakfast, brushing teeth, making final preparations for school, going to school by oneself or with a parent, and entering the school building and classroom.

If a child is unable to attend school, then the therapist and parents establish a supervised daytime routine. This involves having the child sit in a boring place during the day (at home or work) under the supervision of a parent or other adult. The child may also be asked to complete homework or dull household chores, but no additional verbal or physical attention should be given beyond that which is absolutely necessary. The child should not receive any satisfaction or gratification from out-of-school activities. A child who misses the entire school day is grounded during evening hours as well. If the child missed school during most of the week, especially on Friday, then weekend grounding or other punishments may be given. The essential message to be conveyed is that school attendance is mandatory and that school absence is a serious problem that parents will address even at night and on weekends.

IMPLEMENTING REWARDS AND PUNISHMENTS

In conjunction with parent commands and routines, rewards are established for compliance and school attendance. Likewise, punishments are established for noncompliance and school refusal behaviors. To do so, therapists are encouraged to ask parents about rewards and punishments they have used in the past. Each parent rates each reward and punishment for its effectiveness, practicality, and potential usefulness. Two or three rewards and punishments are chosen that greatly impact the child and that can be given by parents immediately and consistently. Because the child is refusing school for attention, orienting rewards toward events such as additional reading time with parents, staying up later, and having a family dinner honoring the child may be best. Conversely, punishments might include verbal reprimands, ignoring and working through misbehavior, time-outs, and grounding in one's bedroom. The child should know ahead of time all the rules, expected appropriate behaviors, inappropriate behaviors, and rewards and punishments.

Parents should link rewards and punishments to compliance or noncompliance, respectively, with parent commands and the morning routine. In addition, parents should link rewards and punishments to the absence or presence, respectively, of five school refusal behaviors that are most problematic (e.g., crying, screaming, hitting, clinging, and refusal to move). Contingencies should be given immediately and perhaps later in the day. When such contingencies are given, the child should be reminded why they are given and what behaviors are appropriate and inappropriate.

As part of this process, parents should be as emotionally neutral and forthright with their child as possible. Parents should communicate in a matter-of-fact way that school attendance is expected and that the child will receive more parental attention for compliant than noncompliant behavior. Parents are also encouraged to work through misbehavior as much as possible. Parents should dress their child and bring him to school despite tantrums and other problems. In addition, these children often exaggerate physical complaints to avoid school. Excess complaints should be ignored by parents and only severe medical conditions such as high fever, vomiting, or other malady should prevent school attendance. If necessary, parents and a therapist should work closely with a school nurse to monitor symptoms, exaggerated or not, that a child shows during the school day.

Forced School Attendance

If a child remains intransigent about going to school, even after the procedures described here, forced school attendance may be considered (Kennedy, 1965). This generally involves some physical intervention in which a child is brought to school and classroom by his parents. This procedure may be considered only under certain circumstances:

- School refusal behavior is motivated only by attention.
- Parents and school officials are willing participants in the procedure.
- Two parents or one parent and another adult can complete the procedure.
- The child understands what the procedure will involve.
- The child is currently missing more school days than not.
- The child is under age 11 years.

Therapists are encouraged to raise the possibility of forced school attendance with parents if desired and solicit feedback from them. In particular, therapists should assess for parental guilt, resistance from school officials, and other circumstances that may interfere with this procedure.

If these conditions are met and a child continues to refuse school, then forced school attendance may be used. Parents should bring the child to school with as little verbal or physical attention as possible. In some cases, parents may initially have to bring a child to school for part of the day, such as the afternoon only, and then gradually increase amount of in-school time. In other cases, parents may initially have to bring a child to a nonclassroom setting such as a school library prior to classroom reintegration.

Children who refuse school for attention will often cease misbehavior once brought to school. If not, a classroom-based system of rewards and punishments may be established with the child's teacher. Forced school attendance should be ended if the child displays severe anxiety or if the situation becomes unbearable for the parents.

CASE STUDY

PRESENTING CLIENT AND PROBLEM

Amy was an 8-year-old girl referred by her mother, Mrs. L., and the principal at Amy's elementary school. During the initial telephone screening, Mrs. L. said Amy had missed 18 of the previous 30 days of school. On most days when Amy attended school, a parent accompanied her and spent at least part of the day in her classroom. If her parents told Amy to go to school by herself, Amy would cry, scream, cling to objects, or become "dead weight." She also complained of mild stomachaches and begged her parents to let her stay home. On most recent days, Mr. and Mrs. L. acquiesced to these demands. However, Amy's schoolwork was suffering considerably, family disruption was becoming substantial, and school officials were pressuring Mr. and Mrs. L. for a solution.

Amy's problems may have been triggered by three key events: (1) movement to a new classroom, (2) the recent birth of Amy's brother, and (3) business travel that required Mr. L. to be out of town extensively. With respect to the latter, Mrs. L. said her husband would be only intermittently available for assessment and treatment sessions.

During assessment, Amy was reluctant to talk in general and especially alone with the therapist. When eventually coaxed to do so, Amy was quiet but said she often cried the night before school and in the morning before rising from bed. She reported stomachaches in the morning and that her parents would let her stay home as a result. When Amy was home, her mother would read to her and allow Amy to help with tasks needed to care for her new baby. Amy said her mother "needs my help because Daddy is always gone." Amy also said she had no problems on weekends except for Sunday night. She also reported several things she liked about school, including recess, her teacher, and reading.

Mrs. L. gave a similar report, but added that Amy's tantrums and other misbehaviors were becoming more frequent even during the day at home. Amy was starting to scream if not allowed to care for the baby in the way she wanted. Mrs. L. also admitted feeling guilty about not spending enough time with Amy since the birth of her brother. She said this may have been one reason she was "quicker" to give in to Amy's demands than her husband, who was encouraging a stricter approach. However, Amy's behaviors had reached the point of intolerability. A telephone interview with Amy's teacher revealed that Amy was generally well behaved at school, though she often complained of wanting to be with her parents and demanded substantial attention from adults at school.

FORMULATION

Based on a comprehensive assessment, the therapist determined that Amy was largely missing school to obtain attention from her parents. This determination was supported by the facts that Amy displayed few physical or other problems on the weekend, had fewer problems attending school if a parent was with her, and was composed when with her teacher for an extended period. In addition, parent and child questionnaire scores and ratings on the SRAS-R indicated that attention was the key function of Amy's school refusal behavior. The therapist recommended that treatment focus on increasing the strength of parent commands, establishing clear guidelines for behavior and daily routines, and instituting a consistent pattern of rewards and punishments for school attendance and absence, respectively. The therapist and parents acknowledged that much of treatment would have to be targeted toward Amy's mother. Mr. L. would attend therapy and contribute to the treatment regimen when possible.

COURSE OF TREATMENT

Treatment was largely parent-based, but Amy was required to attend each session and was told what to expect in coming days. Initially, Amy's parents provided a list of commands given during the past 2 weeks. Many of the commands concerned chores and bedtime, with few directed toward school attendance. The therapist restructured parent commands regarding household tasks and helped build new parent commands about Amy's school attendance. For example, a consistent parent command was "Please clean your room." Mr. and Mrs. L. were asked to restate this and similar commands more clearly and directly. One restatement of this command was "Go into your bedroom now, pick up all clothes from the floor, and hang them up in your closet." In addition, specific commands were designed for the morning, such as "Get out of bed now," "Eat your breakfast in the next ten minutes," and "Put on your jacket now and walk to the car." The therapist also addressed issues such as Mrs. L.'s guilt that interfered with command effectiveness and allowed acquiescence to Amy's demands.

The therapist then established a routine for the morning. Amy was to be awakened at 7:00 and required to rise by 7:10. She would then be required to go to the bathroom and wash by 7:30, dress and eat breakfast by 8:00, brush her teeth and make final preparations for school by 8:15, and get in the car to go to school by 8:30. Compliance or noncompliance to this routine would result in rewards or punishments, respectively. Specific school refusal behaviors were also identified. In this case, rewards and punishments were applied to the presence or absence, respectively, of screaming, clinging, and refusal to move (other behaviors were added later in therapy). If Amy still refused to attend school, then her daytime routine would consist of sitting on her bed without parental attention. She would also be grounded in her room at night and mostly on the weekends but would still complete homework sent by her teacher.

Rewards and punishments were attention-based. Rewards consisted of verbal praise, more reading time with a parent, special dinners, and staying up later with the family at night. Punishments included short verbal reprimands, ignoring, and grounding for twice the amount of time spent refusing school in the morning. Rewards and punishments were given immediately and during the evening and weekends. In addition, Mr. and Mrs. L. were asked to ignore Amy's inappropriate behaviors, such as exaggerated stomachaches, and work through misbehaviors such as tantrums to complete the morning routine. Amy was reminded that receiving rewards or punishments was solely her choice and depended on whether she went to school.

OUTCOME AND PROGNOSIS

During the first week of treatment, Amy's school refusal behavior increased substantially. This was not unexpected, as many children deliberately worsen their behavior to force parental acquiescence to their demands. In this case, Mr. and Mrs. L. held firm, though Mr. L. was required to leave work and physically bring Amy to school on some occasions. After 1 week, Amy's behavior improved somewhat. Full-time school attendance was achieved after 3 weeks. Long-term functioning was generally good, though Amy experienced some minor slips following long weekends and extended vacations.

PARENT-FAMILY THERAPY IN CONTINGENCY CONTRACTING FOR YOUTHS REFUSING SCHOOL FOR TANGIBLE REINFORCEMENT

For children refusing school for tangible reinforcement outside school, parent-family therapy in contingency contracting can be quite helpful. Key components of contingency contracting for this population include (a) establishing times and places for negotiating problem solutions and communicating appropriately, (b) defining a problem, (c) designing a written contract between parents and child to resolve the problem, and (d) implementing the contract.

ESTABLISHING TIMES AND PLACES FOR NEGOTIATION AND COMMUNICATION

Parents and family members are initially encouraged to establish times at home for regular discussions of unresolved problems. Although the formal contracting process should be largely done in-session at the beginning of treatment, family members should talk to one another more in natural settings. These talks may first involve general issues and possible changes in the contracts. Later in treatment, these talks should center on developing contracts independent of the therapist's help. During each family discussion, parents are encouraged to allow each family member to voice concerns and provide solutions to family problems. In addition, family members should practice communication skills described next.

Communication skills training is often crucial for families of children who refuse school for tangible reinforcement. This is so because these families are often conflictive and do not properly communicate during many problem-solving discussions. Initially, therapists should concentrate on having parents and family members eliminate negative speech patterns. Parents may be asked to discourage name-calling, insults, yelling, silence, sarcasm, interruptions, and inappropriate suggestions.

Later in treatment, therapists may focus on developing more positive interactions between parents and children. Parents should convey messages to children in a simple, straightforward, and positive manner, such as "I like it a lot when you go to school all day." Subsequently, the youth should paraphrase or repeat what was said to confirm the child heard the message. Problems should be addressed at this point. Family members then participate in this process with one another. If successful in the office and home, the therapist then models short conversations for the family. The therapist may have a brief conversation with one parent before other family members. Feedback is then given to everyone about appropriate messages, listening, and nonverbal behaviors such as eye contact. Over time, family members practice short, positive conversations at home and audiotape some of them for the therapist to study. By the end of therapy, parents and family members should conduct more extensive, productive, and problem-solving-oriented conversations.

DEFINING A PROBLEM

Before a formal contract can be written, parents and family members must define a specific problem. To do so, the therapist identifies an irritating but fairly minor problem that faces the family. This problem may have little to do with school refusal behavior, such as an unfinished chore, incomplete homework, or missed bedtime. Each family member should agree that the problem is appropriate. Therapists should avoid problems that are unsolvable, long-standing, or overly complicated.

After choosing the problem, parents and family members are asked for definitions of the problem. In the beginning, vast differences in definitions may be the norm, and the therapist must forge a compromise. A parent might define a problem as "He never washes the dishes," whereas a child might define it as "I have to do the dishes all the time." In this case, the therapist may derive a more precise and blameless definition: "The dishes are not being washed regularly." Following any problem definition, family members state whether the definition is acceptable.

More complicated problems such as those related to school refusal behavior may be defined as therapy progresses. School attendance and absence, curfew, completed homework, required chores, and other items may be key to future contracts and must be defined as exactly as possible by everyone. Parents and other family members should provide these definitions more independently of the therapist over time. To test their ability in this area, therapists can give family members hypothetical, vague problems to define and give constructive feedback about their performance when doing so.

Designing a Written Contract to Resolve the Problem

After a problem is defined, the child and parents separately list as many solutions as possible. About 5 to 10 solutions should be solicited from each party and ranked in order of desirability. Determine whether the solution is practical, realistic, specific, and potentially agreeable to everyone. The lists are then compared and the therapist chooses the more desirable solution. Parents and family members are asked whether they agree to the choice. If so, the therapist may proceed.

The next step involves establishing tangible rewards and punishments for completing or not completing the contract. Again, each party gives input and the therapist focuses on blending everyone's viewpoint. The first contract is then formally negotiated by the therapist with the parents and child separately. The first contract, which should be quite simple so the family experiences early success, may read as follows for the problem described earlier: "(Child) agrees to wash the dishes on Thursday and Sunday if asked. If (child) completes this chore correctly, then (child) will receive an extra half-hour with friends on Friday night and 1 day during the week. If (child) does not wash the dishes when asked on these days, then (child) is grounded for a 24-hour period determined by parents."

Therapists must close loopholes in the contract. In this contract, for example, one should define exactly when the dishes will be washed, who

Table 6.1
Sample Contract (Kearney & Albano, 2000)

Privileges	Responsibilities
General In exchange for decreased family conflict and a resolution to school refusal behavior, all family members agree to	try as hard as possible to maintain this contract and fully participate in therapy.
Specific In exchange for the privilege of being paid to complete household chores between now and the next therapy session, (child) agrees to	attend school full-time between now and the next therapy session.
Should (child) not complete this responsibility,	he will be required to complete the household chores without being paid.
In exchange for the privilege of possessing an iPod and television in his room, (child) agrees to	rise in the morning at 7:00, dress and eat by 7:40, wash and brush teeth by 8:00, and finalize preparations for school by 8:20.
Should (child) not complete this responsibility,	he will lose the iPod and television and will be grounded for one day.
In exchange for compensation of five dollars, (child) agrees to	vacuum the living room and clean the bathroom between now and the next therapy session.
Should (child) not go to school, not complete this responsibility, or complete the responsibility inadequately (to be determined by parents),	he will not be paid.

(Child) and his parents agree to uphold the conditions of this contract and read and initial the contract each day.

Signature of (Child) and parents:

_____

_____   Date: _____

will say the dishes were washed acceptably, and when the youth can be with friends. Parents are generally given more say when closing loopholes. In addition, the contract should last no longer than a few days. In this way, the therapist can address problems as soon as possible.

Contracts can become more complicated at a later point and focus directly on a child's school refusal behavior. The main goal of these contracts is to increase tangible rewards for school attendance and decrease rewards (or add punishments) for school absence. A key way of doing this is to require the youth to attend school for the privilege of finishing household chores for money. If the child misses school, the chores would still be required but with no compensation. A sample contract (Table 6.1) from Kearney and Albano (2007) illustrates this point.

IMPLEMENTING THE CONTRACT

Once the contract has been written, family members read the contract and rate its acceptability. Unacceptable contracts must be renegotiated. Once the final contract is drawn, family members sign and post the contract in an open area of the house. Family members should immediately contact the therapist if problems arise. In addition, therapists should contact parents and children almost daily to assess compliance.

Therapists should be aware that some youths will comply to contracts until school attendance is addressed. If sudden noncompliance arises for contracts involving school attendance, then parents or others may have to accompany the child to school and from class to class. In this way, school attendance is assured and the child remains eligible for tangible rewards in the contract. Punishments may still be given for excessive behaviors such as running out of the school building. This process requires substantial effort from parents and must be done in cooperation with school officials. In addition, parents must gradually fade themselves from the school setting.

Therapists are also encouraged to have parents closely monitor their child's school attendance so absences may be addressed immediately. Developing relationships with teachers, principals, attendance officers, and nurses is helpful. Finally, youths in this group often have substantial schoolwork to complete, so future contracts could address this issue as well. Good academic competence is often antithetical to school refusal behavior.

CASE STUDY

PRESENTING CLIENT AND PROBLEM

Kevin was a 14-year-old boy referred by his mother, Mrs. K., and the attendance officer at Kevin's high school. As a ninth grader, Kevin had missed 26 of the previous 42 days of school and was experiencing a severe decline in his grades. During the initial telephone screening, Mrs. K., a single mother of three children, said Kevin had missed school intermittently in previous years. However, his entry into high school this year seemed to be difficult and his school refusal behavior was more intense than before. Mrs. K. also complained that Kevin had "fallen in with the wrong crowd" and was skipping school with his new friends. Because school officials were considering expulsion if a solution was not found soon, an assessment session was scheduled for that week.

The first two scheduled sessions were postponed because Kevin refused to attend. After much pleading by his mother, Kevin agreed to speak with the therapist briefly. He said he needed more independence and did not see the point of attending school, which he saw as unproductive and boring. On days that Kevin missed, he would usually watch television at a friend's house. He acknowledged some concern about his grades and their effect on his ability to graduate, but said he could make up the work any time.

Kevin's mother largely confirmed this report. She added information about Kevin's father, who was living in another state, and gave the therapist recent police reports of vandalism and illicit purchases of alcohol by Kevin. She feared she was losing control of her son and that he would become delinquent. Mrs. K. also admitted that her work responsibilities and demands of caring for her other children left her little time for Kevin. Discussions with Kevin's teachers revealed little additional information because of their lack of contact with him.

FORMULATION

Based on a comprehensive assessment, the therapist determined that Kevin was missing school largely for tangible reinforcement outside school. This determination was supported by the facts that Kevin displayed no major internalizing symptoms, no desire to be constantly near his mother, fewer problems attending school if his mother bribed him to do so, and strong motivation to be with his friends during the school day. In addition, parent and child questionnaire scores and ratings on the SRAS-R indicated that tangible reinforcement was the key function of Kevin's school refusal behavior. The therapist recommended that treatment focus on increasing appropriate rewards for Kevin's school attendance and completed homework, increasing punishments and decreasing out-of-school activities for Kevin's school absences, and giving Mrs. K. a strategy for working with her son to negotiate solutions to family problems.

COURSE OF TREATMENT

Treatment in this case focused almost exclusively on Kevin and his mother, though siblings and important others were included as necessary. Initially, the therapist spent time developing a strong rapport with Kevin, who needed to be convinced that his input was as valuable as anyone's. In doing so, the therapist explained that a contract would involve privileges and responsibilities for all parties. Kevin acknowledged the possible usefulness of the contract but said his conditions would have to include some free time with friends.

The first contract involved a simple chore, reward, and punishment similar to that described earlier. Because this contract was successful and because of the urgent nature of Kevin's poor attendance, the therapist proceeded quickly to a more complex contract. This contract required Kevin to (a) attend school full-time for 4 of the next 5 school days, (b) refrain from illicit activity, and (c) obey an 11:00 P.M. curfew. In exchange, Kevin would be allowed to (a) vacuum the house on Saturday for $10, (b) be driven by his mother to a friend's house of his choice on Sunday afternoon, and (c) go out with his friends on Friday and Saturday nights. Each party accepted the conditions of the 1-week contract, signed it, and agreed to discuss the contract with one another daily. The therapist also spent time discussing Kevin's relationship with his mother, the family's communication skills, and Kevin's academic work. Finally, Mrs. K. was asked to call the school daily to check Kevin's school attendance and class assignments.

In the next session, Mrs. K. said the contract was only partially successful. Kevin did adhere to curfew and avoided legal trouble, but missed 4 of 5 school days. Mrs. K. allowed Kevin to see his friends on Saturday night but prohibited other social activities or payments. The next three contracts over the next 3 weeks were modified so Kevin would experience some success with school attendance and Mrs. K. would follow through more thoroughly on all aspects of the contract, especially punishments. These three contracts were largely successful in the latter, but Kevin's school attendance did not improve.

At this point, the therapist and Mrs. K. recruited a family friend to accompany Kevin to school and escort him from class to class for the next 2 weeks. Kevin was told he would be escorted in this manner. After missing 2 more days of school, this procedure was implemented. Kevin then received tangible rewards for attending school and was not punished. Kevin's school attendance was perfect for 2 weeks, after which the escort was gradually faded. This was done by escorting Kevin in the morning up to lunchtime and then monitoring his afternoon attendance via conversations with school officials. Over 2 weeks, the escort was faded until Kevin showed he could attend school on his own. In the meantime, the therapist continued to work on other areas of conflict within the family as well as Kevin's academic status.

OUTCOME AND PROGNOSIS

Kevin attended school on a fairly regular basis, though slips were common. Teenagers who refuse school often challenge their parents' resolve by occasionally skipping school. Vigilance and consistent follow-through are thus crucial. In addition, therapists should focus on developing communication skills and reducing conflict inherent to many families of youths who refuse school. In this case, the therapist tried to develop a partnership between Kevin and his mother that focused on taking care of the family, negotiating problem solutions, and easing tension. The therapist also worked to increase Mrs. K.'s social support network to reduce her parenting burden. Prognosis for this type of case depends highly on the final quality of the parent-child relationship, ongoing use of contracts, and improvements in academic work.

CONCLUSION

Parents must generally be involved in many aspects of assessment and treatment of youths with school refusal behavior. Parents are one of the richest sources of information about a child refusing school, particularly a younger child. Parental participation is thus crucial during screening conversations, interviews, questionnaire administration, and direct observations of behavior. Initial parent reports can be frantic and overstated, but this often reflects the crisis-like nature of these problems. In particular, parents often overemphasize overt behavior problems in their children and minimize potentially severe problems such as anxiety and depression. Therapists should bear in mind as well that discrepancies between parent and child reports are common to this population. A comprehensive assessment involving multiple sources of information is highly recommended.

Clinicians are also encouraged to rely on a functional model for assessing and treating school refusal behavior. This includes using the inclusive definition of school refusal behavior presented earlier and examining functions in addition to forms of school refusal behavior. The major functions discussed in this chapter included (a) negative reinforcement (avoidance of school-based stimuli provoking negative affectivity or escape from aversive social/evaluative situations at school), (b) pursuit of attention from significant others, and (3) pursuit of tangible reinforcement outside school.

The functional model is linked to a prescriptive treatment approach that involves substantial parental input and training. Such procedures involve training parents to (a) help their child implement and maintain compliance to relaxation training, modeling, role-play, cognitive therapy, and exposure techniques; (b) implement major components of contingency management such as restructured parent commands, regular daytime routines, and rewards and punishments for compliance and noncompliance; and (c) better monitor a child's school attendance and use contracts to define problems clearly, negotiate solutions without conflict, increase appropriate tangible rewards for school attendance, and restrict activities for school absence. Preliminary work regarding this prescriptive treatment approach is promising (Chorpita, Albano, Heimberg, & Barlow, 1996; Kearney, 2002a; Kearney, Pursell, & Alvarez, 2001; Kearney & Silverman, 1990, 1999).

Parental involvement in treatment for youths with school refusal behavior goes beyond mere use of techniques. Clinicians should take care to enlist the support of both parents, even if one is separated from daily family life; provide substantial support to parents enduring this difficult time with their child; maintain almost daily contact with parents to encourage follow-through with treatment; alleviate parental guilt, conflict, psychopathology, pessimism, and ineffective disciplinary practices that arrest treatment progress; and provide parents with a long-term strategy to remedy future occurrences of school refusal behavior. Finally, therapists are encouraged to prevent more serious school refusal problems by working closely with school officials to secure early referrals and urge parents to seek treatment sooner rather than later.

REFERENCES

Baker, H., & Wills, U. (1978). School phobia: Classification and treatment. *British Journal of Psychiatry, 132,* 492–499.

Berg, I. (1970). A follow-up study of school phobic adolescents admitted to an inpatient unit. *Journal of Child Psychology and Psychiatry, 11,* 37–47.

Berg, I., & Jackson, A. (1985). Teenage school refusers grow up: A follow-up study of 168 subjects, 10 years on average after inpatient treatment. *British Journal of Psychiatry, 147,* 366–370.

Berg, I., Marks, I., McGuire, R., & Lipsedge, M. (1974). School phobia and agoraphobia. *Psychological Medicine, 4,* 428–434.

Chorpita, B. F., Albano, A. M., Heimberg, R. G., & Barlow, D. H. (1996). A systematic replication of the prescriptive treatment of school refusal behavior in a single subject. *Journal of Behavior Therapy and Experimental Psychiatry, 27,* 281–290.

Flakierska, N., Lindstrom, M., & Gillberg, C. (1988). School refusal: A 15 to 20-year follow-up study of 35 Swedish urban children. *British Journal of Psychiatry, 152,* 834–837.

Hampe, E., Miller, L., Barrett, C., & Noble, H. (1973). Intelligence and school phobia. *Journal of School Psychology, 11,* 66–70.

Hibbett, A., & Fogelman, K. (1990). Future lives of truants: Family formation and health-related behavior. *British Journal of Educational Psychology, 60,* 171–179.

Hibbett, A., Fogelman, K., & Manor, O. (1990). Occupational outcomes of truancy. *British Journal of Educational Psychology, 60,* 23–36.

Kahn, J. H., & Nursten, J. P. (1962). School refusal: A comprehensive view of school phobia and other failures of school attendance. *American Journal of Orthopsychiatry, 32,* 707–718.

Kazdin, A. E. (1991). Effectiveness of psychotherapy with children and adolescents. *Journal of Consulting and Clinical Psychology, 59,* 785–789.

Kearney, C. A. (2001). *School refusal behavior in youth: A functional approach to assessment and treatment.* Washington, DC: American Psychological Association.

Kearney, C. A. (2002a). Case study of the assessment and treatment of a youth with multifunction school refusal behavior. *Clinical Case Studies, 1,* 67–80.

Kearney, C. A. (2002b). Identifying the function of school refusal behavior: A revision of the School Refusal Assessment Scale. *Journal of Psychopathology and Behavioral Assessment, 24,* 235–245.

Kearney, C. A. (2003). Bridging the gap among professionals who address youth with school absenteeism: Overview and suggestions for consensus. *Professional Psychology: Research and Practice, 34,* 57–65.

Kearney, C. A. (2005). *Social anxiety and social phobia in youth: Characteristics, assessment, and psychological treatment.* New York: Springer.

Kearney, C. A. (2006). Confirmatory factor analysis of the School Refusal Assessment Scale-Revised: Child and parent versions. *Journal of Psychopathology and Behavioral Assessment, 28,* 139–144.

Kearney, C. A., & Albano, A. M. (2000). *When children refuse school: A cognitive-behavioral therapy approach/Therapist's guide.* San Antonio, TX: The Psychological Corporation.

Kearney, C. A., & Albano, A. M. (2007). *When children refuse school: A cognitive-behavioral therapy approach/Therapist's guide* (2nd ed.). New York: Oxford University Press.

Kearney, C. A., Pursell, C., & Alvarez, K. (2001). Treatment of school refusal behavior in children with mixed functional profiles. *Cognitive and Behavioral Practice, 8,* 3–11.

Kearney, C. A., & Silverman, W. K. (1990). A preliminary analysis of a functional model of assessment and treatment for school refusal behavior. *Behavior Modification, 14,* 340–366.

Kearney, C. A., & Silverman, W. K. (1995). Family environment of youngsters with school refusal behavior: A synopsis with implications for assessment and treatment. *American Journal of Family Therapy, 23,* 59–72.

Kearney, C. A., & Silverman, W. K. (1996). The evolution and reconciliation of taxonomic strategies for school refusal behavior. *Clinical Psychology: Science and Practice, 3,* 339–354.

Kearney, C. A., & Silverman, W. K. (1999). Functionally-based prescriptive and nonprescriptive treatment for children and adolescents with school refusal behavior. *Behavior Therapy, 30,* 673–695.

Kennedy, W. A. (1965). School phobia: Rapid treatment of 50 cases. *Journal of Abnormal Psychology, 70,* 285–289.

Last, C. G. (1991). Somatic complaints in anxiety disordered children. *Journal of Anxiety Disorders, 5,* 125–138.

Last, C. G., & Strauss, C. C. (1990). School refusal in anxiety-disordered children and adolescents. *Journal of the American Academy of Child and Adolescent Psychiatry, 29,* 31–35.

Nichols, K. A., & Berg, I. (1970). School phobia and self-evaluation. *Journal of Child Psychology and Psychiatry, 11,* 133–141.

Silverman, W. K., & Kurtines, W. M. (1996). *Anxiety and phobic disorders: A pragmatic approach.* New York: Plenum Press.

Tyrer, P., & Tyrer, S. (1974). School refusal, truancy, and adult neurotic illness. *Psychological Medicine, 6,* 313–332.

PART FOUR

EXTERNALIZING DISORDERS

DISORDERS THAT are characterized as externalizing may include features such as acting-out, antisocial and oppositional behaviors, Attention-Deficit/Hyperactivity Disorder, and childhood aggression. These are behaviors that typically turn against society. Part Four focuses on state-of-the-art intervention programs that help parents to identify, assess, and modify maladaptive and dysfunctional externalizing disorders. These programs assist parents in changing the behaviors of children that not only disrupt the fabric of the family but also impact the various aspects of society, such as school, relationships, agencies that work for the well-being of children and parents, and the community, in general.

In Chapter 7, Sanders introduces an empirically-based and highly systematic treatment, the Triple P–Positive Parenting Program. This is a unique multilevel system of parenting and family support that can be implemented as a strategy to support parents in the task of raising their children. It is a public health approach that was developed by Sanders and it aims to enhance family protective factors and reduce the risk factors associated with behavioral and emotional problems. The Triple P–Positive Parenting Program promotes a parent's capacity for self-regulation. This involves teaching parents skills that allow them to become independent problem solvers. The self-regulatory framework used in this program is operationalized to include self-sufficiency, parental self-efficacy, and self-management. The aim of the intervention process is to help parents become increasing autonomous agents of change, foster greater confidence in the parents, and improve the parents' abilities to select effective parenting and child management techniques.

The Triple P–Positive Parenting Program employs five core positive parenting principles: (1) It instructs parents in the methods of forming a safe and engaging environment for their children; (2) it establishes a positive learning environment; (3) it helps parents develop assertive discipline strategies that are an alternative to coercive and ineffective discipline practices; (4) it shows parents how to set realistic and attainable expectations and goals for their children, goals that are developmentally appropriate; and (5) since the disruptive behaviors of children with externalizing disorders can leave parents with low self-esteem and a faltering sense of self-worth, the program also teaches parents how to take care of themselves, become more resourceful, and, in general, improve their own well-being. These five principles translate into a series of specific parenting strategies that form the basis of the Triple P–Positive Parenting Program. It involves several different types of intervention approaches depending on the severity of the presenting problem and its associated risk and protective factors. The protocol is tailored to the unique presenting needs of each case. The author also offers research outcome studies as well as an insightful discussion of moderator, mediator variables. A case study illustrates the format and successful implementation of this creative intervention modality.

Chapter 8 presents Herschell and McNeil's intervention strategy, a parent-child interaction therapy with physically abusive families. They present research that demonstrates a high correlation between child physical abuse and disruptive behavior such as aggression and noncompliance. The Parent-Child Interaction Therapy (PCIT) approach is an empirically-based parent training program that was originally developed by Eyberg in the late 1960s and early 1970s. The program has been updated and revisioned. The program involves coaching and coding parents as they interact with their children, ages 2 to 6. Although this intervention strategy does not have any time constraints, it is designed to be a short-term parent management strategy that typically involves approximately 12 one-hour treatment sessions.

The Parent-Child Interaction Therapy includes two treatment phases, the Child-Directed Interaction (CDI) phase and the Parent-Directed Interaction (PDI) phase. During the CDI phase, parents are taught to use the PRIDE skills. This acronym refers to Praise, Reflection, Imitation, Description, and Enthusiasm. These skills are selected, designed, and implemented to increase appropriate child behaviors and decrease undesirable child behaviors. During the PDI phase, parents are taught the importance of structure, consistency, and predictability. The parents learn to use nonaggressive behavior management skills. The authors discuss the importance and use of mastery criteria to guide the therapist regarding when to move from one treatment phase to the next. To complete treatment, this program requires parents to master discipline skills and children's behavior must be within normal limits as measured by select standardized assessment tools.

Herschell and McNeil share an extremely thorough, systematic, and interesting case that offers valuable insights into the content and objectives of the various sessions. Practical approaches are utilized. These include some of the following: relaxation techniques, home practice assignments, time-out procedures, and instructing caregivers how to generalize discipline procedures in a variety of situations. The authors address the implications of current research assessments of the program. They also discuss a significant challenge for Parent-Child Interaction Therapy, the difficulty encountered in attempting to transport the program from university-based clinics to community settings. Despite many challenges, PCIT has proven to be an effective, widely used, and promising approach for treating families with young children who have experienced physical abuse.

In Chapter 9, Ducharme offers an intervention strategy that is designed to reduce the need for punishment and power assertion in the treatment of children who exhibit severe oppositional behavior and related problems. The author describes some of the traditional approaches to compliance training, such as the use of requests and reinforcements. However, parents often encounter high levels of resistance and confrontation when they use power-assertive interventions. As such, a success-focused and noncoercive intervention approach to treatment is presented. This incorporates "errorless" approaches to managing severe behavioral problems and is derived from the principles of operant conditioning. The essential goal of any compliance training program is to induce children to respond to "low probability" requests in the same way they respond to "high probability" requests. That is to say, the children comply and cooperate even when given requests that are typically met with noncompliance.

Ducharme demonstrates that errorless compliance training can be conducted in either an individual or group format, depending on the resources available to the clinician as well as the specific needs of the family. The group format has proven to be more efficient. This approach allows several parents to be trained simultaneously. Parents can learn by observing other parents modeling successful strategies. Furthermore, this group approach fosters mutual support. The author gives an in-depth and detailed description of the format and content of the various group sessions. He clearly illustrates how the errorless approach to parent training can be implemented. In these sessions, parents learn how to assess compliance probabilities through the use of a Compliance Probability Checklist. Parents also learn how to collect data on the probability of compliance to specific requests. Throughout the sequence of sessions, parents also learn to issue requests to their children that are less likely to meet with resistance and noncompliance. Parents are instructed in the value of data collection and the use of compliance records. This data-collecting process allows for the development of successful compliance probability levels that are essential to activating treatment and a development of a compliance probability hierarchy.

The intervention program trains parents in crucial treatment skills. These skills include praise and reinforcement for child compliance to parental requests, avoidance of attention and other reinforcers for non-compliance, and avoidance of requests from subsequent probability levels. Following descriptions of the various sessions, the author presents a review of key outcome studies with a broad range of populations of children with severe oppositional behavior. These include children with developmental disabilities, children who have witnessed and been victims of family violence, children of parents with an acquired brain injury, and children with autistic spectrum disorders. Ducharme describes and addresses the unique challenges to parenting as well as the specific behavioral and noncompliance problems offered by each of these populations. Studies are also presented that demonstrate the benefits of using the errorless approaches in the classroom as well as home-based intervention strategies.

In Chapter 10, Webster-Stratton elucidates an innovative treatment procedure. She offers a thorough and illuminating discussion of the Incredible Years Program. This is an evidence-based program that has been shown to significantly reduce oppositional defiant disorders and internalizing problems and strengthen positive parent-child relationships. The program has also been effective with families of children struggling with many other disorders and risk factors. The Incredible Years Training Program includes a number of child training options. The program allows for flexibility and can be tailored to meet the needs of various families and their specific problem areas, including children with comorbid diagnoses or family risk factors. Parents are taught how to identify goals for themselves and their children as well as how to apply child development and behavioral management principles when working on individual intervention plans and strategies. While implementing programs such as preschool and school-age versions of BASIC parenting and BASIC Play Program, for instance, parents learn valuable coping skills, effective communication skills, and problem-solving strategies. These and other skills help the parents and the children control and reduce various problems and risk factors.

The author discusses the problems of parenting children with oppositional defiant disorder or conduct disorder and the added difficulties of parenting children who are comorbid with Attention Deficit Disorder (ADD) or an Attention-Deficit/Hyperactive Disorder (ADHD). For example, child training programs, such as the Dinosaur Program, help children with ADHD learn play and social skills, problem solving, and anger management. Children with these disorders typically encounter difficulties with self-reflection. Therefore, the author offers specific and concrete aids, such as sticker charts and behavior plans with clearly defined goals and incentives to help children remember their behavior goals and concretely measure their successes. Parents are instructed to give children immediate consequences for their misbehaviors and reinforcements for their desirable behaviors. Parents learn the entire compliance training regime in order to help their children comply and become more cooperative. In addition to helping parents grasp developmentally appropriate discipline strategies, the Incredible Years Parent Program also helps parents in teaching their children problem-solving strategies and the practice of more appropriate solutions to problems.

Children with oppositional defiant disorders may have ambivalent or avoidant attachment patterns with the biological, foster, or adoptive parents. Webster-Stratton discusses the various classifications of attachment problems and the ways in which the intervention program can address these issues. The chapter presents substantial and invaluable lists of objectives for parents of children with attachment problems as well as objectives for the children. Similar lists of objectives are also offered for divorcing parents and for parents of children with internalizing problems such as fear and depression. These objectives, like the approach in general, demonstrate the manner in which the Incredible Years Program can be tailored to the individual needs of parents and children. The program teaches parents a common set of parenting and management principles and skills that can be applied according to the parents' target goals for their children and themselves.

In Chapter 11, Danforth addresses the challenges of training parents of children with comorbid disorders. He focuses on an intervention program designed to address and ameliorate the problems of comorbid Attention-Deficit/Hyperactivity Disorder and Oppositional Defiant Disorder (ODD). The parent training program offers a therapeutic environment to the child. The structure and content of the program are grounded in research on ADHD and the subsequent development of ODD. Following a review of major alternative treatment modalities, medication, and cognitive-behavioral procedures, the author poses theoretical and empirically-based evidence for the effectiveness of parent training. He discusses an approach that focuses on a didactic presentation on ADHD and family interactions and a stepwise behavior management skills training program. He, then, shares an extremely useful and systematic description of the format, purpose, and content of the various parent training sessions. He clearly illustrates the topics and schedules for eight parent-training sessions. Therapists can adjust the schedule based on the needs of the individual child and family. The goal is to develop specific parenting skills that alter the inter-action with the child. These are skills that promote prosocial compliance and decrease disruptive behaviors in the child. Parents are offered opportu-nities to adapt to and cope with ADHD behaviors while modifying defiant and disruptive behaviors.

To help parents understand the relationship between ADHD and defi-ant/disruptive behavior, Danforth presents a three-term contingency (also known as the ABCs) that helps parents identify and correct their own behavioral patterns that may unwittingly contribute to the development of ODD. A Behavior Management Flow Chart (BMFC) depicts a chain of skilled responses that adults are to emit throughout the day in an effort to help manage the disruptive and disturbing behaviors of ADHD/ODD children. Supplementary written materials are given to parents in each of the sessions. These materials encompass steps that correspond to the steps of the BMFC. There is enough flexibility in the design to generalize and use the same flow charts in a variety of settings. Training with the BMFC is one component of the treatment package tailored to individual needs. It is one element of a larger treatment plan that might include an array of ser-vices and train parents in specific skills. The author gives a detailed de-scription of specific and practical parent management skills, such as instructions in giving practical commands, praise, reprimand, and time-out. A compelling case illustration demonstrates the application and effec-tiveness of the parents' newly acquired management skills. These are research-validated and time-tested skills that the parents learn and prac-tice within this systematic and creative parent training method.

In Chapter 12, Cavell and Elledge provide an in-depth discussion and treatment approach for the challenges involved in working with parents of aggressive, school-age children. They present a conceptual framework as well as practical guidelines for working with this population in light of what is known about children's long-term socialization. They describe a socialization-as-intervention frame that is in contrast to many traditional parent training models. The socialization-as-intervention view introduces an integrated life course-social learning approach to understand the de-velopment and treatment of antisocial behavior. The authors discuss eight basic assumptions that link diverse areas of research, including the interaction of nature with nuture, the significance of and interdepen-dence among multiple social contexts, the importance of individual dif-ferences in risk and proneness for crime, and the critical role of social contingencies in the development of antisocial behavior. These assump-tions address many of the key factors that affect the development of pro-social skills and diminish antisocial or aggressive behaviors.

The authors discuss and distinguish some of the underlying premises between parent management training (PMT) and responsive parent training (RPT). RPT is not a specific treatment package but an organized framework and a set of guiding principles for working with parents of aggressive children. It seeks to enhance the emotional quality of the parent-child relationship while establishing firm generational boundaries and adaptive family structure. Clinically, the parent-based RPT borrows heavily from PMT. The authors point out that the parent-child relationship is an important vehicle for socializing aggressive children. The socializing relationships provide aggressive children, over time, with emotional acceptance, an implicit message of belonging. Positive parenting is viewed in terms of emotional acceptance. It also offers children behavioral containment as well as prosocial values that begin with explicit statements against antisocial behavior.

Those who use this intervention program are encouraged to listen long and carefully to what parents say about their child, about themselves, and about their parenting style. In closing, Cavell and Elledge offer an illuminating fictional exchange between parent and practitioner that illustrates the art of listening and focuses on the issue of parental self-care. Therapists who are responsive to parents help parents become more responsive to their children.

CHAPTER 7

The Triple P–Positive Parenting Program: A Public Health Approach to Parenting Support

MATTHEW R. SANDERS

THE FAMILY provides the first and most important, social, emotional, interpersonal, economic, and cultural context for human development and, as a result, family relationships have a pervasive influence on the well-being of children. Evidence from behavior genetics research, as well as epidemiological, correlational, and experimental studies, show that parenting practices have a major influence on children's development (Collins, Maccoby, Steinberg, Hetherington, & Bornstein, 2000). The strongest potentially modifiable risk factor contributing to the development of behavioral and emotional problems in children is the quality of parenting a child receives. Disturbed family relationships are generic risk factors, and positive family relationships are protective factors that are related to a wide variety of mental health, social, and economic problems that occur from infancy to old age (Chamberlain & Patterson, 1995; Patterson, 1982; Sanders, 1995; Sanders & Duncan, 1995). Epidemiological studies indicate that family risk factors such as poor parenting, family conflict, and marriage breakdown strongly influence children's development (e.g., Cummings & Davies, 1994; Dryfoos, 1990; Robins, 1991). Specifically, the lack of a warm positive relationship with parents; insecure attachment; harsh, inflexible, rigid, or inconsistent discipline practices; inadequate supervision of and involvement with children; marital conflict and breakdown; and parental psychopathology (particularly maternal depression) increase the risk that children develop major behavioral and emotional problems, including substance abuse, antisocial behavior, and juvenile crime (e.g., Coie, 1996; Loeber & Farrington, 1998).

The recognition that the adverse effects of inadequate or dysfunctional parenting practices are associated with the development of a range of mental health and social problems in children has led to calls for the widespread implementation of parenting interventions to help prevent serious mental health problems in young people (e.g., Biglan, 1995). This chapter outlines a unique multilevel system of parenting and family support that can be implemented as a population level strategy to support parents in the challenging task of raising their children.

Triple P aims to enhance family protective factors and to reduce risk factors associated with behavioral and emotional problems in children and adolescents. Specifically the program aims to: (a) enhance the knowledge, skills, confidence, self-sufficiency, and resourcefulness of parents; (b) promote nurturing, safe, engaging, nonviolent, and low conflict environments for children; and (c) promote children's social, emotional, language, intellectual, and behavioral competencies through positive parenting practices.

The Triple P–Positive Parenting Program (Triple P; Sanders, 1999) is a public health parenting and family support strategy developed by Sanders and his colleagues at the University of Queensland in Brisbane, Australia. The program aims to prevent severe behavioral, emotional and developmental problems in children by enhancing the knowledge, skills, and confidence of parents. It incorporates five levels of intervention on a tiered continuum of increasing strength and narrowing population reach (see Table 7.1) for parents of children and adolescents from birth to age 16 years.

Level 1, a universal parent information strategy, provides all interested parents with access to useful information about parenting through a coordinated media and promotional campaign. This includes print and electronic media, user-friendly parenting tip sheets, videotapes that demonstrate specific parenting strategies, and professional seminars. This level of intervention aims to increase community awareness of parenting resources, to increase receptivity of parents to participation in programs, and to create a sense of optimism by depicting solutions to common behavioral and developmental concerns. Level 2 is a brief primary health care intervention providing early anticipatory developmental guidance to parents of children with mild behavior difficulties. This level of intervention can be delivered individually (one- to two-sessions), or to large groups of parents as three 90-minute seminars. Level 3 targets children with mild to moderate behavior difficulties and includes an

Table 7.1

The Triple P Model of Parenting and Family Support

Level of Intervention	Target Population	Intervention Methods	Practitioners
Level 1 Media-based parent information campaign Universal Triple P	All parents interested in information about parenting and promoting their child's development.	Coordinated media and health promotion campaign raising awareness of parent issues and encouraging participation in parenting programs. May involve electronic and print media (e.g., community service announcements; talk-back radio, newspaper and magazine editorials).	Typically coordinated by area media liaison officers or mental health or welfare staff.
Level 2 Health promotion strategy/brief selective intervention Selected Triple P Selected Teen Triple P	Parents interested in parenting education or with specific concerns about their child's development or behavior.	Health promotion information or specific advice for a discrete developmental issue or minor child behavior problem. May involve a group seminar process or brief (up to 20 minutes) telephone or face-to-face clinician contact.	Parent support during routine well-child health care (e.g., child and community health, education, allied health, and childcare staff).
Level 3 Narrow focus parent training Primary Care Triple P Primary Care Teen Triple P	Parents with specific concerns as above who require consultations or active skills training.	Brief program (about 80 minutes over four sessions) combining advice, rehearsal, and self-evaluation to teach parents to manage a discrete child problem behavior. May involve telephone or face-to-face clinician contact or group sessions.	Same as for Level 2.

(continued)

Table 7.1 *(Continued)*

Level of Intervention	Target Population	Intervention Methods	Practitioners
Level 4			
Broad focus parent training	Parents wanting intensive training in positive parenting skills. Typically parents of children with behavior problems such as aggressive or oppositional behavior.	Broad focus program (about 10 hours over 8 to 10 sessions) focusing on parent-child interaction and the application of parenting skills to a broad range of target behaviors. Includes generalization enhancement strategies. May be self-directed or involve telephone or face-to-face clinician contact or group sessions.	Intensive parenting interventions (e.g., mental health and welfare staff, and other allied health and education professionals who regularly consult with parents about child behavior).
Standard Triple P			
Group Triple P			
Group Teen Triple P			
Self-Directed Triple P			
Self-Directed Teen Triple P			
Stepping Stones Triple P	Families of preschool children with disabilities who have or are at risk of developing behavioral or emotional disorders.	A parallel 10-session individually tailored program with a focus on disabilities. Sessions typically last 60 to 90 minutes (with the exception of three practice sessions which last 40 minutes).	Same as above.
Level 5			
Behavioral family intervention modules	Parents of children with behavior problems and concurrent family dysfunction such as parental depression or stress, or conflict between partners.	Intensive individually tailored program with modules (60 to 90 minute sessions) including practice sessions to enhance parenting skills, mood management and stress coping skills, and partner support skills.	Intensive family intervention work (e.g., mental health and welfare staff).
Enhanced Triple P			
Pathways Triple P	Parents at risk of maltreating their children. Targets anger management problems and other factors associated with abuse.	Modules include attribution retraining and anger management.	Same as above.

individually tailored parenting plan to manage a specific behavioral or developmental concern. It involves four sessions and incorporates active skills training for parents. Level 4 is an intensive 8- to 10-session broad-focused parent training program for children with more severe behavioral difficulties and Level 5 is an enhanced 12- to 16-session behavioral family intervention program for families where parenting difficulties are complicated by other sources of family distress (e.g., marital conflict, parental depression, high levels of stress or anger).

HISTORY

Triple P is a form of behavioral family intervention (BFI). As such, its development is linked to the history of behavioral approaches to working with parents and families as a field. Behavioral family intervention has traditionally emphasized the importance of involving parents, teachers, and significant others as change agents to bring about lasting change in children's behavior (e.g., Patterson, 1969). Many of the principles and behavior change techniques used in Triple P were derived from contemporary learning theory, particularly models of operant behavior, and informed by developmental theory (e.g., Baer, Wolf, & Risley, 1968; 1987). Triple P was also influenced by cognitive social learning theory (Bandura, 1995) that emphasizes the importance of self-regulation.

Four stages in the development of the program have occurred:

1. *Initial program development and testing of core parenting procedures (1977–1981).* During this early period, the author was strongly influenced by the excellent work of Professor Todd Risley originally from the University of Kansas and more recently from the University of Alaska. Risley's groundbreaking ecological or contextual approach to designing "living environments" for children and other dependent people (which had been applied to young children in various child care environments, those in residential facilities for the mentally handicapped and the elderly in nursing homes) was extrapolated to the task of supporting parents through the creation of "family friendly" environments. This early interaction between the author and Risley in 1978, then a visiting professor at the University of Auckland where the author undertook his undergraduate, masters, and initial doctoral studies before moving to the University of Queensland in 1979, had a profound impact on the design of Triple P as a system of intervention as distinct from an individual program. It inspired the author to think in terms of the broader social ecology of parenthood including the impact of the media, the systems of primary health care, and social structures in the

community that could be used to support parents. A second influence during this period was the work of educational psychologist Professor Ted Glynn. His research on the use of self-management procedures in classroom settings provided the impetus to the author to apply similar principles to working with parents (Sanders & Glynn, 1981). Self-regulation subsequently became a central theoretical underpinning of the Triple P system. A third major influence was the work of Gerald Patterson at the Oregon Social Learning Center and in particular his pioneering observational studies that described the intricacies of coercive family processes that maintain conduct problems in children (Patterson, 1982). These early influences convinced the author that the quality of parenting children receive has a profound effect on all children and that better preparation for parenthood was essential to prevent serious behavioral and emotional problems in children.

2. *Extension of the core program to a wider range of child problems and more complex parental problems (1981 to present).* Over the next 25 years, a series of studies demonstrated the robustness of the core parenting intervention methods developed during the previous period in managing a wide range of clinical problems, including children with developmental disabilities with serious challenging behaviors (Plant & Sanders, in press; Sanders & Plant, 1989); children with recurrent pain syndromes (Sanders et al., 1990); children with feeding disorders (Turner, Sanders, & Wall, 1994); and children with ADHD (Bor, Sanders, & Markie-Dadds, 2002). Studies were also conducted to show how diverse types of family problems could benefit including maritally discordant couples (Dadds, Schwartz, & Sanders, 1987); depressed parents (Sanders & McFarland, 2000); stepparents (Nicholson & Sanders, 1999); and parent with anger management difficulties (Sanders, Pidgeon, et al., 2004). This phase of development continues and Triple P has been further extended to other parenting problems including the parenting of children who are overweight or obese, children who have experienced the breakdown of their parents' relationships, and teenagers experiencing conflictual relationships with their parents.

3. *Development of a public health framework for the delivery of parenting interventions (1992 to present).* It became apparent that not all parents either wanted or required the same level or intensity of intervention to solve a behavior problem or address a parenting issue (see Sanders, 1992a). The term *Triple P* was first used in 1993 to describe an early intervention project, the Positive Parenting of Preschoolers that provided intensive early parenting interventions for parents of preschool children who were at high risk for serious conduct problems.

From 1995 onward, the term was applied to all behavioral family intervention programs developed at the Parenting and Family Support Center at the University of Queensland. The shift from considering parenting programs as a form of treatment or early intervention for children with well-established problems to conceptualizing parenting programs in a broader public health framework represented a major shift in focus. A series of studies was conducted that showed that briefer, more cost-effective parenting programs were feasible and could produce meaningful outcomes. These studies included clinical trials examining the impact of the television programs on parenting (Sanders, Montgomery, & Brechman-Toussaint, 2000), small and large group parenting programs (Zubrick et al., 2005), and self-directed (Markie-Dadds & Sanders, 2006) and telephone-assisted programs (Connell, Sanders, & Markie-Dadds, 1997). The ultimate aim of this work was to develop a suite of flexible evidence-based delivery options that would increase the population reach of parenting programs.

4. *Development of a comprehensive training and accreditation system to disseminate Triple P (1996 to present).* The establishment of the Parenting and Family Support Center at the University of Queensland in Brisbane in 1996 heralded a new stage in the evolution of Triple P, namely the development of a system to disseminate Triple P to service providers and agencies, initially within Australia and subsequently to a number of other countries. The need to establish a comprehensive system of training and accreditation also provided an opportunity to develop a model of dissemination and to examine the impact on professional practices of the training and dissemination process itself (Sanders, Murphy-Brennan, & McAuliffe, 2003; Sanders & Turner, 2002; Turner & Sanders, 2006). As of early 2007, 15 countries were involved in the implementation of Triple P programs and over 20,000 service providers had been trained to deliver Triple P interventions to parents in their communities.

PARENTAL SELF-REGULATION: A UNIFYING CONCEPTUAL FRAMEWORK

The development of a parent's capacity for self-regulation is viewed as a central goal of Triple P with parents. This involves teaching parents skills that enable them to become independent problem solvers. Karoly (1993) defined self-regulation as follows: "Self-regulation refers to those processes, internal and or transactional, that enable an individual to guide his or her goal directed activities over time and across changing circumstances (contexts). Regulation implies modulation of thought, affect, behavior, and attention via deliberate or automated use of specific mechanisms and supportive metaskills. The processes of self-regulation are initiated when routinized activity is impeded or when goal directedness is otherwise made salient (e.g., The appearance of a challenge, the failure of habitual patterns) . . . " (p. 25). This definition emphasizes that self-regulatory processes are embedded in a social context that not only provides opportunities and limitations for individual self-directedness, but implies a dynamic reciprocal interchange between the internal and external determinants of human motivation. Self-regulation is a process whereby individuals are taught skills to modify their own behavior.

This self-regulatory framework used in Triple P is operationalized to include:

- *Self-sufficiency:* As a parenting program is time limited, parents need to become independent problem solvers so they trust their own judgment and become less reliant on others in carrying out basic parenting responsibilities. Self-sufficient parents are viewed as having the necessary resilience, personal resources, knowledge, and skills they require to parent with confidence with minimal or no additional support. It is hypothesized that the more self-sufficient parents become, the more likely they are to seek appropriate support when they need it, to advocate for children, become involved in their child's schooling, and to protect children from harm (e.g., by managing conflict with partners, and creating a secure low-conflict environment). The intervention process seeks to help parents become increasingly autonomous of the service providers in making parenting decisions.
- *Parental self-efficacy:* This refers to a parent's belief that they can overcome or solve a specific parenting or child management problem. Parents with high self-efficacy have more positive expectations that change is possible. Parents of children with behavior problems tend to have lower task specific self-efficacy in managing their daily parenting responsibilities (Sanders & Wooley, 2005). A central goal of the intervention process is to foster greater confidence.
- *Self-management:* Self-management refers to the tools or skills that parents use to enable them to change their parenting practices and become self-sufficient. These skills include self-monitoring, self-determination of performance goals and standards, self-evaluation against some performance criterion, and self-selection of parenting strategies. As each parent is responsible for the way they choose to raise their children, parents select which aspects of their own and their child's behavior they wish to work on. They learn to set developmentally appropriate goals, choose specific parenting and child

management techniques they wish to implement, and self-evaluate their success with their chosen goals against self-determined criteria. Triple P aims to help parents make informed decisions by sharing knowledge and skills derived from research into effective child rearing practices. An active skills training process, involving a self-regulation framework, is incorporated into Triple P to enable skills to be modeled and practiced. Parents are observed interacting with their child and receive feedback regarding their implementation of skills using a self-regulation framework (see Sanders & Dadds, 1993).

- *Personal agency:* Here parents are encouraged to own the change process. This involves attributing changes or improvements in their family situation to their own or their child's efforts rather than to chance, age, maturational factors, or other uncontrollable events (e.g., spouses' poor parenting or genes). This outcome is achieved by prompting parents to identify causes or explanations for their child's or their own behavior and encouraging parents to challenge and change negative or dysfunctional attributions that blame the child (e.g., "He's is deliberately doing this just to upset me").

Triple P teaches parents strategies to encourage self-regulation in children. It does this by teaching parents strategies that foster children's social and language skills, emotional self-regulation, independence, and problem-solving ability. It is hypothesized that attainment of these skills promotes family harmony, reduces parent-child conflict, fosters successful peer relationships, and prepares children for school.

PRINCIPLES OF POSITIVE PARENTING

Five core positive parenting principles form the basis of the program. These principles address specific risk and protective factors known to predict positive developmental and mental health outcomes in children. Tables 7.2 and 7.3 show how these core principles are operationalized into 18 basic parenting skills.

A Safe and Engaging Environment

Children of all ages need a safe, supervised, and therefore protective environment that provides opportunities for them to explore, experiment, and play. This principle is essential to promote healthy development and to prevent accidents and injuries in the home (Peterson & Saldana, 1996; Risley, Clark, & Cataldo, 1976; Wesch & Lutzker, 1991). It also is relevant to older children and adolescents who need adequate supervision and

Table 7.2
Promoting Social Competence in Children

Type of Strategy	Description	Recommended Ages	Applications
Spending quality time with children	Involves spending frequent brief (30 sec to 3 minutes) uninterrupted time involved in child preferred activity.	All ages	Conveys interest and caring for the child; provides opportunities for child to self-disclose and practice conversational skills.
Conversing with children	Brief conversations with children about an activity or interest of the child.	All ages	Vocabulary, conversational and social skills.
Giving plenty of physical affection	Providing contingent positive attention following prosocial or other appropriate behavior.	All ages	Holding, touching, cuddling, tickling, kissing, or hugging.
Praising children	Using descriptive praise to encourage a behavior that a parent would like to see repeated.	All ages	Showing appreciation for appropriate child behavior; motivating the child and developing the child's self-esteem.
Giving attention	Providing contingent positive attention following prosocial or other appropriate behavior.	All ages	Speaking in a pleasant voice, playing cooperatively, sharing, reading, compliance.
Providing engaging activities for children	Involves arranging the child's physical and social environment with people, objects, materials, and age-appropriate toys.	All ages	Board games, paper, paints, pens, tapes, books, construction toys, balls, and so on.
Setting a good example through modeling	Providing the child a demonstration of desirable behavior through the use of parental modeling.	All ages	Social skills, self-help skills, self-management skills.
Using incidental teaching	Using a series of graded prompts to respond to child-initiated language interactions.	All ages	Language utterances, problem solving, cognitive ability.
Encouraging independence through Ask, Say, Do	Using verbal, gestural, and manual prompts to teach children self-care skills.	3 to 12 years	Self-care skills (brushing teeth, making bed, tidying up).
Good behavior charts	Providing social attention and backup rewards contingent on the performance of a desired behavior (or the absence of an undesirable behavior).	2 to 12 years	Doing homework, chores, sleeping in own bed, eating appropriately, playing cooperatively.

Table 7.3

Reducing Problem Behavior

Type of strategy	Description	Recommended Ages	Applications
Establishing clear ground rules	Negotiating in advance a set of fair, specific, and enforceable rules that apply in particular situations.	3 to 12 years	Watching TV, shopping trips, visiting relatives, going out in the car.
Directed discussion	Identifying the problem behavior, identifying an alternative, and rehearsing the correct behavior, contingent on rule breaking.	3 to 12 years	Leaving the school bag on floor in kitchen, leaving a mess on the table, walking in the house with boots on.
Planned ignoring	Withdrawal of attention while minor problem behavior continues.	1to 7 years	Answering back, protesting after a consequence, crying and whining.
Giving clear calm instructions	A clear, specific instruction to the child to engage in a specific behavior, carry out some task or activity, or cease incorrect behavior.	2 to 12 years	Daily tasks, dangerous play.
Logical consequences	Providing a specific consequence that involves either the removal of an activity from the child or the child from an activity.	2 to 12 years	Leaving a bike in the drive, toys in the hall, fighting over television programs.
Quiet time	Involves placing the child in a chair or bean-bag in the same environment as other family members for a specific time period, contingent on a problem behavior.	18 months to 10 years	Squealing, temper outburst, whining, demanding, hitting, noncompliance.
Time-out	The removal of a child to an area away from other family members for a specified time period, contingent on a problem behavior.	2 to 10 years	Aggressive behavior, severe tantrums.
Planned activities	Providing engaging activities in specific high-risk situations.	All ages	Out of home disruptions (e.g., shopping trips, visiting, traveling in a car, bus, train).

213

monitoring in an appropriate developmental context (Dishion & McMahon, 1998; Forehand, Miller, Dutra, & Chance, 1997).

A Positive Learning Environment

Although this involves educating parents in their role as their child's first teacher, the program specifically targets how parents can respond positively and constructively to child-initiated interactions (e.g., requests for help, information, advice, attention) through incidental teaching and other techniques to assist children learn to solve problems for themselves. Incidental teaching involves parents being receptive to child-initiated interactions when children attempt to communicate with their parents. The procedure has been used extensively in the teaching of language, social skills, and social problem solving (e.g., Hart & Risley, 1975). A related technique known as "Ask, Say, Do" involves parents breaking down complex skills into discrete steps and teaching children the skill sequentially (in a forward fashion) through the use of graded series of prompts from the least to the most intrusive.

Assertive Discipline

Triple P teaches parents specific child management and behavior change strategies that are alternatives to coercive and ineffective discipline practices (such as shouting, threatening, or using physical punishment). These strategies include: selecting ground rules for specific situations; discussing rules with children; giving clear, calm, age-appropriate instructions and requests; logical consequences; quiet time (nonexclusionary time out); time-out; and planned ignoring. Parents are taught to use these skills in a variety of home and community settings (e.g., getting ready to go out, having visitors, and going shopping) to promote the generalization of parenting skills to diverse parenting situations (see Sanders & Dadds, 1993, for more detail).

Realistic Expectations

This involves exploring with parents their expectations, assumptions, and beliefs about the causes of children's behavior and choosing goals that are developmentally appropriate for the child and realistic for the parent. There is evidence that parents who are at risk of abusing their children are more likely to have unrealistic expectations of children's capabilities (Azar & Rohrbeck, 1986). Developmentally appropriate expectations are taught in the context of parent's specific expectations concerning difficult and prosocial behaviors rather than through the more traditional age and stages approach to teaching about child development.

TAKING CARE OF ONESELF AS A PARENT

Parenting is affected by a range of factors that impact on a parent's self-esteem and sense of well-being. All levels of Triple P specifically address this issue by encouraging parents to view parenting as part of a larger context of personal self-care, resourcefulness, and well-being and by teaching parents practical parenting skills that both parents are able to implement. In more intensive levels of intervention (Level 5), couples are also taught effective marital communication skills and are encouraged to explore how their own emotional state affects their parenting and consequently their child's behavior. Parents develop specific coping strategies for managing difficult emotions including depression, anger, anxiety, and high levels of parenting stress.

These five principles are translated into a series of specific parenting strategies. The program content draws from:

1. Social learning models of parent-child interaction that highlight the reciprocal and bidirectional nature of parent-child interactions (e.g., Patterson, 1982). This model identifies learning mechanisms, which maintain coercive and dysfunctional patterns of family interaction and predicts future antisocial behavior in children (Patterson, Reid, & Dishion, 1992). As such, the Triple P program specifically teaches parents positive child management skills as an alternative to coercive parenting practices.

2. Research in child and family behavior therapy and applied behavior analysis that has developed many useful behavior change strategies, particularly research which focuses on rearranging antecedents of problem behavior through designing more positive engaging environments for children (Risley et al., 1976; Sanders, 1992a, 1996).

3. Developmental research on parenting in everyday contexts. The program targets children's competencies in naturally occurring everyday contexts, drawing heavily on work which traces the origins of social and intellectual competence to early parent-child relationships (e.g., Hart & Risley, 1995). Children's risk of developing severe behavioral and emotional problems is reduced by teaching parents to use naturally occurring daily interactions to teach children language, social skills and developmental competencies, and problem-solving skills in an emotionally supportive context. Particular emphasis is placed on using child-initiated interactions as a context for the use of incidental teaching (Hart & Risley, 1975). Children are at greater risk for adverse developmental outcomes, including behavioral problems, if they fail to acquire core language competencies and impulse control during early childhood (Hart & Risley, 1995).

4. Social information processing models that highlight the important role of parental cognitions such as attributions, expectancies, and beliefs as factors that contribute to parental self-efficacy, decision making, and behavioral intentions (e.g., Bandura, 1977; 1995). Parent's attributions are specifically targeted in the intervention by encouraging parents to identify alternative nonblaming social interactional explanations for their child's behavior.

5. Research from the field of developmental psychopathology has identified specific risk and protective factors that are linked to adverse developmental outcomes in children (e.g., Emery, 1982; Grych & Fincham, 1990; Hart & Risley, 1995; Rutter, 1985). Specifically the risk factors of poor parent management practices, marital family conflict, and parental distress are targeted risk factors. Because parental discord is a specific risk factor for many forms of child and adolescent psychopathology (Grych & Fincham, 1990; Rutter, 1985; Sanders, Nicholson, & Floyd, 1997), the program fosters collaboration, teamwork, and good communication between caregivers in raising children. Improving couples communication is an important vehicle to reduce marital conflict over child-rearing issues, and to reduce personal distress of parents and children in conflictual relationships (Sanders, Markie-Dadds, & Turner, 1998).

A PUBLIC HEALTH APPROACH TO PARENTING

A public health perspective to parenting and family intervention involves the explicit recognition of the role of the broader ecological context for human development (e.g., Biglan, 1995; Mrazek & Haggerty, 1994; National Institute of Mental Health, 1998). A public health perspective introduces notions such as the reach of interventions, their cost effectiveness, and the need for the community context for parenting to change (Biglan, 1995).

The case for adopting a public health approach to parenthood preparation is a compelling one. Large numbers of children develop potentially preventable behavioral and emotional problems. In a large scale survey of parenting practices in Australia, nearly half of the parents reported using discipline strategies for dealing with children's misbehavior that are considered ineffective or coercive (Sanders et al., in press). Only a minority of parents (14%) had completed any sort of parenting program. Although there is clear evidence that parenting programs work, evidence-based parenting programs are underutilized and reach relatively few parents.

The majority of the workforce who parents turn to for guidance and advice regarding children's development and who are potentially in a position to support parents (e.g., family doctors and teachers), are not trained to use evidence-based parenting interventions or to do so effectively. Existing approaches to parent education simply do not reach enough parents to make any real difference at a population level and large numbers of children continue to develop potentially preventable behavioral and emotional problems.

There are several other public health concepts that differentiate Triple P as a system of parenting intervention:

- *Principle of program sufficiency:* This concept refers to the notion that parents differ in the strength of intervention they may require to enable them to independently manage a problem. Triple P aims to provide the minimally sufficient level of support parents require. For example, parents seeking advice on a specific topic (e.g., tantrums) receive clear high-quality, behaviorally specific advice in the form of a parenting tip sheet on how to manage or prevent a specific problem. For such a parent Levels 1 or 2 of Triple P would constitute a sufficient intervention.
- *Flexible tailoring to identified risk and protective factors:* The program enables parents to receive parenting support in the most cost-effective way possible. Within this context, a number of different programs of varying intensity have been developed. For example, Level 5 provides intervention for additional family risk factors, such as marital conflict, mood disturbance, and high levels of stress.
- *Varied delivery modalities:* Several of the levels of intervention in Triple P can be delivered in a variety of formats, including individual face-to-face, group, telephone-assisted, self-directed programs, or a combination. This flexibility enables parents to participate in ways that suit their individual circumstances and allows participation from families in rural and remote areas who typically have less access to professional services.
- *Wide reach:* Triple P is designed to be implemented as an entire integrated system at a population level (Table 7.4). However, the multilevel nature of the program enables various combinations of the intervention levels and modalities within levels to be used flexibly as either universal, indicated, or selective prevention strategies depending on local priorities, staffing, and budget constraints. Some communities using Triple P use the entire multilevel system, while others may focus on getting the Level 4 group program implemented at a population level, while seeking funding support for the other levels of intervention.
- *A multidisciplinary approach:* Many different professional groups provide counsel and advice to parents. Triple P was developed as a professional resource that can be used by a range of helping professionals. These professionals include community nurses,

Table 7.4

Core Parenting Skills Introduced in Triple P

Basic Skills	
Parent-child relationship Enhancement skills	Spending brief quality time Talking with children Showing affection
Encouraging desirable behavior	Giving descriptive praise Giving nonverbal attention Providing engaging activities
Teaching new skills and behaviors	Setting a good example Using incidental teaching Using ask, say, do Using behavior charts
Managing misbehavior	Establishing ground rules Using directed discussion Using planned ignoring Giving clear, calm instructions Using logical consequences Using quiet time Using time-out
Anticipating and planning	Planning and advanced preparation Discussing ground rules for specific situations Selecting engaging activities Providing incentives Providing consequences Holding follow-up discussions
Self-regulation skills	Monitoring children's behavior Monitoring own behavior Setting developmentally appropriate goals Setting practice tasks Self-evaluation of strengths and weaknesses Setting personal goals for change
Enhanced Skills	
Mood and coping skills	Catching unhelpful thoughts Relaxation and stress management Developing personal coping statements Challenging unhelpful thoughts Developing coping plans for high risk situations
Partner support skills	Improving personal communication habits Giving and receiving constructive feedback Having casual conversations Supporting each other when problem behavior occurs Problem solving Improving relationship happiness

family doctors, pediatricians, teachers, social workers, psychologists, psychiatrists, and police officers to name a few. At a community level, rigid professional boundaries are discouraged and an emphasis is put on providing training and support for a variety of professionals to become more effective in their parent consultation skills.

PROGRAM DESCRIPTION

Triple P involves several different types of interventions depending on the severity of the presenting problem and its associated risk and protective factors. Each program variant in the Triple P system has its own intervention protocol and extensive program resources. These resources include practitioner kits that include a practitioner manual that provides detailed session guidelines, power point presentations, parent workbooks, and, depending on the level of intervention, a companion DVD or video for use with parents. Separate practitioner manuals have been developed for the following individual programs: Selected Triple P, Primary Care Triple P, Standard Triple P, Enhanced Triple P, Pathways Triple P, Group Triple P, Selected Teen Triple P, Primary Care Teen Triple P, and Group Teen Triple P. Each protocol is written with extensive information on how the protocol can be tailored to the needs of the presenting case.

SESSION PROTOCOL

Table 7.5 provides an example of the session content and therapeutic goals and tasks from one of the Triple P programs, namely the Group Triple P program (a Level 4 program).

RESEARCH FINDINGS

Triple P has a large and growing evidence base to support its efficacy and effectiveness (Sanders, 1999; Sanders, Markie-Dadds, Turner, & Ralph, 2004; Sanders & Turner, 2002). Twenty-five years of research involving a large number of randomized controlled trials evaluating the different levels and delivery modalities in the Triple P system show that the suite of programs comprising the system are effective in reducing disruptive behaviors in young children. The program has been evaluated in culturally, racially, and linguistically diverse contexts, involving several different regions and language groups in Asia, Europe, North America, and Australasia (see Leung, Sanders, Leung, Mak, & Lau, 2003). It has also been evaluated with many different family types (e.g., two-parent, single-parent, stepparent) and with quite diverse SES groups. The age of target children have ranged from toddlers to teenagers, who have had a range of different behavior problems.

Collectively, these studies (see Sanders, 1999, for a review) consistently show that children of parents receiving Triple P engage in less problem behavior after intervention, and the effects typically maintain over time. Many studies have also shown other familywide benefits, including reduced coercive discipline, parental depression, stress, and

Table 7.5

Overview of Session Content for Group Triple P

Session	Core Content Covered	Therapeutic Goals and Tasks	Duration (Minutes)
1 Positive parenting	Working as a group What is positive parenting? Causes of child behavior problems Goals for change Keeping track of children's behavior	Establishing a commitment and climate for change Introduction to the five main principles of positive parenting Helping parents identify possible causes for their child's behavior problem Establishing age appropriate goals Monitoring and keeping track of child's behavior	120
2 Promoting children's development	Developing positive relationships with children Encouraging desirable behavior Teaching new skills and behaviors	Video modeling, discussion, and practicing of 10 positive parenting strategies including: brief quality time; talking to children; affection; praise; attention; behavior charts; Ask, Say, Do; incidental teaching; activities	120
3 Managing misbehavior	Managing misbehavior Developing parenting routines Behavior charts	Video modeling, discussion, and practice of seven basic discipline strategies including: ground rules, directed discussion, planned ignoring, clear instructions, logical consequences, quiet time, time-out	
4 Planning ahead	Family survival tips High risk situations Planned activities routines Preparing for telephone sessions	Introduction of teamwork Introduction to planned activities training Planning for commencement of individual phone calls	120

Session		Content	Time (min)
5 Implementing parenting poutines 1	Preparing for the session Update on progress Other issues	Using telephone consultation via self-regulation approach to foster independent problem solving Parent prepares agenda Therapist prompts parent to review goals and report on progress Therapist prompts parent to set new goals to select strategy for goal attainment Therapist helps parent to set specific homework tasks and asks parent to summarize their action plan	15–30
6 Implementing parenting poutines 2	Preparing for the session Update on progress Other issues		15–30
7 Implementing parenting poutines 3	Preparing for the session Update on progress Other issues		15–30
8 Program close	Preparing for the session Update on progress Maintaining changes Other issues	Parent reviews program to date Parent undertakes exercise to promote generalization and transfer of knowledge and problem solving skills to future and nontargeted child behaviors Completion of post assessment Celebration of course completion	15–30

marital conflict, increased parental self-efficacy and satisfaction, and high consumer satisfaction.

Research concerning the efficacy of Triple P has met a number of important scientific criteria:

- *Replicated findings:* The primary intervention effects of Triple P, showing that decreases in parents' negative disciplinary behavior and increases in their use of positive attention and other relationship enhancing skills lead to improved child behavior, have been replicated in different studies, involving different investigators, in several different countries, with a diverse variety of client populations (Sanders, 1999).

- *Demonstrations of effectiveness with varied clinical problems:* The empirical basis of Triple P is strengthened by evidence that the basic approach to working with parents can be successfully applied to many clinical problems and disorders, including conduct problems (e.g., Zubrick et al., in press), attention deficit hyperactivity disorder (Bor et al., 2002), persistent feeding difficulties (Turner et al., 1994), recurrent pain syndromes (Sanders, Shepherd, Cleghorn, & Woolford, 1994), developmental disabilities (Plant & Sanders, in press), habit disorders (Christensen & Sanders, 1987), as well as everyday problems of normal children (see Sanders, 1996; Taylor & Biglan, 1998, for reviews of this literature).

- *Impact on other areas of family functioning:* It is also becoming evident that the benefits of these interventions are not restricted to children, with several studies reporting beneficial effects in other areas of family functioning, including reduced maternal depression, stress, and anger; increased parental satisfaction and efficacy; reduced couple conflict over parenting issues; and improved functioning at work (e.g., Martin & Sanders, 2003; Nicholson & Sanders, 1999; Sanders, Markie-Dadds, Tully, & Bor, 2000; Sanders & McFarland, 2000; Sanders, Pidgeon, et al., 2004).

- *The effectiveness of different delivery modalities:* There is increasing evidence showing that a variety of delivery modalities can produce similar positive outcomes for children, including individual programs (e.g., Sanders & Dadds, 1982; Sanders, Markie-Dadds, et al., 2000), group programs (e.g., Sanders, Pidgeon, et al., 2004; Zubrick et al., in press), telephone-assisted programs (e.g., Connell et al., 1997; Markie-Dadds & Sanders, 2005; Morawska & Sanders, 2006), and completely self-directed programs (Markie-Dadds & Sanders, 2005, 2006; Sanders, Montgomery, et al., 2000).

- *High levels of consumer acceptability:* High levels of consumer satisfaction have been repeatedly demonstrated in different controlled evaluations of Triple P and for specific parenting techniques advocated (e.g., Sanders, Markie-Dabbs, et al., 2000).

- *Effectiveness with a range of family types:* Triple P has been successfully used with two biological parent families, stepparents, and single parents.

MODERATOR, MEDIATOR VARIABLES

Triple P studies have been conducted with a wide range of parents from diverse socioeconomic and cultural backgrounds. McTaggart and Sanders (in press) examined the role of sociodemographic and family risk factors as mediators or moderators of the success of parents undertaking a universal group parent training program for preschool children. The results showed that parent's capacity to change their dysfunctional parenting practices were not moderated by the child's gender, family income, family type, or preintervention level of parental stress, but were partially mediated by changes in parental satisfaction and efficacy. Irrespective of their sociodemographic background, parents who completed Triple P were equally likely to succeed in changing their parenting practices.

Overall, few pretreatment characteristics of parents have differentiated between families who do well in Triple P compared to those who do not, at least in parents who complete the program. However, there is some evidence that sociodemographic characteristics are related to program completion. Zubrick et al. (2005) found that parents who received less than 7 hours of Triple P (low participation) were significantly more likely than those who received 7 or more hours (high participation) to be in blended or sole parent families, have less than year 10 schooling, earn less than $20,000 per year in family income, and to be single or in a de facto relationship rather than in a first marriage. Parents with lower levels of Triple P participation were also more likely to report significantly higher levels of depression, anxiety, and stress. There were no statistically significant differences in the proportion of children with clinically elevated behavior problems.

Information concerning factors that moderate or mediate intervention outcomes in cross-cultural samples is relatively limited. However, some research is emerging. For example, Leung, Sanders, Ip, and Lau (in press) examined the response of 661 parents of preschool and primary-school-aged children to Group Triple P. There were significant decreases in disruptive child behaviors, levels of parenting stress, general stress, and anxiety and an increase in parenting sense of competence. Greater change in reports of child behavior problems was related to lower levels of family income, new immigrant family status, and higher preintervention levels of parenting stress.

CASE STUDY

The Family
Target child: Jamie (aged 3 years 4 months)
Sibling: Sarah (aged 5 years 5 months)
Mother: Jane (aged 32)
Father: Tom (aged 33)

PRESENTING CONCERNS

Jane and Tom signed up to do the Triple P Group Program because of their 3-year-old son Jamie's behavior. Jane complained of a variety of behavior problems, the most concerning of which were violence toward both his parents and his older sister (including hitting, punching, kicking, and head butting), swearing, temper tantrums both at home and in public, and bedtime problems. At home, his tantrums often involved ransacking his room and destroying his toys in anger in response to being reprimanded or prevented from having what he wanted. According to Jane, Jamie's behavior in public was so bad and embarrassing that shopping trips and outings were often cut short or avoided altogether because they were so traumatic. One of the biggest concerns for Jane was Jamie's bedtime behavior. Jamie had a TV and video player permanently set up in his room and refused to go to bed without the TV on. Once in bed, Jamie would repeatedly call out and get up throughout the night, asking for food, drinks, and toys. For Jane and Tom, keeping Jamie in bed all night was almost impossible, and as a consequence the entire family's sleep was disrupted with Jane only able to get approximately 4 hours of sleep per night. Jane and Tom felt that they had tried everything to try to control Jamie and handle his behavior but said that nothing except "bribery" worked. This "bribery" involved giving Jamie little presents whenever he was behaving badly so that he would change his mood and calm down, allowing his mother a brief moment of peace. By the time the family presented to the clinic, this strategy was costing them a great deal of money per month because Jane was buying Jamie a couple of presents every day. She reported finding it very difficult to say no to him, because she knew how he would react if she did. Jane and Tom presented to the clinic feeling extremely stressed, tired, and out of control, as though their lives were being ruled by their 3-year-old child. They were very motivated to bring about significant changes to their home life.

Assessment

Initial assessment of the family involved an intake interview, an observation of parent-child interaction in the home, and the completion of standardized questionnaires. Interview and parent-child observation data revealed a number of important maintenance factors contributing to Jamie's behavior problems (e.g., accidental reward for aggressive behavior, inconsistent bedtime routine, vague instructions, disagreement between parents regarding discipline, and some coercive punishment). Jane and Tom completed a series of questionnaires both before and after the Triple P program to ascertain change. Results are presented in Table 7.6. The following measures were completed: the Eyeberg Child Behavior Inventory (ECBI), the Problem Setting Checklist (PSC), the Depression Anxiety Stress Scale (DASS), the Parent Problem Checklist (PPC), and the Parenting Scale (PS). On almost all of these measures, both Jane and Tom scored in the clinical range of severity at pretesting. The ECBI scores for parental perceptions of frequency of disruptive behavior were extremely high before the program. Jane and Tom scored 186 and 177 respectively on this measure, far exceeding the clinical range cutoff of 132. Also, out of 36 potential behavioral problems, Jane reported 26 and Tom reported 20 of these as consistent difficulties for them, with a score of 15 being the cutoff for clinical severity. While measures of depression and stress were within the normal to mild range for both parents on the DASS, scores for dysfunctional parenting styles as measured by the Parenting Scale were clinically elevated for both parents. On the Parent-Problem Checklist, Jane and Tom both reported a high degree of interparental conflict over child-rearing and family management scoring 8 and 10 respectively,

Table 7.6
Clinical Outcomes for Jamie and His Parents

Measure	Pre	Post	Showed Reliable Change	Moved Out of Clinical Range
Mother				
ECBI intensity	186	99	Yes	Yes
ECBI problem	26	5	Yes	Yes
Problem setting checklist	66.43	94	Yes	Yes
Depression	6	0	Yes	
Stress	16	1	Yes	Yes
Parent problem checklist	8	3	Yes	Yes
Parenting scale	4.4	2.4	Yes	Yes
Father				
ECBI intensity	177	86	Yes	Yes
ECBI problem	20	1	Yes	Yes
Problem setting checklist	55	91.4	Yes	Yes
Depression	0	0	No	
Stress	7	2	Yes	
Parent problem checklist	10	0	Yes	Yes
Parenting scale	3.1	1.2	Yes	Yes

exceeding the clinical range cutoff score of 5. Their PSC scores showed that both parents had a very low level of confidence in dealing with Jamie in various daily situations.

INTERVENTION

Jane and Tom participated in the Group Triple P Program conducted by the author, delivered over an 8-week period. Parents participating in Group Triple P are provided with specific developmental and child management advice to optimize their child's development. The program is an eight-session training program delivered in groups of 10 to 12 parents who have children between the ages of 2 to 12 years. There are four 2-hour group sessions and four 15- to 30-minute telephone sessions with each participant following the completion of the group sessions. Telephone sessions are used to provide additional support to parents as they put into practice what they have learned in the group sessions. Both parents are encouraged to participate and to discuss their participation in the program with relevant staff if their child attends daycare, kindergarten, or preschool. (See Table 7.3 for a summary of the major program content for each session.)

OUTCOMES

As shown in Table 7.6, Jane's postprogram assessment scores revealed a substantial improvement on all measures Anecdotal reports taken from an interview with the mother following the program indicated the kinds of changes experienced by the family. "Everything we wanted to achieve, we have. We can go out more often and people comment on how well behaved Jamie is. He now sleeps throughout the night, with no TV in his room and we sleep better ourselves. He is getting presents as rewards for good behavior now as opposed to before when he was getting presents to divert his attention from a tantrum. Family life is generally much more pleasurable. One of things that has made the biggest difference is that everyone speaks nicely to each other at home. Relations between all of us have improved. There is a stronger bond between Jamie and us as parents. I feel in control now. Being firm, decisive, calm, and consistent are the keys for me."

TRAINING AND DISSEMINATION MODEL

Triple P has been widely disseminated both in Australia and overseas to health, education, and welfare professionals through a professional training and accreditation system (Sanders, 1999). An ecological approach is taken to the dissemination of Triple P (Sanders, Markie-

Dadds, & Turner, 2003). This perspective views changing professionals' consulting practices as being a complex interaction between the quality of the intervention itself (i.e., Triple P), the quality of the skills training and the practitioner's posttraining support environment. The dissemination process combines two complementary perspectives: (1) a systems-contextual organizational intervention that aims to promote and support practitioners' program use; and (2) a self-regulatory approach that promotes professional behavior change through self-directed learning. The systems-contextual approach views the attitudes, knowledge, receptivity to innovation, and consulting practices of professionals as being embedded within the broader organizational environment within which the practitioner works (Biglan, Mrazek, & Carnine, 1999). Specifically, professional change is thought more likely to occur when supervisors, managers, and professional colleagues support the adoption or change process (Bacher, Liberman, & Kuehnel, 1986; Parcel, Perry, & Taylor, 1990); when peer supervision, feedback, and support is available (Henggeler, Melton, Brondino, Scherer, & Hanley, 1997), and where computer technologies such as the Web and email services are used to support and provide consultative backup to professionals (Sanders, 2001). As argued by Ash (1997), in organizations where a culture of innovation is supported by management through the provision of resources and attention, a greater success in establishing and implementing new projects is predicted.

CONCLUSION

Parenting interventions are among the most powerful and cost-effective tools available to improve children's health and well-being. Good parenting should be the centerpiece of public health efforts to promote children's well-being and prevent major mental health, social, and educational problems in children and young people. However, evidence-based parenting programs need to be much more widely available if the prevalence of serious behavioral and emotional problems in children is to be reduced.

An evidence-based parenting program should always be a work in progress. We have tried to adhere closely to the principle that all programs that become part of the suite of Triple P interventions are subjected to close empirical scrutiny. This has seen the evolution of several derivative programs to meet the needs of particular parents including the development of Stepping Stones Triple P for parents of a child with a disability (Sanders, Mazzucchelli, & Studman, 2004), and Pathways Triple P for children involved in the child protection system (Sanders & Pidgeon, 2005). Other programs under development include an Indigenous version of Group Triple P, Lifestyle Triple P for parents of overweight and obese children (West & Sanders, in press), Teen Triple P (Sanders & Ralph, 2001), and Family Transitions Triple P for divorcing parents. A commitment to ensuring that all programs have a strong evidence base means that a close working relationship is required between program developers, evaluators, agencies, service providers, and consumers (including children and adolescents) to ensure that a program continues to evolve and respond to evidence stemming from service base use of disseminated programs.

ACKNOWLEDGMENTS

Triple P is the result of the dedication, hard work, and creativity of many staff and students at the Parenting and Family Support Center at the University of Queensland. There are several key contributors who have coauthored Triple P materials including Karen Turner, Alan Ralph, Carol Markie-Dadds, Trevor Mazucchelli, Lisa Studman, and Aileen Pidgeon. Other important research collaborators in research projects relating to parenting interventions Mark Dadds, Jan Nicholson, Margaret McFarland, Karen Plant, Bill Bor, Ross Shepherd, Clare Wall, and Geoffrey Cleghorn.

REFERENCES

Ash, J. (1997). Organizational factors that influence information technology diffusion in academic health science centers. *Journal of the American Information Association, 4,* 102–111.

Azar, S. T., & Rohrbeck, C. A. (1986). Child abuse and unrealistic expectations: Further validation of the Parent Opinion Questionnaire. *Journal of Consulting and Clinical Psychology, 54,* 867–868.

Bacher, T. E., Lieberman, R. P., & Kuehnel, T. G. (1986). Dissemination and adoption of innovative psychosocial interventions. *Journal of Consulting and Clinical Psychology, 54,* 111–118.

Baer, D., Wolf, M., & Risley, T. (1968). Some current dimensions of applied behavior analysis. *Journal of Applied Behavior Analysis, 1*(1), 91–97.

Baer, D., Wolf, M., & Risley, T. (1987). Some still-current dimensions of applied behavior analysis. *Journal of Applied Behavior Analysis, 20*(4), 313–327.

Bandura, A. (1977). Self-efficacy: Toward a unifying theory of behavioral change. *Psychological Review, 84,* 191–215.

Bandura, A. (1995). Exercise of personal and collective efficacy in changing societies. In A. Bandura (Ed.), *Self-efficacy in changing societies* (pp. 1–45). New York: Cambridge University Press.

Biglan, A. (1995). Translating what we know about the context of antisocial behavior into a lower prevalence of such behavior. *Journal of Applied Behavior Analysis, 28,* 479–492.

Biglan, A., Mrazek, P. J., & Carnine, D. (1999). *Strategies for translating research into practice.* Unpublished manuscript.

Bor, B., Sanders, M. R., & Markie-Dadds, C. (2002). The effects of the Triple P–Positive Parenting Program on preschool children with co-occurring disruptive behavior and attentional/hyperactive difficulties. *Journal of Abnormal Child Psychology, 30,* 571–587.

Chamberlain, P., & Patterson, G. R. (1995). Discipline and child compliance in parenting. In M. H. Bornstein (Eds.), *Handbook of parenting: Vol. 4. Applied and practical parenting* (pp. 205–225). Mahwah, NJ: Erlbaum.

Christensen, A. P., & Sanders, M. R. (1987). Habit reversal and differential reinforcement of other behavior in the treatment of thumbsucking: An analysis of generalization and side-effects. *Journal of Child Psychology and Psychiatry, 28*(2), 281–295.

Coie, J. D. (1996). Prevention of violence and antisocial behavior. In R. D. Peters & R. J. McMahon (Eds.), *Preventing childhood disorders, substance abuse, and delinquency* (pp. 1–18). Thousand Oaks, CA: Sage.

Collins, W. A., Maccoby, E. E., Steinberg, L., Hetherington, E. M., & Bornstein, M. H. (2000). Contemporary research on parenting: The case for nature and nurture. *American Psychologist, 55,* 218–232.

Connell, S., Sanders, M. R., & Markie-Dadds, C. (1997). Self-directed behavioral family intervention for parents of oppositional children in rural and remote areas. *Behavior Modification, 21,* 379–408.

Cummings, E. M., & Davies, P. (1994). *Children and marital conflict: The impact of family dispute and resolution.* New York: Guilford Press.

Dadds, M. R., Schwartz, S., & Sanders, M. R. (1987). Marital discord and treatment outcome in behavioral treatment of child conduct disorders. *Journal of Consulting and Clinical Psychology, 55,* 396–403.

Dishion, T. J., & McMahon, R. J. (1998). Parental monitoring and the prevention of child adolescent problem behavior: A conceptual and empirical foundation. *Clinical Child and Family Psychology Review, 1,* 61–75.

Dryfoos, J. G. (1990). *Adolescents at risk: Prevalence and prevention.* New York: Oxford University Press.

Emery, R. E. (1982). Interparental conflict and the children of discord and divorce. *Psychological Bulletin, 92,* 310–330.

Forehand, R., Miller, K. S., Dutra, R., & Chance, M. W. (1997). Role of parenting in adolescent deviant behavior: Replication across and within two ethnic groups. *Journal of Consulting and Clinical Psychology, 65,* 1036–1041.

Grych, J. H., & Fincham, F. D. (1990). Marital conflict and children's adjustment: A cognitive-contextual framework. *Psychological Bulletin, 108,* 267–290.

Hart, B., & Risley, T. R. (1975). Incidental teaching of language in the preschool. *Journal of Applied Behavior Analysis, 8*(4), 411–420.

Hart, B., & Risley, T. R. (1995). *Meaningful differences in the everyday experience of young American children.* Baltimore: Paul H. Brookes.

Henggeler, S. W., Melton, G. B., Brondino, M. J., Scherer, D. G., & Hanley, J. H. (1997). Multisystemic therapy with violent and chronic juvenile offenders and their families: The role of treatment fidelity in successful dissemination. *Journal of Consulting and Clinical Psychology, 65,* 821–833.

Karoly, P. (1993). Mechanisms of self-regulation: A systems view. *Annual Review of Psychology, 44,* 23–52.

Leung, C., Sanders, M. R., Ip, F., & Lau, J. (in press). Implementation of Triple P–Positive Parenting Program in Hong Kong: Predictors of program completion and clinical outcomes. *Journal of Children's Services.*

Leung, C., Sanders, M. R., Leung, S., Mak, R., & Lau, J. (2003). An outcome evaluation of the implementation of the Triple P–Positive Parenting Program in Hong Kong. *Family Process, 42,* 531–544.

Loeber, R., & Farrington, D. P. (1998). Never too early, never too late: Risk factors and successful interventions for serious and violent juvenile offenders. *Studies on Crime and Crime Prevention, 7,* 7–30.

Markie-Dadds, C., & Sanders, M. R. (2005). *An evaluation of an enhanced self-directed behavioral family intervention for parents of children with conduct problems in rural and remote areas.* Manuscript submitted for publication.

Markie-Dadds, C., & Sanders, M. R. (2006). Self-directed Triple P (Positive Parenting Program) for mothers with children at-risk of developing conduct problems. *Behavioral and Cognitive Psychotherapy, 34*(3), 259–275.

Martin, A. J., & Sanders, M. R. (2003). Balancing work and family: A controlled evaluation of the Triple P–Positive Parenting Program as a work-site intervention. *Child and Adolescent Mental Health, 8*(4), 161–169.

McTaggert, P. G., & Sanders, M. R. (in press). *Mechanisms of change in a school-based universal application of the Triple P–Positive Parenting Program.* Manuscript submitted for publication.

Morawska, A., & Sanders, M. R. (2006). Self-administered behavioural family intervention for parents of toddlers: Effectiveness and dissemination. *Behaviour Research and Therapy, 44*(12), 1839–1848.

Mrazek, P. J., & Haggerty, R. J. (1994). *Reducing risks for mental disorders.* Washington, DC: National Academy Press.

National Institute of Mental Health. (1998). *Priorities for prevention research at NIMH: A report by the national advisory mental health council workgroup on mental disorders prevention research* (NIH Publication No. 98-4321). Washington, DC: U.S. Government Printing Office.

Nicholson, J. M., & Sanders, M. R. (1999). Randomized controlled trial of behavioral family intervention for the treatment of child behavior problems in step-families. *Journal of Divorce and Remarriage, 30*(3/4), 1–23.

Parcel, G. S., Perry, C. L., & Taylor, W. C. (1990). Beyond demonstration: Diffusion of health promotion innovations. In N. Bracht (Ed.), *Health promotion at the community level* (pp. 229–251). Thousand Oaks, CA: Sage.

Patterson, G. R. (1969). Behavioral techniques based on social learning: An additional base for developing behavioral technologies. In C. M. Franks (Ed.), *Behavior therapy: Appraisal and status* (pp. 29–62). New York: McGraw-Hill.

Patterson, G. R. (1982). *Coercive family process.* Eugene, OR: Castalia.

Patterson, G. R., Reid, J. B., & Dishion, T. J. (1992). *Antisocial boys.* Eugene, OR: Castalia.

Peterson, L., & Saldana, L. (1996). Accelerating children's risk for injury: Mother's decisions regarding common safety rules. *Journal of Behavioral Medicine, 19,* 317–331.

Plant, K., & Sanders, M. R. (in press). Reducing problem behavior during caregiving in families of preschool-aged children with developmental disabilities. *Journal of Intellectual and Developmental Disability.*

Risley, T. R., Clark, H. B., & Cataldo, M. F. (1976). Behavioral technology for the normal middle-class family. In E. J. Mash, L. A. Hammerlynch, & L. C. Handy (Eds.), *Behavior modification and families* (pp. 34–60). New York: Brunner/ Mazel.

Robins, L. N. (1991). Conduct disorder. *Journal of Child Psychology and Psychiatry and Allied Disciplines, 32*(1), 193–212.

Rutter, M. (1985). Resilience in the face of adversity: Protective factors and resistance to psychiatric disorder. *British Journal of Psychiatry, 147,* 598–611.

Sanders, M. R. (1992a). Enhancing the impact of behavioral family intervention with children: Emerging perspectives. *Behavior Change, 9,* 115–119.

Sanders, M. R. (1992b). *Every parent: A positive approach to children's behavior.* Sydney, Australia: Addison-Wesley.

Sanders, M. R. (1995). *Healthy families, healthy nation: Strategies for promoting family mental health in Australia.* Bowen Hills, Brisbane: Australian Academic Press.

Sanders, M. R. (1996). New directions in behavioral family intervention with children. In T. H. Ollendick & R. J. Prinz (Eds.), *Advances in clinical child psychology* (pp. 283–330). New York: Plenum Press.

Sanders, M. R. (1999). Triple P–Positive Parenting Program: Towards an empirically validated multilevel parenting and family support strategy for the prevention of behavior and emotional problems in children. *Clinical Child and Family Psychology Review, 2,* 71–90.

Sanders, M. R. (2001). Helping families change: From clinical interventions to population based strategies. In A. Booth, A. Crouter, & M. Clements (Eds.), *Couples in conflict* (pp. 185–219). Mahwah, NJ: Erlbaum.

Sanders, M. R., & Dadds, M. R. (1982). The effects of planned activities and child management procedures in parent training: An analysis of setting generality. *Behavior Therapy, 13,* 452–461.

Sanders, M. R., & Dadds, M. (1993). *Behavioral family intervention.* Needham Heights, MA: Allyn & Bacon.

Sanders, M. R., & Duncan, S. B. (1995). Empowering families: Policy, training, and research issues in promoting family mental health in Australia. *Behavior Change, 12,* 109–121.

Sanders, M. R., & Glynn, T. (1981). Training parents in behavioral self-management: An analysis of generalization and maintenance. *Journal of Applied Behavior Analysis, 14,* 223–237.

Sanders, M. R., Markie-Dadds, C., Rinaldis, M., Firman, D., & Boag, N. (in press). Using household survey data to inform policy decisions regarding the delivery of evidenced-based parenting interventions. *Child: Care, Health and Development.*

Sanders, M. R., Markie-Dadds, C., Tully, L. A., & Bor, W. (2000). The Triple P–Positive Parenting Program: A comparison of enhanced, standard and self-directed behavioral family intervention for parents of children with early onset conduct problems. *Journal of Consulting and Clinical Psychology, 68,* 624–640.

Sanders, M. R., Markie-Dadds, C., & Turner, K. M. T. (1998). *Practitioner's manual for Enhanced Triple P.* Brisbane, Australia: Families International.

Sanders, M. R., Markie-Dadds, C., & Turner, K. M. T. (2003). Theoretical, scientific and clinical foundations of the Triple P–Positive Parenting Program: A population approach to the promotion of parenting competence. *Parenting Research and Practice Monograph, 1,* 1–21.

Sanders, M. R., Markie-Dadds, C., Turner, K. M. T., & Ralph, A. (2004). Using the Triple P system of intervention to prevent behavioral problems in children and adolescents. In P. Barrett & T. H. Ollendick (Eds.), *Handbook of interventions that work with children and adolescents: Prevention and treatment* (pp. 489–516). Chichester, West Sussex, England: Wiley.

Sanders, M. R., Mazzucchelli, T. G., & Studman, L. (2004). Stepping Stones Triple P: The theoretical basis and development of an evidence-based positive parenting program for families with a child who has a disability. *Journal of Intellectual and Developmental Disability, 29,* 265–283.

Sanders, M. R., & McFarland, M. (2000). Treatment of depressed mothers with disruptive children: A controlled evaluation of cognitive behavioral family intervention. *Behavior Therapy, 31,* 89–112.

Sanders, M. R., Montgomery, D. T., & Brechman-Touissant, M. L. (2000). The mass media and the prevention of child behavior problems: The evaluation of a television series to promote positive outcomes for parents and their children. *Journal of Child Psychology and Psychiatry, 41,* 939–948.

Sanders, M. R., Morrison, M., Rebgetz, M., Bor, W., Dadds, M. R., & Shepherd, R. W. (1990). Behavioral treatment of childhood recurrent abdominal pain: Relationships between pain, children's psychological characteristics and family functioning. *Behavior Change, 7*(1), 16–24.

Sanders, M. R., Murphy-Brennan, M., & McAuliffe, C. (2003). The development, evaluation, and dissemination of a training programme for general practitioners in evidence-based parent consultation skills. *International Journal of Mental Health Promotion, 5*(4), 5–12.

Sanders, M. R., Nicholson, J. M., & Floyd, F. (1997). Couples' relationships and children. In W. K. Halford & H. Markman (Eds.), *Clinical handbook of marriage and couples interventions* (pp. 225–253). Chichester, West Sussex, England: Wiley.

Sanders, M. R., & Pidgeon, A. (2005). *Practitioner manual for Pathways Triple P.* Milton, Queensland, Australia: Triple P International.

Sanders, M. R., Pidgeon, A. M., Gravestock, F., Connors, M. D., Brown, S., & Young, R. W. (2004). Does parental attributional retraining and anger management enhance the effects of the Triple P–Positive Parenting Program with parents at risk of child maltreatment? *Behavior Therapy, 35,* 513–535.

Sanders, M. R., & Plant, K. (1989). Programming generalization to high and low risk parenting situations in families with oppositional developmentally disabled preschoolers. *Behavior Modification, 13,* 283–305.

Sanders, M. R., & Ralph, A. (2001). *Practitioner manual for Primary Care Teen Triple P.* Milton, Queensland, Australia: Triple P International.

Sanders, M. R., & Ralph, A. (2004). Towards a multi-level model of parenting intervention. In M. Hoghughi & N. Long (Eds.), *Handbook of parenting: Theory and research for practice* (pp. 352–368). London: Sage.

Sanders, M. R., Shepherd, R. W., Cleghorn, G., & Woolford, H. (1994). The treatment of recurrent abdominal pain in children: A controlled comparison of cognitive-behavioral family intervention and standard pediatric care. *Journal of Consulting and Clinical Psychology, 62,* 306–314.

Sanders, M. R., & Turner, K. M. T. (2002). The role of the media and primary care in the dissemination of evidence-based parenting and family support interventions. *Behavior Therapist, 25,* 156–166.

Sanders, M. R., & Woolley, M. L. (2005). The relationship between global, domain, and task-specific self-efficacy and parenting practices: Implications for parent training. *Child: Care, Health and Development, 31*(1), 65–73.

Taylor, T. K., & Biglan, A. (1998). Behavioral family interventions for improving child-rearing: A review of literature for clinicians and policy makers. *Clinical Child and Family Psychology Review, 1,* 41–60.

Turner, K. M. T., & Sanders, M. R. (2006). Dissemination of evidence-based parenting and family support strategies: Learnings from the Triple P–Positive Parenting Program system approach. *Aggression and Violent Behavior, 11*(2), 176–193.

Turner, K. M. T., Sanders, M. R., & Wall, C. R. (1994). Behavioral parent training versus dietary education in the treatment of children with persistent feeding difficulties. *Behavior Change, 11,* 242–258.

Wesch, D., & Lutzker, J. R. (1991). A comprehensive 5-year evaluation of Project 12-Ways: An ecobehavioral program for treating and preventing child abuse and neglect. *Journal of Family Violence, 6,* 17–35.

West, F., & Sanders, M. R. (in press). *Practitioner manual for Lifestyle Triple P.* Milton, Queensland, Australia: Triple P International.

Zubrick, S. R., Ward, K. A., Silburn, S. R., Lawrence, D., Williams, A. A., Blair, E., et al. (2005). Prevention of child behavior problems through universal implementation of a group behavioral family intervention. *Prevention Science, 6,* 287–304.

CHAPTER 8

Parent-Child Interaction Therapy with Physically Abusive Families

AMY D. HERSCHELL and CHERYL B. MCNEIL

PARENT-CHILD INTERACTION THERAPY (PCIT; Eyberg & Calzada, 1998; Hembree-Kigin & McNeil, 1995) is an intervention designed to treat children aged 2 through 6 who are exhibiting a disruptive behavior disorder. Parent-Child Interaction Therapy incorporates two discrete phases: Child-Directed Interaction (CDI), which emphasizes the quality of the parent-child relationship; and Parent-Directed Interaction (PDI), which concentrates on establishing a structured and consistent discipline program. For each phase of treatment, parents attend one didactic session. Afterward, parents and their child attend weekly coaching sessions together. During these coaching sessions, parents wear a bug-in-the-ear hearing device and are coached on their use of the skills by a therapist who is observing the parent-child interaction from behind a one-way mirror. Coaching is somewhat unique to PCIT and requires therapists to be extremely active, directive, and assertive (Hembree-Kigin & McNeil, 1995). For most families, the full course of treatment is completed in 10 to 16 weekly, one-hour sessions.

HISTORY

Parent-Child Interaction Therapy was originally developed by Sheila Eyberg in the late 1960s and early 1970s, and formalized in 1974 when Dr. Eyberg submitted a grant application to the Alcohol, Drug Abuse, and

Mental Health Administration to conduct a pilot study of PCIT's efficacy. As PCIT's efficacy became clearer, Dr. Eyberg began training her doctoral students (e.g., E. Brestan, B. Funderburk, T. Hembree-Kigin, C. McNeil, K. Newcomb), at the University of Florida to conduct and further study the intervention. As those students moved on, many of them established PCIT clinical and research programs at universities (e.g., Auburn University, West Virginia University) and medical centers (e.g., University of Oklahoma Health Sciences Center). As the empirical evidence for PCIT mounted, national panels of experts began to recognize PCIT's efficacy, and investigators (e.g., C. McNeil) began to train community agencies in the clinical application of PCIT.

Parent-Child Interaction Therapy first gained attention as an empirically supported treatment for externalizing behavior problems with a review completed by Division 53 of the American Psychological Association (Society of Clinical Child and Adolescent Psychology) and subsequent publication in the *Journal of Clinical Child and Adolescent Psychology* (e.g., Brestan & Eyberg, 1998).

Later, PCIT was identified as a "Best Practice" in treating child physical abuse by the Kauffman Foundation's Best Practices Project (Kauffman Best Practices Project, 2004) as well as a "supported and acceptable" intervention for child physical abuse by the National Crime Victims Research and Treatment Center and the Center for Sexual Assault and Traumatic Stress.

THEORY

The content of PCIT was influenced most notably by Virginia Axline, Bernard Guerney, Diana Baumrind, Gerald Patterson, and Constance Hanf (Eyberg, 2004). The first phase of PCIT, Child-Directed Interaction, integrates traditional play therapy with behavioral principles of differential social attention. The play therapy base and emphasis on reflections and descriptions of children's behavior reflects Axline's play therapy. Guerney extended play therapy ideas to parent training groups and taught parents to use play therapy with their children at home. Parent-Child Interaction Therapy reflects these ideas by incorporating parents as a main focus of treatment and empowering them to be the agents of change for their child's behavior.

Baumrind's work on how different parenting styles (authoritarian, permissive, and authoritative) affect children has demonstrated that authoritative parenting achieves the healthiest outcomes (e.g., Baumrind, 1966). Authoritative parents are nurturing and responsive to their children and at the same time can set and follow through with reasonable limits. Social learning theory recognizes that child behavior problems are sometimes inadvertently established or maintained by dysfunctional parent-child interactions. Patterson's *coercion hypothesis* (Patterson, 1976, 2002) suggests that difficult child behaviors are part of the developmental process for all children. However, specific parent behaviors (e.g., a parent's failure to reinforce appropriate prosocial skills and instead respond to the child's difficult behavior) may exacerbate and extend difficult child behavior beyond what would be developmentally appropriate. Interaction patterns are then established between the parent and child in which each person seeks to control interactions, and in turn, each person's (the child's and the parent's) behavior escalates. For abusive mother-child dyads, patterns of behavior in which they reinforced each other's aversive behaviors have been found; Mothers were likely to reinforce their child's negative behavior and children were likely to reinforce their mother's negative behavior (Lorber, Felton, & Reid, 1984).

The two-phase format of PCIT was influenced by Constance Hanf, who developed an intervention for mothers and their developmentally disabled children to improve child compliance (Hanf, 1969). Much like PCIT, Dr. Hanf's intervention had two phases: *Child's Game* and *Mother's Game*. During Child's Game, mothers were taught to use play therapy skills and differential social attention. During Mother's Game, mothers were taught to use direct commands, praise compliance, and provide a consequence (time-out) for noncompliance. Throughout these phases, mothers were coached through a bug-in-the-ear device (Eyberg, 2004). The goals of this program were to increase parent nurturance by improving responsiveness and building the number of positive parent-child experiences as well as to increase the parent's ability to set and follow through with limits.

PARENT-CHILD INTERACTION THERAPY

GENERAL DESCRIPTION OF THE TREATMENT

As in some other parent management training programs (e.g., Barkley, 1987; Forehand & McMahon, 1981; Webster-Stratton, 1984, 1994), there are two phases to PCIT: Child-Directed Interaction (CDI) and Parent-Directed Interaction (PDI). For each phase, parents attend one didactic session without their child present during which the PCIT therapist reviews with the parent specific skills that will be coached in subsequent sessions. This didactic session builds rapport as well as provides detailed descriptions and rationales for each skill. In fact, each skill is modeled for and role-played with parents to facilitate their learning. Following the initial didactic session, parents attend weekly sessions with their child, and they are coached in applying the skills taught.

During CDI, parents are taught to use the PRIDE (Praise, Reflection, Imitation, Description, and Enthusiasm) skills and to avoid questions, commands, and criticism. Parents are coached in how to apply the skills so that they can increase appropriate child behaviors (e.g., sharing, using good manners) and decrease inappropriate child behaviors (e.g., grabbing, being bossy or rude) by providing attention to appropriate and ignoring mildly inappropriate behaviors. Once parents' skill level meets a predetermined set of criteria, typically in six or seven sessions, the second phase of PCIT begins, PDI. During PDI, parents are taught to provide clear, direct commands, assess compliance versus noncompliance, and to provide consistent consequences for both compliance (labeled praise) and noncompliance (time-out). In response to repeated noncompliance, parents are taught a sophisticated time-out procedure that emphasizes shaping and teaching appropriate behavior. Critical clinical components of PCIT have been identified and include involving the child and parents together in treatment, coaching parents, using assessment to guide treatment, and tailoring treatment to the child's developmental level (Herschell, Calzada, Eyberg, & McNeil, 2002a).

For most families, the full course of treatment is conducted in 10 to 16 weekly, 1-hour, clinic-based sessions. These sessions include a pretreatment assessment of child and family functioning and feedback, teaching CDI (behavioral play therapy) skills to the parents, coaching the parents in CDI skills, teaching PDI (discipline) skills to the parents, coaching PDI skills, conducting posttreatment assessment of child and family functioning and feedback, and providing booster sessions as needed. Booster sessions are recommended at 1, 3, 6, and 12 months to enhance maintenance of parenting skill and to address new problems.

DETAILED DESCRIPTION OF EACH SESSION

Pretreatment Assessment (Session 1)

Parent-Child Interaction Therapy begins with a thorough, multimodal, and multiinformant assessment. Standardized measures such as the Eyberg Child Behavior Inventory (ECBI; Eyberg & Pincus, 1999), Parenting Stress Index (Abidin, 1995), Child Abuse Potential Inventory (CAPI; Milner, 1980; Ondersma, Chaffin, Mullins, & LeBreton, 2005), and Brief Symptom Inventory (Derogatis, 1975, 1993) are routinely collected to understand the clinical significance of the child's behavior as well as parents' stress, parenting practices, and mental health concerns, respectively. A comprehensive intake interview and structured behavioral observations, coded using the Dyadic Parent-Child Interaction Coding System-III (DPICS-III; Eyberg, Nelson, Duke, & Boggs, 2005), also are completed. If the child attends school, Head Start, or day care, teachers are asked to complete standardized behavioral measures such as the Sutter-Eyberg Child Behavior Inventory (SESBI; Eyberg & Pincus, 1999). If PCIT is determined to be an appropriate treatment, parents are provided with educational information about PCIT and asked to commit to attending a specific number of sessions on particular dates. Often, a written contract is developed and signed between the therapist and client to increase treatment compliance and attendance (McNeil & Herschell, 1998). This type of contracting has been found to be particularly helpful with physically abusive families (Wolfe & Sandler, 1981).

Child-Directed Interaction Didactic (Session 2)

Following completion of the evaluation, parents are asked to attend one session without their child. During this teaching time, parents are instructed about the PRIDE skills and how to apply them with their child. Parents are encouraged to use *Praise, Reflection, Imitation, Description,* and *Enthusiasm*, while avoiding questions, commands, and criticisms (see Table 8.1). In addition, parents are taught to allow their child to lead the play as well as to use selective attention and strategic ignoring for appropriate and inappropriate behavior, respectively. This combination of skills is designed to focus the parent on the child's strengths as well as to facilitate warm, positive, and nurturing parent-child interactions, which often are lacking in abusive families (Kolko, 2002; Milner & Chilamkurti, 1991). Parent-child interactions in abusive families often are characterized by parent verbal aggression such as whining, yelling, criticizing, threatening, and screaming (Lahey, Conger, Atkeson, & Treiber, 1984) rather than the warm, supportive interaction patterns that PCIT tries to establish.

Parents also are asked to complete 5 minutes of "special playtime" with their child each day at home. For the parent, particularly abusive parents, these 5 minutes serve as a time for him or her to (a) practice and refine skills learned in session, (b) increase the number of positive parent-child interactions, (c) begin to establish a new way of interacting with the child, and (d) invest time in teaching the child. For the child, these 5 minutes serve as a time to receive positive attention from the parent in the home environment as well as develop social (e.g., sharing, turn taking), decision-making, and leadership skills through a developmentally appropriate medium—play.

Child-Directed Interaction Coaching (Sessions 3 through 8)

The ultimate goal of this treatment phase is to enhance the parent-child relationship and decrease minor child behavioral concerns (e.g., whining, not sharing) by changing the way parents interact with their children. During these 5 to 6 sessions, parents and their child attend

Table 8.1

Child-Directed Interaction Skills

Skill	Definition	Rationale	Example
Skills to Use			
Praise (Labeled)	Specific verbalization that expresses a favorable judgment on an activity, product, or attribute of the child	Adds warmth to the relationship Causes the behavior to increase Increases self-esteem	Parent: "You are doing a great job of coloring in the lines."
Reflection	Statement that immediately repeats back the child's verbalization	Allows the child to control the conversation Shows the child that the parent is interested Demonstrates acceptance and understanding	Child: "The horse is going to be friends with the cow." Parent: "Oh—I see. The horse is going to be friends with the cow."
Imitation	Physical act that mimics or accompanies the behavior in which the child is engaged	Permits the child to lead the play Teaches the child how to play with others	Child: "I'm making a circle." Parent: "I'm going to draw a circle, too—just like you."
Description (Behavioral)	Sentence that gives a neutral account of the child's behavior	Teaches concepts Models speech Holds the child's attention Organizes the child's thoughts and activities	Parent: "You are driving the car into the garage."
Enthusiasm	Excitement or interest in the child	Keeps the child interested Helps to distract the child when ignoring	Voice has lots of inflection.
Skills to Avoid			
Questions	Comment expressed in a question form	Creates an unpleasant interaction (leads the conversation) Puts the child on the spot	Parent: "What are you making?"
Commands	Order, demand, or direction for a behavioral response	Takes the lead away from the child Sets up the interaction to be unpleasant	Parent: "Put the blocks in the box."
Criticism	Verbalization that finds fault with the child's behavior, products, or attributes	Often increases the criticized behavior Lowers child's self-esteem Creates an unpleasant interaction	Parent: "That's not how you should do that. You know better."

Adapted from "Parent Training for Oppositional-Defiant Preschoolers" (pp. 105–132), by S. M. Eyberg and S. R. Boggs, in *Handbook of Parent Training: Parents as Co-Therapists for Children's Behavior Problems,* C. E. Schaefer and J. M. Briesmeister (Eds.), 1989, New York: Wiley. Copyright 1989 by John Wiley & Sons, Inc. Adapted with permission. Definitions adapted from "Dyadic Parent-Child Interaction Coding System-II: A Manual," by S.M. Eyberg, J. Bessmer, K. Newcomb, D. Edwards, and E. A. Robinson, 1994, *Social and Behavioral Sciences Documents,* Ms. No. 2897. San Rafael, CA: Select Press.

sessions together and parents are coached, usually using a bug-in-the-ear hearing device and one-way mirror, in the appropriate use of the skills with their child. Each session begins with a brief check-in during which the therapist inquires about the parent and child's week, confirms the completion of homework, and problem-solves any difficulties that were noted during special playtime. Next, the therapist observes and codes the parent's skills using the DPICS-III coding system (Eyberg et al., 2005) for 5 minutes to determine the parent's current skill level. This assessment guides the therapist's coaching of the parents for that session. If the coding reveals that the parent is not using labeled praise, then the therapist will focus on coaching the parent to use more specific praises during the session. Afterward, the therapist coaches the parent for a minimum of 30 minutes. A checkout time is then completed during which the therapist meets with the parent and child to briefly process the session and assign home practice (special playtime). Once parents' skill levels meet a predetermined set of mastery criteria, the second stage of PCIT (PDI) is initiated.

Parent-Directed Interaction Didactic (Session 9)

Like the CDI didactic session, this session includes only the parent. Parents are taught the importance of structure, consistency, predictability, and follow-through as well as specific skills such as giving good directions, determining compliance, and providing specific, appropriate consequences for compliance (labeled praise) and noncompliance (time-out). For parents with a history of physical abuse, care is taken during this session to discuss what previously led up to abusive interactions (antecedents of abuse) given that precipitants to violence often can be a combination of child behavioral difficulty and parent emotion dysregulation. The discussion also focuses on the parents' ability to regulate their emotions as well as their willingness (and sometimes fear) to discipline the child. This information is considered in coaching the parent, and parents are often taught emotion-regulation skills such as anger management and relaxation procedures before initiating emotionally charged discipline sessions with the child.

Parent-Directed Interaction Coaching (Sessions 10 through 16)

The ultimate goal of this treatment phase is to help parents effectively discipline their child by acquiring nonaggressive behavior management skills and to reduce remaining child behavior problems so that the child's behavior is within normal limits by the end of therapy. Parents and their child are strategically guided through this treatment phase by the therapist. Once compliance improves to within normal limits, other misbehaviors are addressed (e.g., throwing toys, talking back). When skills are mastered in a controlled therapy room, the therapist coaches the parent in less controlled situations (e.g., clinic waiting room, hallways, playground near the clinic) and assigns homework to practice progressively more difficult scenarios at home, and ultimately in public settings.

Ending and Booster Sessions

Just as mastery criteria guide the therapist in moving from the first to second phase of treatment, predetermined mastery criteria clarify when treatment should end. To complete treatment, parents must master discipline skills and children's behavior must be within normal limits as measured by standardized assessment tools (e.g., DPICS-III, ECBI). In the final session, treatment gains are reviewed, anticipated future behavior difficulties are discussed, and parents are taught to use problem-solving skills to match discipline techniques with potential behavior problems. The last session typically includes a graduation ceremony in which both parents and children receive recognition for their accomplishments (e.g., certificates of completion, ribbons).

RESEARCH FINDINGS

Consistent with a scientist-practitioner approach, studies of PCIT seek to answer clinically meaningful questions: How is PCIT helpful for parents and their children who are exhibiting behavior problems? Do the results generalize to untreated settings and children? How long do treatment benefits last? Can the model be adapted to help other families? A significant body of literature is now available to support that PCIT is an effective intervention for changing parenting skills and improving disruptive child behavior.

Treatment outcome studies demonstrate improvements in parent skill and child behavior (for reviews see Gallagher, 2003; Herschell, Calzada, Eyberg, & McNeil, 2002b). More specifically, behavior observations of parent-child interactions indicate pre-post changes in parent behavior such as increased rates of praise, descriptions, reflections, and physical proximity as well as decreased rates of criticism and sarcasm (e.g., Eisenstadt, Eyberg, McNeil, Newcomb, & Funderburk, 1993). Additionally, parents report lower parenting stress, more internal (rather than external) locus of control, and increased confidence in parenting skills after completing PCIT. Similarly, observations of child behavior have demonstrated decreases in disruptive behavior and overactivity as well as increases in compliance. Pre- to posttreatment compliance rates have been reported to change as follows: 29% to 43%; 41% to 72%; 21% to 46%; 39% to 89%; 21% to 70%; 64% to 81% (Herschell & McNeil, 2005). Parents report their child's behavior to improve from the clinical range to within normal limits on multiple parent report measures including the Eyberg Child Behavior Inventory (both problem and intensity scales; McNeil, Clemens-Mowrer, Gurwitch, & Funderburk, 1994; Schuhmann, Foote, Eyberg, Boggs, & Algina, 1998) and the Child Behavior Checklist (both internalizing and externalizing scores; Eisenstadt et al., 1993). In addition to being highly satisfied with the outcome of treatment, parents also report high satisfaction with the process of PCIT (e.g., Schuhmann et al., 1998).

GENERALIZATION: DO THE RESULTS GENERALIZE TO UNTREATED SETTINGS AND CHILDREN?

Studies have indicated that the treatment results of PCIT generalize to untreated siblings (Brestan, Eyberg, Boggs, & Algina, 1997) as well as school settings (McNeil, Eyberg, Eisenstadt, Newcomb, & Funderburk, 1991). Brestan and colleagues (1997) found that both mothers and fathers of treated children reported improvement in the behavior of untreated siblings. These improvements were not reported by the comparison group (wait-list control parents).

Children who experience behavioral difficulties at home often experience these same difficulties as school. Some have suggested that school problems have to be directly addressed to successfully reduce them (Breiner & Forehand, 1981); however, McNeil et al. (1991) found that preschool children who completed PCIT demonstrated behavioral improvements at school without any direct classroom intervention. In a follow-up study, Funderburk et al. (1998) found that these school gains maintained up to 12 months posttreatment; however, at 18 months posttreatment, only compliance gains maintained.

MAINTENANCE: HOW LONG DO TREATMENT BENEFITS LAST?

A series of studies have been conducted to understand the endurance of treatment benefits (Boggs et al., 2004; Eyberg et al., 2001; Funderburk et al., 1998; Hood & Eyberg, 2003). Two years after treatment, the majority of children (69%) maintained gains on measures of child behavior problems, child activity level, and parenting stress as well as remained free of disruptive behavior disorder diagnosis (54%; Eyberg et al., 2001). Compared with completers of treatment, those who did not complete treatment reported significantly more symptoms of disruptive behavior disorders 10 to 30 months after pretreatment assessment. Treatment completion was associated with decreased parenting stress and higher satisfaction (Boggs et al., 2004). At 3 to 6 years posttreatment, mothers reported the frequency of child externalizing behavior and their confidence to be unchanged compared with posttreatment (Hood & Eyberg, 2003).

ADAPTATIONS: CAN THE MODEL BE ADAPTED TO HELP OTHER FAMILIES?

Parent-Child Interaction Therapy has been applied to a wide array of childhood disorders including Separation Anxiety Disorder (Choate, Pincus, Eyberg, & Barlow, 2005), chronic pediatric illness (cancer; Bagner, Fernandez, & Eyberg, 2004), developmental disorders (Eyberg & Matarazzo, 1975), Attention-Deficit/Hyperactivity Disorder (Matos, Torres, Santiago, Jurado, & Rodríguez, 2006), general child maltreatment (Fricker-Elhai, Ruggerio, & Smith, 2005), and child physical abuse (Chaffin et al., 2004). It also has been adapted to fit younger (Dombrowski, Timmer, Blacker, & Urquiza, 2005) and older (McCoy, Funderburk, & Chaffin, in press) children. To fit different treatment modalities, PCIT has been successfully abbreviated (Nixon, Sweeney, Erickson, & Touyz, 2003, 2004) and adapted for use as a group intervention (Niec, Hemme, Yopp, & Brestan, 2005).

CHILD PHYSICAL ABUSE AND PCIT

RATIONALE

Research has demonstrated a high correlation between child physical abuse and disruptive behavior such as aggression and noncompliance (e.g., Kolko, 2002). The rate of abuse is inversely related to age. Younger children (ages birth through 7 years) have the highest victimization rates (51.8% of cases), suffer the most severe injuries, and are the most likely to experience a recurrence of maltreatment (U.S. Department of Health and Human Services, 2003). The most common scenario is for a biological mother to perpetrate physical abuse against her child (U.S. Department of Health and Human Services, 2003). A number of studies have compared maltreating and nonmaltreating parents. In those studies, abusive parents have been found to be less positive when interacting with their children (Bousha & Twentyman, 1984). Abusive parents also tend to display fewer appropriate care-giving behaviors, a high degree of negative emotions (Crittenden, 1981), and an overall lack of empathy in responding to their children's cues (Frodi & Lamb, 1980) and understanding emotional issues in general (Shipman & Zeman, 1999).

PROGRESSION OF RESEARCH

Though children with histories of physical abuse were not the focus of initial PCIT outcome studies, it is likely that some children with histories of or at high risk for child physical abuse (CPA) were included, given the co-occurrence between extreme behavior problems (like aggression) and CPA. Similarly, in the late 1980s and early 1990s clinicians began applying PCIT to physical abuse populations (e.g., The Center on Child Abuse and

Neglect at the University of Oklahoma Health Sciences Center) and recognized its potential utility. Urquiza and McNeil first documented the conceptual rationale for applying PCIT to child physical abuse in a grant application to the National Institute of Mental Health (1995) and a publication that followed shortly thereafter (Urquiza & McNeil, 1996). Afterward, a series of single-subject design studies and case reports documented the application and utility of PCIT with physically abusive families (Borrego, Urquiza, Rasmussen, & Zebell, 1999; Filcheck, McNeil, & Herschell, 2005; Herschell, Calzada, Eyberg, & McNeil, 2002a).

In 2004, Chaffin and colleagues at the University of Oklahoma Health Sciences Center published the first large-scale treatment outcome study (effectiveness trial) of PCIT with child abuse populations in the community. A 4-year, randomized trial with 110 physically abusive parent-child dyads tested the efficacy and sufficiency of PCIT in preventing re-reports of physical abuse. Included parent-child dyads were all involved with the child welfare system and many were financially disadvantaged; 62% reported incomes below the poverty line. Participants were primarily single (58%), Caucasian (52%) mothers (65%) with an average of four prior child welfare reports: two for physical abuse and two for neglect.

The study compared three treatments, each of which was structured and lasted approximately 6 months: (a) PCIT; (b) PCIT with individualized, enhanced services; and (c) treatment as usual, a community-based parenting group. The PCIT condition included a 6-week motivational enhancement group treatment for parents, standard PCIT, and a 4-session follow-up group treatment for parents and children. The second condition, PCIT with individualized, enhanced services, included the same treatment with the addition of individualized services targeting parental depression, substance abuse, and marital or domestic violence problems. The third group, treatment as usual, included the parenting skills group typically provided by a local nonprofit community-based agency.

Findings supported the effectiveness of PCIT for reducing rates of repeated abuse. At follow-up (median time of 850 days), 19% of participants in the PCIT condition had another report of physical abuse, compared with 36% of participants in the PCIT plus individualized, enhanced services condition, and 49% of participants in the community group. Repeated report rates of neglect were not different across groups, suggesting that PCIT did not influence child neglect outcomes. Instead, PCIT appeared to be helpful in reducing the previously discussed, negative, coercive process underlying CPA (e.g., Patterson, 1976). All conditions were helpful in increasing positive parent behaviors. Only the groups that included PCIT were associated with reductions in negative parent behaviors. Interestingly, additional services did not improve the efficacy of PCIT. In fact, the addition of treatment services for other parent mental health needs (the PCIT with individualized, enhanced services condition), indicated a trend (although not statistically significant) for these services to attenuate efficacy.

Timmer, Urquiza, McGrath, and Zebell (2005) completed a quasi-experimental study of 126 biological parents and their children who completed PCIT. Parent-child dyads with high versus low risks of abuse were compared on pre- and postmeasures of child behavior, parent functioning, and parent satisfaction. Results indicated decreases in child behavior problems, child psychopathology, and parent stress from pre- to posttreatment. However, parents with histories of physical abuse showed smaller reductions on a measure of psychopathology than parents with no history of physical abuse and children with histories of physical abuse showed smaller reductions in child behavior problems than children with no history of physical abuse.

EMPIRICALLY SUPPORTED MODIFICATIONS TO PCIT FOR CPA

Modifications have been made to PCIT for CPA populations based on descriptive studies of CPA and extensive clinical experience (McCoy, Funderburk, & Chaffin, in press). Most notable is the intensive focus on the parent. Child behavior, including behavior problems, is not considered in determination of the appropriateness of treatment for physically abusive families. Instead, families are included in treatment if the *parent* has demonstrated aggressive or abusive behavior toward one or more of their children. In traditional PCIT, treatment focuses on changing the child's behavior through change in the parent's parenting skills. In PCIT with physically abusive families, the focus is on reducing harsh parenting practices. Accordingly, children's behavior is considered, but it is not the main focus nor is it emphasized as "difficult" or "problematic."

During the Parent-Directed Interaction phase of PCIT, parents are taught specific skills that are then practiced with the therapist. Once parents have demonstrated good self-control and skill use, the therapist then coaches them as they interact with their child. For example, parents are first taught relaxation skills and behavior management skills. Then, as parents interact with their child, the relaxation skills are integrated with child behavior management skills. Similarly, parents are taught and directly coached in the use of multiple nonphysical discipline procedures, responsivity to the child's needs, self-control, and development of appropriate expectations for their child (McCoy, Funderburk, & Chaffin, in press). These modifications were tested in the previously mentioned randomized clinical trial (Chaffin et al., 2004).

While PCIT is primarily used and researched as a clinic-based model, it also has been applied to school, home, and primary care settings. Bahl and McNeil (2001) describe a modification, Teacher-Child Interaction Training, for training teachers in PCIT skills (e.g., PRIDE, commands, time-out) and then coaching them in their classrooms. In a study by Tiano and McNeil (2006), seven Head Start classrooms were randomized to receive PCIT or no treatment. The teachers receiving PCIT used praise much more frequently following the intervention than the control group. Similarly, Filcheck, McNeil, Greco, and Bernard (2004) found that coaching a teacher in PCIT resulted in greater teacher praise and less teacher criticism, as well as improvements in child behavior. A case report of TCIT included a 2-year-old African American girl referred with her teacher. Completion of TCIT resulted in an increased number of positive interactions between child and teacher, increased child compliance, decreased child disruptive behavior, and less need for teacher commands (McIntosh, Rizza, & Bliss, 2000). Similarly, Querido and Eyberg (2001) implemented a school-based PCIT model for low-income, Head Start families.

Clinically, PCIT has been used as an in-home program primarily for families involved in the child welfare system. Recently, Ware (2006) completed a single-subject study demonstrating the utility of an in-home model of PCIT that included 5 families with preschoolers who displayed disruptive behavior. Three of the 5 families completed PCIT. Each of these families had clinically significant improvements in observed parenting skills, parent report of child behavior problems, and observed child compliance and disruptive behavior following PCIT. Modifications that were conducted for this in-home trial included the following: (a) coaching in a room of the client's home (no bug-in-the-ear device), (b) conducting sessions twice per week, and (c) using two therapists for all sessions. Improvements with in-home PCIT were comparable to those found in traditional clinic-based outcome studies.

In an effort to provide psychosocial care within the pediatric primary care setting, Harwood and colleagues (Harwood, O'Brien, Carter, & Eyberg, 2006) developed an abbreviated, group-based version of PCIT and completed a small randomized controlled trial to evaluate the treatment's efficacy. Thirty mother-child dyads were randomized to receive either the treatment or a comparison condition that included handouts on child behavior management. Both groups reported improvements that were maintained at 6 months; however, there were no group differences.

THERAPIST VARIABLES

Research also has been initiated to understand whether certain PCIT therapist styles are more effective than others. Borrego and Urquiza (1998) have discussed the utility of PCIT's use of social reinforcement with parents as models for parent-child relationships. Recent research has indicated that initial therapist-parent interactions predict treatment dropout. The use of questions, facilitative comments, and supportive statements predicted treatment dropout versus completion for 73% of families (Harwood & Eyberg, 2004). An analog study that controlled for therapist style (positive, neutral, constructive) indicated that mothers acquire skills more efficiently when coaches balance positive with constructive feedback. No associations were found between therapist style and maternal compliance or treatment satisfaction (Herschell, Capage, Bahl, & McNeil, 2006).

CAREGIVERS

While the majority of PCIT studies have included biological mothers and their children, other caregivers such as fathers (Tiano & McNeil, 2005) and foster parents have been considered. In a study examining the impact of fathers' participation on treatment outcome, Bagner and Eyberg (2003) found that while fathers may not affect immediate treatment outcome, they do affect maintenance of treatment gains. Children who have been removed from their parents' care and placed in foster care often demonstrate the type of behavior that PCIT is designed to treat. In fact, 50% to 61% of children in foster care demonstrate clinically significant behavior problems, and children with disruptive behavior in foster care often display higher rates of hyperactivity, noncompliance, and aggression compared with other children with disruptive behavior who are not in foster care (e.g., Clausen, Landsverk, Ganger, Chadwick, & Litrownik, 1998). Parent-Child Interaction Therapy has been successfully applied to foster parents and children in their care (McNeil, Herschell, Gurwitch, & Clemens-Mowrer, 2005) and differences have not been found in the effectiveness of PCIT for foster parents compared with nonabusive biological parents (Timmer, Urquiza, & Zebell, 2005).

CULTURAL CONSIDERATIONS

The role of cultural issues in behavioral parent training programs has received relatively little attention over the years (Forehand & Kotchick, 1996). As such, the literature on cultural considerations in PCIT is limited. Given the strong relationship between culture and parenting attitudes and behaviors (e.g., Harkness & Super, 1995), it is reasonable to expect that PCIT would need to be adapted to be as effective as possible with families from a variety of cultural backgrounds (e.g., McNeil, Capage, & Bennett, 2002). In an attempt to make PCIT more sensitive to the Mexican American population, McCabe, Yeh, Garland, Lau, and Chavez (2005) have suggested a program called GANA in which PCIT is tailored to be more acceptable to Mexican American families. Outcome data from this project are not yet available to determine whether such cultural adaptations to PCIT enhance its efficacy. With African American parent-child dyads, preliminary work suggests that PCIT's emphasis on an authoritative parenting style may be appropriate with this population (Querido, Warner, & Eyberg, 2002). Additionally, two outcome studies have demonstrated that PCIT may be as effective (or perhaps even more effective) with African American families as with Caucasian participants (Fernandez & Eyberg, 2004), particularly when socioeconomic status (SES) is held constant (Capage, Bennett, & McNeil, 2001). At this point, however, only a few studies have addressed cultural issues with PCIT, and the wide range of cultural groups has not been examined. Therefore, conclusions currently cannot be drawn regarding the cultural sensitivity of PCIT or the appropriateness of tailoring the treatment to better meet the needs of ethnic minority families.

CASE STUDY

BACKGROUND INFORMATION

Doug, a 6-year-old African American boy, was removed from his mother's care after he was found wandering the streets alone. When found, he reported that his mother had locked him out of the house as a punishment because he had hit his younger sister (aged 3 years) when she tried to take one of his toys. A policewoman took Doug to the local Child Advocacy Center after picking him up and hearing this account. At the Child Advocacy Center, Doug received a physical examination, which revealed medical findings of physical abuse (e.g., bruise patterns consistent with belt marks—evidence on buttocks of hyperpigmented linear scars; multiple injuries in various states of healing; the pattern and extent of injuries indicated that they would have caused severe pain). He also met with a forensic interviewer and his disclosure matched the physical findings. During his interview, Doug described being hit by his mother with a belt, switch, and electrical cord. When asked about other things that happened when he got in trouble, Doug mentioned several other physical forms of discipline such as (a) having to do push-ups, (b) being made to stand in the corner with his arms out (if his arms dropped, he would get hit), (c) being kicked up the stairs, and (d) having to lie on the floor on his back with his heels held off the floor (if his heels touched the floor, he would get hit).

After an investigation, Child Protective Services (CPS) substantiated the physical abuse. Doug and his younger sister were placed in kinship foster care, with their maternal aunt. As part of the family service plan, Doug's mother, Ms. Anderson, was required to complete weekly drug screens, attend anger management classes, complete a psychological evaluation, and participate in PCIT. She also was required to obtain appropriate housing and furnishings. As part of this larger family service plan, PCIT was initiated after successful completion of all other requirements, and approximately 1 month prior to the anticipated reunification date.

PRETREATMENT ASSESSMENT (SESSION 1)

Session Objectives

1. Obtain parental consent and child assent for treatment.
2. Build rapport.
3. Obtain detailed information about the child's behavior and family history.
4. Determine appropriateness of PCIT.
5. Explain the rationale, structure, and logistics for PCIT.
6. Agree on attendance contract.

Session Content

As planned, the mother, Ms. Anderson, arrived for her 2-hour appointment at 3:00 P.M. Her son, Doug, arrived one hour later at 4:00 P.M. Because Doug was in the care of his maternal aunt, Ms. Jackson, the therapist purposefully staggered the arrival times to allow some individual time with Ms. Anderson and to keep the session time at a reasonable length for a preschooler. During the 1-hour meeting with Ms. Anderson, the therapist first reviewed several administrative forms (e.g., consent to treatment, office policy, insurance information) and then carefully discussed confidentiality and limitations to confidentiality. The therapist shared what information she already knew about the abuse incident and clarified that only new concerns about abuse could be reported. What had been reported was already investigated and part of the past. The therapist specifically discussed this as a way to alleviate some of Ms. Anderson's mistrust and concern that discussing those incidents would negatively impact her case and potentially keep her children in care longer.

Ms. Anderson brought with her a packet of uncompleted questionnaires that the therapist had mailed to her and apologized that she did not have time to complete them prior to the appointment. When asked if she would prefer to complete questionnaires on her own or with the therapist, Ms. Anderson reported that she did not mind completing them with the therapist. Together, the therapist and Ms. Anderson completed the Child Behavior Checklist (CBCL), Eyberg Child Behavior Inventory (ECBI), Parenting Stress Index (PSI), and Child Abuse Potential Inventory (CAPI). Later in the session, the therapist learned that Ms. Anderson stopped attending school in eighth grade, and before dropping out, she had missed a considerable number of days because she stayed home to help her mother care for her siblings. The lack of schooling affected her ability to read some of the questionnaires.

Once Doug arrived, he and his mother were observed in the three parent-child interaction tasks of the DPICS-III (Child-Directed Interaction, Parent-Directed Interaction, and Clean-Up situations). As his aunt waited in the waiting room, the therapist asked her to complete the same behavior ratings that Doug's mother completed (Child Behavior Checklist, Eyberg Child Behavior Inventory, Parenting Stress Index, Child Abuse Potential Inventory) so that the therapist would have a comparison of his behavior with different caregivers and a report of current behavior while Doug was living with his aunt.

Given that Doug had not been in Ms. Anderson's care for many months and the potential that Ms. Anderson would want to (understandably) present favorably, results of this assessment were interpreted cautiously. These results indicated that Doug exhibited significant oppositionality and conduct problems. Both his mother and his aunt reported clinical elevations on the CBCL for the Externalizing and Total Problems Scales (Ms. Anderson's scores were Externalizing T = 74 and Total Problems T = 73; Ms. Jackson's scores were Externalizing T = 80 and Total Problems T = 81). Similarly, Ms. Anderson obtained an Intensity Score of 146 and Problem Score of 19 on the ECBI, and mentioned particular behavioral concerns for Doug including teasing other children, physically fighting with his sister, lying, and repeatedly not listening. Ms. Jackson obtained an Intensity Score of 154 and Problem Score of 20 on the ECBI. Collectively, these scores and both caregivers' reports suggested that Doug was experiencing a clinically significant level of disruptive behavior. When asked if a teacher could complete a behavioral rating scale (Sutter-Eyberg Child Behavior Inventory-Revised), Ms. Anderson decided not to sign a consent form for the therapist to contact the teacher. She reported that she was concerned about the school already labeling Doug as a troublemaker and did not want to make things worse.

The CAPI scores for both Ms. Anderson and Ms. Jackson could not be interpreted. Each revealed an elevated "Faking-Good index" rendering the results invalid. During the DPICS-III behavioral observations, Ms. Anderson initially appeared overly concerned with Doug's appearance. She mentioned that his pants looked too tight, and his shirt too big; complaining to him that his aunt should take better care of him. Initially, she also appeared uncomfortable; however, over the course of the observation, Ms. Anderson appeared more comfortable in her interaction with Doug. In the CDI observation, Ms. Anderson gave 0 behavioral descriptions, 2 reflective statements, 0 labeled praise statements, 10 questions, 9 indirect commands, and 7 criticisms. During the PDI and Clean-Up situations, similar patterns were observed; the majority of her statements were indirect commands and criticisms. Doug complied with approximately 48% of Ms. Anderson's commands. Despite these scores, Doug appeared to enjoy spending time with his mother and was disappointed when the session was over.

Once it was clear that Doug and his mother were appropriate for PCIT, the therapist explained the expectations for treatment (e.g., weekly 1-hour sessions, 5 minutes of home practice each day they were together) as well as the attendance and cancellation policies. Together, Ms. Anderson, Ms. Jackson, and the therapist developed and signed a treatment contract so that it was clear when appointments were scheduled and who was to attend. The therapist explained that treatment would involve two phases, the first focused on relationship enhancement (CDI), and the second focused on discipline (PDI). At the beginning of each phase, the parent would meet with the therapist alone to review skills. Afterward, Doug and Ms. Anderson would attend sessions together so that Ms. Anderson could be coached in the skills.

CHILD-DIRECTED INTERACTION DIDACTIC (SESSION 2)

Session Objectives

1. Continue to build rapport with the parent.
2. Review parent's behavioral concerns and differentiate which types of behaviors will be targeted in Child-Directed Interaction versus in Parent-Directed Interaction.
3. Teach the PRIDE Skills.
4. Discuss strategic attention and selective ignoring (differential attention) as well as the value of letting the child lead the interaction.
5. Discuss the value of play as a medium for children to learn skills.
6. Provide a rationale and multiple examples for each skill.
7. Model, role-play, and provide feedback on each skill.
8. Assign and discuss home practice.

Session Content

After explaining why CDI precedes PDI and giving an overview of CDI, the therapist provided a rationale for having the child in the lead during

CDI. Next, the therapist presented the skills to avoid (questions, commands, and criticism) and to use (praise, reflection, imitation, description, and enthusiasm). The therapist explained, provided a rationale, modeled, and role-played each skill. She also frequently asked Ms. Anderson questions and checked with her to determine her understanding and level of acceptance of the information presented. After it was clear that Ms. Anderson understood each skill, the therapist demonstrated how to use them in combination and how to manage misbehavior within the session. The therapist also reviewed and demonstrated strategic attention and selective ignoring skills. Throughout this session, the therapist highlighted Ms. Anderson's strengths and discussed how they would work together to improve Doug's behavior. Ms. Anderson was asked to complete 5 minutes of special playtime with Doug during each of her visits with Doug during the week. The therapist reviewed appropriate (e.g., creative and constructive) versus inappropriate (e.g., dangerous and destructive) toys to use during this time. Ms. Anderson was given a form to use to record whether she completed the home practice at each visit as well as questions or problems that came up during the playtime.

CHILD-DIRECTED INTERACTION COACHING (SESSIONS 3 TO 8)

Session Objectives

1. Review home practice assignment and overview of the week (5 to 10 minutes).
2. Check skill level with a 5-minute behavior observation of the parent-child interaction before initiating coaching.
3. Coach Ms. Anderson in the use of the CDI skills for at least 30 minutes.
4. Conduct a brief checkout to process session and assign home practice (5 to 10 minutes).
5. Assist Ms. Anderson in mastering CDI skills.

Session Content

Both Ms. Anderson and Doug attended the next session, the first CDI coaching session. The session began with the therapist asking Ms. Anderson about completion of the home practice. Ms. Anderson reported completing the special playtime with Doug during three of their four visits the previous week. The therapist complimented Ms. Anderson on her ability to complete the home practice at nearly every visit. After reviewing questions and concerns that had come up during the special playtime, the therapist asked if Ms. Anderson could practice on four out of four times the next week. The therapist explained that more frequent practice would lead to a quicker treatment, given that advancing through treatment stages is based on skill acquisition rather than a set number of sessions. Ms. Anderson agreed to try to complete the special playtime during each visit.

Next, the therapist explained to Doug why he and his mom were attending sessions, what he could expect during session, and then showed him the treatment room, including the observation room, one-way mirror, and bug-in-the ear device. As the therapist reviewed skills with Ms. Anderson, Doug played with toys and interrupted periodically. In reviewing the skills, Ms. Anderson mentioned that behavioral descriptions were particularly difficult for her; therefore, they decided to focus coaching on that skill during the session. After helping Ms. Anderson secure the bug-in-the ear device, the therapist exited the therapy room, and went into the observation room to conduct the 5-minute coding and 30-minute coaching. During the 5-minute coding, the therapist noted that Ms. Anderson demonstrated a slight increase in behavioral descriptions (2) and praise (1) as well as a decrease in criticisms (2). Immediately after the coding time, the therapist complimented Ms. Anderson on these improvements, reminded her about the goal of increasing behavioral descriptions, and began coaching.

THERAPIST: That was amazing. You are already increasing your skills. Compared to the initial assessment, you got in more behavioral descriptions and praise this time and decreased your critical statements. That's excellent. I can tell that you must have been working on this during your special playtime.

DOUG: Mom, will you draw a dinosaur?

MS. ANDERSON: I don't know how, but I'll try.

THERAPIST: That's a great way to model trying for him. Even when we initially don't know how to do something, it's important to try—that's a great lesson to teach him.

MS. ANDERSON: What kind of dinosaur would you like me to make?

THERAPIST: [Intentionally Silent. Ignoring the question and waiting for a statement.]

DOUG: The green kind.

MS. ANDERSON: Okay—I'll make the green kind.

THERAPIST: Great reflection.

MS. ANDERSON: This is a funny looking dinosaur.

DOUG: [Giggles as he looks at the picture.]

THERAPIST: It looks like he's having fun and likes what you made.

After 30 minutes of coaching, the therapist congratulated Ms. Anderson on what a great job she did with increasing her behavioral descriptions and reflections, and then ended the coaching part of the session. The therapist returned to the room to process the session with Ms. Anderson and Doug as well as to review and assign home practice.

The next five sessions progressed similarly with a 5- to 10-minute check-in, 5-minute coding, 30-minute coaching, and 5- to 10-minute checkout. Over the course of the sessions, Ms. Anderson's skills increased, she became more confident in her abilities, and appeared to become more comfortable playing with and talking to Doug. During the check-in of Session 5, Ms. Anderson asked if it might be a good idea to include Ms. Jackson in sessions, given that Doug was currently living with her and she had always been an important part of his life. Ms. Anderson thought it might be a good idea for everyone to "be on the same page." The therapist agreed knowing that a consistent parenting style across caregivers would help Doug and that Ms. Jackson's support would also help Ms. Anderson to continue using her new skills after treatment ended. Following a discussion with Ms. Anderson about how to include Ms. Jackson in sessions without detracting from the mother-child focus, the therapist met with Ms. Jackson to discuss her interest in participating. Ms. Jackson agreed to be involved in PCIT. The therapist met with her to complete a separate didactic session (CDI teaching session). In subsequent sessions, Ms. Jackson observed sessions with Ms. Anderson and Doug. After a full coaching with Ms. Anderson, Ms. Jackson was coached in her skill use with Doug for a shorter period. Essentially, the focus remained on Ms. Anderson and Doug, and treatment progressed based on Ms. Anderson's skills.

The most challenging skill for Ms. Anderson was ignoring mild misbehaviors that Doug engaged in to obtain negative attention (e.g., whining, bossiness). Ms. Anderson was quick to criticize ("Don't be so mean, Doug") and to give commands to Doug when he misbehaved. The therapist had to coach ignoring in a very directive way at first to get Ms. Anderson to try the skill (e.g., "Go ahead and turn around. It's okay. He is just doing that to get a reaction out of you. Just turn around and ignore. Great job of removing your attention. You can see that he does not like that. Okay, he has been quiet for a couple of seconds. Go ahead and look at him again and give him a big praise for playing so quietly. I like the way you stayed calm and improved his behavior without any negative words. Well done"). After approximately eight episodes of ignoring across several sessions, Ms. Anderson began to ignore on her own, without prompting from the therapist.

Throughout sessions, the therapist maintained contact with the CPS caseworker, who confirmed Ms. Anderson's report that she was completing weekly drug screens and had remained drug free. At the 8th appointment, Ms. Anderson reached mastery on the CDI skills during the 5 minutes of coding at the beginning of the session (10 labeled praises, 10 behavioral descriptions, and 10 reflections, with fewer than 3 questions, commands, and criticisms), allowing the family to move on to the PDI phase of treatment. Ms. Anderson and Ms. Jackson were asked to complete the ECBI again. Both Ms. Anderson's (Intensity = 138; Problem = 16) and Ms. Jackson's (Intensity = 144; Problem = 15) scores indicated improvements in Doug's behavior, though his behavior remained in the clinically significant range.

PARENT-DIRECTED INTERACTION DIDACTIC (SESSION 9)

Session Objectives

1. Emphasize the value of consistency, predictability, and follow-through.
2. Discuss how to give an effective command.
3. Differentiate compliance versus noncompliance.
4. Review consequences for compliance (praise) and noncompliance (time-out).
5. Discuss, role-play, and troubleshoot the time-out procedure.
6. Discuss and role-play how to stay calm when setting limits and following through with consequences.

Session Content

Ms. Anderson and Ms. Jackson attended this session without Doug to learn the discipline skills. The therapist explained that to be consistent with setting limits, it is important to have just a few rules. By having a small number of rules, neither the child nor the parent becomes overwhelmed with too many rules to follow or enforce. The therapist discussed the importance of beginning with compliance as the first rule. Once Doug could follow instructions consistently ("to do" behaviors), then it would be much easier to follow through with a few rules for the behaviors that the caregivers wanted to decrease ("stop" behaviors). A rationale was provided for starting with simple "play" instructions (e.g., handing the mother a toy), using compliance practice and working up to real-life instructions (e.g., cleaning up) that could be used throughout the day. The therapist taught the caregivers the eight rules for giving effective instructions (e.g., tell rather than ask, be specific, be positive, one at a time) and emphasized the importance of using an enthusiastic labeled praise each time the child complies with a command. For noncompliance, the caregivers were taught to give a warning about time-out. For Doug's refusal to comply with the time-out warning, the caregivers were taught to put Doug in a time-out chair for 3 minutes. Specific time-out information that was taught to the family included the following: safely getting Doug to the time-out chair, having a backup consequence for refusing to stay in the chair (e.g., going to a time-out room for 1 minute plus 5 seconds of silence), handling aggression from Doug on the way to time-out, teaching Doug to be quiet in time-out, handling time-out problems such as scooting the chair and cursing, and requiring Doug to comply with the original instruction after time-out. For a detailed description of the PCIT time-out procedure, please see Eyberg (1999) or Hembree-Kigin and McNeil (1995).

Because Ms. Anderson had a history of child maltreatment, approximately 25 minutes of anger management and relaxation training was added to the standard PCIT protocol. Ms. Anderson was taught to identify her bodily cues, both the subtle (e.g., heart racing) and more obvious signs (raising her voice) that she was becoming angry and stressed. Given that the therapist might not know how Ms. Anderson was feeling during sessions, an agreement was made that Ms. Anderson would raise one finger in the air if she ever felt herself becoming angry or upset during discipline coaching sessions in the clinic. Then the therapist would help her use some skills to calm down. In particular, Ms. Anderson was taught to use breathing techniques, self-talk, and muscle relaxation to regulate her emotions during conflict-laden discipline interactions with Doug.

The overarching theme for Ms. Anderson was that she remain calm and robotic when following through with discipline procedures. She was encouraged to memorize the words that she had been taught to say during time-out procedures (e.g., "You didn't do what I told you to do so you have to sit on the chair") so that she could talk to her son in a calm and neutral tone of voice. The therapist told her that it was her job as the parent to "take the high road" when Doug was having a tantrum. Rather than screaming and arguing with Doug ("getting on his level"), she would have to work hard to underreact to his misbehavior (stay at the "higher" adult level). She was told that the louder he became, the quieter she should become. Examples were provided to help her to see that negative attention is fun and rewarding to a child who is having a tantrum.

A role-play was conducted to help Ms. Anderson and Ms. Jackson understand the importance of underreacting to child misbehavior. In the first scenario, Ms. Jackson (Doug's aunt) was instructed to play the parent and to try to get the child (played by Doug's mother) to put a crayon in the box. As the child, Ms. Anderson was told to refuse to listen no matter what Doug's aunt said or did. Then, Doug's aunt was instructed to yell and argue and try to convince Ms. Anderson to put the crayon away. During the role-play, Ms. Anderson enjoyed playing the "bad child," and Ms. Jackson did a good job of arguing and screaming back at "Doug" (getting on the child's level). Ms. Anderson then was asked how it felt to misbehave, and she said, "It was fun!" She seemed to gain a better understanding of how rewarding negative attention (e.g., arguing) is to a child who is having a tantrum. In the second scenario, Ms. Anderson was asked to play the child again. This time, Doug's aunt was asked to respond differently. She was told to memorize the words that she would say to Doug in advance. And, she was encouraged to pretend she was an actress in a play, just saying her lines, disciplining her son using a predetermined script. In this way, it would be easier to stay objective and calm. She was reminded that the goal is to take the adult high road rather than escalating with the child and reacting on the child's level. The role-play began with Doug's aunt telling Ms. Anderson, "Please put the crayon in the box." She then was instructed to simply point to the crayon and stay quiet for 5 long seconds. When Ms. Anderson did not comply, Doug's aunt was coached to give the warning in a calm and neutral tone of voice: "If you don't put the crayon in the box, you're going to have to sit on the chair." Then, she was coached to simply point to the crayon and to the time-out chair, while staying quiet for 5 more seconds. Ms. Anderson was told to keep pretending to be "bad" and not to listen. At the end of the role-play, Ms. Anderson was asked how it felt to be the child the second time. She immediately understood that it was much less fun because she did not have someone yelling and arguing with her. When receiving no reaction from "the parent," being defiant was a lot less rewarding.

After that role-play, Ms. Anderson was given the chance to play the parent. She was coached to recite her lines like an actress, take deep breaths, relax her muscles, and to underreact and remain calm even though her child was escalating into a full-blown temper tantrum. She was encouraged to talk to herself throughout the role-play with reminder cues like "stay calm" and "take the high road." During the debriefing from the role-play, Ms. Anderson said that it was a lot easier to stay calm when she had a plan to follow rather than just winging it. For home practice, Ms. Anderson and Ms. Jackson were instructed to continue with their 5 minutes of special playtime (CDI practice) each day. The therapist emphasized that they should not try the time-out procedure at home this week. Instead, they were told to wait until they received coaching in the clinic before trying the new time-out procedure elsewhere, as it would be critical for Doug's first time-out to be done exactly as taught to set a positive precedent for future time-outs.

PARENT-DIRECTED INTERACTION COACHING (SESSIONS 10 TO 16)

Session Objectives

1. Practice time-out procedures with intensive coaching to ensure that they are implemented properly.
2. Practice relaxation techniques with mother to the point that they become habits that occur automatically when faced with child misbehavior.

3. Code caregivers' discipline skills to determine whether they can perform the procedures independently at the level required for mastery.
4. Provide home practice assignments in a gradual and systematic way so that the parent and child can achieve goals each step of the way.
5. Continue to monitor CDI skills to ensure that parent continues to display mastery of the play therapy techniques.
6. Teach the caregivers how to generalize the discipline procedures to handle multiple children, public places, and "stop" behaviors (e.g., hurting others).

Session Content

At the first PDI coaching session, Ms. Anderson volunteered that she had worked on taking the high road during the week by staying calm and ignoring misbehavior when Doug whined or screamed. Ms. Anderson smiled with pride when describing that Doug calmed down more quickly when she stayed neutral instead of behaving at his level (e.g., arguing, raising her voice, throwing objects). The therapist praised Ms. Anderson for being willing to try some new approaches to parenting. The first PDI coaching session began by having Ms. Anderson review the time-out rules with Doug while Ms. Jackson observed behind the mirror. Ms. Anderson also encouraged Doug to role-play the time-out procedure ("just pretend . . . you're not in trouble") and gave him stickers for cooperating. In the beginning, the therapist provided Ms. Anderson with some simple instructions that she could simply repeat to Doug (e.g., "Please hand me the cat."). Later, the therapist prompted Ms. Anderson to come up with her own instructions. When Ms. Anderson phrased her first instructions as a question ("Doug, could you hand Mama the cow?"), the therapist quickly reminded Ms. Anderson that it is more effective to "tell" rather than "ask" Doug to listen during these compliance sessions. The therapist then asked Ms. Anderson to re-phrase the instruction in a more direct way. Ms. Anderson often responded to Doug's compliance by saying, "That's a good boy." The therapist helped Ms. Anderson to be more specific with her praise and to use a variety of different praise statements to keep it interesting, and therefore reinforcing, for Doug. Although the therapist made a point of increasing the difficulty of the instructions throughout the first session, Doug complied with all commands and never required a time-out in the clinic.

During the checkout time, the therapist did a role-play with Ms. Anderson to determine whether she remembered the time-out sequence. The therapist played the child and instructed Ms. Anderson to put "the child" in time-out for noncompliance. Ms. Anderson showed that she had learned the words and the sequence of events quite well. As a result, the therapist assigned a 10-minute per day home practice in which Ms. Anderson would do compliance practice with Doug using "play" commands only (e.g., "Please make a ball with the clay."). Ms. Anderson and Ms. Jackson were told to use the time-out procedure only during compliance practice, not for misbehavior during the rest of the day. They also were instructed to discontinue the assignment and call the therapist if Doug became aggressive or defiant during any of the daily practice sessions. As always, the caregivers were asked to have special playtime with Doug for 5 minutes each day.

During Sessions 11 and 12, Doug continued to comply with all instructions provided by both Ms. Anderson and Ms. Jackson in the clinic and during their home practices. Because time-outs were not needed, the therapist spent time each session role-playing the time-out procedure with the family (e.g., using a stuffed animal). The first 10 minutes of each session was spent coding CDI skills and PDI skills. Ms. Anderson continued to master the CDI skills. But, she did not reach mastery in PDI skills because she had a tendency to use indirect commands (i.e., asking rather than telling) and to repeat the instruction (forgetting to wait 5 seconds). In the 13th session, Doug refused a command to clean up a toy that he was playing with. He also refused to listen when given the warning about the time-out chair. As a result, Ms. Anderson took Doug to time-out. On the way to the time-out chair, Doug pulled his mother's hair and attempted to bite her. The therapist coached Ms. Anderson to ignore his aggression and calmly place him in the chair. And, the therapist reminded Ms. Anderson to take deep breaths and "stay in character" (reciting her lines and under-reacting to misbehavior). While on the chair, Doug shouted that he hated Ms. Anderson and wished that Ms. Jackson was his mother. The therapist normalized this behavior for Ms. Anderson, reminding her that it is common for children to use cruel words in time-out to try to get attention from their parents. Ms. Anderson was praised for staying calm and ignoring Doug's whining and screaming while in the time-out chair.

During Session 14, Ms. Anderson mastered the PDI skills during the 5 minutes of coding at the beginning of the session. Another discipline coaching session was scheduled, however, because Ms. Anderson's report on the ECBI suggested that Doug's behavior was still in the clinical range. By Session 16, all the criteria for termination were met, as Doug's ECBI scores improved to within normal limits and the mother continued to display mastery of both the CDI and PDI skills.

ENDING AND BOOSTER SESSIONS

Session Objectives

1. Conduct a posttreatment assessment.
2. Provide caregiver a certificate of completion.

3. Provide child with a blue ribbon for good behavior.
4. Emphasize the importance of continuing CDI on a daily basis, remaining consistent with the PDI skills, and always underreacting to child misbehavior.
5. Review signs of regression in the child's behavior or parenting skills and encourage the parent to call for a booster session before problems get worse.
6. Review pre- to posttreatment changes on measures and observed behavior, and congratulate the parent for the improvements.

Session Content

On the last session, Ms. Anderson and Ms. Jackson completed the pretreatment measures again. Additionally, Ms. Anderson was observed and coded in the three 5-minute situations of the DPICS (child leads, parent leads, clean-up). The results of the assessment were reviewed with the family, and the therapist showed Ms. Anderson some video clips of the pretreatment DPICS. The therapist paused the video at several points to ask Ms. Anderson about her thoughts and feelings. Ms. Anderson was surprised at how critical and unresponsive she had been to her son before treatment. The therapist also paused the video at several points to ask Ms. Anderson what she would do differently now that she had completed PCIT. Ms. Anderson was congratulated and given a certificate of completion. Additionally, Doug received a blue ribbon for good behavior. Ms. Anderson was reminded of the importance of continuing her daily special playtime sessions with Doug. And, she was encouraged to contact the clinic right away if she noticed herself losing her temper with Doug or felt that Doug's behavior problems were returning.

CONCLUSION

In the past 15 years, PCIT has been the subject of many research investigations, and PCIT's visibility has grown significantly with its inclusion on various lists that identify evidence-based treatments for young children (see Table 8.2). The interest in PCIT has expanded even further with the recent evidence suggesting that PCIT is effective for reducing future abuse reports in families with histories of child physical abuse (e.g., Chaffin et al., 2004). Currently, the greatest challenge for PCIT is transporting the program from university-based clinics to community settings (Herschell, McNeil, & McNeil, 2004). Franco, Soler, and McBride (2005) described some of the issues and challenges associated with an ongoing treatment effectiveness study exploring whether the addition of

Table 8.2
Websites with Additional Information

Website	Description
PCIT Specific	
http://www.pcit.org	Primary PCIT website; Dr. Eyberg's lab at the University of Florida
Evidence-Based Practice Sites That Include PCIT	
http://www.NCTSNet.org	The National Child Traumatic Stress Network
http://www.cachildwelfareclearinghouse.org	The California Evidence-Based Clearinghouse for Child Welfare
http://www.effectivechildtherapy.com	Society of Clinical Child and Adolescent Psychology, Division 53, American Psychological Association and the Network on Youth Mental Health
http://www.musc.edu/cvc/kauffman.html	The Kauffman Best Practices Report
http://www.musc.edu/cvc/guide1.htm	Child Physical and Sexual Abuse: Guidelines for Treatment

PCIT to a comprehensive system-of-care delivery results in better outcomes than system-of-care alone. The authors highlighted that a significant concern with transporting PCIT into community mental health is ensuring treatment integrity through training, fidelity checklists, and ongoing consultation. The training requirements of PCIT are extensive and costly. Research has demonstrated that a 2-day intensive training workshop and testing on required readings do not lead to mastery of the skills necessary to conduct just the first phase of PCIT (Herschell, McNeil, et al., 2006). The PCIT Advisory Board has grappled with the minimum requirements for training PCIT therapists and is in general agreement that the process requires at least 40 hours of initial training, as well as some type of advanced training or supervision once several PCIT cases have been completed (Eyberg & Brestan, 2006). Additionally, there are special equipment and room requirements for PCIT. An ideal setup involves a one-way mirror with bug-in-the-ear equipment, videotaping options, and a sound system in a nearby observation room. A small time-out room also is needed to provide the intervention with fidelity. Therefore, to implement PCIT in community mental health requires a significant commitment of therapist time, money, and space, which is difficult for many agencies to secure. Yet, efforts are underway to disseminate PCIT widely and evaluate those dissemination efforts, as

PCIT is a promising approach for treating families with young children who have experienced physical abuse and associated problems with disruptive behavior.

REFERENCES

Abidin, R. (1995). *Parenting stress index: Professional manual* (3rd ed.). Lutz, FL: Psychological Assessment Resources.

Bagner, D. M., & Eyberg, S. M. (2003). Father involvement in parent training: When does it matter? *Journal of Clinical Child and Adolescent Psychology, 32,* 599–605.

Bagner, D. M., Fernandez, M. A., & Eyberg, S. M. (2004). Parent-child interaction therapy and chronic illness: A case study. *Journal of Clinical Psychology in Medical Settings, 11,* 1–6.

Bahl, A. B., & McNeil, C. B. (2001). *Adapting parent-child interaction therapy to train Head Start teachers in behavior management.* Unpublished manuscript, West Virginia University.

Barkley, R. A. (1987). *Defiant children.* New York: Guilford Press.

Baumrind, D. (1966). Effects of authoritative parental control on child behavior. *Child Development, 4,* 887–907.

Boggs, S. R., Eyberg, S. M., Edwards, D. L., Rayfield, A., Jacobs, J., Bagner, D., et al. (2004). Outcomes of parent-child interaction therapy: A comparison of treatment completers and study dropouts 1 to 3 years later. *Child and Family Behavior Therapy, 26,* 1–22.

Borrego, J., Jr., & Urquiza, A. J. (1998). Importance of therapist use of social reinforcement with parents as a model for parent-child relationships: An example with parent-child interaction therapy. *Child and Family Behavior Therapy, 20,* 27–54.

Borrego, J., Jr., Urquiza, A. J., Rasmussen, R. A., & Zebell, N. (1999). Parent-child interaction therapy with a family at high-risk for physical abuse. *Child Maltreatment, 4,* 331–342.

Bousha, D. M., & Twentymen, C. T. (1984). Mother-child interactional style in abuse, neglect, and control groups: Naturalistic observations in the home. *Journal of Abnormal Psychology, 93,* 106–114.

Breiner, J., & Forehand, R. (1981). An assessment of the effects of parent training on clinic-referred children's school behavior. *Behavioral Assessment, 3,* 31–42.

Brestan, E. V., & Eyberg, S. M. (1998). Effective psychosocial treatment of conduct-disordered children and adolescents: 29 years, 82 studies, and 5,272 kids. *Journal of Clinical Child Psychology, 27,* 180–189.

Brestan, E. V., Eyberg, S. M., Boggs, S., & Algina, J. (1997). Parent-child interaction therapy: Parent perceptions of untreated siblings. *Child and Family Behavior Therapy, 19,* 13–28.

Capage, L. C., Bennett, G. M., & McNeil, C. B. (2001). A comparison between African American and Caucasian children referred for treatment of disruptive behavior disorders. *Child and Family Behavior Therapy, 23,* 1–14.

Chaffin, M., Silovsky, J. F., Funderburk, B., Valle, L. A., Brestan, E. V., Balachova, T., et al. (2004). Parent-child interaction therapy with physically abusive parents: Efficacy for reducing future abuse reports. *Journal of Consulting and Clinical Psychology, 72,* 500–510.

Choate, M. L., Pincus, D. B., Eyberg, S. M., & Barlow, D. H. (2005). Parent-child interaction therapy for treatment of separation anxiety disorder in young children: A pilot study. *Cognitive and Behavioral Practice, 12,* 126–135.

Clausen, J. M., Landsverk, J., Ganger, W., Chadwick, D., & Litrownik, A. (1998). Mental health problems of children in foster care. *Journal of Child and Family Studies, 7,* 283–296.

Crittenden, P. M. (1981). Abusing, neglecting, problematic, and adequate dyads: Differentiating by patterns of interaction. *Merrill-Palmer Quarterly, 27,* 201–218.

Derogatis, L. R. (1975). *Brief symptom inventory.* Baltimore: Clinical Psychometric Research.

Derogatis, L. R. (1993). *BSI Brief Symptom Inventory: Administration, scoring, and procedures manual* (4th ed.). Minneapolis, MN: National Computer Systems.

Dombrowski, S. C., Timmer, S. G., Blacker, D. M., & Urquiza, A. J. (2005). A positive behavioral intervention for toddlers: Parent-child attunement therapy. *Child Abuse Review, 14,* 132–151.

Eisenstadt, T. H., Eyberg, S. M., McNeil, C. B., Newcomb, K., & Funderburk, B. (1993). Parent-child interaction therapy with behavior problem children: Relative effectiveness of two stages and overall treatment outcome. *Journal of Child Clinical Psychology, 22,* 42–51.

Eyberg, S. M. (1999). *Parent-child interaction therapy: Integrity checklists and session materials.* Unpublished manuscript, University of Florida, Gainesville. Retrieved July 27, 2006, from www.pcit.org.

Eyberg, S. M. (2004). The PCIT story: Conceptual foundation. *PCIT Pages: Parent-Child Interaction Therapy Newsletter, 1,* 1–2.

Eyberg, S. M., Bessmer, J., Newcomb, K., Edwards, D., & Robinson, E. A. (1994). Dyadic parent-child interaction coding system-II: A manual. *Social and Behavioral Sciences Documents* (Ms. No. 2897). San Rafael, CA: Select Press.

Eyberg, S. M., & Boggs, S. R. (1989). Parent training for oppositional-defiant preschoolers. In C. E. Schaefer & J. M. Briesmeister (Eds.), *Handbook of parent training: Parents as co-therapists for children's behavior problems* (pp. 105–132). New York: Wiley.

Eyberg, S. M., & Brestan, E. V. (2006, January). *Advisory board review.* Paper presented at the 6th annual meeting of the Parent-Child Interaction Therapy Conference, Gainesville, FL.

Eyberg, S. M., & Calzada, E. J. (1998). *Parent-child interaction therapy: Procedures manual.* Unpublished manuscript, University of Florida.

Eyberg, S. M., Funderburk, B. W., Hembree-Kigin, T., McNeil, C. B., Querido, J., & Hood, K. K. (2001). Parent-child interaction therapy with behavior problem children: One and two year maintenance of treatment effects in the family. *Child and Family Behavior Therapy, 23*(4), 1–20.

Eyberg, S. M., & Matarazzo, R. G. (1975, April). *Efficiency in teaching child management skills: Individual parent-child interaction training versus group didactic training.* Paper presented at the annual meeting of the Western Psychological Association, Sacramento, CA.

Eyberg, S. M., Nelson, M. M., Duke, M., & Boggs, S. R. (2005). *Manual for the dyadic parent-child interaction coding system* (3rd ed.). Unpublished manuscript, University of Florida.

Eyberg, S. M., & Pincus, D. (1999). *Eyberg child behavior inventory and Sutter-Eyberg behavior inventory-Revised professional manual.* Odessa, FL: Psychological Assessment Resources.

Fernandez, M. A., & Eyberg, S. M. (2004). *Race matters: Treatment outcome for African American families in parent-child interaction therapy.* Manuscript submitted for publication.

Filcheck, H. A., McNeil, C. B., Greco, L. A., & Bernard, R. S. (2004). Using a whole-class token economy and coaching of teacher skills in a preschool classroom to manage disruptive behavior. *Psychology in the Schools, 41,* 351–361.

Filcheck, H. A., McNeil, C. B., & Herschell, A. D. (2005). Parent interventions with physically abused children. In P. Talley & A. J. Urquiza (Eds.), *Handbook for the treatment of abused and neglected children* (pp. 285–314). Boston: Allyn & Bacon.

Forehand, R. L., & Kotchick, B. A. (1996). Cultural diversity: A wake-up call for parent training. *Behavior Therapy, 27,* 187–206.

Forehand, R. L., & McMahon, R. (1981). *Helping the noncompliant child.* New York: Guilford Press.

Franco, E., Soler, R. E., & McBride, M. (2005). Introducing and evaluating parent-child interaction therapy in a system of care. *Child and Adolescent Psychiatric Clinics of North America, 14,* 351–366.

Fricker-Elhai, A. E., Ruggiero, K. J., & Smith, D. W. (2005). Parent-child interaction therapy with two maltreated siblings in foster care. *Clinical Case Studies, 4,* 13–39.

Frodi, A. M., & Lamb, M. E. (1980). Child abusers' responses to infant smiles and cries. *Child Development, 51,* 238–241.

Funderburk, B. W., Eyberg, S. M., Newcomb, K., McNeil, C. B., Hembree-Kigin, T., & Capage, L. (1998). Parent-child interaction therapy with behavior problem children: Maintenance of treatment effects in the school setting. *Child and Family Behavior Therapy, 20,* 17–38.

Gallagher, N. (2003). Effects of parent-child interaction therapy on young children with disruptive behavior disorders. *Bridges Practice-Based Research Syntheses, 1,* 1–17.

Hanf, C. (1969). *A two stage program for modifying maternal controlling during mother child interaction.* Paper presented at the meeting of the Western Psychological Association, Vancouver, B. C.

Harkness, S., & Super, C. (1995). Culture and parenting. In M. Bornstein (Ed.), *Handbook of parenting* (Vol. 2, pp. 211–234). Hillsdale, NJ: Erlbaum.

Harwood, M. D., & Eyberg, S. M. (2004). Therapist verbal behavior early in treatment: Relation to successful completion of parent-child interaction therapy. *Journal of Clinical Child and Adolescent Psychology, 33*(3), 601–612.

Harwood, M. D., O'Brien, K. A., Carter, C. G., & Eyberg, S. M. (2006). *Early identification and intervention for disruptive behavior in primary care: A randomized controlled trial.* Unpublished manuscript.

Hembree-Kigin, T. L., & McNeil, C. B. (1995). *Parent-child interaction therapy.* New York: Plenum Press.

Herschell, A. D., Calzada, E. J., Eyberg, S. M., & McNeil, C. B. (2002a). Clinical issues in parent-child interaction therapy. *Cognitive and Behavioral Practice, 9,* 16–27.

Herschell, A. D., Calzada, E. J., Eyberg, S. M., & McNeil, C. B. (2002b). Parent-child interaction therapy: New directions in research. *Cognitive and Behavioral Practice, 9,* 9–16.

Herschell, A. D., Capage, L., Bahl, A. B., & McNeil, C. B. (2006). *The role of therapist communication style in parent-child interaction therapy.* Manuscript submitted for publication.

Herschell, A. D., & McNeil, C. B. (2005). Theoretical and empirical underpinnings of parent-child interaction therapy with child physical abuse populations. *Education and Treatment of Children, 28*(2), 142–162.

Herschell, A. D., McNeil, C. B., & McNeil, D. W. (2004). Clinical child psychology's progress in disseminating empirically supported treatments. *Clinical Psychology: Science and Practice, 11*(3), 267–288.

Herschell, A. D., McNeil, C. B., Urquiza, A. J., McGrath, J. M., Zebell, N. M., Timmer, S., et al. (2006). *Evaluation of two strategies for training therapists in parent-child interaction therapy.* Manuscript submitted for publication.

Hood, K. K., & Eyberg, S. M. (2003). Outcomes of parent-child interaction therapy: Mothers' reports of maintenance 3 to 6 years after treatment. *Journal of Clinical Child and Adolescent Psychology, 32,* 419–429.

Kauffman Best Practices Project. (2004). *Closing the quality chasm in child abuse treatment: Identifying and disseminating best practices—The findings of the Kauffman Best Practices Project to help children heal from child abuse.* Kansas City, MO: Ewing Marion Kauffman Foundation.

Kolko, D. J. (2002). Child physical abuse. In J. E. B. Myers, L. Berliner, J. Briere, C. T. Hendrix, C. Jenny, & T. Reid (Eds.), *APSAC handbook of child maltreatment* (2nd ed., pp. 21–54). Thousand Oaks, CA: Sage.

Lahey, B. B., Conger, R. D., Atkeson, B. M., & Treiber, F. A. (1984). Parenting behavior and emotional status of physically abusive mothers. *Journal of Consulting and Clinical Psychology, 52,* 1062–1071.

Lorber, R., Felton, D. K., & Reid, J. B. (1984). A social learning approach to the reduction of coercive process in child abuse families: A molecular analysis. *Advances in Behavior Research and Therapy, 6,* 29–45.

Matos, M., Torres, R., Santiago, R., Jurado, M., & Rodríguez, I. (2006). Adaptation of parent-child interaction therapy for Puerto Rican families: A preliminary study. *Family Process, 45,* 205–222.

McCabe, K. M., Yeh, M., Garland, A., Lau, A. S., & Chavez, G. (2005). The GANA program: A tailoring approach to adapting parent-child interaction therapy for Mexican Americans. *Education and Treatment of Children, 28,* 111–129.

McCoy, C. J., Funderburk, B., & Chaffin, C. (in press). Modifying PCIT as a treatment for physically abusive parents. *PCIT Pages: Parent-Child Interaction Therapy Newsletter, 1*(2).

McIntosh, D. E., Rizza, M. G., & Bliss, L. (2000). Implementing empirically supported interventions: Teacher-child interaction therapy. *Psychology in the Schools, 37*, 453–462.

McNeil, C. B., Capage, L. C., & Bennett, G. M. (2002). Cultural issues in the treatment of young African American children diagnosed with disruptive behavior disorders. *Journal of Pediatric Psychology, 27*, 339–350.

McNeil, C. B., Clemens-Mowrer, L., Gurwitch, R. H., & Funderburk, B. W. (1994). Assessment of a new procedure to prevent time-out escape in preschoolers. *Child and Family Behavior Therapy, 16*(3), 27–35.

McNeil, C. B., Eyberg, S. M., Eisenstadt, T. H., Newcomb, K., & Funderburk, B. W. (1991). Parent-child interaction therapy with behavior problem children: Generalization of treatment effects to the school setting. *Journal of Clinical Child Psychology, 20*, 140–151.

McNeil, C. B., & Herschell, A. D. (1998). Treating multi-problem, high-stress families: Suggested strategies for practitioners. *Family Relations: Interdisciplinary Journal of Applied Family Studies, 47*, 259–262.

McNeil, C. B., Herschell, A. D., Gurwitch, R. H., & Clemens-Mowrer, L. (2005). Training foster parents in parent-child interaction therapy. *Education and Treatment of Children, 28*(2), 182–196.

Milner, J. S. (1980). *Child abuse potential inventory: Manual.* Webster, NC: Psytec.

Milner, J. S., & Chilamkurti, C. (1991). Physical abuse perpetrator characteristics: A review of the literature. *Journal of Interpersonal Violence, 6*, 345–366.

Niec, L. N., Hemme, J. M., Yopp, J. M., & Brestan, E. V. (2005). Parent-child interaction therapy: The rewards and challenges of a group format. *Cognitive and Behavioral Practice, 12*, 113–125.

Nixon, R. D. V., Sweeney, L., Erickson, D. B., & Touyz, S. W. (2003). Parent-child interaction therapy: A comparison of standard and abbreviated treatments for oppositional defiant preschoolers. *Journal of Consulting and Clinical Psychology, 71*, 251–260.

Nixon, R. D. V., Sweeney, L., Erickson, D. B., & Touyz, S. W. (2004). Parent-child interaction therapy: One- and two-year follow-up of standard and abbreviated treatments for oppositional preschoolers. *Journal of Abnormal Child Psychology, 32*, 263–271.

Ondersma, S. J., Chaffin, M. J., Mullins, S. M., & LeBreton, J. M. (2005). A brief form of the Child Abuse Potential Inventory: Development and validation. *Journal of Clinical Child and Adolescent Psychology, 34*, 301–311.

Patterson, G. R. (1976). The aggressive child: Victim and architect of a coercive system. In E. J. Mash, L. A. Hamerlynck, & L. C. Handy (Eds.), *Behavior modification and families* (pp. 267–316). New York: Brunner/Mazel.

Patterson, G. R. (2002). The early development of coercive family process. In J. B. Reid, G. R. Patterson, & J. Snyder (Eds.), *Antisocial behavior in children and adolescents: A developmental analysis and model for intervention* (pp. 25–44). Washington, DC: American Psychological Association.

Querido, J. G., & Eyberg, S. M. (2001, June). *Parent-child interaction therapy with Head Start families.* Poster session presented at the second annual PCIT meeting, Sacramento, CA.

Querido, J. G., Warner, T. D., & Eyberg, S. M. (2002). Parenting styles and child behavior in African American families of preschool children. *Journal of Clinical Child Psychology, 31,* 272–277.

Schuhmann, E., Foote, R., Eyberg, S. M., Boggs, S., & Algina, J. (1998). Parent-child interaction therapy: Interim report of a randomized trial with short-term maintenance. *Journal of Clinical Child Psychology, 27,* 34–45.

Shipman, K. L., & Zeman, J. (1999). Emotional understanding: A comparison of physically maltreating and nonmaltreating mother-child dyads. *Journal of Clinical Child Psychology, 28,* 407–417.

Tiano, J. D., & McNeil, C. B. (2005). The inclusion of fathers in behavioral parent training: A critical evaluation. *Child and Family Behavior Therapy, 27,* 1–28.

Tiano, J. D., & McNeil, C. B. (2006). Training Head Start teachers in behavior management using parent-child interaction therapy: A preliminary investigation. *Journal of Early and Intensive Behavior Intervention, 3,* 220–233.

Timmer, S. G., Urquiza, A. J., McGrath, J. M., & Zebell, N. M. (2005). Parent-child interaction therapy: Application to maltreating parent-child dyads. *Child Abuse and Neglect, 29,* 825–842.

Timmer, S. G., Urquiza, A. J., & Zebell, N. M. (2005). Challenging foster caregiver-maltreated child relationships: The effectiveness of parent-child interaction therapy. *Child and Youth Services Review, 28,* 1–19.

Urquiza, A. J., & McNeil, C. B. (1996). Parent-child interaction therapy: An intensive dyadic intervention for physically abusive families. *Child Maltreatment, 1,* 134–144.

U.S. Department of Health and Human Services, Administration on Children, Youth, and Families. (2003). *Child maltreatment 2001.* Washington, DC: U.S. Government Printing Office.

Ware, L. M. (2006). *Efficacy of in-home parent-child interaction therapy.* Unpublished doctoral dissertation, West Virginia University, Morgantown.

Webster-Stratton, C. (1984). Randomized trial of two parent-training programs for families with conduct-disordered children. *Journal of Consulting and Clinical Psychology, 52,* 666–678.

Webster-Stratton, C. (1994). Advancing videotape parent training: A comparison study. *Journal of Consulting and Clinical Psychology, 62,* 299–315.

Wolfe, D. A., & Sandler, J. (1981). Training abusive parents in effective child management. *Behavior Modification, 5,* 320–335.

CHAPTER 9

Success-Based, Noncoercive Treatment of Oppositional Behavior

THIS CHAPTER provides a description and discussion of an intervention that was designed to reduce the need for punishment and power assertion in the treatment of children who exhibit severe oppositional and other problem behaviors. The paper presents the rationale for development of the approach before describing the treatment protocol and the research supporting its use.

BEHAVIOR MANAGEMENT AND COERCION

Several years ago, I worked for an agency that provided intensive supports, including behavior management services, to children, adolescents, and adults with developmental disabilities and their families. Among the strategies used at this agency for management of severe problem behavior, the therapists and their supervisors sometimes employed and recommended the use of decelerative consequences (i.e., punishment procedures designed to reduce the frequency of the target behaviors they followed) that required forceful physical constraint of the individual. The clinical team conscientiously conducted systematic research and evaluation on use of these highly restrictive interventions to assess the effects on client behavior. The evaluation data showed that such consequences effectively reduced severe aberrant behaviors, such as aggression, self-injury and destruction that often stigmatized these clients, reduced learning opportunities, and presented serious management challenges in the community. The suppression of these problem behaviors potentially provided opportunities for teaching new skills to these individuals that could increase their autonomy and quality of life.

Notwithstanding this compelling justification for the use of these physically coercive forms of punishment, many of us at the agency and within the clinical research community had serious misgivings about such approaches for individuals with and without developmental disabilities. Concerns centered around a few key issues, particularly the ethicality of using physical force to compel individuals to terminate behaviors that had developed as adaptations to their cognitive, emotional, and communication deficits. Research evidence shows that persons with such deficits use problem behavior to communicate needs that they are unable to express in more prosocial ways (Carr et al., 1994).

Another concern involved the high levels of resistance and confrontation that sometimes occurred with the use of power-assertive interventions, leading to interactions that were dangerous and distressing for both the intervention agent (e.g., parent, therapist) and the client (e.g., Persi & Pasquali, 1999). With children, such interventions are likely to be deleterious to the parent-child relationship. Moreover, the use of physical force to change behavior has the potential to result in modeling effects, with the child learning that physical force is an effective strategy for gaining compliance from others. This concern is especially relevant to the often-noted intergenerational nature of family violence; children who experience or observe family violence are more likely to become perpetrators of such violence in adulthood (e.g., Avakame, 1998; Doumas, Margolin, & John, 1994).

There were also concerns common to most punishment procedures, including those that did not require physical force. Most research evidence shows that behavior change brought about by means of punishment rarely generalizes to settings where the threat of punishment is not present (Lerman & Vorndran, 2002; Sidman, 1989). Thus, children who have been punished for disruptive behavior in the home may discontinue the problem responses in that setting but not where the authority figure is absent or punishment is not possible (e.g., in the schoolyard or at the grocery store).There is potential for punitive or power-assertive consequences that are intended to reduce problem behaviors to actually serve as reinforcers for aberrant responding (e.g., Kern, Delaney, Hilt, Bailin, & Elliot, 2002; Martens, Witt, Daly, & Vollmer, 1999). Some children may be deprived of adequate levels of stimulation, attention, and praise from their parents. Under such circumstances, youngsters may seek less positive forms of stimulation and attention (e.g., scolding, reprimands, and even physical struggles) and may use undesirable responses to initiate such interaction.

Given concerns such as these, many behavioral researchers, particularly in the field of developmental disabilities, began investigating the potential for developing more positive approaches to behavioral intervention (Horner et al., 1990). Concurrent with these efforts, developmental researchers were documenting the relationship between responsive, sensitive parenting styles and positive behavioral outcomes in children (e.g., Ainsworth & Marvin, 1995; Baumrind, 1971). In Baumrind's (1971) examination of parenting styles, she found that authoritative parents (i.e., those who believed in the reciprocal rights of children, listened to their children's point of view, controlled their children through reasoning and explanations of rules, and were less likely to use physical punishment) had children who were self-reliant, willing to explore, and generally content. In contrast, an authoritarian parenting style (i.e., the parent emphasizes obedience to authority and uses punitive measures to gain behavioral control) was most often associated with less positive behavioral outcomes (Baumrind, 1971). Recent research has demonstrated a correlation between power-assertive or harsh parenting and behavioral difficulties in children (e.g., Gershoff, 2002; Nicolson, Fox, & Johnson, 2005).

TIME-OUT: BENEFITS AND LIMITATIONS

Notwithstanding the potential advantages of positive parenting and intervention approaches, the reality for parents of a child who has developed severe conduct difficulties is that demonstrating warmth, listening to the child's point of view, and reasoning with the child are not likely to be effective short-term options for managing and decreasing out-of-control behavioral outbursts. The child's behavior may be highly disruptive and even dangerous without strategies that serve to contain and limit child responding. Without such constraints, child behavior may trigger anger and frustration in care providers that could increase the potential for child maltreatment.

For this reason, certain punishment procedures, particularly various forms of time-out (i.e., removal of the child to an area that is free of reinforcement for a preset time contingent on the occurrence of a target problem behavior), are commonly used and recommended for controlling and reducing problem behavior in children (Turner & Watson, 1999). In conjunction with a range of skill- and relationship-building strategies, virtually all of the empirically supported parent management training approaches include time-out as an essential component (e.g., Barkley, 1997; Eyberg & Boggs, 1998; Forehand & McMahon, 1981; Webster-Stratton &

Hancock, 1998). Moreover, apart from serving to reduce the probability of future incidents of the targeted behavior, some forms of time-out provide an element of containment that prevents continued confrontation and struggle with the disruptive episode.

For the child with minor behavioral issues, a time-out consequence can be a very useful addition to the parenting arsenal, particularly if it is infrequently required and the child is willing to go to time-out when asked without additional intervention from the parent. However, concerns with time-out arise with children who are more severely oppositional, and who may offer strong resistance to the use of time-out and other constraining procedures.

Under these circumstances, some of the concerns cited earlier with power-assertive parenting come into play. The opposition of the child can result in potentially dangerous confrontations (Roberts, 1982). Parents who need to use such force are likely to end up modeling for the child the use of coercion as a strategy for gaining compliance from others. The consequence can inadvertently serve a reinforcement rather than punishment function (i.e., time-out conditions may provide escape from aversive conditions or demands present before time-out). Thus, the use of time-out with highly defiant children could feasibly do more harm than good.

THE IMPORTANCE OF COMPLIANCE

Child compliance involves the willingness of children to carry out the requests of their parents and other care providers or authority figures. Compliance is one of the most important targets for intervention in children, as cooperation with parents and other adults is essential to successful achievement of almost any goal, including positive parent-child relationships and academic or other accomplishments in the classroom. Moreover, researchers have established the "keystone" nature of compliance—intervention to improve compliance in children with oppositional difficulties can produce positive effects on a broad range of other problem behavior (Ducharme & Popynick, 1993; Parrish, Cataldo, Kolko, Neef, & Egel, 1986). It would appear from these studies that learning to follow through with the requests of authority figures has some overlap with learning to follow general rules of behavior (i.e., adult expectations that are not explicitly stated). Noncompliance is one of the most prevalent of all referral problems, being commonplace in virtually all externalizing diagnoses in children and one of the defining criteria for Oppositional Defiant Disorder. If untreated, severe noncompliance and oppositionality present risk factors for psychiatric disturbances in adolescence and adulthood (Gross & Wixted, 1987).

Traditional approaches to compliance training (Barkley, 1997; Forehand & McMahon, 1981) involve, among other components, teaching parents how to issue effective requests, how to provide reinforcement for child compliance, and how to deliver a consequence, typically time-out, contingent on noncompliant responses. Given the earlier cited concerns with intervention procedures that could potentially become confrontational and power assertive, we sought to develop a compliance training approach that precluded the use of such consequences and focused behavioral treatment on the positive aspects of parent-child interaction (e.g., contingent praise).

ERRORLESS COMPLIANCE TRAINING

Drawing from applied behavior analysis research and other effective compliance training approaches (e.g., Forehand & McMahon, 1981), we developed a success-focused and noncoercive approach to treatment of severe oppositional behavior. Research evidence and our own clinical experience with the severe behavior problems of children indicated that the punishment component of intervention could not simply be discontinued without significant loss of treatment gains (Ducharme, Harris, Milligan, & Pontes, 2003; Lerman & Vorndran, 2002). Clearly, time-out would need to be replaced with another strategy if significant treatment effects were to be preserved. The substitute component we decided to incorporate was graduation—the systematic and hierarchical introduction of conditions that are most commonly associated with the problem responses of the child.

The intervention was named Errorless Compliance Training (Ducharme, 2005) because it incorporates the same learning principles as those employed in errorless discrimination teaching (see the following section, *Theoretical Underpinnings*). In errorless discrimination teaching, early discriminations are made simple through the use of prompts that are gradually and systematically withdrawn at a pace that promotes correct responding throughout the learning process and after all prompts have been faded (e.g., Terrace, 1963; Touchette, 1968). Errorless Compliance Training involves a similar graduated and success-focused approach, but is applied to child behavior rather than discrimination learning. With this intervention, the environment is arranged to ensure the lowest possible probability of noncompliant responses during intervention.

The treatment process begins with an observational probability assessment of child compliance to parental requests to determine a hierarchy of child compliance. Requests are then divided into four probability levels, from requests that are highly likely to yield compliance (Level 1) to those that rarely do (Level 4). During the initial phase of treatment, parents are taught to deliver a high proportion of Level 1 requests and to immerse the child in praise and warm physical contact after each compliant response. Lower probability requests (Levels 2, 3, and 4) are gradually and sequentially introduced at a slow enough rate to ensure continued high rates of compliance. By the end of treatment, the child is typically complying at a high rate even to low probability requests.

Thus, through gradual introduction of challenging requests made by parents, which are often the primary triggers for problem behavior, children are taught to tolerate difficult compliance situations that were previously associated with defiance. The approach makes it easy for parents to obtain cooperative and prosocial behavior from their children and to provide warmth, praise, and other forms of positive interaction contingent on these responses. Improvements in generalized compliance are accomplished with virtually no use of punitive consequences for noncompliance throughout treatment.

THEORETICAL UNDERPINNINGS

Errorless approaches to managing severe problem behavior are derived from principles of operant conditioning, especially stimulus control, stimulus fading, positive reinforcement, and extinction. A stimulus condition is said to have stimulus control over a response or behavior when that behavior is much more likely to occur in the presence of that stimulus than in its absence. The stimulus develops control over the response because the response has been reinforced in the presence of that stimulus and not other stimuli. Thus, a person is much more likely to pick up the telephone after a ring than at other times because the ring has acquired stimulus control over the response of picking up the receiver. This occurs because the ring signals the presence of a potential reinforcer for the "picking up" response—someone on the other end of the line who wants to talk (Martin & Pear, 1978).

Many stimuli can develop stimulus control over specific behaviors of children. A parental request (e.g., "turn off the television") may develop stimulus control over a child tantrum because, in the past, the parents have inadvertently reinforced (given in to) the tantrum by allowing the child to leave the television on. Parents may acquiesce to the child's desire because it may lead to a quick termination of the child's disruptive response. Thus, parental requests to complete demanding tasks may develop stimulus control over noncompliance and other problem behavior because the child has learned to respond in ways that are likely to provide escape from the demand (it should be noted that other possible outcomes could maintain the child's aberrant behavior).

Some requests acquire stimulus control over more prosocial responding, even for children who often respond with opposition to their parents' demands. They are sometimes referred to in the clinical-research literature as "high probability" requests because the probability of the child completing the requested behavior is high (Mace et al., 1988). Requests such as "give me five," "throw me the ball," "eat your cookie," and "turn on the television" are much more likely to yield compliance than more demanding requests because the child's response often leads to natural sources of reinforcement (e.g., an enjoyable interaction, a playful activity, a cookie, a television program) and there is no reason for the child to seek escape from the requested task.

The goal of any compliance training program is to somehow induce children to respond to "low probability" requests (i.e., those that are often associated with noncompliance) in the same way that they respond to high probability requests—to demonstrate cooperation with most or all of the requests made by care providers. This is where the concept of stimulus fading becomes useful. Stimulus fading is the gradual change of the stimulus controlling a response or behavior, until the response eventually occurs in the presence of a different stimulus (Martin & Pear, 1978). With Errorless Compliance Training, the process of stimulus fading is used to gradually alter the stimulus conditions associated with child cooperative responses (i.e., high probability requests), such that compliance eventually occurs with all requests, including low probability requests. We begin the process by exposing the child to a high density of high probability requests and eventually progress stepwise through slightly lower probability requests until eventually the lowest probability requests (i.e., those that presented serious management problems to parents before treatment) are introduced. By the end of treatment, stimulus control has been expanded to include all of the requests that parents need children to follow.

An essential part of this process is the use of positive reinforcement by the care provider in the form of praise, positive social interaction, or other rewards that are contingent on child compliance to requests. Positive reinforcement is included to increase the likelihood that the child will cooperate with the gradually changing requests and to help broaden the range of requests that acquire stimulus control over cooperative responding. During intervention, children quickly learn that compliance with parental requests leads to desired outcomes.

Another operant principle that can play a role in Errorless Compliance Training is extinction—the operation of terminating reinforcement for a previously reinforced response. Extinction results in the eventual decrease in frequency and termination of the response because the response no longer serves the function of accessing reinforcement (Ducharme & van Houten, 1994). During Errorless Compliance Training, we ask parents to pay little attention to episodes of noncompliance because some behaviors may have been reinforced and maintained by parental attention in the form of scoldings and angry retorts (and even physical intervention).

In Errorless Compliance Training, the extinction component involves trying to ensure that noncompliance is not functional for accessing desirable social outcomes for the child.

This combination of learning principles provides parents with the opportunity to improve child compliance in a graduated, nonintrusive manner. The approach provides an alternative to the more conventional use of a combination of reinforcement for desirable responses to demanding conditions and punishment for inhibition of undesirable responses to theses conditions.

ERRORLESS COMPLIANCE TRAINING PROTOCOL

Errorless Compliance Training can be conducted in an individual or group format, depending on the resources available to the clinician and the specific needs of the family. The group format is more efficient, permitting several parents to be trained simultaneously in approximately the same amount of time required for individual training. Moreover, parents are able to observe other parents exhibiting the skills being taught during group training workshops, providing additional modeling effects. The group format also encourages mutual support among the parents by providing them with opportunities to share problems and solutions with one another. In some cases, however, especially for some parents with severe cognitive or emotional difficulties (e.g., parents with brain injuries or developmental disabilities), individual training will be required to provide them with the needed support to conduct the intervention. For the purposes of this chapter, we provide guidelines for conducting the treatment in a group format, given that only minor alterations are required to transform this content into an individualized protocol.

GROUP SESSION 1

The first training session is conducted to provide parents with an overview of the errorless approach. The workshop starts with introductions of all group members. Parents provide some brief comments on the behavior problems of their children and previous attempts at behavior management. Instructors then describe traditional approaches to treatment of problem behavior that involve the use of decelerative consequences (e.g., time-out) to reduce the frequency of these responses. They also discuss advantages and disadvantages of such approaches.

Parents sometimes note during this discussion that they have been raised on punitive strategies (e.g., scoldings, spankings) and are convinced that such approaches are the most effective way to discipline their own children (i.e., "my parents punished me and I turned out okay"). A compassionate and understanding approach to such comments is best for eventually changing parent perceptions about the nonpunitive strategies that we endorse in this workshop. We inform parents that we understand the rationale for using reprimands and constraining approaches to manage problem behavior and note that we have used them ourselves with our own children at times. Parents who use such approaches are often trying the best they can to stop problem behaviors that they know are not going to be in the future best interests of their child. We then describe the differences we see in our own children and the children we have treated when we use the more success-focused and positive strategies that will be part of the training for the workshop. We also point out that kids are much more likely to cooperate with their parents and feel good about themselves when parents focus on and acknowledge the things they do right rather than constantly noticing, criticizing, and punishing their failings.

This discussion is often enough to convince parents to give our new approach a try. However, with parents who continue to believe that "sparing the rod will spoil the child," more time may be needed outside of the group format to gain greater understanding of the parent's need to use punishment and eventually to alter their beliefs about the necessity for intrusive approaches for disciplining children.

We then provide an overview of Errorless Compliance Training and some potential benefits of the approach. The following information is presented verbally and on overheads:

What Is Errorless Compliance Training?

- Parents use the Errorless Compliance Training approach to teach their children to cooperate with their requests. With this approach, the parent focuses much more on child success and pays less attention to child failure.
- Parents start treatment by asking their child to complete tasks that they enjoy or are easy for them to do. By starting with such easy requests, parents greatly increase child compliance and opportunities to reward the child for cooperation.
- Parents praise and reward their children for compliance to these requests.
- After children have successfully completed many easy tasks requested by their parents for several days, tasks that are slightly more difficult are introduced. Task difficulty is introduced gradually to ensure that children continue to respond to requests with the same high rate of cooperation. Parents continue to praise and reward the children for compliance with these more challenging requests.
- By the end of treatment, children typically continue to comply with requests that they may have refused to cooperate with before treatment.

- Errorless Compliance Training provides an alternative to more conventional treatment approaches because it does not require disciplinary consequences for child problem behavior.

What Are the Benefits of Errorless Compliance Training?

- Because noncompliance is greatly reduced throughout treatment, parent frustration with child behavior is reduced, and parents do not need to struggle with use of disciplinary consequences to decrease problem behavior.
- The approach has the potential to reduce other behaviors such as aggression and disruptive behavior.
- The approach increases opportunities for parents to provide praise and warmth to their children following cooperative responses, thereby improving the parent-child relationship.
- The approach involves learning a very simple set of skills to produce improvements in child behavior.
- Improvements in child compliance to parental requests included in treatment typically generalize to other requests that are problematic for parents.

ASSESSMENT PROCEDURES

BASELINE ASSESSMENT OF COMPLIANCE PROBABILITIES

After the overview of Errorless Compliance Training is provided to parents in Group Session 1 and questions about the approach have been answered, we initiate the Baseline Assessment of Compliance Probabilities, a process that will eventually result in the four compliance probability levels necessary to activate treatment. During assessment of probability levels, we use both a checklist and observational assessment of child compliance.

Compliance Probability Checklist

In Group Session 1, parents complete the Compliance Probability Checklist (Ducharme, Atkinson, & Poulton, 2000; Ducharme & Popynick, 1993; Ducharme, Popynick, Pontes, & Steele, 1996; Ducharme, Pontes, et al., 1994) to assist in the selection of specific requests to include in treatment. When completed, this checklist provides an indication of parent perceptions of child compliance to specific parental requests. The checklist comprises approximately 120 requests involving everyday tasks from several different compliance domains, including hygiene (e.g., "wash your face," "brush your teeth"), dressing (e.g., "put on your pants," "button your shirt"), leisure (e.g., "throw me the ball," "do a somersault"), and social interaction (e.g., "give me five," "shake my hand").

The checklist includes columns for rating the request as either "almost always" complies (Level 1: 76% to 100% of the time), "usually" complies (Level 2: 51% to 75% of the time), "occasionally" complies (Level 3: 26% to 50% of the time), and "rarely" complies (Level 4: 0% to 25% of the time). Requests rated as Level 1 typically are those that involve activities the child finds enjoyable (e.g., "turn on the television," "give me five"). Level 4 requests are often associated with unpleasant or demanding tasks (e.g., "put away your toy," "wash your hands"). Levels 2 and 3 requests are those that fall between the previous two extremes; requests in these levels might yield compliance when the child is in a good mood or well rested, but might be associated with noncompliance at other times.

The checklist also has a column for indicating that the child has not yet learned the skill or task represented by the request (i.e., failure of the child to complete the request would represent a skill deficit rather than a compliance problem). The final column provides the opportunity for parents to indicate that a request is important to them. We make an effort to include such requests in treatment when possible.

At Group Session 1, we work through several of the requests on the checklist with the parents to ensure that they understand how to fill it out and provide them with time to complete it. If parents have more than one child with oppositional behavior, we ask them to fill out a separate checklist for each child.

BETWEEN GROUP SESSIONS 1 AND 2

Assessment Data Sheet Preparation

To enable parent collection of data on the probability of compliance to specific requests, the clinician prepares assessment data sheets (see Table 9.1) from the information provided by the parents in the completed Compliance Probability Checklist. For each child in the group, the clinician reviews the completed checklist and selects approximately 6 requests from each of the four probability levels (as rated by the parent) to include on the data sheet (24 requests in total). For lower probability requests (Levels 3 and 4), the clinician should include requests designated as important by the parent because these requests will be the primary target for intervention. The requests selected for observational assessment should sample the diverse range of domains covered by the questionnaire (e.g., dressing, hygiene, leisure), to increase the likelihood of treatment generalization to all relevant areas (Stokes & Baer, 1977). Requests are listed in random order on the assessment data sheet. The data sheet has space for the parent to indicate whether the child was compliant or noncompliant to several repetitions of each of the requests when provided over several days

Table 9.1
Sample Assessment Data Sheet

Child's Name: _____   Start Date: _____

Requests		Dates											Totals
1	Come here.												
2	Give me a hug.												
3	Wash your hands.												
4	Dry your hands.												
5	Go get your ___ (toy).												
6	Play with your ___ (toy).												
7	Give ___ to ___.												
8	Come to the table.												
9	Go to the kitchen.												
10	Pass the ___.												
11	Put it in the garbage.												
12	Get your brush/comb.												
13	Brush/comb your hair.												
14	Tell me what time it is.												
15	Put your ___ away.												
16	Pick up your ___.												
17	Sit down.												
18	Bring me the ___.												
19	Fold the ___.												
20	Push your chair in.												
21	Put your dish in the sink.												
22	Give me the ___.												
23	Put away your books/toys.												
24	Turn off the TV.												

or weeks. Individualized assessment data sheets will be provided to each parent in Group Session 2.

GROUP SESSION 2

In Group Session 2, we teach parents to conduct the observational probability assessment, which requires them to learn the definition of compliance and noncompliance, how to deliver requests effectively, and how to collect data on child compliance.

Observational Probability Assessment

This phase of the baseline assessment of compliance probabilities is required to empirically determine the probability of child compliance to specific requests so that they can be designated to one of the four compliance probability levels used in treatment. Many parents have difficulty accurately predicting the probability of child compliance using a self-report measure such as the Compliance Probability Checklist. The observational probability assessment provides a much more precise measure of child compliance probabilities.

During Session 2, the clinician teaches parents the skills required to complete the observational probability assessment, including request delivery and data collection procedures. Performance-based training procedures, including modeling, role-playing, and performance feedback are used to promote optimal training effects for these and all other intervention procedures.

Request Delivery Training

During this segment of the session, we teach parents how to issue requests that are easily understood and interpreted as requiring immediate compliance by the child. Some children are noncompliant primarily because they have difficulty processing or understanding parental requests due to improper request delivery. In such cases, teaching parents to deliver requests effectively may result in immediate improvements in child compliance. Parents are taught several guidelines for request delivery.

- *Issue requests in the imperative.* We teach parents to use the imperative ("Tommy, brush your teeth") rather than the interrogative format ("Tommy, would you like to brush your teeth?") for request delivery, to ensure that the child is aware that the parent is seeking compliance without delay. Although the question format is often viewed as the more polite option for gaining compliance (and is perfectly acceptable for children without a compliance problem), the imperative format is more appropriate for oppositional children.
- *Use simple requests.* Children may be noncompliant because the requests they are asked to follow are too complex. Parents should keep requests short and simple to ensure comprehension and ease of completion, saying, for example, "Tommy, set the table," rather than "Tommy, set the table, wash your hands, and go get your brother for dinner."
- *Maintain proximity and eye contact.* Parents need to ensure that the child has heard and processed the requests they deliver. Children may be noncompliant because they were preoccupied with or distracted by other tasks (e.g., watching television) and were unable to focus on the parents' words. Parents should move close to the child and gain eye contact before request delivery.
- *Use a polite but firm tone.* Parents often become irritated with children because of their oppositional responses and may, at times, de-

liver requests in an angry or militaristic tone of voice. A polite but assertive tone conveys a more collaborative and conciliatory message. Such a request indicates that compliance is expected but that parents will work cooperatively with the child (without confrontation or coercion) to obtain it.

- *Do not repeat the request or provide prompts/discussion.* Parents of children with compliance difficulties often repeat requests several times, hoping that eventually the child will get the point and comply. Children may habituate to frequent request repetitions and cease to respond readily to them. Further, children sometimes learn to avoid or delay compliance to requests by asking questions or drawing parents into an argument about the need to complete the desired response. For these reasons, parents are asked to provide only one statement of the request. With this strategy, requests become more salient to children and they learn that ignoring or failing to comply to specific requests will momentarily reduce their access to parental praise and positive attention. With regard to children's questions or arguments about the appropriateness of the request, we ask parents to provide all explanations prior to issuing the request and to avoid such discussion after request delivery. This procedure will help to ensure that such child-initiated discussion does not become a strategy for avoiding or delaying tasks. The parent can say, "Tommy, we need to go to the store to get groceries" before delivering the request "Tommy, please put on your shoes."

- *Provide time for the child to respond.* Parents sometimes provide little time for a child to respond before becoming angry and repeating the request, or giving up and completing the requested task themselves. We teach parents to wait calmly for child compliance after request delivery. Usually around 10 seconds is a reasonable duration to wait for response initiation for most children, although at times we have recommended longer latencies for children with physical or cognitive difficulties.

- *Be natural.* Parents are asked to be as natural as possible when issuing requests. Children will make greater gains with the program if they are unable to distinguish between requests delivered as part of this program and requests that are delivered as a normal part of everyday interactions.

Compliance Record

Data collection on child compliance is an important component of Errorless Compliance Training. A record of child responses to parental requests provides a means for development of the compliance probability levels that are essential for activating treatment. Data on child compliance before, during, and after intervention also provide a strategy for evaluating the efficacy of the intervention. In some of our early studies examining Errorless Compliance Training, we used research assistants to collect data as a means of ensuring accuracy of measurement. More recently, however, we have found that parents can be taught to collect data that are just as accurate as those provided by trained research staff (e.g., Ducharme et al., 2000). During Group Session 2, we teach the following operational definition of child compliance and noncompliance to parents:

> Children are considered compliant if they begin the requested response within about 10 seconds of the request and complete the response in a reasonable period of time, based on the nature of the requested task.
>
> Children should be considered noncompliant if they fail to respond to the request at all, fail to respond within about 10 seconds, or fail to complete the requested task within a reasonable period of time. Responding to the request with problem behavior, such as verbal or physical opposition, is also considered noncompliance.

During the performance-based training of data collection, we model how behaviors should be coded in real and contrived compliance situations and provide parents with feedback on their efforts to record compliance and noncompliance during the training session.

Observational Probability Assessment Data Collection by Parents

During Group Session 2, we provide parents with the assessment data sheet (see Table 9.2) that includes a listing of the approximately 24 requests equally sampling the four probability levels of the Compliance Probability Checklist. Parents are instructed to deliver these requests to the child over the next several days or weeks until data is collected for 5 to 10 repetitions of each request. We teach parents to respond as they normally do to child compliance and noncompliance during this phase so that we can obtain a representative picture of how children react to parental requests before intervention.

BETWEEN GROUP SESSION 2 AND 3

At some point during the observational probability assessment, the clinician should make phone contact with the parent to provide prompts and support around the assessment process and data collection. Parents with emotional or cognitive difficulties may require additional prompt procedures (e.g., signs on the walls, scheduling in a memory book or calendar, alarms on a watch) to assist them in implementation of the required procedures.

Table 9.2
Sample Treatment Data Sheet

Child's Name: _____   Start Date: _____

Phase Levels □1 □2 □3 □4 □ Transition	Responses (📄 or ⏳)										
Dates											
Repetition 1											
1. Give me a hug.											
2. Play with your ___ (toy).											
3. Go get your ___ (toy).											
4. Come here.											
5. Pass the ___.											
6. Dry your hands.											
Repetition 2											
1. Give me a hug.											
2. Play with your ___ (toy).											
3. Go get your ___ (toy).											
4. Come here.											
5. Pass the ___.											
6. Dry your hands.											
Repetition 3											
1. Give me a hug.											
2. Play with your ___ (toy).											
3. Go get your ___ (toy).											
4. Come here.											
5. Pass the ___.											
6. Dry your hands.											
Totals											
Compliance (%)											

TREATMENT PROCEDURES

GROUP SESSION 3

During this session, we collect observational assessment data from parents, construct the treatment hierarchy and data sheets, and provide parents with training in all treatment procedures.

Development of Compliance Probability Hierarchy
and Treatment Data Sheets

At the beginning of Group Session 3, the observational probability assessment data collected by parents over the past few weeks should be gathered from them by the clinician. During this session, we often have an assistant available who collects the observational assessment data sheets and constructs the compliance probability hierarchy and all treatment data sheets for each child on the spot. With this strategy, parents can be provided with everything they need to initiate treatment at this training session (data sheets can also be constructed after the session is over and either mailed or emailed to parents—this procedure is more practical if there are a large number of parents in the treatment group or no one to assist in construction of the data sheets).

The compliance probability for each request on the data sheet can be calculated by dividing the total number of compliant responses to that request by the total number of request deliveries. Requests can then be arranged in order of the probability of child compliance and divided into four categories, roughly approximating the four compliance probability levels: Level 1 (76% to 100% compliance), Level 2 (51% to 75% compliance), Level 3 (26% to 50% compliance), and Level 4 (0% to 25% compliance). These percentages provide only a general guideline; levels for some children may be skewed in the positive (i.e., more compliant) or negative direction and still meet the requirements of the errorless approach.

From this analysis, treatment data sheets (see Table 9.2) for each child are constructed for each of the four treatment phases and for the three transitions. All requests from Level 1 should be copied onto the Phase 1 treatment data sheet, all requests from Level 2 onto the Phase 2 data sheet, and so on. Transition data sheets involve a combination of requests from the two adjoining levels (see the following section *Transition Sessions*). A selection of approximately three requests can be taken from each of the adjoining levels for each transition sheet. Thus, the Transition 1 sheet would have a combination of requests from Level 1 and Level 2; the Transition 2 sheet, a combination of requests from Levels 2 and 3; and the Transition 3 sheet, a combination of requests from Levels 3 and 4.

Training in Treatment Skills

During Parent Group Session 3, parents learn the three discrete skill sets that are required to conduct treatment across all treatment phases (these skills are in addition to the request delivery and data collection procedures that parents learned previously). The skills include praise and reinforcement for child compliance to parental requests, avoidance of attention and other reinforcers for noncompliance, and avoidance of requests from subsequent probability levels.

As with pretreatment skills, we use modeling, role-playing, and performance feedback procedures to train parents in the use of all treatment procedures. For parents with cognitive deficits, we have used prompt procedures (e.g., timers, posted signs) to remind parents to use the following three procedures:

1. *Provide praise and reinforcement for child compliance.* Opportunities for parents to deliver warmth, praise, and other reinforcers to their child contingent on prosocial responses are greatly increased with Errorless Compliance Training due to the initial presentation of requests that commonly yield compliance. Parents are often surprised at how easy it becomes to provide the child with positive attention in the early phases of treatment, given that these same parents often complained before intervention about the difficulty of finding praiseworthy behavior in their oppositional child. We teach parents to follow certain guidelines when providing praise and reinforcement after each child-compliant response to ensure optimal effectiveness.

   First, parents should provide reinforcement immediately following every incident of child compliance. The goal of intervention is to teach children that cooperative responses will reliably lead to positive outcomes, so immediacy and consistency are essential. Second, parents should provide enthusiastic praise and warm physical contact (e.g., pat on the back, a hug or kiss) after completion of the requested task. We teach parents to be as varied in their praise statements as possible to ensure that parental attention does not lose its potency as a reinforcer. Third, when parental attention does not serve as a reinforcer, other types may be necessary (e.g., points, stars, tokens, stickers that can be exchanged for toys, desired activities, privileges). In one study that involved children with autism (Ducharme & Drain, 2004), we used puzzle pieces as token reinforcers that could be exchanged for activity rewards when the final piece was added to the puzzle. We often provide parents with a reinforcer survey that requires them to list some of their children's favorite foods, toys, entertainment activities (e.g., movies, music), sports and games (e.g., basketball, billiards, cards, video games), excursions (e.g., to the mall, beach, park, arcade), personal appearance items (e.g., running shoes, T-shirt, jewelry, make-up), token reinforcers (e.g., stickers, certificates, points to be exchanged), time with specific persons (e.g., having friends over, going on an outing with a relative), or any other potential reinforcer. Parents can then include their children in the process of deciding on additional rewards that they are willing to work for.

2. *Avoid desirable outcomes following noncompliance.* Many parents are highly reactive to child problem behaviors, which are often much more salient to them than child-cooperative and prosocial responses. A parent may deliver reprimands, threats, or other forms of negative interaction in their frustration at trying to manage the child's behavior, and may pay little heed when the child is more appropriately engaged. One of the problems with negative attention provided in this manner is that, in some cases, it may inadvertently serve as a reinforcer for problem responses. Children are often so deprived of parental contact that virtually any attention, even scoldings and reprimands, can be much more rewarding to the child than no interaction at all. Under such circumstances, children may learn that the easiest way to gain parental attention is to exhibit oppositional or other problem behavior.

Thus, in addition to noticing and reinforcing cooperative responses, parents should avoid reacting to child problem behavior, especially noncompliance, with threats, criticism, reprimands, scolding, or any other statements, as well as facial expressions that indicate to the child that the parent is angry or distressed (even subtle reactions by the parent may be sufficient to maintain the child's problem behavior). Although parents may have difficulty fighting their instinctive reactions to child misbehavior, the process is made much easier by the graduated nature of request delivery in the errorless approach, rendering child oppositional responses much less frequent.

3. *Avoid request delivery from subsequent levels.* To increase the probability of high compliance levels throughout treatment, thereby maintaining the errorless nature of intervention, parents should avoid premature delivery of requests from lower probability levels. When parents maximize the proportion of requests that yield compliance throughout treatment, the child experiences frequent interactive successes that can be praised and acknowledged by parents. This process ensures that children begin to see request delivery as a positive process that leads to compliance and subsequent reinforcement. Premature introduction of low probability requests would compromise this process and increase the likelihood of noncompliant responses from the child. Thus, lower probability requests should be faded in gradually over several weeks, rather than introduced early in treatment.

For tasks that must be completed (e.g., getting dressed, coming for dinner), the parent should make statements such as "it's time for us to get ready for school" and then use prompting or gentle guidance to help the child complete the task. The parent may also simply complete the task for the child (e.g., "I'm going to turn off the television now") rather than asking the child to do it. It is important, particularly in early phases of the program, to minimize requests that are likely to lead to noncompliance. Parent avoidance of requests from subsequent levels is typically required only for a few weeks, after all phases of treatment have been introduced. By this time, the probability of child compliance to any request delivered by the parent will have increased substantially over baseline levels.

INITIATION OF TREATMENT PHASE 1 (LEVEL 1 REQUESTS)

As soon as the parents have been provided with treatment data sheets, they can initiate Phase 1 of treatment. The Phase 1 treatment data sheet includes three repetitions of the six requests from Level 1 (those requests that yield the highest rates of compliance). Parents should deliver each of the requests on the sheet at least once per day and as many as three times, and continue to keep a record of child compliance or noncompliance to the requests on the data sheet.

With children who demonstrate high levels of oppositionality, compliance may be difficult to obtain even to Level 1 requests. In such cases, we provide parents with specific guidelines for ensuring that compliance occurs at a high level, such as asking parents to deliver requests when the child is not involved in highly desirable activities that would make engagement in other tasks difficult. Similarly, requests should not be delivered when the child is tired, hungry, or in an agitated state as compliance probability may be adversely affected by such conditions. Simplifying task conditions is another option for increasing compliance probability (e.g., asking the child to bring an object that is within his reach rather than one that requires more effort to access). If needed at all (for most children, Level 1 requests will reliably lead to cooperative responses), these procedures are typically required only in Phase 1.

Phase 1 treatment sessions should continue for at least 1 week, and may require several weeks before the child learns that compliant responses reliably lead to enjoyable outcomes. For this and all subsequent phases of treatment, we use a criterion of 75% or greater child compliance over approximately 3 consecutive days of request delivery before the transition phase is introduced.

TRANSITION SESSIONS

During or following Group Session 3, parents are provided with data sheets for conducting transition sessions that involve delivery of requests from the two adjacent probability levels. Transitions are designed to make passage from one phase of treatment to the next less abrupt (e.g., Ducharme & Popynick, 1993). Thus, in the first transition sessions (those following Phase 1), parents deliver requests from both Level 1 and Level 2. Once compliance is consistently high to the Level 2 requests delivered during these sessions (over 75%), parents can move on to Phase 2 requests. Typically, only two or three transition sessions are required before moving on to the next phase of treatment. Parents should use similar transition procedures between all subsequent phases.

TREATMENT PHASES 2, 3, AND 4 (LEVEL 2, 3, AND 4 REQUESTS)

Requests from the remaining three request levels are introduced sequentially in Phases 2, 3, and 4. Parents are informed that once they shift to a new phase of treatment, they can continue to use requests from all previously trained request levels, but should continue to avoid requests from subsequent phases.

GROUP SESSION 4

Group Session 4 is conducted at some point during the treatment process (ideally during Phase 3). During the first half of the session, the clinician discusses treatment progress with the parents, answers any questions they may have, and helps to problem solve any treatment issues that have come up. During the remainder of the session, the clinician can conduct brief refresher training on the key skills required to conduct treatment: request delivery, praise and reinforcement for child compliance, and avoidance of reactions to noncompliance.

GROUP SESSION 5

Group Session 5 is used to discuss child progress, review treatment concepts and procedures, answer parent questions, and problem solve any behavioral difficulties that were not resolved in treatment. Parents should be commended for their efforts in implementing the approach and encouraged to exchange phone numbers and to remain in touch with each other for support. In addition to the preceding content, the clinician should review the following maintenance guidelines for parents:

- *Praise cooperation and rule following in all situations and settings.* Parents should praise the cooperative behavior and compliance with general rules of behavior of their child in all situations and settings (e.g., with grandparents, siblings, at the playground, at the mall). For example, the parent could (a) praise the child for acquiescing to the wishes of a peer rather than insisting on having things his own way (e.g., "I'm really happy with the way you let that little girl have a turn pushing the train"), (b) commend the child for staying within a reasonable proximity when walking around at the mall (e.g., "thank you for staying close to me while we're shopping—that really helps me a lot"), or (c) acknowledge the child for staying at the table while eating (e.g., "do you realize that you haven't gotten down from your chair once while we've been eating? I'm so proud of you"). Children are much more likely to demonstrate prosocial behavior when parents are constantly noticing them for following rules rather than scolding them for infractions.

- *Use activity and tangible rewards for exceptional behavior.* Occasionally, parents should accompany praise statements and acknowledgment with tangible rewards (e.g., toys, snacks, activities) to let the child know that their improved behavior is greatly appreciated. For example, the parent could take the child out for an ice cream cone or buy an inexpensive toy after completion of a particularly challenging task (e.g., "I'm so happy with how you helped me clean up the basement; let's go get a milkshake to celebrate all the work you did").
- *Do not expect perfection.* Parents are often unaware that it is perfectly normal for children to be uncooperative occasionally. No child is 100% compliant; parents should be tolerant of minor forms of noncompliance and not return to focusing on and criticizing child problem responses rather than emphasizing and acknowledging the child's prosocial behaviors.
- *Play with your child.* Parents should be taught that simply playing with their child in a warm and affectionate manner can greatly improve cooperation and enhance the parent-child relationship (e.g., Ducharme & Rushford, 2001). Parents should be encouraged to schedule a time every day that is dedicated solely to enjoyable parent-child activity (e.g., playing a game, building with blocks, drawing pictures, telling stories). During the play period, the parent should make an effort to notice and comment on the child's successes (e.g., "what an interesting flower you drew," "that's a funny story"). Even a few minutes a day can produce powerful positive effects on child behavior and affection for the parent.

REVIEW OF OUTCOME STUDIES

Over more than a decade, we have been conducting time-series evaluations (typically using multiple baseline designs) of errorless approaches with a broad range of populations of children with severe oppositional behavior, including children with developmental disabilities, children who have witnessed and been victims of family violence, children of parents with an acquired brain injury, and children with autistic spectrum disorders. More recently, we have been examining the efficacy of classroom-based errorless approaches to managing severe problem behavior.

DEVELOPMENTAL DISABILITIES

Behavior problems are much more common in children with developmental disabilities than in typically developing youngsters (Baker, Blacher, Crnic, & Edelbrock, 2002; Baker et al., 2003). These children may use aberrant responses to communicate their needs (Carr et al., 1994) given their often-deficient levels of communication (e.g., exhibiting problem behavior when exposed to demands that they wish to escape, Carr & Newsom, 1985; Weeks & Gaylord-Ross, 1981).

In Ducharme and Popynick (1993), the first study conducted to examine Errorless Compliance Training, we focused on building up the tolerance levels to parent-issued demands of four children with developmental disabilities (two 5-year-olds; two 8-year-olds). During individual training sessions, we taught the parents of the four children to conduct baseline and treatment in the family home. Parents then conducted compliance sessions with their children that were videotaped by therapists. Data on child compliance and other problem behavior were coded from these videotapes.

As described earlier, assessment involved the use of the Compliance Probability Checklist to obtain parents' initial perception of the compliance of their children to a broad range of household requests from several domains of compliance (e.g., dressing, cleaning up). Parent responses to this checklist were used to develop a list of requests that parents delivered to their children over the next few weeks, with approximately 10 repetitions of each of 48 requests. After determining the probability of child compliance to each request, we categorized the requests for each child into the four probability levels (from high to low probability of compliance).

During the first phase of treatment, parents issued several repetitions of seven Level 1 requests (i.e., those that yielded the highest compliance during baseline) over several sessions and praised child compliance following each request. After several weeks of sessions using Level 1 requests, parents gradually introduced Level 2 requests and continued with praise for compliant responses. Eventually all four request levels were presented sequentially. Throughout treatment, children continued to comply at high levels (typically over 80%) to requests from each probability level, including Level 4 requests that had been associated with severe noncompliance before treatment.

There were several other findings of note. First, we ran generalization probe sessions throughout all phases of intervention. During these sessions, parents presented the child with requests from all four levels that had not been included in treatment sessions. We found that, during the generalization sessions, children showed improved compliance to non-treatment requests from the same level as those being trained. However, children showed low levels of compliance to generalization requests from untrained levels, indicating that generalized compliance to all requests did not occur until all four probability levels had been introduced.

In addition, results showed a substantial reduction in problem behaviors (i.e., aggression, screaming, crying, verbal opposition, and disruptive behavior) that had not been specifically targeted for treatment. This result confirmed the keystone effects that have been demonstrated with other forms of compliance training and suggested that compliance may be one of the most important targets for intervention with problem behavior.

In the first replication study (Ducharme, Pontes, et al., 1994), we investigated whether Errorless Compliance Training could be made more efficient along several treatment parameters without compromising treatment effects. The study was run with four children with developmental disabilities and two of their nondelayed siblings, all with severe noncompliance. We reduced the number of sessions used to conduct the probability assessment and decreased the duration of sessions. We also reduced the time required for the entire course of intervention by approximately 50%. Compliance results were comparable to the more labor-intensive version of the approach assessed in Ducharme and Popynick (1993). In Ducharme, Pontes, et al. (1994), we also replicated the generalization findings and reduction of maladaptive behavior that were found in the first investigation.

In the third study (Ducharme et al., 1996), Errorless Compliance Training was again conducted by parents of children with developmental disabilities. This study was the first in which we incorporated parent-collected data as the primary means of evaluation (parent data were as accurate as those collected by trained therapists). We also used a parent group format for teaching parents to use Errorless Compliance Training and collected long-term data on the compliance of the children. Compliance and generalization results in this study were comparable to those obtained in the previous two investigations, suggesting that the approach can be taught in the more efficient group context without loss of effects. Similarly encouraging were the follow-up results. Children maintained their improved compliance for up to 15 months posttreatment.

FAMILY VIOLENCE

The next stage in the systematic replication of the Errorless Compliance Training protocol involved evaluation of the approach in circumstances of family violence. Witnessing or experiencing family violence can produce wide-ranging internalizing and externalizing effects on children (Sternberg, Baradaran, Abbott, Lamb, & Guterman, 2006). Family violence is transgenerational in nature: Men who have experienced child abuse are more likely to be aggressive or abusive parents (Doumas et al., 1994).

Abused mothers often have difficulty disciplining their children and may resort to intrusive verbal or physical strategies that can escalate levels of tension in the family (Giles-Sims, 1985). Such coercive interactions could further the difficulties with these children as they learn, both through observation of violent family interactions and their parents' power-assertive disciplinary style, that the only way to gain cooperation from others is through force. We therefore felt that a strategy for securing child cooperation without physical coercion was particularly relevant for this population and anticipated that Errorless Compliance Training would increase opportunities for parents to be warm and responsive with their children while decreasing the likelihood of confrontation and abuse.

In Ducharme et al. (2000), we used the errorless approach to build cooperation between mothers who had been abused by their partners and their severely oppositional children who had witnessed or experienced the violence. The study included 9 mothers, who were trained in a group format to use the errorless approach, and their 15 children. With this approach, we were able to produce substantial improvements in child compliance to maternal requests (i.e., approximately 50 percentage point mean improvement over baseline levels to Level 4 requests). Similar improvements were seen on generalization requests that had not been included in treatment, indicating that the approach had produced generalized compliance gains. Follow-up data indicated that these improvements in compliance maintained for up to 6 months after treatment completion. Pre- and postmaternal reports on the Child Behavior Checklist (CBCL) showed significant improvements in internalizing, externalizing, and total behavior problems. The intervention also appeared to decrease maternal stress.

This study demonstrated that Errorless Compliance Training was an effective approach with mothers who were victims of but generally not the perpetrators of family violence. In a small follow-up study (Ducharme, Atkinson, & Poulton, 2001), we conducted Errorless Compliance Training with two mothers who acknowledged that their interactions with their children often became abusive when the child showed opposition to their requests. Both mothers were involved with child welfare agencies because of their use of physical punishment (i.e., hitting) to discipline their children. Our goal was to reduce child noncompliance without the use of punishment or constraining approaches, thereby eliminating the most prominent antecedent to child abuse.

The results of the study were comparable to those of Ducharme et al. (2000) with mothers producing substantial, generalized, and durable improvements in child compliance in their children. With regard to abuse, there were no reports of maltreatment or child injury throughout intervention or follow-up. The demonstrated improvements in parenting skills and reductions in child noncompliance provided ancillary evidence that abuse was no longer occurring (Isaacs, 1982).

These two studies suggest that Errorless Compliance Training may provide benefits to parents and children in violent families that extend beyond those commonly obtained with more traditional parent management training approaches. The graduated, success-focused, and nonpunitive nature of the errorless approach seems particularly appropriate for altering the vicious cycle of power-assertive interactions that are commonplace in violent families and that have the potential to produce deleterious long-term outcomes.

PARENTS WITH BRAIN INJURY

Persons who have sustained brain injuries may encounter a broad range of difficulties, including cognitive, behavioral, and emotional impairments. These individuals often show low levels of motivation, noncompliance to recommendations of clinicians and others, high levels of agitation under demand conditions, impulsivity, disinhibition, anxiety, depression, and low self-esteem (Ducharme, 1999, 2000). Some of these behavioral difficulties are the direct result of the physiological injury to the brain, but most result from an interaction between the acquired impairments and an environment that the individuals find excessively challenging after the injury. For this reason, persons with acquired brain injury often use disruptive and aggressive responses in an attempt to escape or avoid postinjury stresses.

Given these difficulties, parenting a child can become a complex and distressing task for an adult with a brain injury. These parents often experience extreme personality changes that can be highly stressful to family members and detrimental to relationships. They are less likely to notice or respond positively to desirable behavior in their children and are more likely to react to problem behavior with threats, bullying, and physical coercion (Devany Serio, Kreutzer, & Gervasio, 1995).

In addition to these parent-focused difficulties, the children often respond differently after the parent has been injured. These youngsters may experience emotional difficulties, become avoidant of and less responsive to the parent, and demonstrate higher levels of disobedience, tantrums, and school difficulties (Pessar, Coad, Linn, & Willer, 1993). This combination of high levels of externalizing behavior in the children and impulsive, disinhibited attempts by the parent to terminate child oppositionality can have a disastrous effect on the parent-child relationship and could result in child physical or emotional maltreatment.

We decided to investigate the potential for Errorless Compliance Training to assist brain-injured parents in managing the behavior of their children and in rebuilding the parent-child relationship. We expected that the graduated nature of the approach would help these parents focus on the cooperative successes of their children rather than on problem responses and would reduce triggers for anger and frustration that could lead to confrontations with their children. The approach also reduces the complexity of the parenting skills that must be taught to activate treatment, an important consideration for parents with cognitive deficits.

In Ducharme, Spencer, Davidson, and Rushford (2002), we used Errorless Compliance Training in a group training format with eight brain-injured parents who were having difficulty managing the oppositional behavior of their children. The parents had a wide range of sequelae including impulsivity, poor anger control, and severe cognitive deficits. Twelve typically developing children (age 2- to 7-years-old) participated. Although the approach took longer to implement with this group than in most of our previous research because of the extra supports needed by individuals with cognitive and emotional difficulties, the parents were able to bring about substantial improvements in the compliance of their children. As in previous studies, mean improvements in compliance to the most challenging parental requests (Level 4) were approximately 50 percentage points. Generalization and follow-up results were encouraging and comparable to earlier studies. There was also suggestive evidence of improvements in parent self-esteem after intervention.

In a second study (Ducharme, Davidson, & Rushford, 2002), we investigated the effects of Errorless Compliance Training on children of two male parents with both brain injuries and severe chronic pain, a common covariate of brain injury (Lahz & Bryant, 1996; Uomoto & Esselman, 1993). Chronic pain often compromises the ability of an individual to fulfill the parenting role, leading to impatience, frustration, anger, guilt, and depression (Barlow, Cullen, Foster, Harrison, & Wade, 1999). We felt that Errorless Compliance Training might be the ideal approach to use with this population because it reduces the need for decelerative consequences that could be extremely difficult to implement for parents in severe pain.

Despite the fact that both fathers experienced major stressors during the course of intervention (e.g., severe depression, deaths of close family members) in addition to their chronic pain, they were able to persevere with intervention procedures and produce substantial treatment effects. Gains in child compliance for the three children (age 2- to 5-years-old) exceeded 40 percentage points for both treatment and generalization requests.

The findings of these studies suggest that Errorless Compliance Training is well matched to parents with brain injuries who may have difficulty performing the parenting role. The simple and nonconfrontational nature of the approach provides an alternative to treatment strategies that may be overly complex and demanding for persons with cognitive, emotional, and physical challenges.

Autistic Spectrum Disorders

Three studies were conducted to evaluate the effects of errorless approaches on children with Autistic Spectrum Disorders, specifically autism and Asperger syndrome. Children with autism are characterized by severe social interaction and communication deficits, and they often have cognitive skill impairments or abnormalities. They also demonstrate restricted and stereotyped behavior, interests, and activities (American Psychiatric Association [APA], 1994). Children with Asperger syndrome have similar diagnostic features with the exception that they have no delays in language or cognitive development. Common to both disorders is the presence of problem behavior and noncompliance, often including severe reactions to the presentation of demands.

Given the behavioral difficulties of these children, we hypothesized that errorless approaches would provide a potential strategy for improving child cooperation and diminishing severe behavioral responses to demands issued by parents. For the Ducharme and Drain (2004) study, we encountered a number of children with autism who were experiencing compliance difficulties in two primary areas: general household compliance to everyday requests (e.g., "pick up your toy"; "turn off the television") and compliance to more academic, tabletop requests (e.g., "draw me a house"; "show me the letter D").

Our approach to treatment of these children involved a modification of the Errorless Compliance Training strategy (i.e., Errorless Academic Compliance Training) to focus the intervention specifically on academic compliance issues. We wanted to determine whether such a treatment emphasis would produce improvements in compliance to academic requests as well as broad enough change to address the general household compliance issues that were of concern to the parents of these children.

We developed a Compliance Probability Checklist that included a wide range of requests associated with academic or tabletop tasks. Similar to the process used with the general Errorless Compliance Training procedure, we used the checklist to facilitate observational assessment and determination of compliance probability levels for academic requests. We also observationally assessed a sample of general household requests that we included to measure generalization of treatment effects after intervention. We trained the four parents (three mothers and one father) to use requests from these four probability levels of academic requests in a hierarchical manner during the four phases of treatment, as with the general Errorless Compliance Training approach.

By Phase 4 of treatment, children showed large improvements (a 50 percentage point increase) in compliance to Level 4 requests (i.e., those that yielded the lowest levels of compliance during baseline). Generalization to academic requests that were not included in treatment was similarly strong (a 50 percentage point improvement for Level 4 generalization requests). The most compelling result, however, was for generalization to general household requests that had not been included in treatment. Gains over baseline compliance levels to these requests were substantial, even though no general household requests had been included in treatment (again, a 50 percentage point gain for Level 4 household requests). These results were maintained up to 6 months posttreatment. Parents' perception of their child's compliance to academic requests was also measured before and after intervention using the Academic Compliance Probability Checklist. Before treatment, parents rated 40% of the requests as Level 1 or 2 (yielding high compliance). After treatment, parents rated 92% of the requests at these high levels.

These results suggest that Errorless Academic Compliance Training may be useful as a nonintrusive intervention for children with autism to resolve both general household and academic compliance issues in the home. Moreover, the approach may be beneficial as an adjunct or precursor to other treatment approaches (e.g., intensive behavioral intervention programs based on applied behavior analysis) that are designed to overcome the broad ranging deficits associated with autism. Children are likely to benefit much more from such programs if they are willing to participate and cooperate fully with therapist and parental requests.

We conducted a second study (Ducharme, Sanjuan, & Drain, in press) for three children with characteristics of Asperger syndrome and their two parents. In this investigation, we used Errorless Compliance Training to assist parents in managing the noncompliance of these children. Mean compliance gains over baseline levels during treatment were over 50 percentage points for both Level 4 treatment and Level 4 generalization requests. Mean compliance levels at 2 months posttreatment were over 80%. With respect to perception of child compliance, mothers rated approximately 40% of requests on the compliance probability checklist as Level 1 or 2 (i.e., high probability of compliance) before treatment, in comparison with 97% of requests following treatment.

One final study for consideration in this section is a study by Ducharme, Lucas, and Pontes (1994). In this investigation, we worked with a 5-year-old girl with autism who showed severe self-injurious and aggressive reactions to interactive and learning activities in the home. We developed an errorless approach that we called "Errorless Embedding" to teach the child to tolerate such tasks without the need for punishment. We initially embedded short intervals of the problem tasks (i.e., those associated with aberrant behavior) into much longer durations of a moderating task that was rarely associated with aberrant reactions (i.e., labeling picture cards). Over several sessions, we gradually increased the length of time the child was exposed to the problem tasks and decreased the duration of the moderating task, until the moderating task was completely faded. Problem behavior was reduced by more than 60% for each of the problem tasks. We also observed improvements in on-task behavior and correct academic responses.

Although the samples in these studies were small, the results are encouraging and suggest that errorless approaches may be beneficial for children with pervasive developmental disorders. The approach appears to be particularly germane to this population because these children so commonly have difficulty managing the daily demands that parents and other care providers must place on them to enable learning experiences and a reasonable quality of life. The errorless approach can be used to build their tolerance to these situations, thereby reducing the need to inhibit aberrant responses that occur in the presence of demanding tasks.

CLASSROOM-BASED APPROACHES

Although intervention with parents and their children in the home can greatly improve child conduct difficulties, there is often need to conduct intervention in the school, where the child spends a large portion of his daytime hours, and where prosocial behavior is a prerequisite of academic performance and achievement. Child problem behavior in the classroom often manifests as noncompliance to teacher requests and other forms of disruptive behavior that can result in decreased levels of work completed and potential academic failure.

We have recently begun to assess the effects of Errorless Compliance Training and Errorless Embedding as potential strategies for remediation of child conduct difficulties in the classroom (Ducharme & DiAdamo, 2005; Ducharme & Harris, 2005). In Ducharme and DiAdamo (2005), we conducted Errorless Compliance Training in a special education classroom. The study involved two 5-year-old girls with Down syndrome who had severe behavior problems and were oppositional to teacher requests. Given the heavy workload on the teacher in the classroom, the intervention was conducted by a graduate student/researcher using typical classroom requests. She implemented both the observational probability analysis (i.e., using requests drawn from a classroom adaptation of the Compliance Probability Checklist) and the four phases of intervention, as in the home-based version of the treatment. Both children made gains of well over 50 percentage points to Level 4 requests in Phase 4 of treatment. Observational evidence suggested that the gains made with the graduate student generalized to the teacher.

In another classroom-based study (Ducharme & Harris, 2005), we used a variation of the Errorless Embedding technique described earlier (Ducharme, Lucas, et al., 1994) to build the on-task skills of five youngsters in a special education classroom for children with severe conduct difficulties. The children had severely disrupted home lives and had experienced foster care, family violence, and neglect. They were commonly noncompliant to requests to complete their work and exhibited high levels of disruptive behavior in the classroom. Given that the academic difficulties of these children were likely exacerbated by the psychosocial problems they were experiencing in the home, we wanted to intervene with a strategy that was sensitive to their home-based problems by reducing negative reactions from teachers around off-task behavior.

We initially observed the children to determine baseline levels of on-task and off-task behavior. In the beginning of treatment, short durations of independent academic work by the children (short enough to render escape behavior unnecessary) were embedded into much longer durations of adult-supported work. During this adult-supported period, instructors used rapport-based interaction and assistance with the child for the task being completed and provided reinforcement (usually in the form of praise) for task-related effort. As treatment progressed, durations of independent work were slowly and gradually increased and adult-supported periods were reduced until adult assistance was completely terminated. All children demonstrated substantially longer durations of on-task behavior following intervention. The results of this study suggested that simple adjustments to the way teachers interact with and support children can result in substantial gains in the child's ability to function effectively in the classroom. These findings have obvious ramifications for parents who are struggling to improve the homework habits of their children.

These studies suggest that errorless approaches may be as beneficial in the classroom as they have been in home-based intervention. We are currently working to make the procedures more practical for classroom usage, given that classroom teachers must deal with a broad range of issues (e.g., curriculum requirements, large numbers of children) that necessitate use of classroom management procedures that are efficient and easy to use.

CONCLUSION

Benefits of Errorless Approaches

In our work with parents and other care providers using these interventions, we have encountered several potential benefits. First, the errorless approach enables parents to focus on child success rather than child failure. Before treatment, parents may tend to notice the more salient problem behavior of their children and spend much of their interaction time attempting to terminate these responses with scoldings, reprimands, and other forms of negative attention. With the errorless approach, conditions are arranged to ensure that prosocial, cooperative child responses occur at a high rate from the beginning of treatment, and parents are taught to provide enthusiastic praise and acknowledgment to the children for such successes. This increase in desirable behavior and parent acknowledgment during and following intervention greatly increases the likelihood of positive interactions between the parent and child and may help promote a warmer and more cooperative relationship (Ducharme et al., 2000). In addition, the increased recognition for desired behavior may have benefits for child self-esteem and self-efficacy.

Second, by virtue of the graduated introduction of demanding conditions, the errorless approach greatly reduces the frequency of child opposition and aberrant responses during treatment and consequently, the need to employ punishment or power-assertive procedures following noncompliance and other problem behavior. Because child problem behaviors can be triggers for parent frustration and potentially aversive reactions, the reduction of child problem responses renders confrontational and potentially abusive responses by the parent much less likely. Moreover, this reduction in use of power-assertive approaches by parents reduces the likelihood that they will model coercion to their child as an acceptable strategy for gaining compliance from others.

Third, many parent training packages require parents to learn an extensive set of parenting skills that are taught over several training sessions. In contrast, the parenting skill set essential for implementation of Errorless Compliance Training is small, requiring parents to learn only three key skills: request delivery, reinforcement for compliant responses, and nonreaction to child noncompliance. All other aspects of the program are implemented through the support of the clinician. For parents with cognitive, physical, or emotional deficits, the greatly reduced learning requirements may increase the probability that they will complete the program successfully, without becoming overwhelmed and frustrated by the complexity of the task.

Fourth, results of most studies indicate that the errorless approach promotes widespread generalization and maintenance of treatment gains, as well as covariation to behaviors that were not specifically targeted for treatment. Moreover, when long-term measurement was possible, studies have indicated that these generalized improvements in child behavior were durable, with gains maintained up to 1 year beyond termination of treatment.

Fifth, much recent research has demonstrated that provision of choices, particularly in persons with developmental disabilities, is associated with substantial decreases in problem behavior (e.g., Dyer, Dunlap, & Winterling, 1990). In errorless approaches, children are not forced to cooperate with the will of the care provider (i.e., sent to time-out when they do not cooperate) but are given the choice of complying or not. Efforts are made, however, to make compliance easy and rewarding for children so that children are likely to choose to cooperate with the wishes of their care providers. The presence of response choices for the child may play a role in the extent of treatment gains that have been demonstrated with these approaches.

Finally, several studies have focused on extending errorless research to a broad range of psychopathologies, parent characteristics, behaviors, and age ranges. This research suggests that the approach is adaptable to a wide range of clinical circumstances surrounding children who exhibit aberrant and oppositional behavior.

LIMITATIONS

The errorless approach is not without significant limitations. For example, the intervention requires a substantial amount of assessment up front to individually determine the probability levels that are necessary to activate treatment. This can be a time-consuming process and may reveal child problem behavior during the baseline process that parents were able to successfully avoid by not delivering low probability requests. Most parent management approaches do not require extensive assessment before initiation of treatment.

Another concern is the occasional perception by parents that the errorless strategy is not initially empowering. With approaches that require parents to follow problem responses with decelerative consequences like time-out, parents often have a strong sense of being in control and actively doing something to stop the problem behavior of their children. With the errorless approach, parents are asked to ignore noncompliance and respond as though it never occurred. This can be a frustrating process for a parent who has been raised on punishment and who feels that it is necessary for disciplining children. We have had some parents drop out of treatment because they felt strongly that their child needed to be dealt with more firmly than our approach advised. It should be noted, however, that the noncompliance that occurs through treatment should be minimal given the graduated introduction of requests. For this reason, we can often work parents through their desire to become power assertive and point out the positive changes in the parent-child interaction that occur.

Summary

Our research on errorless intervention has indicated that severe behavior problems can be successfully treated using a success-focused approach that involves gradual introduction of challenging conditions associated with problem behavior and reinforcement of child prosocial responses in the presence of these increasing demands. This model contrasts with more traditional approaches in which desirable behaviors are increased with reinforcement and problem responses are inhibited using punishment. Given that children gradually learn to tolerate demand conditions, errorless strategies can render problem behavior unnecessary for the individual and thereby greatly reduce the need for decelerative consequences to inhibit these responses.

REFERENCES

Ainsworth, M., & Marvin, R. S. (1995). On the shaping of attachment theory and research: An interview with Mary D. S. Ainsworth (1994, Fall). *Monographs of the Society for Research in Child Development, 60*(2/3), 3–21.

American Psychiatric Association. (1994). *Diagnostic and statistical manual of mental disorders* (4th ed.). Washington, DC: Author.

Avakame, E. F. (1998). Intergenerational transmission of violence and psychological aggression against wives. *Canadian Journal of Behavioral Science, 30*(3), 193–202.

Baker, B. L., Blacher, J., Crnic, K., & Edelbrock, C. (2002). Behavior problems and parenting stress in families of 3-year-old children with and without developmental delays. *American Journal on Mental Retardation, 107*(6), 433–444.

Baker, B. L., McIntyre, L. L., Blacher, J., Crnic, K., Edelbrock, C., & Low, C. (2003). Pre-school children with and without developmental delay: Behavior problems and parenting stress over time. *Journal of Intellectual Disability Research, 47*(4/5), 217–230.

Barkley, R. A. (1997). *Defiant children: A clinician's manual for assessment and parent training* (2nd ed.). New York: Guilford Press.

Barlow, J. H., Cullen, L. A., Foster, N. E., Harrison, K., & Wade, M. (1999). Does arthritis influence perceived ability to fulfill a parenting role? Perceptions of mothers, fathers, and grandparents. *Parent Education and Counseling, 37,* 141–151.

Baumrind, D. (1971). Current patterns of parental authority. *Developmental Psychology Monographs, 4*(1, Pt. 2), 1–103.

Carr, E. G., Levin, L., McConnachie, G., Carlson, J. I., Kemp, D. C., & Smith, C. E. (1994). *Communication-based intervention for problem behavior.* Baltimore: Paul H. Brookes.

Carr, E. G., & Newsom, C. (1985). Demand-related tantrums: Conceptualization and treatment. *Behavior Modification, 9,* 403–426.

Devany Serio, C., Kreutzer, J. S., & Gervasio, A. H. (1995). Predicting family needs after brain injury: Implications for intervention. *Journal of Head Trauma Rehabilitation, 10*, 32–45.

Doumas, D., Margolin, G., & John, R. S. (1994). Intergenerational transmission of aggression across three generations. *Journal of Family Violence, 9*(2), 157–175.

Ducharme, J. M. (1999). A conceptual model for treatment of externalizing behavior in acquired brain injury. *Brain Injury, 13*, 645–668.

Ducharme, J. M. (2000). Treatment of maladaptive behavior in acquired brain injury: Remedial approaches in post-acute settings. *Clinical Psychology Review, 20*, 405–426.

Ducharme, J. M. (2005). Errorless compliance training. In M. Hersen & J. Rosqvist (Eds.), *Encyclopedia of behavior modification and cognitive behavior therapy: Vol. 2. Child clinical applications* (pp. 822–823). Thousand Oaks, CA: Sage.

Ducharme, J. M., Atkinson, L., & Poulton, L. (2000). Success-based, non-coercive treatment of oppositional behavior in children from violent homes. *Journal of the American Academy of Child and Adolescent Psychiatry, 39*, 995–1003.

Ducharme, J. M., Atkinson, L., & Poulton, L. (2001). Errorless compliance training with physically abusive mothers: A single-case approach. *Child Abuse and Neglect, 25*, 855–868.

Ducharme, J. M., Davidson, A., & Rushford, N. (2002). Treatment of oppositional behavior in children of parents with brain injury and chronic pain. *Journal of Emotional and Behavioral Disorders, 10*(4), 241–248.

Ducharme, J. M., & DiAdamo, C. (2005). An errorless approach to management of child noncompliance in a special education setting. *School Psychology Review, 34*, 107–115.

Ducharme, J. M., & Drain, T. (2004). Treatment and generalization effects of errorless academic compliance training for children with autism. *Journal of the American Academy of Child and Adolescent Psychiatry, 43*, 163–171.

Ducharme, J. M., & Harris, K. (2005). Errorless embedding for children with conduct difficulties: Rapport-based success-focused intervention in the classroom. *Behavior Therapy, 36*, 213–222.

Ducharme, J. M., Harris, K., Milligan, K., & Pontes, E. (2003). Sequential evaluation of reinforced compliance and graduated request delivery in the treatment of child noncompliance. *Journal of Autism and Developmental Disorders, 33*(5), 519–526.

Ducharme, J. M., Lucas, H., & Pontes, E. (1994). Errorless embedding in the reduction of severe maladaptive behavior during interactive and learning tasks. *Behavior Therapy, 25*, 489–501.

Ducharme, J. M., Pontes, E., Guger, S., Crozier, K., Lucas, H., & Popynick, M. (1994). Errorless compliance to parental requests II: Increasing clinical practicality through abbreviation of treatment parameters. *Behavior Therapy, 25*, 469–487.

Ducharme, J. M., & Popynick, M. (1993). Errorless compliance to parental requests: Treatment effects and generalization. *Behavior Therapy, 24*, 209–226.

Ducharme, J. M., Popynick, M., Pontes, E., & Steele, S. (1996). Errorless compliance to parental requests III: Group parent training with parent observational data and long-term follow-up. *Behavior Therapy, 27*, 353–372.

Ducharme, J. M., & Rushford, N. (2001). Proximal and distal effects of play on child compliance with a brain-injured parent. *Journal of Applied Behavior Analysis, 34,* 221–224.

Ducharme, J. M., Sanjuan, E., & Drain, T. (in press). Errorless compliance training: Success-focused behavioral treatment for children with characteristics of Asperger syndrome. *Behavior Modification.*

Ducharme, J. M., Spencer, T., Davidson, A., & Rushford, N. (2002). Errorless compliance training: Building a cooperative relationship between brain-injured parents at risk for maltreatment and their oppositional children. *American Journal of Orthopsychiatry, 72*(4), 585–595.

Ducharme, J. M., & van Houten, R. (1994). Operant extinction in the treatment of severe maladaptive behavior: Adapting research to practice. *Behavior Modification, 18,* 139–170.

Dyer, K., Dunlap, G., & Winterling, V. (1990). Effects of choice-making on the serious problem behaviors of students with severe handicaps. *Journal of Applied Behavior Analysis, 23,* 515–524.

Eyberg, S. M., & Boggs, S. R. (1998). Parent-child interaction therapy: A psychosocial intervention for the treatment of young conduct-disordered children. In J. Briesmeister & C. E. Schaefer (Eds.), *Handbook of parent training: Parents as cotherapists for children's behavior problems* (pp. 61–97). Hoboken, NJ: Wiley.

Forehand, R., & McMahon, R. J. (1981). *Helping the non-compliant child: A clinician's guide to parent training.* New York: Guilford Press.

Gershoff, E. T. (2002). Corporal punishment by parents and associated child behaviors and experiences: A meta-analytic and theoretical review. *Psychological Bulletin, 128*(4), 539–579.

Giles-Sims, J. (1985). A longitudinal study of battered children of battered wives. *Family Relations, 34,* 205–210.

Gross, A. M., & Wixted, J. T. (1987). Oppositional behavior. In M. Hersen & V. B. Van Hasselt (Eds.), *Behavior therapy with children and adolescents: A clinical approach* (pp. 301–324). New York: Wiley.

Horner, R. H., Dunlap, G., Koegel, R. L., Carr, E. G., Sailor, W., Anderson, J., et al. (1990). Toward a technology of "nonaversive" behavioral support. *Journal of the Association for Persons with Severe Handicaps, 15,* 125–132.

Isaacs, C. D. (1982). Treatment of child abuse: A review of the behavioral interventions. *Journal of Applied Behavior Analysis, 15,* 273–294.

Kern, L., Delaney, B. A., Hilt, A., Bailin, D. E., & Elliot, C. (2002). An analysis of physical guidance as reinforcement for noncompliance. *Behavior Modification, 26*(4), 516–536.

Lahz, S., & Bryant, R. A. (1996). Incidence of chronic pain following traumatic brain injury. *Archives of Physical Medicine and Rehabilitation, 77,* 889–891.

Lerman, D. C., & Vorndran, C. M. (2002). On the status of knowledge for using punishment: Implications for treating behavior disorders. *Journal of Applied Behavior Analysis, 35,* 431–464.

Mace, F. C., Hock, M. L., Lalli, J. S., West, B. J., Belfiore, P., Pinter, E., et al. (1988). Behavioral momentum in the treatment of noncompliance. *Journal of Applied Behavior Analysis, 21,* 123–141.

Martens, B., Witt, J., Daly, E., III, & Vollmer, T. (1999). Behavior analysis: Theory and practice in educational settings. In C. Reynolds & T. Gutkin (Eds.), *The handbook of school psychology* (pp. 638–663). New York: Wiley.

Martin, G., & Pear, J. (1978). *Behavior modification: What it is and how to do it.* Englewood Cliffs, NJ: Prentice-Hall.

Nicholson, B. C., Fox, R. A., & Johnson, S. D. (2005). Parenting young children with challenging behavior. *Infant and Child Development, 14,* 425–428.

Parrish, J. M., Cataldo, M., Kolko, D., Neef, N. A., & Egel, A. (1986). Experimental analysis of response covariation among compliant and inappropriate behavior. *Journal of Applied Behavior Analysis, 19,* 241–254.

Persi, J., & Pasquali, B. (1999). The use of seclusions and physical restraints: Just how consistent are we? *Child and Youth Care Forum, 28*(2), 87–103.

Pessar, L. F., Coad, M. L., Linn, R. T., & Willer, B. S. (1993). The effects of parental traumatic brain injury on the behavior of parents and children. *Brain Injury, 7,* 231–240.

Roberts, M. W. (1982). Resistance to time-out: Some normative data. *Behavioral Assessment, 4,* 237–246.

Sidman, M. (1989). *Coercion and its fallout.* Boston: Author's Cooperative.

Sternberg, K. J., Baradaran, L. P., Abbott, C. B., Lamb, M. E., & Guterman, E. (2006). Type of violence, age, and gender differences in the effects of family violence on children's behavior problems: A mega-analysis. *Developmental Review, 26*(1), 89–112.

Stokes, T. F., & Baer, D. M. (1977). An implicit technology of generalization. *Journal of Applied Behavior Analysis, 10*(2), 349–367.

Terrace, H. S. (1963). Errorless transfer of a discrimination across two continua. *Journal of the Experimental Analysis of Behavior, 6*(2), 223–232.

Touchette, P. E. (1968). The effects of graduated stimulus change on the acquisition of a simple discrimination in severely retarded boys. *Journal of the Experimental Analysis of Behavior, 17,* 175–188.

Turner, H. S., & Watson, T. S. (1999). Consultant's guide for the use of time-out in the pre-school and elementary classroom. *Psychology in the Schools, 36*(2), 135–148.

Uomoto, J. M., & Esselman, P. C. (1993). Traumatic brain injury and chronic pain: Differential types and rates by head injury severity. *Archives of Physical Medicine and Rehabilitation, 74*(1), 61–64.

Webster-Stratton, C., & Hancock, L. (1998). Training for parents of young children with conduct problems: Content, methods and therapeutic processes. In J. M. Briesmeister & C. E. Schaefer (Eds.), *Handbook of parent training* (pp. 98–152). New York: Wiley.

Weeks, M., & Gaylord-Ross, R. (1981). Task difficulty and aberrant behavior in severely handicapped students. *Journal of Applied Behavior Analysis, 14,* 449–463.

CHAPTER 10

Tailoring the Incredible Years Parent Programs according to Children's Developmental Needs and Family Risk Factors

CAROLYN WEBSTER-STRATTON

OPPOSITIONAL DEFIANT DISORDER (ODD) and conduct problems (CP) are the most common reasons that young children (aged 3 to 8 years) are taken to mental health clinics (Hinshaw & Anderson, 1996). Parents bring their children for treatment because of difficulties in managing their children's social, emotional, and behavioral problems. Approximately 50% of these children are comorbid for Attention-Deficit/Hyperactivity Disorder (ADHD; Campbell, Shaw, & Gilliom, 2000) and for language/learning and developmental delays. Many of these children are also comorbid for internalizing problems (e.g., anxiety or depression) and are suffering from somatic complaints (Webster-Stratton & Hammond, 1998). Frequently, internalizing symptoms are overlooked because of the immediacy of handling the children's aggressive and oppositional defiant behavior. These children also experience higher than normal rates of stressful family circumstances such as divorce, child abuse, or neglect that compound their behavioral or adjustment problems. In a sample of more than 450 families referred to the Parenting Clinic at the University of Washington for children's ODD or conduct problems, over 76% had additional family or child risk factors (see Table 10.1). Although these comorbid diagnoses and

Table 10.1
Children with Oppositional Defiant Disorder Who
Experienced Additional Family Risk Factors or
Comorbid Child Behavior Problems

Family Risk Factor	Percentage
Divorce	38
Child abuse/neglect report filed	16
Language delay	7
CBCL internalizing T score > 60	34
CBCL attention problems T score > 60	44

Note: n = 450; 33% of the sample reported one of the above risk factors, 28% reported two, and 15% experienced three or more in addition to the ODD diagnoses.

family circumstances often are not the presenting problem for a child with ODD, they convey additional risk in short- and long-term treatment outcomes and may be directly or indirectly contributing to the externalizing behavior problems (Webster-Stratton, 1985, 1990). Thus, treatments that target children's oppositional and aggressive behaviors, such as the *Incredible Years Parent Program*, must be flexible enough to meet the needs of children with complicated profiles. Since young children cannot easily communicate their feelings or worries and the reasons for their misbehavior, it is important for therapists to look beyond the aggressive symptoms to the underlying reasons for the misbehavior and address other, less obvious symptoms such as anxiety, fears, or depression. The skilled therapist will develop a working model for every child and their parents based on knowledge of the child's family background and parenting experiences, biological makeup, and functional analyses of the behavior problems (Webster-Stratton & Herbert, 1994).

The Incredible Years (IY) Parent Program is an evidence-based program that has been shown in over nine randomized control group trials to significantly reduce ODD and internalizing problems and to strengthen positive parent-child relationships. (For a review of these studies, see Webster-Stratton & Reid, 2003a.) Although the presenting problem for all children in our evaluation studies was ODD or conduct problems, these program evaluations represent treatment for families and children who struggled with many other complicated diagnoses and risk factors (see Table 10.1). To use the IY treatment model successfully, the therapist must understand how to tailor the manual's treatment protocol to fit each family's risk factors and each child's developmental needs and social and emotional goals. Therapists can achieve flexible applications of the manual when there is understanding of the treatment on multiple levels, including the treatment model, content, and methods as well as the elements involved in adapting or tailoring the treatment to the individual needs of each child and family. This chapter summarizes this treatment model with special attention to the way the model is tailored to meet the particular goals of each family in the parent group.

The leader's manual (Webster-Stratton, 1984, 2001) provides recommended protocols for offering the BASIC Parenting Program in 12 to 14 two-hour sessions with groups of 10 to 14 parents. These protocols are considered the minimal number of core sessions, vignettes, and content required to achieve results similar to those in the published literature. However, the length of the program, the number of vignettes shown, and the emphasis given to certain components of the program will vary according to the particular needs of the parents and children in each group. It is recommended that for diagnosed children with comorbid problems, it can be helpful to supplement the BASIC Parent Program with other IY parent programs such as the ADVANCE, School, or Interactive Reading and School Readiness Programs. The Incredible Years Training Series also includes a number of Child Training options. When working with children with diagnosed conduct problems and other emotional or developmental problems or stressful life circumstances, it is recommended that the *Child Dinosaur Small Group Treatment Program* be offered in conjunction with the Parent Program, as the strongest long-term follow-up results have been found when the parent and child programs are offered together (Webster-Stratton & Hammond, 1997; Webster-Stratton, Reid, & Hammond, 2004). The child programs are described in detail elsewhere (Webster-Stratton & Reid, 2003b; Webster-Stratton, Reid, & Hammond, 2001). In addition, the child programs should be tailored to meet the particular needs of the children. The modifications are outlined in Webster-Stratton (Webster-Stratton & Reid, 2005a). This chapter summarizes the standard treatment model and objectives for children with ODD and then highlights the ways the model is adapted to meet the needs of specific groups of parents and children.

OVERVIEW OF THE BASIC PARENTING PROGRAM

For therapists to begin tailoring the program for children with comorbid diagnoses or family risk factors, it is extremely important to understand the core content of the program and the teaching methods and therapeutic process of the program delivery. This program is described in great detail in the program leader's manual, in a book for therapists (Webster-Stratton & Herbert, 1994), and in several summary chapters by Webster-Stratton and colleagues (Webster-Stratton, 1998, in press; Webster-Stratton & Hancock, 1998). Therapists with a thorough understanding of the program quickly see that it is designed to allow for tailoring the learning process according to the individual goals and needs of the parents and children.

In the first group session, the therapist helps parents identify their goals for themselves and their children as well as understand how to apply child development and behavior management principles when working on individual behavior plans for their children. While therapists collaborate with parents to formulate plans for each individual family according to their needs and the children's temperament, they highlight common themes, concerns, and connections among all the parents in the group. In this way, the parents not only feel the program is tailored to their unique issues but find immense support from the other parents who may be addressing similar issues.

Originally, this parent program was developed for children diagnosed with ODD, and then it was adapted for use as a prevention program for high-risk children as well as for use with children who have other problems. First, I discuss the basic program and the parent program objectives that apply to children with conduct problems. I then describe the additional objectives for children with special needs such as ADHD, attachment problems, and internalizing problems, and for those experiencing family stress such as divorce.

CHILDREN WITH OPPOSITIONAL DEFIANT DISORDER, CONDUCT PROBLEMS, AND EMOTIONAL REGULATION OR ANGER MANAGEMENT DIFFICULTIES

Children with conduct problems are often difficult to parent because they are noncompliant and oppositional to parents' requests. When children refuse to do as they are told, parents cannot socialize or teach them. Often parents respond to defiant behavior by criticizing, yelling, or hitting disobedient children. Other parents, fearing escalation of their defiance, give in to their children's demands. Many times, parents argue and fight with each other over how to discipline their children, resulting in inconsistent responses or a lack of follow-through. These responses not only model aggressive behavior, but give the children's oppositional behavior powerful emotional attention, thereby reinforcing its occurrence. Children who are oppositional with adults are usually aggressive with peers and have few friends because of being uncooperative, bossy, and critical of other children's ideas and suggestions. These negative responses and subsequent rejections by peers compound the children's problems and result in social isolation, giving them even fewer opportunities to learn how to make friends.

RECOMMENDED IY PROGRAMS

For parents of children with diagnosed ODD or conduct problems, the BASIC Parent Programs (early childhood or school-age versions) and the ADVANCE Parent Programs 5 to 7 are recommended; they take 20 to 24 weeks to complete. While the parents are in the parent group, it is recommended that the small group child treatment program (Dinosaur Program) be offered to their children to promote their social, emotional, and problem-solving skills. This program also takes 20 to 24 weeks to complete.

ALTERNATIVE TEACHER TRAINING PROGRAM

Instead of offering the Dinosaur Program, the teacher classroom management training program may be offered. This program takes 35 to 42 hours to complete, preferably on 5 to 6 separate days spread over several months. Training teachers will promote consistency in management approaches from home to school (see Tables 10.2 and 10.3 for description of programs by age group and type of child problem).

OBJECTIVES OF THE IY PARENTING PROGRAM

Strengthen Parent-Child Relationships and Bonding

- Increase parents' understanding, empathy, and acceptance of the needs of children with conduct problems.
- Increase parents' positive attributions of their child and decrease their negative attributions. Encourage parents' understanding of their children's temperament.
- Teach parents how to do social, emotional, and academic coaching during child-directed play interactions with their children.
- Encourage parents to give more effective praise and encouragement for targeted prosocial behaviors and for their children's efforts to self-regulate and stay calm.
- Strengthen positive parent-child relationships and attachment.

Promote Effective Limit Setting, Nonpunitive Discipline, and Systematic Behavior Plans

- Help parents set up behavior plans and develop salient rewards for targeted prosocial behaviors.
- Help parents use nonpunitive and less harsh discipline approaches for misbehavior.
- Teach parents anger management skills so they can stay calm and controlled when disciplining their children.
- Teach parents how to do compliance training with their children.

Table 10.2

Recommended IY Programs for Preschool Children (Aged 3–5)

	Children With				
	Externalizing Problems	ADHD	Attachment Disorder	Divorcing Parents	Internalizing Problems
Parent Programs					
Play Program 1	X	X	X	X	X
Child-Directed Play	X	X	X	X	X
Interactive Reading	Optional	X			
Praise and Incentives Program 2	X	X	X	X	X
Limit Setting Handling Misbehavior Programs 3 and 4	X	X	X	X	X
ADVANCE Programs 6–7	X	5–6 optional 7 recommended		X	7 recommended
Other					
Dina Dinosaur Treatment Program or Teacher Training	Both	Both	Optional	Optional	Optional

- Teach parents how to help their children self-regulate, manage their anger and problem solve.
- Help parents learn how to provide children with joyful and happy experiences and memories and reduce exposure to violent TV, computer games, and a diet of fear or depression.

Strengthen Parents' Interpersonal Skills and Supportive Networks

- Teach parents coping skills, such as depression and anger management, effective communication skills, and problem-solving strategies.
- Teach parents ways to work with teachers to develop home-school behavior plans.
- Teach parents how to give and get support to enhance supportive networks.

10.3
Recommended IY Programs for Early School-Age Children (Aged 6–8)

	Children With				
	Externalizing Problems	ADHD	Attachment Disorder	Divorcing Parents	Internalizing Problems
Parent Programs					
Play Program 1 or Child-Directed Play*	X	X	X	X	Optional
Promoting Positive Behaviors Program 9	X	X	X	X	X
Reducing Inappropriate Behaviors Program 10	X	X	X	X	X
Education Program 8	X	X			
ADVANCE Program 5–7	X	X		X	7 recommended
Other					
Dina Dinosaur Treatment Program or Teacher Training	Both	Both	Either optional	Dina program	Dina program

* Either of these programs provides added emphasis on relationship building.

Focus—Strengthening Parent-Child Relationships
and Encouraging Child Cooperation
(Parent BASIC Program 1: 3 to 8 Years)

No matter whether the preschool or school-age version of the BASIC parenting program is being used, the entire BASIC Play Program 1 should be shown first. This emphasis on teaching parents child-directed play concepts is important for parents in helping their children learn to be more compliant and to encourage their social skills. Often parents of these children have responded to their defiance and disrespect by becoming more controlling and oppositional, thereby compounding their problems. Instead, parents learn how to coach their children's compliant and prosocial behaviors while ignoring their inappropriate behaviors. During play, parents model compliance to their children's requests as long as they are behaving appropriately. Parents learn the value of noncompetitive and child-directed play skills. This parent social coaching helps the children learn basic friendship skills such as how to take turns, wait, share during play, accept a friend's ideas, and give a compliment. Not only will this child-directed play help children to learn valuable social skills, but it will also promote a more positive attachment or stronger bonds between the parent and child. Often, parents of such children are feeling angry with them because of their disruptive behavior, and they have experienced very few positive times together. These playtimes will begin to build up the positive bank account between the parent and child.

Focus—Increasing Parents' Nurturing and Positive Parenting Skills (Parent BASIC Program 2: 3 to 6 Years, or BASIC Program 9: 6 to 8 Years)

Children with conduct problems usually get less praise and encouragement from adults than other children. When they do get praise, they are likely to reject it because of their oppositional responses. For some children, this oppositional response to praise and encouragement is actually a bid to get more attention and to keep the adult focusing on them longer. Parents can help these children by giving the praise frequently and then ignoring the protests that follow. Over time with consistent encouragement, the children will become more comfortable with this positive view of themselves.

Sticker charts and incentive programs to encourage compliance to requests and rules are the first priority, because once compliance is increased, it is easier to teach other social behaviors. Therefore, parents learn to set up behavior plans and charts for the targeted positive behaviors that they would like to see more of.

Focus—Parents Learning Effective Limit Setting and Establishing Clear Household Rules (Parent BASIC Program 3: 3 to 6 Years, and Program 10: 6 to 8 Years)

Children with conduct problems refuse to do what they are asked to do by parents or teachers 70% to 100% of the time (whereas the normal child obeys approximately 65% of the time). This has occurred because the refusal has resulted in a lot of adult attention and power. Parents have learned to expect this noncompliance and oppositional behavior and may have responded by avoiding giving commands or making requests, by repeating the same command over and over (because they don't expect compliance), or by escalating their hostile responses because of anticipating their child's defiance. Therefore, the first step in this program is to help the parents set clear limits, predictable routines and household rules and to stay calm. Parents will then learn to reduce excessive and unnecessary commands and to give necessary commands clearly, politely, and without fear of their children's responses.

Once this has been accomplished, parents are taught a compliance training procedure in which they follow through with a brief time-out if children don't comply with commands.

Focus—Nonviolent Discipline Strategies and Ways to Teach Children Self-Regulation Skills (Parent BASIC Program 4: 3 to 6 Years, and Program 10: 6 to 8 Years)

Next, parents learn how to successfully ignore many of the annoying defiant behaviors that children with conduct problems exhibit such as tantrums, whining, arguing, sarcastic backtalk, and swearing. They also are trained to use a "Time-Out for Calming Down" procedure, which is really an extended ignore procedure. When they initially explain time-out to their children, parents talk about the location of time-out and how long it will last and rehearse with their children (when their children are calm) how to go to time-out. The children practice going to time-out, taking three deep breaths and telling themselves, *"I can calm down, I can do it, I can try again."* Once the children have been taught time-out, then parents reserve its use for physically aggressive behavior or extreme oppositional behavior.

Other discipline strategies that work well for other kinds of behavior problems are consequences that are immediately tied to their misbehavior, such as loss of a privilege or loss of the object involved in the conflict for a brief period. In addition to discipline strategies, parents learn how to help their children self-regulate and control anger as well as how to teach them problem-solving strategies. Parents learn how to help their children identify that they have a problem and then to use a self-regulation skill such as expressing their feelings with words, using a calm-down strategy, taking a personal time-out or taking three breaths, thinking a happy thought or imagining their happy place. Once children have learned these calming strategies, then they can be prompted by parents to think of other prosocial solutions such as waiting, sharing, asking, trading, and apologizing. It is important to give these angry children the tools to calm down before engaging them in problem-solving discussions. It is also important not to do the problem solving at the very time children are behaving aggressively, or the misbehavior will be reinforced with parental attention.

FOCUS—PARENTS PROMOTING CHILDREN'S ACADEMIC COMPETENCE (SUPPORTING EDUCATION PROGRAM 8)

Because children with conduct problems may have had less instruction and positive feedback at school from teachers, and because they may have reading, learning, and academic delays as well, it is recommended that Program 8: Supporting Your Child at School be shown as a supplement to the BASIC Parent Program for children aged 6 to 10 years. In this program, parents learn how to set up predictable homework schedules, to coach their children successfully in their academic skills, and to have productive parent-teacher conferences where behavior plans are shared. For children aged 3 to 5 years, the Interactive Reading Program is recommended as a supplement because it emphasizes how interactive reading skills can promote children's social, emotional, and academic competence. It takes three to four extra sessions to complete the Education program and two to three sessions for the Interactive Reading programs, which are offered later in the Basic Series.

FOCUS—PROMOTING POSITIVE FAMILY COMMUNICATION AND SUPPORT (ADVANCE PROGRAMS 5 AND 6)

Families of children with conduct problems often experience parental depression, marital conflict, high levels of stress, anger-management problems, and sense of isolation or stigma because of their children's behavior problems as well as the lack of family, school, or community support. Therefore, the ADVANCE Parent Program is an essential part of the therapy for the parents of children with conduct problems. This program focuses on helping parents learn effective communication skills with partners and with teachers, ways to cope with discouraging and depressive thoughts, anger management strategies, ways to give and get support from family members and other parents, and effective problem-solving strategies. The ADVANCE program is offered after the BASIC program has been completed and takes another eight sessions. It is especially important to include this program when working with multiply stressed families who have interpersonal issues.

FOCUS—TRAINING CHILDREN IN ANGER MANAGEMENT AND SOCIAL SKILLS (DINOSAUR SCHOOL)

The BASIC Parent Program focuses on helping parents coach peer play, which will help children learn social skills. However, it is also recommended that children with conduct problems attend the Dinosaur Small Group Treatment Program where they can get specific practice with other children learning social and self-regulation skills. In this child training program, children practice behaviors needed to be successful at school, build a rich vocabulary for expressing emotions, learn how to identify their own and others' emotions, and practice anger management, problem solving, and effective communication skills. Our studies indicate that combining this training with parent training enhances children's outcomes in terms of better peer relationships and classroom behavior with peers and teachers (Webster-Stratton & Hammond, 1997; Webster-Stratton, Reid, & Hammond, 2004).

CHILDREN WITH ATTENTION-DEFICIT/ HYPERACTIVITY DISORDER

Children with ODD are difficult to parent but those who are comorbid with Attention Deficit Disorder (ADD) with or without Hyperactivity (ADHD) are even more difficult to parent because they are impulsive, inattentive, distractible, and hyperactive. They have difficulty attending to, hearing, or remembering parental requests and anticipating consequences, and therefore don't seem to be cooperative or to learn from negative consequences. Because of their distractibility, they have difficulty completing schoolwork, homework, chores, or other activities that require sustained concentration. If this lack of cooperation is given a lot of attention or criticism by parents, it may be inadvertently reinforced, especially if little parental attention is given for the child's prosocial behaviors. Children with attention difficulties also are so distracted they miss their parents' praise and may seem unresponsive to parental encouragement as well as their limit-setting efforts.

Many children with ADD/ADHD have trouble making friends (Coie, Dodge, & Kupersmidt, 1990). Because of their impulsivity, it is hard for them to wait for a turn when playing, or to concentrate long enough to complete a puzzle or game. They are likely to grab things away from other children or to disrupt a carefully built tower or puzzle because of their activity level and lack of patience. In fact, research has shown that these children are delayed in their play and social skills (Barkley, 1996). A 6-year-old with ADHD plays more like a 4-year-old and has difficulty with sharing, waiting, taking turns, and focusing on a play activity for more than a few minutes; the child is more likely to be engaged in solitary play (Webster-Stratton & Lindsay, 1999). Because these children are annoying to play with, they have few friends, and other children frequently reject them. They are usually the children who are not invited to birthday parties or playdates—a problem that further compounds their social difficulties and affects their self-esteem.

About 40% to 50% of children with ODD also have ADD/ADHD and other problems such as language delays and learning disabilities. Academic and developmental problems are intertwined with social and emotional problems. Poor attention, hyperactivity, and language or reading difficulties limit children's ability to engage in learning and result in less encouragement and instruction from teachers as well as parents. This negative feedback and lack of instruction makes their problems worse. Thus, a cycle is created whereby one problem exacerbates the other.

RECOMMENDED IY PARENT PROGRAMS

For parents of children with ADD/ADHD, recommended programs are the BASIC Parent Programs (early childhood and school-age versions) and Supporting Your Child's Education Program (for children aged 6 to 8 years) or Child Directed Play and Interactive Reading Programs (for children aged 3 to 6 years) that focus on helping parents to promote their children's academic competence. The ADVANCE Program 7, which focuses on children's problem-solving skills, is also recommended. The ADVANCE Programs 5 and 6, which focus on communication and family meetings, are optional but may be helpful for somewhat older children. It will take 22 to 26 weeks to complete these programs.

COMBINING PARENT PROGRAM WITH IY CHILD DINOSAUR TREATMENT PROGRAM OR TEACHER CLASSROOM MANAGEMENT PROGRAM

The child training program (Dinosaur School) will help children with ADHD to learn play and social skills, to make good friends, and to practice problem-solving and anger-management strategies. Instead of offering the Dinosaur Program for the children, an optional approach is to provide the teacher classroom management training program for the teachers of these children. This program takes teachers 28 to 42 hours to complete, preferably on 4 to 6 separate days spread over several months. When teachers are trained, they are reinforcing the same behaviors as parents, and there is more consistency from home to school in management approaches. Our research suggests that offering either the child or the teacher training program will enhance outcomes in terms of improvements in children's classroom behavior and peer relationships (Webster-Stratton, Reid, & Hammond, 2004).

Additional Objectives for Parent Program for Children with ADD/ADHD

- Increase parents' understanding and knowledge about the parenting needs of children with ADD/ADHD.
- Teach parents how to do academic, persistence, social, and peer coaching.

- Encourage parents to give more effective praise and encouragement for targeted prosocial and academic behaviors.
- Help parents set up behavior plans and develop salient rewards for targeted prosocial and academic behaviors.
- Teach parents ways to work with teachers to coordinate home-school behavior plans.
- Help parents understand how they can support their children's academic learning at home.
- Enhance parents' support networks.

Additional Objectives for Children

- Increase children's social skills, such as group entry skills, cooperative play skills, and friendship skills (e.g., teamwork, sharing, taking turns, complimenting).
- Increase children's emotional self-regulation skills, such as waiting, concentrating, using stop-think-check, and calming down with deep breathing, positive self-talk, or happy images.
- Increase children's coping skills, such as problem solving, generation of positive solutions for conflict situations, and ability to think ahead to consequences of particular behaviors.
- Decrease children's disruptive behaviors, such as blurting out, interrupting, and noncompliance.
- Increase children's academic skills, such as putting up a quiet hand, listening to their teacher, and concentrating on work (e.g., stop, think, look, check).

FOCUS—PARENTS LEARNING HOW TO COACH THEIR CHILDREN'S FRIENDSHIP SKILLS AND HELP SUSTAIN THEIR ATTENTION ON PLAY ACTIVITIES (PARENT BASIC PROGRAM 1: 3 TO 8 YEARS)

No matter whether the preschool or school age version of the BASIC parenting program is being used, the entire BASIC Play Program (including all the vignettes) should be covered first. This program emphasizes parents learning child-directed play concepts so that they can help their children develop friendship skills. It is critical that parents of children with ODD + ADD/ADHD become highly skilled as academic, persistence, social, and emotional coaches. First, the academic and persistence coaching during parent-child play interactions helps the parents scaffold their children's play so that they can sustain their play activities for longer periods. During *persistence coaching,* the parent is commenting on the child's attention to the task. A parent might say to his child who is working with blocks, *"You are really concentrating on building that tower;*

you are really staying patient; you are trying again and really focusing on getting it as high as you can; you are staying so calm; you are focused; there, you did it all by yourself." With this persistence coaching, the child begins to be aware of his internal state when he or she is calm, focused, and persisting with an activity. Next, the parents learn how to do *emotion and social coaching* during child-directed play. During social coaching, the parents describe the children when they take turns, wait, share, make a suggestion, follow another's ideas, or give a compliment. Parents begin practicing this during dyadic play with their children; they model appropriate social skills and prompt their children's use of those skills. Later, they are encouraged to arrange playdates with other children at their home and to provide peer coaching during these visits to further their children's social learning experiences. The added child-directed peer play vignettes and extra practice coaching several children not only will enhance children's social skills, but also will help parents understand and accept developmental, temperamental, and biological differences in their children such as variation in distractibility, impulsiveness, and hyperactivity.

FOCUS—PARENTS LEARNING TO INCREASE THE SALIENCY OF THEIR PRAISE AND TANGIBLE REWARDS (PARENT BASIC PROGRAM 2: 3 TO 6 YEARS, OR BASIC PROGRAM 9: 6 TO 8 YEARS)

Children with ODD + ADHD get less praise and encouragement from adults than less active or less disruptive children. When such children do get praise, however, they are even less likely to notice or comprehend that they were praised. In fact, parents of these children frequently remark that their children are unresponsive to their praise and encouragement. Because of their inattentiveness, distractibility, and failure to read nonverbal facial cues, children with ADD/ADHD need praise that is highly pronounced and combined with visual and tactile cues. Before giving praise to a distractible child, the parent needs to move close and establish eye contact and a connection to capture attention. Next, the parent must give the praise with a genuine smile, lots of emotional enthusiasm, and a pat on the back or hug. Finally, the parent describes the social behavior that is being encouraged. For these children, behaviors targeted for praise may include concentrating hard on an activity, waiting a turn, problem solving, asking for something (rather than grabbing), staying calm, and politely asking to be part of a game. Because it is not normal to praise in such an exaggerated way, parents of these children need extra training in these skills as well as extra encouragement to keep praising even when their children don't seem to be responsive to their praise.

It is also hard for children with ADD/ADHD to evaluate their own progress in the social arena since self-reflection is difficult for them. Sticker charts and behavior plans with clearly established behavioral goals and incentives can help children remember the behaviors they are working on and also serve as concrete markers depicting their success. Incentive systems provide more salient and immediate rewards as well as a visual reminder to the children of their accomplishments and a continual reminder of the positive consequences of working toward their goal. Behavior charts and incentive programs are covered in detail when working with parents of children with ADHD and are refined over time so that parents can continually motivate and challenge their children in novel ways. Charts also offer structure and positive scaffolding that provide a sense of safety and security for distractible children.

Focus—Parents Learning about Clear Limit Setting and Predictable Schedules (Parent BASIC Program 3: 3 to 6 Years, and Program 10: 6 to 8 Years)

Just as children with ADD/ADHD frequently fail to hear vague praise statements, they also fail to focus on or remember parental instructions. They may not comprehend the parental request if it is unclear, negatively stated, embedded in a great deal of distracting verbal content and negative emotion, or if too many commands are strung together. Therefore, parents of such children need to learn how to make a positive request that is clear, calm, and specific. As when giving praise, parents must get their child's attention before making the request. Moreover, because children with ADD/ADHD live in the present moment and have difficulty thinking ahead to future consequences (positive or negative), they are not motivated by delayed consequences. Therefore, they need consequences that are immediate and as closely related to the misbehavior as possible. This means that child compliance to a parental request requires immediate praise, and noncompliance needs immediate follow-through.

Because these children are frequently disruptive and don't seem to respond to commands, adults are more likely to speak loudly and to repeat many commands. Parents need help reducing their commands to those that are the most important, giving them in a positive and clear manner, and then being prepared to follow through if the command is not obeyed. Children then will learn that when a parent makes a request, they are expected to comply and will be helped to do so.

Another way to help children follow the rules and to limit the number of commands given is to have clearly articulated schedules for the children. Therapists help parents set up a predictable after-school routine such as hanging up their coat, having a snack, doing their homework activity, having a play activity, and dinner; or a predictable morning routine (and bedtime routine) such as getting dressed, making the bed, eating breakfast, brushing teeth, washing face and hands, and getting their book bag and lunch. Group leaders work out these schedules with parents and then help them use picture cues for each activity on laminated boards (or magnets for the refrigerator) so children can move each activity to the "done" side of the board. These visual cues and schedules help children know what is required of them during these difficult transition times. The difficulty for young children with ADHD is that they get distracted easily and forget what they are to do next. These schedule boards with pictures describing each step, which can be moved or checked by the child, help them to remember what to do, thereby increasing their independence and reducing parents' need to remind them. Parents can also add chores to these picture boards contributing to their children's sense of responsibility in the family.

Focus—Parents Learning about Immediacy of Consequences
(Parent BASIC Program 4: 3 to 6 Years, and Program 10:
6 to 8 Years)

Children with ADD/ADHD need immediate consequences for their misbehavior. Having children on medication or with a diagnosis of ADD/ADHD should not be an excuse to avoid holding them accountable for their actions. However, parents need to have developmentally appropriate expectations for their children's behavior. Since children with ADD/ADHD are delayed about 30% in their social and emotional competence, the 5-year-old with ADHD cannot be expected to wait easily for a turn, or sit still at a table for any extended period, or concentrate on a complex puzzle or LEGO set. Parents will need to plan for activities that are developmentally appropriate for their child's abilities and learn to ignore distractible, hyperactive, fidgety, and noisy behaviors as long as they are not hurtful to others. Parents also learn the value of redirecting distractible children to another task to keep them from losing their interest or from disrupting others. However, aggressive and oppositional behavior requires time-out so that the children do not get reinforced for the misbehavior. Parents learn the entire compliance training regime to help their children be more cooperative. Before doing this training, several sessions in Program 3 (Limit Setting) will be spent on reducing commands to those that are most necessary. Other discipline strategies that work well for children with ADD/ADHD are consequences that are immediately tied to the misbehavior. Scissors are removed for a brief period if the children are using them inappropriately, or children must clean up the floor because they made a mess with the paint, and so forth.

In addition to focusing on helping parents understand developmentally appropriate discipline strategies such as ignoring and redirecting, using logical and natural consequences, and time-out for aggression, parents also learn how to teach their children problem-solving strategies and to practice more appropriate solutions. The school-age version of BASIC, Parent Program 10, helps parents learn how to teach their children to identify a problem and how to stop and think about the best choice or solution to the problem. Parents help young children learn and practice prosocial and self-regulating solutions (e.g., trade, ask first, get parent, take a deep breath, share, help one another, apologize, use words, tell self to calm down, ignore) using a children's problem-solving book. For older children, parents help them learn how to make the best choice and to evaluate the outcome of their solutions.

FOCUS—PARENTS LEARNING HOW TO COACH HOMEWORK AND
PROMOTE THEIR CHILDREN'S READING SKILLS

Because about 30% of children with ADD/ADHD often have reading, learning, and academic delays, we recommend that Program 8: Supporting Your Child's Education at School be shown as a supplement to the BASIC Parent Program. In this program, parents are helped to set up predictable homework schedules, coach children successfully with their homework, have productive parent-teacher conferences, and practice interactive reading skills with their children. It takes two to four extra sessions to complete this program, which is offered at the end of the BASIC Series. For children aged 3 to 5 years, the Interactive Reading Program is recommended.

FOCUS—CHILD TRAINING IN FRIENDSHIP SKILLS, PROBLEM SOLVING, AND
POSITIVE PEER PLAY SKILLS (CHILD DINOSAUR TREATMENT PROGRAM)

The BASIC Parent Program focuses on training parents to coach peer play, which will help their children learn social and problem-solving skills. It is also helpful if children attend the Dinosaur Treatment Program where they get specific practice with other children learning social and self-regulation skills. In this child program, children practice behaviors needed to be successful at school such as putting up a quiet hand, waiting a turn, ignoring distractions, staying focused on an activity, and following teacher's directions. In addition they learn a vocabulary for expressing a range of positive and negative emotions, learn how to identify another's emotions, and are taught anger management, problem solving, and effective communication skills. The children learn how to play appropriately with other children through modeling and many guided practice experiences with one and then two children. Three studies have indicated that combining this child training with parent training enhances children's outcomes in terms of better peer relationships and classroom behavior (Webster-Stratton & Hammond, 1997; Webster-Stratton, Reid, & Hammond, 2001, 2004).

CHILDREN WITH ATTACHMENT PROBLEMS

Children with ODD may also have ambivalent or avoidant attachment patterns with their biological, foster, or adoptive parents (Bakermans-Kranenburg, Van Ijzendoorn, & Juffer, 2003). Insecure attachment may develop because children have experienced abandonment, neglect, death of a parent, trauma, or physical abuse during their early childhood years. It may also occur because parent or caregiver responses have been unpredictable, inconsistent, harsh, and dismissive of children's emotional needs. Parents with these parenting difficulties may have attachment difficulties due to their own childhood experiences. They may be preoccupied with their own feelings, needs, and life stressors including the stress of poverty. Such parents may be only sporadically emotionally available to their children. They are often characterized as chaotic, neglectful, emotionally unavailable, and disorganized. Children who have experienced such stressful and inconsistent parenting learn not to trust the world or their relationships with other adults. Their insecure attachment, in turn, affects how they process information, solve problems, and behave with others. Some children with insecure attachment may be angry with adults and oppositional, suspicious, or rejecting of caregiver attention or attempts to nurture them. Other children may have an insatiable need for adult attention and be resentful and clingy whenever adult attention is given to someone other than themselves. These children may have difficulty separating from their parent or caregiver for fear of abandonment, or they may sulk and cry whenever attention is given to another child. Still other children with insecure attachment may be frightened of adults and become emotionally absent or disassociated to escape their fears. They may appear independent and grown up when in fact, this is masking their intense need for nurturing and support.

Children's attachment classifications are not permanent and may become more secure by parenting interactions and caregiver relationships that are predictable and consistent, sensitive to their cues, comforting when they are hurt or frightened, calming and nurturing when they are distressed, and accepting of their emotions (Van Ijzendoorn, 1995).

RECOMMENDED IY PARENT PROGRAMS

For parents of children with attachment disorders, the BASIC Parent Program (early childhood and school age versions) is recommended and will take 16 to 18 weeks to complete because of the added emphasis on child-directed play and social and emotional coaching. These programs may be offered to the biological parents, adoptive parents, or foster parents of these children.

COMBINED PARENT PROGRAM WITH IY CHILD DINOSAUR
TREATMENT PROGRAM

While the parents are in the parent group, it is recommended that the small group child treatment program (18 to 22 sessions) be offered to their children. This program will help these children learn to make friends, to build their self-esteem, to express their emotions in more appropriate ways, and to learn ways to solve some of their problems. See Tables 10.2 and 10.3 for descriptions of recommended programs by age and nature of child problems.

Additional Objectives for Biological, Foster, or Adoptive Parents

- Increase parents' empathy for the child and understanding of why insecure attachment is affecting their child's behavior and relationships.
- Encourage parents to understand ways to promote a secure attachment.
- Encourage parents to participate in pretend and fantasy play with their children.
- Teach parents how to do social and emotional coaching during child-directed play interactions with children.
- Encourage parents to provide consistent and calm comforting for children when they are hurt, frightened, ill, or lonely.
- Encourage parents to give love, attention, praise, and encouragement whenever possible for prosocial behaviors.
- Encourage parents to have consistent rules and clear limit setting, to be honest about where they are going and when they will be back, and to provide predictable, nonpunitive, and nonrejecting discipline responses for misbehavior.
- Help parents learn ways to give their children a sense of trust in the world and the people in it.
- Encourage parents to focus on joyful memories and positive emotions, as well as family traditions.

Additional Objectives for Children

- Promote secure attachment with parents or caregivers.
- Promote children's positive self-esteem, self-confidence, and sense of security.
- Increase children's ability to regulate their emotional responses.
- Increase children's ability to identify and talk about their own feelings (positive and negative).

FOCUS—PARENTS LEARNING EMOTIONAL COACHING AND WAYS TO STRENGTHEN ATTACHMENT (PARENT BASIC PROGRAM 1: 3 TO 8 YEARS; AND PROMOTING CHILDREN'S SOCIAL, EMOTIONAL, PROBLEM-SOLVING, AND ACADEMIC SKILLS THROUGH CHILD-DIRECTED PLAY)

All the vignettes from the two programs focused on child-directed play are shown to parents, and parents are provided with many practice experiences. Instead of taking two to three sessions to cover this material, it may take four to five sessions. These programs teach parents how to provide emotional and social coaching during their playtimes with their children to strengthen their attachment and positive relationships. Parents learn to provide consistent, positive attention for prosocial behaviors. To promote empathy for their children's needs, they learn to see the world from the perspective of a child. Parents learn about their children's developmental needs for contingent attention, predictable responses, and positive emotional experiences. Moreover, this undivided parental attention results in children feeling valued and respected and leads to increased self-esteem.

Parents are taught to be "emotion coaches" for their children. They are asked to play at home and to participate in pretend play so as to encourage their children's imaginary worlds. When parents encourage fantasy during play, children have opportunities to express their anxious feelings, frustration, and anger in legitimate and nonhurtful ways. Some children may explore aggressive themes in their play, such as adults hitting each other, violent car crashes, or death scenes. Other children may regress to more baby roles and want to be fed and cuddled. Often they will enact the same play theme repeatedly. When children act out these upsetting or fearful emotions symbolically through fantasy play, they are gaining mastery and control over the emotional situation. Still other children may seem unable to initiate any play at all and find it difficult to engage in fantasy. Encouraging parents' sustained child-directed play approaches even when their children's play is boring, repetitive, babyish, and unimaginative is critical, for it helps children to feel safe and to begin to form a bond with the parent before they risk sharing their inner world with an adult. This is particularly likely if their experience in the past has been with an adult who has neglected, abandoned, or abused them. Parents need reassurance that the children will not always remain in these stages of play.

In addition to encouraging fantasy play, emotion coaching also involves parents naming the children's feelings and providing support for expression of positive emotions such as joy, love, happiness, curiosity, and calmness, as well as negative emotions. This emotion coaching will help children recognize and express a wide range of emotions and begin to understand others' emotions. Some of these children may be reluctant to share feelings at all until the parent-child play interactions have increased their feelings of security or attachment in their relationship. Understanding that this takes time will help parents become more sensitive and patient when interacting with their child.

FOCUS—PARENTS PROMOTING CHILDREN'S SELF-CONFIDENCE AND JOYFUL TIMES THROUGH PRAISE AND CONSISTENT LOVE (PARENT BASIC PROGRAM 2: 3 TO 6 YEARS, OR BASIC PROGRAM 9: 6 TO 8 YEARS)

Children with attachment problems who have been blamed or abused in the past may be suspicious of praise and uncomfortable with physical touch. They may respond by rejecting it, getting overexcited, or misbehaving (e.g., the child tears up his math report when his parent praises him, or the child who goes out of her way to be disruptive after her teacher has praised her for being helpful). These children are uncomfortable with a positive self-image and seem to want to convince the adult they are not really worthy of this praise. Their self-concept is that they are worthless, and they are more comfortable with this negative image than with the new positive image being presented to them. This rejection of praise, attempts at encouragement, or resistance to being physically touched could cause parents or caregivers to stop giving praise or hugs to avoid the negative response. In fact, these children need *much more* praise, encouragement, and physical warmth than typical children. In this program, parents and caregivers are helped to understand why children might reject praise and are encouraged to keep providing praise and physical comfort so that the child will accept a more positive self-image. Instead of giving exuberant praise, parents may provide it in quiet, personal moments or with physical signals, such as a thumbs-up; and any rejection or arguments from the child are ignored. Instead of big hugs, caregivers may start with small pats on the arm combined with a smile, thumbs-up, or high five and gradually increase the length of time the physical contact lasts. Some of the targeted behaviors that may get praise include staying calm when the parent leaves, doing independent work, appearing confident about an activity, verbalizing feelings, or recognizing another's feelings and being friendly to someone else.

Children who have experienced many negative and traumatizing events will also be helped by their caregivers to develop their happy thoughts and positive emotional memory banks. Parents or caregivers are encouraged to talk with their children about a favorite place they lived, or pleasurable experience, or fun person they spent time with. Likewise parents share with their children positive memories of when they were born, or special events. Over time, these joyful memories can be referred to, written down as stories, and recounted until they become alive as family traditions.

Sticker charts and behavior plans with clearly established behavioral goals and incentives can be very helpful for these children. In fact, sometimes children with attachment problems respond more readily in the beginning to tangible incentives and sticker charts than to parent or caregiver praise and encouragement, which can be frightening to them. Setting up a sticker and reward program helps the children to experience its predictability and see that they can safely trust the plan. It can serve as a structure to help them with their behaviors while the parents and caregivers are working on strengthening their emotional relationship and their child's attachment status and self-esteem through praise and physical touch.

In addition to praise, encouragement, and incentive programs, parents are encouraged to show unconditional love and commitment to their children. The message behind this love is that no matter what happens or how the child behaves, the parent or caregiver is there for the child. Communications such as "I'm going to send you to another foster home," or, "I should never have adopted you. You ruined my life and caused my divorce," or, "You are just like your delinquent father," are harmful to the child. Instead, messages should recognize their children's positive behaviors and unique qualities and share expressions of concern, as well as loving and caring feelings. The positive messages include "I care about you and will help you learn to make better choices," or, "You will be able to do it next time," or, "I am sure you can succeed," or, "I will always care about you," and "I am frustrated about this, but I still care about you, and we will work this out together."

FOCUS—PARENTS LEARNING HOW TO HELP THEIR CHILDREN FEEL SAFE THROUGH PREDICTABLE SCHEDULES, LIMITS, AND SEPARATION AND REUNION RITUALS (PARENT BASIC PROGRAM 3: 3 TO 6 YEARS, AND PROGRAM 10: 6 TO 8 YEARS)

Children with insecure attachment classifications need to learn the family household rules and experience their predictability. Knowledge of rules and expectations for their behavior will help them to feel safe and more secure in their relationship. Parents are encouraged to be aware of and set limits on exposure to aggressive and tragic events on television, aggressive computer games, and exposure to parental conflict.

Parents learn the importance of being honest with their children about where they are going and when they will be back—even though the children may tantrum and cling when parents tell them they are leaving. Good-bye rituals are rehearsed, and parents are prepared for how to respond if their child tantrums at separations. They learn about the destructive effect of leaving in secretive ways or threatening to leave if their children don't comply with their requests. They are helped to understand and rehearse the importance of a joyful reunion when they are reunited. Other separation rituals such as bedtime rituals are also planned for. Once children experience the repeated predictability of their parents' return at the time when they said they would, their children's fears of abandonment eventually subside.

During the limit-setting program, parents learn how to give clear, positive commands and to follow through with their limits. Parents are taught the importance of providing a family schedule that is as predictable as possible (e.g., setting up a consistent routine after school, as well as for bedtime and getting up in the morning). For some parents, it will be helpful to map out the day and determine the sequence of events in a similar way as that described for children with ADHD.

FOCUS—STRENGTHENING PARENTS' POSITIVE DISCIPLINE STRATEGIES
(PARENT BASIC PROGRAM 4: 3 TO 6 YEARS, AND PROGRAM 10:
6 TO 8 YEARS)

Parents or caregivers first work hard over many sessions to establish a positive relationship and more secure attachment status with their child before starting the discipline program. Because children with attachment problems send out distorted signals to their parents, it can be hard for their parents to read their cues. They will need extra child-directed play sessions focused on emotional coaching and a great deal of positive feedback before starting to use the discipline strategies in this program. It is also important that the positive replacement behaviors (e.g., sharing, helping, cooperating with rules) have been taught to the children and that they have learned some vocabulary for expressing their emotions before parents begin the discipline program.

Parents learn to briefly ignore (with no eye contact or verbal or physical contact) the particular target negative behavior that they have identified as problematic or attention getting (e.g., whining, swearing, pouting, pestering, sulking, tantrumming). Parents are prepared for the worsening of misbehavior as children test their parents' consistency. This ignoring is brief, however, and parents are ready to give back their attention as soon as their child calms down or is behaving appropriately. Children with insecure attachment status will want their parents' positive attention so desperately that they usually stop the misbehavior pretty quickly when it is ignored. For children with a history of neglect, it is particularly important that the ignoring strategy be used briefly for the target negative behavior and that parents consistently give heavy doses of positive attention whenever the children are behaving appropriately. In this program, parents learn about the value of combining ignoring with a redirect or distraction, which often works well to avoid giving attention to the misbehavior while diverting the child's attention to something else. This approach helps the children not to feel abandoned. It is important to help parents understand the difference between planned ignoring for a target negative behavior and emotionally withdrawing from them.

Time-out is taught as a way of helping children self-regulate and helps parents avoid giving attention to aggressive behavior. Because parents or caregivers feel badly about the child's prior traumas, they may be inclined to give in to the aggression or hold a child who has been aggressive. Both of these approaches reinforce the misbehavior. Parents are helped to understand that time-out is not used to humiliate children or threaten loss of their love but rather to help them learn to self-regulate and become more independent. They are taught to use this procedure only for aggressive or destructive behavior or for compliance training if their child is oppositional and defiant. Parents decide what behavior (primarily aggressive behavior toward another person) will result in time-out. At a time when children are calm, parents explain what behaviors will result in a time-out, where time-out will take place, how long time-out will last, and how to calm down while in time-out. They rehearse this procedure with their children when they are calm by practicing going to time-out and saying to themselves *"I can calm down; I can take three deep breaths; I can do it; I can try again."* This teaching helps the children learn how to help themselves to self-regulate when they are angry. During group sessions, parents practice these steps and are prepared for all possible responses that their children may give them so that they can stay calm and predictable themselves. Parents also learn to take personal time-outs when they feel they are losing control and understand the importance of regulating their own emotional and negative responses with their children.

Children who attend the Dinosaur School program also have direct practice going to time-out and learning the breathing and self-talk strategies to help them calm down.

Focus—Supporting Children's Academic Skills (Program 8: Supporting Your Child's Education—6 to 8 Years, or Interactive Reading Program—3 to 6 Years)

Sometimes these children have experienced many moves and missed quite a bit of school. They may not have had much experience with adults reading to them or providing academic stimulation in the home. If this is true, parents or caregivers may need more information about working with teachers, setting up predictable homework routines, and providing interactive reading experiences. These two programs will be helpful to parents in providing this academic coaching at home and coordinating with teachers.

Focus—Child Training in Friendship Skills, Problem Solving, and Emotion Language (Incredible Years Dinosaur Treatment Program)

While the parents or caregivers are receiving the parent program, the children may be enrolled in the small group child treatment program. This program augments what the parents are learning by providing the children with direct coaching and small group experiences with building feelings literacy, learning anger management and problem-solving skills, and practicing friendship and communication skills. Throughout this training, children receive heavy doses of adult attention, praise, and acceptance to promote their self-esteem and self-confidence in their abilities, as well as their trust in adults who care about them.

CHILDREN WITH DIVORCING PARENTS

Children react to divorce in a variety of ways. Some children become aggressive and angry about the family disruption in routine and households; others become sad and anxious about being abandoned by one parent; others are confused about who to be loyal to; others feel lonely and different because of their family circumstances; and still others seem to show no feelings at all and act as if nothing has changed. Because children aged 3 to 8 years are still vacillating between fantasy and reality, most will have fantasies about their parents getting back together again and will have difficulty accepting the permanency of the divorce. Many children worry about whether they are partially to blame for the divorce. They may remember arguments concerning them that lead them to think they have caused their parents' divorce. In addition, they may fear that their parents will abandon them. (If it is possible for one parent to leave another parent, why not their child?) Therefore, most children will feel insecure in their relationship with their parents, worried that their parent might not return, and concerned about when they will see him or her. If the divorcing parent moves away or lives with someone else, this can add complexity to the fears of abandonment or reasons for anger.

RECOMMENDED IY PARENT PROGRAMS

For parents who are divorcing, the BASIC Parent Program (Early childhood or school-age versions) is recommended as well as the Advance Parent program. In addition, it is recommended that the children attend the Dinosaur Program while the parents are in the parenting program. It will take 20 to 24 weeks to complete these programs.

Additional Objectives for Divorcing Parents

- Increase parents' understanding and awareness of their children's feelings concerning their divorce and encourage their children's appropriate expression.
- Teach parents how to provide emotional support, reassurance, and extra time through child-directed play interactions.
- Help parents to reassure their children that they are not responsible for the divorce and will not be abandoned.
- Encourage parents to give added praise and encouragement to increase their children's self-esteem and sense of security in their relationship.
- Help parents to provide predictable routines and visitation schedules that make children feel more secure.
- Help parents understand the importance of following through with promises and visit dates and times.
- Help parents set up consistent and regular communication and visits with their children.
- Help parents understand the importance of keeping their children out of the conflict between parents.

Additional Objectives for Children

- Increase children's accurate attributions for divorce.
- Increase adjustment to family changes.
- Decrease anxiety and divorce-related concerns.
- Increase problem-solving skills.

- Increase ability to talk about feelings, self-regulate, and cope with anger.
- Increase friendships and support.

FOCUS—PARENTS STRENGTHENING THEIR RELATIONSHIP WITH THEIR CHILDREN (CHILD-DIRECTED PLAY SKILLS, PARENT BASIC PROGRAM 1: 3 TO 8 YEARS)

Teaching parents child-directed play skills is a central component for parents who want to help their children cope with their divorce because it assures children that they are still cared for and are important to their parents. Because divorcing parents are preoccupied with the stress of the divorce, financial changes, legal issues, and new housing needs, they may be giving their children less attention than usual. Children may mistakenly attribute this lack of attention to their parents not loving them. Taking the time to engage in *daily* play can be one of the most reassuring things parents can do for their children because it lets them know how important they are in their lives. By using the child-directed play principles taught in this program, parents will provide emotional coaching, enter into their child's fantasy world, and discover what their children are thinking and feeling about their divorce. A child may act out her parents' fights with puppets, or indicate that the baby in her make-believe family is worried his parent won't ever come back. Other themes of fear of abandonment, or feelings of guilt or blame because the parents are divorcing, or lack of power may be symbolically revealed in parent-child play interactions. When this happens, parents can work to correct inaccurate attributions and to gently reassure their children that they will be cared for and loved no matter what happens. Also by using the emotion coaching principles taught in this program, parents will provide their children with ways to talk with them about their feelings.

In addition to helping children talk about their unhappy feelings during play, this is also a time when parents need to encourage their children's expression of positive feelings, such as allowing them to talk about things and times that make them feel confident, happy, calm, curious, and joyful. Parents should predict happier times for their family and be sure to share their own feelings of happiness about spending time with their children. It is important for parents to support their children's expression of a range of feelings, particularly during child-directed playtimes. During a time when children feel stressed and powerless and parents seem preoccupied, these intimate playtimes together can be the medicine that will help children cope successfully with their parents' divorce.

FOCUS—PARENTS GIVING EXTRA ENCOURAGEMENT AND ASSURING
CHILDREN THEY ARE WANTED (PARENT BASIC PROGRAM 2:
3 TO 6 YEARS, OR BASIC PROGRAM 9: 6 TO 8 YEARS)

Giving extra encouragement and planning some fun family outings during these stressful times can be immensely reassuring to children. Divorce is naturally stressful to parents and results in parents' feelings of anger as well as depression and fear about the future. Children worry about their parents' unhappiness and emotional distance. Sometimes parents' anger and stress spill over into their parenting causing them to be more critical, impatient, and hostile toward their children. In this program, parents are encouraged to make an effort to notice their children's helpful behaviors and to praise their cooperation with changing routines. For children who are acting out with misbehavior, parents set up behavior plans with stickers and incentives for targeted positive behaviors.

Parents' guilt about their divorce also can lead them to give their children gifts, to comply with all their requests, and to avoid limit setting, perhaps as a way to get their children to like them better. These incentives are not encouraged and can result in children becoming manipulative and oppositional to get a payoff.

In some families, one parent may be less available or less involved in the children's lives. When children have infrequent and unpredictable contact with a parent, they tend to internalize a belief that they are bad or not lovable. Therefore, the primary parent needs to help the child know that the problem is not with the child's lovability but rather with the parent's own issues. Here the goals will be for the parent to provide praise, love, and nurturing to build the child's self-esteem.

FOCUS—PARENTS LEARNING THE IMPORTANCE OF CONSISTENT LIMIT
SETTING, MONITORING, AND PREDICTABLE ROUTINES (PARENT BASIC
PROGRAM 3: 3 TO 6 YEARS, AND PROGRAM 10: 6 TO 8 YEARS)

Because divorce results in changing routines, and perhaps children changing households each week, it is important that the custody plan be set up for young children in as predictable a routine as possible. It is important for parents to agree on a visitation or shared custody plan and, when necessary, set limits with the children to follow through with the plan. A child may resist going to one parent's house on the night that he is supposed to move home. The parent should avoid giving in to this noncompliance and calmly follow through with the plan letting the child know parents are in charge of the schedule and not the child.

Sometimes, because parents feel guilty about their divorce and the distress it is causing their children, they don't follow though with household rules. Or, because they are stressed and depressed, they are inconsistent about enforcing the consequences for misbehavior. Thus, children learn they can manipulate the rules or get away with noncompliance. In this program, parents are helped to understand the long-term consequences of this inconsistency or failure to monitor rules. Moreover, they learn that by providing consistency in rules and limit setting, they are actually helping their children feel safer because the rules are predictable.

FOCUS—CONSISTENT DISCIPLINE (PARENT BASIC PROGRAM 4: 3 TO 6 YEARS, AND PROGRAM 10: 6 TO 8 YEARS)

For children who are reacting to divorce with misbehavior, it will be important for both parents to agree on a behavior management plan and decide which negative behaviors to target and the appropriate discipline strategy. This can be especially important if there is shared custody and children are changing homes frequently (e.g., an 8-year-old child may have lost his TV privileges that evening because he did not do his homework, but because he is going to the other parent's house that evening, it will be necessary for the second parent to carry out this consequence). When possible, coordination between parents on a behavior plan will help children improve their misbehaviors more quickly.

It is ideal if both parents can attend the parenting program so that there is consistency in responses to misbehavior from one home to another. In this part of the training program, parents are reminded of the importance of not fighting in front of the children and not saying disparaging remarks about the other parent.

FOCUS—HELPING DIVORCED PARENTS TO LEARN POSITIVE COMMUNICATION AND EFFECTIVE PROBLEM-SOLVING SKILLS (ADVANCE PARENT PROGRAM: 4 TO 8 YEARS)

For divorcing parents, it can be immensely helpful to include the Advance program after the BASIC program. Although the parents are divorcing each other, they are not divorcing the child and will still need to communicate and negotiate with each other regarding such things as parent-teacher meetings, parent care during holidays or work trips, changes in pickup and drop-off at houses, medical issues, sports events, and finances. The Advance program focuses on effective communication and problem-solving skills for adults as well as anger and depression management. This program can help divorcing couples have a structured format for discussing issues and making plans for their children.

FOCUS—CHILD TRAINING TO PROMOTE PEER SUPPORT,
COMMUNICATION, AND PROBLEM SOLVING
(CHILD DINOSAUR TREATMENT PROGRAM)

It can also be helpful, while divorcing parents are in a parent group, to offer their children the small group Dinosaur Treatment Program. Children make friends with other children who have similar experiences and have opportunities to share their feelings with each other. This group support normalizes the divorce experience and provides children with friends who can help them talk about their problems and can make them feel less lonely. During the first components of this program, children learn the *emotional vocabulary* to express a variety of feelings and are given opportunities to talk about how the divorce is affecting them. Puppets, games, and books engage the children and enable them to safely express feelings. These games and group discussions can help children understand that all feelings are acceptable as well as to clarify common misconceptions and loyalty conflicts. For example, the child who fears deep down that he is responsible for his parents' breakup will find comfort and relief from another child who expresses exactly the same feelings.

Another component of the program focuses on teaching the children problem-solving skills. These skills will help them learn how to cope with some of the issues that their parents' divorce is presenting them: *"Who will I spend my birthday with? What will I do when one of my parents doesn't call at the agreed upon time? Which house do I keep my bike or Nintendo at? How can I behave better so my parents will get back together? What do I do when I'm lonely and miss my parent? What do I do when my parents fight?"*

These discussions of problems often reveal children's fears or self-blame and magical thinking. An important aspect of solving these problems is for the therapist to clarify misconceptions about the cause of divorce ("divorce is a grown-up problem") and to increase the child's ability to separate adult responsibilities from child concerns. When discussions reveal that children have witnessed domestic violence, the group will focus on how to keep themselves safe and where to go for help if this should happen again. For many children, explaining a parent's absence and lack of involvement in their lives is a central issue. Therapists help these children understand that their parent's absence has nothing to do with their own fantasized unlovability but rather with the parent's problems or guilt. The goal here is to promote the self-esteem of these children.

The anger management component of this program helps the children learn how to calm down when they are frustrated, disappointed, or angry with their parent or family situation, so that they can think about possible ways to solve the problem. Because feeling powerless can lead to escalating anger, these calming strategies can help children with their capacity to cope. They are also helped to sort out "green light" problems that they can try to solve and "red light" problems that they cannot solve. This distinction is important in helping them disengage from interparental conflicts and from issues that they cannot resolve. Puppets are used to present some of these common divorce-related scenarios, and the children participate in teaching the puppet how to solve the problem (e.g., Wally the puppet tells the children he is lonely with his dad gone and asks them to help him with two things that will help him feel better).

Many children are embarrassed when they learn their parents are getting divorced and don't know how to talk about it to their friends. By the time the children participate in the friendship and communication components of this program, they will have the communication and language skills to talk about their feelings and problems, not only with other children, but with their parents as well. The group format includes a great deal of role-playing and practice activities in friendly talk and asking for help so that children have opportunities for developing important coping skills.

CHILDREN WITH INTERNALIZING PROBLEMS SUCH AS FEARS AND DEPRESSION

In our studies of young children with conduct problems, we find over 60% of the children are also comorbid for internalizing problems (Webster-Stratton & Hammond, 1988, 1999; Webster-Stratton & Reid, 2005b). Internalizing problems encompass a wide variety of conditions such as fears, social or school phobia, separation anxiety, and depression. Young children may not recognize these feelings or be able to talk about them with others. Consequently, their anxieties may be expressed in symptoms that include crying, clinging behavior, stomachaches, headaches, irritability, and withdrawal. Depressed children may misbehave or even express their sadness in the form of aggression and anger in their interactions with others. The goal of the treatment is help the parents understand how they can help their children manage their distress by teaching them social skills, problem solving, and emotional vocabulary so that their children can recognize and cope successfully with their uncomfortable feelings.

RECOMMENDED IY PROGRAMS

For parents of children with internalizing problems, the BASIC Parent Program (early childhood and school-age versions) is recommended and will take 16 to 18 weeks to complete.

While the parents are in the parent group, it is also recommended that the small group child treatment program be offered to their children, which takes 18 to 22 weeks to complete. This program will help these children learn to make friends, to build their self-esteem, to express their emotions, and to learn ways to solve some of their problems.

Additional Objectives for Parents

- Educate parents on the nature and causes of social fears and anxieties.
- Encourage parents to understand ways to respond to children's expression of fear or depression.
- Teach parents how to do social and emotional coaching during child-directed play interactions with children so that children can express their emotions.
- Encourage parents to provide consistent and calm comforting for children but not to reinforce fears through modeling or undue attention.
- Encourage parents to give love, attention, praise, and encouragement whenever possible for prosocial behaviors.
- Encourage parents to have consistent rules and clear limit setting and not to reinforce their children's avoidance behaviors.
- Encourage parents to focus on joyful memories and positive emotions, as well as family traditions.

Additional Objectives for Children

- Promote children's positive self-esteem, self-confidence, and sense of security.
- Increase children's social competence and ability to make friends.
- Increase children's ability to cope with their emotional responses through problem solving.
- Increase children's ability to identify and talk about their own feelings (positive and negative).

FOCUS—PARENTS LEARNING HOW TO PROMOTE THEIR CHILDREN'S SELF-CONFIDENCE AND EXPRESSION OF EMOTION (CHILD-DIRECTED PLAY SKILLS, PARENT BASIC PROGRAM: 3 TO 8 YEARS, AND PROMOTING CHILDREN'S SOCIAL, EMOTIONAL, PROBLEM-SOLVING, AND ACADEMIC SKILLS THROUGH CHILD-DIRECTED PLAY)

These programs teach parents how to provide emotion and social coaching during their playtimes with their children that will strengthen their positive relationships and teach children the emotion language for expressing their feelings. Parents learn to provide consistent, positive attention for prosocial behaviors and to strengthen their children's self-esteem and confidence in making friends and coping with peer problems. They are encouraged to set up playdates for their children and to coach these peer interactions when friends visit. This experience gives the children added practice in social interactions and builds their confidence in their friendship skills. In so doing their social phobia decreases.

Parents are encouraged to challenge their children's expression of negative emotions especially when they are unrealistic. Parents help their children understand that is normal sometimes not to be asked to join in a game or to be told that they can't play with a peer. They can help their children understand how to respond to this perceived rejection and encourage them to "be brave" and try again, either with the same group or a different friend. It is important that parents not encourage children's avoidant strategies or withdrawal from social activities. Instead, parents might say, "Those kids didn't mean to leave you out, they were already half way through the game, and it was difficult to add another player. You need to stay calm, wait, watch, and try again when they start the next game." This approach helps the parents challenge the child's negative thinking that she has no friends or is not liked. Parents make lists of the kinds of things their children worry about and talk about ways to help their children challenge those negative thoughts. In addition, they are encouraged to provide discussions of positive emotions by pointing out times when their friends seem to enjoy playing with them, or they seem happy, or they successfully stayed calm in a frustrating situation.

Research has indicated that rates of anxiety and depression are high in parents of anxious and depressed children. Therefore, parents learn about the *modeling principle* and how their own anxieties, sadness, and fears can be modeled for children. They are cautioned to keep control of their own anxious talk or negative expression of affect with their children. They are also helped to avoid giving undue attention to their children's expression of negative emotion, which inadvertently reinforces this expression (see ADVANCE portion of Parent Curriculum where parents learn how to manage their depression and anger with relaxation, self-talk, and problem-solving approaches).

FOCUS—PARENTS ENCOURAGING THEIR CHILDREN'S INDEPENDENCE THROUGH PRAISE AND TANGIBLE REWARDS (PARENT BASIC PROGRAM 2: 3 TO 6 YEARS, OR PARENT BASIC PROGRAM 9: 6 TO 8 YEARS)

Children who are anxious or fearful are praised for their courage in trying to cope with their problems and working out peer relationship problems. In the first parent group session, parents make a list of target goals for themselves and for their children. They identify the target child behaviors they want to decrease (e.g., clinging to them when they leave or resisting going to bed or withdrawing from social events) and the positive replacement behaviors (e.g., separating easily). Parents are asked to take a coaching role and are told that their job is to encourage their children's "growing up behaviors." This means giving them praise for taking a risk, or trying something new, or doing something independently. A parent might say, "I'm so proud of you for staying overnight at your friend's house; you are really growing up." Or, "You were scared to present your Show and Share toy at school, but you were brave and really showed how strong you are."

Incentive plans are also set up for children facing feared situations, such as sticker charts for staying in their bed all night, going to swimming lessons, or separating at school without a fuss. These behavior plans become the focus of group sessions and home assignments. Parents are also encouraged to work with teachers to set up a system at school whereby the withdrawn and fearful child is praised and reinforced for interacting with others or presenting at "Show and Tell." If a child is afraid of a particular situation or activity (e.g., dogs or swimming), parents learn how to set up gradual exposure in small doses. First the parent might read books about dogs with their child, then stop to watch other children pet a dog and make positive comments about the dog. Later they gradually get closer to a gentle dog while the parent models petting the dog. The child is praised for getting closer despite her fear.

FOCUS—ESTABLISHING CLEAR LIMITS (PARENT BASIC PROGRAM 3: 3 TO 6 YEARS, AND PROGRAM 10: 6 TO 8 YEARS)

If parents are anxious or depressed, they may lack the confidence or energy to set effective limits or to follow through with consequences for their children's misbehavior. Moreover, they may be more likely to find fault with their children and to respond negatively to misbehaviors than to their positive behaviors because of their own sadness. Consequently, in addition to practice looking for something positive in their children, parents are helped to clarify the important rules for their households and to be confident when they follow through with them. By establishing clear household rules and practicing how to state them clearly and positively, not only do they help their children feel less anxious, but the parents will find they spend less energy worrying about how they should respond.

For the child who has school phobia and uses somatic symptoms to avoid going to school, the parents are encouraged to have their child checked by a pediatrician to reassure themselves that there is no medical problem. After taking this step, parents learn to express their optimism about their child's ability to return to school. They might say, "I know school is scary now, but I am sure you can be brave, and it will get easier every day. I bet you will make some nice friends." Parents learn that it is normal for children to react adversely with clinging and crying when they leave them at school, or with a babysitter, or when tucked in bed at night. They are encouraged to set up a predictable routine for leaving as follows:

- Express confidence and happiness about the experience the child is about to have.
- Let children know clearly they will be leaving (don't sneak away).
- Remind child of when they will return.
- Ignore child's protests and tantrums.

Similarly, parents are helped to set up a predictable routine for their reunion with their child:

- They return when they say they will.
- They look excited about seeing their child (leave worries about work behind).

Focus—Parents Learning Effective Discipline to Promote Persistence and Avoidance Responses (Parent BASIC Program 4: 3 to 6 Years, and Program 10: 6 to 8 Years)

Parents learn a variety of strategies, including ignoring, redirecting, warning, logical and natural consequences, and problem solving. The approach taken will depend on the child's problems. If the child is not aggressive or noncompliant, the emphasis will be on what somatic behaviors can be ignored, such as excessive complaining. Parents learn when they should problem-solve with the children and why it is important to encourage children to keep trying, to go right back to cope with the situation. Of course, all somatic complaints need to be checked out by a physician before starting the program.

For children who have difficulty separating from their parents, it is important to get the right balance between being supportive and not giving expressions of fear too much attention. Parents are encouraged to confidently say good-bye with a hug, to explain when they will be back and to walk away and ignore the ensuing tantrum. Fear of going to bed can be handled in a similar way. After finishing the bedtime routine, parents say "good night" and express their belief that their child can be brave and stay in bed and then leave the room, ignoring any crying.

FOCUS—PARENTS MODELING POSITIVE COMMUNICATION AND PROBLEM SOLVING (ADVANCE PARENTING PROGRAM 5, 6, AND 7)

This program can be helpful for these parents because it focuses on communication skills, depression and anger management, and ways to give and get support. It also teaches parents problem-solving strategies. With these skills, they will be better equipped to cope with their own anxieties and fears. Moreover, the parent group provides immense support and an ongoing network even after the program is completed.

FOCUS—CHILD TRAINING IN FEELINGS LANGUAGE AND PROBLEM SOLVING (INCREDIBLE YEARS DINOSAUR TREATMENT PROGRAM)

One of the first components of the Dinosaur Program is focused on the children learning to recognize their own feelings and to put words to those feelings. Through the use of a relaxation thermometer, children identify what kinds of things make them tense, fearful, or sad and how their body reacts to these feelings. They draw body outlines and color in feelings in certain parts of the body. Using blue for sadness, they identify their feeling fingerprints—that is the places in their body that signal a happy or distressed feeling (e.g., racing heart, sweaty palms, stomachache). This helps children recognize when they are feeling tense. Once children recognize and have words for these feelings, they learn how to reduce their tenseness on the thermometer through relaxation exercises and bring their body temperature down into the "relaxed" zone. Large poster-size pictures of the thermometer with arrows marking the change in stress are used to help children visualize the concept of changing feelings and help them understand that all feelings are okay.

Some of the strategies that the children learn for coping with their stressful or problem feelings include taking three deep breaths, visualizing a happy place where they can go in their imaginations, tensing and relaxing their muscles, and challenging their negative self-talk with positive thoughts. Many games and small group activities are played to practice these self-soothing responses.

After the children develop a vocabulary for talking about feelings and some self-regulating skills, they learn a set of problem-solving steps. Beginning with the first step of recognizing their problem through their problem feelings, they learn to generate possible solutions to these problems and to evaluate the best solution. Many of the solutions for these children will include cognitive strategies such as "Compliment yourself," "Tell yourself you can try again," "Take a deep breath and blow your bad feelings out of your fingers," "Use your teasing shield," "Throw away bad feelings," "Tell a parent how you feel," "Have a calming thought," "Be brave and keep going," "Do something that makes you feel happy," "Tell yourself to keep trying," and "Stop fearful thoughts." There are over 40 laminated solution cards that children learn and can use to cope with problems when they are feeling their stress build up on their worry thermometer. The children also learn how to evaluate their choices and how to give themselves praise for their efforts.

In addition to learning problem solving, another component of the program focuses on friendship skills and communication skills. Since many of these children are social phobic, they need help in making friends and knowing how to enter in play or to play cooperatively with another child. In the Dinosaur Program, children have weekly coached practice sessions in play interaction skills with the other children.

Active participants in the Dinosaur Program are large child-size puppets known as Wally Problem Solver, Molly Manners, and Freddy and Felicity Feelings. Children find these puppets easy to talk to and are more likely to talk with them than with therapists. These puppets are present at every session and disclose to the children their personal examples of stressful situations that are similar to the children's difficulties. The children help the puppets solve their problems by teaching them the skills of relaxing, staying calm, and coming up with solutions. The puppets, in turn, learn from the children and provide models for how they have successfully coped with their anxiety. Together with the puppets, the children engage in role-plays, imagery, and many practices of coping skills.

CONCLUSION

In this chapter, I have described how the Incredible Years Parenting Program focuses on teaching parents a common set of parenting and child-management principles and then applies these principles according to the parents' target goals for their children or themselves. Parents of children who are impulsive, hyperactive, and inattentive learn about temperament and how their children's biological makeup makes it more difficult for them to listen, follow directions, and play appropriately with other children. They learn the importance of clear limit setting and consistent follow-through and ways to help coach their children's academic and social skills during play with other children.

Adoptive or foster parents are more likely to be focused on helping their children develop trusting relationships with them. This means they will spend more time on child-directed play, emotional coaching, and building the relationship or attachment-building components of the curriculum.

Divorcing parents will be working on achieving consistency from one home to another, keeping their children out of their adult conflict, and providing them with consistent reassurance they are loved.

Parents with children who have somatic complaints will be sorting out which behaviors can be ignored and which ones need extra support or limit setting to keep the child from withdrawing from stressful situations.

In this discussion, I have provided examples of ways the program is tailored to help parents learn how to respond to children with differing needs. In some cases, I have recommended additional small group training for the child to augment the parents' efforts as well as teacher training to promote consistency from home to school. The value of parents working in groups together to address their children's varying problems cannot be overestimated. The group support helps normalize and destigmatize their situation. When single or divorcing parents befriend couples in the group who have similar difficulties, they realize it is not because they are single that their child has a problem. Or, foster parents may meet other foster parents and discover similar worries and issues in their attempts to parent a child who seems to reject their love. This sharing of similar experiences provides a supportive network that for some parent groups can last for years after the formal training. The therapists who have the privilege of facilitating these groups and their sharing will find this to be an ever-challenging process and a highly rewarding experience.

REFERENCES

Bakermans-Kranenburg, M. J., Van Ijzendoorn, M. H., & Juffer, F. (2003). Less is more: Meta-analyses of sensitivity and attachment interventions in early childhood. *Psychological Bulletin, 129,* 195–215.

Barkley, R. A. (1996). Attention deficit/hyperactivity disorder. In E. J. Mash & R. A. Barkley (Eds.), *Child psychopathology* (pp. 63–112). New York: Guilford Press.

Campbell, S. B., Shaw, D. S., & Gilliom, M. (2000). Early externalizing behavior problems: Toddlers and preschoolers at risk for later maladjustment. *Development and Psychopathology, 12,* 467–488.

Coie, J. D., Dodge, K. A., & Kupersmidt, J. B. (1990). Peer group behavior and social status. In S. R. Asher & J. D. Coie (Eds.), *Peer rejection in childhood* (pp. 17–59). New York: Cambridge University Press.

Hinshaw, S. P., & Anderson, C. A. (1996). Conduct and oppositional defiant disorders. In E. J. Mash & R. A. Barkley (Eds.), *Child psychopathology* (pp. 108–149). New York: Guilford Press.

Van Ijzendoorn, M. H. (1995). Adult attachment representations, parental responsiveness, and infant attachment: A meta-analysis on the predictive validity of the Adult Attachment Interview. *Psychological Bulletin, 177,* 387–403.

Webster-Stratton, C. (1984, 2001). *The incredible years parent training manual: BASIC program.* 1411 8th Avenue West, Seattle 98119.

Webster-Stratton, C. (1985). Predictors of treatment outcome in parent training for conduct disordered children. *Behavior Therapy, 16,* 223–243.

Webster-Stratton, C. (1990). Stress: A potential disruptor of parent perceptions and family interactions. *Journal of Clinical Child Psychology, 19,* 302–312.

Webster-Stratton, C. (1998). Parent training with low-income clients: Promoting parental engagement through a collaborative approach. In J. R. Lutzker (Ed.), *Handbook of child abuse research and treatment* (pp. 183–210). New York: Plenum Press.

Webster-Stratton, C. (in press). The incredible years parents, teachers, and children training series: Early intervention and prevention programs for young children. In P. S. Jensen & E. D. Hibbs (Eds.), *Psychosocial treatments for child and adolescent disorders: Empirically based approaches.* Washington, DC: American Psychological Association.

Webster-Stratton, C., & Hammond, M. (1988). Maternal depression and its relationship to life stress, perceptions of child behavior problems, parenting behaviors and child conduct problems. *Journal of Abnormal Child Psychology, 16*(3), 299–315.

Webster-Stratton, C., & Hammond, M. (1997). Treating children with early-onset conduct problems: A comparison of child and parent training interventions. *Journal of Consulting and Clinical Psychology, 65*(1), 93–109.

Webster-Stratton, C., & Hammond, M. (1998). Conduct problems and level of social competence in Head Start children: Prevalence, pervasiveness and associated risk factors. *Clinical Child Psychology and Family Psychology Review, 1*(2), 101–124.

Webster-Stratton, C., & Hammond, M. (1999). Marital conflict management skills, parenting style and early-onset conduct problems: Processes and pathways. *Journal of Child Psychology and Psychiatry, 40,* 917–927.

Webster-Stratton, C., & Hancock, L. (1998). Parent training: Content, methods and processes. In E. Schaefer (Ed.), *Handbook of parent training* (2nd ed., pp. 98–152). New York: Wiley.

Webster-Stratton, C., & Herbert, M. (1994). *Troubled families—Problem children: Working with parents: A collaborative process.* Chichester, England: Wiley.

Webster-Stratton, C., & Lindsay, D. W. (1999). Social competence and early-onset conduct problems: Issues in assessment. *Journal of Child Clinical Psychology, 28,* 25–93.

Webster-Stratton, C., & Reid, M. J. (2003a). The incredible years parents, teachers and child training series: A multifacted treatment approach for young children with conduct problems. In A. E. Kazdin & J. R. Weisz (Eds.), *Evidence-based psychotherapies for children and adolescents* (pp. 224–240). New York: Guilford Press.

Webster-Stratton, C., & Reid, M. J. (2003b). Treating conduct problems and strengthening social emotional competence in young children (ages 4 to 8 years): The Dina Dinosaur treatment program. *Journal of Emotional and Behavioral Disorders, 11*(3), 130–143.

Webster-Stratton, C., & Reid, M. J. (2005a). *Adapting the incredible years child dinosaur social, emotional, and problem-solving intervention to address co-morbid diagnoses and family risk factors.* Seattle: University of Washington.

Webster-Stratton, C., & Reid, M. J. (2006). Treatment and prevention of conduct problems: Parent training interventions for young children (2 to 7 years old). In K. McCartney & D. A. Phillips (Eds.), *Blackwell handbook on early childhood development* (pp. 616–641). Malden, MA: Blackwell.

Webster-Stratton, C., Reid, M. J., & Hammond, M. (2001). Social skills and problem solving training for children with early-onset conduct problems: Who benefits? *Journal of Child Psychology and Psychiatry, 42*(7), 943–952.

Webster-Stratton, C., Reid, M. J., & Hammond, M. (2004). Treating children with early-onset conduct problems: Intervention outcomes for parent, child, and teacher training. *Journal of Clinical Child and Adolescent Psychology, 33*(1), 105–124.

CHAPTER 11

Training Parents of Children with Comorbid Attention-Deficit/Hyperactivity Disorder and Oppositional Defiant Disorder

JEFFREY S. DANFORTH

CHILDREN WITH Attention-Deficit/Hyperactivity Disorder (ADHD) demonstrate developmentally inappropriate degrees of overactivity, impulsiveness, and inattention (American Psychiatric Association, 1994). In 1966, pioneers in behavioral parent training (Hawkins, Peterson, Schweid, & Bijou, 1966) presented a successful case study of home based parent training for a mother of a child described as "hyperactive." Today, there is considerable evidence that parent training for families of children with ADHD results in improved parenting behavior, reduced parent stress, and reduced disruptive child behavior (Chronis, Chacko, Fabiano, Wymbs, & Pelham, 2004). Behavioral parent training for ADHD meets the American Psychological Association Division 53 criteria for well-established, evidence-based treatment (Lonigan, Elbert, & Johnson, 1998). Nonetheless, there are limitations in research design and factors that moderate the role of parent training for ADHD. Diagnoses of hyperactivity are difficult to compare across studies. Most research has examined short-term outcome and has not evaluated generalization over time or across settings. Much of the research is conducted in university-based or medical school settings, not in traditional clinic-based settings. Lower

SES families, single parents, and fathers are not adequately represented. Risk factors that may contribute to poor outcome include maternal depression, parental ADHD, marital problems, low SES, lack of father participation, and comorbidity (Chronis et al., 2004; Smith, Barkley, & Shapiro, 2006).

Recently, interest in children with comorbid ADHD/Oppositional Defiant Disorder (ODD) has developed. At least 55% of children with ADHD also have behavior characteristic of ODD, and a large proportion of these children will subsequently develop conduct disorder (CD) where overall prognosis is worse yet again (Barkley, 2006). ODD and CD are the most common forms of comorbidity with ADHD (Angold, Costello, & Erkanli, 1999). This is important because children with co-occurring ADHD/ODD have a distinctive pattern of dysfunction dissimilar to ADHD alone and ODD alone children. The etiology of familial transmission is likely different with an additive effect leading to outcome that is generally worse than seen in children with ADHD or ODD alone (Barkley, 2006; Hinshaw, 1994; Kuhne, Schachar, & Tannock, 1997; Lynam, 1996). For example, Gomez and Sanson (1994) found qualitative differences in the tone of the noncompliant episodes. The comorbid group, "openly expressed defiance . . . (e.g., appearing indifferent, and threatening angrily to discontinue the activity)" whereas the ADHD group, "appeared to have some difficulties moving from one task to another, and were slow in responding to maternal commands" (p. 484).

THEORY SUPPORTING PARENT TRAINING

Parent training is the preferred mode of treatment for children with ADHD/ODD. Medicine and cognitive behavior therapy are also used. Although proven effective, there are limitations to stimulant medication and the deficit in behavioral inhibition that characterizes ADHD is incompatible with the skills necessary for a child's successful participation in cognitive talk therapy.

PARENT TRAINING

The parent training program described next presents a therapeutic environment to the child. The structure and the content are influenced by a theory of ADHD and theories about subsequent development of ODD. The program acknowledges and accommodates for the essential disability of ADHD and holds the child accountable for ODD behavior.

A Theory of ADHD

The parent training program is informed by the theory of ADHD presented by Barkley. A brief summary is presented here (for detail, see

Barkley 1994, 1997a, 2001, 2006). Research indicates that characteristics of ADHD are associated with neurophysiological impairment in the prefrontal cortex and its associated networks. This, in turn, is associated with a delay in the development of behavioral inhibition characterized by three deficiencies. Children with ADHD have difficulty inhibiting (a) prepotent responses that leads to immediate positive or negative reinforcement, (b) an ongoing sequence of behavior, and (c) the influence of interfering external and internal stimuli. The failure of inhibition prevents a necessary delay between the child's response and the overwhelming influence of antecedent, concurrent, and consequent stimulus events. This short latency between the environmental events and the child's response limits the opportunity for self-directed behavior, characterized as executive functions, which regulate behavior directed toward the future. Thus, the executive functions are not impaired, but rather rendered less effective by the disabled behavioral inhibition.

Barkley described four categories of executive functions that typically assist children to control their subsequent behavior. He contends that these functions are diminished in children with ADHD. Nonverbal working memory is the ability to maintain internal representations of sensory-motor information. Verbal working memory is the internal representation of speech. Self-regulation of affect and arousal refers to the ability to delay or modulate emotional reactions elicited by stimulus events. Reconstitution refers to verbal and nonverbal analysis/synthesis skills that contribute to the flexibility and creativity necessary for planning solutions. The self-directed, internalized executive functions generate motor behavior that is more planned and goal directed. However, lacking the requisite behavioral inhibition that allows for and protects executive function, the behavior of children with ADHD tends to be unplanned, unreasoned, and emotional, seemingly lacking organization, purpose, and intent. The outcome is poor goal-directed inattentive behavior, impulsive responses, and nondirected hyperactivity, as well as associated features including poor adaptive functioning, academic functioning, and learning disabilities.

The Development of Oppositional Defiant Disorder

Approximately 55% of children with ADHD develop ODD (Barkley, 2006) with characteristics such as active defiance, angry tantrums, and arguments with adults. How does ADHD, a biologically based neurological disorder (Nigg, 2006) that precedes the onset of ODD, develop to include ODD, the specific responses of which are often learned? Three synergistic models describe how faulty development in subtle but critical child skills could contribute to disturbed parent-child interactions that further exacerbate faulty development, the stepping stone model, the failure of rule-governed behavior, and coercion. This discussion does not address comorbid ADHD/CD, which together may constitute a distinct subtype (Barkley, 2006, pp. 191–192; Lynam, 1996).

Stepping Stone Model. One explanation acknowledges that ADHD is causally related to ODD. Children with ADHD may not pay attention or listen to instructions. They may not follow directions for a long duration, they may respond quickly and carelessly, or they may not finish the assigned task. Impulsive misbehavior includes rudeness and disobeying. Lynam (1996) termed this the *stepping stone model.*

A Failure of Rule-Governed Behavior. As noted, one result of the impairment in behavioral inhibition is the adverse effect on the internalization of speech (verbal working memory). This impairment leads to delays in the development of rule-governed behavior, including self-speech. Barkley (1997a) proposes that an essential behavioral deficit is the failure of children with hyperactive behavior to use private speech to regulate their behavior. Influenced by Vygotsky (1962), Luria (1961), and Skinner (1953), Barkley postulates that during the development of typical children, the influence of language over behavior occurs in three stages: (1) the control of language by others, (2) the progressive control of behavior by self-directed and subsequently private speech conditioned by the verbal community, and (3) the creation of new rules by the child, which come about through self-directed questions. The child with ADHD is unlikely to master control of their behavior by self-directed private speech, and thus requires control by the language of others. The deficiency is more problematic in the comorbid subgroup where the child does not follow rules, much less generate rules, that guide behavior toward future goals. Thus, the rules need to be generated by others.

Coercion. A behavior analysis helps explain the development of ODD in children with ADHD. The analysis is influenced by a review of direct observation research of interactions between parents and their hyperactive children (Danforth, Barkley, & Stokes, 1991). The review reveals that the chronic intensity of ADHD behavior can set the occasion for adults to give in earlier when their children protest. Coercion (Patterson, 1976, 1982; Patterson & Bank, 1986) is more common when adults interact with ADHD children than with typical children. For example, in their verbal interactions parents present repeated commands, verbal reprimands, and correction more often to children with hyperactive behavior. However, when children with ADHD behave well, their parents give fewer rewards for compliance, initiate fewer verbal interactions, and attend less to appropriate behavior and vocalizations initiated by the child. Ironically, such parent behavior can be characterized as both lax and overreactive (Harvey, Danforth, Ulaszek, & Eberhardt, 2001). Parent behavior may be, in part, an outcome of their child's disruptive, intrusive repertoire (Danforth et al.), and parent nonresponsiveness and overreactivity seems more pronounced in families of children with comorbid ADHD/ODD (Seipp & Johnston, 2005). The aversive properties of the hyperactive behavior may generalize to the child him/herself, as parents tend to avoid children with ADHD behavior when they behave well. Lynam (1996) termed this the *risk factor model*, and consistent with Danforth et al., recommended parent training to break the cycle of negatively reinforced parent-child interactions.

Parent over-reaction followed by acquiescence may be more functional for adults reacting to children with ADHD than for adults reacting to typical children. Such a pattern is a common way for parents (and teachers; DuPaul, McGoey, Eckert, & VanBrakle, 2001) to react to ADHD behavior. The child influences the adult (e.g., Bell, 1968; Bell & Harper, 1977), the adult influences the child, so the unit of analysis is the interaction between the two. The ongoing intensity of ADHD behavior can lead to parent fatigue and stress that facilitates coercion. Parent stress has been associated with ADHD (Anastopoulos, Guevremont, Shelton, & DuPaul, 1992) and disruptive child behavior (Eyberg, Boggs, & Rodriguez, 1992). Evidence suggests that the stress, resulting from the child's intense, impulsive, overactive, and disruptive behaviors adversely affects parental functioning (Anastopoulos, Shelton, DuPaul, & Guevremont, 1993).

Coercion and the Failure of Rule-Governed Behavior. Recall that the influence of language over behavior is a developmental progression from control of language by others and then control by self-directed speech. Effective self-directed speech might also be less typical in children with hyperactive behavior because their verbal environment is less likely to provide the context to condition self-directed speech. Children with hyperactive behavior have parent (and teacher) interactions that are different from the parent interactions of typical children. Direct observation data (Danforth et al., 1991) suggest that when the children are well behaved and perhaps prone to attend, their verbal community is less likely to question them about past, present, or future behavior, or the variables and contingencies of which their behavior is a function. The verbal community of children with hyperactive behavior is far more likely to engage them when they are particularly overactive and disruptive, but children are not prone to attend when overactive (i.e., when the child is most active is not a good teaching moment). The form of the interaction when the child is disruptive is more likely to be harsh discipline, unlikely to condition self-directed speech and self-directed questions.

OTHER TREATMENTS

Medication

Central nervous system stimulant medication is the most common treatment for ADHD, and its efficacy has been demonstrated for children with

ADHD (Multimodal Treatment Study of Children with ADHD Coopera-tive Group, 1999) and co-occurring aggression (D. F. Connor, Glatt, Lopez, Jackson, & Melloni, 2002). Controversy surrounds the overuse of psychostimulant medication (LeFever, Arcona, & Antonuccio, 2003). There is the potential for negative short-term and long-term side effects, the failure of research to demonstrate enduring change after the cessation of medication, and 23% to 27% of children with ADHD do not have a pos-itive initial response to stimulant medication (D. C. Connor, 2006). This demonstrates the need for improved parent training programs. The ef-fects of the typical immediate-release regimen of stimulant medication wear off by evening (Garland, 1998), so even parents whose children are on an effective dose of medication may benefit from parent training. As noted by Connor, "the stimulants should rarely be the only form of ther-apy provided to individuals with ADHD" (2006, p. 609).

Child-Directed Cognitive Therapy

Cognitive-behavioral procedures are effective for many child disorders (Kendall, 2006). However, Barkley (1997a; see also Douglas, 1999) posits that the neurobiological deficits that account for core behavioral charac-teristics of children with ADHD mean that cognitive strategies that focus on teaching the child self-directed speech should fail to increase the rate of compliance behavior among children with hyperactive behavior. Barkley writes that children with ADHD behavior have an essential deficit in behavioral inhibition that adversely effect executive function. He contends that even if self-speech precedes behavior, such speech has less stimulus control over the motor behavior of children with ADHD (Barkley, 1997a; Smith et al., 2006). This is because the deficit in behavioral inhibi-tion precludes effective control by self-stated verbal rules. Specifically, "The control of motor action by verbal thought is weakened by the defi-ciency in inhibition characterizing ADHD, such that knowing what to do is not so much the problem as doing what one knows" (Barkley, 1997a, p. 245). Barkley refers to ADHD as a disorder of performance not skill, children with ADHD know how to behave well, but they do not perform what they know. Hinshaw writes that, "Procedures based on cognitive self-instructional methods are not sufficiently powerful to influence the symptomotology or course of ADHD; their use is not empirically sup-ported" (2006, p. 104). Therefore, interventions to increase compliant be-havior among children with ADHD should not rely on self-speech.

Theory and Parent Training

The characteristics and theory of ADHD, the environment of the ADHD child and their parents, and the etiology of comorbid ODD are reflected in the parent training program presented in this chapter. The skills taught allow the parent to accommodate the child's ADHD disability while using behavior management to help with active defiance. Knowledge of ADHD can help a parent learn appropriate expectations and attributions and set a healthy tone in the family. Parents can respond to the immediate context of the conflict, not the historical context. The parent is the therapist because the therapy is most salient, and hence influential, when presented in the immediate context of their child's behavior. Preventative parent responses immediately preceding child behavior can modify the affect of antecedent stimuli. Quality instructions, rewards, and disciplinary consequences provide external controls to compensate for the child's lack of internal controls. The trained parent can provide such a therapeutic milieu in the home and community; the therapist cannot provide a therapeutic milieu from the office.

PARENT TRAINING PROGRAM

This chapter presents the program details of parent training therapy for families of children with comorbid ADHD/ODD. Table 11.1 presents the topics and schedule for eight parent training sessions. Group parent training takes 10 sessions and therapists can adjust the schedule at their discretion. The goal is to develop specific parenting skills that alter the interaction with a child, thus promoting prosocial compliance and decreasing disruptive child behavior. Parents will adapt to and cope with ADHD behavior while modifying defiance and aggressive disruptive behavior.

We present supplemental written materials to the parents to read during and after training sessions.* These materials provide a detailed outline for two parts of parent training. Part I is a didactic presentation on ADHD and family interactions. Part II is a stepwise behavior management skills training program.

PART I. INTERACTIONS BETWEEN ADULTS AND DEFIANT
HYPERACTIVE CHILDREN

During the first parent training session, describe the interactions between parents and their hyperactive children. Present this training before teaching the behavior management skills. Describe the behaviors associated with ADHD, give a very brief review of etiology, discuss relevant technical terms, and analyze why many children with ADHD also develop ODD. Parents will then understand how the relationship between

---

*A complete copy of the supplemental written materials that correspond to each session and step of the BMFC is available from the author.

Table 11.1

Proposed Schedule for Training Adults to Use the BMFC

Hour Number	BMFC Step	Training Topic	Homework/Application
1	N/A	Didactic instruction on social learning principles, ADHD, ODD, and coercion.	Read handout on social learning principles, ODD, ADHD, and coercion.
2	1	Commands.	Read. Implement step 1.
3	2–6	Wait five seconds after command. Praise. Reprimand.	Read. Implement steps 1–6.
4	7–26	Warning for time-out. Time-out. Backup for time-out refusal.	Read. Select time-out location. Option to select two target behaviors, in addition to non-compliance for time-out. Create a menu of backup consequences for time-out refusal. Implement only steps 1–6, *not 1–26.*
5	7–26	Same as Hour 4. Also, review time-out location, target behaviors, and backup consequences.	Read. Preview program with child. Implement steps 1–26 in home setting using flowchart as a guide.
6	1–26	Review specific difficulties and rehearse all BMFC steps.	Read. Implement steps 1–26 using flowchart as a guide. Implement BMFC steps in community using wallet-sized copies of BMFC as a guide.
7	Same.	Review specific difficulties and rehearse all BMFC steps.	Same.
8	Same.	Didactic instruction on social learning principles, ODD, ADHD, and coercion. Review specific difficulties and rehearse all BMFC steps.	Same.

Note: BMFC steps correspond to the steps in Figure 11.1 on page 356.

the nature of ADHD and the development of ODD logically leads to the parenting steps. When teaching parenting skills in subsequent sessions, constantly refer back to this didactic material.

Attention-Deficit/Hyperactivity Disorder

First, present characteristics of ADHD to the parents. For each characteristic, present examples from your own experiences. The conceptual basis for understanding the nature of ADHD is Barkley's (1997a) analysis. ADHD children have delays or disabilities in three areas: impulse control, overactivity, and attention. The *DSM* (American Psychiatric Association, 1994) presents descriptions of how such characteristics are manifested and what parents can expect. The distinctive feature of

ADHD is impulsiveness, or a lack of behavioral inhibition. There may be an inability to delay a response (e.g., there may be a short latency between antecedent events and behavior) or sustain an inhibited response. Executive functions (e.g., rules) may have little control over behavior. For example, children may act as if they are not thinking about the consequences of their behavior or be unduly influenced by immediate rewards and escape opportunities.

Overactive motor behavior seems linked in nature to the impulsive behavior and poor inhibition. Compared with other same-age children, children with hyperactive behavior have far higher rates of motor behavior, including vocal behavior. Hyperactive behavior is described as "generally unnecessary" and "often irrelevant to the task or situation . . . at times purposeless" (Barkley, 1998, p. 82). Hyperactive behavior does not result in observable consequences that alter the strength of the behavior. Because parents often attribute such behavior to the child's efforts to annoy them (e.g., "he runs around crazy like that just to bother me"), helping parents with accurate attributions may enhance parent training (Johnston & Ohan, 2005). Emphasize that such behavior is likely functional only in that it is automatically strengthened by internal sensory positive reinforcement (see Martin & Pear, 2007, p. 289).

Poor attention can be manifested in two ways. Children may present with shorter sustained attention, particularly in the context of long, repetitive, and passive tasks. Children with ADHD are readily distracted by events and opportunities around them, particularly stimuli embedded within the task with which they are engaged (Zentall, 2005). Parent instruction on speaking with the children focuses on concise structured vocalizations that are not distracting themselves.

Etiology

Present a very brief review of etiology, with a mention of possible genetic, neurological, and congenital factors. The goal is for parents to learn that it is unlikely that their parenting behavior shaped the constellation of ADHD behavior. We acknowledge that environmental factors such as disorganized and loud environments, harsh parenting, harsh adult reactions, and coercion can escalate ADHD behavior (see the next section).

Basic Terms

To understand better the relationship between ADHD and defiant/disruptive behavior, present five basic terms. It is more important for parents to understand the concept behind the term than it is to remember the name of the term. Give examples when presenting these five terms: the three-term contingency (also known as the ABCs), positive reinforcement, punishment, negative reinforcement, and the impact of immediate consequences. Emphasize the functional nature of behavior. Negative reinforcement seems the most difficult concept for parents and it would not be discussed except that negative reinforcement is essential to the concept of coercion, which in turn is important to understanding the emergence of defiant behavior. When aversive events such as parent directives are escaped (negative reinforcement), the impact of the immediate consequence is usually relevant (Hineline, 1977, 1984), and the prepotent response style of the child with ADHD will manifest with quick actions to escape the undesired parent directive.

The Development of Oppositional Defiant Disorder

Describe how many children with ADHD present with another separate childhood disorder called Oppositional Defiant Disorder. Describe ODD characteristics such as active defiance, angry tantrums, and arguments with adults. For many parents, this is the first time the comorbid issue is presented explicitly. Then discuss how ADHD, which is generally considered a biologically based neurological disorder, might develop to include ODD, the specific responses of which are often learned. The models explained earlier, stepping stone, failure of rule-governed behavior, and coercion, describe how faulty development in subtle but critical child skills could contribute to disturbed parent-child interactions that further exacerbate faulty development. Define and explain coercion (Patterson, 1976, 1982; Patterson & Bank, 1986). An example of a coercion analysis of child behavior that might grow to ODD follows:

> A = Parent tells a child to put toy away.
> B = Child whines noisily.
> C = Parent does not make the child put the toy away.
> Future = Child cries and whines more when told to put fun things away.

Many parents recognize this pattern ("That's me"). It is helpful when parents identify how their own behavior contributes to the development of ODD. The risk is that attributions of self-blame can be associated with emotional responses (e.g., guilt, sadness, crying) that interfere with subsequent learning. Acknowledge evidence showing that a child's hyperactive behavior may be aversive to adults in whose presence such behavior frequently occurs. Explain how coercion, with parent overreaction followed by acquiescence may be more functional for adults reacting to children with ADHD than for adults reacting to typical children. Parents should attend to the bidirectional effects of child and adult behavior. Explain that good parents engage in coercive behavior when they are around children with ADHD because the parents can avoid or escape loud angry children by letting them have their way. Here is an example of a coercion analysis of parent behavior; in this case, the B is a parent response:

A = Child is loud, or cries, or whines, or argues.
B = Parent allows child to "have their way."
C = Child stops being loud, or crying/whining, or arguing.
Future = Parent allows child to have their way and this functions to avoid/ escape loud, whining, or arguing.

PART II. THE BEHAVIOR MANAGEMENT FLOW CHART AND SKILLS TRAINING

The specific skills learned by parents are informed by two sources. One is the theory of ADHD and the development of ODD described earlier. The second source is a review of representative published child behavior management research (Danforth, 1998a).

THE BEHAVIOR MANAGEMENT FLOW CHART

A task analysis of the research was conducted. The chain of responses required of parents was broken into precise individual components, in their proper order. This task analysis subdivided behavior management into individual, discrete, and orderly steps. The Behavior Management Flow Chart (BMFC) is a diagram, based on the task analysis, of the child behavior management steps taught to parents (Figure 11.1). The flow chart synthesizes the research on child management into a cohesive unit that allows a clear portrayal of child behavior management steps (ongoing review, feedback from parents, and research data has resulted in ongoing refinements to the BMFC). The BMFC is the unit that provides structure for the synthesis of the literature. The flow chart depicts a chain of skilled responses that adults are to emit throughout the day in an effort to help ADHD/ODD children.

The key in the lower left-hand box of the BMFC describes the function of each geometric figure. Rectangles describe a parent response. Diamonds describe a yes/no option. The word or phrase in the diamond is followed by a question mark. Two lines emerge from each diamond. One line indicates that "yes," the condition in the diamond was met, and a second line indicates that "no" the condition described was not met. Finally, circles indicate that the interaction is complete.

There are critical differences between the BMFC parenting steps and well-known parent training programs based on the two-stage Hanf model (Anastopoulos, Hennis-Rhoads, & Farley, 2006; Barkley, 1997b; Eyberg & Boggs, 1998; Forehand & McMahon, 2003). During training, the visually

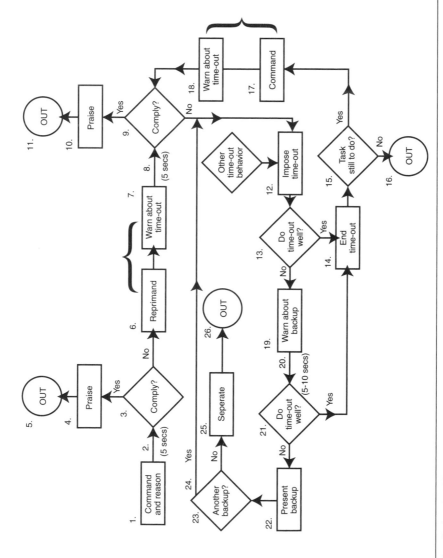

Figure 11.1 The Behavior Management Flow Chart Is a Flow Chart of Steps Taught to Parents. (Rectangles indicate an adult response, diamonds indicate a yes/no option, and circles indicate that the interaction is over.)

depicted BMFC serves as the basis for discussion and as a guide to parenting in the home and community. Decision diamonds in the BMFC reflect flexibility and allow the parent options to adapt the program to situational demands. Teach the parenting skills in a forward chaining fashion (see Martin & Pear, 2007, p. 141), in the same order that they are presented in the flow chart and consistent with how the parent is to utilize the strategies in the context of child misbehavior. That is, the first response emitted by parents when they want to direct their child is a command or instruction, and this is the first skill taught; the second response emitted by the parent is to wait 5 seconds, and this is the second skill taught, and so on.

When teaching behavior management skills, present the parents with a copy of the flow chart as a visual aid. The supplemental written materials that we give to parents each session have steps that correspond to the steps of the BMFC. Present portions of the BMFC as chunks. When parents practice step 1, the only visual guide is the rectangle for step 1. When parents are practicing steps 1 to 6, an abbreviated flow chart illustrating just steps 1 to 6 is used. When parents subsequently apply the entire program, the entire BMFC is used. Individual trainers can further subdivide the BMFC. When parents first practice the program, they use the flow chart as a prompt to decrease errors during learning trials. Then flow-chart use is faded. When parents implement the program in the home setting after session five (see Table 11.1), give them copies of the BMFC to post for reference. When parents implement the program in the community after session six, give them wallet-sized laminated copies of the BMFC to keep in the car and on their person. Generalization across settings and over time is facilitated because parents have copies of the BMFC to which to refer. The parent has constant access to a visual representation of the empirical literature on child behavior management.

There is enough flexibility in the design to use the same flow chart in many settings. To enhance generalization, parents follow the general parameters of the program across settings because the program can be adapted to different settings. For example, the time-out setting at home may be the couch whereas the time-out setting at the grandparents' house may be the back porch. Praise can be presented anywhere.

In the written outline presented to parents, each step begins with a description of the procedures the parent performs in the context of child behavior, followed by exemplars and in many cases, nonexemplars. To ensure appropriate parent expectations, emphasize that no one action by a parent will change the child. Instead, each interaction is one learning trial, and over many learning trials, the child's behavior will improve. The child's behavior will not suddenly change.

A parsimonious explanation for the difficulties of parent training is evident when the BMFC is examined. Trainers are asking parents to do something that is very hard. The flow chart elucidates a 26-step procedure that requires conditional discriminations in the context of acute child misconduct. Child antisocial behavior itself is likely to have a negative impact on parental discipline practices (Vuchinich, Bank, & Patterson, 1992). Disruptive ADHD behavior likely elicits adult emotional responses that are incompatible with recall and implementation of complex tasks. Behavior management for children with ADHD is difficult under any circumstances, and perhaps this difficulty is underestimated (Sajwaj & Dillon, 1977). Furthermore, idiographic assessment is likely to reveal that management skills are not uniform across or within adults. Rather than assuming that all adults will need an equal degree of training on all steps, trainers need to concentrate on parents' individual difficulties (Richman, Harrison, & Summers, 1995). The mode of presentation, with the task analysis leading to the use of a flow chart, may enhance the training program (O'Dell, Mahoney, Horton, & Turner, 1979). Use the flow chart and supplemental written materials in conjunction with verbal explanation, trainer modeling, and role-play with trainer feedback.

Training with the BMFC is one component of a treatment package tailored to individual families of children with ADHD/ODD. This is not an entire treatment program; it is one element of a treatment plan that might include an array of services. The remainder of this chapter describes the specific skills taught to parents. Each step described corresponds to the steps in the flow chart.

The principal target behavior of the BMFC is child noncompliance. Psychometric research has identified noncompliance as a fundamental element of disruptive behavior patterns (e.g., Achenbach & Rescorla, 2001), so compliance is a response relevant to many settings and occasions. Functional analyses have shown that noncompliance serves as the cornerstone response in the development of disruptive behavior (Patterson, 1976; Wahler, 1975), and such behavior consistently covaries with important parameters such as peer rejection (Coie & Kupersmidt, 1983) and academic failure (Wilson & Herrnstein, 1985). Parents are most inconsistent when an interaction sequence begins with a parent command requesting child compliance (Gardner, 1989), so the command/instruction is the logical place to start.

THE FLOW CHART STEPS

Step 1. Practical Commands or Instructions

First, parents decide if the child is required to follow a directive. Presenting the child with choices is encouraged, often in the form of questions or favors, but only if the child really has a choice. If it is hot outside, you may ask, "Do you want to wear shorts?" This is encouraged only if the child really has a choice about wearing shorts because he or she can learn to experience the natural consequences of the decision and there is not an extrinsic parent disciplinary consequence. However, if it is very hot and parents decide the child must wear shorts then do not ask. Do not give a choice in a no-choice situation. Therefore, the first parent response is a decision, and if they decide the child must do something, then parents present the command in the imperative form, indicating that the behavior is required.

Do not present commands that must be followed as favors or questions. Consequences are contingent on a child's compliance to instructions presented in the imperative form. Consequences are not presented contingent on a child's adherence to requests framed as questions or favors. Parents often frame this decision as "picking your battles," and one result is that fewer required commands are presented. This is good because when fewer commands are presented then the probability of escalating coercive exchanges is decreased (Patterson, 1982) and the probability of compliance is increased (Lobitz & Johnson, 1975).

Second, preview commands, but only hold children accountable for directives that require compliance at the present. Parents can predict commands they will be presenting later, either in a few minutes or perhaps even hours later. If parents know they will be presenting a command, preview this with the child. Only present consequences contingent on a child's compliance to instructions requiring an immediate response, so commands focus on behavior that the child has to do now, not later on. For example, rather than instructing a child to, "feed the dog after you eat breakfast," forewarn the child that the dog will have to be fed after breakfast, and then after breakfast say, "feed the dog now, please."

Third, as part of the command, include the reasons why the child is to do something. Vague explanations such as, "I really need you to do this" are not reasons.

Fourth, before presenting the command, make sure the child is oriented or observing. Get reasonably close, within three meters, use the child's name, and establish eye contact.

Fifth, clearly label or describe the required behavior (i.e., operationalize). Note that declarations describe the state of things, but they do not tell a child what behavior to do. For example, "It's raining" informs the child of the weather conditions, but it does not tell the child to put on a raincoat. Declarations do not label a response.

Sixth, when a child is likely to disobey, present short instructions that have few steps (i.e., chunking).

Seventh, if the child is emitting an undesirable behavior, it is preferable to tell the child to do something else (e.g., "Pat, please give me the ball") rather than to tell the child to stop an ongoing response (nonexample, "Pat, please stop bouncing that ball"). This takes into account the ADHD child's difficulty inhibiting an ongoing sequence of behavior.

Finally, encourage patience and acknowledge that mistakes are inevitable. When the child must follow the command, but the command is presented in a way that does not meet the criteria for a good instruction, do not move on to step 2. The likelihood of compliance is too low. First, restate the instruction correctly. Example: if Ken must dry the dishes now because you are washing them now, but you ask, "Do you want to dry the dishes?" while you are looking in the refrigerator, then Ken is less likely to wash the dishes. So, start over. Go to Ken and get eye contact while you restate the command directly, "Ken, I'm washing the dishes so you need to dry now." Whereas hyperactive children can be quick and active, parents are encouraged to take their time. The importance of quality commands is illustrated in lag analysis research on adolescents with ADHD illustrating that the first event in the interaction in most likely to influence the behavior of the other member of the parent/child dyad (Fletcher, Fischer, Barkley, & Smallish, 1996).

Step 2. Wait Silently

Allow the child 5 seconds to start following directions. After presenting the command, be silent and do not interfere with the child until they either begin to follow directions, or 5 seconds passes. Parents report that is the most difficult step, but this is an essential step because children with ADHD have difficulty with the dimension of interference control (one of the processes of behavioral inhibition), so parents must not contribute to this by adding external competing information. Parents remain with the child and stay within three meters. Do not glare at the child, but do look toward him. If the child begins to argue here, which is expected, it is very important that parents not engage in debate or argument that escalates the intensity of the aversive interaction. If the parent begins to engage in an aversive argument, there is an increased probability that the child's subsequent responses will be more aversive (Patterson, 1982). In negative reinforcement, the rate of learning is a function of the magnitude of reduction of the aversive stimuli (Hineline, 1977, 1984). Therefore, if the parent presents progressively aversive statements and then gives in, then the child is more likely to argue in the future because the consequence for arguing was escape from strongly aversive parent behavior.

If the child asks a legitimate question, or makes a legitimate plea to postpone the task, parents may suspend the command. For example, after being told to put the Legos in the bin, a child may say, "Can I finish building this house?" If the parent decides to let the child finish, then exit the BMFC and begin with step 1 again when ready to have the child put their

Legos away. Caution parents because few guidelines are available to distinguish legitimate postponement from coercion.

Step 3. Decide if the Child Has Started to Follow Directions

Decide if the child has started to follow directions. Base the decision on what the child has done, not what the child says he is going to do.

Step 4. Praise

If the answer to step 3 was "yes," the child complied, then without delay, the moment the child starts to follow directions, praise him in an effort to strengthen (reinforce) following directions. The target behavior is beginning to follow directions, not completing the task. We anticipate that the child will not finish many tasks because that is a defining feature of ADHD.

Praise is an essential component of the program. First, as noted above, children with ADHD are praised less when they behave well and adults are less responsive to their needs. A lack of maternal warmth and responsiveness is correlated with comorbid ADHD/conduct disorder (Pfiffner, McBurnett, Rathouz, & Judice, 2005). Time-out (see step 12) might not work because of a lack of praise and other reinforcers in the child's time-in setting. Finally, the children have not demonstrated the response class of compliance. When teaching a new behavior, a dense schedule of reinforcement is most effective.

Practical praise has six parts: (1) Praise when the child begins to follow directions, not when she has finished. (2) Make a positive comment about the child or her behavior. (3) Name the good behavior (or the outcome of the behavior). (4) Present it with positive emotion. Parents should smile and use a nice physical touch if they want to. Parents do not praise if they are angry, and this is anticipated in the context of some intense hyperactive behavior that many people find aversive. (5) Parents do not scold the child for past responses while at the same time praising the child for what she is doing now. This scolding may diminish the reinforcing effect of praise, and it is too late to punish the undesired response. For example, "When I asked you to wash the dishes today you did a good job, why couldn't you do that yesterday?" (6) If the child starts to follow directions, but then she gets off task and does not finish, the parent starts at step 1 and presents a command to start again. Otherwise, we strongly urge parents to "catch 'em being good" whenever the child stays with her assigned task.

Step 5. Out

The interaction is complete.

Step 6. Reprimand

If the answer to step 3 was "no," the child did not comply, present a verbal reprimand. Eight characteristics of a reprimand help make it effective. Name the target behavior or describe it. Second, present the reprimand immediately, at the fifth second. This is important when the behavior of other children reinforces the child's misbehavior. Make eye contact. Use a firm steady voice; do not be soft and apologetic. Do not yell. This is better said as "try as best you can to yell as little as possible." Be firm. It is best if other children do not hear the reprimand. Stay within three meters of the child. The reprimand is short and to the point. For parents who like to lecture, it helps them to know that for children with ADHD extra narrative and detail can reduce comprehension and performance (Edmonds & Smith, 1985; Shroyer & Zentall, 1986), and the children pay attention less to long tasks (Zentall, 1985; Zentall & Zentall, 1976). Preceding the child's attention skills and angry emotional behavior associated with disruptive defiance are incompatible with the skills necessary to comprehend and respond effectively to long parent explanation.

This is a good place to stop so parents can practice steps 1 through 6 at home.

Step 7. Warning about Time-Out

As part of the reprimand, present the child with one firm warning that if he does not follow directions he will have to go to a time-out. Name the desired response and what will happen if the child does not emit that response. "Time-out" is an adult phrase; it is not necessary. Instead, tell the child what he will be required to do if he does not comply. An example, "Carlos, if you don't shut the door like I said, you will have to go to your room." The purpose of the warning, or the second chance, is to weaken time-out resistance and accommodate for attention problems. Time-out details are explained in step 12.

We are repeating the command here to accommodate for attention problems. We do not hold children accountable for their ADHD characteristics. Not following directions is an anticipated inattentive defining feature of ADHD. We accommodate for ADHD by clearly restating the instruction paired with a warning. If the instruction is presented twice, as defined under practical command, with 5 seconds to allow time to respond, then we have accommodated for ADHD and any ongoing disobedience is defiance, for which the child is accountable. Hence, the importance of distinguishing ADHD and ODD in earlier sessions.

Step 8. Wait Silently

Allow the child 5 seconds to begin to comply with the command as directed in the warning. Parents remain silent and do not interfere with the child until he or she has begun to comply with the command.

Step 9. Decide if the Child Has Started to Follow Directions

Step 10. Praise

If the answer to step 9 was "yes," the child complied, then the moment the child starts to follow directions, praise him. Present praise when the child follows the first command or the command after a warning.

Step 11. Out

The interaction is complete.

Step 12. Time-Out (Time-Out from Positive Reinforcement)

If the answer to step 9 was "no," the child did not comply, then time-out is presented. Time-out is a complex procedure that takes at least 2 hours to teach. Consequences for noncompliance are an essential part of the treatment protocol (Danforth, 1998a). This is important because time-out is an ethical, noncorporal consequence that is an effective punishment, and it can only take a few minutes. Most parents report that they have used time-out before and it does not work. There is a great discrepancy between research (with literally hundreds of published articles, see Roberts, 1988) and popular practice of time-out.

The idea behind time-out is to make the behavior it follows happen less often; time-out is punishment. It is wise to review basic terms in context. Knowledge of the principle of punishment, and distinguishing time-out from intense discipline makes parents more effective. Then, explain how time-out works. Time-out might work because the child moves from a more reinforcing to a less reinforcing place. This provides another opportunity to discuss the importance of praise. Time-out is most effective when the tone of family interaction is positive because the child loses positive interaction. Time-out might work because it interrupts arguments and yelling between children and adults and fosters separation during conflict. This might reduce the ADHD child's vulnerability to external sources of emotional interference. Finally, time-out might be effective because the child with ADHD finds boring activities particularly aversive.

Three Decisions.   Describe time-out, but before using time-out for the first time, parents go home and make three decisions to discuss at the next session. First, parents decide exactly what behaviors result in time-out. Parents have the option of selecting up to two individually defined target behaviors (in addition to noncompliance after the warning) for which time-out will be the consequence. Typically, parents choose responses such as physical aggression, tantrums, property destruction, and verbal abuse. Sometimes, parents choose not to add additional target behaviors. A time-out warning does not precede intense misbehavior such as this. Instead, see the diamond above step 12. When these additional time-out target behaviors occur, parents immediately move to the diamond above step 12 on the BMFC and send the child directly to time-out without a warning. Help parents operationalize clear target behaviors and focus on responses indicative of ODD (e.g., aggression) and not ADHD (e.g., fidgeting). Do not use disciplinary consequences to punish hyperactive motor behavior.

Second, parents go home and select a place for time-out that does not have reinforcing value, a "dull" place. A physical feature required of the time-out location is a clear demarcation of whether a child is "in" or "out" of time-out. For practical purposes, parents may choose more than one location, and typical sites include the bottom of a staircase, the end of a hallway, a boring room, or a bedroom if pleasant toys do not dominate it. Although a chair is available should the child choose to sit, we never require the child to sit in the chair. This is because children with hyperactive behavior may find required sitting aversive. We want to avoid setting the occasion for time-out resistance. We do not arrange a contingency wherein standing and moving are disciplined when we can rightly predict that the child with hyperactivity will probably move, stand, and leave the chair. There is no empirical evidence that sitting in a chair is a critical component of time-out success. Review time-out locations with parents. Remain vigilant for impractical locations (e.g., bathrooms) and aversive locations (a cold dark basement). In the community, time-out can be in a car, on a bench, or right where the child is standing.

Third, parents create an individualized menu of possible backup consequences, one of which is presented if the child refuses to go to time-out (step 22). Back-up consequences generally consist of the loss of a privilege. Review back-up consequences for practical utility and parent willingness to administer the backup. Detail about the back-up consequence is presented in step 22. This is a good place to stop so parents can go home and make the three decisions.

Time-Out Preview. The next session is a review and clarification of the three decisions about the target behaviors, the location, and the back-up consequence. Then parents go home and conduct a time-out preview. Conduct the preview daily, and then fade it. Calmly explain to the child (a) the target behaviors (b) where time-out is, (c) what is expected of the child when they are told to go to time-out, and (d) the back-up discipline if they do not do the time-out correctly (see Step 22). All the adults who will be implementing time-out are part of this preview. For example, both parents, or a parent and a grandparent participate in the preview. The preview is a teaching and instructing moment, like previewing a command, not a reprimand. Conduct the preview when the child is behaving well. A paraphrased script from the parent handout follows, designed for a single mother for use with her 5-year old boy: "You are being a good boy right now, but sometimes you have a hard time following directions and hitting, and mommy is going to help you with that. So, every time you don't follow directions or you hit, you will have to go to your room for 5 minutes. I will not talk to you when you are in your room. Don't come out by yourself; I will tell you when you can come out. If you don't follow directions or you hit, and then you won't go to your room when I say to, you will be in big trouble (parent describes some of the back-up consequences, see step 22). But you are following directions right now so you are doing a good job now."

Conducting a Time-Out. (a) At home and then later in the community, when the target behavior occurs, parents label it and tell the child that he must go to time-out. For example, "Luis I told you to put the cereal away and you didn't listen so you have to sit on the steps." (b) Parents stay calm and say it only once. Parents do not talk, debate, or quarrel with the child, a task that parents report is difficult. If the child starts to follow the original command after parents tell them to go to time-out, it is too late; he still has to go to time-out. (c) When the child arrives at the time-out site, parents tell him, "Stay there for x minutes, I will decide when you can leave." The stay is 1 minute per year of developmental age. (d) Parents do not talk to the child again until the time-out is over. (e) Parents do not "guard" the child, or stare at the child; they move away and do something else. (f) Wait until the child has been in time-out for the specified duration, and has been composed and not agitated for the last few minutes of time-out. (g) Ignore the child's behavior unless it is disruptive to the house (more on this shortly).

If the child is loud and disruptive at the end of his time-out, do not end the time-out. Parents do not adventitiously teach the child that disruptive behavior is consequated by time-out cessation. Instead, end time-out after the child has been quiet for a few (1 to 3) minutes. Parents are teaching the child that when he is calm, the time-out will end. Still, do not talk to the child. Do not wait until the child is quiet to start the time-out. Do not start the time-out all over if he is disruptive. Do not use time-out for other misbehavior until it is previewed with the child.

Step 13. Is the Child Completing the Time-Out Correctly?

Decide whether the child has completed the time-out well. The child should stay in the time-out setting, and behave in a manner that does not disrupt others.

Step 14. End Time-Out

If the child completes the time-out well, then the time-out is over. Tell the child what he did that resulted in time-out and it is over and he may come out now if he wants. An example is, "Ronaldo, you didn't put away your soccer ball when I told you, so you had to go to your room. Your time-out is over and you can come back out now." Then, drop the subject and start fresh with the child. Reminders here about what the child did that resulted in time-out do not help. The discipline was the time-out, and it is over.

Some parents are concerned because they want to speak with their children about misbehavior now. We address this issue here. Encourage parents to problem solve with their children (Hinshaw, 2006). Encourage parents to seek information about antecedents to misbehavior. Encourage parents to tell their child calmly about the natural consequences of his or her disruptive behavior. Discourage parents from engaging in these conversations while their child is disruptive or shortly (within minutes) thereafter. Such dialog at that time is more likely to evolve into a coercive exchange. The dysregulated emotion associated with the disruptive behavior is incompatible with productive dialog. First, after time-out get the child back into his routine and praise the next successful enterprise.

Step 15. Does the Child Still Have to Do the Task from Step 1?

If the child is in time-out as a result of defiance, then after the child successfully completes time-out, decide if the child still has to do the task that they were told to do in the first place (from the original command in Step 1).

Step 16. Finish

If, for whatever reason, the child no longer has to do the task, then the interaction is complete; drop the subject. There are many occasions where repeating a directive is impractical.

Steps 17 and 18. Command and Warning

If there is a remaining task that needs completion, present a command (step 1) instructing the child to complete the task, paired with a warning (step 7) that if he does not follow directions, he must return to time-out. The purpose is to prevent time-out from functioning as negative reinforcement that allows the child to avoid the requirements of the instruction. Anecdotal reports by parents indicated that repeated time-outs (i.e., steps 15 to 18 leading to another time-out for ongoing noncompliance) were rare, and no child was reported to go through this loop more than three times in succession.

Step 9, Again. Decide if the Child Has Started to Follow Directions

If the child follows directions now, praise him (step 10). Direct the child to time-out if he or she does not follow directions (step 12).

Step 19. Disruptive Behavior during Time-Out, the Warning about the Time-Out Backup

From step 13. If parents decide that the child is not doing time-out well in step 13, go to step 19. If a child (a) refuses to do time-out, (b) leaves time-out or, (c) disturbs others during time-out, then parents give one warning that the child will receive a back-up consequence if they do not complete their time-out correctly. The backup is a major consequence for refusal to do time-out. Parents select one back-up consequence from the menu developed earlier. An example might be, "Taylor, if you do not stay on the steps, you cannot play in the pool for the rest of the day."

This step illustrates the importance of decisions made earlier. The time-out location needs features that clearly demark when a child is "in" time-out verses when they have "left" time-out. A door jam, a line on the floor or rug, the bottom of the stairs, can all serve as salient boundaries. Defiance is a serious behavior problem and the treatment is a serious endeavor. If a child is in time-out in his room and mockingly stands with one foot out of the room, then the child is out of the room. Therefore, present the back-up warning. The phrase "disturbs others during time-out" is deliberately ambiguous because the standards change depending on the setting. We encourage parents to tolerate as much "disturbing" behavior as possible, but the criteria will change. For example, if the child is at his grandparents, a moderate degree of noise might be disturbing, but if the child is home, an intense degree of noise might not be disturbing.

Step 20. Wait Silently

Give the child 5 to 10 seconds to make his choice as indicated by his behavior. Some parents have tried to help the child make a good decision by clarifying the potential consequences. For example, "If you stay on the porch (for time-out), it will be for 5 minutes. If you do not stay on the porch, you cannot ride your bike for the rest of the day. Five minutes is a lot shorter than all day."

Step 21. Is the Child Completing the Time-Out Correctly?

This is the same as step 13. Decide whether the child has completed the time-out well. The child should stay in the time-out setting and behave in a manner that does not disrupt others.

Step 22. Back-Up Consequence

If the child continues to refuse time-out, leaves time-out, or continues to disturb others, present the back-up consequence. Individualize the consequence for each child. The purpose of this consequence is to prevent time-out refusal. The back-up consequence needs to be strong so that parents will not have to use it often. If the backup is weak, it may have to be used frequently, and time-out becomes less effective. This consequence is the most severe one parents are willing to use, but they must be willing to use it. The sooner the back-up consequence occurs, the better. Back-up consequences must occur the same day as time-out refusal. Examples of back-up consequences include grounding, no playing outside, privileges removed (e.g., bike riding, television, computer, video games, handheld electronic devices, fishing, the telephone, favorite toy, special dessert food treat), early bedtime, loss of opportunity to engage in special event such as a school field trip, soccer, little league, sleep over, or after school sports or activity. As part of their back-up menu, all parents include the consequence of not allowing the child to continue the activity in which the child is currently engaged (e.g., playing with cars). The logic is that if a child is currently engaged in an activity, then the activity is acutely reinforcing.

Step 23. Are Parents Willing to Present Another Back-Up Consequence?

After applying the back-up consequence for incorrect time-out, parents decide if they are willing, or have time, to give another back-up consequence for this episode of misbehavior. The question for parents is, "Am I willing to give another back-up punishment if this child continues to refuse time-out?" This is an adult decision and the issue is practical. Parents have concurrent work and community obligations, other children, and other stresses. If the parent training program is structured so that parents do not have time to meet these other obligations, then parents are less likely to follow through across time (months, perhaps years) and over settings (home and community). Parents need options within the framework of treatment programs.

Step 24. Time-Out

If the answer to step 23 was "yes," then parents are willing to give another back-up consequence for failure to do time-out correctly. Therefore, go to step 12 and direct the child to time-out again. Only send a child to time-out if parents are willing to present a back-up consequence for time-out refusal. Parents reported that they never used a back-up consequence more than two times in 1 day, by either choice or circumstance.

Step 25. Separate

If the answer to step 23 was "no," then parents were not willing to give the child another back-up consequence for refusing to do time-out. So, defuse the situation without giving in entirely. First, isolate the child from other children and adults in the setting. Since the child with ADHD is less likely to comply in the midst of a disruptive episode, it is best to ask other children to move away than to expect the child with ADHD to begin following instructions now. An example provided by a parent directed to a sibling was, "Sally is having a hard time right now so let's leave her alone." Second, walk gently to the child with ADHD, perhaps place a hand calmly on her shoulder, and say, "We will keep on working together to help you learn to" (name the behavior that resulted in time-out; e.g., follow directions, not to hit). Do not apologize; do not be conciliatory. Finally, parents separate from the child, walk away. Do not speak to the child until she has calmed down. If the child is still in the time-out setting, leave her there.

RESEARCH FINDINGS

OUTCOME STUDIES

The effects of this parent-training program on parent behavior and on the disruptive behavior of children were evaluated in four outcome studies (Danforth, 1998b, 1999, 2001; Danforth, Harvey, Ulaszek, & McKee, in press). In this research, the children's' ages ranged from 4 to 12 and each met the *DSM-IV* criteria for ODD and ADHD, either combined type or predominantly hyperactive/impulsive type (American Psychiatric Association, 1994). Each child also met diagnostic research criteria for ADHD (Barkley, 1988) with average intelligence scores. T-scores on standardized rating scales assessing ADHD and oppositional defiant/aggressive behavior were typically more than two standard deviations above the mean. Almost every baseline direct observation session revealed clinically significant noncompliance, below 60% (Forehand, 1977). Child problem behavior measured at prescreening and baseline was strong. At least three types of outcome measures were used in each study. Disruptive child behavior was assessed with standardized rating scales and home telephone interviews. Dimensions of parenting behavior and parent stress were assessed with standardized parent self-report scales. Direct observations of mother/child interaction were videotaped or home-based audio recordings were made. Following the baseline, parent-training sessions were conducted with individual families or in a group format with 10 families per group. Overall results reveal that parent training significantly improved parenting behavior, reduced parent stress, and reduced oppositional child behavior and aggression. Limited follow-ups revealed that parenting and child behavior remained stable.

Analysis of clinical significance data suggested that parent training brought child and parent behavior within the nonclinical range of functioning. The results from the direct observation are comparable to other parent training research that used ADHD/ODD children with direct observation documenting parenting and child behavior (Pisterman et al., 1989, 1992). Data suggest that parent behavior changed very quickly, but significant improvement in child behavior did not emerge until 5 to 8 weeks after parent training was initiated. Parents also reported that as weeks progressed, the back-up consequence (step 22) was used less often and then time-out (step 12) became less necessary whereas warnings about time-out (step 7) remained common. Clinical significance data for the children suggest demanding behavior even after parent training. Sometimes ADHD behavior was prevalent during the course of treatment. This may reflect relentless hyperactivity across household, school, and community settings. The intervention did not target ADHD behavior. The etiology of ADHD has a considerable biological component and research has illustrated the persistence of ADHD characteristics over time (Barkley, 2006), so we expected that some children might still emit ADHD behavior at the conclusion of treatment. Sometimes oppositional behavior continued to present across a significant number of settings, but the intensity of such behavior was diminished. Some t-scores from standardized rating scales assessing disruptive behavior remained above 60 as did scores assessing child-based stress. Physical aggression almost always decreased, but did not always end. The impact of the parent training was evaluated in isolation of other forms of treatment, but in applied practice parent training is typically just one component of a treatment package.

Moderating Variables

Using data from the outcome research reported, two studies examined the relation between parenting styles and child behavior. Harvey, Danforth, McKee, Ulaszek, and Friedman (2003) found that parent inattention and impulsivity were associated with unsuitable, overreactive, and lax parenting. High levels of father inattention and impulsivity and high levels of mother inattention diminished the impact of the parent training program. However, mothers with moderate degrees of inattention showed the greatest improvements as demonstrated by less arguing and fewer repetitive commands. The authors conclude that parent training was most beneficial for mothers with moderate levels of inattention. In baseline, moderate mother inattention appeared to disrupt parenting, but it did not interfere with their ability to implement the parenting training strategies. In contrast, high levels of maternal inattention disrupted parenting in the baseline and interfered with the implementation of the parenting training strategies. High levels of inattention might impede mothers from learning during the parent training sessions or it may impede them from implementing strategies they learned, or both.

McKee, Harvey, Danforth, Ulaszek, and Friedman (2004) examined the relation between four parental coping styles and parent-child interactions before and after parent training. Before parent training, measures of avoidance-focused coping, seeking social support, and venting emotions were associated with lax and overreactive parenting as well coercive parent-child exchanges, externalizing child behavior, and general child misbehavior. Before parent training, adaptive-focused coping (e.g., planning) was negatively correlated with lax and overreactive parenting.

After parent training, these relations did not hold for mothers, suggesting that regardless of the coping style, the program was effective for mothers. The authors conceptualize dysfunctional parenting as a maladaptive coping style that is a potential target for change. The stresses associated with poor parenting (e.g., impulsive/hyperactive child behavior) are not always malleable, but the ways in which parents cope with the stress may be amenable to change. All of these data are limited by small sample sizes for fathers and resulting limited power.

CASE STUDY

Guy, a 7-year-old second-grade boy, was referred to a psychologist by his pediatrician secondary to concerns about ADHD and aggressive behavior. Assessment included three, 1-hour clinical interviews (see Barkley & Murphy, 2006) with parents at home, completion of standardized rating scales by parents and teacher, a review of school and treatment records, a brief telephone conversation with the referring pediatrician, and a telephone conversation with the second-grade teacher. Following a 1-hour meeting with parents to describe the assessment outcomes and present a treatment plan, four, 2-hour parent-training sessions as described earlier were conducted in the home while Guy was supervised at his grandparents. Following this, a brief summary of the same training program was presented to Guy's teacher. Guy's mother attended all training sessions. His father attended the first 1-hour assessment, the assessment outcome meeting, and half of the parent training sessions. When fathers do not regularly attend, this therapist strongly encourages attendance minimally at the outcomes assessment meeting.

Prenatal history indicated that Guy's mother smoked one pack of cigarettes per day. There was no fetal distress during labor or birth, and no health complications following birth. Guy was described as an irritable baby who cried a lot when he did not get his way, yet he was very sociable with other people, smiling and easily making eye contact. Speech milestones were within normal limits. His mother described his motor activity as a toddler as, "up and running." Mild asthma was diagnosed at age 2, and a prescribed inhaler was used as needed, discarded 2 years ago. Otherwise, medical history is within normal limits. Guy is the natural child of a couple who has been married 8 years. The father, age 34, works full time in business and the mother, age 32, is a part-time professional, home when Guy arrives after school. Two younger sisters are doing well, but three children under 8-years-old, "give us a run for our money." In kindergarten, Guy was reported to be "distractible" and "lacking self-control," but there were no episodes of aggression. In first grade, his grades were good. He finished his work quickly but then disrupted class. In this, his second-grade year, the theme of parent-teacher conferences has been Guy hitting and pushing other children. Disruptive behavior is apparent, "he pokes other kids a lot . . . he can't calm himself down . . . he has trouble completing his work, but if he does it, the work is good." His mother drives him to school to avoid problems on the bus. A previous psycho-educational evaluation, revealed average IQ scores. Previous treatment included an "herbalist" who recommended a change in diet, a brushing program by the occupational therapist at school, and an 8-week social skills training group in school. No changes were observed.

During interviews, his parents described a boy who angrily yelled at them and "stomped" his feet at least once a day, and then cried as the episode passed. This has progressed over 3 to 4 years. He argues, "about anything, he always wants the last word." He actively defied parent direction, "You're always telling me to do something." He was easily annoyed and jealous when sisters got attention, and he was beginning to bully and threaten his sisters. Attention-Deficit/Hyperactivity Disorder characteristics were described, especially the hyperactive/impulsive symptoms. He was fidgety, often leaving his seat (he ate supper standing up), "he's always saying something, he's always doing something . . . loud and boisterous," "constantly" interrupting, and, "he can't wait in line, he has to be first." Symptoms of inattention were less compelling because he, "is okay when he is interested in something." Most notable was a high degree of distractibility, "He's always looking around." When spoken to directly, he, "looks away as if he's bored . . . he doesn't stick with anything, bounces from one activity to another." He loses his toys, his glove, and when asked about organizational skills, his parents said, "What organizational skills?" Parents also reported subclinical features of anxiety. He is a perfectionist who worries about missing the bus home, being blamed for things, being late, getting the wrong lunch at school. He throws his schoolwork in the trash and announces, "I'm not good at anything." It was hard to assess whether Guy could control the worry, but associated features included fatigue and irritability. A descriptive functional assessment revealed that most common antecedents to angry tantrums and arguments were directions or occasions where Guy did not get his way. Parents presented most commands repeatedly, and then either acquiesced and/or yelled.

Before the intervention, Guy was briefly interviewed three times and he completed two self-report scales. On the Children's Depression Inventory (Kovacs, 1980), all factors were within normal limits. On the Multidimensional Anxiety Scale for Children (March, 1997) all factors were within normal limits albeit the total t-score was just under 60. The teacher completed standardized rating scales for assessment and parents completed standardized rating scales before and after training. On the BASC-II (Reynolds & Kamphaus, 2004) before treatment, the hyperactivity and aggression factors were in the clinically significant range. On the parent report, the anxiety factor was in the at risk range, and on the teacher report, social skills and leadership skills factors were in the at-risk range. After treatment, BASC aggression was within normal limits and hyperactivity and anxiety were at risk. The Home Situations Questionnaire (Breen & Altepeter, 1991) measure of disobedience showed that before training, his t-scores were two standard deviations above the mean on the severity and pervasiveness factors. After training, the severity of oppositional behavior was within normal limits, but the pervasiveness of oppositional behavior was still more than 1.5 standard deviations above the mean. All scores on the Conners' Rating Scales-R (2001) completed by parent and teachers indicated, "an above average correspondence with *DSM-IV* criteria for combined inattentive and hyperactive-impulsive type ADHD." The Social Skills Rating System (Gresham & Elliot, 1990) revealed "fewer" overall social skills than average, particularly in cooperation and self-control. On the Parenting Scale (Arnold, O'Leary, Wolff, & Acker, 1993), the overreactive and lax parenting factors were more than 1.5 standard deviations above the mean at pretreatment, but within normal limits after treatment.

CONCLUSION

Ongoing efforts to develop parent-training programs to help children with ADHD and ODD are warranted. The disorder is a worthy target for treatment. Children with hyperactive behavior are at risk for clinically significant oppositional and disruptive behavior. It is important for therapists to understand the relationship between ADHD and ODD. Trainers must be well versed in diagnosis and theory of ADHD, as well as the behavior analysis of coercion. Understanding the bidirectional nature of parent and child behavior is critical. Furthermore, parent training is time consuming and deceptively complicated and difficult for parents to perform. Formats that simplify the procedure without losing the necessary technical nuances should be explored.

REFERENCES

Achenbach, T. M., & Rescorla, L. A. (2001). *Manual for the ASEBA school-age forms and profiles.* Burlington: University of Vermont, Research Center for Children, Youth, and Families.

American Psychiatric Association. (1994). *Diagnostic and statistical manual of mental disorders* (4th ed.). Washington, DC: Author.

Anastopoulos, A. D., Guevremont, D. C., Shelton, T. L., & DuPaul, G. J. (1992). Parenting stress among families of children with attention deficit hyperactivity disorder. *Journal of Abnormal Child Psychology, 20,* 503–520.

Anastopoulos, A. D., Hennis-Rhoads, L., & Farley, S. E. (2006). Counseling and training parents. In R. A. Barkley (Ed.), *Attention-deficit hyperactivity disorder:*

A handbook for diagnosis and treatment (3rd ed., pp. 453–479). New York: Guilford Press.

Anastopoulos, A. D., Shelton, T. L., DuPaul, G. J., & Guevremont, D. C. (1993). Parent training for attention-deficit hyperactivity disorder: Its impact on parent functioning. *Journal of Abnormal Child Psychology, 21,* 581–596.

Angold, A., Costello, E. J., & Erkanli, A. (1999). Comorbidity. *Journal of Child Psychology and Psychiatry, 40,* 57–88.

Arnold, D. S., O'Leary, S. G., Wolff, L. S., & Acker, M. A. (1993). The Parenting Scale: A measure of dysfunctional parenting in discipline situations. *Psychological Assessment, 5,* 137–144.

Barkley, R. A. (1988). Attention deficit disorder with hyperactivity. In E. J. Mash & L. G. Terdal (Eds.), *Behavioral assessment of childhood disorders: Selected core problems* (2nd ed., pp. 69–104). New York: Guilford Press.

Barkley, R. A. (1994). Impaired delayed responding: A unified theory of attention-deficit hyperactivity disorder. In D. K. Routh (Ed.), *Disruptive behavior disorders in childhood* (pp. 11–57). New York: Plenum Press.

Barkley, R. A. (1997a). *ADHD and the nature of self-control.* New York: Guilford Press.

Barkley, R. A. (1997b). *Defiant children: A clinician's manual for assessment and parent training* (2nd ed.). New York: Guilford Press.

Barkley, R. A. (1998). *Attention-deficit hyperactivity disorder.* New York: Guilford Press.

Barkley, R. A. (2001). The executive functions and self-regulation: An evolutionary neuropsychological perspective. *Neuropsychology Review, 11,* 1–29.

Barkley, R. A. (2006). *Attention-deficit hyperactivity disorder: A handbook for diagnosis and treatment* (3rd ed.). New York: Guilford Press.

Barkley, R. A., & Murphy, K. R. (2006). *Attention-deficit hyperactivity disorder: A clinical workbook* (3rd ed.). New York: Guilford Press.

Bell, R. Q. (1968). A reinterpretation of the direction of effects in studies of socialization. *Psychological Review, 75,* 81–95.

Bell, R. Q., & Harper, L. (1977). *Child effects on adults.* New York: Wiley.

Breen, M. J., & Altepeter, T. S. (1991). Factor structures of the Home Situations Questionnaire and the School Situations Questionnaire. *Journal of Pediatric Psychology, 16,* 59–67.

Chronis, A. M., Chacko, A., Fabiano, G. A., Wymbs, B. T., & Pelham, W. E., Jr. (2004). Enhancements to the behavioral parent-training paradigm for families of children with ADHD: Review and future directions. *Clinical Child and Family Psychology Review, 7,* 1–27.

Coie, J. D., & Kupersmidt, J. B. (1983). A behavioral analysis of emerging social status in boy's groups. *Child Development, 54,* 1400–1416.

Conners, C. K. (2001). *Conners' Rating Scales-Revised: Technical manual.* North Tonawanda, NY: Multi-Health Systems.

Connor, D. C. (2006). Stimulants. In R. A. Barkley (Ed.), *Attention-deficit hyperactivity disorder: A handbook for diagnosis and treatment* (3rd ed., pp. 608–647). New York: Guilford Press.

Connor, D. F., Glatt, S. J., Lopez, I. D., Jackson, D., & Melloni, R. H., Jr. (2002). Psychopharmacology and aggression: Pt. I. A meta-analysis of stimulant affects on over/covert aggression-related behaviors in ADHD. *Journal of the American Academy of Child and Adolescent Psychiatry, 41,* 253–261.

Danforth, J. S. (1998a). The behavior management flow chart: A component analysis of behavior management strategies. *Clinical Psychology Review, 18,* 229–257.

Danforth, J. S. (1998b). The outcome of parent training using the behavior management flow chart with mothers and their children with oppositional defiant disorder and attention-deficit hyperactivity disorder. *Behavior Modification, 22,* 443–473.

Danforth, J. S. (1999). The outcome of parent training using the behavior management flow chart with a mother and her twin boys with oppositional defiant disorder and attention-deficit hyperactivity disorder. *Child and Family Behavior Therapy, 21,* 59–80.

Danforth, J. S. (2001). Altering the function of commands presented to boys with oppositional and hyperactive behavior. *Analysis of Verbal Behavior, 18,* 31–49.

Danforth, J. S., Barkley, R. A., & Stokes, T. R. (1991). Observations of parent-child interactions with hyperactive children: Research and clinical implications. *Clinical Psychology Review, 11,* 703–727.

Danforth, J. S., Harvey, E., Ulaszek, W. R., & McKee, T. E. (in press). The outcome of group parent training for families of children with attention-deficit hyperactivity disorder and defiant/aggressive behavior. *Journal of Behavior Therapy and Experimental Psychiatry.*

Douglas, V. I. (1999). Cognitive control processes in attention-deficit/hyperactivity disorder. In H. C. Quay & Anne E. Hogan (Eds.), *Handbook of disruptive behavior disorders* (pp. 105–138). New York: Kluwer Academic.

DuPaul, G. J., McGoey, K. E., Eckert, T., & VanBrakle, J. (2001). Preschool children with attention-deficit/hyperactivity disorder: Impairments in behavioral, social, and school functioning. *Journal of the American Academy of Child and Adolescent Psychiatry, 40,* 508–515.

Edmonds, E. M., & Smith, L. R. (1985). Students' performance as a function of sex, noise, and intelligence. *Psychological Reports, 56,* 727–730.

Eyberg, S. M., & Boggs, S. R. (1998). Parent-child interaction therapy: A psychosocial intervention for the treatment of young conduct-disordered children. In J. M. Briesmeister & C. E. Schaefer (Eds.), *Handbook of parent training: Training parents as co-therapists for children's behavior problems* (2nd ed., pp. 61–97). New York: Wiley.

Eyberg, S. M., Boggs, S. R., & Rodriguez, C. M. (1992). Relationships between maternal parenting stress and child disruptive behavior. *Child and Family Behavior Therapy, 14,* 1–9.

Fletcher, K., Fischer, M., Barkley, R. A., & Smallish, L. (1996). A sequential analysis of the mother-adolescent interactions of ADHD, ADHD/ODD, and normal teenagers during neutral and conflict discussions. *Journal of Abnormal Child Psychology, 24,* 271–297.

Forehand, R. (1977). Child noncompliance to parent commands: Behavioral analysis and treatment. In M. Hersen, R. M. Eisler, & P. M. Miller (Eds.), *Progress in behavior modification* (Vol. 5, pp. 111–147). New York: Academic Press.

Forehand, R. J., & McMahon, R. L. (2003). *Helping the noncompliant child: Family-based treatment for oppositional behavior* (2nd ed.). New York: Guilford Press.

Gardner, F. E. M. (1989). Inconsistent parenting: Is there evidence for a link with children's conduct problems? *Journal of Abnormal Child Psychology, 17,* 223–233.

Garland, E. J. (1998). Pharmacotherapy of adolescent attention deficit hyperactivity disorder: Challenges, choices, and caveats. *Journal of Psychopharmacology, 12,* 385–395.

Gomez, R., & Sanson, A. V. (1994). Mother-child interactions and noncompliance in hyperactive boys with and without conduct problems. *Journal of Child Psychology and Psychiatry, 35,* 477–490.

Gresham, F. M., & Elliot, S. N. (1990). *Social skills rating system manual.* Circle Pines, MN: American Guidance Service.

Harvey, E., Danforth, J. S., McKee, T. E., & Ulaszek, W. R., & Friedman, J. L. (2003). Parenting of children with attention-deficit/hyperactivity disorder (ADHD): The role of parental ADHD symptomotology. *Journal of Attention Disorders, 7,* 31–41.

Harvey, E. A., Danforth, J. S., Ulaszek, W. R., & Eberhardt, T. L. (2001). Validity of the parenting scale for parents of children with attention-deficit/hyperactivity disorder. *Behavior Research and Therapy, 39,* 731–743.

Hawkins, R. P., Peterson, R. F., Schweid, E., & Bijou, S. W. (1966). Behavior therapy in the home: Amelioration of problem parent-child relations with the parent in the therapeutic role. *Journal of Experimental Child Psychology, 4,* 99–107.

Hineline, P. N. (1977). Negative reinforcement and avoidance. In W. Honig & J. E. Staddon (Eds.), *Handbook of operant behavior* (pp. 364–414). Englewood Cliffs, NJ: Prentice-Hall.

Hineline, P. N. (1984). Aversive control: A separate domain? *Journal of the Experimental Analysis of Behavior, 42,* 495–509.

Hinshaw, S. P. (1994). *Attention deficits and hyperactivity in children.* Thousand Oaks, CA: Sage.

Hinshaw, S. P. (2006). Treatment of children and adolescents with attention-deficit/hyperactivity disorder. In P. C. Kendall (Ed.), *Child and adolescent therapy: Cognitive-behavioral procedures* (3rd ed., 82–113). New York: Guilford Press.

Johnston, C. J., & Ohan, J. L. (2005). The importance of parental attributions in families of children with attention-deficit/hyperactivity and disruptive behavior disorders. *Clinical Child and Family Psychology Review, 8,* 167–182.

Kendall, P. C. (2006). *Child and adolescent therapy: Cognitive-behavioral procedures.* New York: Guilford Press.

Kovacs, M. (1980). Rating scales to assess depression in school-age children. *Acta Paediatrica, 46,* 305–315.

Kuhne, M., Schachar, R., & Tannock, R. (1997). Impact of comorbid oppositional or conduct problems on attention-deficit hyperactivity disorder. *Journal of the American Academy of Child and Adolescent Psychiatry, 36,* 1715–1725.

LeFever, G. B., Arcona, A. P., & Antonuccio, D. O. (2003). ADHD among American schoolchildren: Evidence of overdiagnosis and overuse of medication. *Scientific Review of Mental Health Practice, 2,* 1–15. Retrieved June 9, 2004, from http://www.srmhp.org/0201-adhd.html.

Lobitz, W. C., & Johnson, S. M. (1975). Parental manipulation of the behavior of normal and deviant children. *Child Development, 46,* 719–726.

Lonigan, C. J., Elbert, J. C., & Johnson, S. B. (1998). Empirically supported psychosocial interventions for children: An overview. *Journal of Clinical Child Psychology, 27,* 138–145.

Luria, A. R. (1961). *The role of speech in the regulation of normal and abnormal behavior.* New York: Liveright.

Lynam, D. R. (1996). Early identification of chronic offenders: Who is a fledging psychopath? *Psychological Bulletin, 120,* 209–234.

March, J. S. (1997). *Multidimensional Anxiety Scale for Children: Technical manual.* North Tonawanda, NY: Multi-Health Systems.

Martin, G. L., & Pear, J. (2007). *Behavior modification: What it is and how to do it* (8th ed.). Upper Saddle River, NJ: Prentice-Hall.

McKee, T. E., Harvey, E., Danforth, J. S., & Ulaszek, W. R., & Friedman, J. L. (2004). The relation between parental coping styles and parent-child interactions before and after treatment for children with ADHD and oppositional behavior. *Journal of Clinical Child and Adolescent Psychology, 33,* 158–168.

The Multimodal Treatment Study of Children with ADHD Cooperative Group. (1999). A 14-month randomized clinical trail of treatment strategies for attention-deficit/hyperactivity disorder. *Archives of General Psychiatry, 56,* 1073–1086.

Nigg, J. T. (2006). *What causes ADHD?: Understanding what goes wrong and why.* New York: Guilford Press.

O'Dell, S. L., Mahoney, N. D., Horton, W. G., & Turner, P. E. (1979). Media-assisted parent training: Alternative models. *Behavior Therapy, 10,* 103–109.

Patterson, G. R. (1976). The aggressive child: Architect of a coercive system. In E. J. Mash, L. A. Hamerlynck, & L. C. Handy (Eds.), *Behavior modification and families* (pp. 267–316). New York: Brunner/Mazel.

Patterson, G. R. (1982). *Coercive family process.* Eugene, OR: Castalia.

Patterson, G. R., & Bank, L. (1986). Bootstrapping your way in the nomological thicket. *Behavioral Assessment, 8,* 49–73.

Pfiffner, L. J., McBurnett, K., Rathouz, P. J., & Judice, S. (2005). Family correlates of oppositional and conduct disorders in children with attention deficit/hyperactivity disorder. *Journal of Abnormal Child Psychology, 33,* 551–563.

Pisterman, S., Firestone, P., McGrath, P., Goodman, J. T., Webster, I., Mallory, R., et al. (1992). The role of parent training in treatment of preschoolers with ADHD. *American Journal of Orthopsychiatry, 62,* 397–408.

Pisterman, S., McGrath, P., Firestone, P., Goodman, J. T., Webster, I., & Mallory, R. (1989). Outcome of parent-mediated treatment of preschoolers with attention deficit disorder with hyperactivity. *Journal of Consulting and Clinical Psychology, 57,* 628–635.

Reynolds, C. R., & Kamphaus, R. W. (2004). *Behavioral assessment system for children manual* (2nd ed.). Circle Pines, MN: American Guidance Service.

Richman, G. S., Harrison, K. A., & Summers, J. A. (1995). Assessing and modifying parent responses to their children's noncompliance. *Education and Treatment of Children, 18,* 105–116.

Roberts, M. W. (1988). Enforcing chair timeouts with room timeouts. *Behavior Modification, 12,* 353–370.

Sajwaj, T., & Dillon, A. (1977). Complexities of an "elementary" behavior modification procedure: Differential adult attention used for children's behavior disorders. In B. C. Etzel, J. M. LeBlanc, & D. M. Baer (Eds.), *New developments in behavioral research: Theory, method, and application* (pp. 303–315). New York: Wiley.

Seipp, C. M., & Johnston, C. (2005). Mother-son interactions in families of boys with attention-deficit/hyperactivity disorder with and without oppositional behavior. *Journal of Abnormal Child Psychology, 33,* 87–98.

Shroyer, C., & Zentall, S. S. (1986). Effects of rate, nonrelevant information, and repetition on the listening comprehension of hyperactive children. *Journal of Special Education, 20,* 231–239.

Skinner, B. F. (1953). *Science and human behavior.* New York: Free Press.

Smith, B. H., Barkley, R. A., & Shapiro, C. J. (2006). Attention-deficit/hyperactivity disorder. In E. J. Mash & R. A. Barkley (Eds.), *Treatment of childhood disorders* (3rd ed., pp. 65–136). New York: Guilford Press.

Vuchinich, S., Bank, L., & Patterson, G. R. (1992). Parenting, peers, and the stability of antisocial behavior in preadolescent boys. *Developmental Psychology, 28,* 510–521.

Vygotsky, L. S. (1962). *Thought and language.* Cambridge, MA: MIT Press.

Wahler, R. G. (1975). Some structural aspects of deviant child behavior. *Journal of Applied Behavior Analysis, 8,* 27–42.

Wilson, R. J., & Herrnstein, R. J. (1985). *Crime and human nature.* New York: Simon & Schuster.

Zentall, S. S. (1985). Stimulus control factors in search performance of hyperactive children. *Journal of Learning Disabilities, 18,* 480–485.

Zentall, S. S. (2005). Theory- and evidence-based strategies for children with attentional problems. *Psychology in the Schools, 42,* 821–836.

Zentall, S. S., & Zentall, T. R. (1976). Activity and task performance of hyperactive children as a function of environmental stimulation. *Journal of Consulting and Clinical Psychology, 44,* 693–697.

CHAPTER 12

Working with Parents
of Aggressive,
School-Age Children

TIMOTHY A. CAVELL and L. CHRISTIAN ELLEDGE

THIS CHAPTER provides a conceptual framework and practice guidelines for working with parents of aggressive, school-age children. We begin by discussing the development of childhood aggression in light of what is known about children's long-term socialization. We propose that parent-based interventions are an opportunity to help parents identify and implement effective, sustainable strategies for socializing their aggressive, high-risk children. We introduce the Responsive Parent Therapy (RPT) model and describe key principles, overall structure, and options for tailoring interventions to fit the needs of individual families. We illustrate these points with a case example.

AGGRESSIVE CHILDREN

In writing about *aggressive, school-age* children, we interchange other, applicable labels. These include *aggressive, antisocial* children and *aggressive, high-risk* children as well as the shorthand versions of *aggressive* or *antisocial* children. We use these labels to refer to children who are older, more aggressive, and more antisocial than the oppositional preschoolers who often are the focus of parent training outcome studies (Serketich & Dumas, 1996). Compared to their younger, less aggressive counterparts (Campbell, Pierce, March, Ewing, & Szumowski, 1994), children whose use of aggression extends beyond the preschool years and beyond the confines of their home are at substantially greater risk for negative outcomes, including delinquency, substance abuse, risky sexual behavior, impaired occupational functioning, and poor romantic relationships (Loeber, 1990; Patterson, Reid, & Dishion, 1992). Highly aggressive, school-age children are likely to meet diagnostic criteria for Conduct Disorder-Child Onset (American Psychiatric Association, 1994; Loeber & Burke, 2000). Other labels used to describe this group of high-risk children are *early starters* (Patterson et al., 1992) and *life-course persistent offenders* (Moffitt, 1993), though neither label indicates where a given child is currently in that trajectory (e.g., school-age, teenager, young adult).

SOCIALIZATION AND THE DEVELOPMENTAL COURSE OF CHILDHOOD AGGRESSION

Aggressive, antisocial youth are often considered socialization failures—clear examples of what can go wrong when the job of inculcating society's younger members is left undone or poorly done (Tremblay, 2003). Socialization researchers routinely cite positive outcomes from parent training programs as strong, experimental evidence that parents affect their children's development (e.g., Collins, Maccoby, Steinberg, Hetherington, & Bornstein, 2000). Less common, however, is for interventionists to view treatments for aggressive children from a socialization perspective (Cavell, Hymel, Malcolm, & Seay, 2006). Ideally, the link between socialization theory and intervention practice is mutually beneficial: Research on normative socialization processes informs the design of interventions for antisocial youth, and well-implemented intervention studies test the putative causal mechanisms of socialization (see Pettit & Dodge, 2003). But is this an accurate or useful frame for working with parents of aggressive children?

We submit that a socialization-as-intervention frame has considerable, practical value. It is also a perspective that stands in contrast to traditional parent-training models (Cavell & Strand, 2003). The more conventional intervention-as-intervention model places greater emphasis on the immediate reduction of problem behavior but eschews the broader, longer-term perspective afforded by a socialization approach. A better fit is afforded by an intervention-as-socialization model that recognizes the need for sustained, preventative efforts but continues to rely on extraordinary psychosocial interventions instead of socialization forces indigenous to children's social and developmental ecology.

Socialization is typically defined from the standpoint of those adults (e.g., parents, teachers) who shape and guide the next generation of citizens. Parents and teachers play a key role in the socialization process (Maccoby, 1992), though sometimes their actions contribute inadvertently to the onset and maintenance of childhood aggression (Hughes, Cavell, &

Jackson, 1999; Patterson et al., 1992). These primary "agents" are but one part of the socialization picture. Also operating are friends and peers, neighborhoods, schools, and communities, as well as larger macrosocial forces (Grusec & Hastings, 2006; Harris, 1995, 1998). Particularly important is the fact that children are active participants in their own socialization experiences (Kuczynski, 2003). Effective parent-based interventions require an appreciation for the range of factors that affect socialization, for the interplay among them, and especially, for the power and influence wielded by aggressive children themselves (Cavell & Strand, 2003).

In making the case for socialization as intervention, we introduce an integrated *life course-social learning* approach to understanding the development and treatment of antisocial behavior (Cavell et al., 2006; Conger & Simons, 1997; J. J. Snyder, Reid, & Patterson, 2003). This model helps to explain the multiple causes and the predictable course of antisocial behavior (ASB). To explicate the model, we present eight basic assumptions that link diverse areas of research, including the interaction of nature with nurture (Collins et al., 2000, 2001; Moffitt, 2005), the significance of and interdependence among multiple social contexts (Harris, 1995, 1998; Parke et al., 2002; Vaillancourt & Hymel, 2004), the importance of individual differences in crime proneness (Caspi et al., 1994; Moffitt, 1993), and the critical role of social contingencies in the development of ASB (Patterson, 1982; Patterson et al., 1992; J. J. Snyder & Patterson, 1995).

ASSUMPTION 1

For children, socialization is the process of actively seeking, routinely accessing, and effectively participating in contexts that provide greater and more reliable benefits than other, competing contexts. There are three key points here: The first is that children are active players in their own development. One way in which children contribute to their socialization experiences is through a process called *niche finding* (Scarr, 1992): Children tend to seek, access, and invest in environmental niches that capitalize on their specific genetic endowments. The second point is that children will perform behaviors and spend time in contexts that offer greater and more reliable benefits than other behaviors or contexts, respectively. This point reflects the basic tenets of the Matching Law (Herrnstein, 1970; McDowell, 1988). The Matching Law is an informational rather than a mechanical conceptualization of reinforcement: "Consequences do not shape behavior; rather, they shape the meaning of objects and events" (DeGrandpre, 2000, p. 726). According to the Matching Law, the probability of a child using coercion in the home should be matched by the probability of coercion being reinforced *relative* to other, competing responses (e.g., cooperation). J. J. Snyder and Patterson (1995) applied this principle in revising Patterson's (1982) original Coercion Hypothesis, which had over-emphasized between individual differences in reinforcement for coercion and had under-emphasized intraindividual differences. Complementing the *relative response* form of the Matching Law is the *time allocation* version of the theory (McDowell, 1988): "In the years since Herrnstein first proposed the Matching Law, several investigators have demonstrated that time spent in an environment will also be relative to the rate of reinforcement provided by that environment" (Conger & Simons, 1997, p. 62). Conger and Simons (1997) suggest this aspect of the Matching Law is more critical than the first because it considers the competing values of social contexts differing in support of prosocial versus antisocial activities. The final point is that socialization—from the vantage of the developing child—is not a process that is inherently prosocial or anti-social. Instead, the moral valence of associated with socialization outcomes is a reflection of the contexts in which children come to invest their time and energy.

ASSUMPTION 2

For parents and other stakeholders, socialization is the process of promoting children's access to and participation in prosocial contexts while limiting their access to and participation in contexts that encourage or condone ASB. Our first assumption highlighted children's capacity to shape their socialization experiences by accessing and investing in specific social contexts. One implication of that assumption is that the family, often considered the fundamental crucible of children's socialization, is but one context among many that competes for the opportunity to influence developing youth. Our second assumption speaks to the role that parents and other responsible adults have when attempting to impact children's socialization experiences. Recognized is the obvious goal of providing children with adaptive, prosocial contexts in which to grow and learn. Less obvious is the fact that primary socialization agents also serve as "gatekeepers," social managers, and supervisors who largely determine where and how children spend their time and energy, especially at younger ages (Parke et al., 2002). Also recognized is the fact that adults are responsible for monitoring children's whereabouts, as well as their activities and their companions. Patterson and colleagues have repeatedly shown that parental supervision is a significant predictor of children's ASB (Patterson et al., 1992; Patterson, Dishion, & Yoerger, 2000; J. J. Snyder et al., 2003).

Assumption 2 also recognizes more subtle aspects of adults' role in the socialization process. Parents who are consistently in the dark about children's whereabouts, their companions, and their activities are, by definition, poor monitors. However, the direction of causality is not always clear in these situations: Some children are simply more difficult to monitor. In fact, it appears the robust relation between parental monitoring and ASB is due in part to children and adolescents actively managing the information they give to parents (Kerr & Stattin, 2000). Thus, to view monitoring solely as a parenting *practice* fails to appreciate the level of influence that children and adolescents wield in this process. Even parents who know where their children are and who they are with can misjudge the nature of their activities. For example, easy access to the Internet and to cell phones has increased dramatically children's capacity to engage surreptitiously in deviant activities (e.g., Ybarra & Mitchell, 2004). Less common but still possible are times when parents' misjudgment or ignorance about children's whereabouts is due to active deceit, either by children themselves or by their deviant companions. An extreme example is the child molester who tries to exploit the limits of parental monitoring (van Dam, 2001), "grooming" children to feel partly responsible for their own victimization (Berliner & Conte, 1990). Fortunately, the majority of children do not suffer such abuses, but similar processes are at work when children are pressured by deviant peers. Just as some children are more likely to be victimized by sexual predators (Elliott, Browne, & Kilcoyne, 1995), some youth are more susceptible to the influence of deviant peers (Fergusson, Woodward, & Horwood, 1999; Steinberg, 1986; Vitaro, Brendgan, & Tremblay, 2001). Even within "normal" peer contexts, youth who are disliked by peers tend to be less discriminating about their companions and about the activities (e.g., delinquency, substance use, sexual interaction) considered "necessary" to maintain companionship (Boivin, Hymel, & Bukowski, 1995; McDougall, Hymel, Vaillancourt, & Mercer, 2001). Indeed, for highly rejected children, affiliating with deviant peers is often not an option as it is a last resort for social interchange.

ASSUMPTION 3

Contexts are prosocial to the extent (a) aggression and other forms of ASB are reliably restricted, (b) prosocial behavior is sufficiently rewarded, and (c) normative beliefs neither encourage nor condone ASB. In this third assumption, we offer a working definition of *prosocial contexts*. It is a definition that emphasizes function over topography (Jacobson, 1992). Knowing that families, schools, and neighborhoods espouse positive virtues and good citizenship is less important than knowing whether prosocial behavior is functional (actually works) within these contexts. In keeping with the tenets of the Matching Law, a prosocial context is one in which the value of performing prosocial behavior consistently exceeds the value of performing ASB (Conger & Simons, 1997; J. J. Snyder et al., 2003). For that to happen, certain conditions are needed.

Foremost among these is the reliable restriction of aggression and other forms of ASB. If the past 30 years of research has taught us anything about the development of aggression, it is that children are at risk when they adopt aggression and other forms of coercion as their dominant influence strategy (Dumas, LaFreniere, & Serketich, 1995; Patterson, 1982; Patterson et al., 1992; J. J. Snyder & Patterson, 1995). Placing strict limits on ASB is a rather obvious socialization strategy, but not all adults recognize its importance and not all contexts provide such limits. Some parents downplay instances of ASB if their child is meeting other, more valued goals (e.g., academic achievement, athletic prowess, musical success), whereas other parents feel powerless and give up trying to control their misbehaving youth (Bugental, Lewis, Lin, Lyon, & Kopeikin, 1999). Other parents adopt a strong disciplinary stance but fail to distinguish between aggressive, ASB, and minor misbehavior (see Cavell, 2001).

Restricting aggression and other forms of ASB is a necessary but insufficient condition for ensuring that contexts are prosocial. In keeping with the tenets of the Matching Law, the value of performing prosocial behaviors should exceed the value of performing ASB (Conger & Simons, 1997; J. J. Snyder et al., 2003). Adequate and reliable rewards are needed to sustain behaviors that are prosocial and not harmful or antisocial. Strict limits can reduce the benefits of ASB but leave unspecified and under-used behaviors that are necessary for adaptive socialization. Parents of antisocial children experience this when they spend time and effort "policing" their child's misbehavior only to find that ASB returns when the threat of immediate sanctions is removed (Patterson, 1982).

The final condition for prosocial contexts is a system of shared beliefs that neither encourages nor condones ASB. When parents (Hanlon et al., 2005), siblings (D. K. Snyder, Castellani, & Whisman, 2006), and peers (Dishion, Capaldi, Spracklen, & Li, 1995; Patterson et al., 2000) actively endorse or routinely model ASB, they place children at risk for later delinquency. Children are also influenced by group norms for ASB (Henry et al., 2000; Salmivalli & Voeten, 2004), and youth who are aggressive and rejected are more likely to overestimate friends' involvement in deviant and risky behaviors (Prinstein & Wang, 2005).

ASSUMPTION 4

Children's access to and active participation in deviant (nonprosocial) contexts represent environmental risks for ASB that limit their opportunity to learn and perform prosocial behavior and promote their opportunity to learn and perform ASB. This assumption emphasizes the influence of social learning processes in children's use of ASB. Violent and chaotic homes, deviant peer groups, and crime-ridden neighborhoods provide numerous opportunities to observe, to practice, and to refine the performance of ASB. Children who participate in deviant social contexts are building skill repertoires that fit poorly the demands of traditional prosocial contexts (e.g., classroom, schools). With few opportunities to learn or perform prosocial skills, with a growing repertoire of ASB, and with contingencies that provide greater payoffs for ASB than for prosocial behavior, aggressive children are unlikely to benefit from the advice of parents and teachers. And because concerned adults have little power to alter this complex set of circumstances, childhood aggression tends to follow a chronic course (Loeber & Hay, 1997).

Creating and sustaining positive deflections in this risk trajectory can be difficult, particularly when interventionists fail to appreciate the contextual factors that maintain aggression and ASB (Eddy & Chamberlain, 2000). The real value of a social learning approach is not in explaining how or why children *acquire* ASB but in explaining why and when children are likely to *perform* ASB (Conger & Simons, 1997; J. J. Snyder & Patterson, 1995). This fact is often lost on interventionists who assume that children's use of ASB stems primarily from a lack of acquired, alternative skills. This is somewhat ironic given that the prevailing models among social learning theorists are used to explain variability in the *performance* of ASB (Patterson, 1982, 1986; Patterson et al., 1992). As a result, a number of interventions place emphasis on teaching children skills thought to be missing from their repertoire (e.g., Goldstein, Sprafkin, Gershaw, & Klein, 1997). If ASB is due to a deficit in children's skill sets (e.g., social cognitions), then skill training is a reasonable intervention option. However, if ASB is a function of prevailing contingencies and normative beliefs, then skill-building efforts will not lead to significant and lasting gains. This is essentially the conclusion reached by Taylor, Eddy, and Biglan (1999) in their review of social and interpersonal skills training interventions for children with externalizing problems. They point out that interventions designed to help parents alter the contingencies that govern children's use of ASB in the home have been shown to be far more successful than child-focused, skills training interventions. Interestingly, proponents of parent-training programs tend to ignore the contextual determinants of parents' performance and assume instead that parents need new, more effective skills (see Cavell, 2000; Cavell & Strand, 2003). Often overlooked is the role of strong child effects and other factors that can greatly influence the quality of parenting in many homes (Lytton, 1990). Needed are intervention models that address the *performance* of poor parenting (Patterson, 1997) and that offer strategies other than the learning of new skills (Strand & Cavell, 2006).

In sum, Assumption 4 is not simply a reminder that environmental factors play a role in the socialization of children and in the development of ASB. It is a reminder that children use ASB because it works in certain contexts (J. J. Snyder et al., 2003). Interventions that teach prosocial skills but fail to change (or restrict access to) contexts that reward and maintain ASB are unlikely to succeed. Effective interventions will require careful appraisal of the contexts in which children spend their time and energy and a clear understanding of the conditions that promote those investments.

ASSUMPTION 5

Deficits in self-regulatory skills represent biogenetic risks for ASB that diminishes children's capacity to participate actively and successfully in prosocial contexts. Scholars recognize the link between biologically based individual difference variables and the onset or course of ASB (Lahey, Moffitt, & Caspi, 2003; Tremblay, Nagin, & Seguin, 2005). They differ in how to label or categorize these variables (Nigg & Huang-Pollock, 2003): Some focus on cognitive or neurological deficits (Moffitt, 2003; Nigg & Huang-Pollock, 2003), some emphasize temperament or personality dimensions (Lahey & Waldman, 2003), and still others are concerned with problems in emotion regulation (Keenan & Shaw, 2003). These differences aside, it is clear that self-regulatory deficits diminish children's capacity to gain access to, mastery in, and acceptance from prosocial contexts (e.g., Conger & Simons, 1997; J. J. Synder et al., 2003). For the practitioner working with parents of aggressive children, it would be hard to over-estimate the significance of this interplay between biogenetic risk and children's participation in available social contexts (Cavell et al., 2006).

Developmental theorists have long posited that child temperament affects the quality of early parent-child interactions and that the goodness of fit between parent and child can affect later development (Thomas & Chess, 1977). A more recent notion is that children gravitate toward ecological niches that fit their genetically endowed strengths and weaknesses (Scarr, 1992). Assumption 5 extends each of these notions in two ways. The first is that the goodness-of-fit criterion is not limited to a particular dyad or to a specific developmental period. Rather, the challenge of entering and participating in available social contexts is a pervasive and recurring task that can span the life course. The second extension highlights the bifurcation of children's socialization experiences. For some children, effective self-regulation allows for successful participation in a host of prosocial contexts and yields a developmental trajectory in which expected transitions are managed rather seamlessly and unexpected perturbations are uncommon, short-lived, or efficiently traversed.

For other children, socialization is a lifelong struggle in which the tendency to react too quickly, too strongly, or for too long narrows tremendously the opportunities to participate in social ecologies that expect and value mutual respect, verbal give-and-take, planned action, and nonviolence. The inherent disconnect between this high-risk self-regulatory profile and the contingencies and norms of most prosocial contexts does not fate vulnerable children to a life of ASB, but it does represent a chronic and significant impediment to socialization (Cavell et al., 2006; Conger & Simons, 1997; J. J. Snyder et al., 2003). In other words, if such children are "socialization failures," it is because they had less chance of succeeding from a very early age.

ASSUMPTION 6

Biogenetic and environmental risks co-contribute to a pattern of coercive transactions that foster and support early onset ASB, an extreme form that begins early, tends to persist, and is often violent. Scholars tend to agree that deficits in cognitive ability, behavioral inhibition, and emotion regulation are key vulnerabilities to ASB (Lahey et al., 2003), but not all view these vulnerabilities as direct determinants of ASB. Rather, these vulnerabilities are thought to interact with environmental factors to contribute to the maintenance of ASB. A rather extreme example comes from research on fledgling psychopaths—that small proportion of antisocial youth who think and feel in ways that diminish the influence of prosocial adults (Frick, 1998; Frick, Stickle, Dandreaux, Farrell, & Kimonis, 2005; Lynam, 1998; Vasey, Kotov, Frick, & Loney, 2005). Frick and colleagues (e.g., Wootton, Frick, Shelton, & Silverthorn, 1997) found that poor parenting failed to predict externalizing problems for children who were callous and unemotional, although it did predict problem behavior for children who lacked those traits (see also Oxford, Cavell, & Hughes, 2003). Research on biogenetic vulnerabilities and fledging psychopathy challenge but do not disprove social learning conceptualizations of ASB. Rather, findings from these studies underscore the need to consider multiple pathways to ASB and the ongoing process of nature interacting with nurture (Moffitt, 2005).

Biogenetic risk factors are differentially linked to early- versus late-onset ASB. Moffitt (1993, 2003) calls the latter type *adolescent-limited* because it emerges during adolescence and does not typically persist into adulthood. Late-onset ASB reflects significant, age-related increases in relatively minor offenses, including truancy, vandalism, shoplifting, underage drinking, and possession and use of marijuana. As adolescents become young adults and take on new roles and added responsibilities (e.g., greater academic challenges, work obligations, family responsibilities), their involvement in ASB decreases accordingly. The relatively benign course of late-onset ASB contrasts sharply with the serious risk trajectory of early starters (Patterson et al., 1992). Early involvement in ASB signals multiple and recurring difficulties within prosocial contexts and portends a greater likelihood that those difficulties will persist into and beyond adolescence (Moffitt, 1993, 2003). Early-onset ASB also predicts a more serious pattern of offending, including a propensity for violence.

Assumption 6 is drawn from research indicating that early onset ASB is multiply determined and often over-determined. Moffitt (1993, 2003) makes a strong case that biogenetic risk factors are key determinants of the early onset, life course-persistent pattern of offending. Other scholars also recognize the role of biogenetic factors (Conger & Simons, 1997; Dodge & Pettit, 2003; Keenan & Shaw, 2003; Lahey & Waldman, 2003; J. J. Snyder et al., 2003), though some (e.g., Tremblay, 2003) have questioned whether these risk factors are distributed dichotomously, as Moffitt (1993) suggests, or continuously. There is also continuing debate about the role of environmental factors in the development of early onset ASB (Lahey et al., 2003), although social learning theorists continue to endorse this view (Conger & Simons, 1997; Keenan & Shaw, 2003; Patterson et al., 1992; J. J. Snyder et al., 2003; Tremblay, 2003).

Assumption 7

Short-term reductions in ASB are possible when antisocial children actively participate in prosocial contexts. In line with the Matching Law, reductions in ASB are expected when children spend time and energy in contexts where the rewards for prosocial acts are greater than the rewards for ASB. There are several ways to create these kinds of contextual changes, including the use of formal intervention strategies. Some children and teens are removed from their current contexts and placed settings that are thought to be therapeutic (e.g., in-patient facilities, treatment foster homes). Treatment settings that effectively control the availability of key reinforcers and limit the possibility of further deviancy training (Dishion, McCord, & Poulin, 1999) can achieve significant reductions in ASB (e.g., Chamberlain & Reid, 1998; Hoefler & Bornstein, 1975). There are also informal ways to remove children from one setting and place them elsewhere. Families can move out of town or to a different neighborhood, or children can transfer to a new school or move in with another family. Little is known about whether such changes actually help or harm aggressive, antisocial children.

A less restrictive strategy is to alter the contexts in which children currently live. This is the core premise underlying parent management training (PMT). Parents learn to issue clear commands, to reinforce obedience (e.g., via praise), to ignore minor misbehaviors, and to punish (e.g., via time-out) noncompliance and serious misbehaviors (Briesmeister & Schaefer, this book; Kazdin, 2005). Outcome studies generally find that PMT leads to significant reductions in problem behavior (Brestan & Eyberg, 1998; Kazdin, 2005; McMahon & Wells, 1998) and that improved parenting predicts treatment gains (Patterson, 2005; Patterson, DeGarmo, & Forgatch, 2004). Some interventions target the entire family and assume that systemwide changes are needed (Minuchin, 1974; Nichols & Schwartz, 2004). It is unclear whether positive outcomes from parent- or family-based interventions are due to improvements in parent-imposed contingencies, to changes in family wide beliefs, to greater cohesion among family members, to structural changes in family hierarchy, or to other unrecognized factors (Cavell & Strand, 2003; Nichols & Schwartz, 2004; Patterson, 2005). Tests of hypothesized mediators are uncommon in studies of family-based interventions; rarer still are studies that test competing mediating mechanisms (Kazdin, 2005). One such study was conducted by DeGarmo, Patterson, and Forgatch (2004). These investigators expected to find that changes in parenting led directly to reduced externalizing problems; instead, they found that parent training resulted in a decrease in children's internalizing symptoms, which then led to therapeutic changes in children's externalizing problems. Apparently, mothers' participation in parent training helped children to feel less sad and anxious, which in turn led to better behavior. As Patterson et al. (2004) note: "It is obvious that we are just beginning to understand how PMT functions as an agent of change in the family system over time" (p. 631).

Strategies for reducing ASB via changes in context offer documented success as well as nagging concerns (Cavell et al., 2006). At least two factors limit the potential benefits of contextual changes on future ASB. The first is difficulty sustaining the changes over time. In-patient and residential facilities usually provide short-term stays, teachers and classrooms change every year, and high-intensity intervention programs eventually fade as financial resources are depleted. Not surprisingly, treatment gains are typically lost when children end their active participation in prosocial, therapeutic contexts (e.g., Kirigin, Braukmann, & Atwater, 1982). Parents of aggressive children can also struggle to maintain changes in the home. Optimism will fade and new parenting strategies will be dropped if parents are overwhelmed by current life demands, a history of antagonistic relationships, and negative expectations for future interactions (Cavell & Strand, 2003; Serketich & Dumas, 1996).

A second, limiting factor is children's capacity to participate effectively in prosocial contexts for an extended period of time. As noted by J. J. Snyder et al. (2003), children's participation in prosocial contexts is not determined unilaterally. Moving to a new community, transferring to a better school, and living with an inviting family are all rich with potential. But children with poor self-regulatory skills and limited success in prosocial contexts are ill-equipped to take advantage of these opportunities. Studies in which aggressive children interact with unfamiliar peers (Dodge, 1983) or with parents of socially competent children (Dumas & LaFreniere, 1993) reveal how quickly aggressive, antisocial children recreate patterns of negative interaction in new contexts that are benign and prosocial. Self-regulatory deficits also hinder children's response to changes in existing environments (e.g., a new system of rewards and rules). This is especially true for children in the early onset ASB pathway. The potential pitfalls include waning enthusiasm for available rewards, growing fatigue from the effort to earn those rewards, and increasing emotional and relational costs associated with their use of coercive strategies. In the end, parents and teachers will likely view early starters as having spoiled their opportunity to participate in prosocial contexts.

If special treatments and costly interventions offer merely short-term solutions, what is their value beyond the effective management of problem behavior and the protection of potential victims? If antisocial children struggle to maintain success in prosocial contexts, what hope is there of long-term reductions in aggression and other forms of ASB?

ASSUMPTION 8

Long-term reductions in ASB are possible when antisocial children (a) experience sustained success in prosocial contexts and (b) invest in systems of shared, prosocial commerce. Our final assumption asserts that achieving long-term reductions in ASB is essentially an exercise in socializing antisocial children into systems of shared, prosocial commerce (Richters & Waters, 1991). Unless antisocial children come to invest time and energy in prosocial contexts, attempts to socialize them will fail or have only short-lived results. This is particularly likely for children in the early onset pathway (Moffitt, 1993, 2003). The challenge of maintaining antisocial children's successful involvement in prosocial contexts requires practical and effective strategies for overcoming numerous, recurring obstacles. Antisocial children are drawn to contexts that actively promote (via peer reinforcement) or passively condone (via modeling) ASB. Restricting access to those contexts is difficult, particularly if children keep secret their activities (Kerr & Stattin, 2000) and engage in covert forms of ASB (J. J. Snyder et al., 2003). Aggressive, antisocial children are also hard to manage and hard to like. They struggle in settings that require prosocial commerce and interacting with them on a daily basis can be costly emotionally, physically, and financially. This is certainly the case for parents who suffer daily the weight of aggressive children's coercive actions and reap few rewards (e.g., Spitzer, Webster-Stratton, & Hollinsworth, 1991). Over time, the task of sustaining a prosocial context becomes increasingly difficult and feelings of frustration, fatigue, and hopelessness can prevail. When this happens, emotional tension in the home rises and the overall level of available reinforcement drops (McDowell, 1982, 1988; Patterson, 1982; Patterson et al., 1992). When this happens, family members look to optimize their own, immediate outcomes instead of aiming for longer-term outcomes that serve the greater good. How can parents resist this tendency and persist in their effort to socialize an aggressive, antisocial child?

From an evolutionary standpoint, parents have the greatest investment in their offspring's future (Clutton-Brock, 1991). It is not surprising, therefore, to encounter parents who carry on despite being repeatedly disappointed and frustrated by their antisocial son or daughter. Even parents who feel hopeless and defeated are still the principle stakeholders in their child's socialization. They have the burden of ensuring that children with early onset ASB access and effectively participate in prosocial contexts; they also have the task of restricting children's use of ASB in the home and their access to contexts that promote ASB. Performing either of these tasks can be difficult, but doing both more or less simultaneously for a period of 18+ years can be almost impossible (Cavell, 2000; Cavell & Strand, 2003). What assortment of strategies can give parents a reasonable chance that their aggressive, antisocial child will grow to become a law-abiding adult? What parent-based interventions should practitioners turn to when working with these beleaguered parents? These are complex questions that defy simple answers. RPT is an attempt to answer those questions.

RESPONSIVE PARENT THERAPY

Responsive Parent Therapy is not a specific treatment package; it is an organizing framework and a set of guiding principles for working with parents of aggressive children (Cavell, 2000; 2001; Cavell & Strand, 2003). It is innovative only in the way it brings together diverse clinical and research traditions. Metaphorically, RPT is neither new wine nor old wine in new bottles; rather, it is a new way to blend grapes from old, proven vines.

RPT: Conceptual Roots and Empirical Base

RPT is a parent-based intervention that attempts to close an important gap—the gap between what is known about childhood aggression and what is typically recommended to practitioners (Cavell, 2000; Cavell &

Strand, 2003). For over 30 years, the core PMT curriculum has remained relatively intact as the study of childhood aggression advanced steadily and impressively forward. The result has been a growing disconnect between what researchers know and what practitioners do. The broad theoretical basis of RPT is founded in social learning, family systems, and attachment theories; more specifically, RPT reflects a strong appreciation for environmental contingencies (Conger & Simons, 1997), for genetically endowed individual differences (Scarr, 1992), for children's capacity to affect their own development (Kuczynski, 2003), and for relationship-based models of socialization (Kuczynski & Hildebrandt, 1997; Richters & Waters, 1991).

Clinically, RPT borrows heavily from PMT (Kazdin, 2005; McMahon & Wells, 1998; Patterson, 2005), structural family therapy (Minuchin, 1974), and Child Relationship Enhancement Family-Therapy (CREFT; Ginsberg, 1989; Guerney & Guerney, 1985, 1987). Specific treatment techniques (e.g., praise, time-out) are used and evaluated based on their function and not their topography (Jacobson, 1992), and intervention decisions are based on robust treatment principles rather than the prescriptive use of a given set of techniques. The application of core principles that transcend a particular treatment program is a growing trend among clinical researchers (e.g., Barlow, Allen, & Choate, 2004; Beutler, 2000; Henggeler, Schoenwald, Borduin, Rowland, & Cunningham, 1998).

Empirical support for RPT comes from three primary sources. One is the vast amount of research examining the causes, correlates, and course of childhood aggression (Cavell et al., 2006; Lahey et al., 2003; Patterson et al., 1992; Tremblay et al., 2005). A second is the plethora of studies evaluating parent-based interventions for children with conduct problems or disruptive behavior disorders (Kazdin, 2005; McMahon & Wells, 1998; Patterson, 2005). Key findings from these two bodies of work have substantially shaped the overarching framework and guiding principles of RPT. Despite this broad base of empirical support, these bodies of knowledge provide only indirect support for RPT.

A more direct test of RPT was a clinical trial comparing Webster-Stratton's (1987) videotaped parenting training series with an alternative model (Cavell, 1996, 2000) that blended aspects of Child Relationship Enhancement Family-therapy (CREFT; Guerney & Guerney, 1985, 1987) and structural family therapy (Minuchin, 1974). Cavell (1996) called this approach Responsive Parent Training and described its goals as enhancing the emotional quality of the parent-child relationship while establishing firm generational boundaries and adaptive family structure. Cavell viewed these goals as closely approximating Baumrind's (1971) concept of authoritative parenting. Also addressed was the critical issue of establishing a strong therapeutic alliance and working through parents' resistance to change (Patterson & Forgatch, 1985; Stoolmiller, Duncan, Bank, & Patterson, 1993). Borrowing from CREFT (Guerney & Guerney, 1985), therapists used *dynamic processing* to encourage parents to reflect on thoughts or feelings that arise as they learn new skills and to support parents as they encountered changing dynamics in the parent-child relationship.

To evaluate this mix of CREFT and structural family therapy, Cavell (1996) randomly assigned parents to the experimental condition or to Webster-Stratton's (1987) PMT video-modeling (PMT-VM) condition. Parents in the PMT-VM used a self-administered format that had yielded significant gains similar to those produced by a therapist-led format (Webster-Stratton, 1989). Responsive Parent Training was conducted in groups of 6 to 8 parents who met for about 2 hours each week for 10 to 12 weeks. Graduate student co-leaders followed a detailed manual and were closely supervised each week.

Outcome analyses were conducted on a sample of 36 children and their parents—24 in the experimental condition and 12 in the comparison condition. Children ranged in age from 3 to 10 years ($M = 6.41$ years) and 74% were boys. The mean pretreatment CBCL Externalizing t-score (Achenbach, 1991) for this sample of children was 63.83 ($SD = 8.22$). Other parent-report measures included the Eyberg Child Behavior Inventory (ECBI; Robinson, Eyberg, & Ross, 1980), the Parenting Stress Index (PSI; Abidin, 1983), the Parent Daily Report (PDR; Chamberlain & Reid, 1987), and a measure of negative attributions used by Dix and Lochman (1990). Children completed Harter and Pike's (1984) measure of self-perceived competence. Parents were also interviewed in the home and videotaped playing with their child and directing a toy clean-up task. Families were assessed at pre- and posttreatment and at 1-year follow-up.

There were three main findings. First, parents were more likely to drop out of the PMT-VM condition (47.8%) than the experimental condition (20.0%). The majority of parents who dropped out of the PMT-VM condition did so before starting the intervention, suggesting the possibility of unmet expectations for therapist contact, for group participation, or for both. Second, both interventions led to gains from pre- to posttreatment and from pretreatment to follow-up on key measures of problem behavior. Finally, differential results across the two conditions were in line with their respective emphases. Parents in the experimental condition were rated as less controlling during play and children were rated as displaying more positive affect. These parents also reported greater use of parent-child play and their children reported greater gains in self-worth. Parents in the PMT-VM group received higher global ratings of effectiveness from home interviewers and reported fewer problem behaviors on the PDR. Overall, the results of this small study showed that RPT is a promising alternative to PMT but that combining the two approaches makes more sense than using either singly. The RPT model (Cavell, 2000) is an effort in that regard, one designed specifically for working with parents of aggressive, school-age children.

RPT: GUIDING PRINCIPLES AND ORGANIZING FRAMEWORK

In presenting the guiding principles of RPT, we use language that is less cautious and more provocative than is perhaps justified given the state of the science (Cavell, 2000, 2001; Strand, 2000). Our goal is to call for a paradigmatic shift in how practitioners (and researchers) think about the therapeutic task of working with aggressive children and their parents.

Principle 1

The long-term socialization of aggressive children takes precedence over the short-term management of their behavior. We begin by stating the obvious: The goal of socializing children into a system of shared, prosocial commerce (Richters & Waters, 1991) is an important goal for parents generally and a paramount goal for parents of aggressive children. We make this point explicitly because parents can err in over-estimating their capacity to influence some child outcomes (e.g., intellectual functioning) while under-estimating the value of pursuing this fundamental parenting goal. Practitioners should also be careful about drawing parents' attention away from the long-term goal of socializing their aggressive child (Cavell, 2001). Parent Management Training, as its name implies, is designed to help parents better manage children's current behavior. It borrows heavily from techniques used by trained behavior modifiers to increase or decrease the rate of child behavior. A reformulated model of parent-based intervention shifts the focus to the long-term and developmentally significant goal of children's socialization. This single shift in emphasis has tremendous implications for the way practitioners approach the task of working with parents of aggressive children. It is a point of view that better reflects the chronic course of childhood aggression and one that breaks set from traditional notions about how to intervene in the lives of conduct disordered youth (Kazdin, 1993). By adopting a long-term socialization focus, it becomes possible to generate new, empirically testable strategies that are not currently a part of the PMT curriculum.

Principle 2

The parent-child relationship is a useful vehicle for socializing aggressive children. What is it that parents should do if committed to the long-term goal of socializing their aggressive children? Where should they put their time and energy in light of other parenting goals and other demands in their life? We propose that parents of aggressive children are well served when they place primary emphasis on the nature and quality of the parent-child relationship. In proposing a relationship-based model of socialization, we are recommending that parents give time and attention to managing the relationship they have with their aggressive child. This recommendation stands in contrast to the dominant theme of PMT, which is that parents learn to use the principles of operant conditioning to manage their child's behavior. Effectively managing the behavior of an aggressive child is important, but how parents respond to a child's behavior in specific situations cannot be understood apart from the overall context of the parent-child relationship (Baumrind, 1971; Cavell, 2000, 2001; Costanzo, 2002; Dumas, 1996; Kuczynski & Hildebrant, 1997; Maccoby, 1980; Richters & Waters, 1991; Strand, 2000). In its most extreme form, a strictly operant model casts parenting as a rather straightforward process of matching the right behavior modification technique with the specific problem behavior (e.g., Christopherson & Mortweet, 2001). Not only are individual differences among parents and children down played, but their shared history and future as co-participants in a close, emotional relationship are ignored. Most PMT programs are not this extreme, but managing child behavior via the principles of operant conditioning continues to be a dominant theme.

By framing parental socialization efforts in this molar, relationship-based manner, we are not dismissing the role of microlevel processes that function as important building blocks in any close relationship. Instead, we are suggesting that researchers and practitioners appreciate the broader, temporal context in which these processes occur. As noted by Kuczynski and Hildebrandt (1997), a relationship-based model of socialization "gives a time dimension to parent-child interactions" (p. 236) and helps explain how parents and children adapt to past interactions and how they think about and approach future interactions. There are multiple factors that influence the outcome of a given parent-child interaction, only some of which exist within the finite space and time immediately before, during, and after an interaction takes place. A relationship-based view of parents' involvement in the socialization of aggressive children helps clarify this multivariate mix (Cook, 2000; Kochanska & Murray, 2000). It also sheds light on the relation between coercive parent-child interactions and (a) the overall level and relative distribution of reinforcement available to parents and children (both within and outside the dyad), (b) the role of individual differences (e.g., maternal depression, child ADHD), and (c) the impact of distal setting events (e.g., aversive adult-adult interactions) and broader ecological factors (e.g., neighborhood violence, deviant peers).

Principle 3

Socializing relationships provide aggressive children, over time, with emotional acceptance, behavioral containment, and prosocial values. Assuming the parent-child relationship is an important vehicle by which aggressive children are socialized, what are the parameters of an effective, socializing relationship? More specifically, what kind of parent-child relationship is likely to alter the negative developmental trajectory that typifies aggressive children? Definitive answers to these questions await further study, but Cavell (2000) offered the following supposition: *Socializing relationships provide aggressive children, over time, with emotional acceptance, behavioral containment, and prosocial values.* There are a number of implications that flow from this statement. One is that the topography of specific parenting behaviors is less important than function (Jacobson, 1992) and practitioners must be careful about assuming that specific parenting techniques will lead invariably to the conditions necessary for socialization. How parents use punishment, how children interpret and respond to punishment, and how this dynamic changes over time, are not always straightforward in families with aggressive children (Patterson et al., 1992; Schneider, Cavell, & Hughes, 2003).

A second implication is that parents who do not provide these relationship conditions, over time, will greatly reduce the odds of socializing their aggressive child. This would explain why childhood aggression is so stable and so resistant to treatment. Parents struggle to accept and discipline their aggressive children. Some parents of aggressive children also model behaviors and espouse beliefs that are decidedly antisocial (Pettit, Dodge, & Brown, 1988; Tapscott, Frick, Wootten, & Kruh, 1996). Cavell (2000) contends that *all* three factors—acceptance, containment, and prosocial values—are integral to socializing relationships. Moreover, parents have to provide these relationship conditions over an extended period of time. Exactly how long is not known, but given the temporal stability of childhood aggression, the parenting model proposed by Cavell (2000) sets a high standard on what must happen if parents are to have a socializing effect on their aggressive child.

The notion that good parenting is multifaceted is certainly not new, and Baumrind's (1971) observation that authoritative parents combine responsiveness and demandingness is but one, well-known case in point. It is also true that PMT programs routinely target both the positive and the disciplinary aspects of parenting, as witnessed by the common pairing of child-directed and parent-directed skills training (Eyberg, 1988; Forehand & McMahon, 1981; Webster-Stratton, 1987). However, the model of parenting that is implied (if not explicitly presented) in PMT is one that treats positive parenting and discipline practices in a piece-meal fashion. Parents are expected to use both, but rarely considered is the challenge of performing both tasks more or less simultaneously over time in service of the parent-child relationship and children's long-term socialization. The temporal and practical separation of these two parenting tasks can be particularly problematic for parents of aggressive children. These parents have to find ways to restrict their child's use of coercion while not resorting to coercion themselves (Patterson et al., 1992). Thus, what is novel about Cavell's (2000) supposition is that it calls for a model of parenting (and for parent-based interventions) that integrates these often opposing tasks into a single, coordinated system over time.

Principle 4

The ratio of emotional acceptance to behavioral containment is a key parameter of the socializing relationship. Effective parents are said to be those who can successfully navigate two competing demands: (1) the need to impose strict limits on unacceptable behavior and (2) the challenge of maintaining an emotionally positive parent-child relationship (Baumrind, 1971; Maccoby & Martin, 1983). Such parents give children the opportunity to learn right from wrong without feeling threatened emotionally or relationally. Parents of aggressive children find it difficult to meet these competing demands. They pursue one but not the other, they switch back and forth depending on their mood, or they simply give up both (Patterson et al., 1992; Wahler & Dumas, 1989; Webster-Stratton & Spitzer, 1996). How can struggling parents address *both* of these demands in an integrated fashion?

Findings from several recent studies converge on the notion that the ratio of positive to negative exchanges is an important parameter for distinguishing between functional and dysfunctional interpersonal relationships. Relationships tend to be more stable and adaptive when the proportion of positive emotional exchanges consistently exceeds the proportion of negative exchanges (Dumas, 1996; Dumas et al., 1995; Friman, Jones, Smith, Daly, & Larzelere, 1997; Gottman, 1994; Hart & Risley, 1995; Latham, 1992; Wahler, Herring, & Edwards, 2001). For example, Dumas (1996) found that mothers of nondisruptive children expressed positive affect toward their children about 80% of the time (i.e., a 4:1 ratio), whereas mothers of disruptive children expressed positive affect only 30% of the time. Hart and Risley (1995) reported that parents of young preschool children maintained a 6:1 ratio of positive-to-negative comments, and Wahler et al. (2001) found that mothers of nonreferred school-age children initiated only one instruction-compliance exchange for every seven positive social exchanges their child initiated. Other studies report similar ratios for teacher-student, staff-resident, and adult couple relationships (Friman et al., 1997; Gottman, 1994; Latham, 1992). From a Matching Law perspective, a positive interaction ratio gives dyadic partners a total level of reinforcement that serves to reduce the relative value of performing aversive behavior (McDowell, 1982).

These findings have significant implications for parents who would use the parent-child relationship as a means of socializing their aggressive child. The validity and specific value of that positive interaction ratio awaits further research, but presumably it falls within the range of published values (4:1 to 8:1). In parent-child dyads, most negative exchanges occur when parents try to discipline or restrict the child's behavior in some way. It would seem, therefore, that parents of aggressive children operate within a kind of "quota system" in which their efforts to manage misbehavior are constrained by the need to maintain a proper balance of positive to negative exchanges. Needed is a disciplinary approach that is forceful enough to counter children's antisocial tendencies but not so forceful that it spoils the affective quality of the parent-child relationship. In other words, parents of aggressive children will need to adhere to a level of discipline that is continually yoked to the level of positive emotional exchanges.

Most parents, including those with aggressive children, can easily generate reasons why their child *should* perform this or that prosocial behavior and why their child *should* stop using certain undesirable behaviors. But parents' expectations can exist separately from what is feasible, from what is necessary, and from what the parent-child relationship can tolerate. And parents' expectations, however reasonable, will matter little if the affective tone of the parent-child relationship becomes overly harsh and punitive. As noted by Stormshak and colleagues (Stormshak, Bierman, McMahon, Lengua, & Conduct Problems Prevention Research Group, 2000), "punitive discipline is clearly a core parenting deficit and may be the most relevant parenting problem to work on with children and families in clinical settings" (p. 27). Even parents who use empirically supported behavior management techniques are likely to find that aggressive children continue to display some level of noncompliant and coercive behavior (Forgatch, 1991; Roberts & Powers, 1988; Webster-Stratton, 1990). Waging too strong a disciplinary campaign can significantly reduce the ratio of positive to negative exchanges and jeopardize the foundation for child's socialization (Dumas, 1996; Kochanska, 1997; Kochanska & Murray, 2000; Richters & Waters, 1991; Wahler, 1994, 1997).

Principle 5

Characteristics of the parent, the child, and the ecology surrounding the parent-child relationship affect the degree to which socializing relationships are established and maintained. In theory, parents whose children are generally cooperative and rarely coercive are under the same quota system as parents of aggressive children. That possibility is likely to go unappreciated, however, when children meet most if not all of parents' expectations. And if their parents are typically calm and deliberate, then the idea that they are working under a "disciplinary quota" seems even less tenable: They set high expectations for their children, their children meet those high expectations, and the parent-child relationship is none the worse. But families with aggressive, high-risk children often operate under a different set of child-rearing circumstances. The parents are inconsistent and emotionally reactive and the children are uncooperative and coercive. Typically added to this mix are marital strife, economic disadvantage, beleaguered schools, and violent neighborhoods. Individual risk factors and environmental stressors affect substantially the degree to which parents can establish and maintain a socializing relationship. Families with aggressive children carry a disproportionate share of those risk factors and stressors.

Principle 6

The primary goal of parent-based interventions for aggressive children is helping parents establish and maintain a socializing relationship. The parent-child relationship is a useful vehicle for socialization, but conditions needed to ensure a socializing relationship can be elusive for parents of aggressive children. As a result, parent-based intervention for aggressive children is a complex and challenging therapeutic undertaking. Indeed, the term *parent training* fails to convey the complexity of this work, inviting a perception that parents need only participate to benefit. Cavell (2000) used the term *parent therapy*, as in *couple therapy*, to emphasize that the goal is one of helping parents and children improve a relationship that is going badly. There are a number of parallels between current approaches to couple therapy and RPT. Earlier forms of behavioral marital therapy emphasized behavioral exchange and the teaching of communication skills; current approaches have expanded to address (a) individuals differences that affect interpersonal goal disputes and relationship quality, (b) strategies for resolving conflict while maintaining relationship satisfaction, and (c) the value of accepting rather than simply changing one's partner (Christensen & Heavey, 1999; Fincham & Beach, 1999; Gottman, 1994; D. K. Snyder et al., 2006).

For the most part, these parallels have had little impact on the conduct of PMT. Assumptions about the vertical nature of the parent-child relationship appear to have created a rarely crossed boundary between couple therapy research and parent intervention research. As a result, proponents of PMT tend to place greater emphasis on parenting skills than on parenting relationships. Parents are considered the sole arbiters of whether a child's behavior is acceptable or unacceptable (assuming the absence of maltreatment) and whether that behavior is deserving of reward or punishment. When parents and children have conflicting goals, and when children refuse to relinquish their goals, they are frequently seen as noncompliant or misbehaving (Dix, 1991). When goal conflicts between parents and children are cast as child misbehavior, parents are expected to discipline children. But when parents cannot manage their child's "misbehavior," they are seen as inept, a view they may come to believe (Webster-Stratton, & Spitzer, 1996).

In RPT, the parent-child relationship is parents' chief ally for helping their aggressive child. Intervention is defined in relationship terms and is designed to answer the following questions, "How can this parent and this child live peaceably together in a way that does not promote the child's use of antisocial behavior?" The chief goal of RPT is to help parents of aggressive children establish and maintain a socializing relationship characterized by emotional acceptance, behavioral containment, and prosocial values. The challenge, of course, is finding a way to accomplish that goal given various characteristics of the parent, the child, and the child-rearing context. Integral to the RPT model are the twin themes of *minimalism* and *sustainability.* Instead of presenting to parents of aggressive children a standard set of behavior management skills, practitioners help parents identify and implement strategies that provide (at least) minimum coverage but maximum sustainability of the relationship conditions necessary for an effective socializing relationship. Because RPT emphasizes minimal coverage but maximum sustainability of the conditions needed for a socializing relationship, it is important to define those lower boundaries.

Principle 7

Behavioral containment begins with strict limits on aggressive, antisocial behavior. Interventions designed to help parents of aggressive children must address this key issue. The core PMT curriculum certainly reflects the importance of teaching parents to be effective disciplinarians. Unfortunately, the task of disciplining children has been poorly integrated with the goal of maintaining parent-child relationships that effectively balance positive and negative emotional exchanges. Consider the common PMT strategy of encouraging parents to punish acts of noncompliance. The rationale for this strategy is that noncompliance is a "keystone" behavior in the development of children's aggression and should be targeted before other misbehaviors (Loeber & Schmaling, 1985). Noncompliance is also a frequent complaint of parents seeking professional help, and there is a well-documented empirical relation between early displays of child noncompliance and later aggression (Patterson et al., 1992).

Cavell (2001) questioned both the strategy and its underlying assumptions, arguing that for some parent-child dyads it could undermine the affective quality of their relationship. He suggested instead that practitioners tailor their recommendations to fit the characteristics of the parents and children involved. Parents who are not overly punitive could probably follow a compliance-based disciplinary strategy without undue damage to the parent-child relationship, especially if their children were not overly aggressive and antisocial. But parents who are harsh and overly punitive, whose children are aggressive and antisocial, will likely need a different strategy, one in which discipline is both effective *and* selective. In considering which behaviors parents should target, Cavell (2001) drew from the work of Patterson and colleagues (1986; Patterson et al., 1992) to show that the progression from nonphysical coercion to physical aggression is more robust than the link between disobedience and fighting. Developmental studies also reveal that children can be noncompliant without being aggressive (Kuczynski, Kochanska, Radke-Yarrow, & Girnius-Brown, 1987) and that some forms of compliance are unrelated to children's internalization of parents' values (Kochanska, Aksan, & Koenig, 1995). It seems that aggression and other forms of coercion are developmentally more significant than child compliance or noncompliance. As such, effectively containing aggression and other forms of ASB is where discipline should begin, especially for overly reactive parents of highly aggressive children.

Principle 8

Emotional acceptance begins with an implicit message of belonging. A strategy of selective behavioral containment should help to reduce occasions when parents of aggressive children are overly punitive. But what can parents do to increase the *positive* aspects of their relationship? Positive parenting has been traditionally defined in one of two ways. In the behavioral parent training literature, positive parenting is the contingent use of positive reinforcement—praising or rewarding children when they behave in prosocial ways. In the developmental literature, positive parenting is often defined as warm involvement (Baumrind, 1971; Maccoby & Martin, 1983). Both approaches to positive parenting have empirical support, but parents of aggressive children could find it difficult to use and sustain either approach. Some parents lack the disposition to be warm and agreeable and others do not attend well enough to child behavior to be contingently reinforcing (Wahler & Dumas, 1989).

An alternative strategy for enhancing the ratio of positive to negative exchanges is to view positive parenting in terms of emotional acceptance (Cavell, 2000). Cavell defined parental acceptance as any behavior that fosters in children a sense of autonomy while not threatening their relationship security. Critical here is the distinction between change and acceptance as ways of improving the quality of close relationships (Jacobson, 1992). As Jacobson (1992) observed, a healthy relationship "involves the ability to accept the inherent unsolvability of some relationship problems" (p. 502). The construct of emotional acceptance is also akin to what Baumeister and Leary (1995) refer to as the *need to belong,* defined as "the need for frequent, nonaversive interactions within an ongoing relational bond" (p. 497). Based on their extensive review of the research literature, Baumeister and Leary argued that the need to belong is a fundamental human motivation. The value of defining positive parenting as emotional acceptance is that parents who are ill equipped to be warm and involved or who fail to track and reinforce good behavior can still adopt and maintain *a posture of acceptance* (Cavell, 2000), essentially a default mode of interacting in which parental intervention and emotional rejection are the exception and not the rule.

Emotional acceptance is certainly easier to maintain if parents have the capacity to tolerate or detach from child behaviors that are unpleasant or annoying. But if that is not possible, then parents may have to avoid interactions that are likely to challenge a child's sense of belonging. Some parents of aggressive children are capable of engaging in frequent parent-child interactions as a way to communicate *explicit* messages of affection, warmth, or praise; other parents cannot or will not do this consistently. Too often, exchanges with their children devolve into negative affectivity and inadvertent messages of emotional rejection for children. To push this latter group of parents to interact more frequently and more positively with an aggressive child could be ill advised. At minimum, they will need to steer clear of interactions that lead predictably to harsh parenting and unnecessary control attempts, aiming instead for more understated ways to convey a sense of belonging. In short, for parents of aggressive children, emotional acceptance begins with a strategy of selective engagement and an *implicit* message of belonging.

Principle 9

Prosocial values begin with explicit statements against antisocial behavior. Children whose parents appropriately balance emotional acceptance and behavioral containment have a great advantage over other children: They are given a clear message that they belong in the relationship and a clear message that certain behaviors do not belong in the relationship. But there are other parental "messages" that are important for socialization. We are referring primarily to the values parents espouse and the behaviors they model. Recent studies document that children are influenced by the explicitly endorsed values and behavioral norms of their family members (e.g., Bogenschneider, Wu, Raffaelli, & Tsay, 1998; Brody, Flor, Hollett-Wright, & McCoy, 1998). For example, Bogenschneider et al. (1998) found that parents' values regarding alcohol use moderated the relation between parenting practices and adolescents' reports of substance use. Specifically, the predicted relation between paternal monitoring and adolescent substance use was stronger among adolescents whose fathers held more disapproving views of alcohol use.

If children's participation in a socializing relationship facilitates the internalization of parental values (Cavell, 2000; Kuczynksi & Hildebrandt, 1997; Richters & Waters, 1991), then it would be helpful if those values were clearly prosocial. That may not be the case, however, especially for aggressive children whose parents have a greater likelihood of evincing antisocial personality disorder or a history of criminal behavior than parents of nonaggressive children (Frick & Jackson, 1993; Tapscott, Frick, Wootton, & Kruh, 1996). Children prone to engaging in ASB also need more than the absence of antisocial norms; they need strong, explicit messages *against* ASB. Brody et al. (1998) found that family norms against alcohol use that departed even slightly from an abstinence-based message were more likely to be misinterpreted by children with high-risk temperaments. Therefore, our recommendation is that parents of aggressive children begin efforts to promote prosocial values by making explicit statements against ASB.

In most PMT programs, the goal of helping parents give voice to prosocial values is more implicit than explicit. The issue of whether parents' own behavior and beliefs are, in fact, prosocial is also rarely addressed (Cavell, 2000). Instead, the prosocial or antisocial nature of parents' behavior is usually treated as background text that sets the upper limit on children's socialization. Reluctance to focus more directly on parents' behavior and beliefs may reflect concerns that such actions are intrusive or should be addressed only in the context of child discipline. Such concerns do not deter clinicians who work from a Multisystemic Therapy (MST; Henggeler et al., 1998) model. In fact, a guiding principle of MST is promoting responsible behavior in both children and parents. Lacking are reliable, nonthreatening, and empirically supported strategies that practitioners can use to highlight the more prosocial aspects of parents' belief system. For example, Cavell (2000) described a procedure in which the topics of family norms and parents' beliefs are broached through an exercise in which children are asked to make a poster displaying the family's household rules. Because families of aggressive children may lack such rules, this exercise provides an opportunity and a prompt for parents to speak openly about their values and beliefs and about their future expectations for their children.

Principle 10

Effective parent-based interventions for aggressive children are multisystemic. To this point, the guiding principles of RPT have centered on helping parents establish and maintain a socializing relationship with their aggressive, antisocial child. But it would be a mistake to conclude that effective parent-based interventions for aggressive children are narrowly dyadic in scope. Other factors influence children's socialization experiences, and the influence is often mediated through perturbations in parenting practices or family functioning (Patterson et al., 1992). Marital conflict, divorce, family violence, parental psychopathology, and economic deprivation are common examples of the disruptive forces that can interfere with parenting and distort how families operate. When issues are addressed in the context of parenting training, it is usually through additional training modules (e.g., communication skills, problem solving, coping, social support) tacked onto the primary PMT curriculum (Cavell, 2000). This approach to enhancing PMT has led to a rather long list of skills that parents theoretically lack and that practitioners should ideally teach. For example, the Triple P program encompasses 40 different parenting skills from 9 different domains of functioning (Sanders, Markie-Dadds, & Turner, 2003). Kazdin and Whitely (2003), who found support for their added-on Parental Problem Solving component, questioned the value of enhancing PMT outcomes in this way:

> One cannot keep adding components to a treatment that might enhance or indeed actually does enhance therapeutic change. . . . The methodological and design constraints limit how much one can add to an evidence-based treatment and expect to show an effect, even if there is one. From a more clinical and service delivery standpoint, the strategy of adding components to treatment has further limitations. Patient attrition, already high in child, adolescent, and adult therapy (40% to 60%) is partially a function of the demands made of the client (Kazdin, Holland, & Crowley, 1997) and duration of treatment (Phillips, 1985). Adding a component to treatment that increases either one of these is quite likely to cause greater attrition so that fewer patients will complete treatment. Also of course, there is the monetary cost. (p. 513)

RPT takes a different approach by integrating into its model the task of enhancing two critical, but nondyadic areas of functioning: *family structure* and *parental self-care.*

If the primary goal of RPT is helping parents establish and maintain a socializing relationship, then the utility of addressing issues of family structure and parental self-care is readily apparent. Relevant here is a recent study by Patterson et al. (2004). These investigators found that PMT led to reductions in *maternal* depression 6 months posttreatment and it was this change that predicted continued gains in parenting and child functioning over the next 18 months. Patterson et al. (2004) offered this observation, "Perhaps for many, simply being enrolled in a structured program is associated with a reduction in depression (i.e., now there is renewed hope)" (p. 631). Parents who are overwhelmed and continually despondent, who rely on their children for emotional support, or who refuse to accept the role of their family's leader cannot provide aggressive children with the kind of relationship they need to develop into law-abiding citizens. But if parents have reliable self-care strategies and adaptive family structures, they can contend for several years with the challenge of providing a relationship that combines emotional acceptance, behavioral

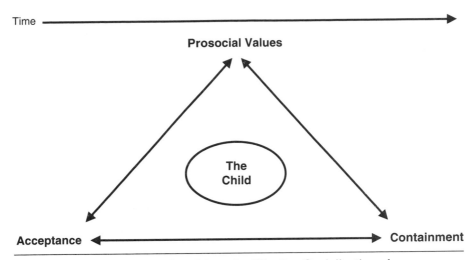

Figure 12.1 Relationship Conditions for Effective Socialization of Aggressive Children.

containment, and prosocial values. Finding reliable ways to refuel and compelling reasons to re-engage in the difficult task of parenting are not luxuries for parents of aggressive children. Similarly, without adequate family structure and organization, parents of aggressive children will fall prey to automatic but less adaptive ways to parent and to cope (Strand & Cavell, 2006).

Figures 12.1 and 12.2 illustrate the RPT approach of working with parents of aggressive children. Figure 12.1 depicts the relationship conditions

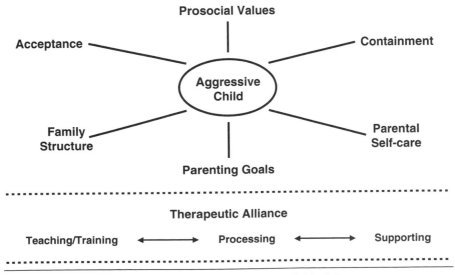

Figure 12.2 The Responsive Parent Therapy (RPT) Model.

considered necessary for a socializing relationship. These relationship conditions are embedded within the larger RPT framework shown in Figure 12.2, which also depicts those aspects that are needed to support and sustain an effective socializing relationship: (a) clearly stated and long-term parenting goals, (b) an organized and adaptive family structure, and (c) a reliable system of parental self-care. Also present in Figure 12.2, but not reflected in the guiding principles of RPT, is the critical issue of establishing a strong therapeutic alliance when working with parents of aggressive children. Illustrated is the tension between teaching or training parents to use skills they might lack and the need to support parents as they struggle to perform their parenting duties day-in an day-out. Understanding and negotiating this tension requires a continual effort to process with parents their reaction to what is happening in parent therapy. Cavell (2000) described processing as the shuttle between teaching/training and supporting and the effective therapist uses this shuttle to go back and forth as needed to move parents forward at a pace that feels safe and collaborative.

Tailoring Responsive Parent Therapy to Meet the Needs of Individual Families

Most parent-training programs follow a standard sequence. For example, a common PMT sequence is to train parents to use positive parenting skills (via the Child's Game or Child-Directed Interaction sessions) before exposing them to disciplinary skills (via the Parent's Game or Parent-Directed Interaction sessions). In the PMT program used by Patterson and colleagues (Patterson, 1975), training begins with a focus on understanding behavioral principles and the importance of tracking a child's behavior and its consequences. In CREFT, child-directed play skills are taught more or less simultaneously with limit setting skills (Guerney, 1983) and as training proceeds, the focus shifts from in-session interactions to weekly home play sessions and then to nonplay interactions between parents and children (Guerney, 1983).

There has been little research to guide practitioners as they decide how to sequence various parent-training components. One exception is a study that evaluated the merits of beginning Parent-Child Interaction Therapy (PCIT) with either the Child's Game or the Parent's Game (Eisenstadt, Eyberg, McNeil, Newcomb, & Funderburk, 1993). No support was found for starting with child-directed interaction training but some evidence emerged for reversing the usual sequence (Eisenstadt et al., 1993). Without further research, practitioners will have to rely on clinical judgment when deciding how to sequence intervention components. The issue is perhaps most relevant to practitioners who work with a group of parents as opposed to individual families. In a group format, each parent is exposed to all training components in a set sequence. With one family, practitioners can set the pace of training depending on the rate at which parents master key skills. This is the format used in PCIT (see Hembree-Kigin & McNeil, 1995).

Tailoring interventions to fit the needs of individual families and parents also requires an understanding of which treatment components are essential and which are perhaps not necessary. In most PMT programs, an abiding assumption is that poor parenting is due to a deficit in proper parenting skills. It is further assumed that the benefits of PMT result from parents' acquisition of new parenting skills, enabling them to manage better their child's behavior. These strong assumptions about parents' skill deficits can be contrasted with a performance model of ineffective parenting (Patterson, 1997). The distinction between acquired skills and observed performance is often subtle and complex (O'Donohue, 2003), but there is evidence that parents of aggressive or conduct problem children have skills and abilities that belie their typically poor performance (Dumas, 1996; Green, Forehand, & McMahon, 1978; Prinz & Miller, 1991; Webster-Stratton, 1994). Parenting, like other kinds of interpersonal behavior, is multiply determined, and skill level is but one part of a larger causal mix that includes other parent variables, child effects, contextual features, and recurring transactions among these factors (Cavell & Strand, 2003; Wahler & Dumas, 1989). Skill level does not appear to be the single, monolithic difference between parents who recognize and avoid a pattern of coercive parent-child interaction and parents who seem stuck in this destructive dance. More accurate is to assume that parents possess a number of useful skills but are failing to use those skills when it is important to do so (Cavell, 2000, 2001; Dumas et al., 1995). This performance-based view of inept parenting also parallels Patterson's (1986) performance model of children's ASB.

If poor parenting is not simply or always due to parents' skill deficits, then what is the job of the parent therapist? Where should practitioners focus their attention and how should they sequence their work? Below we describe two different approaches to implementing the RPT model. Each approach assumes that parents possess some basic skills and that skills training should proceed only after it is clear that parents lack the necessary skills.

Minimal Treatment Approach

With this approach, practitioners present a truncated version of RPT designed to be brief, problem-focused, and minimally taxing of parents. This approach is best suited for parents with relatively intact relationship skills whose child is less severely aggressive and whose family is not experiencing extreme levels of stress and chaos. Such parents usually need help because of a recent disruption in their life (e.g., divorce) or because their children possess characteristics that make them particularly hard to manage. Paradoxically, the minimal treatment approach can also be useful when working with parents who are difficult to engage in treatment or who are unwilling to do extensive therapeutic work. By paring down RPT to this minimal core, such parents could benefit despite their refusal to participate more fully.

The minimal treatment approach to RPT comprises three steps. Therapists begin by fostering an alliance with parents based on emotional support and understanding. Second, therapists help parents to identify parent-child relationship goals that are realistic given the child's dispositional characteristics. And third, therapists help parents establish a clear and finite set of rules about those child behaviors that are strictly prohibited. Using this minimal treatment approach, practitioners can address a number of significant issues without pursuing extensive skills training that may not be warranted. Retained in this truncated model of RPT is the importance of working collaboratively (albeit briefly) with parents (Webster-Stratton & Herbert, 1994). Attention is also given to the degree of fit between parents' goals and the type of child with whom they are trying to live and socialize (Sheeber & Johnson, 1994). Establishing an explicit set of rules about prohibited behaviors infuses several aspects of the RPT model. Insisting that certain behaviors are not allowed is designed to augment parents' efforts at containment, but the finite nature of the list can also help parents curtail their use of nattering and harsh criticism while increasing the overall level of acceptance in the parent-child relationship. Greater selectivity in containment also means less overall work by parents who are prone to feeling fatigued and in need of self-care, and creating and announcing explicit rules is an example of endorsing prosocial values. Finally, establishing a clear set of rules involves a level of planning, organization, and stability that can enhance overall family structure. If problems persist after using the minimal treatment approach, then practitioners will need to work closely with parents to reaffirm the therapeutic alliance and to reconcile any discrepancies that may exist between practitioners' goals and parents' goals. Once this is done, then other intervention components can be phased in as needed.

Outside-In Treatment Approach

This approach to implementing RPT assumes the need for more extensive intervention than that provided by the minimal treatment approach. A more extensive regimen of parent therapy would be indicated if, for example, the target child and siblings were all fairly aggressive and the sole head of the house was a young parent with a history of problematic relationships. As in the minimal treatment approach, therapists begin the outside-in approach by attending to the overlapping issues of the working alliance and the goals for parenting and parent therapy. Therapists would then shift their attention to the RPT components of family structure and parental self-care. These components address issues that fall "outside" the parent-child dyad but are critical to effective parenting. Obvious gaps in these areas can be addressed in a targeted fashion. For example, psychological boundaries separating parents from children may be diffuse, daily and weekly routines may be absent, or parents may be overlooking the importance of scheduling needed self-care. Of course, helping parents develop rules about prohibited behaviors, as is done in the minimal treatment approach, should also be a part of the focus on family structure in the outside-in approach. Each of these concerns involves a systemic issue that transcends a direct focus on dyadic skills. Only after considerable work in the areas of family structure and self-care would therapists address remaining issues related to parental acceptance and containment. It is in these areas that parents will likely require specific skills training.

The idea here is one of working outside-in when it comes to righting the parent-child relationship. By addressing systemic issues first, practitioners do not assume automatically that parents are deficient in dyadic parenting skills (Webster-Stratton, 1994). The early emphasis on system changes may well produce what family therapists call second-order or nonlinear changes in the parent-child relationship (Nichols & Schwartz, 2004). From a social learning point of view, systemwide changes can also affect the contingencies that influence the performance of key parenting practices. By restructuring the family hierarchy, by establishing clear rules and routines, or by creating a periodic respite from the toils of parenting, parents can create qualitative shifts in how they interact with their children. Once these systemwide components are implemented, practitioners can discern if parents need additional help learning to execute the dyadic skills of emotional acceptance and behavioral containment. Training in these two areas requires more extensive work and progress tends to occur in a more linear and incremental fashion than work in other, systemic areas. Use of the outside-in approach to RPT does have the disadvantage that parents lacking critical dyadic skills must first undergo treatment components that may or may not be relevant. Of course, if practitioners were to learn that family structure and parental self-care are pockets of strength for parents, then it would be important to move quickly to dyadic skills training.

CASE STUDY

The RPT model views parent-based interventions as opportunities to help parents identify and implement effective strategies and sustainable strategies for socializing their aggressive, high-risk children. Responsive Parent

Therapy also assumes that parents' best ally in this campaign is a parent-child relationship that provides children, over time, with minimum coverage but maximum sustainability of the conditions necessary for effective socialization (emotional acceptance, behavioral containment, and prosocial values). An important task facing practitioners is to discern what that relationship would look like for any given parent and child. Hopefully, the principles discussed earlier will serve as a useful guide for practitioners.

That being said, it would be grossly misleading to suggest that effective parent therapy is simply about being clever and knowledgeable. The real challenge when working with parents of aggressive children is being responsive to their needs, to their concerns, and to their current parenting goals. The successful therapist draws inspiration from parents' existing skills and resources and continually strives to work collaboratively, even if those parents are hanging on to ill-advised goals and resisting the help they need. When parent therapy is not collaborative and parents are not fully engaged, it will not be productive. Conversely, when therapists and parents work through bouts of resistance and parents remain hopeful and engaged in therapy, their children are likely to show significant and lasting gains (Stoolmiller et al., 1993).

It would be hard to over emphasize the value of working in a responsive and collaborative manner with parents of aggressive children (Cavell, 2000; Webster-Stratton & Herbert, 1994). The term *responsive* in Responsive Parent Therapy signals not only the need for parents to be responsive to children, but also the need for therapists to be responsive to parents. Finding and implementing the strategies by which parents can provide a long-term, socializing relationship is not only a core goal of RPT; it is also critical to the child's later adjustment. However, it is not the kind of goal that parents bring to therapy.

How can practitioners foster and sustain a collaborative alliance with parents while also moving forward with the guiding principles of RPT? Both common sense and empirical research on common factors in psychotherapy (Snyder, Scott, & Cheavens, 1999; Wampold et al., 1997) would suggest that a good place to start is giving parents hope that things will be better for them and for their children (see also Patterson et al., 2004). Kashdan et al. (2002) found that parental hope predicted parenting quality family functioning, even when controlling for child symptoms. Unfortunately, hope emanates from "trust in the reliability of self-initiated cause-and-effect relationships" (Shorey, Snyder, Rand, Hockemeyer, & Feldman, 2002, p. 323) and parents of aggressive children see little evidence that parenting has an effect on their child's behavior. Shorey et al. (2002) also found that high-hope individuals "do not persevere in pursuing untenable goals, but instead disengage and regoal when emotional feedback or contradictory environmental inputs indicate that positive outcomes are no longer probable" (p. 328). Thus a useful tactic for promoting hope in parents is to offer them new goals. In PMT, the goals tend to be the promise of new parenting skills and a well-managed child, but if these goals are a poor fit for parents of aggressive children, failure will ensue and hope will erode.

In RPT, therapists help parents identify realistic parenting goals that offer minimal coverage but maximum sustainability of the conditions needed for a socializing relationship. Therapists help parents to find new, more adaptive goals when they first offer opportunities to reflect on current goals, many of which are automatic and unstated. The task here is to listen long and carefully to what parents say about their child, about themselves, and about parenting (Harwood & Eyberg, 2004). What would that look or sound like? In the following (fictional) exchange between parent and practitioner, the focus is on the issue of parental self-care, although many other issues could have been used. It is presented as but one example of how therapists can be responsive to parents as a way to help parents be more responsive to their children.

PRACTITIONER: It doesn't sound like you have any time to yourself—time when you can stop, catch your breath, and think.

PARENT: Are you kidding? I don't have time to go to the bathroom!

PRACTITIONER: Would it help if you had some time-off? A lot of parents with hard-to-manage children tell me it helps, especially if they know when the breaks are going to be and if they don't have to wait too long for the next one.

PARENT: Oh, I'd love to go to a movie, or to the mall, or just watch TV without being interrupted every 5 seconds, but it's not going to happen.

PRACTITIONER: Is that because it can't happen or because you would feel too guilty doing it—or both?

PARENT: I might feel a little guilty, but mainly it would be that my kids and my schedule won't allow it.

PRACTITIONER: So you're stuck.

PARENT: That's right. Trapped!

PRACTITIONER: Do you feel trapped? If so, how do you do it? How do you keep going day-in and day-out with all you have to do?

PARENT: Beats the hell out of me! Some days I can't do it. I might call in sick to work or if I go to work, I'll be so tired and mean by the end of the day that I know I can't be good for my kids.

PRACTITIONER: And I bet on the weekend you're exhausted and that's when your kids need you.

PARENT: That's right. In fact, sometimes I think I get more rest at work than at home!

PRACTITIONER: Who knows how rough it is for you?

PARENT: No one, really. Maybe my mom and my sister, but they got their own problems and half the time all they do is tell me what I'm doing is wrong. I don't need that.

PRACTITIONER: No, you don't. Do they ever help?

PARENT: Every once in a while, if I'm desperate, I'll ask my mom to keep the kids, but it's usually not worth the hassle.

PRACTITIONER: Is your time at work rewarding at all? Is it a break from parenting or just another source of stress?

PARENT: I have some good days at work and I get along with a couple of the women who work there. But it's a long day and we don't get many chances to rest. It's hard.

PRACTITIONER: Do you see things getting better any time soon or do you think it will be a while before you'll have some time to yourself and a less stressful life.

PARENT: I don't expect it to change right away unless I win the lottery! Otherwise, I'm stuck with waiting for the kids to get older and stay out of trouble—or get locked up because they finally went too far with all their stuff.

PRACTITIONER: Will you make it till then?

PARENT: I'll have to.

PRACTITIONER: How? Is there something about you as a person or as a parent that keeps you going?

PARENT: I do love my kids and I want them to have a better life than I did. But it's hard, you know.

PRACTITIONER: You've certainly convinced me of that! But I'm not sure if you can make things better for them unless things get better for you first. Does that make sense?

PARENT: Maybe, but I don't see how that'll happen.

PRACTITIONER: You're right: Whatever changes you can make to take better care of yourself are probably not going to be very big and they won't be easy—at least at the start. But I'm still wondering if you even think it even makes sense to say, "If I help myself, I help my children"?

PARENT: I'm not sure.

PRACTITIONER: Children respect and take after adults who are strong and caring. I've seen how caring you can be, but your kids also need you to be strong and healthy. So, one of the best ways to help your kids is to be the healthiest person you can be. That means taking care of your self physically, emotionally, and for some parents, spiritually.

PARENT: Hmmm . . .

PRACTITIONER: I'm not talking about an occasional break to go shopping or take a bubble bath. I'm talking about changing the way you take care of yourself, the way you see yourself, and, eventually, the way your children see you.

PARENT: I don't know about all that.

PRACTITIONER: Hard to imagine, huh?

PARENT: You got that right.

PRACTITIONER: How about some examples of what I've seen other parents do to take better care of themselves? Some of these won't fit your situation, but at least you'll have a better idea of what I'm talking about. For example, one mother . . .

REFERENCES

Abidin, R. (1983). *Parenting stress index manual.* Charlottesville, VA: Pediatric Psychology Press.

Achenbach, T. M. (1991). *Manual for the child behavior checklist and revised child behavior profile.* Burlington, VA: Author.

American Psychiatric Association. (1994). *Diagnostic and statistical manual of mental disorders* (4th ed.). Washington, DC: Author.

Barlow, D. H., Allen, L. B., & Choate, M. L. (2004). Toward a unified treatment for emotional disorders. *Behavior Therapy, 35,* 205–230.

Baumeister, R. T., & Leary, M. R. (1995). The need to belong: Desire for interpersonal attachments as a fundamental human motivation. *Psychological Bulletin, 117,* 497–529.

Baumrind, D. (1971). Current patterns of parental authority. *Developmental Psychology Monographs, 4,* 1–103.

Berliner, L., & Conte, J. R. (1990). The process of victimization: The victims' perspective. *Child Abuse and Neglect, 14,* 29–40.

Beutler, L. E. (2000). David and Goliath: When empirical and clinical standards of practice meet. *American Psychologist, 55,* 997–1007.

Bogenschneider, K., Wu, M., Raffaeli, M., & Tsay, J. C. (1998). Parental influences on adolescent peer orientation and substance use: The interface of a parenting practices and values. *Child Development, 69,* 1672–1688.

Boivin, M., Hymel, S., & Bukowski, W. M. (1995). The roles of social withdrawal, peer rejection, and victimization by peers in predicting loneliness and depressed mood in childhood. *Development and Psychopathology, 7,* 765–786.

Brestan, E. V., & Eyberg, S. M. (1998). Effective psychosocial treatments of conduct-disordered children and adolescents: 29 years, 82 studies, and 5,272 kids. *Journal of Clinical Child Psychology, 27,* 180–189.

Brody, G. H., Flor, D. L., Hollett-Wright, N., & McCoy, J. K. (1998). Children's development of alcohol use norms: Contributions of parent and sibling norms, children's temperaments, and parent-child discussions. *Journal of Family Psychology, 12,* 209–219.

Bugental, D. B., Lewis, J. C., Lin, E. K., Lyon, J., & Kopeikin, H. (1999). In charge but not in control: The management of teaching relationships by adults with low perceived power. *Developmental Psychology, 35,* 1367–1378.

Campbell, S. B., Pierce, E. W., March, C. L., Ewing, L. J., & Szumowski, E. K. (1994). Hard-to-manage preschool boys: Symptomatic behavior across contexts and time. *Child Development, 65,* 836–851.

Caspi, A., Moffitt, T. E., Silva, P. A., Stouthamer-Loeber, M., Krueger, R. F., & Schmutte, P. S. (1994). Are some people crime prone? Replications of the personality-crime relationship across nation, gender, race, and method. *Criminology, 35*(2), 163–195.

Cavell, T. A. (1996, August). *Responsive parent training: A preliminary trial.* Paper presented at the 14th biennial meeting of the International Society for the Study of Behavioral Development, Quebec City, Canada.

Cavell, T. A. (2000). *Working with parents of aggressive children: A practitioner's guide.* Washington, DC: American Psychological Association.

Cavell, T. A. (2001). Updating our approach to parent training: Pt. I. The case against targeting noncompliance. *Clinical Psychology: Science and Practice, 8,* 299–318.

Cavell, T. A., Hymel, S., Malcolm, K., & Seay, A. (2006). Socialization and the development of antisocial behavior: Models and interventions. In J. E. Grusec & P. D. Hastings (Eds.), *Handbook of socialization* (pp. 42–67). New York: Guilford Press.

Cavell, T. A., & Strand, P. S. (2003). Parent-based interventions for aggressive, antisocial children: Adapting to a bilateral lens. In L. Kuczynski (Ed.), *Handbook of dynamics in parent-child relations* (pp. 395–419). Thousand Oaks, CA: Sage.

Chamberlain, P., & Reid, J. B. (1987). Parent observation and report of child symptoms. *Behavioral Analysis, 9,* 97–109.

Chamberlain, P., & Reid, J. B. (1998). Comparison of two community alternatives to incarceration for chronic juvenile offenders. *Journal of Consulting and Clinical Psychology, 66,* 624–633.

Christensen, A., & Heavey, C. L. (1999). Interventions for couples. *Annual Review of Psychology, 50,* 1165–1190.

Christophersen, E. R., & Mortweet, S. L. (2001). *Treatments that work with children: Empirically supported strategies for managing childhood problems.* Washington, DC: American Psychological Association.

Clutton-Brock, T. H. (1991). *The evolution of parental care.* Princeton, NJ: Princeton University Press.

Collins, W. A., Maccoby, E., Steinberg, L., Hetherington, E. M., & Bornstein, M. (2000). Contemporary research on parenting: The case for nature *and* nurture. *American Psychologist, 55,* 218–232.

Collins, W. A., Maccoby, E., Steinberg, L., Hetherington, E. M., & Bornstein, M. H. (2001). Toward nature WITH nurture. *American Psychologist, 56,* 171–173.

Conger, R. D., & Simons, R. L. (1997). Life-course contingencies in the development of adolescent antisocial behavior: A matching law approach. In T. P. Thornberry (Ed.), *Advances in criminological theory* (pp. 55–99). New York: Aldine.

Cook, W. L. (2000). Interpersonal influence in family systems: A social relations model analysis. *Child Development, 72,* 1179–1197.

Costanzo, P. (2002). Social exchange and the developing syntax of moral orientation. In W. G. Graziano & B. Laursen (Eds.), *Social exchange in development* (pp. 41–52). San Francisco: Jossey-Bass.

DeGarmo, D. S., Patterson, G. R., & Forgatch, M. S. (2004). How do outcomes in a specified parent training intervention maintain or wane over time? *Prevention Science, 5*(2), 73–89.

DeGrandpre, R. J. (2000). A science of meaning: Can behaviorism bring meaning to psychological science? *American Psychologist, 55,* 721–739.

Dishion, T. J., Capaldi, D., Spracklen, K. M., & Li, F. (1995). Peer ecology of male adolescent drug use. *Development and Psychopathology, 7,* 803–824.

Dishion, T. J., McCord, J., & Poulin, F. (1999). When interventions harm: Peer groups and problem behavior. *American Psychologist, 54,* 755–764.

Dix, T. (1991). The affective organization of parenting: Adaptive and maladaptive processes. *Psychological Bulletin, 110,* 3–25.

Dix, T., & Lochman, J. E. (1990). Social cognition and negative reactions to children: A comparison of mothers of aggressive and nonaggressive boys. *Journal of Social and Clinical Psychology, 9,* 418–438.

Dodge, K. (1983). Behavioral antecedents of peer social status. *Child Development, 53,* 1386–1399.

Dodge, K. A., & Pettit, G. S. (2003). A biopsychosocial model of the development of chronic conduct problems in adolescence. *Developmental Psychology, 39,* 349–371.

Dumas, J. (1996). Why was this child referred? Interactional correlates of referral status in families of children with disruptive behavior problems. *Journal of Clinical Child Psychology, 25,* 106–115.

Dumas, J. E., & LaFreniere, P. J. (1993). Mother-child relationships as sources of support or stress: A comparison of competent, average, aggressive, and anxious dyads. *Child Development, 64,* 1732–1754.

Dumas, J. E., LaFreniere, P. J., & Serketich, W. J. (1995). "Balance of power": A transactional analysis of control in mother-child dyads involving socially competent, aggressive, and anxious children. *Journal of Abnormal Psychology, 104,* 104–113.

Eddy, J. M., & Chamberlain, P. (2000). Family management and deviant peer association as mediators of the impact of treatment condition on youth antisocial behavior. *Journal of Consulting and Clinical Psychology, 68,* 857–863.

Eisenstadt, T. H., Eyberg, S., McNeil, C. B., Newcomb, K. N., & Funderburk, B. (1993). Parent-child interaction therapy with behavior problem children: Relative effectiveness of two stages and overall treatment outcome. *Journal of Clinical Child Psychology, 22,* 42–51.

Elliott, M., Browne, K., & Kilcoyne, J. (1995). Child sexual abuse prevention: What offenders tell us. *Child Abuse and Neglect, 19,* 579–594.

Eyberg, S. (1988). Parent-child interaction therapy: Integration of traditional and behavioral concerns. *Child and Family Behavior Therapy, 10*(1), 33–45.

Fergusson, D. M., Woodward, L. J., & Horwood, L. J. (1999). Childhood peer relationship problems and young people's involvement with deviant peers in adolescence. *Journal of Abnormal Child Psychology, 27,* 357–369.

Fincham, F. D., & Beach, S. R. H. (1999). Conflict in marriage: Implications for working with couples. *Annual Review of Psychology, 50,* 47–77.

Forehand, R. L., & McMahon, R. J. (1981). *Helping the noncompliant child: A clinician's guide to parent training.* New York: Guilford Press.

Forgatch, M. S. (1991). The clinical science vortex: A developing theory of antisocial behavior. In D. J. Pepler & K. H. Rubin (Eds.), *The development and treatment of childhood aggression* (pp. 291–315). Hillsdale, NY: Erlbaum.

Frick, P. J. (1998). Conduct disorders. In T. Ollendick & M. Hersen (Ed.), *Handbook of child psychopathology* (3rd ed., pp. 213–237). New York: Plenum Press.

Frick, P. J., & Jackson, Y. K. (1993). Family functioning and childhood antisocial behavior: Yet another reinterpretation. *Journal of Clinical Child Psychology, 22,* 410–419.

Frick, P. J., Stickle, T. R., Dandreaux, D. M., Farrell, J. M., & Kimonis, E. R. (2005). Callous-unemotional traits in predicting the severity and stability of conduct problems and delinquency. *Journal of Abnormal Child Psychology, 33,* 471–487.

Friman, P. C., Jones, M., Smith, G., Daly, D. L., & Larzelere, R. (1997). Decreasing disruptive behavior by adolescent boys in residential care by increasing their positive to negative interactional ratios. *Behavior Modification, 21,* 470–486.

Ginsberg, B. G. (1989). Training parents as therapeutic agents with foster/adoptive children using the filial approach. In C. E. Schaefer & J. M. Briesmeister (Eds.), *Handbook of parent training: Parents as co-therapsits for children's behavior problems* (pp. 442–478). Oxford, England: Wiley.

Goldstein, A. P., Sprafkin, R. P., Gershaw, N. J., & Klein, P. (1997). *Skill streaming the adolescent.* Champaign, IL: Research Press.

Gottman, J. M. (1994). *What predicts divorce?* Hillsdale, NJ: Erlbaum.

Green, K. D., Forehand, R., & McMahon, R. J. (1978). Parental manipulation of compliance and noncompliance in normal and deviant children. *Behavior Modification, 3,* 245–266.

Grusec, J. E., & Hastings, P. D. (2006). *Handbook of socialization: Theory and research.* New York: Guilford Press.

Guerney, L. F. (1983). Introduction to filial therapy: Training parents as therapists. In P. A. Keller & L. G. Ritt (Eds.), *Innovations in clinical practice: Vol. 2. A source book* (pp. 26–39). Sarasota, FL: Professional Resource Exchange.

Guerney, L. F., & Guerney, B. G., Jr. (1985). The relationship enhancement family of family therapies. In L. L'Abate & M. Milan (Eds.), *Handbook of family therapy* (pp. 506–524). New York: Wiley.

Guerney, L. F., & Guerney, B. G., Jr. (1987). Integrating child and family therapy. *Psychotherapy, 24,* 609–614.

Hanlon, T. E., Blatchley, R. J., Bennett-Sears, T., O'Grady, K. E., Rose, M., & Callaman, J. M. (2005). Vulnerability of children of incarcerated addict mothers: Implications for preventive intervention. *Children and Youth Services Review, 27,* 67–84.

Harris, J. R. (1995). Where is the child's environment? A group socialization theory of development. *Psychological Review, 102,* 458–489.

Harris, J. R. (1998). *The nurture assumption.* New York: Free Press.

Hart, B., & Risley, T. R. (1995). *Meaningful differences in the everyday experience of young American children.* Baltimore: Paul H. Brookes.

Harter, S., & Pike, R. (1984). The pictorial scale of perceived competence and social acceptance for young children. *Child Development, 55,* 1962–1982.

Harwood, M. D., & Eyberg, S. M. (2004). Therapist verbal behavior early in treatment: Relation to successful completion of parent-child interaction therapy. *Journal of Clinical Child and Adolescent Psychology, 33*(3), 601–612.

Hembree-Kigin, T., & McNeil, C. B. (1995). *Parent-child interaction therapy.* New York: Plenum Press.

Henggeler, S. W., Schoenwald, S. K., Borduin, C. M., Rowland, M. D., & Cunningham, P. B. (1998). *Multisystemic treatment of antisocial behavior in children and adolescents.* Pacific Grove, CA: Brooks/Cole.

Henry, D., Guerra, N., Huesmann, R., Tolan, P., VanAcker, R., & Eron, L. (2000). Normative influences on aggression in urban elementary school classrooms. *American Journal of Community Psychology, 28*(1), 59–81.

Herrnstein, R. J. (1970). On the law of effect. *Journal of the Experimental Analysis of Behavior, 13,* 243–266.

Hoefler, S., & Bornstein, P. (1975). Achievement place: An evaluative review. *Criminal Justice and Behavior, 2*(2), 146–168.

Hughes, J. N., Cavell, T. A., & Jackson, T. (1999). Influence of teacher-student relationships on childhood conduct problems: A prospective study. *Journal of Clinical Child Psychology, 28,* 173–184.

Jacobson, N. S. (1992). Behavioral couple therapy: A new beginning. *Behavior Therapy, 23,* 493–506.

Kashdan, T. B., Pelham, W. E., Lang, A. R., Hoza, B., Jacob, R. G., Jennings, J. R., et al. (2002). Hope and optimism as human strengths in parents of children with externalizing disorders: Stress is in the eye of the beholder. *Journal of Social and Clinical Psychology, 21,* 441–468.

Kazdin, A. E. (1993). Treatment of conduct disorder: Progress and directions in psychotherapy research. *Development and Psychopathology, 5,* 277–310.

Kazdin, A. E. (2005). *Parent management training: Treatment for oppositional, aggressive, and antisocial behavior in children and adolescents.* London: Oxford University Press.

Kazdin, A. E., Holland, L., & Crowley, M. (1997). Family experience of barriers to treatment and premature termination from child therapy. *Journal of Consulting and Clinical Psychology, 65,* 453–463.

Kazdin, A. E., & Whitley, M. K. (2003). Treatment of parental stress to enhance therapeutic change among children referred for aggressive and antisocial behavior. *Journal of Consulting and Clinical Psychology, 71*(3), 504–515.

Keenan, K., & Shaw, D. S. (2003). Starting at the beginning: Exploring the etiology of antisocial behavior in the first years of life. In B. Lahey, T. Moffitt, & A. Caspi (Eds.), *Causes of conduct disorder and juvenile delinquency* (pp. 153–181). New York: Guilford Press.

Kerr, M., & Stattin, H. (2000). What parents know, how they know it, and several forms of adolescent adjustment: Further support for a reinterpretation of monitoring. *Developmental Psychology, 36*(3), 366–380.

Kirigin, K. A., Braukmann, C. J., & Atwater, J. D. (1982). An evaluation of teaching-family (achievement place) group homes for juvenile offenders. *Journal of Applied Behavior Analysis, 15*(1), 1–16.

Kochanska, G. (1997). Mutually responsive orientation between mothers and their young children: Implications for early socialization. *Child Development, 68,* 94–112.

Kochanska, G., Aksan, N., & Koenig, A. L. (1995). A longitudinal study of the roots of preschoolers' conscience: Committed compliance and emerging internalization. *Child Development, 66*(6), 1752–1769.

Kochanska, G., & Murray, K. T. (2000). Mother-child mutually responsive orientation and conscience development: From toddler to early school-age. *Child Development, 71,* 417–431.

Kuczynski, L. (2003). Beyond bidirectionality: Bilateral conceptual frameworks for understanding dynamics in parent-child relations. In L. Kuczynski (Ed.), *Handbook of dynamics in parent-child relations* (pp. 1–24). Thousand Oaks, CA: Sage.

Kuczynski, L., & Hildebrandt, N. (1997). Models of conformity and resistance in socialization theory. In J. E. Grusec & L. Kuczynski (Eds.), *Parenting and the internalization of values: A handbook of contemporary theory* (pp. 227–256). New York: Wiley.

Kuczynski, L., Kochanska, G., Radke-Yarrow, M. O., & Girnius-Brown, O. (1987). A developmental interpretation of young children's noncompliance. *Developmental Psychology, 23,* 799–806.

Lahey, B. B., Moffitt, T., & Caspi, A. (2003). *Causes of conduct disorder and juvenile delinquency.* New York: Guilford Press.

Lahey, B. B., & Waldman, I. D. (2003). A developmental propensity model of the origins of conduct problems during childhood and adolescence. In B. Lahey, T. Moffitt, & A. Caspi. *Causes of conduct disorder and juvenile delinquency* (pp. 76–117). New York: Guilford Press.

Latham, G. I. (1992). Interacting with at-risk children: The positive approach. *Principal, 72,* 26–30.

Loeber, R. (1990). Development and risk factors of juvenile antisocial behavior and delinquency. *Clinical Psychology Review, 10,* 1–42.

Loeber, R., & Burk, J. D. (2000). Oppositional and conduct disorder: A review of the past 10 years, Part 1. *Journal of the American Academy of Child and Adolescent Psychiatry, 39*(12), 1468–1484.

Loeber, R., & Hay, D. (1997). Key issues in the development of aggression and violence from childhood to early adulthood. *Annual Review of Psychology, 48,* 371–410.

Loeber, R., & Schmaling, K. B. (1985). The utility of differentiating between mixed and pure forms of antisocial child behavior. *Journal of Abnormal Child Psychology, 13,* 315–336.

Lynam, D. R. (1998). Early identification of the fledgling psychopath: Locating the psychopathic child in the current nomenclature. *Journal of Abnormal Psychology, 107,* 566–575.

Lytton, H. (1990). Child and parent effects in boys' conduct disorder: A reinterpretation. *Developmental Psychology, 26,* 683–697.

Maccoby, E. E. (1980). Comment and reply. In G. R. Patterson (Ed.), Mothers: The unacknowledged victims. *Monographs of the Society for Research in Child Development, 45*(5, Serial No. 186).

Maccoby, E. E., & Martin, J. (1983). Socialization in the context of the family: Parent-child interaction. In P. H. Mussen (Series Ed.) & E. M. Hetherington (Vol. Ed.), *Handbook of child psychology: Vol. 4. Socialization, personality, and social development* (pp. 1–101). New York: Wiley.

McDougall, P., Hymel, S., Vaillancourt, T., & Mercer, L. (2001). The consequences of early childhood rejection. In M. Leary (Ed.), *Interpersonal Rejection* (pp. 213–247). New York: Oxford University Press.

McDowell, J. (1982). The importance of Herrnstein's mathematical statement of the law of effect for behavior therapy. *American Psychologist, 37,* 771–779.

McDowell, J. (1988). Matching theory in natural human environments. *Behavior Analyst, 11,* 95–109.

McMahon, R. J., & Wells, K. C. (1998). Conduct problems. In E. J. Mash & R. A. Barkley (Eds.), *Treatment of childhood disorders* (2nd ed., pp. 111–207). New York: Guilford Press.

Minuchin, S. (1974). *Families and family therapy.* Cambridge, MA: Harvard University Press.

Moffitt, T. E. (1993). Adolescence-limited and life-course-persistent antisocial behavior: A developmental taxonomy. *Psychology Review, 100,* 674–701.

Moffitt, T. E. (2003). Life-course-persistent and adolescence-limited antisocial behavior: A 10-year research review and a research agenda. In B. B. Lahey, T. E. Moffitt, & A. Caspi (Eds.), *Causes of conduct disorder and juvenile delinquency* (pp. 49–75). New York: Guilford Press.

Moffitt, T. E. (2005). The new look of behavioral genetics in developmental psychopathology: Gene-environment interplay in antisocial behavior. *Psychological Bulletin, 131*(4), 533–554.

Nichols, M. P., & Schwartz, R. C. (2004). *Family therapy: Concepts and methods* (6th ed.). Boston: Allyn & Bacon.

Nigg, J. T., & Huang-Pollock, C. L. (2003). An early-onset model of the role of executive functions and intelligence in conduct disorder/delinquency. In B. Lahey, T. Moffitt, & A. Caspi. *Causes of conduct disorder and juvenile delinquency* (pp. 227–253). New York: Guilford Press.

O'Donohue, W. (2003). Psychological skills training: Issues and controversies. *Behavior Analyst Today, 4,* 331–340.

Oxford, M., Cavell, T. A., & Hughes, J. N. (2003). Callous/unemotional traits moderate the relation between ineffective parenting and child externalizing problems: A partial replication and extension. *Journal of Clinical Child and Adolescent Psychology, 32,* 577–585.

Parke, R., Simpkins, S., McDowell, D., Kim, M., Killian, C., Dennis, J., et al. (2002). Relative contributions of families and peers to children's social development. In P. Smith & C. Hart (Eds.), *Blackwell handbook of childhood social development* (pp. 156–177). Oxford, England: Blackwell.

Patterson, G. R. (1975). *Families: Applications of social learning to family life.* Champaign, IL: Research Press.

Patterson, G. R. (1982). *Coercive family process.* Eugene, OR: Castalia.

Patterson, G. R. (1986). Performance models for antisocial boys. *American Psychologist, 41,* 432–444.

Patterson, G. R. (1997). Performance models of parenting: A social interactional perspective. In J. E. Grusec & L. Kuczynski (Eds.), *Parenting and children's internalization of values* (pp. 193–226). New York: Wiley.

Patterson, G. R. (2005). The next generation of PMTO models. *Behavior Therapist, 28,* 27–33.

Patterson, G. R., DeGarmo, D., & Forgatch, M. S. (2004). Systematic changes in families following prevention trials. *Journal of Abnormal Child Psychology, 32,* 621–633.

Patterson, G. R., Dishion, T. J., & Yoerger, K. (2000). Adolescent growth in new forms of problem behavior: Macro- and micro-peer dynamics. *Prevention Science, 1,* 3–13.

Patterson, G. R., & Forgatch, M. S. (1985). Therapist behavior as a determinant for client noncompliance: A paradox for the behavior modifier. *Journal of Consulting and Clinical Psychology, 53,* 846–851.

Patterson, G. R., Reid, J. B., & Dishion, T. J. (1992). *Antisocial boys: A social interactional approach.* Eugene, OR: Castalia.

Pettit, G. S., & Dodge, K. A. (2003). Violent children: Bridging development, intervention, and public policy. *Developmental Psychology, 39,* 187–188.

Pettit, G. S., Dodge, K. A., & Brown, M. M. (1988). Early family experiences, social problem solving patterns, and children's social competence. *Child Development, 59,* 107–120.

Phillips, E. L. (1985). *Psychotherapy revised: New frontiers in research and practice.* Hillsdale, NJ: Erlbaum.

Prinstein, M. J., & Wang, S. S. (2005). False consensus and adolescent peer contagion: Examining discrepancies between perceptions and actual reported levels of friends' deviant and health risk behaviors. *Journal of Abnormal Child Psychology, 33,* 293–306.

Prinz, R. J., & Miller, G. E. (1991). Issues in understanding and treating childhood conduct problems in disadvantaged populations. *Journal of Clinical Child Psychology, 20,* 379–385.

Richters, J. E., & Waters, E. (1991). Attachment and socialization: The positive side of social influence. In M. Lewis & S. Feinman (Eds.), *Social influences and socialization in infancy* (pp. 185–214). New York: Plenum Press.

Roberts, M. W., & Powers, S. W. (1988). The Compliance Test. *Behavioral Assessment, 10,* 375–398.

Robinson, E. A., Eyberg, S. M., & Ross, A. W. (1980). The standardization of an inventory of child conduct problem behaviors. *Journal of Clinical Child Psychology, 9,* 22–28.

Salmivalli, C., & Voeten, M. (2004). Connections between attitudes, group norms, and behavior in bullying. *International Journal of Behavioral Development, 28,* 246–258.

Sanders, M. R., Markie-Dadds, C., & Turner, K. M. T. (2003). Theoretical, scientific and clinical foundations of the Triple P–Positive Parenting Program: A population approach to the promotion of parenting competence. *Parenting Research and Practice Monograph, 1,* 1–21.

Scarr, S. (1992). Developmental theories for the 1990s: Development and individual differences. *Child Development, 63,* 1–19.

Schneider, W. J., Cavell, T. A., & Hughes, J. N. (2003). A sense of containment: Potential moderator of the relation between parenting practices and children's externalizing behaviors. *Development and Psychopathology, 15,* 95–117.

Serketich, W. J., & Dumas, J. E. (1996). The effectiveness of behavioral parent training to modify antisocial behavior in children: A meta-analysis. *Behavior Therapy, 27*(2), 171–186.

Sheeber, L. B., & Johnson, J. H. (1994). Evaluation of a temperament-focused, parent training program. *Journal of Clinical Child Psychology, 23,* 249–259.

Shorey, H. S., Snyder, C. R., Rand, K. L., Hockemyer, J. R., & Feldman, D. B. (2002). Authors' Response: Somewhere over the rainbow: Hope theory weathers its first decade. *Psychological Inquiry, 13*(4), 322–331.

Snyder, C. R., Scott, M., & Cheavens, J. S. (1999). Hope as a psychotherapeutic foundation of common factors, placebos, and expectancies. In M. A. Hubble, B. L., Duncan, & S. D. Miller (Eds.), *The heart and soul of change: What works in therapy* (pp. 179–200). Washington, DC: American Psychological Association.

Snyder, D. K., Castellani, A. M., & Whisman, M. A. (2006). Current status and future directions in couple therapy. *Annual Review of Psychology, 57,* 317–344.

Snyder, J. J., & Patterson, G. R. (1995). Individual differences in social aggression: A test of a reinforcement model of socialization in the natural environment. *Behavior Therapy, 26,* 371–391.

Snyder, J. J., Reid, J., & Patterson, G. (2003). A social learning model of child and adolescent antisocial behavior. In B. B. Lahey, T. E. Moffitt, & A. Caspi (Eds.), *Causes of conduct disorder and juvenile delinquency* (pp. 27–48). New York: Guilford Press.

Spitzer, A., Webster-Stratton, C., & Hollinsworth, T. (1991). Coping with conduct-problem children: Parents gaining knowledge and control. *Journal of Clinical Child Psychology, 20,* 413–427.

Steinberg, L. (1986). Latchkey children and susceptibility to peer pressure: An ecological analysis. *Developmental Psychology, 22,* 433–439.

Stoolmiller, M., Duncan, T., Bank, L., & Patterson, G. R. (1993). Some problems and solutions in the study of change: Significant patterns in client resistance. *Journal of Consulting and Clinical Psychology, 61,* 920–928.

Stormshak, E. A., Bierman, K. L., McMahon, R. J., Legua, L. J., & Conduct Problems Prevention Research Group. (2000). Parenting practices and child disruptive behavior problems in early elementary school. *Journal of Clinical Child Psychology, 29,* 17–29, 169–182.

Strand, P. S. (2000). Responsive parenting and child socialization: Integrating two contexts of family life. *Journal of Child and Family Studies, 9,* 269–281.

Strand, P. S., & Cavell, T. A. (2006). *Updating our approach to parent training: The case for parenting goals and family structure.* Unpublished manuscript.

Tapscott, M., Frick, P. J., Wootton, J., & Kruh, I. (1996). The intergenerational link to antisocial behavior: Effects of paternal contact. *Journal of Child and Family Studies, 5,* 229–240.

Taylor, T. K., Eddy, J. M., & Biglan, A. (1999). Interpersonal skills training to reduce aggressive and delinquent behavior: Limited evidence and the need for an evidence-based system of care. *Clinical Child and Family Psychology Review, 2,* 169–182.

Thomas, A., & Chess, S. (1977). *Temperament and development.* Oxford, England: Brunner/Mazel.

Tremblay, R. E. (2003). Why socialization fails: The case of chronic physical aggression. In B. Lahey, T. Moffitt, & A. Caspi (Eds.), *Causes of conduct disorder and juvenile delinquency* (pp. 182–224). New York: Guilford Press.

Tremblay, R. E., Nagin, D. S., & Seguin, J. R. (2005). Physical aggression during early childhood: Trajectories and predictors. *Canadian Child and Adolescent Psychiatry Review, 14*, 3–9.

Vaillancourt, T., & Hymel, S. (2004). The social context of children's aggression. In M. M. Moretti, C. L. Odgers, & M. A. Jackson (Eds.), *Girls and aggression: Contributing factors and intervention principles* (pp. 57–73). Kluwer Academic.

van Dam, C. (2001). *Identifying child molesters: Preventing child sexual abuse by recognizing the patterns of the offenders.* Binghamton, NY: Haworth Press.

Vasey, M. W., Kotov, R., Frick, P. J., & Loney, B. R. (2005). The latent structure of psychopathy in youth: A taxometric investigation. *Journal of Abnormal Child Psychology, 33*, 411–429.

Vitaro, F., Brendgen, M., & Tremblay, R. E. (2001). Preventive intervention: Assessing its effects on the trajectories of delinquency and testing for mediational processes. *Applied Developmental Science, 5*(4), 201–213.

Wahler, R. G. (1994). Child conduct problems: Disorders in conduct or social continuity? *Journal of Child and Family Studies, 3*, 143–156.

Wahler, R. G. (1997). On the origins of children's compliance and opposition: Family context, reinforcement, and rules. *Journal of Child and Family Studies, 6*, 191–208.

Wahler, R. G., & Dumas, J. E. (1989). Attentional problems in dysfunctional mother-child interactions: An interbehavioral model. *Psychological Bulletin, 105*, 116–130.

Wahler, R. G., Herring, M., & Edwards, M. (2001). Co-regulation of balance between children's prosocial approaches and acts of compliance: A pathway to mother-child cooperation? *Journal of Clinical Child Psychology, 30*, 473–478.

Wampold, B. E., Mondin, G. W., Moody, M., Stich, F., Benson, K., & Ahn, H. (1997). A meta-analysis of outcome studies comparing bona fide psychotherapies: Empirically, "all must have prizes." *Psychological Bulletin, 122*, 203–215.

Webster-Stratton, C. (1987). *The parents and children series.* Eugene, OR: Castalia.

Webster-Stratton, C. (1989). Systematic comparison of consumer satisfaction of three cost-effective parent training programs for conduct problem children. *Behavior Therapy, 20*, 103–115.

Webster-Stratton, C. (1990). Long-term follow-up of families with young conduct problem children: From preschool to grade school. *Journal of Clinical Child Psychology, 19*, 144–149.

Webster-Stratton, C. (1994). Advancing videotape parent training: A comparison study. *Journal of Consulting and Clinical Psychology, 62*, 583–593.

Webster-Stratton, C., & Herbert, M. (1994). *Troubled families: Problem children.* New York: Wiley.

Webster-Stratton, C., & Spitzer, A. (1996). Parenting a young child with conduct problems: New insights using qualitative methods. In T. H. Ollendick

& R. J. Prinz (Eds.), *Advances in clinical child psychology* (Vol. 18, pp. 1–46). New York: Plenum Press.

Wootton, J. M., Frick, P. J., Shelton, K. K., & Silverthorn, P. (1997). Ineffective parenting and childhood conduct problems: The moderating role of callous-unemotional traits. *Journal of Consulting and Clinical Psychology, 65,* 301–308.

Ybarra, M. L., & Mitchell, K. J. (2004). Online aggressor/targets, aggressors, and targets: A comparison of associated youth characteristics. *Journal of Child Psychology and Psychiatry, 45,* 1308–1316.

OTHER COMMON CHILDHOOD DISORDERS

PART FIVE of this book addresses some frequently occurring childhood disorders that do not readily fit into the "internalizing/externalizing" categories or a specific developmental disorder. In Chapter 13, Mellon and Houts introduce the concept of a home-based intervention for primary enuresis, a multicomponent treatment that they developed and modified, called Full Spectrum Home Treatment (FSHT). This home-based approach was designed to provide parents and children with an inexpensive, practical, and effective treatment for uncomplicated nocturnal enuresis. Families are provided with a detailed manual that offers step-by-step guidance and support through treatment components, including (a) basic urine alarm treatment, (b) cleanliness training, (c) retention control training, and (d) overlearning.

In their discussion of FSHT, the authors point out that enuresis has been conceptualized as a "biobehavioral" problem involving both environmental and physiological etiologies. Thus, the ideal management requires the collaboration of behaviorally trained psychologists and physicians. Mellon and Houts have developed the strongest possible combination of behavioral procedures and have created a complete set of support materials for FSHT that go beyond merely pacifying and reassuring the parents that the child will outgrow the bed-wetting. Their sophisticated and empirically-based approach uses a thorough and careful assessment to determine the contributing factors in the enuresis. If the problem does not involve medical complications, then the parents can assist the child to overcome the problem through the home-implemented program, involving a collaborative, working alliance between the parents and professionals. The authors do not recommend implementing home training without the assistance of a qualified professional, even if this only involves some guidance and follow-up via phone. Their intervention strategy offers consistent and ongoing guidance, support, and problem-solving techniques.

The authors clearly offer a detailed explanation of a wide range of possible causes for enuresis and discuss the success and failure of various and alternative treatment strategies to control this disorder. Although medication is not a permanent solution to enuresis, it is acknowledged that, in some instances, this may be a viable alternative, especially for those children who have experienced major barriers to social development and self-esteem related to enuresis. This may be particularly the case for those families who have been unable to implement a program of behavioral intervention strategies. The aim, however, is to find a permanent solution to the problem. The FSHT program for primary enuresis offers just such a solution and gives the parents and the child mastery over the problem of enuresis.

In Chapter 14, Branstetter, Masse, and Greene discuss and demonstrate the effectiveness of a program designed for parents of adolescents with substance use and delinquent behavior problems. The authors review and compare some essential family-based programs that have been developed to treat adolescent delinquent behaviors, including functional family therapy (FFT), multidimensional family therapy (MDFT), and multisystemic therapy (MST). Despite the variance in these empirically supported family-focused intervention programs, they each adhere to a common theme that stresses the importance of family involvement and recognizes the necessity of parent inclusion to protect children from adolescent substance use and delinquent behavior. The authors then present an interesting and systematic discussion of the Parents as Partners for Adolescent Behavior Change (PPABC) training program. This is a creative and resourceful intervention strategy that has been adapted from a variety of empirically supported, family-based interventions for substance-abusing adolescents with delinquent behaviors. This approach can be easily implemented by clinicians working in community agencies, small clinics, or private practice because it is a cost-effective strategy, bringing together essential elements identified by theory, empirical research, and clinical practice. It gives parents the skills necessary to help their adolescent children experiencing problems associated with substance use and delinquency. The authors offer a detailed description and explanation of the 11 separate modules used in PPABC that fall into four board domains: (1) assessment, (2) education, (3) motivation enhancement, and (4) intervention. The modules, presented in sequential order, allow each successive module to build on the preceding module.

Branstetter, Masse, and Greene point out that because of their adolescents' substance abuse and delinquent problems, parents often feel out of control. An important aspect of the PPABC program is restoring a parent's sense of control and responsibility. Parents receive instruction in techniques for negotiating clear and exact rules for addressing and controlling problematic areas. The authors present practical and invaluable tables that delineate and explore specific strategies for controlling and modifying adolescent substance use and delinquent problems. In all, the program emphasizes the importance of clarity and precision in the development of rules and consequences to help parents reduce and control the problems that often ensue from the interaction and overlap of adolescent substance use and delinquent behaviors.

CHAPTER 13

Home-Based Treatment for Primary Enuresis

MICHAEL W. MELLON and ARTHUR C. HOUTS

AN EFFECTIVE treatment approach for childhood bed-wetting requires close collaboration between behavioral psychologists, pediatricians, and parent(s). We have previously described this approach from a biobehavioral perspective in that the physical problem of bed-wetting or nocturnal enuresis is best managed through a social learning-based treatment (Houts, 1991; Mellon & Houts, 2006). Recent findings that highlight specific neurophysiological delays provide a more complete account of the causes of bed-wetting. However, the interaction of these physiological mechanisms within the context of respondent and operant processes and child development suggest exciting areas of needed research to push this already well-established and empirically supported intervention to even higher levels of effectiveness. Therefore, nocturnal enuresis may represent a prototypical example of how the collaboration between pediatric psychologists, medical professionals, and parents leads to the best outcome for this common childhood disorder.

This chapter reflects the authors' 45 years of collective experience in treating children with monosyptomatic nocturnal enuresis or bed-wetting. We discuss our separate clinical experiences from the first author's program at the Mayo Clinic in Rochester, Minnesota, and the second authors' experience in the development of a multicomponent program developed and validated in the psychology laboratory and delivered and further field-tested in a real-world clinical setting. Notable differences in the two programs are highlighted when pertinent to the discussion, but otherwise, the two programs are essentially the same.

429

HISTORY AND THEORY OF BED-WETTING

When a child of at least 5 years of age has accidental wetting in their clothes or bedding, occurring with a frequency of twice a week for at least 3 consecutive months, or the presence of wetting accidents produces considerable distress and impairment in the child's psychosocial and/or academic functioning, and it is not attributable to organic causes, it is called *nocturnal enuresis* (American Psychiatric Association, 1994). *Diurnal Enuresis* refers to daytime wetting and is distinguished from nocturnal enuresis, which applies to children who only wet the bed. This distinction is important because of a significantly higher incidence of medical problems such as urinary tract infection and abnormal urodynamics in diurnal enuresis (Arnold & Ginsberg, 1973; Bakker, van Sprundel, van der Auwera, van Gool, & Wyndaele, 2002; Jarvelin, Huttunen, Seppanen, Seppanen, & Moilanen, 1990). Children with daytime wetting often require further medical evaluation and treatment. However, the focus of this chapter is nocturnal enuresis without daytime wetting. Fortunately, most children who wet the bed should be considered physiologically healthy and should be reassured of this fact.

Bed-wetting has been associated with problems of emotional and social adjustment among enuretic children, though the nature of this association remains unclear. The association appears to be greatest in girls, in diurnal enuretics, and in secondary or onset enuresis, but it is important to emphasize that psychiatric disturbance is present in only a minority of enuretic children (Essen & Peckham, 1976; Kaffman & Elizur, 1977; Rutter, Yule, & Graham, 1973; Stromgren & Thomsen, 1990). Experimental studies have demonstrated that enuretic children treated for bed-wetting improve more than untreated controls on measures of self-concept and peer relations (Baker, 1969; Lovibond, 1964; Moffatt, Kato, & Pless, 1987). Continued recommendations to parents by health professionals to wait for their child to outgrow the disorder may now be considered inappropriate due to the potential psychosocial consequences of continued bed-wetting and in light of effective treatments. Although the reported prevalence of enuresis varies (DeJonge, 1973), it is conservatively estimated that about 10% of school-age children (i.e., age 5 years to 16 years) wet their beds, with most of them doing so every night of the week (Fergusson, Horwood, & Shannon, 1986; Jarvelin, Vikevainen-Tervonen, Moilanen, & Huttunen, 1988). An average-sized school of 1,000 students would be estimated to have 100 children that wet the bed each night of the week.

Epidemiological studies indicate the prevalence of enuresis declines with age and this has contributed to the belief among professionals and parents that children will outgrow the problem (Vogel, Young, & Primack, 1986). Although the spontaneous remission rate is estimated to be

16% per year, cessation of bed-wetting without treatment can take several years (Forsythe & Redmond, 1974). Moreover, it has been reported as many as 3% of all enuretic children may continue bed-wetting into adulthood (Forsythe & Redmond, 1974; Levine, 1943). Primary nocturnal enuresis accounts for approximately 80% of all children who wet the bed and describes the child who has been wetting continuously since birth and evidencing less than 6 consecutive months of dryness (Rawashde, Hvistendahl, Kamperis, & Djurhuus, 2002). Less than 10% of these children have some sort of physical abnormality of the urinary tract (American Academy of Pediatrics Committee of Radiology, 1980; Jarvelin et al., 1990; Kass, 1991; Redman & Seibert, 1979; Rushton, 1989; Stansfeld, 1973) that would lead to the symptoms of day and/or night wetting. Bed-wetting has an established genetic component, and enuretic children may show signs of delayed maturation of the nervous system (Jarvelin, 1989; Jarvelin et al., 1991; Von Gontard, Schaumburg, Hollman, Eiberg, & Rittig, 2001). Up to age 11 years, more than twice as many males as females suffer from enuresis.

BED-WETTING CAUSES

The specific causes of nocturnal enuresis after ruling out an organic etiology are still largely unknown, and several hypotheses have been proposed to explain the problem. Investigators have demonstrated considerable etiological variability among enuretic children (Houts, 1991; Watanabe & Azuma, 1989) rather than assuming that enuretic children are a homogeneous group who should be treated in the same manner. Thus, several of the hypothesized causes may combine to explain the problem for a particular child, whereas some hypothesized causes may be in reality only correlates of the problem. Nevertheless, factors that are significant correlates of enuresis may aid clinicians in identifying specific treatment components that may be warranted for some children depending on the presence or absence of these factors.

Enuresis is most likely the result of complex interactions between genetically transmitted physiological factors and exposure to different environments during growth and development. The major etiological hypotheses that support such a conclusion include family history, delays in physical development, and ineffective learning history. Enuresis is often found in families, which was supported by one of the most recent studies that considered family history. Fergusson et al. (1986) found that the strongest predictor of the age of attaining nocturnal bladder control was the number of first-order relatives having a known history of enuresis. When both parents have a history of bed-wetting, 77% of children are enuretic, as opposed to 44% when one parent has a positive history, and

15% if neither parent does (Bakwin, 1973). Basic genetic research has begun to uncover the specific markers for enuresis, but the practical application of this knowledge to develop better treatments is as yet unknown (Eiberg, Berendt, & Mohr, 1995). Family history findings point to delays in physical development as the genetically transmitted mechanism that plays a causal role in continued bed-wetting (Jarvelin, 1989).

Considerable research efforts have been dedicated to investigating the etiological hypotheses regarding delays in physical development as being those focused on deficiencies in nocturnal antidiuretic hormone (ADH) secretion and on deficiencies in muscular responses needed to inhibit urination. According to the first hypothesis, enuretic children continue bed-wetting because their kidneys do not adequately concentrate urine (i.e., a mechanism of action of ADH) at night, which leads to excess nighttime urine production that exceeds ordinary bladder capacity. This failure of the kidneys to concentrate urine is believed to be caused by a lack of normal cyclic increase in ADH during sleep (George et al., 1975; Klauber, 1989; Norgaard, Rittig, & Djurhuus, 1989). However, studies with larger samples of bed wetters suggest that the nocturnal deficiency of ADH hypothesis accounts for only about 20% of all bed wetters (Watanabe, Kawauchi, Kitamori, & Azuma, 1994).

A Danish research group has also reported important evidence for the second physiological hypothesis regarding deficiencies in muscular responses needed to inhibit urination. Norgaard (1989) observed that during artificial filling of the bladder while enuretic children were asleep, episodes of arousal to bladder filling were preceded by increased pelvic floor activity (i.e., a Kegel contraction). In contrast, bed-wetting without waking was preceded by relaxation of the pelvic floor. In other words, when nighttime wetting was avoided, children appeared to be inhibiting bladder contractions by spontaneously contracting the muscles of the pelvic floor. When nighttime wetting occurred, no such inhibitory responses were observed. Instead, the relatively relaxed pelvic floor was similar to that observed in normal daytime voiding. This phenomenon of bladder-pelvic floor interaction that leads to a wet or dry bed can also be demonstrated in nonbed wetters (Hunsballe, 1999).

Consistent with these hypotheses about delays in physical development, learning theorists have hypothesized that incomplete learning from certain conditions is what causes children to continue bed-wetting. By reasoning backward from the success of conditioning treatments, behavioral psychologists have speculated that simple bed-wetting is caused by children's failure to learn to attend and respond to the need to urinate while asleep (see review by Scott, Barclay, & Houts, 1990). If for any number of reasons (e.g., sleeping for long periods of time, habituating to the discomfort of a wet bed) a child repeatedly fails to respond to the natural conditions of a wet bed, the child will fail to learn the responses necessary to avoid wetting the bed. Thus, continued bed-wetting is viewed as a failure to learn how to be dry from the naturally occurring experiences of development. The enuretic child may pass through a critical period related to gaining nighttime continence, becoming the passive victim of numerous trials of learning to *not* make the appropriate response (i.e., pelvic floor contraction) due to these delays.

In this regard, the etiological hypothesis of ineffective learning history is complemented by hypotheses about delays in physical development. One recent investigation suggested that the delay in development might be at the level of the brain stem where signals from the bladder failed to be adequately processed during sleep (Ornitz, Hana, & de Traversay, 1992). This brain-bladder connection is further exemplified in a study by Kawauchi, Watanabe, Kitamori, Imada, and Ohne (1993). They demonstrated that artificially filling the bladders of normal adult volunteers elicited greater plasma ADH levels than before filling, suggesting that stimulation of the bladder produces vasopressin secretion.

Other hypothesized causes of enuresis that in reality may only be correlates include psychological problems, functional bladder capacity (FBC), and sleep/arousal difficulties. The hypothesis that bed-wetting is caused by emotional problems is still commonly believed by parents and many health care professionals (Haque et al., 1981). Nevertheless, when compared to their nonenuretic peers, enuretic children do not exhibit more emotional or behavioral problems (Friman, Handwerk, Swearer, McGinnis, & Warzak, 1998; Moffatt, 1994). For children who have stopped bed-wetting for a period of 6 months or more and then resumed bed-wetting (secondary enuretics), the onset of bed-wetting may be precipitated by a traumatic event or other significant distress. In these instances, resolving the distress may be a priority. Otherwise, any emotional difficulties experienced by children with enuresis are most likely a result and not a cause of bed-wetting, and treating the enuresis may alleviate problems such as social anxiety and low self-appraisal (Moffat, 1989). At most, the child with emotional problems may only need extra support and encouragement during treatment.

Another hypothesized cause of enuresis is low FBC, or the volume of urine voided when a child has voluntarily postponed urination for as long as possible after first experiencing the urge to go. Functional bladder capacity should not be confused with actual physical bladder capacity, which is a measure of bladder capacity derived from artificial filling of the bladder during catheterization. Researchers have speculated that a smaller FBC and/or overproduction of urine are the primary causes of bed-wetting (Hjälmås, 1997; Hjälmås et al., 2004). However, there are many inconsistencies in the evidence for a low FBC. Kawauchi et al. (2003)

have reported normal FBCs at the time of enuresis in bed wetters and suggest that bladder capacity may be a function of the child's voiding habits rather than the determinant of those habits. Others have even demonstrated that bladder capacity in bed wetters can be increased with urine alarm treatment (Oredsson & Jorgensen, 1998; Taneli et al., 2004). Most likely, a low FBC is a correlate rather than a cause of bed-wetting.

Finally, given that bed-wetting obviously occurs during sleep, parents and professionals have declared "deep sleep" as an important precipitating factor in enuresis, although research has never confidently confirmed this relationship (Friman, 1986). Parents of enuretic children often report that their child is difficult to wake, cannot be awakened at night, or is a "deep sleeper." However, an important distinction between depth of sleep and arousability from sleep should be made as current research suggests the latter is related to the problem of bed-wetting. Depth of sleep has been operationalized in terms of sleep stages recorded on an electroencephalogram (EEG), whereas arousability refers to a behavioral measure of how easily a child can be awakened, which are not the same phenomenon.

Although some of the first studies of sleep recordings in enuretic patients suggested that enuretic events occurred in deep sleep (Pierce, Whitman, Mass, & Gay, 1961), research has since shown that enuretic episodes may occur equally in any sleep stage once the relative proportion of time spent in various sleep stages is taken into account (Mikkelsen et al., 1980; Norgaard, Hansen, et al., 1989). Thus, at least as measured by EEG, depth of sleep is not a reliable correlate of wetting episodes in enuretic children. With regard to the data on arousability, most research has compared enuretics with nonenuretic controls. Recent studies suggest that children who wet the bed demonstrate higher thresholds for arousal from sleep with auditory stimulation (Wolfish, 1999; Wolfish, Pivik, & Busby, 1997). Evidence of neurological delay in bed-wetting children is indicated with findings of longer latencies in P300 signals suggesting immaturity in auditory stimulus evaluation and reduced prepulse inhibition of the startle response (Ornitz, Russell, Gabikian, Gehricke, & Guthrie, 2000). These differences in the neurological functioning of enuretic children may represent the background noise that prevents the child from detecting the signal of a filling bladder. These studies are consistent with a hypothesis that arousal may be an issue in the treatment for some subgroup of enuretic children.

Finally, a study of nearly 1,500 bed wetters using overnight simultaneous monitoring of EEG and bladder pressures (i.e., cystometry) obtained results that led the researchers to propose a classification system of enuresis in which two of the proposed three types are thought to be due to a disturbance in awakening (Watanabe & Azuma, 1989). The classification types Watanabe and Azuma proposed are based on the following findings:

- *Type I (61% of cases):* The first bladder contraction was noticed on cystometrogram during Stage IV sleep when the bladder was full. Evidence of arousal in EEG appeared and EEG changed to a Stage I or II sleep pattern; enuresis occurred without waking.
- *Type IIa (11% of cases):* The first bladder contraction was again noticed in Stage IV sleep, but no EEG arousal response was observed, and enuresis occurred.
- *Type IIb (28% of cases):* Cystometry showed uninhibited contraction of the bladder only during sleep (not on awakening). There was no change in either first bladder contraction or EEG, but enuresis occurred.

The authors consider Type I to represent a mild disturbance in awakening and Type IIa, a more serious grade of awakening problem. Type IIb is thought to be due to occult abnormal bladder function in children that were deemed urologically normal based on medical evaluation. In their review of sleep research, Djurhuus, Norgaard, and Rittig (1992) speculated that the work of Watanabe and Azuma points to a dysfunction in the pathways leading from the pontine micturition center of the brainstem to upper cortical areas of the cortex's brainstem. This hypothesis is based on previous studies of nighttime voiding, suggesting that enuretic episodes reflect normal bladder function and therefore are not the result of dysfunction between the bladder and spinal cord. Watanabe, Imada, Kawauchi, Koyama, and Shirakawa (1997) have implicated the hypothalamus as the source of the inhibition of arousal in response to a bladder signal. This hypothesis is supported by the aforementioned findings of abnormal neurophysiological findings in the area of the brain stem near the pontine micturition center (Ornitz et al., 2000) and may soon account for the Kawauchi et al. (1993) finding of how centripetal stimulation of the bladder elicits ADH secretion in normal adults.

TREATMENTS FOR BED-WETTING

Medication Approaches

Medication therapy for *nocturnal enuresis* began in the early 1960s when imipramine (brand name Tofranil) was found to reduce urinary incontinence in adult psychiatric patients treated for depression (MacLean, 1960). The 1970s saw the introduction of a bladder antispasmodic medication known as oxybutynin chloride (brand name Ditropan). This drug has been shown to reduce spasms of the bladder and to increase bladder capacity, in addition to being a treatment for bed-wetting (Buttarazzi, 1977; Thompson & Lauvetz, 1976). Finally, a synthetic version of the naturally occurring hormone known as vasopressin was introduced to the United States from Europe in the late 1980s. Desmopressin (brand name DDAVP) is currently taken intranasally or in oral tablets to treat excessive urine production by stimulating the kidney to concentrate urine so the bladder capacity during sleep is not exceeded. A quantitative review by Houts, Berman, and Abramson (1994) reported that although pharmacological treatments produce a better outcome than no treatment, these gains are nearly lost at follow-up, and barely exceeded the spontaneous remission rate.

Because of the numerous and potentially dangerous side effects of imipramine (Werry, Dowrick, Lampen, & Vamos, 1975), and indications that oxybutynin chloride may not be more efficacious than the spontaneous cure rate of 16%, we believe DDAVP is the most viable of the current pharmacological treatments for nocturnal enuresis. Imipramine, which has a slightly lower efficacy than DDAVP, might be worth considering in cases resistant to all other treatments, or in children with the added diagnosis of depression. The toxicity of the drug in overdose must be emphasized to the family. Imipramine has also been found to reduce the effectiveness of urine alarm treatment (Houts, Peterson, & Leibert, 1984).

A review of all controlled trials of DDAVP indicated that only 24.5% of patients achieve short-term dryness and only 5.7% remained dry after stopping treatment (Moffatt, Harlos, Kirshen, & Burd, 1993). Houts et al. (1994) reported a more promising figure of 21% remaining dry by follow-up. Hjälmås (1999) reported that the results of the Swedish Enuresis Trial indicated that 22% of children treated with DDAVP remained dry after 1 year of treatment, with 61% of all treated children showing a <50% reduction in wet nights. However, these figures are far less impressive than the 45% lasting cure for behavioral treatments using the urine alarm alone. Therefore, the use of DDAVP for anything more than the management of bed-wetting until the child spontaneously remits is not supported by current scientific knowledge.

Behavioral Approaches

The primary goal of behavioral treatments is to try to eliminate bed-wetting by directly training the child to control bladder functions while asleep. Such training is introduced by a therapist in a clinical setting and then carried out at home by parents and children. Preparing and motivating a family to carry out training procedures is a major component of these approaches and requires a collaborative effort between therapist, parent, and child. The effectiveness of these approaches depends on the willingness and ability of parent and child to follow correctly the procedures for a full course of treatment.

Three types of behavior therapy used to treat bed-wetting include: (1) urine alarm training, (2) retention control training, and (3) dry-bed training. All three approaches have received rather extensive evaluation individually or in quantitative reviews, and it is now possible to draw conclusions about their overall effectiveness as well as their practical feasibility. Our Full Spectrum Home Training (FSHT) program (which is discussed later) has incorporated features of the previous methods that seemed both useful and practical. The first author has incorporated many of the components of FSHT in his Enuresis Conditioning program at the Mayo Clinic except for the retention control training portion as he has not found it to be clinically relevant.

Urine alarm training, sometimes called *bell-and-pad training,* is the oldest form of behavior therapy and was developed by Mowrer and Mowrer (1938) over 60 years ago. Subsequent research has shown the urine alarm to be an essential ingredient in other effective behavior therapy treatment packages as excluding it drastically reduces their effectiveness. The treatment relies on a urine alarm device that consists of a urine sensor with an absorbent pad to detect wetting attached to a battery-operated alarm. A newer type of device, which is worn on the child's bed clothing, replaces the bed pad with an alligator-style clip or small absorbent strip that is placed inside the child's underwear. Both alarm types are very reliable and can be used with any training programs that incorporate the use of a urine alarm. The bell-and-pad alarm and body-worn alarm devices are typically available in most drug stores or can be purchased online at http://www.bedwettingstore.com.

The basic idea of urine alarm training is to wake the child as soon as possible after wetting starts. When the child wets the bed, the alarm sounds and the child is startled awake. The mechanism of action is thought to involve dual-process learning with a pelvic floor contraction being classically conditioned through a startle response to the alarm after a wet. The conditioned response is thought to be maintained through negative reinforcement as the child learns to avoid the activation of the alarm by contracting the pelvic floor when the bladder is perceived as being full. Numerous controlled scientific investigations and empirical reviews of the research literature have demonstrated that basic urine alarm training is very effective with about 75% of children treated with this method for an 8- to 14-week period achieve an initial arrest of bed-wetting, and by follow-up approximately 41% experience a relapse (Houts et al., 1994; Mellon & McGrath, 2000). The most common cause of failure to achieve an initial arrest with this treatment is not following the procedures completely, with the child habituating to the alarm and no longer waking. If the child is permitted to sleep through the alarm, as many children are able to do, then the child never develops the sensitivity to wake up to this stimulus. The procedures are demanding on the family, and single parents who have problems of their own as well as couples with marital problems have been less successful than families without such problems (Dische, Yule, Corbett, & Hand, 1983).

A second common cause of failure is that parents permit the child to get up, turn off the alarm, and return to bed without becoming fully awake and going to the bathroom. A third cause of failure is not continuing long enough and abandoning treatment before optimal learning has occurred. About 12 weeks is typically required, and for children who wet more than once a night as many as 16 weeks may be needed. The first author asks families to be prepared to make a commitment of at least 20 weeks for a "full dose" of treatment. Several studies show that parents who are intolerant of a child's bed-wetting and find it difficult to carry out detailed instructions tend to drop out of this training before its beneficial effects can be realized (James & Foreman, 1973; Morgan & Young, 1975). Others have found that children who construe the wetting as an advantage, or if they believe the wetting is not a problem, have a greater likelihood of failure and dropping out prematurely (Butler, Redfern, & Forsythe, 1994).

If children become dry because of urine alarm training and then experience a relapse, they usually do so within the first 6 months of the end of treatment. Children who relapse after this training can be successfully retrained with a 2- to 4-week reapplication of the urine alarm regimen (Doleys, 1977), but such retraining is not always successful. The first author's enuresis conditioning program has experienced a slightly lower success rate with a subsample of children re-treated with the urine alarm (i.e., 60%). Due to the lack of success with re-treatment, some investigators have emphasized relapse prevention over relapse remediation (Houts, Peterson, & Whelan, 1986). It is unclear why some children relapse and others remain dry, although family problems have been associated with relapse (Dische et al., 1983).

Researchers have devised a powerful method for preventing relapse from the outset. *Overlearning,* as the method is called, requires the child to drink a large quantity of fluid during the hour before bedtime. Overlearning is usually started after the child has been dry for 2 consecutive weeks. It is continued with the urine alarm in place until the child is dry for another 2 consecutive weeks. The overlearning procedure has been shown to cut the relapse rate in half (Young & Morgan, 1972). With the addition of overlearning, the lasting cure rate of urine alarm training for simple bed-wetting is more than 60%, with this component of treatment now considered a standard of care.

The concept that bed-wetting children have smaller bladder capacities than nonbed-wetting children is debatable (Kawauchi et al., 2003; Yeung et al., 2002). The goal of retention control training is to increase the child's bladder capacity, defined as the urine amount the child produces after holding for as long as possible (Kimmel & Kimmel, 1970). The training is done once a day with the parent and child doing the exercises for a 2-to 3-hour period. The child drinks 8 to 16 ounces of fluid and then practices holding for as long as possible after first feeling the need to urinate. The child is given rewards for holding for longer and longer periods, up to 45 minutes. Although retention control training by itself produces a lasting cure in less than 30% of enuretic children with simple bed-wetting (Houts & Liebert, 1984), some evidence suggests that it may be a useful adjunct to standard urine alarm training either by reducing the chance of a relapse or by speeding the child's initial arrest rate (Fielding, 1980; Houts et al., 1986).

Dry-bed training is a behavior therapy program developed by Nathan Azrin and his colleagues (Azrin, Sneed, & Foxx, 1974) that has been described in detail in a self-help book (Azrin & Besalel, 1979). Dry-bed training consists of four procedures. First, the *nightly waking schedule,* which is started by a professional who spends the night in the child's home, requires that the child be awakened every hour during the first night of training. At each waking, the child is taken to the bathroom and asked to urinate, given fluids to drink, and then encouraged to withhold urinating for the next hour. On the second night, the child is awakened by the parents 3 hours after going to bed. If the child is dry, then the next night, the parents wake the child 2.5 hours after bedtime. The waking time is moved ahead by 30 minutes each night following a dry bed and is stopped when the child is scheduled to be awakened 1 hour after going to bed. If the child wets twice in 1 week, the cycle of the nightly waking schedule starts over.

The second procedure, called *positive practice,* requires the child to lie down in the bed, count to 50, and then get up and go to the bathroom and try to urinate. The process is repeated 20 times. Twenty trials of positive practice are done in the middle of the night immediately after a wet bed and also before bedtime the next night. The third procedure of dry-bed training is the *urine alarm,* used as described earlier. The alarm is introduced after the first night of waking the child every hour. If the alarm signals that the child has wet, the child is awakened and reprimanded for wetting the bed. The fourth procedure, called *cleanliness training,* is done immediately after wetting the bed and requires the child to change his or her wet clothes and bed linens. The child places all wet linens in the laundry and remakes the bed with clean sheets. After completing 20 trials of positive practice, the alarm is reactivated and the child goes back to sleep.

The general trend to make treatments more cost-effective led later research on dry-bed training to eliminate the alarm (Azrin & Thienes, 1978) and the use of a professional in the home (Azrin, Thienes-Hontos, & Besalel-Azrin, 1979). Two important conclusions can be drawn from research on dry-bed training. First, the inclusion of a urine alarm in this treatment package should not be considered optional, because the overall effectiveness of dry-bed training is reduced substantially if an alarm is not used. Second, there does not appear to be any appreciable gain in treatment effectiveness when a professional trainer conducts the first night of treatment than when parents do it by themselves (Houts & Liebert, 1984). Relapse after dry-bed training (39%) is virtually identical to that following simple urine alarm training (41%; Bollard, 1982) and dry-bed training is more difficult to carry out than simple urine alarm training. The requirements of the nightly waking schedule and the demands of positive practice are rather severe.

For simple, uncomplicated nocturnal enuresis, we prefer multicomponent treatments that have been demonstrated to impact the problems of speed of treatment response and relapse in urine alarm therapy by adding other behavioral procedures to the basic urine alarm treatment. Our research group has developed and modified one such multicomponent treatment program called Full Spectrum Home Treatment (FSHT). This method has been slightly modified by the first author in his enuresis treatment program, although the main components remain in the treatment. Full Spectrum Home Treatment was designed to provide parent(s) and child(ren) with an inexpensive, easy-to-use, and effective treatment for uncomplicated nocturnal enuresis. Families are provided with a detailed manual and support materials. Treatment has been demonstrated to be most effective if delivered by a trained professional (Houts, Whelan, & Peterson, 1987). The treatment components are (a) basic urine alarm treatment, (b) cleanliness training, (c) retention control training, and (d) overlearning. For basic urine alarm treatment, the second author recommends the newer urine alarm devices that are worn on the body and that are more reliable than the older devices that required use of a bed pad and freestanding alarm box. The first author utilizes the bell-and-pad method with alarm boxes, specially made by engineers at Mayo Clinic, that allow for varying volume intensities to meet the needs of any given child. The newer alarms are produced with a preset alarm volume (e.g., @ 85 decibels) and this may not be loud enough to awaken some children. Most of the newer alarm devices are turned off by removing the urine sensitive probe from the child's underwear and drying it off compared to a switch on the freestanding alarm box.

The effectiveness of the urine alarm has been empirically demonstrated at the level of single case methodology, in uncontrolled group studies, in randomized clinical trials compared to wait-list control groups or against other established treatments, and discussed in narrative and quantitative reviews of the literature. The predominant conclusion in the research literature at each level of experimental rigor is that the urine alarm treatment leads to approximately 60% to 80% of enuretic children becoming completely dry regardless of age and gender. This conclusion has been argued since the first major review of the research literature by Doleys (1977), empirically argued in a meta-analytic review by Houts et al. (1994), and summarized in a review utilizing criteria for defining empirically supported treatments (Mellon & McGrath, 2000). Similar findings were reported in a recent systematic review of studies that included urine alarm treatment alone, combined with other behavioral components, and compared to medication treatments with inclusion criteria involving only studies with randomized or quasi-randomized designs (Glazener & Evans, 2003). Finally, Kristensen and Jensen (2003) completed a meta-analysis comparing various statistical models to test the effectiveness of alarm treatment from 1938 to 1996 and accounting for the influences of reporting practices, the use of various success criteria, and frequency of bed-wetting. These reviews consistently indicate that basic urine alarm treatment cures between 59% and 78% of children and multicomponent treatments that include the urine alarm cures 64% to 86% of children. At the time of follow-up, the success rates fall to between 34% and 43% for the former, and between 45% and 75% for the latter. None of the reviewers reported significant differences although trends were suggested for greater efficacy for the enuresis conditioning treatment combined with other behavioral procedures and with greater durability of the treatment gains at follow-up. Perhaps the lack of reliable differences between the basic urine alarm compared to the multicomponent treatments promoted additional variations to find the "ultimate evidence-based treatment package." However, any intervention, assessed at the end of treatment or at follow-up, should be measured against the reported spontaneous remission rate of 16% (Forsythe & Redmond, 1974). Currently, the most confident conclusion is that behavioral treatments that include the use of the urine alarm alone or in combination with other treatment components are the treatments of choice.

FULL SPECTRUM HOME TRAINING PROGRAM

NECESSARY QUALIFICATIONS FOR THERAPISTS

Because enuresis has been lucidly conceptualized as a biobehavioral problem (Houts, 1991) involving both environmental and physiological etiologies, its ideal management requires the collaboration of behaviorally trained psychologists and physicians. Each of these health care providers offers a unique expertise in the diagnosis and treatment of this multifaceted, yet common childhood problem.

As was previously explained, interventions based on learning processes clearly lead to the best long-term outcomes for bed-wetting. Thus, psychologists or other mental health providers who have been trained in the clinical application of learning principles are well suited to implement FSHT. Ideally, a pediatric psychologist who has had direct training experience with the urine alarm approach and a sensitivity to the medical aspects of the disorder could optimally manage the treatment through collaboration with a physician as needed. These professionals work closely with the parent and child in a collaborative effort to optimize the deliver of the treatment. Based on our years of experience, the parent-child dyad must be provided with a minimal amount of professional guidance to assure a satisfactory outcome.

A small percentage of children with nocturnal enuresis suffer from organic pathologies that can promote or prolong the wetting. Therefore, it has been recommended that all children presenting with bed-wetting have a basic physical exam that includes a urinalysis and culture, and ideally, an ultrasound of the kidneys and bladder (Von Gontard, 1998). In approximately 3% to 5% of children, diseases such as nephritis or diabetes cause the presenting symptoms of day- and nighttime urinary incontinence. Further, in a study of 3,556 children presenting with urinary symptoms at 7 years of age, 8.4% of girls and 1.7% of boys had at least one prior urinary tract infection (Hellstrom, Hanson, Hansson, Hjalmas, & Jodal, 1991). These medical problems and their differential diagnosis from simple bed-wetting clearly require the services of a physician. Fortunately, examination of the urine, reliable cultures, and careful questioning about medical histories and current symptoms can be performed quickly and inexpensively in an outpatient setting by a general pediatrician or family physician. Additional collaboration with a physician would also be necessary if medication treatments are to be combined with the urine alarm and other behavioral approaches.

NECESSARY PATIENT INFORMATION

Barring medical problems as a cause of bed-wetting, the treatment of choice for nocturnal enuresis includes some version of urine alarm therapy. However, this treatment requires a large investment of time from both the child and parent(s). An in-depth clinical interview of the parent and child will determine whether they are able to implement a rather demanding treatment and help identify any associated psychopathology. Factors that have been associated with bed wetters who will successfully complete treatment and maintain those gains include information about history of enuresis, prior treatments, parental attitudes and beliefs, family and home environment, behavioral problems, and the child's current wetting pattern (Butler, 1998). The presence of relevant psychiatric symptoms or significant psychosocial stressors in the family may make a stronger argument for considering the use of a medication treatment to manage the bed-wetting. Our collective clinical experience has suggested that until psychosocial stressors can be reduced to subclinical levels or eliminated, behavioral treatment is unlikely to be effectively delivered.

A thorough history of a child's wetting pattern will reveal whether their wetting occurred after a period of nighttime continence (6 months to a year), which is referred to as secondary enuresis. Medical or emotional factors may have precipitated the wetting. If the onset of bed-wetting has coincided with stressful events or the presence of psychiatric symptoms, it may be useful to focus initially on minimizing current stressful events or treating psychiatric problems prior to implementing urine alarm treatment.

Carefully reviewing prior behavioral and medication interventions will often identify the reasons those treatments failed and how implementation issues might be resolved in the future. Often, previous failure with the urine alarm is due to inadequate parental instruction, preparation, and establishment of appropriate expectations for treatment. In cases of prior failed urine alarm treatment, we have found that parents were not properly instructed to awaken the child, and they did not realize the treatment can require 16 weeks of effort to be successful. Frequent and careful monitoring by an experienced behavioral psychologist during treatment can prevent repeating a disappointing experience. Previous drug treatment failures are the norm rather than the exception, and parents can be reassured that the continued bed-wetting is not due to inadequate parenting.

Because some research has suggested that extremely noncompliant children are more likely to experience relapse following successful treatment (Dische et al., 1983; Sacks & DeLeon, 1973), a screening questionnaire such as the Child Behavior Checklist (CBCL; Achenbach & Edelbrook, 1983) or the Behavior Assessment System for Children (BASC; Reynolds & Kamphaus, 1998) can identify children who need additional attention. Children with externalizing behavioral problems (Externalizing T score of greater than 70) are likely to be noncompliant with any parental requests, let alone the significant demands of waking to the urine alarm in the middle of the night. Likewise, internalizing behavior problems such as significant levels of anxiety and depression may interfere with the enuretic child's capacity to handle the rigors of urine alarm treatment. A clinical decision has to be made whether to train parents in contingency management prior to beginning behavioral treatment for enuresis. Failure to identify child noncompliance and internalizing problems prior to urine alarm treatment can lead to a poor outcome, further contributing to a child's already lowered sense of confidence and self-esteem that is typically associated with bed-wetting (Moffatt, 1994).

Parental attitudes and beliefs have implications for those families that enter treatment. A large survey of parents of bed wetters (Haque et al., 1981) indicated that as many as 35% dealt with the enuresis by punishing the child when bed-wetting occurred. Butler, Brewin, and Forsythe (1986) found that a greater perceived burden on the mother and attributing the cause of bed-wetting to the child were associated with greater parental intolerance as assessed by Morgan and Young's (1975) Tolerance for Enuresis Scale, and this has been predictive of treatment dropout. Informing parents that bed-wetting is a deficit in physical learning rather than a willful act can lead to the family support necessary for behavioral treatment to be implemented.

Because of the genetic contribution to enuresis, the problem of bed-wetting may be a common experience within the family. Young and Morgan (1972) reported a relationship between treatment dropout and positive family history of enuresis, and Fielding and Doleys (1989) have suggested that these findings may be indicative of complacency or poor motivation in these families. The potentially large demands of behavioral treatment can be disrupted by a lack of motivation for complete implementation and a lack of cooperation in the family. We use a behavioral contracting approach designed to increase cooperation and understanding of each family member's responsibilities with treatment. If the family is unable to agree to the goals of treatment, it does not begin.

Assessment of family stress and disturbance, and the physical home environment, is important because they have been associated with slow response to treatment, treatment failure, and relapse. Couchells, Johnson, Carter, and Walker (1981) reported that families seeking help for bed-wetting are more likely to be experiencing stress than those families who do not seek treatment. Family disturbances and high maternal anxiety have been associated with slow response to treatment (Morgan & Young, 1975). Researchers (Devlin & O'Cathain, 1990; Dische et al., 1983) have reported that marital discord, mental or physical handicap of family members, poor maternal coping skills, and unusual family living arrangements and stress were predictors of behavioral treatment failure and relapse.

Having the parents complete the Locke-Wallace Marital Adjustment Test (MAT; Locke & Wallace, 1959) may indicate significant marital distress (MAT scores below 85 for either spouse) that could interfere with urine alarm treatment. Among single parents, typically mothers, the Beck Depression Inventory (BDI; Beck, Rush, Shaw, & Emery, 1980) may identify significant parental distress (scores above 15) that may require therapeutic attention prior to starting behavior therapy for enuresis. Finally, the Symptom Checklist (SCL-90-R; Derogatis, 1977) is useful in screening for significant levels of global psychiatric distress. Clinically significant elevations in any of the previous areas of psychological functioning would allow the health care provider to judge whether prior marital or family therapy is necessary to prevent a negative outcome when the urine alarm is used for enuresis.

Table 13.1

Treatment Outcome and Symptom Reduction

Clinical Subsample	Total Sample	At Least 20 Weeks of Treatment Completed	Patients Who Requested Retreatment after Relapsing
Sample size	*N* = 333	*N* = 261	*N* = 73
Percent cured	65	80	60
Percent failed* and/or dropped out#	35*#	20*	40*
Percent reduction in wets per week by end of treatment	88	57	82

Note: Mayo Clinic Enuresis Conditioning Program (1990–2001).

A 2-week baseline of wetting frequency should be collected. Parents can complete record forms that include wet or dry nights, the size of the wet spot, and whether the child spontaneously awakened to void in the toilet. Generally, the more frequently the child wets, the longer it will take the child to stop bed-wetting (Houts et al., 1994). Thus, it is important to determine if a child wets more than once per night. This may not be apparent until urine alarm treatment begins, as there is often only one large wet spot in the morning. Multiple wetters typically require more time to reach the success criterion of 14 consecutive dry nights, and informing parents accordingly contributes to realistic expectations about progress and avoids discouragement and possible dropout.

Although knowledge of patient and family information that has been associated with a poorer outcome is important, the most accurate guess is that 60% of bed wetters treated with FSHT will cease wetting. However, being aware of correlates of treatment outcome may further improve the odds of success. The first author makes this argument in the outcome of his enuresis conditioning program, indicating that the success rate of those enuretic children who completed 20 weeks of treatment was 80%, but including children who dropped out prior to 20 weeks a success rate of 65% was realized (Table 13.1).

DEFINING FULL SPECTRUM HOME TRAINING

This FSHT program was designed to provide parents and children with an inexpensive, easy-to-use, and effective treatment package for simple bed-wetting. Our goal was to develop the strongest possible combination of behavioral procedures, and we created a full set of support materials for the package that would facilitate its home use. The treatment program has been described in detail in a self-help book for parents and teachers (Houts & Liebert, 1984) and includes urine alarm training, cleanliness training, retention control training, and overlearning, as well as several additional features designed to enhance its effectiveness and simplify its use.

From its inception, FSHT has been done in a single group session to minimize the financial cost to families. Parents and children filled out an explicit behavioral contract together as a trainer modeled each of the procedures point by point. A manual containing explanations and support materials was provided to parents (*Parent Guide*), and a wall chart (*Daily Steps to a Dry Bed*) was given to the child. Through systematic research previously reviewed, the program has evolved to include the addition of overlearning and then the "graduated" overlearning to address our dissatisfaction with a 24% relapse rate. This addition has reduced the relapse rate to approximately 10% today.

Our research with this treatment program has also sought to deliver the treatment in a single session via a didactic video tape to further minimize costs to families. Compared to delivery by a professional, the delivery by videotape was considerably less effective (Houts et al., 1987). Therefore, we do not suggest that parents administer this treatment without having some assistance from a professional who can monitor the child's progress and make minor modifications to the program where needed. Nevertheless, the program can be carried out with minimal professional assistance, and in our current clinical work, we typically follow a four-visit protocol. The first author's enuresis conditioning program begins with a group didactic session in which the child and parent learn about enuresis, its treatment, and a behavioral contract is jointly completed. The remaining four sessions are done on an individual basis and are designed to have face-to-face contact with the child and parent at critical points in treatment (i.e., actual start of treatment, 2-weeks after start of treatment, when overlearning is to be initiated, and at the end of treatment). However, the child and family are informed that any additional contact with the therapist can be requested at any time.

IMPLEMENTING FULL SPECTRUM HOME TRAINING

All children who receive this treatment should be initially screened by a physician to rule out organic causes for their bed-wetting. The program is appropriate and most effective for children whose problem is primary nocturnal enuresis. Provided children meet these screening criteria, the treatment program can generally be administered in their own home after an initial training session.

At the first visit, the Family Support Agreement is completed and all aspects of the training are demonstrated. It is also important to demystify the problem by pointing out to the child and family how common the disorder is and emphasizing that the problem is not a willful or defiant act. The stage must be set for effective collaboration between the child, parent, and therapist. The first author has added a brief second visit after the initial didactic presentation to allow the family to make an informed decision about whether they are ready to begin treatment versus pursuing an alternative such as medication. If the child and family are interested in doing the urine alarm treatment, they begin the program at the second visit.

At the second visit, which occurs the following week, the procedures are reviewed to insure that the family is doing everything correctly and keeping accurate records. After the second visit, the family is contacted by telephone to track the child's progress and to solve any minor problems of implementation. The third visit occurs when the child attains 14 dry nights in a row. At this visit, the procedures for overlearning are introduced, and the family returns for the fourth visit when the child attains 14 consecutive dry nights in overlearning, which is the designated end of treatment. Children are followed for 1 year to monitor relapse, and if a child returns to regular wetting they are instructed to contact the therapist to reinstate the urine alarm until the child is dry for 14 consecutive dry nights. Re-treatment often progresses at a quicker pace.

In the following discussion of FSHT training, we have emphasized some of our more recent modifications to the procedures based on clinical experience. We are in the process of collecting systematic research data on the efficacy of these modifications, and they are presented here as suggestions for parents and professionals who may want to implement the training that has been described in more detail in *Bed-Wetting: A Guide for Parents and Children* (Houts & Liebert, 1984).

The Family Support Agreement is a behavioral contract completed by the parents and child, with the assistance of the trainer, at the initial training session. The contract specifies exactly what the child and parents must do to carry out all of the procedures of FSHT. We have found that having parents and child sign this written agreement and refer back to it during the training, helps remind them of their mutual commitment and obligations, especially at those points when they get discouraged or confused about what to do. Table 13.2 shows the Family Support Agreement of FSHT.

As shown in Item 9 of the Family Support Agreement, FSHT includes a version of retention control training that we call *self-control training*. Parents and children do this procedure once a day during a specified 2-hour period. The child begins by drinking a large glass of water. If the child feels the need to urinate, the child tells the parent about this, and the parent instructs the child to postpone going to the bathroom for 3 minutes. If the child can wait 3 minutes and then use the toilet, the child is given a

Table 13.2

Family Support Agreement (Used in Full Spectrum Home Training)

1. _____ & _____ to carry out the training procedures exactly as described in order to accomplish the mutually desired goal of a dry bed.

2. Training will be carried out for at least 112 days (16 weeks).

3. Parents and family agree not to punish, scold, ridicule, or refer to "bed-wetting" in a negative way during the training.

4. Both parents and child understand that training is most effective when the child is not overtired or stressed. Therefore _____ & _____ agrees that _____ P.M. is a reasonable bedtime, and _____ agrees to go to bed at that time every night.

5. NO RESTRICTIONS ON LIQUIDS. _____ will be allowed to drink as much liquid as desired at all times. However, parents will decide which liquids their child will drink.

6. Parents and family agree to provide support, help, and understanding to _____ . They will praise him/her when dry and provide encouragement that progress will be made. However, they understand that the training itself includes sufficient pressure and agree they will not urge him/her to try harder or do better.

7. Parents and family agree not to complain about the effects of the training on them or about the urine alarm, but to support and help instead. _____ also agrees not to complain about the training and to cooperate fully.

8. The family will provide a relatively stress-free environment at home during training.

9. _____ & _____ agree to participate in Self-Control Training once a day during the hours of _____ & _____ as explained in the Parent Guide.

   Parents will give _____ money for each success according to the Reward Schedule for Self-Control Training.

10. _____ agrees to follow the procedure of Cleanliness Training as outlined on the wall chart and to put wet sheets and underwear in _____ .

    Parents agree to keep clean sheets and clean underwear in the _____ in the child's room for him/her to use when remaking the bed.

11. Parents agree to wake _____ immediately if the buzzer rings and he/she does not wake up.

    IT IS ESSENTIAL THAT THE PERSON RESPONSIBLE FOR WAKING THE CHILD WILL BE ABLE TO HEAR AND BE AWAKENED BY THE ALARM. NOTHING ELSE SHOULD BE DONE TO WAKE THE CHILD DURING THE NIGHT. THE ALARM MUST DO THIS.

12. Parents agree to check the batteries regularly and to have replacement batteries ready when needed. Parents will also check the absorbent pockets for wear and replace these when needed.

Table 13.2 *(Continued)*

13. _____ & _____ agree that only _____ will touch the alarm, except for alarm testing as described earlier.

14. Parents agree to assume all responsibilities associated with training for a dry bed as spelled out in the Parent Guide. _____ agrees to follow the Daily Steps to a Dry Bed outlined on the wall chart.

15. OVERLEARNING. When _____ has been dry for 14 consecutive nights, the Overlearning procedures will be followed until the child is dry for 14 more nights in a row. Overlearning will be explained when the child returns for the second follow-up appointment.

16. It is understood that every child has an occasional wet bed, especially when sick or under stress. Do Not Worry About This. Tell Your Child Not To Worry.

_____

(Child's Signature)

_____

(Parent's Signature)

_____

(Parent's Signature)

_____

(Witness or Other Family Member)

nickel. When the child completes a holding goal, the next day a new goal of 3 minutes longer is set and the reward increases by a nickel for each new goal. This part of the training is completed when the child successfully completes a 45-minute goal in a step-by-step fashion. It is helpful to the family that partial or inconsistent implementation of self-control training will only lengthen treatment and may reduce its overall effectiveness.

Parents make some common mistakes in implementing self-control training. For example, the father of a 6-year-old boy mistakenly allowed his son to hold for as long as possible rather than follow the step-by-step procedure of increasing the holding time in 3-minute increments. This defeated the purpose of training the child to discriminate between the different sensations associated with varying levels of bladder filling. This child had little difficulty holding for 3 minutes, but he did not know his own bodily feelings well enough to be able to urinate at the end of 3 minutes after first feeling the need. In the early stages of self-control training, the challenge is for the child to be able to urinate at a specified time. Only later, as the holding time approaches 45 minutes, does the challenge become one of holding back and thereby increasing functional bladder capacity. Another common mistake is for parents to forget to time the child. This can be easily overcome by setting a kitchen or oven timer with an alarm that can signal when the holding time is past.

Full Spectrum Home Training also includes cleanliness training (see Item 10 in Table 13.2) that requires the child to remake the bed after the alarm has sounded. The steps involved in cleanliness training are displayed on a wall chart (*Daily Steps to A Dry Bed*) in the child's room and colored either "wet" or "dry" for each day of the training, displaying a record of the child's progress. We have found that parents and children may not comply with cleanliness training, especially if the child has wet just enough to make the alarm sound but not so much as to get the bed wet. This can occur with the newer body-worn alarm devices that will sound immediately when the child wets the underpants and stops any further urination. To make sure that the child is fully awake after a wetting episode, we instruct parents to have the child go through with the full procedure of remaking the bed even if the sheets are not wet.

Item 11 of the Family Support Agreement emphasizes the importance of waking the child immediately after the alarm sounds. This is the most important part of urine alarm training and must be done consistently for the first 3 weeks of the training so that the child can learn to respond to the alarm and wake without assistance from parents. There is nothing magical about using an alarm, and parents and children are told that the alarm is used solely for waking the child immediately after wetting starts. Parents must be able to hear the alarm sound, so using a "baby monitor" device or temporarily sleeping in a room closer to the child's can be helpful. Waking up as a reaction to the wetting episode, not just to the alarm, is the important response. Children are instructed to follow the rule of getting out of bed and standing up before turning off the alarm. Parents are told never to turn off the alarm for the child. Parents are also asked to record each wet (e.g., its time of occurrence, the size of the wet spot) and whether children awoke on their own to urinate in the toilet. This information is useful to the therapist in monitoring progress and the need to use other behavioral interventions such as a waking schedule for children not arousing to the alarm. This information is important for the child and parent to document improvements in wetting and to reinforce perseverance during as many as 20 weeks of treatment.

Full Spectrum Home Training incorporates overlearning (Item 15 of Table 13.2) to prevent relapse once a child attains 14 consecutive dry nights. In our previous work, we implemented overlearning by having the child drink 16 ounces of water during the hour before bedtime once the child had attained 14 consecutive dry nights. This nightly drinking continued until the child attained 14 more consecutive dry nights while drinking the water. Although this method of implementing overlearning has consistently resulted in reducing relapse by 50% compared to basic urine alarm training excluding overlearning, we have noted that some children who failed to achieve 14 more dry nights in overlearning also failed to recover from the relapse induced by overlearning. Therefore, we have modified the implementation of overlearning by gradually increasing the amount of water that a child drinks before going to bed. Our preliminary results from this gradual approach to overlearning suggest that the rate of relapse can be reduced yet another 50%. The gradual approach to overlearning has been adopted by the Mayo Clinic Enuresis Conditioning Program.

The incrementally increasing approach to overlearning begins by determining a maximum amount of water a child should drink based on the child's estimated FBC. The child's FBC is determined with the formula, 1 ounce for each year of age plus 2 ounces (Berger, Maizels, Moran, Conway, & Firlit, 1983). Thus, for an 8-year-old child, the maximum amount would be 10 ounces. We have all of our patients begin the overlearning process by drinking 4 ounces of water 15 minutes before bedtime. If they remain dry for two nights while drinking the 4-ounce amount, then the amount of water increases to 6 ounces. If they remain dry for two nights at the 6-ounce amount, then the water is increased by 2 more ounces to 8 ounces. The 2-ounce increase continues in this fashion until the child's maximum amount is reached. The child continues to drink this maximum amount until 14 consecutive dry nights are attained as measured from the beginning of overlearning. About one third of the children who achieve an initial arrest (14 consecutive dry nights) go on to complete this form of overlearning without having a wet night in overlearning. Most, however, do experience some wetting during overlearning, typically as they approach the goal of drinking their maximum amount. When a child has a wet night during overlearning, the child is instructed to drink the amount of water previously consumed on the most recent preceding dry night. The child then drinks this amount until dry for 5 consecutive dry nights, after which time the amount increases by 2 ounces for every 2 consecutive dry nights until the maximum amount is reached. Obviously, parents must keep accurate records to implement this procedure correctly. Because of the complexity of this portion of the treatment, we insist that the child and parent have a follow-up visit with us to assure their full understanding of the procedure and determine appropriate expectations.

Most children can attain the goal of a "lasting cure" for bed-wetting by following the basic steps of FSHT. Parents should seek professional assistance to monitor their child's progress and to determine what modifications of the basic procedures, if any, are needed for their child to be successful. Discussed in the following section are the most common implementation problems with FSHT or any other urine alarm-based approach to treating bed-wetting. These problems include waking difficulties and delayed attainment of the success criteria that can lead to increased frustration and hopelessness in the child if not attended to by the therapist in a prompt and effective way. Our clinical observations suggest that perhaps only 2 out of 10 children will become disenchanted with the treatment and want to quit following a wet just short of the 14 consecutive dry night success criteria. Assisting the child to set realistic expectations and highlighting treatment progress documented in the treatment records is one of the most important things a professional can do and it represents a critical element in effective treatment of bed-wetting. Our research (Houts et al., 1987) and clinical observations lead us to believe that a family report of prior urine alarm treatment failures are the result of the absence of needed therapist supervision and guidance. The importance of proper therapist guidance to prevent or manage premature quitting of the treatment is described in the following section.

Common Implementation Problems

The two most important difficulties with implementing FSHT are problems in waking the child and problems in the delayed response of some children, each of which can lead to frustration and termination of treatment before the child becomes dry. When the therapist recognizes and intervenes early, the bed-wetting child has a greater chance of benefiting from treatment.

Waking Problems.   Urine alarm treatments such as FSHT will only work if a child is systematically awakened immediately after the onset of wetting. Although numerous studies have failed to find a reliable relationship between depth of sleep (as measured by EEG) and enuresis, we have found that some children are more difficult to arouse from sleep than others. Occasionally, a child will fail to wake up to the sound of the urine alarm, so it is crucial to establish a waking routine early in the treatment. This requires having the child get out of bed and get to his or her feet before disconnecting and turning off the urine alarm. With younger children who are especially difficult to arouse, it may be necessary for one parent to sleep in this child's room to ensure that the child is awakened immediately when the alarm sounds and that the child is awake and alert. To assure the child is fully awake, parents should ask the child to perform short-term memory tasks. For example, asking the child to repeat the home phone number backwards or remembering an agreed-on wake-up password is good evidence that the child is fully awake. We have also suggested that the parent wash the child's face if there is still doubt about the child's alertness.

If, within the first 2 weeks of treatment, a child is still not waking to the urine alarm, it is useful to implement a waking schedule (Azrin et al., 1974) to disrupt the child's sleep pattern so that he or she becomes sensitized to the alarm. During the first night of the waking program, parents are instructed to wake the child hourly using minimal prompts. At each awakening, the child is praised for a dry bed and encouraged to void in the toilet. The second night forward, the waking schedule continues with the child being awakened once each night. Following a dry night, the parents wake the child 30 minutes earlier than the previous night. If the child wets during the night, then the time of waking remains the same as the previous night. The nightly waking ends when the scheduled time for waking the child has move forward to within 30 minutes immediately following bedtime. The procedure is very demanding for the whole family and should be used only if absolutely necessary to train a child to awaken to the alarm. Close supervision by the therapist is essential. It should also be remembered that urine alarm treatments for bed-wetting are not perfect, and 1 or 2 of every 10 children will fail to cease bedwetting with this treatment.

Delayed Response Problems. Most children reach the first goal of 14 consecutive dry nights within 8 weeks of treatment. After overlearning is initiated, the second goal of an additional 14 straight dry nights will be attained on the average of 4 more weeks. Some children will not attain the first 14 consecutive dry nights even after 14 weeks of treatment, and their delayed response is often frustrating to them and to their parents.

One way to deal with the problems of delayed response is to keep parents and children focused on the progress being made. This requires regular follow-up and supportive therapy sessions with a family. Even though children may not complete the first goal of treatment within 8 weeks, they usually show evidence of progress, which is clearly documented in the treatment records. The therapist points out the signs of progress such as (a) a reduction in the number of nights that the child needed adult assistance to awaken, (b) a reduction in wetting to once per night among children who started out wetting two or three times each night, (c) a reduction in wetting frequency, (d) a reduction in the size of the wet spot, and (e) an increase in the interval between bedtime and the first wetting episode. Additional interventions include a simple token economy in which the child receives credits or points for adhering to the treatment procedure to earn rewards. This procedure can increase enthusiasm in younger children who tend to lose sight of their stated goal of a dry bed.

Delayed responding can also be related to children who wet multiple times each night. These children may also be good candidates for combined behavioral and pharmacotherapy and would require close collaboration with a physician. Given the occurrence of side effects of other drug treatments for enuresis (i.e., imipramine or oxybutynin chloride), we focus the discussion exclusively on DDAVP. To date, five studies have examined the combined effectiveness of DDAVP and the urine alarm. The initial investigations of this combined urine alarm and DDAVP treatment indicated that these children experienced significantly less wetting during the initial stages of treatment and also suggested more children became dry compared to the urine alarm alone (Bradbury & Meadow, 1995; Sukhai, Mol, & Harris, 1989). Three recent studies (Fai-Ngo Ng & Wong, 2005; Gibb et al., 2004; Leebeek-Groenewegen, Blom, Sukhai, & van der Heijden, 2001) in the context of well-controlled investigations have been less encouraging. These studies continue to demonstrate less wetting at the start of treatment with the combination of DDAVP and the urine alarm, but the number of children who ultimately stop wetting is no better than the urine alarm combined with placebo. It still may be advantageous to those children who wet multiple times each night as they are more likely to drop out of basic urine alarm treatment. However, more research is needed to test the efficacy of such combinations in reducing drop-outs, especially with difficult cases such as multiple wetters. Both authors have treated patients with a combination of FSHT and DDAVP for multiple wetters and found that it seems to reduce the frustration of parents and children who would otherwise be at risk for treatment dropout due to delays in reaching the success criteria. How and at what point to withdraw the medication from FSHT is a question that needs to be answered by future research.

RESEARCH FINDINGS

We have systematically investigated FSHT at the University of Memphis since the early 1980s. Table 13.3 summarizes 1-year follow-up results from six observations of FSHT, four of which are from published studies (Houts, Liebert, & Padawer, 1983; Houts et al., 1986, 1987; Whelan & Houts, 1990). The 1991 sample shows outcomes from an unpublished randomized trial that compared FSHT to imipramine and oxybutynin.

The 137 cases from 2,000 were accumulated in a private enuresis clinic over a period of 14 years and represent effectiveness data from a real-world clinical sample. About three out of every four children treated with this approach can be expected to stop bed-wetting at the end of the average of 12 weeks needed to complete the treatment.

Table 13.1 on page 445 summarizes the treatment outcome of the Enuresis Conditioning Program at the Mayo Clinic from 1990 to 2001.

This Mayo Clinic Enuresis Conditioning Program is quite similar to FSHT except that bell-and-pad urine alarm designs are utilized, and the retention control component of FSHT is not used. The initial cure rate of 65% for the total sample is consistent with the published literature. Those children who failed treatment or dropped out prior to 20 weeks still showed a 49% reduction in wets per week. A subsample of children who were re-treated showed a 60% success rate.

Table 13.3
Children Who Ceased Bed-Wetting or Relapsed at One-Year
Follow-Up with Full Spectrum Home Training

Date of Observation	1983	1986	1987	1990	1991	2000
Sample size	$N = 59$	$N = 15$	$N = 20$	$N = 17$	$N = 68$	$N = 137$
Percent cured at one year	62	47	56	53	65	68
Percent relapsed at one year	24	14	20	22	11	11

At the 1-year follow-up for children treated with FSHT, 6 out of every 10 children are permanently dry. The lower relapse rates observed in the 1988 and 1991 samples were from children who did our modified overlearning where they gradually increased nighttime drinking in 2-ounce increments adjusted for their age. In the other samples, overlearning was done in the original fashion of having children consume 16 ounces of water regardless of age. We now consistently find that only about 10% of children relapse. This may be compared to 40% without overlearning and 20% with the original type of overlearning. We have not completely solved the problem of relapse, but we have come some distance in preventing relapse after successful treatment with the urine alarm.

A current review of the literature has not revealed any significant innovations in the use of the basic urine alarm or packaged multicomponent approaches. Mellon and McGrath (2000) concluded that the multicomponent dry-bed training was an evidence-based treatment for enuresis as long as it included the use of the urine alarm. Recently, this treatment was successfully delivered in a group format with 80% of patients becoming completely dry and this outcome is consistent with prior reviews. Further, even enuretic children with borderline to clinically significant behavior problems were successful with dry-bed training and their behavior problems diminished following successful treatment (HiraSing, van Leerdam, Bolk-Bennink, & Koot, 2002). This finding by itself is unique in that behavior problems were thought to interfere with the implementation of basic urine alarm treatment (Wagner & Johnson, 1988). Van Kampen et. al. (2004) studied a modified, and subsequently inadequate, version of FSHT (Houts et al., 1983) that was considered to be a "Probably Efficacious" treatment for enuresis (Mellon & McGrath, 2000). This study is notable for the fact that an independent researcher studied its efficacy and identified predictors of relapse within the year after treatment such as bladder instability and behavior problems, both of which are consistent with the literature. Three other studies examined the effectiveness of the urine alarm alone, compared to desmopressin or combined with other behavioral treatments

(Butler & Robinson, 2002; Jensen & Kristensen, 2001; Longstaffe, Moffatt, & Whalen, 2000). These studies highlighted positive changes in self-esteem with treatment and identified that bladder dysfunction is associated with a poor outcome and that, contrary to prior research, more frequent wetting at baseline is associated with a better outcome with the urine alarm treatment. Finally, El-Anany, Maghraby, Shaker, and Abdel-Moneim (1999) utilized an alarm clock with a waking schedule as treatment and reported an initial success rate comparable to basic urine alarm treatment. Pennesi, Pitter, Bordugo, Minisini, and Peratoner (2004) reported on a treatment that involved a physician-suggested reinforcement plan for dry nights and the use of pelvic floor exercises, providing an excellent example of how therapist attention will have some therapeutic effects in any treatment without any experimental controls. Caution is advised until other researchers can replicate the treatment findings of these studies.

As previously mentioned, the urine alarm treatment alone, or combined with other behavioral interventions, is the most effective means of treating nocturnal enuresis or bed-wetting. Given that this treatment approach is considered an evidenced-based intervention, the research regarding nocturnal enuresis would be better served by focusing on etiologic and psychosocial factors involved in the development and maintenance of enuresis and the differential effectiveness of urine alarm treatment in subcategories of enuretic children. Rosen and Davison (2003) argue that psychology would be better served by uncovering "empirically supported principles" (ESPs) of behavior change versus "certifying" empirically supported treatments (ESTs) as the latter only promotes the propagation of new therapies simply by adding inert components to already effective treatments. Research that further investigates the physiologic mechanisms that cause enuresis in the context of the child's developmental and learning history has the potential of pushing a proven effective psychosocial treatment closer to a success rate of 100% by unifying these bodies of knowledge. Given that the urine alarm and the mechanism(s) of action through which it likely works is able to transcend a multitude of likely etiologies and still be successful in treating the majority of a heterogeneous population of children who wet the bed, we propose that studying enuresis in the context of learning principles would be scientifically rewarding.

CASE STUDY

HISTORY

William was a 9-year-old male who had been wetting since infancy. He was the third child of four in a two-parent home. William attained daytime bladder and bowel control by the age of 2.5 and had no indication of urinary tract infection or other physical anomaly based on a medical examination. There was a positive family history of bed-wetting in the paternal grandfather, father, and William's 15-year-old brother, all of whom spontaneously remitted bed-wetting at about 13 years of age. William suffered from no apparent psychological problems, but expressed his frustration with the bed-wetting and the interference it caused in his desire for sleepovers with peers.

CLINICAL ASSESSMENT

During the clinical interview with William and his mother, it was reported that William was a very well-behaved child who was also an exceptional student and athlete (i.e., honor role, traveling soccer team). The parent's responses to the Child Behavior Checklist in fact revealed no significant clinical elevations for William in any area. However, both William and his mother admitted that he was embarrassed by his bed-wetting given his 6-year-old brother no longer wets. William was also unwilling to participate in sleepovers with his friends for fear of wetting or being discovered to be wearing a disposable diaper. William's mother reported that he wet the bed on the average of five out of seven nights of the week and had done so since he was toilet trained. Two weeks of baseline recording of wet nights prior to the clinical interview confirmed this reported frequency. William was described as a deep sleeper, but was usually dry when sleeping away from home.

William's parents completed the Enuresis Tolerance Scale and the Locke-Wallace Marital Adjustment Test, neither of which revealed extreme beliefs, harsh attitudes about William's bed-wetting, or significant dissatisfaction with their marriage. Both parents were very concerned about William's self-esteem being affected because of the continued wetting and did not punish him for the problem.

TREATMENT

A week later, William and his parents attended a 1-hour training session for FSHT during which the problem of enuresis was demystified, each component of treatment was reviewed, and all treatment materials were given to the family. This session involved the completion of the Family Support Agreement as described previously. William and his parents agreed to carry out all components of treatment for a minimum of 16 weeks, and they all signed the contract. In addition, the parents were provided with a treatment manual and wall chart, instructed in how to keep treatment records, and given a body-worn urine alarm. Many reliable and relatively inexpensive urine alarms are available on the market, and William's parents were informed about www.thebedwettingstore.com to consider other urine alarm models if they were interested.

The following week William and his parents met the therapist to review treatment progress. William was well into his self-control training and had achieved 5 out of 7 dry nights. The therapist praised William for his progress and emphasized the need to adhere to all treatment components and maintain a patient and persistent attitude in treatment. William was then scheduled to return to the clinic every 2 to 3 weeks to monitor progress.

During the next 8 weeks, William obtained 12 consecutive dry nights on two separate occasions. However, he also failed to complete Self-Control Training. Problem solving with the parents revealed that the onset of the school year and the mother returning to the workforce contributed to a disruption in treatment and the need to reestablish treatment schedules and closer supervision. Another 10 consecutive days of dryness followed by a wet seemed to overwhelm William, and he began to deny he had wet and hid his underwear. William's parents scheduled an impromptu follow-up meeting with the therapist in hopes of preventing William from quitting prematurely. Praising William for his perseverance, reviewing his progress to date, and highlighting his overall accomplishments (i.e., honor student, traveling soccer team) that resulted from not giving-up seemed to rejuvenate his enthusiasm and commitment to be successful. At this point, William immediately obtained his 14-day success criteria and began overlearning. William completed overlearning in 3 more weeks of treatment with only two additional wets. Though the treatment lasted a total of 19 weeks, both William and his parents were extremely pleased with his success and eager to participate fully in future sleepovers. William remained dry at the 1-year follow-up.

CONCLUSION

When parents are concerned about a child who has enuresis, the close collaboration between a behavioral psychologist and a physician is critical for the proper treatment of the child. Given that there are effective treatments for enuresis, the parent should not just be reassured that the child will outgrow the problem as this risks lowered self-esteem and embarrassment. It is important to get a careful assessment to determine contributing factors in the enuresis. Children who have daytime wetting or those whose nighttime wetting has resumed after a period of 1 year or more of consecutive dry nights may require rather extensive medical examination and treatment. All children, even those who are simple bed wetters without apparent complications, should first be examined by their physician. If the problem is simple bed-wetting, or primary nocturnal enuresis without medical complications, then the parent can assist the child to overcome the problem through home-implemented behavioral treatment. However, we do not recommend implementing home training without the assistance of a qualified and knowledgeable professional as this person plays a vital role in providing guidance and support and solving problem that will increase the likelihood of success.

Full Spectrum Home Training is the treatment of choice in most cases. If the family is intact and the parents are generally supportive and understanding of the child, this program can be carried out by having the parents follow the detailed instructions provided in the *Parent Guide*. For such families, weekly consultation may not be necessary, though the professional should provide some support and follow-up even if only via telephone contact. For other families, weekly consultation with a professional may be necessary to keep the family motivated and to insure that the procedures are followed carefully. Most cases of simple bed-wetting can be successfully treated with these methods.

Whereas medication treatment is not generally a permanent solution to enuresis, it may be the best alternative for some children, especially those for whom the enuresis has become a major barrier to social development and self-esteem and whose families are unable to implement a program of behavior therapy. In such cases, desmopressin or DDAVP may provide some temporary and safe control over the problem and enable the child to participate in activities that require sleeping over such as camping trips or summer camp.

Because prolonged, uncontrolled wetting can result in damage to self-esteem, a permanent solution to the problem is needed. When families are experiencing difficulties such as marital problems or excessive stress due to parents' work schedules, they should get help to solve these problems to prepare them to implement behavioral treatment for a child's bed-wetting. Like most parent training approaches to child problems, FSHT for primary enuresis requires that parents work together to support the child and provide a consistent environment where the child can learn new skills.

When a child wets the bed, there is no substitute for a caring and concerned family that understands children rarely choose to be enuretic. In the United States, some 5 to 7 million school-aged children exhibit enuresis, and given the availability of effective treatments for simple bed-wetting, it is possible that parents and professionals can become partners in providing the help needed to deal with this age-old problem of childhood.

REFERENCES

Achenbach, T. M., & Edelbrock, C. (1983). *Manual for the child behavior checklist*. Burlington: University of Vermont, Department of Psychiatry.

American Academy of Pediatrics Committee on Radiology. (1980). Excretory urography for evaluation of enuresis. *Pediatrics, 65*, 644–655.

American Psychiatric Association. (1994). *Diagnostic and statistical manual of mental disorders* (4th ed.). Washington, DC: Author.

Arnold, S. J., & Ginsberg, A. (1973). Enuresis, incidence and pertinence of genitourinary disease in healthy enuretic children. *Urology, 2,* 437–443.

Azrin, N. H., & Besalel, V. A. (1979). *A parent's guide to bedwetting control.* New York: Simon & Schuster.

Azrin, N. H., Sneed, T. J., & Foxx, R. M. (1974). Dry-bed training: Rapid elimination of childhood enuresis. *Behavior Research and Therapy, 12,* 147–156.

Azrin, N. H., & Thienes, P. M. (1978). Rapid elimination of enuresis by intensive learning without a conditioning apparatus. *Behavior Therapy, 9,* 342–354.

Azrin, N. H., Thienes-Hontos, P., & Besalel-Azrin, V. (1979). Elimination of enuresis without a conditioning apparatus: An extension by office instruction of the child and parents. *Behavior Therapy, 10,* 14–19.

Baker, B. L. (1969). Symptom treatment and symptom substitution in enuresis. *Journal of Abnormal Psychology, 74,* 42–49.

Bakker, E., van Sprundel, M., van der Auwera, J., van Gool, J., & Wyndaele, J. (2002). Voiding habits and wetting in a population of 4,332 Belgian schoolchildren aged between 10 and 14 years. *Scandinavian Journal of Urology and Nephrology, 36,* 354–362.

Bakwin, H. (1973). The genetics of enuresis. In I. Kolvin, R. C. MacKeith, & S. R. Meadow (Eds.), *Bladder control and enuresis* (pp. 73–77). London: William Heinemann.

Beck, A. T., Rush, A. J., Shaw, B. F., & Emery, G. (1980). *Cognitive therapy of depression.* New York: Guilford Press.

Berger, R. M., Maizels, M., Moran, G. C., Conway, J. J., & Firlit, C. F. (1983). Bladder capacity (ounces) equals age (years) plus 2 predicts normal bladder capacity and aids in diagnosis of abnormal voiding patterns. *Journal of Urology, 129,* 347–349.

Bollard, J. (1982). A 2-year follow-up of bedwetters treated with dry-bed training and standard conditioning. *Behavior Research and Therapy, 20,* 571–580.

Bradbury, M., & Meadow, S. (1995). Combined treatment with enuresis alarm and desmopressin for nocturnal enuresis. *Acta Paediatrica, 84*(9), 1014–1018.

Butler, R. (1998). Annotation: Night wetting in children—Psychological aspects. *Journal of Child Psychology and Psychiatry, 39,* 453–463.

Butler, R. J., Brewin, C. R., & Forsythe, W. I. (1986). Maternal attributions and tolerance for nocturnal enuresis. *Behavior Research and Therapy, 24,* 307–312.

Butler, R., Redfern, E., & Forsythe, W. (1994). The child's construing of nocturnal enuresis: A method of inquiry and prediction of outcome. *Journal of Child Psychology, 34,* 447–454.

Butler, R., & Robinson, J. (2002). Alarm treatment for childhood nocturnal enuresis: An investigation of within-treatment variables. *Scandinavian Journal of Urology and Nephrology, 36,* 268–272.

Buttarazzi, P. J. (1977). Oxybutynin chloride (ditropan) in enuresis. *Journal of Urology, 118,* 46.

Couchells, S. M., Johnson, S. B., Carter, R., & Walker, D. (1981). Behavioral and environmental characteristics of treated and untreated enuretic children and matched nonenuretic controls. *Journal of Pediatrics, 99,* 812–816.

DeJonge, G. A. (1973). Epidemiology of enuresis: A survey of the literature. In I. Kolvin, R. C. MacKeith, & S. R. Meadow (Eds.), *Bladder control and enuresis* (pp. 39–46). London: William Heinemann.

Derogatis, L. R. (1977). *SCL-90: Administration, scoring and procedures manual for the revised version.* Baltimore: Clinical Psychometric Research.

Devlin, J., & O'Cathain, C. (1990). Predicting treatment outcome in nocturnal enuresis. *Archives of Disease in Childhood, 65,* 1158–1161.

Dische, S., Yule, W., Corbett, J., & Hand, D. (1983). Childhood nocturnal enuresis: Factors associated with outcome of treatment with an enuresis alarm. *Developmental Medicine and Neurology, 25,* 67–80.

Djurhuus, J. C., Norgaard, J. P., & Rittig, S. (1992). Monosymptomatic bedwetting. *Scandinavian Journal of Urology and Nephrology Supplementum, 141,* 7–19.

Doleys, D. M. (1977). Behavioral treatments for nocturnal enuresis in children: A review of the recent literature. *Psychological Bulletin, 84,* 30–54.

Eiberg, H., Berendt, I., & Mohr, J. (1995). Assignment of dominant inherited nocturnal enuresis (ENUR1) to chromosome 13q. *Nature Genetics, 10,* 354–356.

El-Anany, F., Maghraby, H., Shaker, S., & Abdel-Moneim, A. (1999). Primary nocturnal enuresis: A new approach to conditioning treatment. *Urology, 53*(2), 405–408.

Essen, J., & Peckham, C. (1976). Nocturnal enuresis in childhood. *Developmental Medicine and Child Neurology, 18,* 577–589.

Fai-Ngo Ng, C., & Wong, S. (2005). Comparing alarms, desmopressin, and combined treatment in Chinese enuretic children. *Pediatric Nephrology, 20,* 163–169.

Fergusson, D. M., Horwood, L. J., & Shannon, F. T. (1986). Factors related to the age of attainment of nocturnal bladder control: An 8 year longitudinal study. *Pediatrics, 78,* 884–890.

Fielding, D. (1980). The response of day and night wetting children and children who wet only at night to retention control training and the enuresis alarm. *Behavior Research and Therapy, 18,* 305–317.

Fielding, D., & Doleys, D. M. (1989). Elimination problems: Enuresis and encopresis. In E. J. Mash & L. G. Terdal (Eds.), *Behavioral assessment of childhood disorders* (pp. 586–623). New York: Guilford Press.

Forsythe, W. I., & Redmond, A. (1974). Enuresis and spontaneous cure rate: Study of 1,129 enuretics. *Archives of Disease in Childhood, 49,* 259–263.

Friman, P. C. (1986). A preventive context for enuresis. *Pediatric Clinics of North America, 33*(4), 871–886.

Friman, P. C., Handwerk, M., Swearer, S., McGinnis, J., & Warzak, W. (1998). Do children with primary nocturnal enuresis have clinically significant behavior problems? *Archives in Pediatric and Adolescent Medicine, 152,* 537–539.

George, C. P. L., Messerli, F. H., Genest, J., Nowaczynski, W., Boucher, R., Kuchel, O., et al. (1975). Diurnal variation of plasma vasopressin in man. *Journal of Clinical Endocrinology and Metabolism, 41,* 332–338.

Gibb, S., Nolan, T., South, M., Noad, L., Bates, G., & Vidmar, S. (2004). Evidence against a synergistic effect of desmopressin with conditioning in the treatment of nocturnal enuresis. *Journal Pediatrics, 144,* 351–357.

Glazener, C., & Evans, J. (2003). Simple behavioral and physical interventions for nocturnal enuresis in children. *Cochrane Database of Systematic Reviews, 1* (CD003637).

Haque, M., Ellerstein, N. S., Gundy, J. H., Shelov, S. P., Weiss, J. C., McIntire, M. S., et al. (1981). Parental perceptions of enuresis: A collaborative study. *American Journal of Diseases of Childhood, 135,* 809–811.

Hellstrom, A., Hanson, E., Hansson, S., Hjalmas, K., & Jodal, U. (1991). Association between urinary symptoms at 7 years old and previous urinary tract infections. *Archieves of Disease in Childhood, 66,* 232–234.

HiraSing, R., van Leerdam, F., Bolk-Bennink, L., & Koot, H. (2002). Effect of dry bed training on behavioral problems in enuretic children. *Acta Paediatrica, 91*(8), 960–964.

Hjälmås, K. (1997). Pathophysiology and impact of nocturnal enuresis. *Acta Paediatrica, 86,* 919–922.

Hjälmås, K. (1999). Desmopressin treatment: Current status. *Scandinavian Journal of Urology and Nephrology*(Suppl. 202), 70–72.

Hjälmås, K., Arnold, T., Bower, W., Caione, P., Chiozza, L., Von Gontard, A., et al. (2004). Nocturnal enuresis: An international evidence based management strategy. *Journal of Urology, 171,* 2545–2561.

Houts, A. C. (1991). Nocturnal enuresis as a biobehavioral problem. *Behavior Therapy, 22,* 133–151.

Houts, A. C., Berman, J. S., & Abramson, H. A. (1994). The effectiveness of psychological and pharmacological treatments for nocturnal enuresis. *Journal of Consulting and Clinical Psychology, 62,* 737–745.

Houts, A. C., & Liebert, R. M. (1984). *Bedwetting: A guide for parents and children.* Springfield, IL: Charles C Thomas.

Houts, A. C., Liebert, R. M., & Padawer, W. (1983). A delivery system for the treatment of primary enuresis. *Journal of Abnormal Child Psychology, 11,* 513–519.

Houts, A. C., Peterson, J. K., & Liebert, R. M. (1984). Effect of prior imipramine treatment on the results of conditioning therapy in children with enuresis. *Journal of Pediatric Psychology, 9,* 505–509.

Houts, A. C., Peterson, J. K., & Whelan, J. P. (1986). Prevention of relapse in full-spectrum home training for primary enuresis: A components analysis. *Behavior Therapy, 17,* 462–469.

Houts, A. C., Whelan, J. P., & Peterson, J. K. (1987). Filmed versus live delivery of full-spectrum home training for primary enuresis: Presenting the information is not enough. *Journal of Consulting and Clinical Psychology, 55,* 902–906.

Hunsballe, J. (1999). Sleep studies based on electroencephalogram energy analysis. *Scandnavian Journal of Urology and Nephrology*(Suppl. 202), 28–30.

James, L. E., & Foreman, M. E. (1973). A-B status of behavior therapy technicians as related to success of Mowerer's conditioning treatment for enuresis. *Journal of Consulting and Clinical Psychology, 41,* 224–229.

Jarvelin, M. R. (1989). Developmental history and neurological findings in enuretic children. *Developmental Medicine and Child Neurology, 31,* 728–736.

Jarvelin, M. R., Huttunen, N., Seppanen, J., Seppanen, U., & Moilanen, I. (1990). Screening of urinary tract abnormalities among day and nightwetting children. *Scandinavian Journal of Urology and Nephrology, 24,* 181–189.

Jarvelin, M. R., Moilanen, I., Kangas, P., Moring, K., Vikevainen-Tervonen, L., Huttunen, N. P., et al. (1991). Aetiological and precipitating factors for childhood enuresis. *Acta Pediatrica Scandinavia, 80,* 361–369.

Jarvelin, M. R., Vikevainen-Tervonen, L., Moilanen, I., & Huttunen, N. P. (1988). Enuresis in 7-year-old children. *Acta Paediatrica Scandinavia, 77,* 148–153.

Jensen, I., & Kristensen, G. (2001). Frequency of nightly wetting and the efficiency of alarm treatment of nocturnal enuresis. *Scandinavian Journal of Urology and Nephrology, 35,* 357–363.

Kaffman, M., & Elizur, E. (1977). Infants who become enuretics: A longitudinal study of 161 kibbutz children. *Monographs of the Society for Research in Child Development, 42*(2, Serial No. 170), 1–54.

Kass, E. J. (1991). Approaching enuresis in an uncomplicated way. *Contemporary Urology, 3,* 15–24.

Kawauchi, A., Tanaka, Y., Naito, Y., Yamao, Y., Ukimura, O., Yoneda, K., et al. (2003). Bladder capacity at the time of enuresis. *Urology, 61*(5), 1016–1018.

Kawauchi, A., Watanabe, H., Kitamori, T., Imada, N., & Ohne, T. (1993). The possibility of centripetal stimulation from the urinary bladder for vasopressin excretion. *Journal of Kyoto Prefectural University of Medicine, 102,* 747–752.

Kimmel, H. D., & Kimmel, E. (1970). An instrumental conditioning method for the treatment of enuresis. *Journal of Behavior Therapy and Experimental Psychiatry, 1,* 121–123.

Klauber, G. T. (1989). Clinical efficacy and safety of desmopressin in the treatment of nocturnal enuresis. *Pediatrics, 114,* 719–722.

Kristensen, G., & Jensen, I. (2003). Meta-analyses of results of alarm treatment for nocturnal enuresis. *Scandinavian Journal of Urology and Nephrology, 37,* 232–238.

Leebeek-Groenewegen, A., Blom, J., Sukhai, R., & van der Heijden, B. (2001). Efficacy of desmopressin combined with alarm therapy for monosymptomatic nocturnal enuresis. *Journal of Urology, 166*(6), 2456–2458.

Levine, A. (1943). Enuresis in the navy. *American Journal of Psychiatry, 100,* 320–325.

Locke, H. J., & Wallace, K. M. (1959). Short marital adjustment and prediction tests: Their reliability and validity. *Marriage and Family Living, 21,* 251–255.

Longstaffe, S., Moffatt, M., & Whalen, J. (2000). Behavioral and self-concept changes after six months of enuresis treatment: Pt. 2. A randomized, controlled trial. *Pediatrics, 105*(4), 935–940.

Lovibond, S. H. (1964). *Conditioning and enuresis.* Oxford, England: Pergamon Press.

MacLean, R. E. G. (1960). Imipramine hydrochloride (Tofranil) and enuresis. *American Journal of Psychiatry, 117,* 551.

Mellon, M. W., & Houts, A. C. (2006). Nocturnal enuresis: Evidenced based perspectives in etiology, assessment and treatment. In W. O'Donohue & C. Fisher (Eds.), *Practitioner's guide to evidence based psychotherapy* (pp. 432–441). New York: Springer.

Mellon, M. W., & McGrath, M. (2000). Empirically supported treatments in pediatric psychology: Nocturnal enuresis. *Journal of Pediatric Psychology, 25,* 193–214.

Mikkelsen, E. J., Rapoport, J. L., Nee, L., Gruenau, C., Mendelson, W., & Gillin, J. C. (1980). Childhood enuresis I: Sleep patterns and psychopathology. *Archives of General Psychiatry, 37,* 1139–1144.

Moffatt, M. E. K. (1989). Nocturnal enuresis: Pt. 2. Psychologic implications of treatment and nontreatment. *Journal of Pediatrics, 114*(4), 697–704.

Moffatt, M. E. K. (1994). Nocturnal enuresis: Is there a rationale for treatment? *Scandinavian Journal of Urology and Nephrology*(Suppl.), 163, 55–66.

Moffatt, M. E. K., Harlos, S., Kirshen, A. J., & Burd, L. (1993). Desmopressin acetate and nocturnal enuresis: How much do we know? *Pediatrics, 92,* 420–425.

Moffatt, M. E. K., Kato, C., & Pless, I. B. (1987). Improvements in self-concept after treatment of nocturnal enuresis: A randomized clinical trial. *Journal of Pediatrics, 110,* 647–652.

Morgan, R. T. T., & Young, G. C. (1975). Parental attitudes and the conditioning treatment of childhood enuresis. *Behavior Research and Therapy, 13,* 197–199.

Mowrer, O. H., & Mowrer, W. M. (1938). Enuresis: A method for its study and treatment. *American Journal of Orthopsychiatry, 8,* 436–459.

Norgaard, J. P. (1989). Urodynamics in enuretics: Pt. 2: A pressure/flow study. *Neurourology and Urodynamics, 8,* 213–217.

Norgaard, J. P., Hansen, J. H., Neilsen, J. B., Rittig, S., & Djurhuus, J. C. (1989). Nocturnal studies in enuretics: A polygraphic study of sleep-stage and bladder activity. *Scandinavian Journal of Urology and Nephrology Supplementum, 125,* 73–78.

Norgaard, J. P., Rittig, S., & Djurhuus, J. C. (1989). Nocturnal enuresis: An approach to treatment based on pathogenesis. *Pediatrics, 14,* 705–710.

Oredsson, A., & Jorgensen, T. (1998). Changes in nocturnal bladder capacity during treatment with the bell and pad for monosymptomatic nocturnal enuresis. *Journal of Urology, 160,* 166–169.

Ornitz, E. M., Hanna, G. L., & de Traversay, J. (1992). Prestimulation-induced startle modulation in attention-deficit hyperactivity disorder and nocturnal enuresis. *Psychophysiology, 29,* 437–450.

Ornitz, E. M., Russell, A., Gabikian, P., Gehricke, J., & Guthrie, D. (2000). Prepulse inhibition of startle, intelligence and familial primary nocturnal enuresis. *Acta Paediatrica, 89,* 475–481.

Pennesi, M., Pitter, M., Bordugo, A., Minisini, S., & Peratoner, L. (2004). Behavioral therapy for primary nocturnal enuresis. *Journal of Urology, 171,* 408–410.

Pierce, C. M., Whitman, R. M., Mass, T. W., & Gay, M. L. (1961). Enuresis and dreaming: Experimental studies. *Archives of General Psychiatry, 4,* 166–170.

Rawashde, Y., Hvistendahl, G., Kamperis, K., & Djurhuus, J. (2002). Demographics of enuresis patients attending a referral centre. *Scandinavian Journal of Urology and Nephrology, 36,* 348–353.

Redman, J. F., & Siebert, J. J. (1979). The uroradiographic evaluation of the enuretic child. *Journal of Urology, 122,* 799–801.

Reynolds, C., & Kamphaus, R. (1998). *Behavior assessment system for children: Manual.* Circle Pines, MN: American Guidance Services.

Rosen, G., & Davison, G. (2003). Psychology should list empirically supported principles of change (ESPs) and not credential trademarked therapies or other treatment packages. *Behavior Modification, 27,* 300–312.

Rushton, H. G. (1989). Nocturnal enuresis: Epidemiology, evaluation, and currently available treatment options. *Journal of Pediatrics, 114,* 691–696.

Rutter, M., Yule, W., & Graham, P. (1973). Enuresis and behavioral deviance. In I. Kolvin, R. C. MacKeith, & S. R. Meadow (Eds.), *Bladder control and enuresis* (pp. 137–147). London: William Heinemann.

Sacks, S., & DeLeon, G. (1973). Case histories and shorter communications: Conditioning of two types of enuretics. *Behavior Research and Therapy, 11,* 653–654.

Scott, M. A., Barclay, D. R., & Houts, A. C. (1990). Childhood enuresis: Etiology, assessment, and current behavioral treatment. In M. Hersen, R. M. Eisler, & P. M. Miller (Eds.), *Progress in behavior modification* (pp. 83–117). Beverly Hills, CA: Sage.

Stansfeld, J. M. (1973). Enuresis and urinary tract infection. In I. Kolvin, R. C. MacKeith, & S. R. Meadow (Eds.), *Bladder control and enuresis* (pp. 102–103). London: William Heinemann.

Stromgren, A., & Thomsen, P. H. (1990). Personality traits in young adults with a history of conditioning-treated childhood enuresis. *Acta Psychiatrics Scandinavia, 81,* 538–541.

Sukhai, R. N., Mol, J., & Harris, A. S. (1989). Combined therapy of enuresis alarm and desmopressin in the treatment of nocturnal enuresis. *European Journal of Pediatrics, 148,* 465–467.

Taneli, C., Ertan, P., Taneli, F., Genc, A., Gunsar, C., Sencan, A., et al. (2004). Effect of alarm treatment on bladder storage capacities in monosymptomatic nocturnal enuresis. *Scandinavian Journal of Urology and Nephrology, 38,* 207–210.

Thompson, I. M., & Lauvetz, R. (1976). Oxybutinin in bladder spasm, neurogenic bladder, and enuresis. *Urology, 8,* 452–454.

Van Kampen, M., Bogaert, G., Akinwuntan, E., Claessen, L., Van Poppel, H., & De Weerdt, W. (2004). Long-term efficacy and predictive factors of full spectrum therapy for nocturnal enuresis. *Journal of Urology, 171,* 2599–2602.

Vogel, M., Young, M., & Primack, W. (1986). A survey of physician use of treatment methods for functional enuresis. *Developmental and Behavioral Pediatrics, 17,* 90–93.

Von Gontard, A. (1998). Annotation: Day and night wetting in children—A pediatric and child psychiatric perspective. *Journal of Child Psychology and Psychiatry, 39,* 439–451.

Von Gontard, A., Schaumburg, H., Hollmann, E., Eiberg, H., & Rittig, S. (2001). The genetics of enuresis: A review. *Journal of Urology, 166,* 2438–2443.

Wagner, W., & Johnson, J. (1988). Childhood nocturnal enuresis: The prediction of premature withdrawal from behavioral conditioning. *Journal of Abnormal Child Psychology, 16*(6), 687–692.

Watanabe, H., & Azuma, Y. (1989). A proposal for a classification system of enuresis based on overnight simultaneous monitoring of electroencephalography and cystometry. *Sleep, 12,* 257–264.

Watanabe, H., Imada, N., Kawauchi, A., Koyama, Y., & Shirakawa, S. (1997). Physiological background of enuresis type I. A preliminary report. *Scandinavian Journal of Urology and Nephrology*(Suppl. 183), 7–9.

Watanabe, H., Kawauchi, A., Kitamori, T., & Azuma, Y. (1994). Treatment system for nocturnal enuresis according to an original classification system. *Pediatric Urology, 25,* 43–50.

Werry, J. S., Dowrick, P. W., Lampen, E. L., & Vamos, M. J. (1975). Imipramine in enuresis: Psychological and physiological effects. *Journal of Child Psychology and Psychiatry, 16,* 289–299.

Whelan, J. P., & Houts, A. C. (1990). Effects of a waking schedule on the outcome of primary enuretic children treated with full-spectrum home training. *Health Psychology, 9,* 164–176.

Wolfish, N. (1999). Sleep arousal function in enuretic males. *Scandinavian Journal of Urology and Nephrology*(Suppl. 202), 24–26.

Wolfish, N., Pivik, R., & Busby, K. (1997). Elevated sleep arousal thresholds in enuretic boys: Clinical implications. *Acta Paediatrica, 86,* 381–384.

Yeung, C., Sit, F., To, L., Chiu, H., Sihoe, J., Lee, E., et al. (2002). Reduction in nocturnal functional bladder capacity is a common factor in the pathogenesis of refractory nocturnal enuresis. *British Journal of Urology, 90*(3), 302–307.

Young, G. C., & Morgan, R. T. T. (1972). Overlearning in the conditioning treatment of enuresis: A long-term follow-up study. *Behavior Research and Therapy, 10,* 419–420.

CHAPTER 14

Parent Training for Parents of Adolescents with Substance Use and Delinquent Behavior Problems

STEVEN A. BRANSTETTER, JOSHUA MASSE, and LISA GREENE

THE CONSEQUENCES of adolescent substance use (ASU) are profound, including diminished physical health, increased risk of suicide, poor academic functioning, risky sexual practices, failure to meet important developmental milestones, and poor relationships with parents and peers (e.g., Dembo et al., 1991; Newcomb & Bentler, 1988). The repercussions of ASU are felt throughout society from criminal activity, violent behaviors, increased health care costs, and the adaptation of school and social policies (Blau, Whewell, Gullotta, & Bloom, 1994; Gullotta, Adams, & Montemayor, 1994). Given the high personal, familial, and societal cost of ASU, understanding the etiology or contributing factors and identifying those at risk has been a priority among researchers and clinicians for many years. Although significant progress has been made in the understanding of the multidimensional nature of ASU and many important risk and protective factors have been recognized, illicit substance use among adolescents continues to be prevalent and problematic. In 1991, 44% of high school seniors had tried illicit drugs at least once; in 2005, half of seniors had tried illicit drugs (Johnston, O'Malley, Bachman, & Schulenburg, 2006). Similarly, in 1991, approximately 16% of high school seniors were active users of at least one illicit substance; by 2005, that number was up to 23% (Johnston, O'Malley, Bachman, & Schulenburg,

2006). With regard to the prevention and treatment of ASU, a great deal of work remains to be done. Nevertheless, a range of interventions for the treatment of ASU has emerged in recent years, many of which have garnered significant empirical support. Although these interventions differ in many respects, they all share an emphasis on the involvement of parents in the recovery process. This chapter details the Parents as Partners for Adolescent Behavior Change (PPABC) training program that recognizes the importance of parental influences in the treatment of ASU and that helps parents assist their adolescents change substance use and delinquent behaviors (DB). The chapter begins with a review of the issues related to the study and treatment of ASU and DB. Next, we review the risk and protective factors related to the onset and maintenance of ASU and DB. This is followed by a review of traditional treatments for ASU and more contemporary models of prevention and intervention. Finally, we provide a comprehensive description of the PPABC training program for parents of substance-abusing, delinquent adolescents.

STUDY AND TREATMENT OF SUBSTANCE ABUSE AND DELINQUENCY IN ADOLESCENCE

Research in the area of adolescent health risk behavior, including substance abuse and delinquent behavior, has made important advances in the identification of risk and protective factors. As an example, a review of the literature identified at least 20 psychosocial factors related to adolescent smoking (Tyas & Pederson, 1998). Although such information is of critical importance, it may also complicate the study and treatment of ASU in several ways. First, researchers face increasingly complex questions and can no longer simply ask if certain psychosocial factors are correlated with ASU or DB; rather, they must examine how certain psychosocial factors interact with other factors and predict additional factors, determining how these factors interact to influence ASU or DB (Rose, Chassin, Presson, & Sherman, 2000). Second, the complex etiology of an adolescent's problematic behavior leaves clinicians with difficult choices regarding where and when to intervene.

Complications for understanding the nature of adolescent problem behavior are often exacerbated when considering the dynamic and rapid transitioning of the adolescent developmental period. Experimental use of substances in adolescence may be somewhat normative and, as some have suggested, may even be related to positive adjustment (Shedler & Block, 1990). Experimental use may undergo rapid changes in short developmental periods or use may fluctuate in "bursts" in response to situational stressors (Dishion, Capaldi, Spracken, & Li, 1995; Dishion & Skaggs, 2000). Moreover, many social, biological, identity, and significant life changes occur during adolescence. These changes coalesce to create a developmental period that is dynamic, multifaceted, and rapidly transforming. Some researchers have characterized the study and treatment of ASU as trying to hit a "moving target" (e.g., Palmqvist, Martikainen, & von Wright, 2003; Schulenberg & Maggs, 2001).

Another factor complicating the study and treatment of ASU is the fact that adolescents who regularly use or abuse substances are rarely monosymptomatic; well over half of all adolescents who are experiencing substance use disorders are also suffering from another diagnosable psychiatric disorder (Armstrong & Costello, 2002). Despite anecdotal reports that adolescents commonly use substances to "self-medicate" anxiety or depressive symptoms, evidence suggests that the prevalence of comorbid substance use disorder and either depression or anxiety is only between 16% and 19% (Armstrong & Costello, 2002). Conversely, the prevalence of comorbidity between substance use disorders and disruptive behavior disorders (e.g., Oppositional Defiant Disorder, Conduct Disorder, or Attention-Deficit/Hyperactivity Disorder) has been reported to be as high as 59% (Chong, Chan, & Cheng, 1999). It may be difficult, if not impossible, to separate ASU and illegal or delinquent activity because all substances, including alcohol and tobacco, are illicit for adolescents below the age of 18. Therefore, it is technically illegal for these individuals to possess or use any substance. Substance use is also often associated with serious delinquent or illegal behavior, such as physical fights, driving while intoxicated, theft, or truancy (e.g., S. C. Duncan, Alpert, Duncan, & Hops, 1997). Because of the significant overlap between ASU and DB, treatment efforts must not solely be sensitive to ASU but also to the associated DB. Many of the behaviors connected with substance abuse problems are also exhibited by those with significant delinquent behavior (e.g., anger problems, truancy, theft); thus, programs developed to address ASU or DB often share many components. Functional family therapy (FFT), a family-based program developed to prevent and treat adolescent delinquent behavior, has identified poor parent-adolescent communication, poor family management or parenting skills, parental behaviors and attitudes, and family conflict as key risk factors for the development of DB in adolescence (Sexton & Alexander, 2000). As reviewed later in this chapter, many family-based programs for ASU contain these components. Thus, many treatment programs find that by treating ASU, there is a corresponding reduction in DB. Likewise, programs that focus on the treatment of DB see similar reductions in ASU.

Despite the complexities associated with the study and treatment of ASU, adolescence remains a critical period to examine substance use; initial use of alcohol or drugs is rarely seen after the age of 20 (Johnston, O'Malley, & Bachman, 1999), and initiation of use by the age of 16 is a significant risk factor for developing substance-related problems in adulthood (Anthony & Petronis, 1995). Despite the ongoing change and transitions characteristic of adolescence, and the increasing influence of peers, parents are still in an ideal position to affect change in their adolescent's behavior. Although many parents feel their influence over their adolescent's behavior—particularly substance-using behavior—has all but waned, studies suggest parents continue to have a significant influence in many areas—over and above that of peers—even into late adolescence (Ary, Tildesley, Hops, & Andres, 1993; Coombs, Paulson, & Richardson, 1991; Wood, Read, & Mitchell, 2004). Beyond their opportunity to serve as agents of change for their adolescents, parental attitudes and behaviors are among the most powerful risk and protective factors of ASU. Moreover, it has been suggested that parents are the most underutilized tool in the battle against ASU (Kelly, Comello, & Hunn, 2002). Therefore, given the critical period of adolescence for the prevention and intervention of ASU and DB, and parents' influence on their adolescent's behaviors, training parents as cotherapists in the treatment of ASU is an advantageous intervention at an optimal developmental period.

DEVELOPMENT OF SUBSTANCE ABUSE AND DELINQUENT BEHAVIORS

Before understanding how to intervene in ASU and DB, it is important to understand the nature of the onset and development of these behaviors. Doing so will help parents appreciate the complexity of the problems they are facing and allow them to approach their role in the treatment of these problems equipped with the knowledge necessary to play a meaningful part in the recovery of their adolescent. This section highlights the empirical and theoretical underpinnings of the development of ASU and DB.

Among the many posited theories regarding the role of social influences on the initiation of substance use, the social control theory and the social development theory have each received a great deal of attention. The social control theory (Elliott, Huizinga, & Ageton, 1985) asserts that a lack of commitment to conventional values is at the root of ASU. According to the theory, failed attempts at close and loving relationships with parents or family results in adolescents who do not subscribe to the conventional values of their family or community. Subsequently, individuals reject conventional values and associate with individuals who support more unconventional standards. It is through association with these peers that deviant behaviors such as drug use and criminal activity are observed, imitated, and rewarded. A similar theory, the social development theory, also emphasizes the failure to connect or lack of commitment to parents and other conventional role models as a potential cause of ASU (J. D. Hawkins & Weis, 1985).

The social development theory believes that adolescents who had poor opportunities for rewarding interactions at home and who received few rewards for interactions with parents will likely reject the importance of a close relationship with parents and conventional standards, associating with peers who share these views. These theories and others (e.g., family stress theory, family systems theory) suggest pathways to ASU that emphasize parental influences and how those influences result in adolescent's association with peers that support substance use. Although it has been noted that interaction with drug-using peers is "clearly the strongest proximal correlate of adolescent substance use" (Dishion et al., 1995, p. 804), evidence is strong that parents create an environment that will increase or decrease the likelihood that adolescents will associate with peers who support drug use (Dishion & Skaggs, 2000).

Although biological influences (e.g., physiological addiction) play an important role in the maintenance of ASU, biology cannot fully account for the perpetuation of substance use among adolescents. Indeed, ASU often serves more functions than simply meeting a biological need. Adolescents may use substances to meet social needs (e.g., belonging), cope with negative emotions or situations, enhance creativity or performance, or simply for pleasure (Novacek, Raskin, & Hogan, 1991). Moreover, a range of factors has been demonstrated to influence an adolescent's ongoing use of substances. If substances are readily available within the community in which an adolescent lives, he or she is at increased risk for use. Similarly, if substance use is common within an adolescent's school, or if the school does not have anti-drug programs or promote anti-drug messages, he or she is more likely to use substances (Wright & Pemberton, 2004).

An adolescent's mental health and personality characteristics are also influential in the use of substances. Adolescents who engage in antisocial behavior, suffer from depression or anxiety, or have another psychiatric diagnosis are at increased risk for ASU (Swadi, 1999). Likewise, an adolescent's attitudes toward academic success, perceptions of peer use, and level of personal religiosity have all been shown to be related to ASU (Wright & Pemberton, 2004). Another important domain influencing ASU is the peer environment. As suggested by both the social control theory and the social development theory, if an adolescent spends time with substance-using peers who have positive attitudes toward substance use, or who regularly engage in delinquent behaviors, that adolescent is at high risk to use substances.

Although a number of potential factors relate to the onset and development of substance use, it may be particularly salient to consider the role of parents in this process, particularly during adolescence, a time when parents still have an influence in important developmental areas. It has been suggested that the family is one of the single most important factors in understanding ASU because many of the other risk or protective factors may be directly influenced by the family. Family management skills (e.g., parental monitoring of adolescent behavior) have been demonstrated to reduce an adolescent's affiliation with substance-using peers (Rodgers-Farmer, 2000). Similarly, parents directly influence an adolescent's ability to cope with stress in an appropriate manner, his or her attitudes toward academic success, as well as attitudes toward the use of substances. Therefore, we turn our attention to the influence of parental attitudes and behaviors in the onset and maintenance of ASU and DB.

PARENTAL INFLUENCES ON ADOLESCENT SUBSTANCE USE AND DELINQUENT BEHAVIOR

A range of factors relating to the parent-child relationship has been shown to be associated with ASU and DB, including parental attitudes toward substance use, parental use of substances, parental support (Marshal & Chassin, 2000), parental monitoring (Griffin, Botvin, Scheier, Diaz, & Miller, 2000), and family communication (Windle, 2000). Nevertheless, clinicians often report that parents are unaware of these factors and how alterations to their own attitudes and behavior may positively impact ASU and DB. Thus, we believe it is critical that parents understand how these factors impact their adolescent's behavior for two reasons: first, as parents become aware of how their own attitudes and behaviors may impact their adolescent's behavior, we often observe an increase in parental motivation and involvement. Next, parental awareness of their own influence is important because many of the modules in the parent training program focus specifically on addressing problems or enhancing skills in these areas.

PARENTAL ATTITUDES AND BEHAVIORS

Parents who use substances have adolescents who are at greater risk for using substances themselves. Although an adolescent's peers have an immediate, direct influence on the initiation of cigarette smoking, parental smoking remains a significant predictor of the onset and escalation of smoking (Flay et al., 1994). Similarly, it has been found that adolescents who have parents who suffer from alcohol use disorders are significantly more likely to drink alcohol and to develop such disorders themselves (e.g., Chassin, Curran, Hussong, & Colder, 1996; Chassin, Pillow, Curran, Molina, & Barrera, 1993). These findings hold true for parental use of illicit substances as well: adolescents whose parents use marijuana are significantly more likely to use marijuana (T. E. Duncan, Duncan, Hops, & Stoolmiller, 1995).

In addition to being influenced by their parents' behavior, adolescents are also clearly influenced by their parents' attitudes and viewpoints.

This transmission of attitudes and values from parents to children, whether intentional or unintentional, may be especially important when it comes to alcohol and drug use. A strong link between parental attitudes toward substance use and adolescent substance use has consistently been demonstrated in the literature (e.g., Hansen et al., 1987). One study found that not only did permissive parental attitudes toward alcohol use predict adolescent drinking, it also predicted the amount of alcohol consumed by the adolescent: the more permissive the parental attitudes, the more alcohol the adolescents drank (G. M. Barnes & Welte, 1986). McDermott (1984) found that favorable parental attitudes toward substance use may be a stronger predictor of adolescent substance use then even parental substance use.

PARENT-ADOLESCENT RELATIONSHIPS

Parent support, defined as encouragement, physical affection, and praise (Anderson & Henry, 1994), has often been found to be a strong protection against pathology and substance abuse (Barber, 1992). Stice and Barrera (1995) found an inverse relation between parental support and ASU such that lower levels of parental support were related to increased ASU, and increased ASU was related to lower parental support. Similarly, Knight, Broome, Cross, and Simpson (1998) concluded that parental support of adolescents can serve as a powerful buffer against antisocial behavior and drug use. Support seems to influence ASU in at least two separate ways: first, parental support appears to be highly related to academic competence and investment—factors that are important in the prevention of ASU (Wills & Cleary, 1996). Second, parental support provides adolescents with improved behavioral coping, which helps them deal with adversity in appropriate ways (Wills & Cleary, 1996).

   Another dimension of the parent-adolescent relationship that has a direct impact on ASU and DB is parent-adolescent conflict. Farrell and White (1998) found that drug use increased as a function of overt conflict between adolescents and their mothers. Similarly, Brody and Forehand (1993) found that high mother-adolescent conflict predicted adolescent drug use problems. Bhatia (1998) noted that adolescent drug users consistently reported higher levels of parental conflict than nondrug users. Furthermore, an empirical study that employed a 12-week training program designed to increase social problem-solving skills between parent and children found that the training reduced family conflict and thus reduced drug use onset risk scores of the adolescents (Corby & Russell, 1997).

PARENT-ADOLESCENT COMMUNICATION

The quality of the communication between parents and their adolescents is another important factor relating to ASU. When a parent has an open style of communication with his or her adolescent, conveys clear and consistent expectations for behavior, and talks with his or her adolescent about ways to manage conflict and stress, those adolescents are more resilient and less likely to be influenced by peers to use substances (D. J. Hawkins & Catalano, 1992; Kafka & London, 1991). In support of both the social control and social development theories, when communication between parents and their adolescents involves both the parent and the adolescent perspective, adolescents are more likely to develop conventional standards of conduct (Brody & Shaffer, 1982). Indeed, open two-way communication between parents and adolescents helps adolescents feel as if rules and values are not simply imposed on them; rather, they feel a connection to those values and are more likely to behave in accordance with those values (Langer, 1983).

FAMILY MANAGEMENT AND MONITORING

All the ways in which parents organize their household, adhere to routines, set boundaries, administer consistent discipline, make informed decisions, and monitor their adolescents behaviors combine to influence ASU (Herman, Dornbusch, Herron, & Herting, 1997). Among these important family management factors, parental monitoring has recently emerged as one of the most powerful preventative factors against ASU. Popular media advertisements sponsored by the National Youth Anti-Drug Media Campaign proclaim parents are the "anti-drug" and many of these advertisements advocate close parental monitoring. The emphasis on monitoring is justified; Chilcoat and Anthony (1996) found a strong association between low parental monitoring and early onset of alcohol, tobacco, and other drug use. One study found that when considering other important factors, such as parent-adolescent attachment and relationship qualities (i.e., support and conflict), only parental monitoring was predictive of changes in substance use over time (Branstetter, 2005). Furthermore, it has been found that parents who know their child's whereabouts after school, know their child's peers, and know their child's activities are significantly less likely to have a child who exhibits DB (Cottrell et al., 2003; Griffin et al., 2000).

In addition to monitoring an adolescent's behavior, parents who have clear, predictable, and consistent rules for adolescent behavior are more likely to have adolescents who are less involved in ASU or DB. Guo and colleagues (Guo, Hawkins, Hill, & Abbott, 2001) found that a combination of monitoring and rule setting in early adolescence was predictive of less alcohol use across adolescence and into early adulthood. Likewise, it has been shown that having reasonable and well-defined rules, with consistent enforcement of those rules, is a strong protective factor against the development of substance use in adolescence (Kosterman, Graham, Hawkins, Catalano, & Herrenkohl, 2001).

TREATMENT OF ADOLESCENT SUBSTANCE ABUSE AND DELINQUENT BEHAVIOR

INDIVIDUAL TREATMENTS

Despite the body of research that demonstrates the importance of parents in the onset and development of ASU and DB, traditional treatments have focused on interventions with an identified patient only (i.e., the adolescent; Kumpfer, Alvarado, & Whiteside, 2003; H. A. Liddle, Rowe, Dakof, & Lyke, 1998). Research suggests that interventions designed to reduce ASU and DB that focus solely on the adolescent (e.g., individual therapy, inpatient services) have not been shown to significantly ameliorate clinical symptoms or reduce the likelihood of juvenile acts (Hinton, Sheperis, & Sims, 2003; Mulvey, Arthur, & Reppucci, 1993). One study that compared motivational enhancement, cognitive-behavioral therapy, and 12-step programs for adolescent alcohol use found that only 3% of the change in alcohol use could be attributed to treatment (Cutler & Fishbain, 2005). Research into the effectiveness of different treatment approaches for ASU is still in its most early stages (Titus & Godley, 1999), and a great deal remains to be learned about these interventions. Nevertheless, programs such as motivational enhancement and cognitive-behavioral therapy have substantial evidence for effectiveness in adult populations (e.g., Bien, Miller, & Boroughs, 1993; Crits-Christoph & Siqueland, 1996). Evidence suggests that an empathetic therapeutic relationship may have a beneficial effect, regardless of the treatment intervention. Thus, the parent training introduced in this chapter highly recommends that while parents participate in the training program, the adolescent struggling with ASU and DB be involved with individual therapy. While the adolescent participates in individual therapy, parents learn ways in which they can help their adolescent recover and how to provide an environmental context that is supportive of the adolescent's individual treatment efforts.

FAMILY-BASED TREATMENTS

Recognizing the shortcomings of individual treatments for ASU and DB, a number of programs designed to prevent or reduce ASU and DB have expanded their scope to examine the adolescent's behavior in a larger context. These programs have taken a multisystemic approach that views ASU and DB within a complex environmental system (Henggeler, 1991; Hinton et al., 2003; H. L. Liddle & Diamond, 1991). More specifically, many of these interventions have focused on familial influence and particular ways in which an adolescent's family may contribute to, or prevent, the development and maintenance of ASU (Stern, 2004). A vast body of literature has demonstrated the importance of involving an adolescent's family and the positive impact such involvement has on the adolescent's prognosis (Stern). Studies comparing family-based interventions with nonfamily-based interventions have demonstrated that family-based interventions show greater reductions in ASU and a higher retention rate (Barrett-Waldron, Brody, & Slesnick, 2001). In the following, we review two such family-based approaches, with a special focus on how parental involvement has emerged as a critical component of ASU and DB treatment.

MULTIDIMENSIONAL FAMILY THERAPY

Multidimensional family therapy (MDFT; Hogue, Liddle, & Becker, 2002) is a family-based outpatient intervention developed for adolescents clinically referred for substance abuse and behavioral problems. This approach examines adolescent drug abuse and its related problems within a complex environment (Liddle, 1992, 2002; Liddle & Diamond, 1991), taking both a developmental and ecological view of adolescent drug use and behavior problems. The treatment is multifaceted and therefore extends beyond the adolescent into other ecologies such as the family, social support networks, and school settings. Multidimensional family therapy is a sequential, three-stage intervention that includes assessment, a "working phase" where both the adolescent and his or her parents engage in individual sessions, and a termination phase that brings all components together (U.S. Department of Health and Human Services, 2004).

In the "working phase" of MDFT, parents begin therapy not only for family issues but also for individual problems (e.g., drug abuse, anger management). Parents are initially educated on developmentally appropriate parenting ideologies, helped to devise operationalized goals of therapy, and encouraged to increase time spent with the adolescent. Therapists then teach parents skills to communicate effectively with their adolescent, specific parenting techniques designed to modify their child's behavior, and developmentally appropriate boundaries surrounding adolescent autonomy. Also during this phase, the parents and adolescent participate in therapy together to generalize skills learned in individual sessions. The overlying goal of this phase is to restructure interaction patterns and create a more comfortable, enriching relationship.

A number of studies have been conducted on MDFT, including research investigating MDFT as an intervention as well as a prevention program. In comparison to other interventions such as multifamily educational intervention (MFEI), adolescent group therapy (AGT), and cognitive behavioral therapy (CBT), MDFT has demonstrated larger gains in a number of domains including substance use, behavioral difficulties, academic performance, and family functioning (Liddle et al., 2001; Liddle, 2002). Multidimensional family therapy was also compared to residential treatment for adolescent substance abusers with comorbid behavioral difficulties, showed a continual decrease in drug use and externalizing behaviors 12 months after treatment, and was demonstrated to be more cost-effective (Liddle et al., 2001). Finally, a study examining an adaptation of MDFT for the prevention of drug use in a population of adolescents at risk for substance use and delinquent behavior found that a MDFT group showed greater gains in comparison to a community control group (Hogue et al., 2002).

MULTISYSTEMIC THERAPY

Multisystemic therapy (MST) is a manualized, empirically-based, intensive therapy that is both family and community oriented, having been applied to an array of clinically significant problems including juvenile delinquency, substance-abusing juvenile offenders, adolescent sexual offenders, and adolescents presenting as a risk to themselves or others (Henggeler & Lee, 2003). Similar to MDFT, MST recognizes the multifaceted nature of ASU and juvenile delinquency and thus places the focus of treatment beyond the scope of the adolescent to include additional ecologies such as family environment, school setting, peer groups, neighborhoods, family social supports, and other agencies such as the juvenile justice system and child welfare system. Stressing the importance of central figures (i.e., parents), MST generalizes learned skills and uses the support attained in therapy to create change across the specific domains relevant to the adolescent (Henggeler, Schoenwald, & Borduin, 1998). Therefore, a great deal of the therapy is concentrated on the family system and enhancing parenting skills and in-family social support.

Guided by assessment, the family component of MST is comprehensive and focuses on a number of parental and adolescent domains. Parents are taught skills to enhance their ability to dispense effective rewards and punishments to their adolescent. In addition, parents learn to watch for good behaviors and provide a tangible or social reward for these behaviors. Additionally, parents are taught methods in which to monitor the child's behavior, learning to recognize and address risk factors such as poor monitoring, low caregiver warmth, dysfunctional communication patterns, parental behavior, and ineffective discipline. However, protective factors such as secure attachment, positive interactions, healthy monitoring, and effective discipline techniques are also addressed with parents.

After rigorous examination in the literature, MFT possesses strong empirical support. Research has demonstrated that MST has strong retention rates among families (Henggeler, Schoenwald, & Munger, 1996), and has shown to be associated with improved overall family functioning, decreased problem behaviors, decreased substance use, significantly lower amounts of drug-related arrests, and decreased psychiatric symptomology (Henggeler, 1986, 1991).

SUMMARY OF FAMILY-BASED INTERVENTION PROGRAMS

Although empirically supported, family-focused intervention programs vary in terms of individual theoretical assumptions and clinical applications, common themes run throughout the core parental components of each intervention. Each intervention stresses the importance of family involvement and recognizes the necessity of parental inclusion to protect children from ASU and DB. Each program recognizes the need for supportive family relationships, stresses the importance of parental monitoring and rule setting, teaches communication skills, and helps parents serve as important agents of change for their adolescent's ASU or DB.

PARENTS AS PARTNERS FOR ADOLESCENT BEHAVIOR CHANGE TRAINING PROGRAM

Parents as Partners for Adolescent Behavior Change (PPABC) is an intervention that has been adapted from a variety of empirically supported, family-based interventions for substance-abusing adolescents with DB. Although ASU is recognized as a multidimensional, multifaceted problem requiring intervention in multiple contexts, PPABC mainly focuses on ways in which parents themselves may assist their adolescents through the process of change. For many families, comprehensive programs such as MDFT and MST may be an ideal intervention to target ASU and DB. Unfortunately, such comprehensive programs are not available in every community, participation in such programs may not be feasible or acceptable to some parents, and many clinics and clinicians are not equipped to administer such intensive interventions. Thus, PPABC was developed as an intervention that can be easily implemented by clinicians working in community agencies, small clinics, or private practice. The PPABC program has the benefit of being an easily implemented, cost-effective, and accessible intervention that brings together key elements identified by theory, empirical research, and clinical practice to help parents assist an adolescent who is struggling with substance use and delinquency problems.

Table 14.1

Components of Parents as Partners for Adolescent
Behavior Change Training Program

1. Assessment
   a. Assessment of adolescent problems related to ASU and DB
   b. Assessment of parental strengths, weaknesses, and mental health issues
2. Education
   a. Education of risk and protective factors related to ASU and DB
   b. Education of the role of parents in adolescent development
   c. Education of the principles of behavior change
   d. Education of developmental issues in adolescence
3. Motivation Enhancement
4. Intervention
   a. Relationship building
   b. Communication training
   c. Rule setting and discipline strategies
   d. Monitoring training

The components of PPABC include 11 separate modules within four broad domains: (1) assessment, (2) education, (3) motivation enhancement, and (4) intervention (see Table 14.1). The modules, presented in sequential order, allow each successive module to build on the previous module. Although most modules can be delivered in one session, they are flexible and can be administered over two or more sessions if parents need more practice, information, or remediation on certain topics.

ASSESSMENT

Adolescent Problem Assessment

In the initial meeting with parents, PPABC clinicians seek to assess the nature and scope of the problems caused by the adolescent's substance use and delinquent behaviors. Given that there are a number of problems with clinical diagnoses of substance use disorders in adolescent populations (i.e., certain symptoms may only be present in small populations of adolescent users and several symptoms are atypical for adolescent users; C. S. Martin & Winters, 1999), initial assessment focuses on problem severity rather than frequency of use or physiological characteristics of addiction (e.g., tolerance or withdrawal). Thus, the clinicians focus assessment on four domains of adolescent functioning: (1) interpersonal functioning, (2) intrapersonal functioning, (3) problems controlling substance use, and (4) negative consequences related to use.

To assess for these problems, PPABC has developed a semi-structured parent interview adapted from the negative outcomes section of the Drug Involvement Scale for Adolescents (DISA; Eggert, Herting, & Thompson, 1996). This semi-structured assessment gives parents an opportunity to express themselves, vent frustrations, and build rapport with the clinician.

The information garnered from this assessment is valuable for both parents and clinicians. Such assessments help parents and clinicians track progress over the course of the training program. Because ASU and DB tend to be "stubborn" behaviors, which can make for a slow process of recovery, giving parents a method by which they can measure the progress of their adolescent is important. These assessments are also valuable in that they allow parents and clinicians to understand areas in which the adolescent may need the most help. If an adolescent is experiencing more of his or her problem in the area of interpersonal relationships, certain aspects of the PPABC program (i.e., relationship building) may be emphasized.

Parental Functioning Assessment

In addition to assessing problems related to the adolescent's use and behaviors, the initial meetings also assess what techniques the parent has used to alter his or her adolescent's behavior. Because a typical response is that the parent has "tried everything," a detailed analysis of the interventions tried is conducted, including what rewards or punishments were used (if any), problems implementing the intervention, and the outcome of each attempted intervention. Information gathered here is useful, especially in the education of behavioral principles, motivation enhancement, and rule setting and discipline strategies modules. When parents see how and where previous intervention efforts have failed (e.g., inconsistent reinforcement, quitting the program during an extinction burst), parents can develop hope that "everything" has not failed because there is promise for a properly developed and administered program of behavior change.

Next, parents are assessed with regard to the quality of their relationship and communication with their adolescent. To assess five characteristics of positive relationships between parents and adolescents (i.e., affection, providing a secure base, intimacy, companionship, and providing a safe haven) the Network or Relationships Inventory (NRI; Furman & Buhrmester, 1985) is used. The NRI is also used to assess five characteristics of negative relationships (i.e., relationship control, relational aggression, criticism, antagonism, and conflict).

To assess the communication between the parent and adolescent, the Parent-Adolescent Communication Scale (PACS; H. Barnes & Olsen, 1985) is used, which allows parents to rate their perceptions of communication with their adolescent in several areas, including their own offers of praise and support and provision of rewards, as well as their perceptions of opportunities for two-way discussion with adolescents, adolescent listening and acceptance during discussions, and adolescent willingness to seek out a parent for discussion. The information garnered from these assessments allows parents and clinicians to evaluate areas of strength or weakness, and clinicians can use this information in later stages of the training program. If the results of the NRI reveal that a parent uses a great deal of antagonism in their relationship with their adolescent, this section of the communication training can be emphasized.

Finally, as parental mental health is important in implementing effective parenting practices, an assessment of the parents current psychological functioning is warranted. It is common for the parent of an adolescent who uses substances and demonstrates DB to also present with clinically significant impairments. Parents may present with substance use or abuse problems of their own, or they may be experiencing problems related to depression, Bipolar Disorder, anxiety disorders, or Attention-Deficit/Hyperactivity Disorder. Each of these disorders may adversely affect a parent's ability to adequately parent their adolescent.

It is worth noting that many stressors and symptoms associated with parental mental health issues may be indirectly addressed in the PPABC training sessions. A parent's depressive symptomology may be perpetuated by her frequent arguments with her daughter. As the parent begins to learn new ways of communicating, and arguments decrease, she may experience fewer depressive symptoms. Therefore, being able to empathize and discuss ways in which ASU and DB may contribute to personal difficulties and stressors is an important aspect of the therapeutic process. Although treating specific parental mental health conditions is beyond the scope of PPABC, therapists should seek to refer individuals to receive therapeutic services in conjunction with PPABC. It is the clinician's responsibility to determine which mental health issues may be directly related to parenting an adolescent experiencing ASU and DB, possibly warranting adjunct services, and which may be unrelated.

EDUCATION

Risk and Protective Factors Related to Adolescent Substance Use and Delinquent Behaviors

As reviewed earlier in the chapter, parents may unwittingly contribute to their adolescent's ASU or DB by having permissive attitudes toward substance use, using substances themselves, or through having poor relationships with their adolescent. Conversely, parents can engage in certain behaviors that may make it less likely that their adolescent will use substances or engage in delinquent behavior. Educating parents on how their attitudes and behaviors may be risk or protective factors gives them new ways to help their adolescent change behaviors related to ASU and DB. Parents are provided a handout (see Table 14.2) that describes specific risk and protective factors, how those factors may lead to ASU or DB, and how parents can reduce these risk factors or increase the protective factors. It is emphasized that these attitudes and behaviors are risk or protective factors. A parent who drinks alcohol does not necessarily *cause* their adolescent's alcohol use. Rather, adolescents with parents who drink alcohol are *more likely* to use alcohol than those adolescents whose parents do not drink. Many parents who drink alcohol or use substances have adolescents who never drink or use, and many adolescents drink or use when their parents do not drink or use.

Role of Parents in Adolescent Development

By the time they seek treatment, parents are often on the verge of "giving up," and often insist that they no longer have control of their adolescent or their household. Parents claim that "there is nothing I can do . . . he won't listen to me anymore." Educating parents that they still matter, that they still have an influence over their adolescent's behavior, and that they do (or they *can*) have control, is an important aspect of the PPABC program. Parents are told how years of empirical research has demonstrated that parents remain a significant influence in their adolescent's lives in a range of important areas. Although peers may influence what music an adolescent listens to or what clothes he or she wears, parents have a strong influence in the adolescent's involvement in romantic relationships (Gray & Steinberg, 1999), academic achievement (Dornbusch, Ritter, Leiderman, Roberts, & Fraleigh, 1987), sexual behavior (Romer et al., 1999), driving safety (Beck, Shattuck, & Raleigh, 2001), quality of peer friendships (Cui, Conger, Bryant, & Elder, 2002), Internet use (Cottrell, Branstetter, Stanton, Cottrell, & Harris, 2006), and religiousness and faith (T. F. Martin, White, & Perlman, 2003). Recent research has suggested that although the influence of peers grows in early adolescence, it peaks in mid-adolescence and then begins to decline (Jang, 1999). Conversely, parental influence remains steady throughout adolescence (Jang) and a significant source of influence into early adulthood. The conclusion is that parents remain important, and adolescents continue to look to parents for guidance, support, and love through adolescence. This information allows parents and PPABC therapists to engage in discussions about how the parents can become influential in the lives of their adolescent and to set the stage for future modules (e.g., relationship building, rule setting).

Table 14.2
Risk and Protective Factors

Risk or Protective Factor	Relation to ASU or DB	What Parents Can Do
Parental attitudes toward substance use	Permissive attitudes toward substance use (e.g., "smoking pot now and then is ok, as long as it does not interfere with school") are directly related to ASU. Conversely, parents with negative attitudes toward substance use (e.g., "no amount of marijuana use is acceptable") are related to less ASU.	Let adolescents know you disapprove of substance use, and *why* you disapprove. Help adolescents dispel myths about substances, and educate them about the negative aspects of use.
Parental use of substances	Parents who use substances (including alcohol and tobacco) have adolescents who are more likely to use. Adolescents, like all of us, learn both by watching others and by our own experience. If you are using, your adolescent is learning to use.	If you use substances, stop using. Get help, if you need it. This sends a strong message that recovery is a worthy goal to pursue. Again, adolescents learn by watching: If you are recovering or quitting, they are more likely to attempt to quit.
Parental-adolescent relationships	When adolescents perceive that parents are interested, involved, and concerned about their activities, they are more likely to make efforts to adhere to parental and conventional values (e.g., not engaging in criminal behavior).	Make efforts to be supportive of your adolescent's goals, ambitions, and show an interest in their lives. (Addressed in Relationship Building Module of PPABC.)
Parental communication	Closed, hostile, critical, or absent communication is related to having adolescents who are more likely to use substances. Alternatively, parents who have open, clear, and reciprocal communication styles have adolescents who are better able to resist substance use.	Don't just talk to your adolescent: Listen. Don't lecture: Listen. At the same time, make your feelings and expectations clear. Ask questions, and ask for feedback. Avoid yelling, interrupting, eye rolling, walking out of the room, and other negative styles of interacting. (Addressed in the Communication Module of PPABC.)

(continued)

Table 14.2 *(Continued)*

Risk or Protective Factor	Relation to ASU or DB	What Parents Can Do
Parental mental health	Mental health issues such as depression, anxiety, or substance use make an already difficult job (parenting a teenager) more difficult. Such problems make monitoring, bonding, communicating, or supporting your adolescent difficult. All of these parenting behaviors are related to ASU and DB.	Seek help for yourself. Being a good parent means taking care of your child *and* taking care of yourself. It is not selfish to seek mental health treatment—in fact, it is selfish *not* to seek treatment. Your child needs the best parenting effort you can give.
Family management (monitoring and discipline)	Adolescents without clear rules and consistent, predictable consequences are far more likely to engage in ASU and DB than teens with such rules and consequences. Additionally, when teens perceive that their parents know about their friends and activities, they are less likely to engage in risky behaviors.	Make rules and enforce them. Don't change rules based on your mood, your adolescent's mood, or other circumstances. The rules are the rules. Ask to talk to your adolescent's friends and their parents. With regard to your adolescent's activities, ask "who, what, when, and where."

Principles of Behavior Change

Prior to introducing specific components of PPABC, we have found it useful to provide parents with a brief overview of basic behavioral principles so that they are better able to conceptualize their own, as well as their adolescent's, actions in a behavioral context. The overview is not exceedingly technical and is designed to educate parents on recognizing and labeling simple behavioral techniques. Parents are taught the difference between a reward (i.e., reinforcing) and a punishment (i.e., aversive) and positive and negative reinforcement. In teaching these principles, we have found using concrete and simple examples and handouts to be a useful way of illustrating the concepts (see Table 14.3). Typically, parents are able to relate to these examples, making it easier to recognize the different techniques. At this point, definitions and examples of each principle are presented and parents are told that specific guidelines associated with administering each will be discussed in further sessions.

A few specific issues with regard to effectively implementing a behavioral treatment are stressed. First, the importance of consistency in all aspects of the program is emphasized. Parents are told that ASU and DB, like most behaviors, are learned. Adolescents learned to engage in these behav-

Table 14.3
Basic Behavioral Principles

Behavioral Principle	Description	Examples
Positive reward	When given in response to a certain behavior, increases the likelihood of repeating the behavior in the future	Praise Food Privileges Money
Negative reward	When taken away in response to a certain behavior, increases the likelihood of repeating the behavior in the future	Parent stops yelling when child completes homework Parent turns off "stupid" music in the car when the child talks
Punishment	When presented in response to a certain behavior, decreases the likelihood of repeating the behavior in the future	Spanking Yelling Extra chores
Negative punishment	When taken away in response to a certain behavior, decreases the likelihood of repeating the behavior in the future	Taking away car keys Restricting TV / video games Grounding
Shaping	To start a training program, individuals may be given rewards for "almost" achieving a certain goal or behavioral outcome	A teen receives a reward for picking up his room, even though he left a number of dirty dishes on his dresser A teen receives verbal praise for calling home, even though she called from the mall instead of before leaving school
Extinction burst	A temporary increase in the occurrence of a behavior after the reward for doing that behavior has stopped	For two weeks after his mother has told him "no more driving on weeknights," a teen begs, argues, and pouts *twice as much as he used to* to be allowed to use the car
Extinction	The gradual decrease in a behavior once the reward for doing that behavior has stopped	For another week or two, the teen begs and pouts now and then to use the car, but eventually stops begging because his mother no longer lets him drive on weeknights

iors because when they did these behaviors, they got something that was consistently rewarding to them in some way. Parents are told of the *law of effect,* a behavioral principle stating that behaviors that result in "satisfaction" are more likely to happen again, and behaviors that result in "discomfort" are less likely to happen again. Because adolescents have learned that substance use and delinquent behavior result in "satisfaction," they must relearn that these behaviors now result in "discomfort" (which does not necessarily mean physical discomfort, rather it could mean not playing a desired video game or going to a friend's party). At the same time, adolescents must learn that other, more acceptable behaviors result in "satisfaction." As with learning anything new, all behaviors (positive and negative) must have a predictable, consistent result. If a certain, undesirable behavior sometimes results in "satisfaction" and other times results in "discomfort," the adolescent is likely to try the behavior again and again hoping for the "satisfaction." Parents are encouraged to think of a slot machine: Despite no payoff (discomfort), 8 or 9 times out of 10, players will continue to put money in the machine in hopes of achieving a large jackpot (satisfaction). However, if an undesirable behavior *always* results in "discomfort," the adolescent will stop that behavior and seek another, more desirable, behavior. Likewise, the slot machine player will eventually quit playing if the machine simply *never* pays off.

Next, the important behavioral phenomenon of the extinction burst is explained in detail. Parents are told that when the result of a behavior (e.g., yelling) changes from "satisfaction" (i.e., getting his or her way) to "discomfort" (i.e., not getting his or her way), the adolescent rarely gives up and tries another behavior. Instead, because the adolescent's learning history states "yelling = getting my way," he will assume he performed the behavior (yelling), incorrectly. He will then attempt variations of the behavior (yelling louder, more frequently, or adding obscenities). This increase in the undesirable behavior is called an "extinction burst." If the adolescent learns that the behavior, in any variation, is no longer effective, the behavior will become extinct. However, if the adolescent learns that a variation of the behavior (yelling louder) *is* effective, he has modified his learning history from "yelling = getting my way" to "yelling (louder) = getting my way." During this extinction burst, many treatment programs fail. Parent often say *"I tried the program, but the behavior got worse . . . so I stopped because it was not working."* During the education of behavioral principles, PPABC clinicians highlight the need to "ride out" the extinction burst: Once the adolescent learns that a behavior *consistently* results in "discomfort," they will no longer demonstrate that behavior.

Developmental Issues in Adolescence

Parents often express frustration that their adolescent either needs to "grow up and act his age," or "is too big for her britches." Each of these complaints reflects the fact that the adolescent is neither an adult nor a child. Parents may expect their adolescent to stop acting like a child and take on more responsibility (i.e., be an adult) or to scale back their involvement with peers, romantic partners, or other activities (i.e., be more child-like). Such expectations may be perfectly appropriate depending on

Table 14.4

Developmental Tasks for Adolescents

1. Establish their own set of values
2. Establish and maintain peer relationships
3. Learn how to express themselves in complex verbal ways
4. Start to develop a personal identity
5. Begin to establish independence from parents
6. Learn to manage increasingly complex emotions
7. Develop ability to plan for the future and control impulses
8. Learn to manage sexual identity
9. Deal with changing bodies
10. Learn to experience the real-world consequences of their behavior
11. Learn about romantic relationships

the adolescent and his or her age and behaviors. However, when parents fail to consider developmentally appropriate behavior, a great deal of conflict, rebellion, or other problems may result. Practitioners of PPABC attempt to help parents understand the major tasks of adolescence, and a normal range of behaviors, and seek to help parents assist their adolescent in meeting these important developmental milestones. The handout seen in Table 14.4 is used as a guideline in this module. The theme of this module is to have conversations with parents to help them understand what behavior is to be expected from an average adolescent. Here is an example of such a conversation:

PARENT: This alcohol use has her emotions all messed up. I mean, anytime she and her boyfriend fight, she acts like the world has completely come to an end. She cries and bites my head off anytime I try to tell her it will pass and there are other fish in the sea. She didn't use to be like that.

THERAPIST: Yes, I see how that might be difficult for you. However, such reactions are not that uncommon for many teens. As we talked about, one major task in adolescence is to learn how romantic relationships work. And for many teenagers, some of the most pervasive and strongest emotions revolve around their romantic partners.

PARENT: Yeah, I know that, but can't she see it's not that big a deal? It's like her fourth boyfriend in a year, so it's not like they are married.

THERAPIST: Well, for her it may be a VERY big deal; especially if she feels like she is failing in a major developmental area. If she is having trouble making a romantic relationship work, maybe her strong emotional reactions are as much about her inability to have an "adult" relationship as it is about the boyfriend himself. Perhaps this issue is independent of her alcohol use?

MOTIVATION ENHANCEMENT

Parents whose children are struggling from ASU or DB often describe themselves as "at wits end." They feel disconnected from their child, like they have exhausted all options and there is no point in trying to help. Although some parents may admit they might have "done some things differently," they often feel that making significant changes in their parenting approach, their attitudes, or other aspects of their lives is not going to have a noteworthy impact on their child's ASU or DB. Additionally, therapists often have a difficult time suggesting that parent's previous parenting practices have failed, and that they may need to alter their approach to parenting. For many therapists, this suggestion feels like they are blaming the parents for their child's ASU or DB. Nevertheless, for a majority of parents seeking help with their adolescent who uses substances and engages in delinquent behavior, previous parenting practices have indeed failed. Therefore, parents often must be motivated to change their own parenting approaches, attitudes, and behaviors. Practitioners of PPABC approach this task not through blaming; rather, they help parents see their strengths and how a child with ASU or DB may need a different parenting approach than another child. Indeed, parents whose practices and behaviors are otherwise excellent, loving, and thoughtful may experience difficulties when faced with ASU or DB from their child.

The methods PPABC clinicians take to motivate parents to change their parenting behaviors are based on the motivational interviewing techniques developed by Miller and Rollnick (1991). These techniques have been used to help individuals change a range of behaviors, including smoking, alcohol use, exercise behaviors, eating behaviors, and increasing adherence to treatment programs (e.g., Zweben & Zuckoff, 2002). The components of this module are based on the six elements of effective brief intervention, or FRAMES, as described by Yahne and Miller (1999). The acronym stands for Feedback, Responsibility, Advice, Menu of options, Empathy, and Self-efficacy. Three additional elements of motivational interviewing are incorporated into the standard PPABC program: (1) develop discrepancies, (2) avoid argumentation, and (3) roll with resistance. It is important for clinicians to remember that although certain aspects of this module are concrete tasks (e.g., providing feedback), other tasks are therapeutic approaches used throughout the PPABC program (e.g., express empathy).

In contrast to the traditional personalized feedback of health-relevant information used in most motivational enhancement programs, PPABC provides parents with specific feedback regarding their parental strengths and weakness as assessed by the NRI and the PACS. This information gives parents an idea of how often they are using certain behaviors, and how these behaviors may serve as risk or protective factors. If a parent scores high on the criticism scale of the NRI, he may be given feedback about how this style of interaction may contribute to his adolescent seeking to identify with peers who oppose conventional standards. Feedback in both positive and negative domains is provided, and discussions are initiated with parents regarding how adolescents with ASU or DB may elicit certain parenting styles. An adolescent who is using substances may frequently be dishonest about her whereabouts, and may be hostile when confronted. This hostility and defensiveness may make otherwise patient parents become more authoritarian, angry, or likely to be critical.

The principle of developing a discrepancy is often useful in the provision of feedback. Parents may argue that direct criticism is the "only way to get through" to their adolescent, and that this approach "has nothing to do" with the adolescent's ASU or DB. Instead of directly confronting such ideas, PPABC clinicians may instead gently point out incidents that conflict with the parent's notion that such interactions "get through" to the adolescent as shown in the following example:

THERAPIST: You said that your son continues to dress for school "like a circus freak," right?
PARENT: Yeah, he leaves the house and I tell him how ridiculous he looks, but for some reason he thinks he looks cool.
THERAPIST: You mentioned when we talked about criticism that it is the only thing that "gets through" to your son; however, he still dresses the same, despite the criticism. I'm wondering if it is not "getting through" as well as another approach might.

Developing a discrepancy is a gentle way of allowing parents to become gradually aware of certain aspects of their parenting approach without becoming defensive as they might if a therapist were to directly point out the shortcoming. Nevertheless, parents may continue to defend their positions that their approach is right and that the adolescent is failing to respond correctly to the parenting behavior (e.g., criticism). In such cases, PPABC clinicians avoid argumentation with the parent. Argumentation is rarely helpful in clinical practice, and may simply result in parents who drop out or dismiss the importance of change. Additionally, PPABC clinicians roll with the parent's resistance, meaning that a parent's resistance to change a certain behavior is not only accepted without argumentation, but it is also acknowledged as important to the parent. At the same time, however, parents are invited to view the situation from an alternative perspective.

An important aspect of the PPABC program is restoring a parent's sense of control and responsibility. Because parents have often felt out of control with their adolescents with ASU or DB problems, it is important to spend time reminding parents that they are responsible for their own parenting behaviors, the success or failure of those behaviors, and for taking control of their households. Parents are praised for taking the responsibility back into their own hands through the simple act of seeking professional assistance and are told that such steps are important in regaining control of their lives and their families. Finally, parents are reminded that they ultimately have the power to change their interactions with their adolescents, change "broken" aspects of their parenting approach (e.g., failed discipline programs), and master new parenting behaviors.

As clinicians progress with parents, they are often faced with direct solicitation for advice. Although some clinicians are trained to avoid giving specific or direct advice, PPABC clinicians are instructed to provide such advice when it is clearly solicited, and when there is a clear reason for the advice. Such advice is helpful on many levels. First, a parent simply may not understand how to implement certain behavioral strategies, or they may need help selecting appropriate rewards or consequences. We have found that having direct advice from a professional serves as a "prescription" for parents to change. A parent who has been advised to stop using alcohol because it is a risk factor for increased use by his adolescent, and because the parent's cessation may serve as a good model for his adolescent's recovery, may be more likely to do so because "the counselor said it would help my son."

As parents begin to change their behavior, they should be provided with a menu of options. Instead of offering only a single way to approach a problem, parents are provided with several ways in which they can change. It is important to allow parents to reject certain approaches, and discover alternate ways to accomplish the same goal. Parents who may be uncomfortable with certain techniques or ways of interacting with their adolescent may become stuck or trapped if there is only one way to implement the technique. Accomplishing the goal of having a range of options may involve problem solving with the parent, role-playing alternative approaches, or helping a parent become more comfortable with a certain approach before asking them to implement it with their adolescent.

Expressing empathy is one of the most important elements of any clinical practice. This remains true in the PPABC training program: The difficulty parents face when a child is suffering with ASU or DB problems may be profound. Clinicians are encouraged to express empathy, avoid direct confrontation with parents, and help parents talk about the sense of failure, helplessness, frustration, anger, and the range of other emotions that accompany having a child with ASU or DB problems. The turmoil ASU and DB cause in virtually every area of parents' lives is recognized, and clinicians take time to help parents explore the many negative, and highly uncomfortable, feelings parents often feel toward their adolescents. For example:

PARENT: I can't believe I am saying this. . . . I mean, I must be the worst parent ever . . . but I just *hate* that kid sometimes! He can be the most dishonest, rude, and mean punk I've ever met! And when I think or say that, I feel worse . . . he's my baby, after all.

THERAPIST: Yes, I can see how you would feel pretty down on yourself for thinking that. However, I can also see why you feel that way sometimes—you have mentioned several examples of his being quite rude and mean to you. I think anyone would feel the way you do right now, and many parents I meet express the same conflicted feelings—you're not alone. However, clearly you still care because you are here, trying to help.

The final step of helping motivate parents to change is enhancing their sense of self-efficacy. Because of repeated failure of discipline programs, or direct defiance of expectations or demands, parents often feel like they are no longer effective parents. They begin to experience a sense of learned helplessness—feeling as if anything they try to change their adolescent's behavior is ineffective. Clinicians help parents recognize their abilities to make changes, find opportunities to help parents build a sense of self-efficacy, and express confidence that the parent is indeed capable of making the changes they wish to make. One method of doing this is finding an example where the parent has already succeeded. The accomplishments may be as simple as getting the adolescent to enter treatment or assisting the parent themselves to seek assistance, as shown in the following example:

THERAPIST: I know you are feeling pretty low because you feel as if your daughter never listens to you. However, you told me she talked to you about looking for a job, and she ended up taking your advice about calling the music store where she wanted to work. Also, she has been seeing the therapist you picked. It seems like some things you are doing are working pretty well.

INTERVENTION

Relationship Building

A crucial aspect of many parent training programs is to foster a warm and enriching relationship between parent and child (Hembree-Kigin & McNeil, 1995; McMahon & Forehand, 2003; Webster-Stratton, 1996). The

PPABC program emphasizes the importance of increasing positive interactions and rewarding experiences between adolescent and parent. To accomplish this, positive time spent between adolescent and parent may need to be increased. Oftentimes, due to time spent with peers, an increased interest in solitary activities (i.e., computer, video games), and parental work demands, parents are not able to spend an adequate amount of time with their children. Therefore, clinicians work with parents to arrange their schedule to afford them the opportunity to spend more time with their adolescent. In the beginning stages, parents establish a brief period of daily time (5 to 10 minutes) set aside for their adolescent. In addition, informal activities are established in which discussing negative events of the past week are avoided. These activities should take place in environments conducive to interaction (i.e., taking a walk, going to a restaurant). It is worth noting that "bonding" times should not be contingent on avoiding negative behavior (i.e., missing curfew, detention). To the contrary, parents should recognize that "bad" weeks require this time more than weeks marked with positive behavior. Parents are given five guidelines for bonding time with their adolescent, as shown in Table 14.5.

Once a consistent time has been established, parents are taught specific skills to foster a more rewarding and engaging interaction. First, the therapist and parent work together on identifying positive behaviors. The

Table 14.5
Basic Rules for Relationship Building Time

1. *Make "dates" with your adolescent well in advance.* Don't "surprise" your adolescent—this may have the result of interfering with other plans and may make the event aversive rather than rewarding. Give reminders that the date is upcoming (e.g., "this Friday is our day out...do you still want to see that movie, or go to the new Thai restaurant?").

2. *All activities should be mutually agreed on.* Don't select the activity for your adolescent. Don't use this time to expose them to art if they hate art. Don't take them someplace you think they should want to go, or where they need to go. Rather, take them someplace they want to go (even if it is not your ideal).

3. *Don't take your friends, your adolescent's friends, other children, cell phones, work, or other distractions along.* Take just you and your adolescent.

4. *Make the time regular and consistent.* Even if things are difficult between you and your adolescent, even if your adolescent is grounded, keep the relationship time sacred.

5. *Issues of negative behavior, substance use, recent fights, or other "problems" are off limits for the relationship-building time.* The point of this time is to get to know your adolescent, understand his/her perspective, appreciate him/her as a person—not to hash out issues, scold your adolescent, or make them feel bad about past behavior.

Table 14.6

Things to Keep in Mind When Praising an Adolescent

1. Always look for something to praise. Remember to praise both good and neutral behaviors.
2. Always praise immediately after the behavior.
3. Try to be as specific as possible when praising.
4. Be sure to praise in the presence of other family members or important individuals in the adolescent's life.
5. Avoid sarcastic or nongenuine praises.
6. Try to be developmentally appropriate when praising your adolescent—avoid embarrassing situations.

parent and therapist may decide that better decision-making skills (e.g., deciding not to associate with a particular individual), positive coping activities (e.g., joining a sports team), or providing honest information (e.g., admitting to substance use) are important behaviors to praise. Then, a parent is taught to recognize these behaviors and offer praise when the behavior occurs. Oftentimes, parents find this task to be initially difficult. Some parents feel like their adolescent does not deserve praise for engaging in appropriate behaviors, or they may feel awkward giving praise for "insignificant" behaviors such as doing chores on time. In this case, the therapist explains the importance and benefits of offering reinforcement for a particular behavior. For these parents, role-plays are set up in which the therapist and parent work together on establishing a style that is comfortable for the parent. Parents are also given basic guidelines for offering appropriate praise (see Table 14.6). The following is a situation where a parent is hesitant about giving praise for a particular behavior:

PARENT: Why should I praise my child for being honest when they should be honest in the first place?

THERAPIST: I realize it seems strange to give praise to something you would normally expect to see. However, when you praise a behavior, it will increase. It lets your child know that he is doing something you like and want to see more of.

PARENT: I just feel so stupid doing it—my kid looks at me like I have three heads. Sometimes it sounds so insincere or sappy.

THERAPIST: He may react this way because he has seldom heard praise for good behavior like this. It will get easier as you do it more and more.

Communication Training

Enhancing effective communication between parents and adolescents is a critical element of PPABC. Not only is communication important in the context of goal-oriented interactions such as arguments and problem-solving situations, it is also an underlying element of many PPABC modules, such as setting and enforcing discipline programs and monitoring adolescent behavior. Oftentimes, maladaptive communication styles, such as the use of emotionally charged, harsh criticisms or the use of inappropriate nonverbal behavior (e.g., eye rolling) can inhibit the resolution of the matter at hand, regardless of the parent's or adolescent's good intentions. Not only can negative communications interfere with the resolution of an argument or finding a solution to a problem, but it can interfere with broader goals such as improving the quality of the parent-adolescent relationship. Unfortunately, when an adolescent is struggling with ASU or DB, communication with parents is often among the first casualties of the relationship. Communication may become characterized by anger, interrupting, accusing, and other negative interaction styles. To help parents begin to communicate with their adolescents, they are provided with the handout shown in Table 14.7. Clinicians systematically work through this handout with parents, provide examples, help parents recognize poor communication habits, and practice improving new skills. Parents are given homework to attempt to implement these techniques with their adolescent. They return the following session to troubleshoot, evaluate what worked and why, and what failed and why.

Rule Setting and Discipline Strategies

Oftentimes, parents have tried a number of discipline strategies with their adolescent—each of which has essentially failed. Because of this, parents are often initially resistant to the introduction of yet another discipline program. Practitioners of PPABC empathize with the parent that disciplining adolescents is a difficult venture while at the same time attempting to have the parent "buy into" the idea of a new discipline program. Drawing on information gathered in the assessment portion of the program, and on the information parents learned in the education of behavioral principles module, clinicians emphasize how and why previous programs may have failed, as shown in the following:

PARENT: We tried taking away video game privileges, but he acted like he didn't care. He doesn't care about anything, so these programs don't really work for us.

THERAPIST: You mentioned in the intake that when you tried that program, your son was not allowed to play video games until his homework was done. Although your son said he didn't care if you took away the video games, he complained about the "stupid rule" constantly. You said that he moped around for a few days, complained, but didn't

Table 14.7

Parent-Adolescent Communication Dos and Don'ts

Do	Don't	Examples
Find a good time to talk	Talk about sensitive issues in public Talk when or where you will be interrupted Try to communicate when your teen is angry, irritated, or tired Wait forever—make a time to talk!	DO: "Hey, is now a good time to chat with me for awhile? Nothing's wrong, I just miss talking with you." DON'T: "I want to talk to you now before I go to work in a half hour."
Listen and be attentive	Interrupt Answer your cell phone when talking with your teen Lecture or close down your teen's efforts to talk to you	DO: "Let's take a walk so your sister won't interrupt." DON'T: "I've heard that before, so I don't want to hear it again!"
Understand what your teen is trying to say	Anticipate or assume you know what your teen is trying to say Dismiss or discount your teen's views or point out how they are "wrong"	DO: "Ok, so I think what you are trying to say is you sometimes feel ignored." DON'T: "That's ridiculous, how could you possibly feel ignored?"
Attend to nonverbal behavior—both yours and your adolescent's	Roll your eyes Sigh heavily or scoff Shake your head	DO: Look your adolescent in the eye. DON'T: Face away from your teen, sit far away, or only talk with folded arms.
Ask open-ended questions	Ask pointed questions with an "agenda" Ask rhetorical questions Ask "what were you thinking?"	DO: "What did you like about that movie?" DON'T: "Do you like messing up all the time? Do you want to end up in jail?"
Share your feelings (appropriately) and make your views clear	Assume your teen knows how you feel Be afraid to be "human"	DO: "I get so sad sometimes when we argue. I feel like I've failed." DON'T: "I've said I care, don't make me repeat myself."
Be respectful and calm	Name call Be sarcastic Raise your voice or yell	DO: Take a deep breath or "count to 10" to avoid an emotional reaction. DON'T: Stand, pace, throw things, or slam things (or slam doors).
Talk about the good	Limit conversations to when things have gone wrong Talk only about your teen's failures	DO: "I saw your new skateboard move: it looked so hard. How long have you been working on that?" DON'T: "You ripped your pants on the skateboard again."

(continued)

Table 14.7 *(Continued)*

Do	Don't	Examples
Use humor	Make fun of your teen Tease	DO: "I could never wear a hat like yours: I would look like a Pez dispenser!" DON'T: "You look like a Pez dispenser in that goofy hat!"
Stick to the facts and the issue at hand	Overgeneralize or use words like "always" or "never" Criticize your teen's intelligence, personality, or character Bring up "dead" issues or issues that have been resolved	DO: "Are you having some trouble with this section of the math book? It seems like it is pretty challenging." DON'T: "How many times have you gotten a 'D' in math? You never, EVER study and then you ALWAYS come home crying because you failed."

do his homework, and that is when you figured that the plan wasn't working?

PARENT: Yeah, it sure didn't make him do his homework.

THERAPIST: But instead of engaging in the desired behavior (homework) to achieve "satisfaction" (playing the video game), he found another behavior that was easier than homework and that resulted in "satisfaction": moping and complaining. What if your son learned that the *only* behavior that would lead to satisfaction is homework? Do you think he might never play a video game again?

PARENT: No way, as much time and money as he has invested in those games, I can't picture him never playing them again.

THERAPIST: So once he learned which behavior (homework) leads to video games, he might eventually do that behavior?

PARENT: Yeah, I suppose eventually he would have to give in. . . .

Once the parent understands how previous efforts may have failed, they often find renewed motivation to engage in the PPABC discipline program.

Once the parents are comfortable and ready to begin designing a new discipline strategy, PPABC clinicians guide them through five separate steps. The first step is to identify a range of potential rewards that are relevant to each adolescent. Parents are encouraged to identify a minimum of 15 rewards: five "small rewards," five "medium rewards," and five "large rewards." Small rewards might be verbal praise, more television, computer or video game time, or small amounts of money.

Medium rewards might be larger privileges (e.g., staying out later on weeknights, using the car), video game rentals, or movie tickets. Large rewards might be larger amounts of money, use of a cell phone, vacations, and so forth. The next step is to have the parent generate a similar list of 15 punishments: five small, five medium, and five large. Punishments can be "positive" punishments (e.g., added responsibilities, but not physical or verbal abuse) or "negative" punishments (e.g., removal of privileges, docking allowances). Parents are reminded that withholding basic necessities such as food, shelter, clothing, and school attendance are not appropriate punishments.

The next step is to help parents negotiate clear, exact rules for the most problematic areas of behavior listed in Table 14.8 with their adolescent. Parents are encouraged to present their adolescents with two or three acceptable choices for the rules in each domain, rather than engage in a "bidding war" with their adolescent. Such exchanges rarely result in both parties being happy with the arrangement. Rather, parents are encouraged to have in mind two choices: The first is their ideal or preferred rule, and the other is a less ideal, but acceptable rule. This allows room for "negotiation" within boundaries acceptable to the parent, and helps the adolescent feel involved, invested, and provides the adolescent with an undeniable working knowledge of the rules.

Finally, rewards from the list generated earlier are matched with positive outcomes for each behavior, and punishments are matched with negative outcomes for each behavior. If parents and adolescents agree that curfew is 8:00 P.M. on weeknights, the adolescent may earn 5% of their overall allowance for each time they are home at or before that time. Conversely, for each night they violate the curfew, they may not only fail to earn the 5% for being on time but also lose an additional 1% for every 10 minutes they are late. Parents are encouraged to complete a specific "family rules contract" and sign it with their adolescents. This document should be placed in an area where all members of the family have access.

Several critical components of the rule-setting module are emphasized. First, not every behavior can be or should be targeted at once. Parents should identify the three of four most problematic behaviors, and target those first; for example, targeting school attendance, alcohol use, negative talk toward parents, and spending money as key areas, and postponing problems like room cleanliness, music volume, and eating food in the living room. Second, parents are told to select rewards and punishments that are both appropriate to the behavior and that are easily enforced; for example, choosing from the "small punishment" list for behaviors that may be annoying but not harmful or particularly problematic. A parent who chooses to ground his or her child for a week

Table 14.8

Suggested Domains for Rule Setting

1. Bedtime (school nights/weekends)
2. Wake-up time (school days/weekends)
3. Weekday nights out (allowed or not? curfew?)
4. Weekend nights out (curfew? only with certain friends?)
5. Calling home when out (yes or no? only when changing locations?)
6. Having friends over (yes or no? only certain friends? only on weekends?)
7. Job (hours)
8. School attendance
9. Off-limit spots (house/hangouts)
10. Food and dishes outside of kitchen
11. Spending of money/savings
12. Sharing of household expenses
13. Room condition
14. Laundry
15. Car use and transportation (advance notice for rides? use of car? who pays for gas, insurance, and other expenses?)
16. Phone usage (length of time/expenses)
17. Music (volume/type/times/etc.)
18. Yelling in the house
19. Swearing/verbal assaults
20. Use of cigarettes
21. Use of drugs/alcohol
22. Testing for drugs (when, under what circumstances?)
23. Lending and borrowing of belongings
24. Selling or giving away belongings
25. Borrowing money
26. Leaving items in common areas of the house

when they have failed to put dishes in the sink is encouraged to select a more appropriate punishment. Likewise, a parent who says he or she will sit at the dinner table beside the adolescent until the homework is complete is told that they are selecting a punishment that may be difficult to enforce, and may be more punishment for the parent than for the adolescent.

Next, although we emphasize the importance of including the adolescent in the process of developing the rules, parents are reminded that they should have the final authority in making decisions, and should not select rewards or punishments that are unreasonable, expensive, or otherwise unrealistic simply because those are the rules the adolescent selects. Finally, the importance of consistency is again emphasized, but this time the need for consistency across caregivers and contexts is addressed. If an adolescent lives in a two-parent household, it is stressed that both parents must adhere to the "family rules contract" and rewards and punishments must be applied in a predictable and consistent manner. When adolescents split their time between households because of divorce, day care arrangements, or other circumstances, the importance of applying the same rules in all contexts is discussed.

Finally, the importance of clarity and precision in the development of rules and consequences is stressed. When rules are ambiguous, adolescents (and often times, parents) have trouble interpreting the rules. Likewise, when there is a lack of clarity, parents often find themselves altering the rules "on the fly." For example, an adolescent goes out on a weeknight and comes home at 7:45 P.M., expecting a reward. However, the parent finds the adolescent has not completed her homework before going out. When the adolescent points out there is no rule saying she can't go out until the homework is done, the parent "interprets" the rule and says, "Well, that rule assumes you have done your homework . . . why else would you be allowed to go out?" This lack of clarity leads to confusion, arguments, and a lack of predictability. Therefore, parents are told to be as specific as possible when developing the rules.

Monitoring Training

Parental monitoring is one of the strongest protective factors against a range of adolescent risk behaviors. However, it is rarely as simple to describe or implement effectively. Many parents assume if they ask where their child is going, and with whom the child will be spending his or her time, the job of monitoring is done. However, not only are there many different aspects of an adolescent's life in which a parent can monitor (e.g., sexual behaviors, peer association, substance use, media use), but there also are many ways in which a parent can go about monitoring these areas (e.g., direct solicitation of information from the child, talking to other parents, going through the child's belongings).

Unfortunately, although research has clearly suggested that parental knowledge of adolescent behavior is associated with a reduction in risky behaviors, less empirical guidance exists about which domains of adolescent behavior are important to monitor or how to gather this information. However, some preliminary evidence suggests that parents who directly ask their adolescents about a range of behaviors, including school behaviors, peer associations, media use, and even health behaviors (e.g., eating habits and exercise), and who use collateral resources to gather information (e.g., talk to neighbors, peer's parents, teachers), have adolescents who perceive their parents to have greater overall knowledge (Branstetter & Cottrell, 2006). This perception of overall knowledge is directly related to a reduction in risk behavior. However, parents are reminded that not all monitoring strategies are effective in reducing risk. Parents are cautioned against intrusive methods of monitoring (e.g., looking through personal journals) because this may have significant detrimental effects on the quality of the overall parent-adolescent relationship.

It should be noted that the literature has thought of parental monitoring in at least two separate ways: as a behavior that reflects (1) parental skills (e.g., Dishion & McMahon, 1998) or (2) a child's willing disclosure of information to parents (e.g., Stattin & Kerr, 2000). In the first view, parents actively track their adolescent's behavior and control their peer associations, and as a result, the adolescent is less likely to engage in delinquent activity. In the second view, however, the question is raised "how do parents know about their child's activities and friends?" It is suggested that the effect of parental monitoring is, in fact, the result of a child's willingness to disclose information to his or her parents, and that regardless of parents attempts to solicit and control an adolescent's activities and peers, the parent can only know what the child is willing to disclose. Stattin and Kerr directly examined if parent's direct solicitation of their children's activities and friends or a child's willing disclosure of information to the parents accounted for lower levels of delinquency. It was found that nearly 45% of variability in the effect of monitoring was accounted for by disclosure by the child. Furthermore, it was found that adding parental solicitation and control accounted for only a small amount of additional variance (3%) over and above disclosure alone. One conclusion of this study was that a positive quality to the relationship between parents and adolescents emphasized communication and prevented the child from engaging in behavior that might disrupt this bond (e.g., delinquency or drug use). This is consistent with both the social control and the social development theories of ASU that suggest that adolescents who establish meaningful relationships with parents are more likely to subscribe to conventional values and reject deviant peers and behaviors. Overall, parents are told that monitoring is a two-way street: They must ask their adolescents about their friends and activities, but their adolescent must be willing to disclose this information to the parent. Thus, the importance of the relationship building and communication modules is stressed. Finally, parents are given a handout that provides concrete advice on monitoring techniques and domains (see Table 14.9).

Table 14.9

Parental Monitoring: Things You Should Know about Your Adolescent

Domain	Suggestions
Peers	
1. Who are your adolescent's friends?	Ask to meet your adolescent's friends.
2. What are they like?	Have them hang out at your house some-
3. Do you trust them?	times.
4. Do you know their parents?	Ask for friend's phone numbers and their
5. Do you know how to get a hold of your adolescent's friends and their parents?	parent's phone numbers.
	Talk with your adolescent's friends. Get to know them.
6. Do your adolescent's friends drive?	Talk to friend's parents. Get to know them, too.
School	
1. Is your adolescent going to school?	Talk about school and how it is going.
2. How is he/she doing in classes?	Ask to help with homework.
3. What activities is he/she involved in?	Talk to teachers. Ask for progress reports.
4. What classes is he/she taking?	Keep a class schedule posted on the
5. Who are his/her teachers?	refrigerator.
Media	
1. What TV programs does your adolescent watch?	Talk about TV shows. Watch what they want to watch.
2. What movies does he/she like?	Talk about the Internet, and favorite sites.
3. Does he/she use the Internet?	Surf the Web together.
4. What websites does he/she visit?	IF USE IS PROBLEMATIC: consider monitor-
5. Does he/she use Instant Messaging or chat rooms?	ing software (with adolescent's knowledge).
Substance Use	
1. Does your adolescent use alcohol?	Talk about use in nonthreatening situation
2. Has he/she tired other drugs?	(e.g., not when the adolescent comes home
3. How often does he/she use?	drunk).
4. Where has he/she been when using in the past?	Talk about drugs and expectations around use.
5. Does he/she tend to use at night, day, parties, or other places?	Ask about use when your adolescent is leaving (e.g., will there be alcohol?).
	Reward honesty, but not the behavior.
Activities	
1. What does your adolescent do after school?	Ask, show an interest, and listen.
	Ask to participate in a favorite activity (e.g.,
2. Where does he/she go to lunch during the week?	video games) sometime.
	Talk to friends and other parents.
3. Where does your adolescent go on week nights? Weekend nights?	Get details before agreeing to let your child participate (don't wait until they are half
4. How does your adolescent get around?	way out the door—they may very well lie
5. Who is attending activities your adolescent is attending (e.g., are parents at the parties)?	just to get out of the house).

(continued)

Table 14.9 *(Continued)*

Domain	Suggestions
Financial	
1. How much money does your adolescent earn each week (from allowance, jobs, or other sources)?	Keep track of how much you are giving them, and ask for an accounting.
	Ask for pay stubs or bank statement.
2. What sorts of things does your adolescent spend his/her money on?	Talk about money, savings, and things your adolescent wants to buy—now, and later.
3. Does your adolescent have savings? How often do they access their savings?	

CONCLUSION

Adolescent substance use and DB are two disorders that often go hand in hand: Adolescents who use illicit substances tend to engage in a high number of delinquent behaviors. Empirical evidence has demonstrated a significant overlap among the factors that cause these disorders, including associating with deviant peers, experiencing other psychiatric disorders, having low academic attachment and achievement, and characteristics of the community in which the adolescent lives. However, perhaps the single most influential risk or protective factor in the development of ASU or DB is the adolescent's parents. Indeed, a number of empirically supported prevention and intervention programs designed to address ASU and/or DB have demonstrated the importance of involving parents in an adolescent's treatment. The PPABC program presented in this chapter has drawn on this body of literature to incorporate key elements of parent training identified in these programs into a single, parent-focused intervention. Although the PPABC program is rooted in theory and empirical research, evidence for this specific program is still in its early stages, and much work remains to be done. Nevertheless, we believe that clinicians will find the program to be of great utility when working with parents who are seeking ways to help their adolescents change. Additionally, the acceptability of the program among parents who have participated has been universal: Parents report the concrete examples, handouts, general information, and sequential structure of the program has led to increased motivation and a feeling that they have the "tools" necessary to help their adolescents change.

REFERENCES

Anderson, A. R., & Henry, C. S. (1994). Family system characteristics and parental behaviors as predictors of adolescent substance use. *Adolescence, 29,* 405–420.

Anthony, J. C., & Petronis, K. (1995). Early-onset drug use and risk of later drug problems. *Drug and Alcohol Dependence, 40,* 9–15.

Armstrong, T. D., & Costello, E. J. (2002). Community studies on adolescent substance use, abuse, or dependence and psychiatric comorbidity. *Journal of Consulting and Clinical Psychology, 70,* 1224–1239.

Ary, D. V., Tildesley, E., Hops, H., & Andrews, J. (1993). The influence of parent, sibling, and peer modeling and attitudes on adolescent use of alcohol. *International Journal of the Addictions, 28,* 853–880.

Barber, B. K. (1992). Family, personality, and adolescent behavior problems. *Journal of Marriage and the Family, 54,* 69–79.

Barnes, G. M., & Welte, J. W. (1986). Patterns and predictors of alcohol use among 7th through 12th grade students in New York State. *Journal of Studies on Alcohol, 47,* 53–62.

Barnes, H., & Olson, D. H. (1985). Parent-adolescent communication and the circumplex model. *Child Development, 56,* 438–447.

Barrett-Waldron, H., Brody, J. L., & Slesnick, N. (2001). Integrative behavioral and family therapy for adolescent substance abuse. In P. M. Monti, S. M. Colby, & T. A. O'Leary (Eds.), *Adolescents, alcohol, and substance abuse: Reaching teens through brief interventions* (pp. 216–243). New York: Guilford Press.

Beck, K. H., Shattuck, T., & Raleigh, R. (2001). A comparison of teen perceptions and parental reports of influence on driving risk. *American Journal of Health Behavior, 25,* 376–387.

Bhatia, S. (1998). Drug abuse in adolescents in relation to their values and perceived family environment. *International Journal of Adolescent Medicine, 10,* 27–37.

Bien, T. H., Miller, W. R., & Boroughs, J. M. (1993). Brief interventions for alcohol problems: A review. *Addiction, 88,* 315–336.

Blau, G. M., Whewell, M. C., Gullotta, T. P., & Bloom, M. (1994). The prevention and treatment of child abuse in households of substance abusers: A research demonstration progress report. *Child Welfare, 73,* 83–94.

Branstetter, S. A. (2005). Parent-adolescent attachment, relationship qualities and monitoring: The influence on substance use and consequences. *Dissertation Abstracts International, 66,* 07B. (ISBN: 0-542-22128-4)

Branstetter, S. A., & Cottrell, L. (2006). *Dimensions and techniques of parental monitoring: The relation to adolescent's perceptions of parental knowledge.* Unpublished manuscript.

Brody, G. H., & Forehand, R. (1993). Prospective associations among family form, family processes, and adolescents' alcohol and drug use. *Behavior Research and Therapy, 131,* 587–593.

Brody, G. H., & Shaffer, D. R. (1982). Contributions of parents and peers to children's moral socialization. *Development Review, 2,* 31–75.

Chassin, L., Curran, P. J., Hussong, A. M., & Colder, C. R. (1996). The relation of parent alcoholism to adolescent substance use: A longitudinal follow-up study. *Journal of Abnormal Psychology, 105,* 70–80.

Chassin, L., Pillow, D. R., Curran, P. J., Molina, B. S., & Barrera, M., Jr. (1993). Relation of parental alcoholism to early adolescent substance use: A test of three mediating mechanisms. *Journal of Abnormal Psychology, 102,* 3–19.

Chilcoat, A. A., & Anthony, J. C. (1996). Impact of parent monitoring on initiation of drug use through late childhood. *Journal of the American Academy of Child and Adolescent Psychiatry, 35,* 91–100.

Chong, M. Y., Chan, K. W., & Cheng, A. T. A. (1999). Substance use disorders among adolescents in Taiwan: Prevalence, sociodemographic correlates, and psychiatric comorbidity. *Psychological Medicine, 29,* 1387–1396.

Coombs, R. H. F., Paulson, M. J. F., & Richardson, M. A. F. (1991). Peer versus parent influence in substance use among Hispanic and anglo children and adolescents. *Journal of Youth and Adolescence, 20,* 73–88.

Corby, E. A., & Russell, J. C. (1997). Substance abuse risk reduction: Verbal mediational training for children by parental and non-parental models. *Substance Abuse, 18,* 145–164.

Cottrell, L., Branstetter, S. A., Stanton, B., Cottrell, S., & Harris, C. (2006). *Navigating the fine balance between perceived parental monitoring and adolescent computer/internet usage.* Unpublished manuscript, West Virginia University.

Cottrell, L., Li, X., Harris, C., D'Alessandri, D., Atkins, M., Richardson, B., et al. (2003). Parent and adolescent perceptions of parental monitoring and adolescent risk involvement. *Parenting, 3,* 179–195.

Crits-Christoph, P., & Siquelan, L. (1996). Psychosocial treatment for drug abuse: Selected review and recommendations for national health care. *Archives of General Psychiatry, 53,* 749–756.

Cui, M., Conger, R. D., Bryant, C. M., & Elder, G. H. (2002). Parental behaviors and the quality of adolescent friendships: A social-contextual perspective. *Journal of Marriage and Family, 64,* 676–689.

Cutler, R. B., & Fishbain, D. A. (2005). Are alcoholism treatments effective? The Project MATCH data. *BMC Public Health, 5,* 75.

Dembo, R., Williams, L., Getreu, A., Genung, L., Schmcidler, J., Berry, E., et al. (1991). A longitudinal study of the relationships among marijuana/hashish use, cocaine use, and delinquency in a cohort of high-risk youths. *Journal of Drug Issues, 21,* 271–312.

Dishion, T. J., Capaldi, D., Spracklen, K. M., & Li, F. (1995). Peer ecology of male adolescent drug use. *Developmental Psychopathology, 7,* 803–824.

Dishion, T. J., & McMahon, R. J. (1998). Parental monitoring and the prevention of child and adolescent problem behavior: A conceptual and empirical formulation. *Clinical Child and Family Psychology Review, 1,* 61–75.

Dishion, T. J., & Skaggs, N. M. (2000). An ecological analysis of monthly "bursts" in early adolescent substance use. *Applied Developmental Science, 4,* 89–97.

Dornbusch, S., Ritter, P., Leiderman, P., Roberts, D., & Fraleigh, M. (1987). The relation of parental style to adolescent school performance. *Child Development, 58,* 1244–1257.

Duncan, S. C., Alpert, A., Duncan, T. E., & Hops, H. (1997). Adolescent alcohol use development and young adult outcomes. *Drug Alcohol Dependence, 49,* 39–48.

Duncan, T. E., Duncan, S. C., Hops, H., & Stoolmiller, M. (1995). An analysis of the relationship between parent and adolescent marijuana use via generalized estimating equation methodology. *Multivariate Behavioral Research, 30,* 317–339.

Eggert, L. L., Herting, J. R., & Thompson, E. A. (1996). The drug involvement scale for adolescents (DISA). *Journal of Drug Education, 26,* 101–130.

Elliott, D. S., Huizinga, D., & Ageton, S. (1985). *Explaining delinquency and drug use.* Beverly Hills, CA: Sage.

Farrell, A. D., & White, K. S. (1998). Peer influences and drug use among urban adolescents: Family structure and parent-adolescent relationship as protective factors. *Journal of Consulting and Clinical Psychology, 66,* 248–258.

Flay, B. R., Hu, F. B., Siddiui, O., Day, L. E., Hedeker, D., Petraitis, et al. (1994). Differential influence of parental smoking and friends' smoking on adolescent initiation and escalation and smoking. *Journal of Health and Social Behavior, 35,* 248–265.

Furman, W., & Buhrmester, D. (1985). Children's perceptions of the personal relationships in their social networks. *Developmental Psychology, 21,* 1016–1022.

Gray, M. R., & Steinberg, L. (1999). Adolescent romance and the parent-child relationship. In W. Furman, B. B. Brown, & C. Feiring (Eds.), *The development of romantic relationships in adolescence* (pp. 235–265). Cambridge: Cambridge University Press.

Griffin, K. W., Botvin, G. J., Scheier, L. M., Diaz, T., & Miller, N. L. (2000). Parenting practices as predictors of substance use, delinquency, and aggression among urban minority youth: Moderating effects of family structure and gender. *Psychology of Addictive Behaviors, 14,* 174–184.

Gullotta, T. P., Adams, G. R., & Montemayor, R. (1994). *Substance misuse in adolescence.* Thousand Oaks, CA: Sage.

Guo, J., Hawkins, J. D., Hill, K. G., & Abbott, R. D. (2001). Childhood and adolescent predictors of alcohol abuse and dependence in young adulthood. *Journal of Studies on Alcohol, 62,* 754–762.

Hansen, W. B., Graham, J. W., Sobel, J. L., Shelton, D. R., Flay, B. R., & Johnson, C. A. (1987). The consistency of peer and parent influences on tobacco, alcohol, and marijuana use among young adolescents. *Journal of Behavioral Medicine, 10,* 559–579.

Hawkins, D. J., & Catalano, R. F. (1992). *Communities that care.* San Francisco: Jossey-Bass.

Hawkins, J. D., & Weis, J. G. (1985). The social development model: An integrated approach to delinquency prevention. *Journal of Primary Prevention, 6,* 73–97.

Hembree-Kigin, T. L., & McNeil, C. (1995). *Parent-child interaction therapy.* New York: Plenum Press.

Henggeler, S. W. (1986). Multisystemic treatment of juvenile offenders: Effects on adolescent behavior and family interaction. *Developmental Psychology, 22,* 132–141.

Henggeler, S. W. (1991). Multidimensional causal models of delinquent behavior and their implications for treatment. In R. Cohen & A. W. Siegel (Eds.), *Context and development* (pp. 211–231). Hillsdale, NJ: Erlbaum.

Henggeler, S. W., & Lee, T. (2003). Multisystemic treatment of serious clinical problems. In A. E. Kazdin & J. R. Weisz (Eds.), *Evidence-based psychotherapies for children and adolescents* (pp. 301–322). New York: Guilford Press.

Henggeler, S. W., Schoenwald, S. K., & Munger, R. L. (1996). Families and therapists achieve clinical outcomes, systems of care mediate the process. *Journal of Child and Family Studies, 5,* 177–183.

Herman, M. S., Dornbusch, S. M., Herron, M. C., & Herting, J. R. (1997). The influence of family regulation, connection, and psychological autonomy on six measures of adolescent functioning. *Journal of Adolescent Research, 12,* 34–67.

Hinton, W. J., Sheperis, C., & Sims, P. (2003). Family-based approaches to juvenile delinquency: A review of the literature. *Family Journal: Counseling and Therapy for Couples and Families, 11,* 167–173.

Hogue, A., Liddle, H. A., & Becker, D. (2002). Multidimensional family prevention for at-risk adolescents. In F. W. Kaslow & T. Patterson (Eds.), *Comprehensive handbook of psychotherapy: Vol. 2. Cognitive-behavioral approaches* (pp. 141–166). Hoboken, NJ: Wiley.

Jang, S. J. (1999). Age-varying effects of family, school, and peers on delinquency: A multilevel modeling test of interactional theory. *Criminology, 37,* 643–653.

Johnston, L. D., O'Malley, P. M., & Bachman, J. G. (1999). *National survey results on drug use from the Monitoring the Future study, 1975–1998: Vol. I. Secondary school students* (NIH Publication No. 99-4660). Bethesda, MD: National Institute on Drug Abuse.

Johnston, L. D., O'Malley, P. M., Bachman, J. G., & Schulenberg, J. E. (2006). *Monitoring the Future national results on adolescent drug use: Overview of key findings, 2005* (NIH Publication No. 06-5882). Bethesda, MD: National Institute on Drug Abuse.

Kafka, R., & London, P. (1991). Communication in relationships and adolescent substance use: The influence of parents and friends. *Adolescence, 26,* 587–598.

Kelly, K. J., Comello, M., & Hunn, L. (2002). Parent-child communication, perceived sanctions against drug use, and youth drug involvement. *Adolescence, 37,* 775–787.

Knight, D. K., Broome, K. M., Cross, D. R., & Simpson, D. D. (1998). Antisocial tendency among drug-addicted adults: Potential long-term effects of parental absence, support, and conflict during childhood. *Drug and Alcohol Abuse, 24,* 361–375.

Kosterman, R., Graham, J. W., Hawkins, J. D., Catalano, R. F., & Herrenkohl, T. I. (2001). Childhood risk factors for persistence of violence in the transition to adulthood: A social development perspective. *Violence and Victims, 16,* 355–370.

Kumpfer, K. L., Alvarado, R., & Whiteside, H. O. (2003). Family-based interventions for substance use and misuse prevention (The Middle Eastern Mediterranean Summer Institute on Drug Use Proceedings) [Special issue]. *Substance Use and Misuse, 38,* 11–13.

Langer, E. (1983). *The psychology of control.* New York: Sage.

Liddle, H. A. (2002). Advances in family-based therapy for adolescent substance abuse: Findings from the Multidimensional Family Therapy research program. In L. S. Harris (Ed.), *Problems of drug dependence 2001: Proceedings of the 63rd Annual Scientific Meeting* (NIDA Research Monograph No. 182, NIH Publication No. 02-5097, pp. 113–115). Bethesda, MD: National Institute on Drug Abuse.

Liddle, H. A., Dakof, G. A., Parker, K., Diamond, G. S., Barrett, K., & Tejeda, M. (2001). Multidimensional family therapy for adolescent drug abuse: Results of a randomized clinical trial. *American Journal of Drug and Alcohol Abuse, 27,* 651–688.

Liddle, H. A., Rowe, C. L., Dakof, G. A., & Lyke, J. (1998). Transplanting parenting research into clinical interventions. *Clinical Child Psychology and Psychiatry, 3,* 419–442.

Liddle, H. L. (1992). A multidimensional model for the adolescent who is abusing drugs and alcohol. In W. Snyder & T. Ooms (Eds.), *Empowering families, helping adolescents: Family-centered treatments of adolescents with alcohol, drug, and other mental health problems* (U.S. Department of Health and Human Services, Office of Treatment Improvement, Alcohol, Drug, and Mental Health Administration, pp. 91–101). Washington, DC: U.S. Public Health Service, U.S. Government Printing Office.

Liddle, H. L., & Diamond, G. (1991). Adolescent substance abusers in family therapy: The critical initial phase of treatment. *Family Dynamics of Addictions Quarterly, 1,* 63–75.

Marshal, M. P., & Chassin, L. (2000). Peer influence on adolescent alcohol use: The moderating role of parental support and discipline. *Applied Developmental Science, 4,* 80–88.

Martin, C. S., & Winters, K. C. (1999). Diagnosis and assessment of alcohol use disorders among adolescents. *Alcohol Health and Research World, 22,* 95–105.

Martin, T. F., White, J. M., & Perlman, D. (2003). Religious socialization: A test of the channeling hypothesis of parental influence on adolescent faith maturity. *Journal of Adolescent Research, 18,* 169–187.

McDermott, D. (1984). The relationship of parental drug use and parents' attitude concerning adolescent drug use to adolescent drug use. *Adolescence, 19,* 89–97.

McMahon, R. J., & Forehand, R. L. (2003). *Helping the noncompliant child: Family-based treatment for oppositional behavior* (2nd ed.). New York: Guilford Press.

Miller, W. R., & Rollnick, S. (1991). *Motivational interviewing: Preparing people to change.* New York: Guilford Press.

Mulvey, E. P., Arthur, M. W., & Reppucci, N. (1993). The prevention and treatment of juvenile delinquency: A review of the research. *Clinical Psychology Review, 13,* 133–167.

Newcomb, M. D., & Bentler, P. M. (1988). Impact of adolescent drug use and social support on problems of young adults: A longitudinal study. *Journal of Abnormal Psychology, 97,* 64–75.

Novacek, J., Raskin, R., & Hogan, R. (1991). Why do adolescents use drugs? Age, sex, and user differences. *Journal of Youth and Adolescence, 20,* 475–492.

Palmqvist, R. A., Martikainen, L. K., & von Wright, M. R. (2003). A moving target: Reasons given by adolescents for alcohol and narcotics use, 1984 and 1989. *Journal of Youth and Adolescence, 32,* 195–203.

Rodgers-Farmer, A. Y. (2000). Parental monitoring and peer group association: Their influence on adolescent substance use. *Journal of Social Service Research, 27,* 1–18.

Romer, D., Stanton, B., Galbraith, J., Geigelman, S., Black, M. M., & Li, X. (1999). Parental influence on adolescent sexual behavior in high-poverty settings. *Archives of Pediatric Adolescent Medicine, 153,* 1055–1062.

Rose, J. S., Chassin, L., Presson, C. C., & Sherman, S. J. (Eds.). (2000). *Multivariate application in substance use research: New methods for new questions.* Mahwah, NJ: Erlbaum.

Schulenberg, J., & Maggs, J. L. (2001). Moving targets: Modeling developmental trajectories of adolescent alcohol misuse, individual and peer risk factors, and intervention effects. *Applied Developmental Science, 5,* 237–253.

Sexton, T. L., & Alexander, J. F. (2000, December). Functional family therapy. *Juvenile Justice Bulletin.*

Shedler, J., & Block, J. (1990). Adolescent drug use and psychological health: A longitudinal inquiry. *American Psychologist, 45,* 612–630.

Stattin, H., & Kerr, M. (2000). Parental monitoring: A reinterpretation. *Child Development, 71,* 1072–1085.

Stern, S. B. (2004). Evidence-based practice with antisocial and delinquent youth: The key role of family and multisystemic intervention. In H. E. Briggs & T. L. Rzepnicki (Eds.), *Using evidence in social work practice: Behavioral perspectives* (pp. 104–127). Chicago: Lyceum Books.

Stice, E., & Barrera, M., Jr. (1995). A longitudinal examination of the reciprocal relations between perceived parenting and adolescents' substance use and externalizing behaviors. *Developmental Psychology, 31,* 322–335.

Swadi, H. (1999). Individual risk factors for adolescent substance use. *Drug and Alcohol Dependence, 55,* 209–224.

Titus, J. C., & Godley, M. D. (1999). *What research tells us about the treatment of adolescent substance use disorders.* Bloomington, IL: Chestnut Health Systems.

Tyas, S. L., & Pederson, L. L. (1998). Psychosocial factors related to adolescent smoking: A critical review of the literature. *Tobacco Control, 7,* 409–420.

U.S. Department of Health and Human Services. (2004). *Multidimensional family therapy (MDFT) for adolescent substance abuse* (Best Practice Initiative, Assistant Secretary of Health). Washington, DC: Author.

Webster-Stratton, C. H. (1996). Early intervention with videotape modeling: Programs for families of children with oppositional defiant disorder or conduct disorder. In E. D. Hibbs & P. S. Jensen (Eds.), *Psychosocial treatments for child and adolescent disorders: Empirically based strategies for clinical practice* (pp. 435–474). Washington, DC: American Psychological Association.

Wills, T. A., & Cleary, S. D. (1996). How are social support effects mediated? A test with parental support and adolescent substance use. *Journal of Personality and Social Psychology, 71,* 937–952.

Windle, M. (2000). Parental, sibling, and peer influences on adolescent substance use and alcohol problems. *Applied Developmental Science, 4,* 98–110.

Wood, M. D., Read, J. P., & Mitchell, R. E. (2004). Do parents still matter? Parent and peer influences on alcohol involvement among recent high school graduates. *Psychology of Addictive Behaviors, 18,* 19–30.

Wright, D., & Pemberton, M. (2004). *Risk and protective factors for adolescent drug use: Findings from the 1999 National Household Survey on Drug Abuse* (DHHS Publication No. SMA 04-3874, Analytic Series A-19). Rockville, MD: Substance Abuse and Mental Health Services Administration, Office of Applied Studies.

Yahne, C. E., & Miller, W. R. (1999). Enhancing motivation for treatment and change. In B. S. McCrady & E. E. Epstein (Eds.), *Addictions: A comprehensive guidebook* (pp. 235–249). New York: Oxford University Press.

Zweben, A., & Zuckoff, A. (2002). Motivational interviewing and treatment adherence. In W. R. Miller & S. Rollnick (Eds.), *Motivational interviewing: Preparing people for change* (2nd ed.). New York: Guilford Press.

Author Index

Subject Index